# Business Law in Canada

### Seventh Edition

**Richard A. Yates**  Simon Fraser University

**Teresa Bereznicki-Korol**  Northern Alberta Institute of Technology

**Trevor Clarke**  Northern Alberta Institute of Technology

PEARSON

Prentice
Hall

Toronto

**National Library Cataloguing in Publication**

Yates, Richard
  Business law in Canada / Richard A. Yates.

Triennial (irregular).
7th ed.– have authors: Richard A. Yates, Teresa Bereznicki-Korol, Trevor Clarke.
Supplements accompany some vols.; some supplements on computer disk.
ISSN 1190-9587
ISBN 0-13-120682-6 (7th edition)

1. Commercial law—Canada.   I. Title.

KE919.Y37                    346.71'07                C95-300897-5  rev
KF889.Y38

**Photo Credits:** p. 1, John Verelst/National Archives of Canada/PA 141503; p. 31, PhotoDisc/Getty; p. 53, Philipe Landreville/© The Supreme Court of Canada; p. 107, PhotoDisc/Getty; p. 129, PhotoDisc/Getty; p. 222, CP/Jeff McIntosh; p. 245, PhotoDisc/Getty; p. 277, CP/Jeff Zelevansky; p. 293, Jon Riley/Getty Images; p. 301, Andreas Pollok/Getty Images; p. 347, The Slide Farm/Al Harvey; p. 363, Richard Pasley/Stock Boston; p. 381, PhotoDisc/Getty; p. 439, V.C.L./Getty Images; p. 442, PhotoDisc/Getty; p. 473, courtesy of TSX; p. 501, Rob Melnychuk/Getty Images; p. 518, Dick Hemingway; p. 546, PhotoDisc/Getty.

ISBN 0-13-120682-6

Vice President, Editorial Director: Michael J. Young
Acquisitions Editor: Laura Forbes
Marketing Manager: Steve McGill
Developmental Editor: Meaghan Eley
Production Editor: Avivah Wargon
Copy Editor: Kelli Howey
Proofreader: Karen Bennett
Production Coordinator: Andrea Falkenberg
Page Layout: Bookman
Photo Research: Marnie Lamb
Art Director: Julia Hall
Interior Design: Miguel Angel Acevedo
Cover Design: Miguel Angel Acevedo
Cover Image: Photodisc / Kevin Jordan

5    09 08 07 06 05

Printed and bound in the United States of America.

# Brief Contents

# Contents

# Preface

The seventh version of anything should reflect change and growth, which can be greatly aided by bringing fresh energy and ideas into the effort. For this reason and many others, I decided to introduce co-authors for this edition of *Business Law in Canada*. Along with their enthusiasm for the task, they also brought insight and expertise. It has been a pleasure and an inspiration to work with Teresa and Trevor in the revision of this book. Both are business law instructors at the Northern Alberta Institute of Technology (NAIT). Both practised law in Edmonton and are dedicated educators. Their interest in this book was manifest several years ago when they agreed to publish an Alberta version of the text. Their commitment to excellence was evident in their attention to detail, their keen awareness of when and where the law was changing, and in their careful response to the needs of business students. Because they worked well together I was confident that they would also work well with me. I have not been disappointed. They have undertaken the revision of half the chapters in the text and have committed to continuing the work as my involvement decreases over the next ten years. Their references to current cases and new legislation have added much to the body of the work. Their writing styles have been remarkably compatible with mine. They have been thoughtful and patient as we shared our views of the law and our goals for this book and I am deeply grateful to them for having made this transition so easy for me.

## Changes to the Seventh Edition

The need to add new material without adding to the length of the text has always been the major challenge of the revision process. It has necessitated both reduction and refinement. While we have not eliminated any topic dealt with previously, we have considered its importance relative to new developments in business law and opted, for example, to reduce the discussion of such topics as negotiable instruments and add to the consideration of electronic commerce. Our approach to property law has evolved as new modes of communication create legal challenges for protecting information—a major factor in modern economies. The text has retained the unit divisions and chapter headings established in the fifth and sixth editions. Dispute resolution has become an all-encompassing topic that recognizes the increasing role being played by methods other than judicial litigation. Government regulation continues to have a growing impact on Canadian business, and environmental law still seems like a useful example of how the government exerts its influence. Chapters 4 to 8 cover the fundamentals of tort and contract law and are designed to be studied together and in order. The other sections can be covered in whatever order the instructor feels is best for the class. The sale of goods and consumer transactions make up Part 3. Employment and agency are covered in Part 4 and business organizations form the subject matter of Part 5. The final division, Part 6, is concerned with personal, real, and intellectual property, ending with an extended discussion of the business and legal implications of electronic information and communication technologies.

In every chapter, we have updated legal information, added new cases and posed thought-provoking questions for students along with strategies for avoiding legal risk. In order to do this and retain a manageable text, we have worked hard to condense information throughout. We think students will find the discussions more succinct, more accessible, and more closely connected to the business environment.

Provincial supplements represent a significant addition to the seventh edition. Legal specialists in the various regions of Canada have prepared additional information spotlighting the differences in the law in the provinces in their region. This information appears on the Companion Website that accompanies this text—**www.pearsoned.ca/yates**. An access code for the Companion Website is included with every copy of the textbook. Marginal icons in the text alert the reader to additional relevant information provided on the Companion Website.

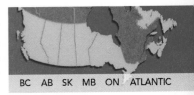

BC  AB  SK  MB  ON  ATLANTIC

We hope that business students will find this new edition of *Business Law in Canada* a stimulating and engaging resource for learning about the law and that it will help you to enter into the world of business with confidence and a heightened respect for the laws that make it workable.

# Features

You will find the following text features in the seventh edition:

**Diagrams** illustrate cases with complex fact patterns.

**"Reducing Risk"** boxes are highlighted throughout the text.

**Case Summaries** appear throughout each chapter. They are used to introduce topics and provide concrete examples that help students understand key legal issues.

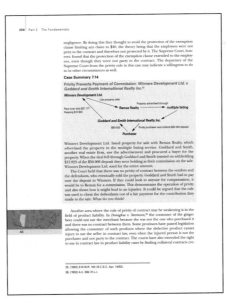

**Key legal terms** appear in bold and full definitions appear in the Glossary and in the Study Guide.

**Icons** direct students to additional information in provincial supplements.

**Summaries** in point form promote quick review and reference.

Finally, we remind all who use this text that it is designed as a tool for learning business law and not as an authoritative source of legal advice. When faced with a specific legal problem, the reader is advised to seek the assistance of a lawyer.

## Supplements

*Business Law in Canada,* Seventh Edition, is accompanied by a complete supplements package:

**Instructor's Resource Manual.** This supplement contains summaries of each chapter, answers to the questions found at the end of each chapter in the text, and solutions to the cases, plus their full citations. The manual also contains the PowerPoint Slides for quick review, in a form that can be copied for overhead transparencies.

**Computerized Test Item File.** This supplement contains over 1600 multiple choice, true/false, and short essay questions with answers. Each question has been checked for accuracy and is available in TestGen EQ test-generating software on the Instructor's CD-ROM. This software package allows instructors to custom design, save, and generate classroom tests. The test program permits instructors to edit, add, or delete questions from the test bank; edit existing graphics and create new ones; analyze test results; and organize a database of tests and student results. This software allows for greater flexibility and ease of use. It provides many options for organizing and displaying tests, along with search and sort features.

**PowerPoint Presentations.** Over 250 transparency masters highlighting key concepts featured in the text are available electronically on the Instructor's Resource CD-ROM.

**Instructor's Resource CD-ROM.** This supplement includes electronic files for the complete Instructor's Resource Manual, the computerized Test Item File, and the PowerPoint Presentations. The materials are provided as MS Word and PowerPoint files, as well as PDF files, allowing the instructor to customize portions and provide them to students as appropriate.

**Student Study Guide and Workbook.** This supplement provides a list of learning outcomes for each chapter, chapter-by-chapter definitions for the key terms highlighted in the text, and student versions of the PowerPoint Presentations, which double as an outline and review of each chapter. The Study Guide includes review questions with answers, and indicates where to find the answers in the text. It also contains guidelines for conducting legal research and briefing a law report.

**Companion Website.** This supplement includes the new Provincial Supplements, a multitude of practice questions, key terms and concepts, weblinks to related sites and more. Check out the *Business Law in Canada* Companion Website at **www.pearsoned.ca/yates.**

**CBC Video Segments.** Current information from CBC programs complements the text and enhances learning by bringing to life practical applications and issues.

**Also Available:** *Business Law in Canada Casebook* by D'Anne Davis (0-13-080597-1). This supplemental text has been updated to correlate with the Seventh Edition of *Business Law in Canada.*

## Acknowledgments

As has been the case in every new edition of *Business Law in Canada,* reviewers have played an important role in correcting, reshaping, and updating the book and we would like to acknowledge their invaluable contribution. In addition to providing encouragement and insight into what instructors want and need, they provide an important connection to the people this book is designed to serve.

We thank all those who have patiently gone over the text and made suggestions for revision, including Douglas H. Beatty, Lambton College of Applied Arts and Technology; Barry Gaetz, Camosun College; Murray Kernaghan, Assiniboine College; Lori Becker, British Columbia Institute of Technology Ethel Lewicki, Southern Alberta Institute of Technology (SAIT); Ronald MacDonald, Mohawk College of Applied Arts and Technology; Peter McKeracher, Durham College; Mike Mann, Malaspina University College; Ronald A. Morrison, Kwantlen University College; Maureen Pellerin, New Brunswick Community College Moncton; Joy Stuart, New Brunswick Community College Moncton; Ronald Gallagher, New Brunswick Community College Moncton; and Patti- Ann Sullivan, Centennial College.

This book truly represents a team effort. Along with my co-authors Teresa and Trevor, I am deeply indebted to the tremendous effort made by the staff at Pearson Education: Kelly Torrance, who brought us together to make this joint endeavour possible; Meaghan Eley, who has worked patiently and persistently with the three of us to coordinate and facilitate our work; and Avivah Wargon, Kelli Howey, and Karen Bennett, who pulled it all together at the end. Without them it would not have been possible.

*Richard A. Yates, LLB, MBA*

We wish to acknowledge Richard Yates for creating and developing a textbook that is easily read and understood by students across Canada. We are grateful to Richard for being extremely gracious in sharing the fruits of his labour with us. It has been a pleasure to work with him. Thank you, Richard, for your insights, support, and encouragement.

The law is constantly changing—politicians continue to create new statutes and regulations and courts continue to decide issues in cases argued before them. It is a real challenge to maintain currency in the law in this day and age. We are extremely grateful to Jennifer Flynn, LLB, for her spirit as a team player and her skills as a researcher. Thank you, Jennifer, for your enthusiasm and for your diligent work in ascertaining and uncovering new developments in the law.

*Teresa Bereznicki-Korol, BA, LLB*
*Trevor Clarke, BSc, MBA, LLB*

## Dedication

First a goal is visualized. Plans are drafted and then the adventure truly begins. Along the way, many sacrifices must be made. We wish to dedicate this text to our respective families whose support was unflinching and to whom we are extremely grateful.

## A Great Way to Learn and Instruct Online

The Pearson Education Canada Companion Website is easy to navigate and is organized to correspond to the chapters in this textbook. Whether you are a student in the classroom or a distance learner you will discover helpful resources for in-depth study and research that empower you in your quest for greater knowledge and maximize your potential for success in the course.

Companion Website

[**www.pearsoned.ca/yates**]

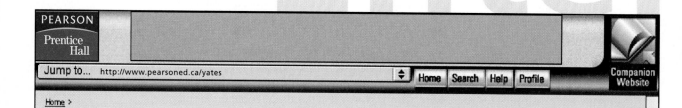

PEARSON
Prentice
Hall

Jump to...    http://www.pearsoned.ca/yates    ⇕    Home | Search | Help | Profile

Companion Website

Home >

## Pearson Companion Website

### *Business Law in Canada*, Seventh Edition, by Yates, Bereznicki-Korol, and Clarke

#### Student Resources

The modules in this section provide students with tools for learning course material. These modules include:
- Chapter Objectives
- Provincial Supplements
- National Supplements
- Quizzes
- Internet Exercises
- Net Search
- Glossary

In the quiz modules students can send answers to the grader and receive instant feedback on their progress through the Results Reporter. Coaching comments and references to the textbook may be available to ensure that students take advantage of all available resources to enhance their learning experience.

#### Instructor Resources

The modules in this section provide instructors with additional teaching tools. Downloadable PowerPoint Presentations and an Instructor's Manual are just some of the materials that may be available in this section. Where appropriate, this section will be password protected.

# Introduction

The study of business law involves an examination of the obligations associated with specialized legal relationships as well as the rights and duties created by various types of commercial transactions. This section lays the foundation essential for understanding the laws related to business activities. It begins by setting the Canadian legal system in its historical context. The institutions that have been developed to resolve legal problems are described. Chapter 1 reviews the sources of our law; the Canadian constitutional structure, including the *Charter of Rights and Freedoms*; and finally the human rights provisions that have important implications for businesspeople. In Chapter 2, we examine the civil court structure and litigation process; because the majority of legal problems are resolved outside the courts, Chapter 2 also looks at alternatives to litigation and the reforms the courts have made to further encourage people to retain control of and resolve their own disputes. Chapter 3 is concerned with the important area of administrative law, or the government regulation of business. When government administrators make decisions that affect individuals or businesses, they must meet procedural standards that are monitored and can be reviewed by the courts. This chapter concludes with an overview of environmental law, demonstrating how the courts, administrative decision-making, and alternative methods have been used to apply and enforce the statutes protecting the environment.

# Introduction to the Legal System

## CHAPTER HIGHLIGHTS

- What is "law" and what types of law exist?
- Distinctions between common law and civil law
- Sources of Canadian law
- Constitutional law and the division of powers
- The parliamentary system
- Protection of rights and freedoms
- The *Charter of Rights and Freedoms*
- Human rights legislation

Why study law? Why should business students, in particular, study law? Laws exist to guide and regulate the interaction of people within society. Businesses exist in order to succeed—to be productive or profitable. But in order to succeed, businesspeople must understand the climate within which they operate. Knowing the law and developing strategies in light of the law can foster success in business. Putting it simply, one has to know the rules of the game if one hopes to win.

# What Is Law?

**No wholly satisfactory definition of law**

**Problems applying theory**

Most of us recognize the rules and regulations that are considered law and understand that law plays an important role in ordering society, but knowing that does not make it easy to come up with a satisfactory, all-inclusive definition. Philosophers have been trying for centuries to determine just what "law" means, and their theories have profoundly affected the development of our legal system. Law has been defined in moral terms, where only good rules are considered law (*natural law theorists*). Others have defined law by looking at its source, stipulating that only the rules enacted by those with authority to do so qualify as law (*legal positivists*). And some have defined law in practical terms, suggesting that only those rules that the courts are willing to enforce qualify as law (*legal realists*). Legal positivism helped shape the concept of law in Canada, where parliamentary supremacy requires that we look to the enactments of the federal parliament or provincial legislatures as the primary source of law. In the United States, however, a more pragmatic approach to law based on legal realism has been adopted. It allows judges to factor in current social and economic realities when they make their decisions.

For our purposes, the following simplified definition is helpful, if we remember that it is not universally applicable. **Law is the body of rules that can be enforced by the courts or by other government agencies.** We are exposed to many rules in our daily activities that do not qualify as law. Courtesy demands that we do not interrupt when someone is speaking. Social convention determines that it is inappropriate to enter a restaurant shirtless or shoeless. Universities and colleges often establish rules of conduct for their students and faculty. These rules do not fall into our definition of law because the courts do not enforce them. But when there is a disagreement over who is responsible for an accident, a question as to whether a crime has been committed, or a difference of opinion about the terms of a contract or a will, the participants may find themselves before a judge. Rules that can be enforced by the courts govern these situations; thus, they are laws within the definition presented here.

A person dealing with government agencies, such as labour relations boards, the Workers' Compensation Board, or city and municipal councils, must recognize that these bodies are also able to render decisions in matters that come before them. The rules enforced by these bodies are also laws within this definition. The unique problems associated with government agencies and regulatory bodies will be discussed in Chapter 3.

While the definition of law as enforceable rules has practical value, it does not suggest what is just or moral. We must not assume that so long as we obey the law we are acting morally. Legal compliance and ethical behaviour are two different things, and people must decide for themselves what standard they will adhere to. Many choose to live by a personal code of conduct demanding adherence to more stringent rules than those set out in the law, while others disregard even these basic requirements. Some think that moral values have no place in the business world, but in fact the opposite is true. There is now an expectation of high ethical standards in business activities, and it is hoped that those who study the law as it relates to business will appreciate and adhere to those higher standards. We must at least understand that whether we are motivated by divine law, conscience, moral indifference, or avarice, serious consequences may follow from non-compliance to the body of rules we call law.

*Definition*

*Do not confuse law and morality*

## Categories of Law

Law consists of rules with different but intersecting functions. The primary categories are substantive and procedural laws. **Substantive law** establishes not only the rights an individual has in society but also the limits on his or her conduct. The rights to travel, to vote, and to own property are guaranteed by substantive law. Prohibitions against theft and murder as well as other actions that harm our neighbours are also examples of substantive law. **Procedural law** determines how the substantive laws will be enforced. The rules governing arrest, investigation, and pre-trial and court processes in both criminal and civil cases are examples. Law can also be distinguished by its public or private function. **Public law** includes constitutional law that determines how the country is governed and the laws that affect an individual's relationship with government, including criminal

*Kinds of law*

law and the regulations created by government agencies. **Private law** involves the rules that govern our personal, social, and business relations, which are enforced by one person suing another in a private or civil action. Knowing the law and how it functions allows us to structure our lives as productive and accepted members of the community and to predict the consequences of our conduct. As business students, we study law because it defines the environment of rules within which business functions. In order to play the game, we must know the rules.

# Origins of Law

Nine of the ten Canadian provinces and the three territories have adopted the common law legal system developed over the last millennium in England. For private matters, Quebec has adopted a system based on the *French Civil Code.* Although this text focuses on common law, understanding it may be assisted by briefly examining the basic differences between the common law and civil law legal systems. It is important to note that the term *civil law* has two distinct meanings. The following discussion is about the civil law legal system developed in Europe and now used in many jurisdictions, including Quebec. The terms *civil court, civil action,* and *civil law* are also used within our common law legal system to describe private law matters and should not be confused with the *Civil Code* or civil law as used in Quebec.

**Quebec civil law; all other provinces common law**

## Civil Law Legal System

Modern civil law traces its origins to the Emperor Justinian, who had Roman law codified for use throughout the Roman Empire. This codification became the foundation of the legal system in continental Europe. Its most significant modification occurred early in the 19th century, when Napoleon revised it. The *Napoleonic Code* was adopted throughout Europe and most of the European colonies. Today, variations of the *Civil Code* are used in all of continental Europe, South America, most of Africa, and many other parts of the world, including Quebec. The most important feature of French civil law is its central *Code*—a list of rules stated as broad principles of law that judges apply to the cases that come before them. Under this system, people wanting to know their legal rights or obligations refer to the *Civil Code.*

**Civil Code used throughout the world**

Quebec courts rely on the *Code* for guidance and solutions in private disputes. While civil law judges are influenced by decisions made in other cases, and lawyers will take great pains to point out what other judges have done in similar situations, the key to understanding the *Civil Code* system is to recognize that ultimately the *Code* determines the principle to be applied. Prior decisions do not constitute binding precedents in a civil law jurisdiction. The most recent Quebec *Civil Code* came into effect on January 1, 1994. One-quarter of the 1994 *Code* is new law, making its introduction a significant event in the evolution of the law of Quebec.

**Civil Code provides predictability**

One of the effects of the new *Code* was to make the doctrine of good faith (recently developed in common law and discussed in Chapter 6) part of Quebec's contract law. Prior to this, the law was similar to the common law, where the obligation to act in good faith toward the person you are dealing with applied only when special relationships existed. Article 1375 of the new *Code* states that contracting parties "shall conduct themselves in good faith both at the time the obli-

## Reducing **Risk** 1.1

If a person were to suffer injury in Quebec because of the careless acts of an employee serving overly hot coffee to a customer at a fast-food restaurant drive-through, the victim would turn to the Quebec *Civil Code*[1] to determine his or her rights. Articles 1457 and 1463 of the most recent *Code* state the following:

*1457. Every person has a duty to abide by the rules of conduct which lie upon him, according to the circumstances, usage or law, so as not to cause injury to another. Where he is endowed with reason and fails in this duty, he is responsible for any injury he causes to another person and is liable to reparation for the injury, whether it be bodily, moral, or material in nature.*

*He is also liable, in certain cases, to reparation for injury caused to another by the act or fault of another person or by the act of things in his custody.*

*1463. The principal is liable to reparation for injury caused by the fault of his agents and servants in the performance of their duties; nevertheless, he retains his recourses against them.*

**You be the judge: (1) In the example above, if the customer suffered burns when the overly hot coffee spilled on her lap, who could the injured party sue? (2) If the customer brought an action against the employer—the owner of the restaurant—could the restaurant then recover damages as against its careless employee?**

gation is created and at the time it is performed or extinguished."[2] This means that the parties can no longer withhold important information or fail to correct erroneous assumptions that they know have been made by the other side without exposing themselves to an action for violating this obligation of good faith.

There are many important differences between civil law and the principles of common law. In this text, we have limited the discussion to common law—while there are many similarities, care should be taken not to assume that the same principles apply to Quebec or other civil law jurisdictions.

## Common Law Legal System

As Roman civil law was taking hold in Europe, relations between the existing English and French kingdoms were frequently strained. It has been suggested that this strain is the reason England maintained its unique common law system of justice rather than adopting the more widely accepted Roman civil law. The early Norman kings established a strong feudal system in England that centralized power in their hands. As long as they remained strong they maintained their power; but, when weak kings were on the throne, power was surrendered to the nobles. The growth of the common law legal system was much affected by this ongoing struggle for power between kings and nobles and later between kings and parliament.

During times when power was decentralized, the administration of justice fell to the local lords, barons, or sheriffs, who would hold court as part of their feudal responsibility. Their courts commonly resorted to such practices as trial by battle or ordeal. Trial by battle involved armed combat between the litigants or their champions, and trial by ordeal involved some physical test. The assumption was made that God would intervene on behalf of the righteous party. Strong kings, especially Henry II, enhanced their power by establishing travelling courts, which provided a more attractive method of resolving disputes. As more people used the king's courts, their power base broadened, and their strength increased. The

**Common law grew from struggle for power**

**Henry II established travelling courts**

---

1. *Civil Code of Quebec,* S.Q. 1991, c. 64.

2. Art. 1375 C.C.Q.

fairer the royal judges, the more litigants they attracted. Eventually, the courts of the nobles fell into disuse. The function of the royal courts was not to impose any particular set of laws but to be as fair and impartial as possible. To this end, they did not make new rules but enforced the customs and traditions they found already in place in the towns and villages they visited. The judges also began to look to each other for rules to apply when faced with new situations.

## Stare Decisis

**Judges follow each other's decisions**

Gradually, a system of justice developed in which the judges were required to follow each other's decisions. This process is called *stare decisis,* or "following precedent." Another factor that affected the development of *stare decisis* was the creation of appeal courts. Although the process of appeal at this time was rudimentary, trial judges would try to avoid the embarrassment of having their decisions overturned and declared in error. Eventually, the practice of following precedent became institutionalized. The most significant feature of our legal system today is that the decision of a judge at one level is binding on all judges in the court hierarchy who function in a court of lower rank, provided the facts in the two cases are similar.[3] Thus, a judge today hearing a case in the Court of Queen's Bench for Alberta would be required to follow a similar decision laid down in the Court of Appeal for Alberta or the Supreme Court of Canada, but would not have to follow a decision involving an identical case from the Court of Appeal for Manitoba. Such a decision would be merely persuasive, since it came from a different jurisdiction. Because the Supreme Court of Canada is the highest court in the land, its decisions are binding on all Canadian courts.

### Case Summary 1.1

#### Precedents in a Federal Landscape: *R. v. Keegstra*[4] and *R. v. Andrews*[5]

The *Keegstra* and *Andrews* cases provide an excellent illustration of how *stare decisis* operates in Canada. In the *Keegstra* case, the Alberta Court of Appeal struck down section 281.2 of the *Criminal Code* as being unconstitutional. This section (now section 319(2)) prohibits dissemination of hate literature. Keegstra had been teaching students that the holocaust was a hoax—a tale created by the Jewish people to attract sympathy. In the *Andrews* case, the accused faced similar charges for spreading white supremacist hate literature. But in this case, the Ontario Court of Appeal upheld the constitutionality of the same charges, even though it had the benefit of the Alberta decision. It simply chose not to follow the Alberta precedent.

These cases demonstrate that courts of similar rank in different provinces are not bound to follow each other. This resulted in a situation where, in Alberta, charges could not be laid under section 281.2, because the section had been declared unconstitutional, but charges could be laid for the same activities in Ontario. These cases also illustrate the importance of access to the Supreme Court of Canada as the final court of recourse. It is undesirable to have opposing

---

3. Strictly speaking, a judge is not bound to follow decisions made by other judges in a court at the same level in that province. However, the practical effect is the same, since these judges must follow their colleagues' decisions "in the absence of strong reason to the contrary." R. ex rel *McWilliam v. Morris* [1942] O.W.N. 447 (Ont. H.C.J.).

4. (1988), 60 Alta. L.R. (2d) 1 (C.A.); [1990] 3 S.C.R. 697.

5. (1988), 65 O.R. (2d) 161 (C.A.); [1990] 3 S.C.R. 870.

rules in different parts of the country, especially in criminal law where national uniformity is desirable.

Both cases were appealed to the Supreme Court of Canada, which delivered its decision on each appeal simultaneously. It declared the sections constitutional, finding that although rights had been violated by the *Code*, these infringements were justifiable under section 1 of the *Charter of Rights and Freedoms*. (In other words, although the charge prohibiting the dissemination of the literature does violate freedom of expression, this violation is justifiable for the good of society as a whole.) Charges for inciting hatred were thus tried as against Keegstra and he was eventually convicted.

Consider these questions: (1) Does following precedent ensure that similar cases will meet similar outcomes? (2) Is it acceptable or fair if laws vary from one province to another?

The role *stare decisis* plays in the English common law legal system is similar to the role the *Civil Code* plays in the French system. It allows the parties to predict the outcome of the litigation and thus avoid going to court. However, a significant disadvantage of following precedent is that a judge must follow another judge's decision even though social attitudes may have changed. The system is anchored to the past, with only limited capacity to make corrections or to adapt and change to meet modern needs. Opposing legal representatives present a judge with several precedents that support their side of the argument. The judge's job is to analyze the facts of the precedent cases and compare them with the case at hand. Since no two cases are ever exactly alike, the judge has some flexibility in deciding whether or not to apply a particular precedent. Judges try to avoid applying precedent decisions by finding essential differences between the facts of the two cases if they feel that the prior decision will create an injustice in the present case. This process is referred to as **distinguishing the facts** of opposing precedents. Still, judges cannot stray very far from the established line of precedents.

*Stare decisis* **provides predictability**

**Results in an inflexible system**

**A judge must choose among precedents**

# Sources of Law

## Common Law

At an early stage in the development of common law, three great courts were created: the court of common pleas, the court of king's bench, and the exchequer court, referred to collectively as the **common law courts**. The rules developed in the courts were called "common law" because the judges, at least in theory, did not create law but merely discovered it in the customs and traditions of the people to whom it was to be applied. However, the foundation for a complete legal system could not be supplied by local custom and tradition alone, so common law judges borrowed legal principles from many different sources. **Roman civil law** gave us our concepts of property and possessions. **Canon or church law** contributed law in relation to families and estates. Another important European system that had an impact on common law was called the **law merchant**. Trading between nations was performed by merchants who were members of guilds (similar to modern trade unions or professional organizations), which developed their own rules to deal with disputes between members. As the strength of the guilds

**Customs and traditions major source of common law**

**Common law borrows from**
• Roman law
• Canon law
• Law merchant

declined, common law judges found themselves dealing increasingly with disputes between merchants. The law merchant was then adopted as part of the English common law, and it included laws relating to negotiable instruments, such as cheques and promissory notes.

## Equity

**Common law rigid**

Common law courts had some serious limitations. Parties seeking justice before them found it difficult to obtain fair and proper redress for the grievances they had suffered. Because of the rigidity of the process, the inflexibility of the rules applied, and the limited scope of the remedies available, people often went directly to the king for satisfaction and relief. The burden of this process made it necessary for the king to delegate the responsibility to the chancellor, who, in turn, appointed several vice-chancellors. This body eventually became known as the **Court of Chancery,** sometimes referred to as the **Court of Equity.** It dealt with matters that, for various reasons, could not be handled adequately or fairly by the common law courts. The Court of Chancery did not hear appeals from the common law courts; rather, it provided an alternative forum. If people seeking relief knew that the common law courts could provide no remedy or that the remedy was inadequate, they would go to the Court of Chancery instead. Initially, the Court of Chancery was unhampered by the rules of precedence and the rigidity that permeated the common law courts, and could decide a case on its merits. The system of law developed by the Court of Chancery became known as the **law of equity.** This flexibility, which was the most significant asset of equity, was also its greatest drawback. Each decision of the Court of Chancery appeared arbitrary; there was no uniformity within the system; and it was difficult to predict the outcome of a given case. This caused friction between the chancery and the common law judges, which was solved, to some extent, by the chancery adopting *stare decisis.* This caused the same problems found in the common law courts. The chancery courts eventually became as formal and rigid as the common law courts. Finally, the two separate court systems were amalgamated by the *Judicature Acts of 1873–1875.*[6] This merger happened in Canada as well, and today there is only one court system in each of the provinces.

**Courts of Chancery provide relief**

**Resulting in the law of equity**

**Conflict results in rigidity in chancery as well**

Although the two court systems merged, the bodies of law they had created did not, and it is best still to think of common law and equity as two distinct bodies of rules. Originally, the rules of equity may have been based on fairness and justice, but when a person today asks a judge to apply equity, they are not asking for fairness: they are asking that the rules developed by the courts of chancery be applied to the case. Equity should be viewed as a supplement to, rather than a replacement of, common law. Common law is complete—albeit somewhat unsatisfactory—without equity, but equity would be nothing without common law. The courts of chancery were instrumental in developing such principles in law as the *trust* (in which one party holds property for another), and also provided several alternative remedies, such as injunction and specific performance, that we will examine later in the text.

**Equity today does not simply mean fairness**

**Equity supplements the common law**

The common law provinces in Canada administer both common law and equity, and judges treat matters differently when proceeding under equity as

---

6. *Judicature Acts* (1873–1875) 31 Geo. III.

opposed to common law rules. Of course, judges must always be alert to the fact that any applicable parliamentary statute will override both.

## Statutes

In many situations, justice was not available in either the common law or chancery courts, and another method was needed to correct these inadequacies. The English Civil War of the 17th century firmly established the principle that Parliament, rather than the king, was supreme, and from that time, Parliament handled any major modification to the law. Parliamentary enactments are referred to as *statutes* or *legislation* and take precedence over judge-made law based on either common law or equity.

**Statutes and regulations override judge-made law**

It is important to remember that government has several distinct functions: legislative, judicial, and administrative. Parliament legislates or creates the law, the judicial branch is the court system, and the executive branch and its agencies administer and implement that law. Organizations such as the RCMP, the Employment Insurance Commission, and the military are part of the executive branch of government. Often, legislation creating such bodies (the enabling statute) delegates power unto them to create regulations (the subordinate legislation). Through those regulations, government agencies implement and accomplish the goals of the enabling statute and enforce its terms. Similarly, municipal bylaws operate as subordinate legislation. A provincial statute, such as Ontario's *Municipal Act, 2001*,[7] may enable municipalities to pass bylaws, but only with regard to matters stipulated in the Act.

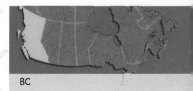

BC

For the businessperson, these statutes and regulations have become all-important, setting out the specific rules governing business activities in all jurisdictions. Although judge-made law still forms the foundation of our legal system, it is statutes and regulations that control and restrict what we can do and determine what we must do to carry on business in Canada today. See Table 1.1 for a summary of the sources of law in Canada.

# The Law in Canada

## Confederation

Canada came into existence in 1867, with the federation of Upper and Lower Canada, Nova Scotia, and New Brunswick. Other provinces followed, with Newfoundland being the most recent to join Confederation. Every jurisdiction except Quebec adopted the English common law legal system. Quebec elected to retain the use of the French *civil law legal* system for private matters falling within provincial jurisdiction.

Confederation was accomplished when the British Parliament passed the *British North America Act (BNA Act)*, now renamed the *Constitution Act (1867)*.[8] The *BNA Act*'s primary significance is that it created the Dominion of Canada and

**BNA Act created Canada and divided powers**

---

7. S.O. 2001, c. 25.

8. *Constitution Act, 1867* (U.K.), 30 & 31 Vict., c. 3, reprinted in R.S.C. 1985, App. II, No.5 (formerly the *British North America Act, 1867*).

## Table 1.1 Sources of Law in Canada

| Branch of Government | Legislative | Executive | Judicial |
|---|---|---|---|
| Who fills these positions? | Federally: Parliament | Prime Minister and Cabinet Ministers together with each department's civil servants/bureaucrats | Judges appointed by the various provinces and federally appointed justices |
| | Provincially: Legislative Assemblies | Premier and the Cabinet together with each department's civil servants/bureaucrats | |
| Type of law made | Statute law (legislation) | Subordinate legislation<br>• regulations made by order-in-council or as authorized by legislation<br>• bylaws made by municipal governments | Case law |
| Examples | (Federal)<br>• *Immigration and Refugee Protection Act*<br>• *Criminal Code* | (Federal)<br>Immigration and Refugee Protection Regulations | The decision of the Supreme Court of Canada in *R. v. Keegstra* |
| | (Provincial)<br>• *Workers' Compensation Act*<br>• *Traffic Safety Act*<br>• *Business Corporations Act* | (Provincial)<br>Workers' Compensation Regulation | The decision of the Ontario Court of Appeal in *Haig v. Canada* |

determined the functions and powers of the provincial and federal levels of government. The preamble to the *BNA Act* says that Canada has a constitution "similar in principle to that of the United Kingdom"; that is, we claim as part of our constitution all the great constitutional institutions of the United Kingdom, such as the *Magna Carta* and the *English Bill of Rights*. Also included are such unwritten conventions as the **rule of law,** which recognizes that although Parliament is supreme and can create any law considered appropriate, citizens are protected from the arbitrary actions of the government. In addition, our constitution

**More to Canadian Constitution than *BNA Act***

includes those acts passed by both the British and Canadian Parliaments subsequent to the *Constitution Act (1867)* that have status beyond mere statutes, such as the *Statute of Westminster* (1931) and the *Constitution Act (1982),*[9] which includes the *Charter of Rights and Freedoms.* The most recent addition to the constitutional statutes is the *Constitution Act, 1999 (Nunavut).*[10]

For the person in business, it must be remembered that the effect of Confederation was not simply to create one country, with one set of rules. Each province was given the power to establish rules in those areas over which it had

---

9.  *Constitution Act, 1982,* being Schedule B to the *Canada Act 1982* (U.K.), 1982, c. 11.

10.  S.C. 1998, c. 15, Part II; (in force April 1, 1999).

jurisdiction. As a consequence, businesses operating within and between provinces must comply with federal, provincial, and municipal regulations. In spite of the opportunity for great divergence among the provinces, it is encouraging to see how similar the controls and restrictions are in the different jurisdictions.

## Constitution and Division of Powers

In Canada, as in Britain, Parliament is supreme and traditionally has had the power to make laws that cannot be overruled by any other body and are subject only to the realities of the political system in which they function. In addition, the *Constitution Act (1867)* and the *Charter of Rights and Freedoms* place some limitations on this supremacy. Unlike the United Kingdom, Canada has a federal form of government with 11 different legislative bodies, each claiming the supreme powers of Parliament.

*Constitution Act* and *Charter* limit power of federal and provincial governments

The *Constitution Act (1867)* assigned different powers to the different levels of government. The powers of the federal government are set out primarily in section 91 of the *Constitution Act (1867)*, and those of the provincial governments in section 92 (see Appendix 1A immediately following this chapter). The federal government has power over such matters as banking, currency, the postal service, criminal law (although not its enforcement), and the appointment of judges in the federal and higher-level provincial courts. The federal government passes considerable legislation affecting such matters as the regulation of all import and export activities, taxation, environmental concerns, money and banking, interprovincial and international transportation, as well as important areas of intellectual property, such as copyrights, patents, and trademarks. The provinces have jurisdiction over such matters as hospitals, education, the administration of the courts, and commercial activities carried on at the provincial level.

*Constitution Act (1867)* divides powers between federal and provincial governments

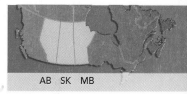

AB  SK  MB

Thus, most business activities that are carried on within the province are governed by provincial legislation or municipal bylaw, including statutes dealing with the sale of goods, consumer protection, employment, workers' compensation, collective bargaining, secured transactions, incorporation, real estate, and licensing. For industries that fall within the federal jurisdiction, such as banking and the railways, there are corresponding federal statutes, such as collective bargaining and incorporation legislation. Under the "Peace, Order, and Good Government" clause (found in the introduction to section 91) the federal government has residual power to make law with respect to things not listed in the *Constitution Act (1867)*, such as broadcasting and air transportation. Under section 92(16), the provinces are given broad powers to make law with respect to all matters of a local or private nature. It is important to note that these assigned areas of jurisdiction are concerned with the nature of the legislation being passed, rather than the individuals or things affected. Thus, the federal government's power to pass banking legislation allows them to control anything to do with banking, including interest rates, deposits, and how those deposits are invested. The division of powers accomplished by sections 91 and 92 of the *Constitution Act (1867)* has been very important in the development of Canada as a nation and, until the recent entrenchment of the *Charter*, was the main consideration of courts when faced with constitutional questions. In these jurisdictional disputes between governments, where competing governments claim to control a particular activity, the courts are called upon to act as a referee. See Table 1.2 for a summary of the division of powers.

Federal powers set out in sec. 91

Provincial powers set out in sec. 92

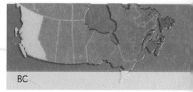

BC

Sections 91 and 92 deal with types of legislations, not things

**Table 1.2 Division of Powers**

| Federal—Section 91 | Provincial—Section 92 |
| --- | --- |
| Trade and commerce | Municipal institutions |
| Employment insurance | Hospitals (and health care) |
| Raising monies by any mode of taxation | Direct taxation within the province |
| Criminal law (although not its enforcement) | Administration of justice within the province |
| Banking; currency; postal service.... | Property and civil rights.... |
| Residual power under the "P.O.G.G." clause | Generally, matters of a local or private nature |

**Case Summary 1.2**

**A Gun Fight between Governments:** *Reference re Firearms Act (Can.)*[11]

In 1995, Parliament amended the *Criminal Code* by enacting the *Firearms Act*.[12] The amendments require all holders of firearms to obtain licences and register their guns. Alberta, backed by the territories, Ontario, Saskatchewan, and Manitoba, challenged the law, arguing it was a brazen intrusion on private property and civil rights, a provincial power according to section 92(13) of the *Constitution Act (1867)*. The opponents argued that the new law would do no more to control gun crimes than registering vehicles does to stop traffic offences. Many gun owners opposed the expense and inconvenience of registration, yet not to register would turn otherwise "law-abiding" citizens into criminals.

The Supreme Court of Canada upheld the *Firearms Act* as *intra vires* Parliament, meaning that it was within its power. It found that the Act constitutes a valid exercise of Parliament's jurisdiction over criminal law because its "pith and substance" is directed to enhancing public safety by controlling access to firearms. Because guns are dangerous and pose a risk to public safety, their control and their regulation as dangerous products were regarded as valid purposes for criminal law. The law further included prohibitions, backed by penalties. In essence, the law was determined to be criminal in focus. The Supreme Court found that the Act impacted provincial jurisdiction over property and civil rights only incidentally. Accordingly, the *Firearms Act* was upheld as a valid exercise of federal power under section 91(27) of the *Constitution Act (1867)*. (Note: the cost of implementing this gun registry has far exceeded initial estimates, leading to calls for its suspension or abandonment.)

How would you characterize the *Firearms Act*? Is it primarily concerned with addressing crime? If it fails to affect crime in Canada, can its constitutionality be re-examined? What do you think?

## Conflicting Powers

On occasion, one level of government passes legislation that may infringe on the powers of another. For example, municipal governments have tried to control prostitution or pornography, using their zoning or licensing power, when in fact these matters are controlled by criminal law, a federal area.[13] Such bylaws have

---

11. [2000] 1 S.C.R. 783.

12. S.C. 1995, c. 39.

13. *R. v. Westendorp,* [1983] 1 S.C.R. 43.

been struck down as *ultra vires* (beyond one's jurisdiction or power) by the courts, as veiled attempts to control moral conduct, matters to be dealt with under criminal jurisdiction. Municipalities sometimes try to increase the licensing fee charged to a business to accomplish the same purpose, often with the same result.

One level of government cannot invade the area given to another by trying to make it look like the legislation is of a different kind. The court simply looks at the substance of what the governing body is trying to do as opposed to what it claims to be doing and asks whether or not it has that power.

**Validity of statute determined by its true nature**

## Case Summary 1.3

### Municipal Bylaw Aimed at Covering Breasts:
### *Maple Ridge (District) v. Meyer*[14]

A quiet B.C. community was shocked to see Ms. Meyer bare her breasts at a public swimming pool—after all, she was no longer a child! The response was an amendment to the Maple Ridge Park bylaw, making it an offence punishable by a fine of $2000 and six months' imprisonment to appear in a park unclothed. "Clothed" was defined to require females over the age of eight years to fully cover their nipples and areolae with opaque apparel. The Court determined that the amendment to the bylaw was motivated by complaints regarding morality, modesty, and embarrassment. The bylaw created a stricter standard regarding nudity than that found in the *Criminal Code*. It imposed strict liability whereas under the *Code* defences were available; further, it criminalized the conduct of girls as young as nine years old. The Court struck the bylaw down as *ultra vires* the legislative competence of Maple Ridge, finding it a "colourable attempt to regulate morality and thus displace the federal jurisdiction in respect of criminal law."

The powers of the federal and provincial governments can overlap considerably. When overlap does take place, the principle of **paramountcy** may require that the federal legislation be operative and that the provincial legislation go into abeyance and no longer apply. If the overlap between provincial and federal legislations is merely incidental, both are valid, and both are operative. An individual must obey both by adhering to the higher standard, whether provincial or federal. It is only when the laws are such that only one can be obeyed that a true conflict exists, and then the federal provision will prevail.

**When provincial and federal laws conflict, follow federal**

## Case Summary 1.4

### Paramountcy Applied Where Laws Conflict:
### *Law Society of British Columbia v. Mangat*[15]

Mangat worked as an immigration consultant through his consulting company, Westcoast. The Law Society of British Columbia sought an injunction preventing Mangat and other Westcoast employees from engaging in the practice of law, as they were not lawyers or members of the B.C. Law Society. The B.C. *Legal Profession Act* prohibits persons other than members in good standing with the society from practising law. Mangat and other Westcoast employees would appear as counsel or advocate on behalf of aliens before the Immigration and Refugee Board; for their services, they would charge a fee. The B.C. Law Society characterized this activity as "practising law."

14. [2000] B.C.J. No. 1154 (B.C.S.C.).

15. [2001] 3 S.C.R. 267.

However, the federal *Immigration Act* granted certain rights to aliens, including the right to be represented in proceedings by either a barrister or solicitor *or* other counsel for a fee. The Supreme Court determined that the provisions of both statutes were valid; but, as there was clearly a conflict and dual compliance with both statutes would be impossible without frustrating Parliament's intent, the *Immigration Act* provisions would be paramount over the provisions of the provincial statute. Accordingly, the injunction was lifted.

## Delegation of Powers

Since neither the federal nor the provincial levels of government are considered inferior legislative bodies, both are supreme parliaments in their assigned areas. Over the years, for various reasons, these bodies have sometimes found it necessary to transfer the powers given to them to other levels of government. However, **Direct delegation prohibited** direct delegation between the federal and provincial governments is prohibited. For example, during the Depression of the 1930s, it became clear that a national system of unemployment insurance was needed. The provinces, which have jurisdiction in this area, attempted to delegate their power to the federal government. The court held that they could not do so, as it was an "abdication" of the "exclusive powers" given to the provinces under the *Constitution Act (1867)*. To make unemployment insurance an area of federal responsibility, the British Parliament needed to amend the constitution. This amendment is now incorporated in section 91, subsection (2A) of the *Constitution Act (1867)*.

Although direct delegation is prohibited, it is possible for the federal and provincial governments to delegate their powers to inferior bodies, such as boards and individual civil servants; in fact, this is usually the only way that governmental bodies can conduct their business. It is also possible for the federal government to delegate its power in a particular area to a provincial board or a provincial civil servant. Similarly, a province can give powers to federal boards, **Indirect delegation permitted** since these are also inferior bodies. In this way, governments overcome the prohibition against delegation.

## Agreements to Share Powers

Another means used to circumvent the constitutional rigidity created by the 1867 division of powers is by federal and provincial government agreements to share powers. These agreements may consist of *transfer payment schemes,* or conditional grants under which the transfer of funds from the federal government is tied to conditions for how the money is to be spent. Through such schemes, the federal government can exercise some say as to how a provincial government operates programs that fall under the province's constitutional area of control. The federal government may set certain national standards to which the funding is tied and in this fashion ensure that all Canadians have access to similar levels of service.

Transfer-payment schemes are evident in the areas of health, social programs, and education. One hundred and thirty years ago, government spending on these services was minuscule. Now, these areas may account for two-thirds of all government spending. The provinces, with their restricted taxing powers, would have difficulty providing these services without federal funding. But in recent years, the federal government has dramatically cut payments under the Canada Health and Social Transfer.

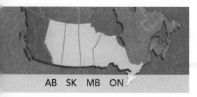

AB   SK   MB   ON

# Legislation

Legislation is introduced to the parliamentary process in the form of a **bill,** which goes through a sequence of introduction, debate, modification, and approval that is referred to as *first, second,* and *third readings.* When a bill is finally enacted, it has the status of a statute (although it may still be referred to as a bill or an act). Such a statute does not have the status of law until it receives the approval (signature) of the governor general at the federal level or the lieutenant-governor in a province, a process referred to as receiving **royal assent.** The governor general and the lieutenant-governors are the Queen's representatives in Canada and can sign on behalf of the Crown. Current convention (practice) in Canada directs the Queen's representatives to sign as the government in power directs them, and such approval is therefore usually a formality. The government may use this requirement to delay the coming into effect of legislation, and care should therefore be taken when examining an act to make sure that it has received royal assent. The statute itself may have provisions for different parts of it to come into force at different times. There are many examples where whole acts, or portions of them, have no legal effect for these reasons. See Figure 1.1 for a summary of the traditional process for passing bills.

**Statutes must receive royal assent**

The Government of Canada publishes a compilation of these statutes annually; the collection can be found in most libraries, under *Statutes of Canada.* The federal government summarized and published all current statutes in the *Revised Statutes of Canada* in 1985, cited as R.S.C. (1985). It is not necessary to go back any earlier than this compilation to find current legislation. Indexes and guides are provided to assist in the process of finding the federal statutes and subsequent amendments.

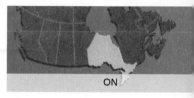

Similarly, each province annually publishes the statutes passed by its legislative assembly and provides a compilation in the form of revised statutes. Unfortunately, there is no uniformity in the timing of the revisions, and each province has revised and summarized its statutes in a different year. Most jurisdictions provide official or unofficial consolidated updates of their statutes online as an ongoing service. These statutes, along with useful commentary about new legislation, are currently available on the Internet at their respective government's website. The Access to Justice Network provides easy access to the laws across the country; see their website at **www.acjnet.org**.

**Federal and provincial statutes summarized and published**

Statutes often empower government agencies to create further rules to carry out their functions. As long as these regulations meet the terms of the statute, they have the effect of law. They are also published and are available to the public as *Regulations of Canada* or of the respective provinces. Cities and municipalities pass bylaws under their statutory authority in the same way, and these too are published and made available by those jurisdictions. Statutes passed within the power of the respective governments as set out in the *Constitution Act (1867)* and other constitutional provisions override any previous law in place, whether judge-made law (common law or equity) or prior legislation. A trial judge required to deal with a statute must first determine what it means. This task is not always easy, since the legislation is not usually drafted by someone who can anticipate all of the situations in which it will be applied or who understands all the legal implications of the wording. The judge must then determine whether, under the *Constitution Act (1867)* and other constitutional provisions, the legislative body that passed the statute in question had the power to do so. When a judge interprets and applies a statute that decision becomes a precedent, and henceforth the statute must be interpreted in the same way by courts lower in the court hierarchy, thus becoming part of judge-made or common law.

**Regulations also published**

**Judges interpret and apply statutes**

**Decisions create precedents**

## Figure 1.1 Traditional Passage of Bills

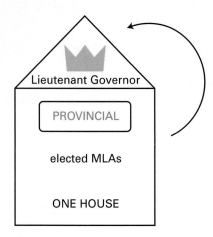

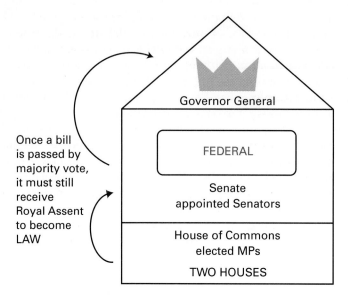

Once a bill is passed by majority vote, it must still receive Royal Assent to become LAW

**First Reading**—Bill is introduced in the Legislative Assembly. Customarily passes first reading without debate.

**Second Reading**—Bill is read again. Now debated. After approval, it may go to Committee of the Whole for review and amendment.
The Committee of the Whole must approve all bills before they can receive a third reading.

**Third Reading**—Bill is read again. Final debate. **VOTE** held.

**First Reading**—Introduction (by government, private member, or possibly by all-party committee*[1]). Bill is printed.
May go to all-party committee after approval.*[2]

**Second Reading**—Bill is debated. After approval in principle, the Bill goes to all-party committee, which may recommend amendments.

**Third Reading**—Final debate and **VOTE**.

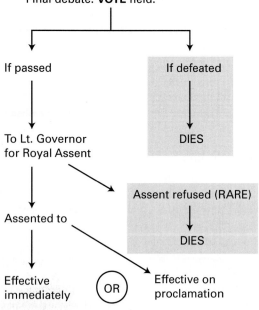

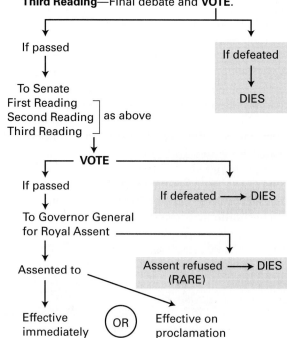

The Federal Government now allows for two variations from the "traditional" passage of bills.*[1] A motion may be tabled for a Committee to prepare and introduce a bill.*[2] Bills may now be referred to Committee BEFORE second reading. In any event, a bill only goes to Committee ONCE.

# Protection of Rights and Freedoms

As noted earlier in this chapter, the preamble of the *Constitution Act (1867)* states that Canada will have "a Constitution similar in principle to that of the United Kingdom." The courts have interpreted that phrase as importing into Canada the unwritten conventions and traditions of government developed in the United Kingdom over the centuries. Among those unwritten conventions are the practices of protecting and preserving fundamental rights and freedoms. Canada has, thus, inherited the British tradition of protecting human rights and individual freedoms through unwritten conventions (practices) as supported by common law.

In the aftermath of the Second World War, concern arose over the adequacy of entrusting the protection of personal rights and freedoms to common law. Two streams of legislation developed, one dealing with protecting human rights against abuses by the government and the second aimed at protecting individuals against discrimination and intolerance by society at large.

## Canadian Bill of Rights

It is important to understand that the basic human rights protections set out in ordinary statutes passed by the federal or provincial governments may not protect people from abuses by government. Because Canada adopted the British method of government, which is based on the supremacy of Parliament, the provincial and federal governments were free to interfere at will with civil rights through legislation. One need look no further than the way the Japanese Canadians were treated during the Second World War to conclude that it could be dangerous for Canadians to leave the protection of their basic rights to the political process.

The first attempt at limiting the federal government's power to pass legislation that violates basic human rights was the passage of the *Canadian Bill of Rights* (in 1960).[16] Because it was not entrenched in the Constitution, the courts viewed the *Bill of Rights* as just another statute that could be repealed, amended, or simply overridden by any subsequent federal statute. Furthermore, when asked to apply the *Bill of Rights*, the courts approached its provisions in the same narrow, restrictive way that they did any other legislation, thus significantly limiting its scope and effect. For example, when subsequently passed federal legislation was found to be in conflict with the provisions of the *Bill of Rights*, instead of applying the *Bill of Rights* and limiting the operation of the new statute, the courts would treat the new legislation as overriding the old and would disregard the provisions that conflicted with the new legislation. This, of course, effectively defeated the purpose of the Canadian *Bill of Rights*, and while it is still considered law in Canada its effectiveness is extremely limited. Something more was needed.

*Bill of Rights* **just another statute**

## *Charter of Rights and Freedoms*

A constitutional guarantee of basic rights and freedoms arose in 1982 following a series of constitutional conferences. The *Constitution Act (1982)*[17] was simultaneously enacted in Canada and England. In England, it was contained in a statute

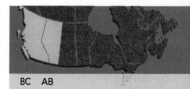

BC   AB

---

16. S.C. 1960, c. 44.

17. Schedule B to the *Canada Act 1982* (U.K.) 1982, c. 11.

called the *Canada Act 1982.*[18] One effect of these enactments was to make a very significant addition to the Canadian Constitution in the form of the Canadian *Charter of Rights and Freedoms.*

**The Constitution includes the *Charter***

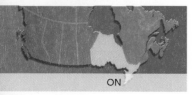

**is the supreme law of Canada**

The effect of including the *Charter* in our Constitution is twofold. First, neither the federal government nor the provinces have the power to modify or otherwise interfere with the basic rights set out in the *Charter* except through constitutional amendment. Ordinary legislation will not override the *Charter* simply because it is passed subsequent to the *Charter.* The provisions are said to be *entrenched* in the Constitution and are, as declared in section 52 of the *Constitution Act (1982),* "*the supreme law of Canada.*" The section goes on to state: "Any law that is inconsistent with the provisions of the Constitution is, to the extent of that inconsistency, of no force or effect." In other words, the *Charter* and the rights protected by it come first.

**Courts are empowered to strike down offending statutes**

Second, the burden of protecting those rights has shifted from the politicians to the judges. Now, an individual who feels that his or her rights have been interfered with by legislation or other forms of government action can seek redress from the courts, relying on the provisions of the *Charter.* The courts can remedy a violation of rights by excluding evidence improperly secured and can grant any remedy deemed just in the circumstances.[19] The courts can even strike down statutes that infringe on rights. Hence, the doctrine of parliamentary supremacy has been to some extent limited, the courts now being able to check the power of Parliament and the legislatures in those areas covered by the *Charter.*

### Case Summary 1.5

**Freedom of Expression versus Pornography: *R. v. John Robin Sharpe*[20]**

Court decisions in the *Sharpe* case caused public outrage. The accused was charged with two counts of simple possession of child pornography and two counts of possession for the purpose of distribution and sale, contrary to the *Criminal Code.* At trial, he successfully argued that the simple possession charge violated his freedom of expression, a freedom guaranteed by section 2(b) of the *Charter.* Further, this infringement could not be justified under section 1 of the *Charter,* for the wording of the charge was so broad that even innocent photos of children in the bath could fall within the *Code*'s definition of pornography.

Section 1 of the *Charter* asserts that the rights and freedoms set out in the *Charter* are guaranteed, subject to justifiable, reasonable limits. It is up to the courts to determine whether a law that violates these rights can be justified (as a reasonable limit on individuals' rights), or whether it should be struck down (because the violation is unjustifiable). Critics argued that the law was so encompassing that even fictional stories concerning imaginary children would be caught. Justice Anne Rowles, of the B.C. Court of Appeal, said that the *Criminal Code* section was "truly only one step removed from criminalizing simply having objectionable thoughts."[21] The potential violation of freedom of expression could not be excused.

---

18. *Canada Act 1982,* (U.K.) 1982, c. 11.

19. *Canadian Charter of Rights and Freedoms,* s. 24, Part I of the *Constitution Act 1982,* being Schedule B to the *Canada Act 1982* (U.K.), 1982, c.11.

20. *R. v. Sharpe,* [2001] 1 S.C.R. 45.

21. *R. v. Sharpe,* B.C.C.A. 1999 416, at paragraph 198.

Demands were made on federal Justice Minister Anne McLellan to invoke the notwithstanding clause if necessary, to enact new legislation that would hold up against a *Charter* challenge. McLellan rejected these demands to override the *Charter*, insisting instead that the matter proceed through the appeal process.

Eventually, the Supreme Court of Canada ruled on the matter and the challenged sections of the *Criminal Code* were upheld. The child pornography law was interpreted in such a manner that any overbreadth would be minimized. Thus, representations of casual intimacy or non-sexual nudity would not be covered by the offence.

As to criminalizing possession of written materials or visual recordings, the Court admitted that there were two problematic applications that bordered on thought control, and so it created an exception for (1) any written material or visual representations created by the accused alone or held by him exclusively for his own use, and (2) any visual recording created by or depicting the accused, provided it does not depict unlawful sexual activity and is held for his private use. Consequently, the Crown can continue to lay charges of unlawful possession of child pornography, and action to protect children from this abuse can proceed.

*Charter* cases present interesting issues. Consider these: (1) Are you comfortable with the courts having the power to declare legislation inoperative if it violates the *Charter*? Who gave the courts this power? (2) Does the court's power to strike down legislation create uncertainty as to what is the law?

## Limitations

There are three important limitations on the entrenchment of these basic rights. Section 1 of the *Charter of Rights and Freedoms* allows "reasonable limits" on those rights and freedoms when limiting them can be "demonstrably justified in a free and democratic society." This gives the courts the power to interpret the provisions of the *Charter* to avoid an unreasonable result. The rights and freedoms set out in the *Charter* are, therefore, not absolute. For example, the *Charter* guarantees freedom of expression, but there would be little dispute that libel, slander, or hardcore pornography must be controlled.

**Government cannot interfere with basic rights and freedoms, except: if reasonable to do so**

The Supreme Court was asked in *Hill v. Church of Scientology of Toronto (1995)*[22] to give effect to the freedom of expression provision of the *Charter* by dismissing a defamation action against the Church and its representative, especially where the remarks were directed at a government official or Crown prosecutor. The Court found that the laws of defamation were, under section 1, a reasonable limitation on the operation of the freedom of expression clause of the *Charter*, thus confirming the lower court's finding of defamation and the highest defamation award up to that time in Canada.

The interests of the public are considered when applying section 1. Nonetheless, a law that restricts *Charter* rights, though apparently justified, will be rejected if it goes too far. For example, section 1 of the *Charter* was used to justify the imposition of reasonable limits on the rights of prisoners; prisoners serving two years or more in jail could not vote in federal elections. The Federal Court of Appeal found that the voting bans violated section 3 of the *Charter* but were justifiable in light of the objectives of the amended *Canada Elections Act*, specifically the foster-

---

22. [1995] 2 S.C.R. 1130.

ing of civic responsibility and respect for the rule of law.[23] These objectives were important enough to warrant (in some cases) a compromise of *Charter* rights. But on further appeal, the Supreme Court of Canada overturned this decision, reasserting prisoners' right to vote. (See Case Summary 1.9 later in this chapter.)

### Case Summary 1.6

#### Law Prohibiting Hate Propaganda Justified Despite Violation of Freedom of Expression: *R. v. Keegstra*[24]

James Keegstra, an Alberta high school teacher, was charged under section 319(2) of the *Criminal Code* with wilfully promoting hatred against an identifiable group by communicating anti-Semitic statements to his students. Before the trial was heard, Keegstra challenged the validity of the charge arguing that section 319(2) violated his freedom of expression. That challenge was dismissed, and Keegstra was tried and convicted. On the appeal, however, Keegstra successfully argued that section 319(2) of the *Code* violated his freedom of expression and, further, that section 319(3)(a) infringed his presumption of innocence. Section 319(3)(a) affords a defence of "truth" to the wilful promotion of hatred, but only where the accused proves the truth of the communicated statements on a balance of probabilities. Keegstra argued that this reverse onus, requiring him to prove the truth of the statements, violated his presumption of innocence.

The matter was appealed to the Supreme Court of Canada. Where the Supreme Court and the Alberta Court of Appeal differed, however, was in their assessments as to whether these infringements were justifiable under section 1 of the *Charter*. Contrary to the Court of Appeal, the Supreme Court of Canada declared them to be constitutional. The objective of preventing the harm caused by hate propaganda was found to be of sufficient importance to warrant overriding a constitutional freedom. Further, the Supreme Court of Canada determined that there was minimal impairment to the presumption of innocence caused by section 319(3)(a), which, in light of the object of preventing the harm caused by hate propaganda, was justifiable.

Should *Charter* rights be absolute, enabling courts to automatically strike down laws that violate these rights? Or, is it preferable to have the courts determine whether such laws are justifiable—perhaps for the good of society as a whole? What do you think?

The second limitation is contained in section 33. It allows each of the provinces and the federal government to override the basic rights contained in section 2 and sections 7 through 15 of the *Charter* simply by stating that the new legislation operates "notwithstanding" (regardless of) the *Charter*. The sections that can be overridden in this way include **fundamental freedoms** (such provisions as freedom of conscience and religion, of thought and belief, of opinion and expression, and of assembly and association); **legal rights** (the right of life, liberty, and security of person; security against unreasonable search and seizure, arbitrary imprisonment and detention); and **equality rights** (the right not to be discriminated against on the basis of gender, age, religion, race, or colour; and the guarantee of equality before the law).

---

23. *Sauvé v. Canada* (Chief Electoral Officer)(C.A.), [2002] 2 F.C.119.

24. *Keegstra, supra* note 4.

It would appear that section 33 weakens the *Charter of Rights and Freedoms* considerably. The supremacy of Parliament appears to have been restored, at least in relation to the designated sections. It was originally hoped that most provinces would find the political cost too great to override the *Charter* in this way and, as a result, would refrain from doing so; for the most part, this has been the case. Quebec, however, used the notwithstanding clause to support language legislation restricting the use of English on business signs in that province. This legislation clearly violates the *Charter*'s guarantee of freedom of expression, but the Quebec government gambled that the majority of the electorate would favour such protection of the French language. There are very few other examples of the clause being used, and Alberta's experiments with invoking the clause have been controversial. The notwithstanding clause does not apply to the sections guaranteeing democratic rights (the right to vote, to elect members to Parliament and the legislative assemblies), mobility rights (the right to enter and leave Canada), or language rights (the right to use both official languages). In addition, the rights of aboriginal people and the rights guaranteed to both genders cannot be overridden by the federal or provincial governments.

**Use of notwithstanding clause may be a political gamble**

A "sunset clause" is applied to the operation of section 33. If the notwithstanding clause is invoked, the statute must be re-enacted by that legislative body every five years. This forces a re-examination of the decision to override the *Charter,* which will likely involve different legislators who may not be as willing to pay the political cost of using the notwithstanding clause.

**Sunset clause**

The third limitation is the restriction of the operation of the *Charter* to government and government-related activities. Section 32(1)(a) declares that the *Charter* applies only to matters falling within the authority of "the Parliament and Government of Canada" and the territories, and section 32(1)(b) makes the *Charter* apply "to the legislature and government of each province." A serious problem facing the courts is determining just where government stops and government institutions acting in a private capacity start. Are government institutions—universities, schools, hospitals, and Crown corporations such as the CBC—affected?

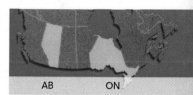

*Charter* **applies only to the government—but where does government stop?**

While there are still many questions, it does seem clear that when such institutions are acting as an arm of government, the *Charter* applies. Certainly the *Charter* applies to the legislation creating these institutions and to the services provided directly by government departments, including the police and military. When government agencies act in their private capacity (for example, in employee relations), the appropriate federal or provincial human rights legislation applies, and such legislation must, in turn, comply with the provisions of the *Charter*. If a section of a statute is in conflict with the provisions of the *Charter,* the offending section will be void, or an appropriate section will be added. In the *Vriend* case[25] (discussed in Case Summary 1.13), the Supreme Court of Canada showed its willingness to interpret into the Alberta statute a provision prohibiting discrimination on the basis of sexual orientation rather than overturning the statute. Occasionally, the courts have declared legislation invalid but have stayed (held in abeyance) their decision in order to give the legislators an opportunity to amend the statutes themselves.[26]

*Charter* **probably applies to private institutions acting as arms of government**

While the *Charter* directly affects an individual's relationship with government, it only indirectly affects the relationships between individuals and between indi-

---

25. *Vriend v. Alberta,* [1998] 1 S.C.R. 493.

26. See *Haig v. Canada* (1992), 9 O.R. (3d) 495 (Ont. C.A.).

viduals and private institutions. Human rights legislation impacts these latter relationships, but these federal and provincial human rights codes must comply with the *Charter*. It is also important to remember that the provisions of the *Charter* apply not only to the regulations and enactments of these government bodies and institutions but also to the conduct of government officials employed by them. These officials derive their authority from provincial or federal enactments. If they are acting in a way that violates the provisions of the *Charter*, either they are not acting within their authority, or their action itself is in violation of the *Charter*. In either case, such offending conduct can be challenged under the *Charter*.

## *Charter* Provisions

A brief summary of the types of rights and freedoms Canadians now enjoy because of the *Charter of Rights and Freedoms* follows. (The complete *Charter* is provided in Appendix 1B, immediately following this chapter.) The *Charter* sets out several rights that are available in some cases only to citizens of Canada and in other cases to everyone in the nation. The extent of these rights and freedoms, their meaning, and the limitations on those rights are still being defined by court decisions. Recourse is available through the courts if the declared rights are interfered with by laws or by the acts of government agents. The courts have been empowered under section 24 of the *Charter* to "provide such remedies as the court considers appropriate and just in the circumstances." These powers are in addition to the inherent power of the court to declare that the offending legislation or conduct is of no effect. This provision allows the courts to award damages, injunctions, and other remedies, when otherwise they would have had no power to do so. Section 24 also gives a judge the power in a criminal matter to exclude evidence that has been obtained in a way that violates the *Charter* rights of the accused, if its admission "would bring the administration of justice into disrepute."

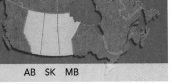

AB SK MB

### Fundamental Freedoms

**Freedom of conscience and religion; thought, belief and opinion; freedom of the press; of peaceful assembly; of association given to everyone in Canada**

Section 2 of the *Charter* declares certain underlying fundamental freedoms available to everyone in Canada. These are freedom of conscience and religion, freedom of belief, opinion, and expression, and freedom of assembly and association. The *Charter* protects the right to believe in whatever we wish, to express that belief, and to carry on activities associated with it free from interference. When the expression of those freedoms or the activities associated with them interferes with the freedoms of others, the courts may restrict those freedoms by applying section 1 of the *Charter*.

**Case Summary 1.7**

#### Sunday Shopping: Does It Prevent Corporations from Going to Church? *R. v. Big M Drug Mart Ltd.*[27]

In this case, the corporation was charged with violation of the *Lord's Day Act*, which required that all such businesses be closed on Sunday. This statute was enacted by the federal government under its criminal law power long before the enactment of the *Charter*. It compelled the observance of a religious duty by means of prohibitions and penalties. This matter went to the Supreme Court of

---

27. [1985] 1 S.C.R. 295.

Canada, which held that the *Lord's Day Act* was invalid and of no effect because it interfered with the right of freedom of conscience and religion. It did not matter that the applicant was a corporation incapable of having a conscience or beliefs. Any accused, whether corporate or individual, may defend a criminal charge by arguing that the law under which the charge is brought is constitutionally invalid. Even after the decision in the *Big M Drug Mart* case, many municipalities have passed bylaws requiring that businesses be closed on Sunday or some other day. Some of these have been overturned for the same reason, but others have been upheld.

## Case Summary 1.8

### Choice of Day of Rest Is Critical: *London Drugs Ltd. v. Red Deer (City)*;[28] *Super Sam Red Deer Ltd. v. Lethbridge (City)*[29]

In the *London Drugs* case, the bylaw requiring closure of retail sales businesses was found to be valid. The Alberta Court of Appeal determined that unlike the impugned law in the *Big M Drug Mart* case (which allowed no alternative day to close operations), the bylaw in question gave full and free choice. Red Deer's bylaw was found to be secular, as opposed to religious, in purpose. It simply required that businesses close for one day per week to allow employees a day of rest. The fact that the bylaw contained a formula, naming Sunday closing unless another day of the week were chosen, did not infringe on religious freedom. The bylaw was found to treat all businesses equally, as each was given the choice as to when to close.

Contrast the above result with that in the *Super Sam* case, where the Lethbridge bylaw required Sunday closure. The Court found this bylaw unconstitutional. It considered the *London Drugs* case decision but found that the bylaws differed in one significant feature. Red Deer allowed a retailer complete freedom of choice in selecting the day for closure. The Lethbridge bylaw provided no choice. The absence of choice indicated that the City of Lethbridge made no attempt to accommodate other religions; thus, the bylaw was declared inoperative.

Freedom of expression, which includes freedom of the press, is an extremely important provision for preserving the democratic nature of Canada, and our courts are very careful to uphold these freedoms. Still, there are many limitations on them, such as the laws of defamation and obscenity. Similarly, the rights to peaceful assembly and freedom of association have been limited when riots may occur; in the field of employment, when employer rights are interfered with by inappropriate trade union activity, limits may be imposed on the right to peaceful assembly. Does freedom of association also include the right not to be forced to associate? The decision of the Supreme Court of Canada in *R. v. Advance Cutting and Coring Ltd.*)[30] suggests a right *not* to associate is implied. The *Quebec Construction Act* required employees to join one of a list of unions. Employers and construction workers could be convicted if the workers did not have competency

---

28. (1987), 55 Alta. L.R. (2d) 56 (Q.B.); aff'd (1988), 61 Alta. L.R. (2d) 1 (C.A.); leave to appeal to S.C.C. refused.

29. (1990), 75 Alta. L.R. (2d) 99 (Q.B.).

30. [2001] S.C.J. No. 68.

certificates. Five of the nine justices of the Supreme Court of Canada found that the legislation did infringe the implied negative right not to associate. But as one of those five found that the infringement could be justified under section 1, the majority concluded that that the legislation should not be struck down as unconstitutional. The decision does support, however, the existence of a right not to associate.

Take note: the rights set out in section 2 can be overridden by the use of the notwithstanding clause (section 33), putting a further limitation on the fundamental freedoms those in Canada enjoy.

### Democratic Rights

**Right to vote, to be elected and to have government sit annually**

Sections 3, 4, and 5 protect our rights to vote and to qualify to be elected to the House of Commons or the provincial legislative assemblies. Reasonable limitations can be put on the right to vote, restricting those who are underage and, most likely, the mentally incompetent. But the abuses of the past, where racial groups were denied the vote, are now prohibited. These rights were protected in the past by constitutional convention, but now they are enshrined in the *Charter*. Section 4 ensures that there will be an election at least every five years, except in times of war, and section 5 requires that the elected body be called into session at least once every 12 months. The government in power still has the right to decide when to call an election within that five-year period and also whether to call the session into sitting more often than the "once every 12 months" minimum. The government also has the power to determine what that session will consist of, which also gives some potential for abuse. These sections cannot be overridden by the notwithstanding clause, a distinction of which the courts have taken notice (see Case Summary 1.9).

**Maximum duration is five years unless crises loom**

### Case Summary 1.9

**Ballot Boxes in Jails:** *Sauvé v. Canada (Chief Electoral Officer)*[31]

All prison inmates were prohibited from voting in federal elections by the former provisions of the *Canada Elections Act*. That Act was held unconstitutional as an unjustified denial of the right to vote guaranteed by section 3 of the *Charter* in *Sauvé v. Canada (Attorney General)*.[32] Parliament responded to this litigation by changing the Act, denying the right to vote to a smaller group—those inmates serving sentences of two years or more. The issue in this case was whether the new provisions were likewise unconstitutional. It was argued that they violated the right to vote (section 3) and equality rights as protected by section 15. The Crown conceded that the Act contravened section 3 of the *Charter*. The key issue was thus whether this restriction could be demonstrably justified under section 1.

The Court decided that the violation was not justified. As stated by Chief Justice McLachlin: "The right to vote, which lies at the heart of Canadian democracy, can only be trammeled for good reason. Here the reasons do not suffice ... *Charter* rights are not a matter of privilege or merit, but a function of membership in the Canadian polity that cannot be lightly set aside. This is manifestly true of the right to vote, the cornerstone of democracy, exempt from the incursion permitted on other rights through s. 33 override."

31. [2002] S.C.J. No. 66.

32. [1993] 2 S.C.R. 438.

## Mobility Rights

Section 6 of the *Charter* ensures that Canadians can travel and live anywhere within the geographic limitations of Canada as well as enter and leave the country at will. It also ensures that all Canadians have the right to earn a livelihood in any part of Canada. But again these assurances are qualified. Programs that are of general application in a province or region can be valid even though they appear to interfere with these rights. In the field of employment, for instance, provincial licensing and educational requirements may prevent people trained and licensed in other parts of the country from carrying on their chosen profession without requalifying in that province. Section 6(4) specifically allows for programs that are designed to better the condition of those "who are socially or economically disadvantaged," even when those programs interfere with the mobility rights of other Canadians who might want to take advantage of the programs but are prohibited from doing so.

**Citizens enjoy right to enter and leave Canada**

### Case Summary 1.10

#### Non-resident Asserts the Right to Earn a Living: *Basile v. Attorney General of Nova Scotia*[33]

Under the *Direct Sellers' Licensing and Regulation Act*,[34] anyone involved in the activity of direct selling (door-to-door sales) in Nova Scotia had to be a resident of that province. Mr. Basile was a bookseller and a resident of Quebec. He applied for a licence to sell in Nova Scotia and was refused because he was not a permanent resident as required by the statute. He challenged this decision as a violation of his mobility rights under the *Charter of Rights and Freedoms*. This was clearly an infringement of the mobility rights under the *Charter*, which gave any Canadian the right to travel to and earn a living in any part of the country. The main difficulty was to decide whether this fell into one of the exceptions set out in either section 6(3)(a) (laws of general application) or the reasonable limitation clause in section 1 of the *Charter*. The Court held that this did not qualify as a law of general application, since it was directed at one specific group—non-residents—and also that no evidence had been presented that would support the argument that this was a reasonable limitation as required under section 1 of the *Charter*. Mr. Basile was successful, and the offending section was declared by the Court to be "of no force and effect."

## Legal Rights

The rights listed under this heading are intended to protect individuals from unreasonable interference from the government or its agents, to ensure that when there is interference, it is done according to the rules of natural justice and that any punishment is neither excessive nor unreasonable. Section 7 states that we have the right to life, liberty, and the security of person and the right not to have these rights taken away, except in accordance with the "principles of fundamental justice." In the *Baker* case, where the Supreme Court examined the procedure followed at the deportation hearings, Justice L'Heureux-Dubé summarized what is required by the principles of fundamental justice—or, in other words, by

**Everyone granted a right to life, liberty and security of person**

---

33. (1984), 11 D.L.R. (4th) 219, N.S.S.C. (A.D.).

34. S.N.S. 1975, c. 9.

the rules of procedural fairness. "The values underlying the duty of procedural fairness relate to the principle that the individual or individuals affected should have the opportunity to present their case fully and fairly, and have decisions affecting their rights, interests, or privileges made using a fair, impartial, and open process, appropriate to the statutory, institutional, and social context of the decision."[35] It is important to note that the protection provided in this section does not extend to interference with property rights. There is no specific reference to property rights in the *Charter*.

Sections 8 and 9 prohibit such activities as unreasonable search and seizure and arbitrary imprisonment. Subsequent sections provide for the right to be informed of the reason for an arrest, the right to retain counsel, the right to be tried within a reasonable time, the presumption of innocence, the right not to be tried twice for the same offence, and the right not to be subjected to any cruel or unusual punishment. The common theme here is to protect people from abusive, arbitrary, or unequal application of police and prosecutorial power. Not only is the individual protected in the event of such an abuse, but the provisions also serve to discourage the police and prosecutors from acting outside the law. The powers given to the courts further help to persuade the law-enforcement community to act properly by allowing the court to exclude evidence obtained in violation of these provisions, where not to do so "would bring the administration of justice into disrepute" (see section 24(2)). These basic legal rights can be overridden by the invocation of the notwithstanding clause.

**Everyone to be secure from unreasonable search, seizure, detention, or imprisonment**

**Everyone entitled to procedural fairness**

### Case Summary 1.11

**A Right to Die?** *Rodriguez v. British Columbia (Attorney General)*[36]

Does the right to life as guaranteed by section 7 of the *Charter* also protect the right to die? Sue Rodriguez, a terminally ill patient, sought the assistance of a physician to commit suicide. The *Criminal Code* of Canada, however, prohibits aiding a person to commit suicide and Rodriguez argued that this violated her rights under sections 7, 12, and 15(1) of the *Charter*. Rodriguez also argued that the guarantee of security of person found in section 7 protected her right to decide what would happen to her body. Control over one's body would be violated if she could not choose to die. She claimed that as her health deteriorated, she would no longer be able to end her own life. The *Code*, to the extent that it precludes a terminally ill person from a "physician assisted suicide," in effect creates inequality. It prevents persons physically unable to end their lives unassisted from choosing suicide, when that option is, in principle, available to other members of the public without contravening the law (since commission of suicide is not a punishable offence or crime). Finally, Rodriguez claimed that forcing her to live in a degenerated body would be cruel and unusual treatment.

In a split decision, the Supreme Court of Canada determined that the right to security of person also had to be viewed in light of the sanctity of life, the right to life also being specifically guaranteed under section 7. Section 12 was not violated by the *Code*, as a prohibition of assisted suicide is not a form of "treatment" by the state. Finally, the majority determined that if equality rights were violated by the *Code*, this violation would be justifiable under section 1. Criminalizing

---

35. *Baker v. Canada (Minister of Citizenship and Immigration)*, [1999] 2 S.C.R. 817, at 841.

36. [1993] 3 S.C.R. 519.

assisted suicide was to protect the sanctity of life and prevent abuses. The Court was not prepared to go down the path toward decriminalization of euthanasia out of concern it might lead to abuses. "Active euthanasia," or doctor-assisted suicide, remains illegal in Canada.

Might the Court address this issue differently in the future as demands on scarce healthcare resources increase with Canada's aging population? Or is it more likely that politicians will be pressured to legislate guidelines for doctor-assisted suicide? What do you think?

## Equality Rights

The equality rights set out in section 15 of the *Charter* prohibit discrimination in the application of the law on the basis of gender, religion, race, age, or national origin and ensure that all people in Canada have the same claim to the protection and benefits of the law. This means that the various provisions of the federal and provincial laws must be applied equally to all. Anytime a distinction is made in any provincial or federal law or by a government official on the basis of one of these categories it can be challenged as unconstitutional. Even where the discrimination relates to a category not listed, there is a general prohibition against such discrimination, and so victims will be protected. The courts tend to interpret the Constitution and its provisions broadly. Thus, even though section 15 makes no reference to sexual preference, the courts have had no difficulty in concluding that a denial of benefits to same-sex couples is prohibited because it discriminates against applicants on the basis of their sexual orientation.

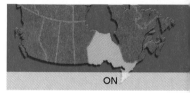

ON

**Every person is to be equal before and under the law**

### Case Summary 1.12

**Courts Prompt Significant Legislative Changes:**
***M. v. H.;*[37] *Halpern v. A.G. of Canada*[38]**

Two women cohabited in a same-sex relationship for 10 years. M. performed many of the household duties, while H. was more involved in business. When their relationship broke down, M. applied for spousal support under Ontario's *Family Law Act.* She argued that the opposite-sex definition of spouse was discriminatory and unconstitutional, as it included married persons and heterosexual couples who had cohabited but had not married, but failed to include same-sex couples. The Courts found the definition violated section 15(1) of the *Charter* as it formally distinguished between M. and others on the basis of sexual orientation. The lower courts favoured "reading in" a non-discriminatory definition of spouse to the legislation, to enable same-sex couples to claim spousal support. The Supreme Court of Canada, however, dismissed the appeal, and chose to sever the offending section from the legislation. It suspended its declaration for six months, to allow the government time to amend the legislation. This would mean that if the government didn't create new legislation, the Supreme Court's decision would result in no spousal benefits being available to either heterosexual or homosexual unmarried couples. In response to this case, the Ontario government amended 67 statutes to extend similar benefits to non-married couples, regardless of their sexual orientation.

---

37. [1999] 2 S.C.R. 3.

38. *Halpern v. Attorney General of Canada* (2003), 65 O.R. (3rd) 161 (C.A.).

The Ontario Court of Appeal later took a different approach when asked to review the common law definition of marriage. It declared the definition of marriage as "one man and one woman" to be invalid as it offends equality rights. It reformulated the definition to the "voluntary union for life of two people to the exclusion of all others," and declared this definition to have immediate effect. Consequently, numerous same-sex couples rushed to secure marriage licences. The federal government responded by referring a proposed bill on same-sex marriages to the Supreme Court of Canada for review.

Which approach do you prefer: the Court rewriting the legislation so that it does not violate the *Charter*, or the Court suspending the operation of its decision when it declares legislation to be unconstitutional to give legislators an opportunity to address the *Charter* violation themselves?

It is important to note that section 15(2) provides for affirmative-action programs. When a provision is intentionally introduced that has the effect of discriminating against one group of people, it may still be allowed if its purpose is to correct an imbalance that has occurred through discrimination in the past. Thus, the government may intentionally set out to hire women or specific ethnic minorities in order to get a better balance in the civil service. This is permissible even though it will have the effect of preventing people of other groups, such as Caucasian men, from having an equal opportunity to obtain those same jobs. Universities often have similar programs to encourage minorities to enter faculties or professions to correct historical imbalance.

In addition to the provisions set out in section 15, there are other provisions in the *Charter* setting out equality rights. Section 28 guarantees that the provisions of the *Charter* apply equally to males and females. Equality rights (protected by section 15) can be overridden by the operation of the notwithstanding clause, but section 28 cannot be overridden.

Section 35 states that the *Charter* in no way affects the aboriginal and treaty rights of the native people of Canada. Although this last provision may have the effect of preserving inequality rather than eliminating it, the object of this section was to ensure that during the process of treaty negotiations and land claim disputes between the provincial governments and the native groups of Canada nothing in the *Charter* would interfere with the special-status rights associated with that group. Section 33 cannot be used to override the protection given to the position of the aboriginal people of Canada.

Although these *Charter* provisions apply only in our dealings with government, it is important for businesspeople to remember that these equality provisions are the essence of most provincial and federal human rights legislation. Since those statutes must comply with the *Charter* provisions, the *Charter* indirectly controls business practices (see Case Summary 1.13, which discusses *Vriend v. Alberta*). In addition, there are many examples of provincial and federal legislation that require all those working on government-funded projects to comply with special federal and provincial programs aimed at correcting past injustices. These special requirements may range from fair-wage policies (where non-union businesses must pay wages comparable with union-negotiated wages) to programs requiring the hiring or promotion of disadvantaged minorities or the correction of gender imbalances in the workforce.[39]

---

39. See, for example, the federal *Employment Equity Act*, S.C. 1995, c. 44.

## Language Rights

The part of the *Charter* headed "Official Languages of Canada" outlined in sections 16 to 22 ensures that French and English have equal status and that the rights of minorities to use those languages are protected.[40] Of the Canadian provinces, only New Brunswick is officially bilingual, and so section 16 of the *Charter* declares that English and French are the official languages of Canada (federally) and of New Brunswick. All federal government activities, including court proceedings, publications, and other services where numbers warrant, must be available in both official languages. Similar rules are established for New Brunswick. Note that some language rights are set out in the *Constitution Act (1867)*. For example, section 3 requires that Quebec provide court services in English as well as French. The *Constitution Act (1867)* also requires that Manitoba provide many government services in both English and French.

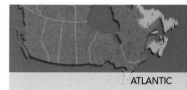

**French and English have equal status—Canada and New Brunswick**

ATLANTIC

Minority-language educational rights, outlined in section 23, are guaranteed for the citizens of Canada, ensuring that those whose first language is English or French and who received their primary education in English or French, or have had one of their children educated in English or French, have the right to have their other children educated in that language. People who are immigrants to Canada have no such rights, no matter what their native language may be. Note that the right to be educated in English or French applies only where community numbers warrant the expense of setting up such a program. Language rights and minority language educational rights cannot be overridden by section 33 of the *Charter*.

## Section 52

The *Constitution Act (1982)* makes other important changes to Canada's Constitution. In addition to declaring that the Constitution is the "supreme law of Canada," section 52 also sets out all the statutes that have constitutional status in an attached schedule. Important amendments are also made to the *Constitution Act (1867)* creating section 92A, which expands the power of the provinces to make law with respect to non-renewable natural resources, including the generation of electric power and forestry resources.

# The Importance of the Changes

The significance of the 1982 additions to the Constitution cannot be overemphasized. The *Charter of Rights and Freedoms* will continue to affect the development of Canadian law over the next century. Traditionally, Canadian courts had adopted the position that their function was to apply the law as it existed. If the law needed to be changed, the judiciary left the job to Parliament and the legislative assemblies. It is clear that the courts have been forced to play a more active role and create new law through their interpretation and application of the provisions of the *Charter*. The broad, generalized nature of the *Charter* provisions contributes to this more expansive role of the courts. Statutes have traditionally been interpreted in a very narrow way, and because of this they are always very carefully and precisely

---

40. For an example, see *R. v. Beaulac*, [1999] 1 S.C.R. 768, where the accused succeeded in appealing his conviction on murder charges and a new trial was ordered because the trial judge refused his request for a trial before a bilingual judge and jury. The trial arose in the province of B.C., and although the accused could express himself in English, his own official language was French.

worded. But the *Charter* provisions are generalizations, and the courts must therefore interpret these broad statements, filling in the gaps and thus making new law.

The *Constitution Act (1982)* also eliminated the requirement that any major change involving Canada's Constitution had to be made by an act of the Parliament of Great Britain. Because the original *BNA Act* was an act of the British Parliament, any changes to it had to be made by that body. When the provinces and the federal government agreed on a formula for amending the Constitution, the British Parliament passed the *Canada Act*,[41] making Canada completely independent of Britain. It should be emphasized that although Canada's ties to the British Parliament have been severed, our relationship with the monarch remains. The Queen remains the Queen of Canada, just as she is the Queen of the United Kingdom, Australia, New Zealand, and other independent nations.

**Quebec did not agree with patriating the Constitution**

Quebec, however, did not assent to this document. Subsequently, another important agreement that attempted to change this amending formula was drawn up; this agreement was known as the *Meech Lake Accord*. However, the Accord did not receive the required unanimous approval by the provinces within the specified time limit. Its failure and the failure of the subsequent *Charlottetown Accord* (which went to a national referendum) have created a constitutional crisis in Canada, with Quebec seeking independence. The pro-separatist government in Quebec took the question of sovereignty to a provincial referendum in 1996, which failed by a margin of only 1 percent. Thereafter, the federal government submitted a Reference to the Supreme Court of Canada[42] to determine whether Quebec could unilaterally secede from Canada. Discussions regarding granting Quebec distinct status in Canada have occasioned much debate and dissension within the federation.

AB

## Human Rights Legislation

Whereas the Canadian *Bill of Rights* and the *Charter* address protecting individuals' rights from abuses by government, various federal and provincial statutes have been enacted with the aim of protecting the rights from abuse by the public. Initially, human rights legislation was designed to stop discrimination against identifiable minority groups in specific areas, such as hotels and restaurants. (See *Racial Discrimination Act, 1944* of Ontario.[43]) Today's statutes are broader in scope, protecting individuals against human rights violations, by the public at large, in a variety of settings. The *Canadian Human Rights Act*[44] is one example.

The *Canadian Human Rights Act (CHRA)* applies to abuses in sectors regulated by federal legislation, such as the broadcast and telecommunication industries; similar provincial statutes apply only in areas controlled by provincial legislation.[45] For example, if one is employed by a bank, any human rights complaints

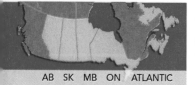

AB  SK  MB  ON  ATLANTIC

41. *Canada Act 1982* (U.K.) 1982, c. 11.

42. *Reference Re Secession of Quebec,* [1998] 2 S.C.R. 217.

43. S.O. 1944, c. 51.

44. R.S.C. 1985, c. H-6.

45. See: *Human Rights Code,* R.S.O. 1990, c. H-5.1; *Charter of Human Rights and Freedoms,* R.S.Q. c. C-12; *Human Rights, Citizenship and Multiculturalism Act,* R.S.A. 2000, c. H-14; *Human Rights Code,* R.S.B.C. 1996, c. 210; *Saskatchewan Human Rights Code,* S.S. 1979, c. S-24.1; *The Human Rights Code,* S.M. 1987-88, c. 45, C.C.S.M. c. H175; *Human Rights Act,* R.S.N.B. 1973, c. H-11; *Human Rights Code,* R.S.N.L. 1990, c. H-14; *Human Rights Act,* R.S.N.S. 1989, c. 214; *Human Rights Act,* R.S.P.E.I. 1988, c. H-12; *Consolidation of Fair Practices Act,* R.S.N.W.T. 1988, c. F-2 (as duplicated for Nunavut by s. 29 of the *Nunavut Act,* S.C. 1993, c. 28); *Human Rights Act,* R.S.Y. 1986, c.11.

concerning activities at work would be brought before the Canadian Human Rights Commission (CHRC), as banks are federally regulated; whereas if one was employed by a provincially regulated retailer, those human rights complaints would be addressed by the provincial human rights commission. These statutes aim at ensuring that individuals will have access to employment (including membership in professional organizations and unions) without facing barriers created through discrimination. Access to facilities and services customarily available to the public, as well as to accommodation (tenancies), is likewise addressed.

Human rights acts protect employees from discrimination in the workplace.

These acts prohibit discrimination relating to gender, religion, ethnic origin, race, age, disabilities, and various other prohibited grounds. The *CHRA* now specifically protects against discrimination on the grounds of sexual orientation and pardoned criminal conviction; not all provincial legislation goes so far. Where protection against discrimination on the basis of sexual orientation has been left out of human rights legislation, the courts have shown a willingness to imply the existence of this protection. The principle applied is that under the *Charter of Rights and Freedoms*, every individual is entitled to the "equal protection and equal benefit of the law"; therefore, such rights ought to have been included. But through such decisions, are the courts in effect rewriting statutes?

**Human rights legislation prohibits discrimination on certain grounds**

## Case Summary 1.13

### Equality Issues Resolved by the Courts: *Vriend v. Alberta*[46]

In 1987, Delwin Vriend was employed by a private religious school in Alberta. His job performance was not in question, but he was dismissed after he "disclosed his homosexuality." He complained under the Alberta *Individual Rights Protection Act* (*IRPA*) to the Alberta Human Rights Commission, claiming that he had been discriminated against because of his sexual orientation. He was told that he could not make such a complaint because the Act did not provide protection against discrimination due to sexual orientation.

This case went to the Supreme Court of Canada, which agreed with the trial court that the protections given by the Act were under-inclusive, protecting some but not all from discrimination. The Supreme Court rewrote the provincial statute so that it complied with section 15 of the *Charter of Rights and Freedoms*. It read sexual orientation into the impugned provisions of the *IRPA*, reasoning that this was the most appropriate way of remedying the under-inclusiveness. In light of the Act's preamble and stated purpose, if the legislature had the choice of

46. *Supra* note 30.

having no human rights statute or having one that extended protection to those historically facing discrimination—such as homosexuals—the latter option would be chosen.

This case is interesting because it raises the issue of how far the courts can go in shaping the law. Can courts merely interpret statutes and enforce them, or does the *Constitution Act (1982)* now empower them to effectively rewrite any legislation that violates *Charter* rights?

What do you think? Is "judicial legislating" proper under Canada's Constitution? Or should the courts merely declare whether legislation is constitutional or not, and then allow the legislators time to amend any contravening legislation?

Even in those provinces where discrimination on the basis of sexual orientation is prohibited, it is still not clear whether the protection given to same-sex relationships will equal that extended to traditional marriages. (See the discussion of the *Halpern* decision in Case Summary 1.12.) For example Alberta, in passing the *Marriage Amendment Act,* invoked the notwithstanding clause (section 33 of the *Charter*) to clarify that, regardless of equality rights, "marriage" means a marriage between a man and a woman.[47] The constitutional validity of this legislation appears doubtful, as defining marriage is a federal matter under section 91 of the *Constitution Act (1867).* The issuance of marriage licences, however, is a provincial matter, and several gay and lesbian couples have recently been married in Ontario following a successful challenge of that province's legislation.[48] It will be interesting to watch how the various provinces grapple with amending their statutes to comply with section 15 of the *Charter.*

**Human rights commissions hear complaints**

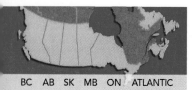

BC  AB  SK  MB  ON  ATLANTIC

Both the federal and the provincial governments have set up special human rights tribunals authorized to hear complaints of human rights violations, to investigate, and, where appropriate, to impose significant sanctions and remedies. There are time limits to consider: a complaint before the CHRC, for example, must be filed within 12 months of the alleged incident. The Commission then proceeds to attempt settlement of the complaint through conciliation and investigation. If all else fails, a panel hearing is convened.

An issue that has arisen since the adoption of the *Charter of Rights and Freedoms* is whether these human rights acts go far enough. The protections extend only to certain areas as identified by the specific federal or provincial legislation—typically, employment, tenancies, public facilities and services, and public signs and notices. Private clubs can still discriminate as to who they will admit as members because discrimination by private facilities is not prohibited by the legislation. This explains why some golf clubs, for example, do not have female members.

Another area addressed by human rights legislation is harassment. The offending conduct in question usually involves the misuse of a position of power or authority to obtain a sexual or some other advantage. Protection against sexual harassment exists because sexual harassment is regarded as a form of discrimination on the basis of gender. Protection against other forms of harassment, although not specifically addressed by legislation, is now being addressed by employers in their policy manuals and in collective agreements. Commission decisions recognize that when there is discrimination in the workplace or where

47. S.A. 1996, c. H-11.7.

48. *Halpern v. Attorney General of Canada* (2003), 65 O.R. (3rd) 161 (C.A.).

public services are provided, there is not only the duty not to discriminate but also the duty to take reasonable steps to accommodate any person who may be discriminated against. This may require anything from creating wider spaces between workstations to accommodate a wheelchair to the provision of a digital reader for a blind person. Failure to accommodate religious beliefs may result in the employer being required to take reasonable steps to rearrange work schedules so that employees are not obligated to work on their Sabbath day. The field of employment is impacted significantly by human rights legislation. This will be treated as a specific topic in Chapter 11.

### Case Summary 1.14

#### Duty to Accommodate Those Facing Discrimination: *Ontario Human Rights Commission et al. v. Simpsons Sears Ltd.*[49]

The clerks employed at a particular branch of Simpsons Sears Ltd. were required to work some Friday nights and two out of every three Saturdays. Mrs. O'Malley, who was a clerk at Sears for three years before joining the Seventh Day Adventist Church, informed her manager that she could no longer work on their Sabbath day (Friday night to Saturday night). Her employment was terminated, and she was hired back part time to accommodate these restrictions. She wanted to continue working full time and laid a complaint with the Ontario Human Rights Commission on the basis of discrimination against her because of her creed. The matter went all the way to the Supreme Court of Canada, which held that discrimination had, in fact, taken place. It was not necessary to show that there was an intention to discriminate, only that there was discrimination in fact. Even where the rule or practice was initiated for sound economic and business reasons, it could still amount to discrimination. The employer was required to take reasonable steps to try to accommodate the religious practices of this employee, short of creating undue hardship on the business. The business had failed to show any evidence of accommodation or that to accommodate would have created undue hardship, and so the complaint was upheld. Simpsons Sears was required to pay Mrs. O'Malley the difference in wages between what she had made as a part-time employee and what she would have made as a full-time employee.

### Case Summary 1.15

#### The Exception for *Bona Fide* Occupational Requirements: *Bhinder et al. v. Canadian National Railway Co.*[50]

Mr. Bhinder was a Sikh who was required by his religion to wear a turban and as a result would not wear a hard hat. His employment was terminated because of this refusal. The Supreme Court held that the requirement that Mr. Bhinder wear a hard hat was not discrimination but rather a bona fide (genuine) requirement of the job. The court held that where such bona fide occupational requirements existed there was no discrimination and therefore no duty to accommodate.

---

49. (1985) 23 D.L.R. (4th) 321 (S.C.C.)

50. (1985) 23 D.L.R. (4th) 481 (S.C.C.)

Part of the mandate of human rights commissions is to promote knowledge of human rights and to encourage people to follow principles of equality. The prohibition of discriminatory signs and notices assists in that end. The federal *CHRA* goes even further and deems it a discriminatory practice to communicate hate messages "telephonically or by means of a telecommunication undertaking within the legislative authority of Parliament."[51] In 2002, Ernst Zundel's internet site was found to have contravened section 13 of the Act. This was Canada's first-ever human rights complaint involving an internet hate site. The Canadian Human Rights Tribunal concluded that the site created conditions that allow hatred to flourish.

Although the *Charter of Rights and Freedoms* has justifiably been given a great deal of attention in recent times, for businesspeople, the human rights codes in force in the various provinces are of greater concern. These codes not only govern how employees are to be treated but also apply to the treatment of customers and those with whom business is conducted. In fact, a significant number of cases before human rights commissions deal with complaints arising from business interactions, usually because of questionable customer-relations practices. A nightclub, for example, that typically demands identification only from customers of certain racial backgrounds may be investigated on allegations of discriminating when granting access to a public facility. Businesspeople are well advised to become familiar with the human rights legislation in place where they do business and to make sure that their activities comply with those regulations.

# Summary

### A workable definition

- Law is the body of rules, made by governments, that can be enforced by courts or government agencies

### Categories of law

- Substantive law governs behaviour
- Procedural law regulates enforcement processes
- Public law comprises constitutional, criminal, and administrative laws
- Private law involves one person suing another

### Origins of law

- Codes in civil law jurisdictions
- Judge-made laws and precedents in common law jurisdictions

### Sources of law

- Common law
- Equity from chancery courts
- Statutes—legislation of federal and provincial governments

### Constitution of Canada

- *Constitution Act (1867)* (*BNA Act*)
- Conventions and traditions of Britain

---

51. *Canadian Human Rights Act,* R.S. 1985, c. H-6, s. 13.

- *Constitution Act* (1982)
- The *Charter of Rights and Freedoms*

## Constitution Act (1867)

- Divides power between federal and provincial governments
- Powers can be indirectly delegated to other levels of government

## Legislative powers

- Set out in *Constitution Act (1867)* sections 91 and 92
- Courts interpret and apply statutes

## Charter

- All legislation must be compliant with *Charter*
- Applies to relationships with government
- Limited by sections 1 and 33

## Human rights

- Federal—provides protection against abuses by businesses within federal jurisdiction
- Provincial—protects individuals in private relationships

--------------------------------------------------------------------------

## QUESTIONS

1. Why is it difficult to come up with a satisfactory definition of law?

2. Where do we look to predict the outcome of a legal dispute:

   a. in a common law system?

   b. in a civil law system?

3. Explain how the use of previous decisions differs in civil law and common law jurisdictions.

4. Describe what is meant by the following statement: "Common law judges did not make the law, they found it."

5. Explain the advantages and the disadvantages of the system of *stare decisis*.

6. Explain which disadvantages in the common law system led to the development of the law of equity.

7. Explain what was accomplished by the *Judicature Acts* of 1873–1875.

8. Explain what is meant by the phrase "the supremacy of Parliament."

9. Explain what effect a properly passed statute will have on inconsistent judge-made law (cases).

10. Explain how a parliamentary bill becomes law.

11. Using the principles of *stare decisis*, explain how judges determine whether or not they are bound by another judge's decision in a similar case.

12. What is included in Canada's Constitution?

13. What is the effect of sections 91 and 92 of the *Constitution Act (1867)*, formerly the *British North America Act*?

14. How did the *Constitution Act (1867)* limit the power of the federal and provincial governments? How is it possible, given the division of powers, to have identical provisions in both federal and provincial legislations and have both be valid? Explain what is meant by the doctrine of paramountcy. When does the doctrine apply?

15. Describe the limitations on the federal and provincial governments' powers to delegate their authority to make laws.

16. Explain the limitations of human rights legislation.

17. Explain how the *Constitution Act (1982)*, including the *Charter of Rights and Freedoms*, affects the doctrine of supremacy of Parliament.

18. Give examples of democratic rights, mobility rights, legal rights, and equality rights as protected under the *Charter*. Give examples of three other types of rights protected under the *Charter*.

19. Explain how the provisions of the provincial human rights codes differ in their application from the *Charter of Rights and Freedoms*.

---

## CASES

### 1. *British Columbia v. Van Gool* (1987), 36 D.L.R. (4th) 481 (B.C.C.A.).

Mr. Van Gool owned property in Surrey, a municipality outside Vancouver, on which he operated an airfield for ultralight planes. His property was in an area designated as an agricultural zone in Surrey, which prevented the use of the property as an airfield except for his own personal use. Since Van Gool rented out space to others, he was in violation of that bylaw. He was also without a permit, licence, or other accreditation or certificate from the federal government to operate an airfield. The problem here is whether the municipal bylaw applies and whether he can be found in violation of it, considering the constitutional division of powers and the jurisdiction of the federal government over aeronautics. Discuss. Would your answer be different if the bylaw in question simply listed what the property could be used for and did not include an airfield? (See *Venchiarutti v. Longhurst* (1992), 92 D.L.R.(4th) 544).)

### 2. *R.B. v. Children's Aid Society of Metropolitan Toronto*, [1995] 1 S.C.R. 315.

In this case, the parents were Jehovah's Witnesses, and when their child was born prematurely with several physical ailments they resisted the recommendations of the doctors to use blood transfusions. An application was made to a Provincial Court judge to make the child a ward of the Court. This was done, and the transfusion was administered. The parents objected to this as an interference with their *Charter* rights. Discuss what sections of the *Charter* they might use in these circumstances as well as the arguments that can be put forward to support the position of the authorities and the likely outcome. Discuss the operation of the *Charter* in these circumstances and whether the transfusion administered to the child violated these basic rights and freedoms.

### 3. *Dartmouth/Halifax (County) Regional Housing Authority v. Sparks* (1993), 101 D.L.R. (4th) 224 (N.S.C.A.).

According to the *Residential Tenancy Act* in place in Nova Scotia, residents who have been renting premises for more than five years have security of tenure, which means that they can be given notice to leave only if they are in violation of their obligations under the lease. The Act, however, specifically excludes people who are living in public housing, and Mrs. Sparks, a single mother with two children, had been living in the public housing for 10 years when she was given one month's notice to leave. She claimed that the *Residential Tenancy Act* provision that makes an exception in the case of public housing discriminated against her. Mrs. Sparks was a black woman, and she argued that because many of the people in public housing were black women on social assistance, they were, as a group, being discriminated against by this provision. What do you think?

### 4. *Roberts v. Ontario* (1994), 117 D.L.R. (4th) 297 (Ont. C.A.).

The Ministry of Health in Ontario started a program to assist disabled children by providing them with various types of devices. That program was gradually expanded to provide services to other disabled people. Part of this service was to assist in providing vision aids for the blind. In 1986, Mr. Roberts, who was legally blind, applied for financial assistance to purchase such a vision aid and was turned down. The reason given was that he was 71 years of age and therefore too old. Mr. Roberts purchased the device himself and filed a complaint under the *Human Rights Code* of Ontario. Explain the likely outcome of that complaint.

# The *Constitution Act, 1867* (formerly the *British North America Act*)

## Sections 91 and 92*
## VI. Distribution of Legislative Powers

### Powers of the Parliament

**Legislative authority of Parliament of Canada**

91. It shall be lawful for the Queen, by and with the Advice and Consent of the Senate and House of Commons, to make Laws for the Peace, Order, and Good Government of Canada, in relation to all Matters not coming within the Classes of Subjects by this Act assigned exclusively to the Legislatures of the Provinces; and for greater Certainty, but not so as to restrict the Generality of the foregoing Terms of this Section, it is hereby declared that (notwithstanding anything in this Act) the exclusive Legislative Authority of the Parliament of Canada extends to all Matters coming within the Classes of Subjects next herein-after enumerated; that is to say,

    1. (Repealed)

1A. The Public Debt and Property (40)

2. The Regulation of Trade and Commerce

2A. Unemployment insurance (41)

3. The raising of Money by any Mode or System of Taxation

4. The borrowing of Money on the Public Credit

5. Postal Service

6. The Census and Statistics

7. Militia, Military and Naval Service, and Defence

8. The fixing of and providing for the Salaries and Allowances of Civil and other Officers of the Government of Canada

9. Beacons, Buoys, Lighthouses, and Sable Island

10. Navigation and Shipping

11. Quarantine and the Establishment and Maintenance of Marine Hospitals

12. Sea Coast and Inland Fisheries

13. Ferries between a Province and any British or Foreign Country or between Two Provinces

14. Currency and Coinage

15. Banking, Incorporation of Banks, and the Issue of Paper Money

16. Savings Banks

17. Weights and Measures

18. Bills of Exchange and Promissory Notes

19. Interest

20. Legal Tender

21. Bankruptcy and Insolvency

22. Patents of Invention and Discovery

23. Copyrights

24. Indians, and Lands reserved for the Indians

25. Naturalization and Aliens

26. Marriage and Divorce

27. The Criminal Law, except the Constitution of Courts of Criminal Jurisdiction, but including the Procedure in Criminal Matters

28. The Establishment, Maintenance, and Management of Penitentiaries

29. Such Classes of Subjects as are expressly excepted in the Enumeration of the Classes of Subjects by this Act assigned exclusively to the Legislatures of the Provinces

And any Matter coming within any of the Classes of Subjects enumerated in this Section shall not be deemed to come within the Class of Matters of a local or private Nature comprised in the Enumeration of the Classes of Subjects by this Act assigned exclusively to the Legislatures of the Provinces.

## Exclusive Powers of Provincial Legislatures

92. In each Province, the Legislature may exclusively make Laws in relation to Matters coming within the Classes of Subject next herein-after enumerated; that is to say,

1. (Repealed)

2. Direct Taxation within the Province in order to the raising of a Revenue for Provincial Purposes

**Subjects of exclusive provincial legislation**

3. The borrowing of Money on the sole Credit of the Province

4. The Establishment and Tenure of Provincial Offices and the Appointment and Payment of Provincial Officers

5. The Management and Sale of the Public Lands belonging to the Province and of the Timber and Wood thereon

6. The Establishment, Maintenance, and Management of Public and Reformatory Prisons in and for the Province

7. The Establishment, Maintenance, and Management of Hospitals, Asylums, Charities, and Eleemosynary Institutions in and for the Province, other than Marine Hospitals

8. Municipal Institutions in the Province

9.   Shop, Saloon, Tavern, Auctioneer, and other Licences in order to the raising of a Revenue for Provincial, Local, or Municipal Purposes

10.  Local Works and Undertakings other than such as are of the following Classes:

 (a) Lines of Steam or other Ships, Railways, Canals, Telegraphs, and other Works and Undertakings connecting the Province with any other or others of the Provinces, or extending beyond the Limits of the Province;

 (b) Lines of Steam Ships between the Province and any British or Foreign Country;

 (c) Such Works as, although wholly situated within the Province, are before or after their Execution declared by the Parliament of Canada to be for the general Advantage of Canada or for the Advantage of Two or more of the Provinces.

11.  The Incorporation of Companies with Provincial Objects

12.  The Solemnization of Marriage in the Province

13.  Property and Civil Rights in the Province

14.  The Administration of Justice in the Province, including the Constitution, Maintenance, and Organization of Provincial Courts, both of Civil and of Criminal Jurisdiction, and including Procedure in Civil Matters in those Courts

15.  The Imposition of Punishment by Fine, Penalty, or Imprisonment for enforcing any Law of the Province made in relation to any Matter coming within any of the Classes of Subjects enumerated in this Section

16.  Generally all Matters of a merely local or private Nature in the Province

# The Constitution Act, 1982

*Charter of Rights and Freedoms**
Schedule B
*Constitution Act, 1982*

## Part I: Canadian Charter of Rights and Freedoms

Whereas Canada is founded upon principles that recognize the supremacy of God and the rule of Law:

### Guarantee of Rights and Freedoms

1. The Canadian Charter of Rights and Freedoms guarantees the rights and freedoms set out in it subject only to such reasonable limits prescribed by law as can be demonstrably justified in a free and democratic society.

   **Rights and freedoms in Canada**

### Fundamental Freedoms

2. Everyone has the following fundamental freedoms:
   (a) freedom of conscience and religion;
   (b) freedom of thought, belief, opinion and expression, including freedom of the press and other media of communications;
   (c) freedom of peaceful assembly; and
   (d) freedom of association.

   **Fundamental freedoms**

### Democratic Rights

3. Every citizen of Canada has the right to vote in an election of members of the House of Commons or of a legislative assembly and to be qualified for membership therein.

   **Democratic rights of citizens**

4. (1) No House of Commons and no legislative assembly shall continue for longer than five years from the date fixed for the return of the writs at a general election of its members.

   **Maximum duration of legislative bodies**

   (2) In time of real or apprehended war, invasion or insurrection, a House of Commons may be continued by Parliament and a legislative assembly may be continued by the legislature beyond five years if such continuation is not opposed by the votes of more than one-third of the members of the House of Commons or the legislative assembly, as the case may be.

   **Continuation in special circumstances**

5. There shall be a sitting of Parliament and of each legislature at least once every 12 months.

   **Annual sitting of legislative bodies**

### Mobility Rights

6. (1) Every citizen of Canada has the right to enter, remain in, and leave Canada.

   **Mobility of citizens**

| | |
|---|---|
| **Rights to move and gain livelihood** | (2) Every citizen of Canada and every person who has the status of a permanent resident of Canada has the right<br><br>   (a) to move to and take up residence in any province; and<br><br>   (b) to pursue the gaining of a livelihood in any province. |
| **Limitation** | (3) The rights specified in subsection (2) are subject to<br><br>   (a) any laws or practices of general application in force in a province other than those that discriminate among persons primarily on the basis of province of present or previous residence; and<br><br>   (b) any laws providing for reasonable residency requirements as a qualification for the receipt of publicly provided social services. |
| **Affirmative action programs** | (4) Subsections (2) and (3) do not preclude any law, program, or activity that has as its object the amelioration in a province of conditions of individuals in that province who are socially or economically disadvantaged if the rate of employment in that province is below the rate of employment in Canada. |

## Legal Rights

| | |
|---|---|
| **Life, liberty, and security of person** | 7. Everyone has the right to life, liberty, and security of the person and the right not to be deprived thereof except in accordance with the principles of fundamental justice. |
| **Search and seizure** | 8. Everyone has the right to be secure against unreasonable search or seizure. |
| **Detention or imprisonment** | 9. Everyone has the right not to be arbitrarily detained or imprisoned. |
| **Arrest or detention** | 10. Everyone has the right on arrest or detention<br><br>   (a) to be informed promptly of the reasons therefor;<br><br>   (b) to retain and instruct counsel without delay and to be informed of that right; and<br><br>   (c) to have the validity of the detention determined by way of habeas corpus and to be released if the detention is not lawful. |
| **Proceedings in criminal and penal matters** | 11. Any person charged with an offence has the right<br><br>   (a) to be informed without unreasonable delay of the specific offence;<br><br>   (b) to be tried within a reasonable time;<br><br>   (c) not to be compelled to be a witness in proceedings against that person in respect of the offence;<br><br>   (d) to be presumed innocent until proven guilty according to law in a fair and public hearing by an independent and impartial tribunal;<br><br>   (e) not to be denied reasonable bail without just cause;<br><br>   (f) except in the case of an offence under military law tried before a military tribunal, to the benefit of trial by jury where the maximum punishment for the offence is imprisonment for five years or a more severe punishment;<br><br>   (g) not to be found guilty on account of any act or omission unless, at the time of the act or omission, it constituted an offence under Canadian or international law or was criminal according to the general principles or law recognized by the community of nations; |

(h) if finally acquitted of the offence, not to be tried for it again and, if finally found guilty and punished for the offence, not to be tried or punished for it again; and

(i) if found guilty of the offence and if the punishment for the offence has been varied between the time of commission and the time of sentencing, to the benefit of the lesser punishment.

12. Everyone has the right not to be subjected to any cruel and unusual treatment or punishment.

**Treatment or punishment**

13. A witness who testifies in any proceedings has the right not to have any incriminating evidence so given used to incriminate that witness in any other proceedings, except in a prosecution for perjury or for the giving of contradictory evidence.

**Self-incrimination**

14. A party or witness in any proceedings who does not understand or speak the language in which the proceedings are conducted or who is deaf has the right to the assistance of an interpreter.

**Interpreter**

## Equality Rights

15. (1) Every individual is equal before and under the law and has the right to the equal protection and equal benefit of the law without discrimination and, in particular, without discrimination based on race, national, or ethnic origin, colour, religion, sex, age or mental or physical disability.

**Equality before and under law and equal protection and benefit of law**

(2) Subsection (1) does not preclude any law, program, or activity that has as its object the amelioration of conditions of disadvantaged individuals or groups including those that are disadvantaged because of race, national, or ethnic origin, colour, religion, sex, age or mental or physical disability.

**Affirmative action programs**

## Official Languages of Canada

16. (1) English and French are the official languages of Canada and have equality of status and equal rights and privileges as to their use in all institutions of the Parliament and government of Canada.

**Official languages of Canada**

(2) English and French are the official languages of New Brunswick and have equality of status and equal rights and privileges as to their use in all institutions of the legislature and government of New Brunswick.

**Official languages of New Brunswick**

(3) Nothing in this Charter limits the authority of Parliament or a legislature to advance the equality of status or use of English and French.

**Advancement of status and use**

16.1 (1) The English linguistic community and the French linguistic community in New Brunswick have equality of status and equal rights and privileges, including the right to distinct educational institutions and such distinct cultural institutions as are necessary for the preservation and promotion of those communities.

**English and French linguistic communities in New Brunswick**

(2) The role of the legislature and government of New Brunswick to preserve and promote the status, rights and privileges referred to in subsection (1) is affirmed.

**Role of legislature and government in New Brunswick**

**Proceedings of Parliament**

17. (1) Everyone has the right to use English or French in any debates and other proceedings of Parliament.

**Proceedings of New Brunswick legislature**

(2) Everyone has the right to use English and French in any debates and other proceedings of the legislature of New Brunswick.

**Parliamentary statutes and records**

18. (1) The statutes, records and journals of Parliament shall be printed and published in English and French and both language versions are equally authoritative.

**New Brunswick statutes and records**

(2) The statutes, records and journals of the legislature of New Brunswick shall be printed and published in English and French and both language versions are equally authoritative.

**Proceedings in court established by Parliament**

19. (1) Either English or French may be used by any person in, or in any pleading in or process issuing from, any court established by Parliament.

**Proceedings in New Brunswick courts**

(2) Either English or French may be used by any person in, or in any pleading in or process issuing from, any court in New Brunswick.

**Communications by public with federal institutions**

20. (1) Any member of the public in Canada has the right to communicate with, and to receive available services from, any head or central office of an institution of the Parliament or government of Canada in English or French, and has the same right with respect to any such institution where

   (a) there is a significant demand for communications with and services from that office in such language; or

   (b) due to the nature of the office, it is reasonable that communications with services from that office be available in both English and French.

**Communications by public with New Brunswick institutions**

(2) Any member of the public in New Brunswick has the right to communicate with, and to receive available services from, any office of an institution of the legislature or government of New Brunswick in English or French.

**Continuation of existing constitutional provisions**

21. Nothing in sections 16 to 20 abrogates or derogates from any right, privilege or obligation with respect to the English and French languages, or either of them, that exists or is continued by virtue of any other provision of the Constitution of Canada.

**Rights and privileges preserved**

22. Nothing in sections 16 to 20 abrogates or derogates from any legal or customary right or privilege acquired or enjoyed either before or after the coming into force of this Charter with respect to any language that is not French or English.

## Minority Language Educational Rights

23. (1) Citizens of Canada

**Language of instruction**

   (a) whose first language learned and still understood is that of the English and French linguistic minority population of the province in which they reside, or

   (b) who have received their primary school instruction in Canada in English or French and reside in a province where the language in which they received that instruction is the language of the

English or French linguistic minority population of the province, have the right to have their children receive primary and secondary school instruction in that language in that province.

(2) Citizens of Canada of whom any child has received or is receiving primary or secondary school instruction in English or French in Canada, have the right to have all their children receive primary and secondary school instruction in the same language.

**Continuity of language instruction**

(3) The right of citizens of Canada under subsections (1) and (2) to have their children receive primary and secondary school instruction in the language of the English or French linguistic minority population of a province

**Application where numbers warrant**

    (a) applies wherever in the province the number of children of citizens who have such a right is sufficient to warrant the provision to them out of public funds of minority language instruction; and

    (b) includes, where the number of those children so warrants, the right to have them receive that instruction in minority language educational facilities provided out of public funds.

## Enforcement

24. (1) Anyone whose right or freedoms, as guaranteed by this Charter, have been infringed or denied may apply to a court of competent jurisdiction to obtain such remedy as the court considers appropriate and just in the circumstances.

**Enforcement of guaranteed rights and freedoms**

(2) Where, in proceedings under subsection (1), a court concludes that evidence was obtained in a manner that infringed or denied any rights or freedoms guaranteed by this Charter, the evidence shall be excluded if it is established that, having regard to all the circumstances, the admission of it in the proceedings would bring the administration of justice into disrepute.

**Exclusion of evidence bringing administration of justice into disrepute**

## General

25. The guarantee in this Charter of certain rights and freedoms shall not be construed so as to abrogate or derogate from any aboriginal, treaty or other rights and freedoms that pertain to the aboriginal peoples of Canada including

**Aboriginal rights and freedoms not affected by *Charter***

    (a) any rights or freedoms that have been recognized by the Royal Proclamation of October 7, 1763; and

    (b) any rights or freedoms that may be acquired by the aboriginal peoples of Canada by way of land claims settlement.

26. The guarantee in this Charter of certain rights and freedoms shall not be construed as denying the existence of any other rights or freedoms that exist in Canada.

**Other rights and freedoms not affected by *Charter***

27. This Charter shall be interpreted in a manner consistent with the preservation and enhancement of the multicultural heritage of Canadians.

**Multicultural heritage**

28. Notwithstanding anything in this Charter, the rights and freedoms referred to in it are guaranteed equally to male and female persons.

**Rights guaranteed equally to both sexes**

| | |
|---|---|
| **Rights respecting certain schools preserved** | 29. Nothing in this Charter abrogates or derogates from any rights or privileges guaranteed by or under the Constitution of Canada in respect of denominational, separate, or dissentient schools. |
| **Applications to territories and territorial authorities** | 30. A reference in this Charter to a province or to the legislative assembly or legislature of a province shall be deemed to include a reference to the Yukon Territory and Northwest Territories, or to the appropriate legislative authority thereof, as the case may be. |
| **Legislative powers not extended** | 31. Nothing in this Charter extends the legislative powers of any body or authority. |

## Application of *Charter*

| | |
|---|---|
| **Application of *Charter*** | 32. (1) This Charter applies |
| |     (a) to the Parliament and government of Canada in respect of all matters within the authority of Parliament including all matters relating to the Yukon Territory and Northwest Territories; and |
| |     (b) to the legislature and government of each province in respect of all matters within the authority of the legislature of each province. |
| **Exception** | (2) Notwithstanding subsection (1), section 15 shall not have effect until three years after this section comes into force. |
| **Exception where express declaration** | 33. (1) Parliament or the legislature of a province may expressly declare in an Act of Parliament or of the legislature, as the case may be, that the Act or a provision thereof shall operate notwithstanding a provision included in section 2 or sections 7 to 15 of this Charter. |
| **Operation of exception** | (2) An Act or a provision of an Act in respect of which a declaration made under this section is in effect shall have such operation as it would have but for the provision of this Charter referred to in the declaration. |
| **Five-year limitation** | (3) A declaration made under subsection (1) shall cease to have effect five years after it comes into force or on such earlier date as may be specified in the declaration. |
| **Re-enactment** | (4) Parliament or the legislature of a province may re-enact a declaration made under subsection (1). |
| **Five-year limitation** | (5) Subsection (3) applies in respect of a re-enactment made under subsection (4). |

## Citation

| | |
|---|---|
| **Citation** | 34. This Part may be cited as the Canadian Charter of Rights and Freedoms. |

## Part VII: General

| | |
|---|---|
| **Primacy of Constitution of Canada** | 52. (1) The Constitution of Canada is the supreme law of Canada, and any law that is inconsistent with the provisions of the Constitution is, to the extent of the inconsistency, of no force or effect. |

# 2

# The Resolution of Disputes— The Courts, Litigation, and Its Alternatives

## CHAPTER HIGHLIGHTS

- The court system in Canada
- The process of litigation
- Problems in the courts
- The alternatives to litigation
- Alternative dispute resolution methods
- Advantages and disadvantages of alternative dispute resolution

In addition to hearing criminal matters, the courts have been charged with the duty of adjudicating civil or private disputes, including assessing liability for injuries and awarding compensation when someone has been harmed by the actions of another. But having the court settle those claims can be an expensive and time-consuming process. While it is always a good idea for the parties to try to resolve their own disputes, when this is not possible they can turn to the courts to adjudicate a resolution. In this chapter, we examine the structure of the courts in Canada and then look at the litigation process, from the initial claim to the enforcement of a judgment. This process is not without its drawbacks, and may result in a decision that neither party is happy with or a judgment that cannot be enforced. The second half of this chapter outlines a variety of alternatives to the litigation process, along with a review of the reasons why businesspeople might choose negotiation, mediation, or arbitration over courts in resolving their disputes.

## The Courts

The process described below outlines the various procedures used at the trial level of the superior courts; students should note that the actual procedure may vary with the jurisdiction. Procedural laws ensure that the hearing will be fair, that all litigants have equal access to the courts, and that parties have notice of an action against them and an opportunity to reply.

**Trials open to public**

As a general rule, Canadian courts are open to the public. The principle is that justice not only must be done but also must be *seen* to be done; no matter how prominent the citizen and no matter how scandalous the action, the procedures are open and available to the public and the press. There are, however, important exceptions to this rule. When the information coming out at a trial may be prejudicial to the security of the nation,[1] the courts may hold **in camera hearings,** which are closed to the public. When children are involved, or in cases involving sexual assaults, the more common practice is to hold an open hearing but prohibit the publication of the names of the parties.[2]

**Both criminal and civil functions**

The courts in Canada preside over criminal prosecutions or adjudicate in civil disputes. While civil matters are the major concern of this text and criminal law is discussed only incidentally, it should be noted that there are some important differences between civil and criminal actions. In civil actions, two private persons use the court as a referee to adjudicate a dispute, and the judge (or, in some cases, the judge with a jury) chooses between the two positions presented. The decision will be made in favour of the side advocating the more probable position. The judge, in such circumstances, is said to be deciding the matter on the *balance of probabilities.*

**Civil test—balance of probabilities**

Criminal prosecutions are quite different. When a crime has been committed, the offence is against the state and the victims of the crime are witnesses at the trial. The government pursues the matter and prosecutes the accused through a Crown prosecutor. Since the action is taken by the government (the Crown) against the accused, such cases are cited as, for example, "*R. v. Jones.*" (The R. stands for either Rex or Regina, depending on whether a king or queen is enthroned at the time of the prosecution.) While a civil dispute is decided on the balance of probabilities, in a criminal prosecution the judge (or judge and jury) must be convinced beyond a reasonable doubt of the guilt of the accused. This is a much more stringent test in that even when it is likely or probable that the accused committed the crime, the accused must be found "not guilty" if there is any reasonable doubt about guilt.

**Criminal test—beyond reasonable doubt**

### Case Summary 2.1

**What Is the Appropriate Burden of Proof?** *Rizzo v. Hanover Insurance Co.*[3]

Mr. Rizzo owned a restaurant that was seriously damaged by fire. When he made a claim under his insurance policy, the insurer refused to pay on the basis of its belief that Mr. Rizzo had started the fire himself. It was clear that the fire was intentionally set and that it was done with careful preparation. Because the restaurant business had not been doing well and Mr. Rizzo was in financial difficulties, the finger of blame was pointed at him. Other evidence damaged his credibility. The Ontario High Court in this case had to decide what burden of proof the insurer should meet. Because the conduct that Mr. Rizzo was being accused of was a crime, he argued that it should be proved "beyond a reasonable doubt." The Court held that because this was a civil action, it was necessary only that the insurer establish that Mr. Rizzo was responsible for setting the fire "on the balance of probabilities" and that it had satisfied that burden. "I have found

---

1. See *Ruby v. Canada,* [2002] S.C.J. No. 73 for a recent discussion of the issue of open courts.

2. *John Doe v. Smith* (2001), 288 A.R. 184 (Q.B.) provides a concise summary of the law on this issue.

3. (1993), 14 O.R. (3d) 98 (C.A.), leave to appeal to S.C.C. refused, [1993] S.C.C.A. No. 488.

on balance that it is more likely than not that the plaintiff did take part in the setting of the fire." As a result, Mr. Rizzo's action against the insurer was dismissed. Note that the fact that Mr. Rizzo had been acquitted of arson in a criminal proceeding was inadmissible in a civil proceeding as proof that he had not committed the arson.

As occurred in this case, even a person who has been acquitted of a crime may be found liable in a civil court for the same conduct. While there may not be enough proof to establish beyond a reasonable doubt that the accused committed the crime, there may be enough evidence to show that he probably committed the wrong. A recent example involves a woman in British Columbia who won a $50 000 judgment against the man she accused of raping her even after he had been acquitted in a criminal prosecution of the sexual assault.[4]

**May face both criminal and civil trial for same matter**

Criminal law is restricted to the matters found in the *Criminal Code,* as well as certain drug control legislation and a few other areas under federal control that have been characterized as criminal matters by the courts. There is a much broader area of law that subjects people to fines and imprisonment but does not qualify as criminal law. This involves regulatory offences, sometimes referred to as *quasi-criminal matters,* and includes such areas as environmental, fishing, and employment offences as well as offences created under provincial jurisdiction, such as motor vehicle, securities, and hunting regulations. Only the federal government has the power to make criminal law, and although people may be punished with fines and sometimes even imprisonment for violations of these regulatory offences, the violations do not qualify as criminal acts. People charged under these provisions usually go through a process similar to prosecution of a summary conviction offence under the *Criminal Code.*[5]

**Regulatory offences**

BC

## Trial Courts of the Provinces

The nature and structure of the courts vary from province to province, but there are essentially four levels, including the Supreme Court of Canada. (Figure 2.1 provides an outline of Canada's court system.) At the lowest level are the provincial courts (their titles vary across Canada). These courts have a criminal jurisdiction over the less serious criminal matters that are assigned to magistrates and judges under the *Criminal Code.* As a separate body, but usually as a division of the provincial courts, most jurisdictions also have small claims courts and family courts. Small claims courts deal with civil matters that involve relatively small amounts of money, usually no more than $10 000.[6] Family courts handle family matters, such as custody issues that arise once the parents have separated. Enforcement of maintenance and alimony can also be dealt with by these courts, but they have no jurisdiction to issue divorces, which must be obtained in the

**Lower and superior courts**

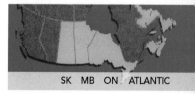

SK   MB   ON   ATLANTIC

4. *J.L.L. v. Ambrose,* [2000] B.C.J. No. 384 (S.C.). The criminal prosecution is unreported in case reports, but was reported in *The Vancouver Sun* (25 February 2000).

5. To view a flowchart depicting the criminal justice process followed when adults are prosecuted for commission of a crime, go to Alberta Justice/Solicitor General, Chart, "Overview of the Justice System: The Criminal Justice Process—Adults," online: Alberta Justice/Solicitor General **http://www.gov.ab.ca/just/lawu/over3.html**.

6. Alberta recently increased the monetary jurisdiction of its small claims court to $25 000. See *Provincial Court Civil Division Regulation,* Alta. Reg. 329/89, s. 1.1.

## Figure 2.1 Outline of Canada's Court System

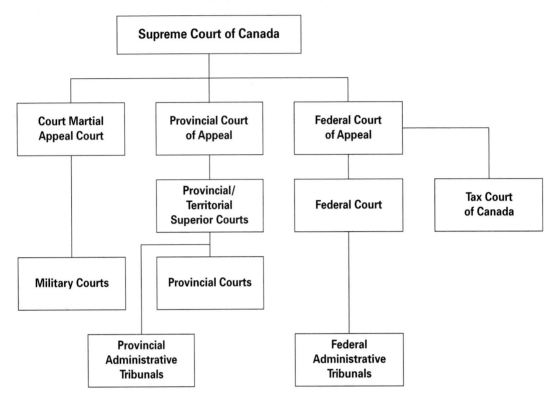

Source: Department of Justice Canada, online: http://canada.justice.gc.ca/en/dept/pub/trib/page3.html.
Note: The Federal Court Trial Division changed its name to Federal Court on July 2, 2003. See explanation on p. 53.

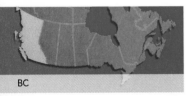

BC

superior trial court.[7] Some provinces maintain separate youth courts. These deal with offences under the *Youth Criminal Justice Act*.[8] In Canada, youth offenders ages 12 to 18 years are subject to the same *Criminal Code* provisions as adults but are subject to a different level of punishment, and so the role of youth courts is very important.

The highest trial level or superior court has an unlimited monetary jurisdiction in civil matters and deals with serious criminal matters. Some provinces have also retained specialized courts, referred to as *surrogate* or *probate courts,* dealing with the administration of wills and estates. In most jurisdictions, however, this is now just a specialized function of the superior court. Similarly, bankruptcy courts operate within the superior court system. These courts deal with the legal aspects of bankruptcy, and must comply with the procedural rules set out in the *Bankruptcy and Insolvency Act*.[9]

It is before the trial courts that the disputing parties in a civil case first appear and testify, the witnesses give evidence, the lawyers make arguments, and a decision is reached. When both a judge and a jury are present, the judge makes find-

7. *Divorce Act,* R.S.C. 1985 (2nd Supp.), c. 3, s. 2(1).

8. S.C. 2002, c.1. This legislation replaced the *Young Offenders Act* on April 1, 2003.

9. R.S.C. 1985, c. B-3.

ings of law, and the jury makes findings of fact. When the judge is acting alone, which is much more common, the judge decides both matters of fact and matters of law. Matters of fact are those regarding the details of an event. For example, was Erasmus at the corner of Portage and Main in the city of Winnipeg at 7:00 a.m. on March 5, 1997? Did a portion of the building owned by Bereznicki fall on Erasmus? Was he paralyzed as a result of his injury? Was Bereznicki aware of the danger? Had she taken steps to correct it? Questions of law, on the other hand, concern the rules or laws that are to be applied in the situation. For example, was Bereznicki obliged to keep the outside of her building in good repair? Would this obligation be affected if Bereznicki were unaware of the danger? The trial itself is discussed in more detail under The Process of Civil Litigation, below.

**Questions of law and fact**

## Recent Developments

Canada's system of courts is dynamic; it is constantly changing to reflect changes in Canadian society. For example, several innovations have recently been made by various governments. For a full understanding of the court system, it is necessary to review these innovations.[10]

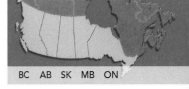

BC  AB  SK  MB  ON

Drug treatment courts have been established in Toronto and Vancouver. The emphasis in these courts is on the treatment of addicts, not incarceration. Non-violent offenders of minor drug offences agree to be bound by the terms of a structured outpatient program designed to reduce their dependence on drugs. They are released on bail, subject to random drug tests, and must appear regularly in court. If they demonstrate control of their addiction, the criminal charges are stayed, or the offender receives a non-custodial sentence. If they cannot demonstrate such control, they are sentenced in the normal way. Research appears to indicate that drug treatment courts are more successful in preventing addicts from reoffending than the traditional court system involving incarceration.[11]

Domestic violence courts have been established in several cities in Canada. (There are 55 such courts in Ontario.[12]) These courts deal with spousal, elder, and child abuse. While the structure and jurisdiction of these courts vary from province to province, most of them offer specialized investigations by police, counselling for first-time offenders, prosecution of repeat offenders by specialized prosecutors, and support services for victims.

Unified family courts have jurisdiction over all legal issues related to the family, and do not deal with any other types of cases. Such courts have been created in several provinces. This simplifies the court process, which can be extremely complicated due to the overlapping jurisdiction of the federal government and the provincial governments. In addition, the court procedures and rules for family cases have been simplified. As is the case with all specialized courts, judges in unified family courts develop expertise in family law.

The Nunavut Court of Justice, established in 1999, is Canada's first single-level court. Judges in this court are given the powers of both the superior trial courts

10. Inspiration and information for this section came from a series of articles included in "Feature on Evolution of the Courts," in *Law Now* 26:4 (February/March 2002) 9, and Department of Justice Canada, "Canada's Court System," online: Department of Justice, Canada **http://canada.justice.gc.ca/en/dept/pub/trib/index.html**.

11. "Canada's First Drug Court Breaks the Cycle of Drugs and Crime" *Law Now, ibid.* at 14–15.

12. Ontario Ministry of the Attorney General, News Release, "Harris Government Expanding Domestic Violence Courts Province-wide" (14 September 2001), online: Canada Newswire **http://www.newswirw.ca/releases/September2001/14/c7592.html**.

and the territorial courts. These judges can therefore hear all of the cases that arise in the territory. The court is a "circuit court," which travels throughout the territory hearing cases.

**Sentencing circles** are found in several provinces, and are used primarily at the provincial court level for cases involving aboriginal offenders and victims. Sentencing circles are not courts. They involve all interested persons meeting in a circle to discuss the offence, including sentencing options. The circle may suggest restorative community sentences, including restitution to the victim and treatment or counselling of the accused. The judge is not bound to accept a circle sentence.

Ontario's Attorney General recently proposed the creation of a specialized court that would deal only with gun-related cases. The province has already trained senior prosecutors to specifically prosecute gun offences. While this proposal has been severely criticized along with the establishment of other specialty courts,[13] it appears that the Canadian court system will continue to evolve in an effort to improve its success in helping Canadians resolve their disputes fairly.

## Courts of Appeal of the Provinces

**Appellate courts**

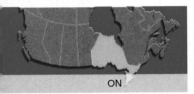

ON

Each province's appellate court hears appeals from the lower courts of that province. They must hear a matter before it can go to the Supreme Court of Canada. In most cases, this is the court of last resort. When one of the parties is dissatisfied with the decision of a provincial trial court and an error in law or procedure is identified, the decision may be successfully appealed. As a general rule, an appeal court will consider a case only when questions of law are in dispute, not questions of fact. But many appeals are based upon questions of mixed law and fact, where the rules that are applied are inseparably connected to the facts that are found. Whether a person lived up to the standards of a reasonable person in a given situation would be an example of such a question of mixed law and fact.

The court exercising an appellate jurisdiction does not hold a new trial. The assumption is that the judge (or judge and jury) who saw and heard all of the evidence presented at trial is (are) best qualified to determine questions of fact. The appeal court judges (usually three) read the transcript of the trial, as well as the trial judge's reasons for decision. They then deal with the specific objections to the trial judge's decision submitted by the appellant's lawyers, hearing the arguments of both the appellant and the respondent.

The judges who serve on provincial superior and appeal courts are appointed by the federal government from a list of candidates supplied by the provinces. Once appointed, the judges have tenure until they retire (by age 75) or are appointed to new positions. They can be removed from the bench only for serious misconduct,[14] but not as the result of a decision that is unfavourable to the federal government, or any other government.

---

13. Dave Brown, "We Don't Need Yet Another Court Freed from the Rules of Fair Trials," *The Ottawa Citizen* (09 January 2003), online: **http://www.ejfi.org/Courts/Courts-8htm**.

14. *Judge's Act,* R.S.C. 1985, c. J-1, s. 65(2).

# Federal Courts

The Federal Court of Canada serves a function similar to that of a provincial superior court. Until July 2, 2003, the Federal Court had a trial division and an appellate division. On that date, the *Courts Administration Service Act*[15] came into effect. The effect of that statute was that the two divisions of the Federal Court became separate courts. The Trial Division became the Federal Court, a trial court. It hears disputes that fall within the federal sphere of power, such as those concerning copyrights and patents, federal boards and commissions, federal lands or money, and federal government contracts. The Federal Court of Appeal kept its previous name; it is an appellate court. It hears appeals from the Federal Court. Both of the federal courts can hear appeals from decisions of federal regulatory bodies and administrative tribunals. The role of these quasi-judicial bodies will be discussed in Chapter 3. An appeal from the Federal Court of Appeal goes directly to the Supreme Court of Canada. The Tax Court of Canada is another very specialized court, which was established in 1983 to hear disputes concerning federal tax matters. This body hears appeals from assessment decisions made by various federal agencies enforcing taxation statutes, such as the *Income Tax Act,* the *Employment Insurance Act,* and the *Old Age Security Act.* Pursuant to the *Courts Administration Service Act,* the Tax Court of Canada became a superior court on July 2, 2003; its powers and jurisdiction did not change. The courts that hear cases involving the military are also specialized courts; a discussion of these courts is beyond the scope of this text.

The Supreme Court of Canada is the highest court in the land.

**Federal Court and
Federal Court of Appeal**

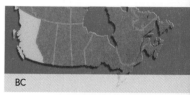

BC

**Supreme Court of Canada**

The Supreme Court of Canada is the highest court in the land. It has a strictly appellate function as far as private citizens are concerned. There are nine judges appointed by the Government of Canada, according to a pattern of regional representation. A quorum consists of five judges, but most appeals are heard by a panel of seven or nine judges. There is no longer an automatic right of appeal to the Supreme Court of Canada (except in criminal cases where a judge in the appellate court dissented on a point of law, or when an appellate court sets aside an acquittal and enters a verdict of guilty[16]). In all other cases, leave to appeal must be obtained from the Supreme Court, and such leave will be granted only if a case has some national significance. The Supreme Court hears both criminal and civil cases. In addition, it is sometimes asked to rule directly on constitutional disputes involving federal and provincial governments. For example, the federal government submitted a Reference to the Supreme Court of Canada in February 1998, asking whether Quebec could unilaterally secede from Canada.[17] Decisions of the Supreme Court set binding precedents for all other courts in Canada.

---

15. S.C. 2002, c. 8.

16. *Criminal Code,* R.S.C. 1985, c. C-46, s. 691.

17. *Reference Re Secession of Quebec,* [1998] 2 S.C.R. 217.

# The Process of Civil Litigation

**Case Summary 2.2**

**Can a Limitation Period Expire Before the Problem Is Discovered?**
*Consumers Glass Co. Ltd. v. Foundation Company of Canada Ltd.*[18]

In 1963, Foundation, a contracting and engineering company, designed and built a warehouse for Consumers Glass. There were no problems with the building, and no indication of any difficulty, until the roof collapsed suddenly in 1981. Consumers Glass sued Foundation for negligence in the design and construction of the building. Foundation claimed that the action should have been brought in contract and within the six-year period set out in the *Limitation Act*. The questions the Ontario Court of Appeal had to resolve were (1) whether the action should be based on negligence—a tort action—or on a breach of contract, and (2) whether the limitation period started running in 1963, when the work was done, or in 1981, when the damage occurred.

The Court, after examining several important precedents, decided that when a person was suing because of a failure to live up to a duty to be careful, that person was free to sue for the tort of negligence even though the relationship that gave rise to that duty was based on a contract between the parties. After the Court decided that Consumers Glass could sue in negligence, it looked at when the limitation period should start to run. The Justices considered several important precedents, but in effect they found that it would be inappropriate if the victim of such negligence were barred from suing before he knew of the damage. The Court also found that this would be equally unjust in contract law.

Case Summary 2.2 is cited here to illustrate how important it is to properly begin the process of suing. You not only have to sue for the right thing—in this case, negligence—but you also have to do so in a timely manner. Failure to sue within the time limits set out in a limitation statute can bar an action from proceeding.

Most of this text deals with matters of **substantive law** (that is, law that summarizes rights and obligations of the "you can" or "you can't" variety) rather than **procedural law** (that is, law that deals with the process by which we enforce those rights and obligations). But it is important to be familiar with the procedures involved in bringing a dispute to trial, if only to understand the function of lawyers and the reasons for the expense and delay involved. Before a decision is made to sue someone, all avenues for settling the dispute outside of litigation ought to be exhausted. Alternative methods for resolving legal disputes have been developed, including negotiation, mediation, and arbitration. Often the court requires the disputing parties to have tried these dispute resolution mechanisms before a trial procedure will be instigated. The litigation procedures may vary somewhat from province to province, but they are substantially the same in all common law jurisdictions. They apply to most superior courts. (One of the distinguishing characteristics of small claims courts is that this involved procedure has been streamlined significantly, eliminating many of the steps described.) The discussion below is based on the procedure followed in British Columbia. Figure 2.2 sets out the process of civil litigation.

**Timely start to action necessary**

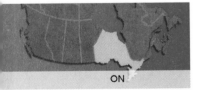

ON

**Should try to settle dispute**

**Some variations from province to province**

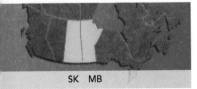

SK   MB

---

18. (1985), 51 O.R. (2d) 385 (C.A.).

**Figure 2.2 Process of Civil Litigation**

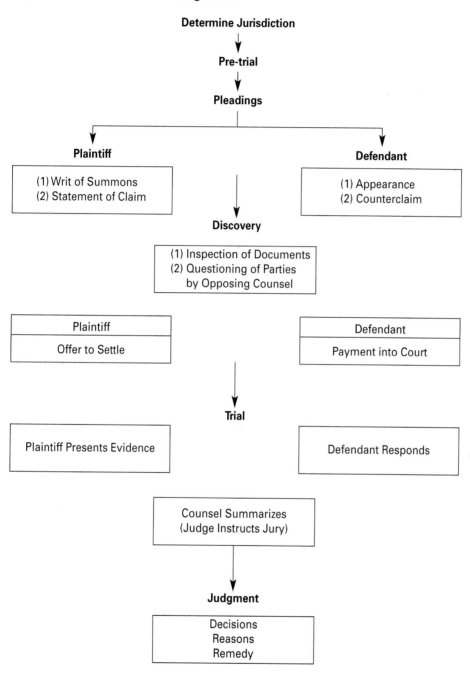

**Determine Jurisdiction**

↓

**Pre-trial**

↓

**Pleadings**

**Plaintiff**

| |
|---|
| (1) Writ of Summons |
| (2) Statement of Claim |

**Defendant**

| |
|---|
| (1) Appearance |
| (2) Counterclaim |

**Discovery**

| |
|---|
| (1) Inspection of Documents |
| (2) Questioning of Parties by Opposing Counsel |

| **Plaintiff** |
|---|
| Offer to Settle |

| **Defendant** |
|---|
| Payment into Court |

**Trial**

| |
|---|
| Plaintiff Presents Evidence |

| |
|---|
| Defendant Responds |

| |
|---|
| Counsel Summarizes (Judge Instructs Jury) |

↓

**Judgment**

| |
|---|
| Decisions |
| Reasons |
| Remedy |

## Jurisdiction

The first step in a legal suit is to determine which court should hear the action. The geographic jurisdiction of a court can be a very difficult question, but generally the plaintiff, or person bringing the action, can choose a court in the area where the defendant resides or in the area where the matter complained about arose. If a traffic accident that happened in Alberta involved one driver from

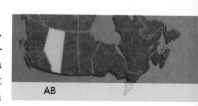

AB

British Columbia and one from Ontario, the Ontario driver would have to sue in British Columbia or Alberta.

The question of selecting the appropriate jurisdiction has become complicated by the prevalence of commercial and other kinds of transactions on the internet. This communication system virtually eliminates distances between people, making it difficult to determine in which jurisdiction litigation should be commenced if the transaction leads to a dispute. Could a retailer be sued (or prosecuted) in every jurisdiction in which its internet message is received? As a rule, the courts seem willing to take jurisdiction where there has been some interaction between the residents in that jurisdiction and the offending corporation.[19] A resident of a province or state who orders or purchases a product or pays a fee for some service over the internet would likely establish the appropriate amount of interactivity to give rise to jurisdiction. Courts have refused to hear cases for which they believed that another jurisdiction would be more appropriate.

**Jurisdiction requires some interaction**

Another problem with respect to jurisdiction is whether, once a province or state has taken jurisdiction, held a trial, and made a judgment, that decision can be enforced in the jurisdiction where the business resides or has assets. Cases in Canada and the United States have demonstrated that the judgment will be enforced only if there is a degree of connectivity or interactivity such that the business in question could clearly be said to be active and functional in the jurisdiction of the court that delivered the judgment.

Once the province has been chosen, the plaintiff must then choose the court in which to commence the litigation. In a civil action, this is either the province's small claims court or superior court. The small claims court in British Columbia has a monetary limit of $10 000 (this amount varies with the province). In several jurisdictions, cases involving amounts above this limit can be tried in the small claims court if the plaintiff waives any claim to a higher amount. Although it is simpler and less expensive to bring an action in the small claims court, a disadvantage is that that court is restricted in the costs it can award. Costs incurred for representation by a lawyer usually cannot be recovered. On the other hand, the procedure followed before the small claims court has been significantly streamlined. It is designed to enable ordinary people to present their legal problems without the need to hire a lawyer. Hiring a lawyer, asking a friend to assist in court, or handling the action on one's own are all options.

## Reducing **Risk** 2.1

In order to avoid problems, those doing business over the internet should specify what law is to apply to transactions entered into with customers. When business is solicited, it would also be wise to include disclaimers limiting the parties with whom transactions will be entered into. Such disclaimers would be similar to those contained in product warranties, namely: "Void where prohibited by law" or "Available only to residents of Canada." If a business creates a website and uses it to do business in other jurisdictions, it will not only be subject to the law of those jurisdictions, but also any resulting litigation may be conducted in the courts of those jurisdictions. See Chapter 16 for a more detailed discussion of this topic.

---

19. *Easthaven Ltd. v. Nutrisystem.com Inc.* (2001), 202 D.L.R. (4th) 560 (Ont. Sup. Ct.).

## Pre-trial

To commence an action in a superior court in British Columbia, the plaintiff must issue a **writ of summons**, have it authorized by a court clerk, pay the appropriate fees, and serve it on the defendant. The writ contains the names and addresses of the parties and a brief summary of the nature of the plaintiff's claim. If the defendant chooses to dispute the claim, he must promptly file an **appearance** with the court clerk. This is an important step, for without it the plaintiff can short-circuit the rest of the procedure and ask for a summary judgment. Once the appearance has been filed and a copy sent to the plaintiff, the plaintiff must prepare a **statement of claim.** The statement of claim sets out in more detail the plaintiff's allegations. It must be filed with the court clerk and served on the defendant. The defendant must then prepare and file a **statement of defence,** in which he provides answers to the claims of the plaintiff. In most jurisdictions in Canada the writ of summons has been eliminated, and civil actions begin with a statement of claim being served on the defendant.

If the defendant believes that he is the real victim, he can also file a **counterclaim.** This is similar to a statement of claim, and requires the filing of a statement of defence from the plaintiff in response. The purpose of this exchange of documents is not to argue and justify positions; rather, the parties are merely stating the claims giving rise to the dispute and establishing the required elements of the legal action. If either party believes that the documents do not make the other party's position completely clear, she may ask for clarification or further information. These documents constitute the **pleadings,** and once they have been closed, the parties have the right to apply to set a date for trial and begin the process of discovery. Throughout the pre-trial process, the parties have the right to—and often do—make applications to the court for direction regarding what details have to be disclosed, what questions have to be answered, and other matters that may arise. These applications are referred to as **chambers applications** because the judge deals with them in a less formal manner; decisions are usually based on affidavit evidence alone. The effect of the resulting court orders, however, can be extremely important to the outcome of the action.

Following the exchange of pleadings, the parties initiate the process of **discovery,** which has two distinct parts:

**1. Discovery of documents.** Each party has the right to inspect any document in the possession of the other party that may be used as evidence in the trial. This includes email and computer files on a disk or a hard drive.

**2. Examination for discovery.** The parties (with their lawyers) meet before a court reporter and, under oath, are asked detailed questions relevant to the problem to be tried. The parties are required to answer these questions fully and truthfully. Everything said is recorded, and may be used later at the trial. This examination process generally applies to only the parties to the action, not to witnesses. When corporations are involved, a representative who has personal knowledge of the matter may be examined. As part of a general reform of the litigation process in some provinces,[20] and in an attempt to

**Writ of summons**

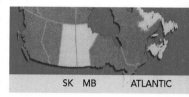

**Appearance**

**Statement of claim**

**Statement of defence**

**Counterclaim**

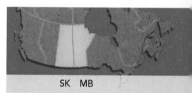

**Discovery**

---

20. For an interesting discussion on the reform of the discovery process in Ontario, see the letter from the Chair of the Advocates' Society Discovery Task Force to the Ministry of the Attorney General Task Force on the Discovery Process in Ontario (9 October 2002), online: **http://www.advsoc.on.ca/pdf/discovery_submission_AG.pdf.**

## Reducing **Risk** 2.2

The discovery stage is an extremely important part of the litigation process, and cases are often won or lost at this point. When parties testify under oath at discovery, they often make admissions or incorrect statements that come back to haunt them at the trial. Admissions of fact that may not seem important at the time may become crucial at the actual trial, and a party is bound by those admissions. A false claim can be investigated before trial, and the party can be forced to recant at the trial, bringing her credibility into question. This means that what is said at the discovery stage often determines the outcome of the case, compelling the parties to come to a settlement. For businesses, it is extremely important that the person who testifies at discovery not only be familiar with the matter, but also be well prepared and appreciate the importance of her testimony and its potential impact on the legal action.

reduce the costs of an action, the examination for discovery has been eliminated in actions involving smaller amounts.[21] Other provinces have limited the amount of time given to the examination process.[22]

**Process encourages settlement by disclosure of information**

In most jurisdictions, a pre-trial conference involving the parties, their lawyers, and a judge is held to determine which issues remain to be tried, and whether the parties can themselves resolve the dispute. In fact, most disputes are resolved by the parties during these pre-trial processes.

**Payment into court**

Another tool often available to parties before a trial is **payment into court.** A defendant being sued for damages may admit liability but think that the amount being demanded by the plaintiff is too high. The defendant can make a payment to the court acknowledging the amount he believes is owed. The judge is unaware of such a payment. If the plaintiff rejects the payment, the matter proceeds to trial. In British Columbia, if the judgment is for less than the amount deposited by the defendant, the plaintiff will not be compensated for any costs incurred after the payment was made, and will have to pay the defendant's costs from that point. If the plaintiff's claim is dismissed, the defendant is entitled to his costs incurred to the time the payment was made, and to double costs from that point.[23] The plaintiff had an opportunity to accept a fair settlement, and failure to do so will result in her being penalized. If the amount awarded is more than the payment into court, the defendant's payment obviously was not sufficient and the plaintiff will be able to claim costs in the normal way. This mechanism encourages the defendant to make a fair offer of payment, and the plaintiff to accept such a fair offer.

**Offer to settle**

A related provision exists for the plaintiff to file an **offer to settle,** which has a similar effect. This mechanism allows the plaintiff to advise the court that she is willing to settle for less than she has claimed. Again, the judge is not advised of such an offer. If the defendant rejects the offer, the matter proceeds to trial. In British Columbia, if the judgment is for more than the offer to settle the defendant will be required to pay double the plaintiff's costs incurred after the offer was made.[24] If the judgment is for less than what was offered, then the defendant will, of course, have to pay the plaintiff's costs in the normal way.

---

21. Under Ontario's Simplified Procedure, for example, examination for discovery is not permitted for actions involving less than $50 000 (Ontario *Rules of Civil Procedure*, r. 76).

22. In British Columbia, there is a 2-hour limit on examinations for discovery for Fast Track Litigation (British Columbia, *Supreme Court Civil Rules*, r. 66), while in Alberta, the Streamlined Procedure for cases involving $75 000 or less sets a 6-hour limit for examinations for discovery (Alberta, *Rules of Court*, r. 662).

23. British Columbia, *Supreme Court Civil Rules*, ibid., r. 37(24).

24. *Ibid.*, r. 37(23).

## Recent Initiatives

While it is obvious that the purpose of this long, involved, and expensive pre-trial process is to encourage the parties to reach a settlement and thereby avoid a trial, it is also clear that such a process results in frustrating delays for the parties. For this reason, the provinces have implemented reforms to speed up the litigation process, especially when smaller amounts are involved. British Columbia and Alberta, for example, allow for summary trials, where evidence is adduced by **affidavit** instead of by the testimony of witnesses.[25] British Columbia also provides for Fast Track Litigation for trials that can be completed within two days;[26] Alberta's Streamlined Procedure applies to trials involving claims of $75 000 or less.[27] Ontario has a Simplified Procedure for claims of $50 000 or less,[28] New Brunswick[29] and Prince Edward Island[30] have procedures for Quick Rulings, and Manitoba has implemented Expedited Trials.[31] Ontario has also introduced a Mandatory Mediation pilot project.[32] Several provinces, including Ontario,[33] have started mandatory case management, which involves judicial supervision of the specific steps in the litigation process. The objectives of reducing costs and delay—and of making the justice system more accessible—have motivated all jurisdictions to dramatically simplify their procedures in small claims courts.[34]

**Recent initiatives**

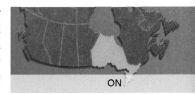

ON

## The Trial

Because the burden of proof at trial rests with the plaintiff, the plaintiff's case and witnesses are presented first. The plaintiff's lawyer assists witnesses in their testimony by asking specific questions, but the types of questions that may be asked are very restricted. For example, the plaintiff's lawyer is prohibited from asking leading questions, in which the answer is suggested (such as, "You were there on

---

### Reducing **Risk** 2.3

The delay and costs associated with litigation, as well as the lack of control over the process and outcome, have contributed to its decreasing popularity. For businesspeople, finding themselves in court should normally be viewed as a failure. Considerable care should be taken to avoid disputes, or to attempt to settle them before litigation becomes necessary. When a settlement cannot be reached by the parties, and both parties are willing, it is sometimes advantageous to explore some of the alternatives to litigation that are available (these are discussed below). However, in some situations—especially when it may be necessary to enforce the court's decision—litigation may be the best option available.

---

25. British Columbia, *Supreme Court Civil Rules, ibid.,* r. 18A, and Alberta, *Rules of Court, supra* note 22, Part 11.

26. British Columbia, *Supreme Court Civil Rules, ibid.,* r. 66.

27. Alberta, *Rules of Court, supra* note 22, Part 48.

28. Ontario, *Rules of Civil Procedure, supra* note 21, r. 76.

29. New Brunswick, *Rules of Court,* Rule 77.

30. Prince Edward Island, *Rules of Civil Procedure,* Rule 75.

31. Manitoba, *Court of Queen's Bench Rules,* Rule 20.

32. Ontario, *Rules of Civil Procedure, supra* note 21, r. 24.1.

33. *Ibid.,* r. 77.

34. Alberta has even increased the monetary jurisdiction of its small claims court to $25 000, and the provincial cabinet has the authority to increase this jurisdiction to $50 000; see *supra* note 6.

Saturday, weren't you?"). When the plaintiff's lawyer completes this direct examination of the witness, the defendant's lawyer is given the opportunity to cross-examine the witness. In cross-examination, the defence has more latitude in the type of questions asked and so is permitted to ask leading questions. When the opposing lawyer believes that the lawyer questioning the witness is abusing the process by asking prohibited questions, she can object to the question. The judge rules on the objection, deciding whether to permit the question or order the lawyer to withdraw it. The rules governing the type of testimony that can be obtained from witnesses—and, indeed, all other types of evidence to be submitted at a trial—are referred to as the **rules of evidence.** (These rules are very complex and beyond the scope of this text.) If something new arises from the cross-examination, the plaintiff's lawyer re-examines the witnesses on those matters. After both sides have finished calling witnesses, the plaintiff's lawyer and then the defendant's lawyer are allowed to summarize the evidence and make arguments to the court. Again, if anything new comes up the other party is given a chance to respond to it.

## Judgment

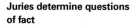
**Juries determine questions of fact**

If a jury is involved (which is not very common in civil cases), the judge will instruct it on matters of law. The jury then retires to consider the case and returns to announce its decision to the judge. The function of the jury is to decide questions of fact; the judge decides questions of law. Where the matter is heard by a judge alone a decision may be delivered immediately; however, it is more common for the judge to hand down a judgment in writing some time later that includes reasons for the decision. These reasons can form the basis for an appeal.

### Costs

The cost of retaining a lawyer to sue someone is often prohibitive; some creditors may decide to write off a debt rather than incur this outlay. In small claims courts the presence of a lawyer is the exception rather than the rule. In higher-level courts lawyers are generally essential, although parties do have the right to represent themselves. Other expenses are often incurred in addition to the lawyer's fees, such as the costs of obtaining transcripts from the discovery process and the fees paid to secure specialized reports from experts.

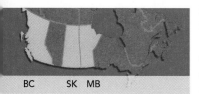
BC    SK  MB

**Legal expenses usually not completely recoverable**

Even the winning party must pay her own legal expenses. She may, however, obtain as part of the judgment an order for "costs." This means that the defendant will be required to compensate the successful plaintiff for at least a portion of her legal expenses. While a judge always has discretion when awarding costs, **party–party costs** are usually awarded to the victorious party in a civil action. Party–party costs are determined using a predetermined scale.[35] Consequently, the plaintiff will usually have to pay some legal expenses even when she is successful. There is, of course, always the risk that a party may lose the action and have to pay all of her own legal expenses as well as the winning party's costs.

---

35. In Alberta, for example, party–party costs are usually awarded for actions in the Court of Queen's Bench pursuant to Schedule C of the *Rules of Court, supra* note 22. In the small claims court, the awarding of costs other than those designed to reimburse the winning party for things such as filing fees is within the discretion of the judge—*Provincial Court Fees and Costs Regulation,* Alta. Reg.18/91.

If the judge finds the conduct of the losing party objectionable (for example, if an action is "frivolous and vexatious"), then he may award the winning party the higher solicitor–client costs.

## Remedies

One of the things that must be decided when a civil suit is begun is what the plaintiff will ask the court to do. The most common remedy requested in a court action is monetary payment in the form of **damages,** which are designed to compensate the victim for any loss suffered. **General damages** are based on estimates, such as when the court awards compensation to a litigant for pain and suffering or for future lost wages. **Special damages,** on the other hand, are calculated to reimburse the litigant for expenses or costs incurred before the trial. **Punitive** or **exemplary damages** are intended not to compensate the victim but rather to punish the wrongdoer for outrageous or extreme behaviour. This may result in a windfall for the victim. Punitive damages will be awarded only in very serious cases, such as a sadistic physical attack, or when an insurer pursued an unfounded allegation of arson against a vulnerable insured.[36]

**Damages**

In rare cases, remedies other than damages may be awarded. The court can order money incorrectly paid to the defendant to be restored to the rightful owner. In some circumstances, it is also possible to obtain an **accounting,** which results in any profits wrongfully obtained by the wrongdoer to be paid over to the victim. The court also has the power to order an **injunction** stopping wrongful conduct or correcting some existing wrong. The court may compel proper performance of a legal obligation by **specific performance.** In some situations, it may be appropriate for the courts to simply make a **declaration** as to the law and the legal rights of the parties.

**Other remedies**

### Case Summary 2.3

#### Is Specific Performance Always an Appropriate Remedy for Land Transactions? *Semelhago v. Paramadevan*[37]

Although damages or monetary compensation is the common remedy in a civil action, sometimes the court will order the equitable remedy of specific performance. In land transactions, it was thought that because all land is unique specific performance would always be available—at least, until this case was decided by the Supreme Court of Canada. Semelhago agreed to purchase from Paramadevan a house that was under construction, for $205 000. When it was time to perform the contract Paramadevan refused, and this action was brought. Semelhago asked for the *remedy of specific performance*—or, as permitted by statute, damages in lieu of specific performance. At the trial he elected to receive damages, and the Court awarded him $125 000 damages in lieu of specific performance. The reason for this high award was that the market value of the house had risen from the $205 000 agreed upon at the time the contract was made to $325 000 at the time of trial. Paramadevan appealed the award, and the Appeal Court reduced it by the amount of the interest that Semelhago would have had to pay to finance the purchase of the house over the period from when the contract was entered into until the trial, saying that damages should reflect not only the increase in the value of

---

36. *Whiten v. Pilot Insurance Co.,* [2002] 1 S.C.R. 595.

37. [1996] 2 S.C.R. 415.

the house from the time of the contract, but also the interest that would have been paid out had the deal closed as required by the contract. This reduced the damages to just less than $82 000.

The purpose of such damages is to put the victim in the position he would have been in had the contract been properly performed—and, so, the interest he would have had to pay should have been taken into consideration. The Supreme Court of Canada refused to further reduce the award, and also refused to take into consideration the increased value of the house that Semelhago had intended to sell to acquire the one in question but which he had instead retained. An important statement that came out of the case was that it should no longer be thought that all land is unique, and that specific performance is therefore not always appropriate in a land transaction.

## Enforcement

**A judgment does not ensure payment**

Even when the litigation process is completed and judgment is obtained, there is no guarantee that the amount awarded will be paid. There may no longer be a dispute over liability, but if the judgment debtor refuses to pay steps must be taken by the plaintiff to enforce the judgment. If the judgment debtor does not own assets (a "dry judgment"), it was likely unwise to have pursued the action in the first place. The successful plaintiff not only will get nothing from the defendant, but also will have to pay his own legal expenses. On the other hand, if the judgment debtor has prospects of owning future assets, the judgment does remain enforceable for several years. The plaintiff must consider all of these factors—as well as the risk of losing the action—when deciding whether to proceed with an action against the defendant.

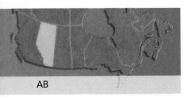

AB

### Enforcing Judgment

**Examination in aid of execution**

The process to follow when enforcing a judgment is set out in Figure 2.3. Once judgment has been obtained, most provinces provide for a further hearing, sometimes called an **examination in aid of execution,**[38] to determine the judgment debtor's assets and income that can be seized or garnished to satisfy the judgment. The plaintiff can question the judgment debtor (who is under oath) about her property, income, debts, recent property transfers, and present and future means of satisfying the judgment. At the conclusion of the process, the plaintiff can take appropriate steps to execute against particular property or income in order to recover the judgment.

### Seizure of Property

**Property may be seized and sold**

The execution process allows for the seizure and eventual sale of the debtor's property to satisfy the judgment. The property is seized by a government official who, after deducting a fee, sells it, usually through public auction.[39] The proceeds

---

38. In Alberta, this hearing is called an examination in aid of enforcement—*Rules of Court, supra* note 22, r. 371–372. Instead of conducting an examination, the plaintiff may attempt to determine the information by requiring the judgment debtor to complete a financial report, verified by statutory declaration—*Rules of Court,* r. 370.

39. In Alberta, seizures and sales of seized property must be conducted by private businesses, civil enforcement agencies, pursuant to the *Civil Enforcement Act,* R.S.A. 2000, c. C-15.

## Figure 2.3 Enforcement of Judgment

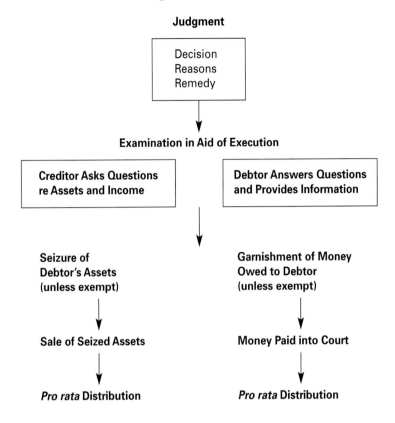

**Judgment**

Decision
Reasons
Remedy

**Examination in Aid of Execution**

| **Creditor Asks Questions re Assets and Income** | **Debtor Answers Questions and Provides Information** |

**Seizure of Debtor's Assets (unless exempt)**

**Garnishment of Money Owed to Debtor (unless exempt)**

**Sale of Seized Assets**

**Money Paid into Court**

*Pro rata* **Distribution**

*Pro rata* **Distribution**

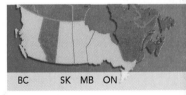

BC    SK   MB   ON

**Proceeds of sale shared by all creditors**

are distributed first to secured creditors, then to preferred creditors, and finally, on a *pro rata* or proportionate basis, to the remaining unsecured creditors. *Secured creditors* used the property in question to secure the loan, and so they have first claim to the proceeds from its sale, up to the amount secured. *Preferred creditors* are those who, by legislation, must be paid before other unsecured creditors. Landlords owed unpaid rent, and employees owed unpaid wages (both for a limited number of months) are examples of preferred creditors. The "necessities of life" are exempt from seizure. Exempt assets vary from province to province, but generally include—within specified limits—food, clothing, household furnishings, tools or other personal property needed to earn income, motor vehicles, and medical and dental aids. It should be noted that real property (land and buildings) can be seized to satisfy a judgment, but that the method employed varies with the jurisdiction. Often, registering the judgment against the real property is enough to pressure the debtor to pay. But when this is not enough, the property can be sold to satisfy the judgment.

**Some properties are exempt from seizure**

## Garnishment

**Garnishment** involves the interception of funds owed to the judgment debtor and the payment of those funds into court. A creditor may garnish funds such as wages earned by the debtor but not yet paid to him, or the balance of the debtor's bank account. The legislation governing garnishment varies from province to province. Once the required documentation is served on the garnishee (the

**Funds owed to debtor can be garnished**

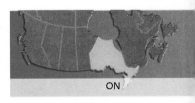

ON

person owing money to the judgment debtor), she must pay the amount owing (less the employment earnings exemption, if applicable) to the court, which then disburses the funds to the creditors. Typically, when wages are garnished, the judgment debtor is entitled to an employment earnings exemption, which will vary depending on such factors as the amount earned and the debtor's number of dependants.[40]

## Judicial Remedies before Judgment

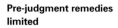

**Pre-judgment remedies limited**

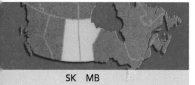

SK MB

Although most methods of execution require that a judgment first be obtained, some judicial remedies may be available to a creditor even before judgment. These are extraordinary remedies that are normally granted only when there is risk that the debtor's property will be removed from the jurisdiction or otherwise made unavailable to the creditor. While bank accounts and other debts can sometimes be attached before judgment, garnishing wages before judgment is usually not permitted.[41] New Brunswick and Nova Scotia do not permit any form of garnishment before judgment. When property other than money is involved, and there is risk of it being removed or sold, the creditor may be able to obtain a court order allowing seizure. This is not a judgment, but rather an interim order granted by the court before the actual trial, to ensure that the goods will be available to satisfy a judgment if one is ultimately granted. Another remedy available in some situations is an **injunction** to prevent a third party from paying out money owed to the debtor. This remedy does not direct those funds to the creditor, but it does prevent them from going to the debtor—who may dissipate or abscond with them.[42]

## Limitation Periods

Whether to remove ongoing uncertainty or to ensure fairness when memories dim or witnesses become unavailable, court action must be brought within a relatively short time from the event giving rise to the complaint. This time is referred

---

## Reducing **Risk** 2.4

The process of collection and enforcement of judgments as described above may appear cumbersome, but it can be quite effective because of the diversity of options available. However, the process can be expensive, and may not be justifiable economically considering the amount of the debt and the likelihood of recovery. Note that when property has been used to secure a debt, and the security has been properly registered, the creditor has a right to repossess the property upon default, without recourse to the courts. Bankruptcy will also affect the debtor's obligation to pay. (Secured transactions involving personal property as well as the bankruptcy process are dealt with in Chapter 10.) A

businessperson should consider the various ways to structure a transaction ("Should I take security or not?") before she enters into a business arrangement. This will require an analysis of whether the other party will be able to fulfill his obligations ("Is his business plan reasonable?"), and if not, whether it will be possible to collect any resulting shortfall through the litigation process ("What other assets does he own that could be used to satisfy the debt?"). An understanding of the process of collection and the enforcement of judgments will enable a prudent businessperson to make better decisions, thereby reducing the risk associated with her business arrangements.

---

40. In Ontario, for example, 80 percent of a person's wages are usually exempt from garnishment —*Wages Act,* R.S.O. 1990, c. W. 1, s. 7.

41. See, for example, s. 3(4) of the *Court Order Enforcement Act,* R.S.B.C. 1996, c. 78.

42. In Alberta, the *Civil Enforcement Act, supra* note 39, Part 3, enables claimants to apply for attachment orders, which can allow both seizure and garnishment before judgment is obtained.

to as a **limitation period.** In most provinces, for example, a person who is owed money from a simple sale of goods transaction must bring an action against the debtor within six years of the failure to pay the debt.[43] The plaintiff must commence an action by filing the appropriate pleading (the *writ*, or the *statement of claim*) with the appropriate court. Failure to fulfill that step within the limitation period will result in the plaintiff being barred from pursuing the action. This time limitation will vary depending on the jurisdiction and the nature of the complaint involved, and may be embodied in several different statutes in a province.

With the expiry of the limitation period and the threat of court action removed, the potential defendant is not likely to settle out of court and the plaintiff is left with no recourse. For this reason, it is important for a person involved in a potential lawsuit to quickly get the advice of a lawyer regarding the relevant limitation period. Whether the limitation period had expired was the problem facing the court in the *Consumers Glass* case discussed in Case Summary 2.2.

**Expiration of limitation period prohibits suing**

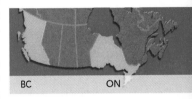

BC          ON

### Case Summary 2.4

**Even Revenue Canada Must Comply with Limitation Periods!**
*Markevich v. Canada*[44]

Markevich accumulated a tax debt of $234 136.04 in the early 1980s. Revenue Canada did nothing to collect the unpaid tax until 1998, long after the relevant limitation period expired. It then sent Markevich a statement of account for $770 583.42: the amount of his original debt, plus accrued interest. The Supreme Court ruled that the relevant limitation period applied. It declared that if the government does not make an effort to collect a tax debt for an extended period of time, a taxpayer may reasonably expect that he will not be called to account for the liability. The federal government estimated that this decision would cost it at least $1.26 billion, as it would not be able to pursue the tax owed from more than 70 000 taxpayers. This case certainly provides more proof of the importance of complying with relevant limitation periods!

# Alternatives to Court Action

Businesspeople involved in private disputes are well advised to avoid litigation whenever possible because of the high costs, the long delays, and the likelihood of dissatisfaction with the results. In this section, we will discuss the various alternatives that can be used instead of—or in conjunction with—the litigation process. It has been suggested that the capacity of the civil justice system has been severely tested in the effort to resolve disputes, and many jurisdictions in Canada are actively supporting the use of alternative mechanisms for avoiding court-

---

43. But in Alberta, the *Limitations Act,* R.S.A. 2000, c. L-12, s. 3 states that most lawsuits (including those for breach of contract and tort) must be commenced within two years of discovering the claim, or within 10 years from the date when the claim arose, whichever period expires first. Ontario adopted a similar system (except that the ultimate limitation period is 15, rather than 10, years) on January 1, 2004, when the *Limitations Act, 2002,* S.O. 2002, c. 24 came into force. Both the Alberta act (ss. 8–9) and the Ontario legislation (s. 13) carry forward the rule that a written acknowledgment, or part payment, of a debt before a limitation period expires revives the limitation period, which begins again at the time of the acknowledgment or part payment. The Alberta legislation (s. 7) also allows the parties to extend a limitation period, by agreement.

44. 2003 S.C.C. 9.

adjudicated settlements. Some of the tools the courts have implemented, and in some cases made mandatory, are very similar to mechanisms that have become increasingly popular. Alternative dispute resolution (ADR) and litigation are neither inconsistent nor rival systems; in fact, each depends on the other. If there is a lack of progress in settling a dispute by an alternate means, the threat of a lawsuit may be enough to make the alternative processes more productive. And, even if the matter does go to court, negotiation and mediation can be used at any stage in the litigation process—including post-judgment, when the parties wish to avoid an appeal. Note that because of the essential privacy of the matters resolved by alternative means, it is difficult to cite actual case examples in this discussion. As a consequence, hypothetical examples of the processes described are used. They should not be relied on as actual case studies.

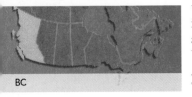

BC

## What Is Alternative Dispute Resolution?

Any strategy that is used as a substitute for court action qualifies as a method of ADR, but there are three main approaches: (1) when the decision making is left in the hands of the disputing parties to work out for themselves (**negotiation**), (2) when a neutral third party assists the parties in coming to a resolution on their own (**mediation**), and (3) when a third party makes a binding decision in the matter under dispute (**arbitration**). Table 2.1 provides a brief comparison of these methods, and they are discussed in more detail later in this section.

**Negotiation**

**Mediation**

**Arbitration**

## Advantages of ADR versus Litigation

### Control

**ADR leaves control in the hands of the parties**

There are some significant advantages in choosing an alternative to litigation. One is the retention of control of the matter by the people most affected by it. When businesspeople turn to the courts to solve their problems, they abdicate their personal responsibility and right to control the decision-making process. Litigants may expend significant amounts of time, money, and personal and business resources pursuing or defending an action. They may feel some satisfaction and relief if the final decision is in their favour, but powerless if the decision goes against them. Rarely does the judgment compensate the parties for all their costs, and because they are not part of the decision-making process they may be unwilling to comply with the decision, making it more difficult to enforce. It is, there-

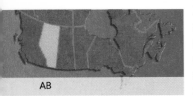

AB

### Table 2.1 Summary and Comparison of Litigation and ADR Methods

|  | Litigation | Arbitration | Mediation | Negotiation |
|---|---|---|---|---|
| **Control** | Low | Low | High | Highest |
| **Delay** | Lengthy | Moderate | Brief | Briefer |
| **Cost** | High | Moderate | Low | Low |
| **Privacy** | Low | Moderate | High | Complete |
| **Flexibility** | Low | Moderate | High | Highest |
| **Good Will** | Unlikely | Possible | Likely | Ensured |
| **Predictability** | High | Reasonable | Low | Low |
| **Appealability** | Usually | Moderate | None | None |
| **Visibility** | High | Moderate | None | None |

fore, vitally important that businesspeople appreciate the advantages of maintaining control over the problem-solving process and the disadvantages of placing it in the hands of others.

## Avoidance of Delay

Most of the delays in litigation are because of the lengthy pre-trial process and the problems of scheduling court personnel and facilities. When other resolution processes are used, there are fewer procedural delays because the structure of the process is determined by the parties themselves. Scheduling has only to involve a meeting time and place convenient to the parties, their representatives, and a mediator or arbitrator, if a third party is involved.

**Less delay with ADR**

## Avoidance of Lost Productivity

An ongoing court battle can be very distracting to a corporation's directors, managers, and employees. Key people may find themselves involved over a considerable period of time in overseeing the process, providing information, or preparing to testify. This is nonproductive time that may cost a corporation its competitive advantage. Other business opportunities may be lost because of this distraction, not to mention the negative publicity that may be given to the case. The much quicker resolution process offered by ADR reduces that problem.

**Less distraction with ADR**

## Lower Cost

ADR is less costly because fewer parties are involved and the procedure is simplified. There is less need for lawyers, and the general expense caused by delay is reduced. The costs of producing documentary evidence and preparing witnesses are largely avoided, as are the unpredictable risks associated with an adverse court decision—no matter how sure a party is of her legal position, it is impossible to be certain of the outcome of an action. Also, there is no danger that punitive damages will be awarded. This is an important consideration, especially in the United States, where the risk of a jury awarding crippling punitive damages exists.

**Less expense with ADR**

In an American case against fast-food chain McDonald's, a woman was injured when a cup of extremely hot coffee spilled on her as she removed the lid to add sugar. She suffered serious burns and spent some time in hospital. She had asked for some small compensation from McDonald's and was rebuffed. When the matter went to trial, the jury awarded more than $2.7 million in punitive damages. (Note that the trial judge later reduced the punitive damages to $480 000; the $160 000 compensatory damages award remained intact.[45]) Even in Canada, there are cases in which the amount of punitive damages has been close to triple the amount of compensatory damages awarded.[46] These cases illustrate the great risk that can be faced by litigants, and why ADR therefore may be much more attractive.

**No risk of unexpected damage awards with ADR**

## Privacy

The fact that ADR is a private process gives it several advantages, not the least of which is that the media can be excluded from the process and the general public will be unaware of the dispute. This protects the public image of the business and

---

45. *Liebeck v. McDonald's Restaurants, P.T.S. Inc.*, 1995 WL 360309 (N.M. Dist. Ct. 1994).

46. See *Whiten v. Pilot Insurance Co., supra* note 36, where the Supreme Court of Canada affirmed the jury's award of about $345 000 in compensatory damages and $1 million in punitive damages.

**Confidentiality retained with ADR**

the reputations of the people involved. Confidential information, trade secrets, profitability, and other sensitive information remains private. Any records of the process that are kept will most likely not be made public, and therefore one agreement cannot set a precedent for subsequent, similar disputes. Other claimants will not be tempted to make a claim against the corporation because they were attracted by the amount of a previous settlement, simply because they will not be aware of it.

## Good Will

One of the costs of a protracted conflict is the breakdown in the relationship between the parties. Litigation—where questioning the opposition's credibility and honesty is routine—is adversarial in nature. The emotional costs can be extreme, leaving bitterness and animosity between the parties. When the parties in conflict have a business relationship and an adjudicated decision favours one party at the expense of the other, it often becomes impossible for them to resume that business relationship. In contrast, when they have worked together to resolve their differences and come to a relatively quick settlement that is mutually agreeable, their relationship may be strengthened. In addition, because they maintain control of the process they may be more likely to abide by the terms of the agreement.

**Good relationship can be retained with ADR**

## International Disputes

Many other trading nations use the civil law system, which is much less adversarial in nature and much more compatible with ADR than the common law system. Canadian corporations accustomed to resolving disputes through cooperation rather than confrontation will function more effectively in the global business environment. There are no international courts that deal with private matters, and it is often difficult to determine the best jurisdiction in which to hear a dispute. Even when the parties agree to specify which country's law will govern their contract, there will likely be a suspicion of bias by a court toward its own nationals. In such circumstances, ADR culminating in international arbitration is the logical alternative. Organizations have been established throughout Canada to assist in the conduct of such processes.[47] Legislation enabling the enforcement of arbitrated awards strengthens their usefulness.[48]

**ADR can resolve conflicts between businesses operating internationally**

## Flexibility

One of the most attractive features of ADR is its flexibility. The processes and methods used to resolve conflicts remain in the control of the parties and can be tailored to the particular dispute. The needs of multiple parties or several competing interests can be accommodated. ADR can consider not only the interests of the corporation, but also those of the shareholders, employees, suppliers, customers, and creditors. Even cultural differences can be taken into consideration. When there are internal conflicts within an organization, such as disputes between different divisions, or between management and employees, ADR may offer a satisfactory solution because it can resolve the matter quickly and allow

47. For example, online: British Columbia International Commercial Arbitration Centre **http://www.bcicac.com**.

48. See, for example, *International Commercial Arbitration Act,* R.S.B.C. 1996, c. 233.

the parties to continue to work together in an improved environment. Litigation, on the other hand, takes place in a very formal atmosphere and must adhere to rigid rules of evidence and procedure.

**ADR less formal than litigation**

## Disadvantages of ADR versus Litigation

ADR is not always the best option. The qualities of judicial fairness and impartiality associated with the litigation process are not always present in ADR. The court has no prior interest in the parties or their problems, but it does have extraordinary powers to extract information from the parties that do not exist outside the litigation process. A mediator cannot ensure that all relevant information has been brought forward. In the court system, there are safeguards and rules in place to ensure that each side gets a fair hearing. Because there are few rules or required procedures, ADR may not be able to provide this assurance. The court strives to balance the process so that neither side can take unfair advantage of the other, although this balance may be compromised when only one side can afford extensive legal help. If parties are using ADR, and there is a power imbalance, there is the danger that the weaker party will be taken advantage of. In contrast, the discovery process does much to level the playing field where such inequality exists and the parties are using the litigation process.

**ADR cannot ensure full disclosure**

Another important advantage of the litigation process over ADR is the consistency of the decisions. A court judgment can establish a precedent that will govern future dealings and avoid disputes between other parties. The doctrine of *stare decisis* requires judges to refer to similar previous cases and base their decisions on earlier judgments; thus, the decisions are quite predictable and can be challenged if they are inconsistent. When disputes are resolved independently and privately through ADR not only is there no precedent created, but also there is no record and no knowledge of the outcome outside of the immediate parties. As a result, each dispute must be dealt with on its own merits, and the same kind of disputes may arise over and over again, with inconsistent results. The availability of effective tools for enforcing the judgment may also be an important consideration in choosing litigation over ADR. Litigation also retains the right of appeal if the loser feels an injustice has taken place.

**ADR cannot ensure consistent outcomes**

**ADR agreements not enforceable or appealable**

The publicity given to high-profile cases makes court decisions an effective deterrent to similar offending conduct. For example, upon discovering that its product is being copied and used without permission, a software corporation might select a particularly blatant offender and initiate an action as a warning to others that such conduct will not be tolerated.

**ADR results unavailable to public**

It must also be emphasized that the public interest may not be served by the privacy of ADR. When there is public scrutiny and businesses are forced to do their business in the plain light of day, they are likely to be much better citizens. It must always be remembered that what is a disadvantage to one party may be the most attractive feature of the chosen process to another. As in all business decisions, sound, properly informed judgment is needed in deciding between ADR and litigation in any given situation.

**Privacy of ADR may not serve public good**

## ADR Mechanisms

Upon concluding that ADR is a viable option, the businessperson must then decide which of the various strategies would be most effective in resolving the dispute.

## Negotiation

**Negotiation should be tried first**

Negotiation should be the first recourse for people who find themselves in a disagreement—too often, it is the last. Negotiation involves the parties meeting to discuss the problem in order to come to an agreement as to how it should be resolved. Both sides must be willing to enter into negotiations, and the goal must be to find a solution even if that means making concessions. Negotiation can be as simple as a phone conversation, an exchange of correspondence, or two people sitting down together in a private meeting; any meeting with the goal of resolving a dispute qualifies as a negotiation. It may take place through agents or legal representatives. The stakes may be very high, as in the treaty negotiations that take place between governments and aboriginal groups. As the size and significance of the meetings increase, so must the formality of the process, to ensure that the position of each side is fairly represented.

Because the process is cooperative and non-binding, either side can withdraw from the negotiations if the other is being unreasonable or intransigent; the parties may then elect to move on to some other means of dealing with the matter. An understanding of the law surrounding the dispute will help the parties recognize the consequences of a failure to settle. This puts pressure on the parties to negotiate a settlement consistent with their legal rights and obligations, but they are free to reach a settlement independent of those legal rights and obligations if it better suits the needs of both parties. This flexibility is one of the great attractions of ADR.

People approach negotiation with a variety of attitudes, skills, and objectives. It is helpful to be aware of these, and to recognize the role each plays in the process. Some parties negotiate determined to secure the best return for their side, even if it is at the expense of the other. This competitive style may be successful in achieving certain goals, but it will do little to resolve underlying problems or to prevent the development of others in the future. In short, it destroys rather than enhances business relationships. Other parties may be too willing to accommodate the other's demands, sacrificing personal interests for the good of the relationship. This, too, can be a pitfall, as it may lead to unfair results that in turn will jeopardize future relations.

**Negotiation requires cooperation and compromise**

The successful model for negotiation requires parties who are acutely aware of their own positions, but who are also capable of understanding the position of the other party. Cooperation and compromise are the central concepts to fruitful negotiation, and the objective is to come to a solution through which both sides win. Coercion has no place in such negotiations. There is some risk of the parties indulging in unethical behaviour, such as withholding essential information or in engaging in deceit. Not everyone is a good negotiator; some are well advised to appoint or employ others to represent them at the table, or to invite a third party to facilitate the process.

**Representatives may conduct negotiation**

Negotiating through representatives has both advantages and disadvantages. It adds to the cost. It creates more formality and less privacy. Relying on third parties, whether they are lawyers, experts in the subject matter, or trained negotiators, puts some distance between the parties and brings another point of view to the dispute. Experts may introduce considerations, or suggest solutions, that were not apparent to the actual parties. This may be more a hindrance than a help if those new points of view simply complicate the picture. The actual parties may also lose some measure of control over the matter. When lawyers are involved and the negotiations fail, they are already up to speed and will be better prepared for the litigation that follows. But if a lawyer is predisposed to the litigation process and approaches the negotiations expecting them to fail, she will not be an effective representative.

While negotiation might involve significant compromise, if the negotiation fails those concessions will not necessarily follow the parties to the next stage. Legal concessions, compromises, and admissions that are given during the negotiation process are generally made **without prejudice**. This means that they cannot be used against the party making the admission or compromise in subsequent litigation. Finally, well-handled negotiations will not harm an ongoing relationship. In fact, they may actually strengthen it, as the parties will have gone through a process of cooperation and compromise, resulting in increased trust and interdependence.

**Relationship may be enhanced**

A failure at negotiation may lead to litigation, but it is also interesting that sometimes a failure to achieve a settlement through litigation can lead to more effective negotiation. Native tribes in British Columbia have long contested their rights to lands and territories in the province. Their demands led to several protracted and unsatisfying legal battles culminating in several hearings before the Supreme Court of Canada. In the *Delgamuukw* decision rendered in 1997,[49] the Supreme Court ordered a new trial but also made it clear that it believed the best approach was the negotiation process. Armed with that endorsement, the provincial government and representatives of the Nisga'a Tribal Council embarked on serious negotiations, accomplishing in a little over a year what had not been accomplished in decades of legal wrangling. A treaty acceptable to both sides resulted—reminding us that negotiation, the most basic of all dispute resolution processes, should hold a significant place in all business relationships.

## Mediation

Mediation also has a long history in resolving disputes. Its use in labour relations has been mandated by statutes for most of the century, and its use in family disputes is commonplace. Mediation has always played a role in commercial relations but has become much more visible in recent years. The main difference between negotiation and mediation is that mediation involves a neutral third party who is trained to assist the parties in coming to an agreement. Her role is to facilitate the discussion, making sure that each side has the opportunity to put his side forward, eliciting information, finding areas of possible compromise, and encouraging settlement. Mediators do not impose decisions, but they may make recommendations if they have some expertise in the matter under dispute.

**Neutral third party facilitates communication**

The mediation process can be very informal or it can be carefully structured with rules of procedure and a set timeframe. Usually, only a few meetings are necessary. The process begins by the mediator summarizing her role and discussing what will occur during the proceedings. Both parties then make an opening statement, describing their positions. One of the main objectives of using a mediator is to find some common ground that can be used as the basis of a settlement. The mediator will meet with both parties together and separately, often forming a communication link between them. By determining which compromises each party is willing to make, the mediator can encourage the parties to move toward a solution.

**Mediator finds common ground**

Many different techniques and variations are available to the mediator. It is this flexibility that makes the process effective in the hands of a skilled mediator.

---

49. *Delgamuukw v. British Columbia,* [1997] 3 S.C.R. 1010.

**Mediator does not make decision**

Because the mediator is so involved in the decision-making process, it is vitally important that she be ethical, free of bias, and highly skilled. The key to understanding the success of mediation is to realize that the persuasiveness, skills, and neutrality of a trained third party are introduced while control of the problem is retained by each party. The mediator does not impose a solution on the parties, but encourages them to come to one on their own. If the parties cannot come to an agreement, they are still free to seek other solutions. If the matter does end up in court before an agreement is concluded, any concessions made at the mediation will not be taken into consideration. Of course, if a settlement is reached and put into an agreement, it can be enforced just like any other contract. In addition to this, a settlement that has been reached by both parties is more likely to be adhered to than one that has been imposed on them. This saves the enforcement costs that often accompany a court order.

Successful mediators require considerable specialized training, and there are organizations that provide membership and certification and that set recognized professional standards. The disputing parties will normally choose a mediator who is a member in good standing with such an organization. They may, in fact, choose a mediator from a list provided by the organization.[50]

**Mediation may be required**

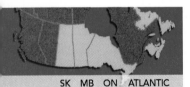

SK  MB  ON  ATLANTIC

In several situations, mediation has been mandated by statute—perhaps the highest-profile of these is in collective bargaining. In most jurisdictions, either party or the government can call for the services of a mediator, selected from a pool of professional labour mediators. While the mediator is trying to help the disputing parties reach a settlement, other forms of labour action, including strikes and lockouts, are prohibited. Mediation in these circumstances is more structured and formal. Still, mediators have many different strategies they can bring to the process and are often successful in bringing the dispute to an end. Even in the litigation process itself, mediation may be mandated before a trial can proceed.[51]

### Fee Mediation

In Alberta, if you think that your lawyer's bill is too high, you may have it reviewed by a court clerk called a "taxing officer"; the review is called a *taxation*.[52] Your lawyer must be given notice of a taxation hearing, and is entitled to make submissions (he may even call witnesses!) at the hearing, which will be recorded and a transcript will be made. A taxation may be appealed to the Court of Queen's Bench.

A taxation, like litigation, is adversarial in nature. It is possible, however, to avoid the process. The Law Society of Alberta offers a fee mediation service.[53] The service is voluntary, and is provided free to both the client and the lawyer. Upon the request of the client or the lawyer, the Law Society will appoint a mediator to

---

50. One example of such an organization is the ADR Institute of Canada, online: **http://www.amic.org/**.

51. Ontario has introduced a Mandatory Mediation pilot project, which requires that a mediation session take place after a statement of defence has been filed. See *supra* note 32. In Alberta, parties involved in small claims litigation may be required to attempt mediation before a trial date will be fixed. See *Mediation Rules of the Provincial Court—Civil Division,* Alta. Reg. 271/1997.

52. See James Christensen and Joe Morin, "Taxation of a Lawyer's Bill" (May 2002), online: Alberta Courts **http://www.albertacourts.ab.ca/cs/taxoffice/TaxationofaLawyers-.pdf**.

53. "Are You Unhappy with Your Lawyer's Account?" Online: Law Society of Alberta **http://www.lawsocietyalberta.com/public_legal/fee_mediation.asp**.

help resolve the fee dispute. Members of the Law Society serve as mediators and, as such, have no power to impose solutions or make decisions. As in all mediation, the mediator in fee mediation simply tries to help the parties come to an agreement. If the mediation is not successful, then the client may begin the taxation process. Other jurisdictions offer similar programs and services.

## Disadvantages of Mediation

In spite of the obvious advantages of mediation (such as being private, less costly, faster, and more flexible), there are some important disadvantages to consider. In the case of mediation involving a client and a professional (such as a doctor or a lawyer) when there has been actual malpractice or negligence, it is unlikely that the full truth of the situation would come out in mediation. Therefore, mediation is not a good forum when blame needs to be established, or when some other legal right or precedent should be set. If it is necessary to obtain confidential or secret information, it is more likely to be forthcoming through the discovery part of litigation. Mediators have little power to compel parties to produce evidence and documentation when they are unwilling to do so. When compensation for loss and damages for injuries are being sought, there is no power provided in the mediation process to enforce such agreements.

**Mediation may be inappropriate**

In other situations, when one of the parties is weaker, mediation may just exacerbate that weakness. This can be a serious problem in family disputes, when the weakness of one of the parties—or his desire to accommodate—leads to an unbalanced result. It is important in such situations for the parties to have legal counsel throughout the process, or at the very least to have their lawyers review the terms of the agreement before they sign it. The job of the mediator is to help the parties reach an agreement, not to ensure that the agreement is fair and balanced. When one of the parties is suspected of acting in bad faith mediation is simply inappropriate, because trust is such an important component of the mediation process.

**Successful mediation requires balance of power**

**and willingness to act in good faith**

Another potential disadvantage of mediation is that there is no public record of a mediated settlement; therefore it cannot become a precedent, and it may not be consistent with past practice. If the settlement is later regretted, there is no appeal to a higher court. Many people find the very flexibility of the mediation process uncomfortable, preferring a more formal and rule-oriented process.

Mediation does work well when highly confidential or sensitive information that should not be disclosed to the public is involved, a speedy resolution is vital,

## Reducing **Risk** 2.5

There are a variety of circumstances in which mediation might be preferable to and more productive than other means of dispute resolution. One example would be where the benefits of a continuing relationship outweigh the benefits of securing a damage award. In the construction industry, the owner of a building may grow disgruntled if the contractor evidently will fail to complete the project on time or is over budget. The owner could sue for damages from the delinquent contractor, but it is likely that work on the project would stop. If the owner is otherwise satisfied with the work, it may make little sense to pursue the matter through the courts. Rather than expending time, energy, and expense on litigation, it may be more reason-

able to call in a mediator who has knowledge of the construction industry. This mediator could help the parties arrive at an understanding of the problems each has faced; possibly, there were unforeseen circumstances that contributed to delays or cost overruns. The mediator may establish the consequences of continuing under new arrangements or breaking off the relationship. The parties can then decide whether new agreements or compromises can be reached. In fact, in the construction sector, it is reported that millions of dollars are saved annually in jurisdictions where the first recourse in the event of problems is to mediate rather than to litigate.

good ongoing relations must be maintained, there is some trust involved, or both parties are desirous of reaching a settlement.

## Variations on Mediation

Mini-trials conducted outside of the judicial system may be valuable as an alternative dispute mechanism, especially in a corporate setting involving internal disputes. In a corporate mini-trial, the senior managers hear the case presented by lawyers, much as it would be presented in a court. Usually, there has been some discovery process and witnesses have been called and cross-examined, or the lawyers have simply summarized what they would have said. It is quite a formal process involving some cost and time. It is, however, still a private process, and still within the control of the parties. This is an effective way to get across the various positions of the parties, as well as their legal ramifications for both the individuals and the corporation. The managers listen to the evidence and the arguments and make a decision as if they were the judges. Because all relevant information can be presented, and both parties have an opportunity to be heard, it is more likely that they will accept the managers' decision. Each party becomes aware of the other's legal position, and can therefore determine whether it would be beneficial to pursue the matter in court. Confidentiality is maintained and adverse publicity is avoided. At the same time, many of the advantages of a trial, such as adherence to due process, are present. This approach is particularly useful when the issues and information are quite technical and require considerable expertise. Expert witnesses are commonly called to testify, and complicated documentation can be introduced.

**Simulated court hearings**

### Case Summary 2.5

#### Mediating Gender Bias by Mini-trial

Gillian had been working with a large and reputable architectural firm for a couple of years as a junior architect. She was a talented designer and had demonstrated a unique ability in the assignments she had been given. Unfortunately, she often found herself drawing up blueprints for the projects of the more senior members of the firm. It eventually became clear to her that younger male architects, even those more recently hired than she, were getting their own interesting projects while she was being kept in the background, busy with the mundane tasks of the firm. She approached her supervisor for an explanation but he brushed her off, claiming that the firm's clients were not interested in having women work for them and that she had better get used to that fact if she wanted a job in the industry at all. Gillian took her complaints to the senior partner. He had not seen her work, nor did he know much about her, but he was not eager to have a gender-discrimination complaint lodged against his firm. After some deliberation, he suggested to Gillian that they deal with the problem through a mini-trial, and he agreed that the firm would cover the costs of legal representation for both sides of the issue. Gillian and her supervisor were allowed the opportunity to prepare their cases. The three senior partners convened a mini-trial at which both sides were able to put forward their evidence, concerns, and arguments. Each side was treated with respect, and each was encouraged to present a full case for themselves. Gillian was able to demonstrate her capabilities; her supervisor brought in the clients who had expressed their disinclination to work with women. At the hearing, all the relevant legal and human rights issues were raised. During their private deliberations, the three-judge panel reconsidered the firm's traditional policies, recognizing that even though it had never been explicitly stated as such, the message was understood by most employees that this was not an environment in which women were encouraged to progress, or were even expected to succeed. Their decision to change that policy, and to demonstrate it by giving Gillian a broader range of responsibilities and assignments, illustrates the unique opportunities given to executives hearing and dealing with sensitive issues within the confines of their own workplace by utilizing the mini-trial format.

## Arbitration

The third major category of alternative dispute resolution involves surrendering the decision making to a third party. In most cases arbitration is voluntary, but in some situations, such as labour relations, the parties are required by statute to agree to some arbitration mechanism as part of the collective agreement process.[54] In other instances, though, the requirement to arbitrate disputes and the method for choosing an arbitrator are contained in the original contract between the parties. In such a case, arbitration is agreed upon before any dispute has arisen. Alternatively, the parties may agree to use arbitration as the best method of resolution after a conflict has developed. Arbitration can be very effective when external disputes arise with creditors, suppliers, or customers, and even internally with employees and shareholders or between departments.

**Arbitration involves third-party decision maker**

Typically, the arbitrator is chosen from a pool of trained and certified professionals. Organizations of professional arbitrators have been established, and the members offer their services like any other professional.[55] These organizations not only provide training and certification, but also set professional and ethical standards requiring that their members be properly trained, avoid conflicts of interest, be free of bias, and keep all information they obtain in strict confidence. Arbitrators are often lawyers, retired judges, or businesspeople with expertise in the particular area in dispute. Sometimes a panel of three arbitrators is chosen, with each side selecting one panelist and then those two choosing a third neutral member. The original agreement between the parties, and the agreement of employment of the arbitrator, will set out fees, time limits, and any restrictions on the decision that can reached. For example, in a hearing to determine whether an employee was improperly dismissed, a decision to reinstate the employee may be beyond the mandate of the decision maker. As well, the power to award punitive damages will likely be withheld.

**Arbitrators may be experts in the field**

**Arbitrators are chosen by parties**

Parties can stipulate in their contract that, should a dispute arise, the matter will be referred to an arbitrator, and that the provincial arbitration legislation will apply to the process. Then, should one party try to commence litigation, a stay of proceedings can be obtained.[56] Alternatively, the procedure to be followed may be set out in the agreement,[57] and sometimes the arbitrators themselves can design the process to meet the needs of the parties and the dispute.

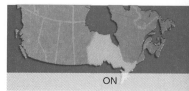

**Procedure often agreed upon, but must be fair**

---

54. See, for example, s. 48 of Ontario's *Labour Relations Act, 1995,* S.O. 1995, c. 1, Sch. A.

55. One such organization is the ADR Institute of Canada, *supra* note 50.

56. See, for example, s. 7 of Ontario's *Arbitration Act, 1991,* S.O. 1991, c. 17.

57. The ADR Institute of Canada recently published National Arbitration Rules, which the parties can agree to use to resolve their contractual disputes. See online: **http://www.amic.org/rules/ national_arb_rules.html**.

Prior to the hearing, some discovery of information usually takes place, which may take the form of a pre-arbitration hearing. At the hearing itself, the lawyers or other representatives begin by introducing their cases. They examine witnesses, present documents, make arguments, and summarize their cases. Formal rules of evidence need not be adhered to, nor is the arbitrator required to follow precedent in reaching the decision. Where the process is mandated by statute, as in labour disputes, the requirements are much more stringent. Arbitration mandated by statute may, in fact, approach a court hearing in its formality and adherence to legal rules of process. The arbitrator(s) then make(s) a decision, usually rendering it in writing, giving reasons. The arbitrator's decision is binding on the parties and is generally not appealable. But because this is a quasi-judicial process, the courts will still exercise supervisory power over the arbitrator. If she has exceeded her powers, or the process used has not provided for a fair hearing, the courts may overturn the decision. If there has been a clear error of law either in the decision or reasons, the decision may also be reviewed.

The unique feature of arbitration is that a third party makes the decision. To be effective, it is vital that the parties be required to honour that decision. Most jurisdictions provide that the decisions reached by arbitrators are binding and enforceable.[58] As a result, arbitration is usually an effective process.

Arbitration is, however, still essentially adversarial in nature. In this sense it is like litigation, with the attendant danger that bitterness and hard feelings may be aggravated. Arbitration is more costly than other forms of ADR, because it is more formal and involves more people, but it is still much less expensive than the litigation process.

Ideally, arbitration should be voluntary, but clauses requiring arbitration are finding their way into standard form contracts at an alarming rate. These contracts often cover consumer transactions, with the consumer unaware that he has surrendered the right to a court hearing until the dispute arises. Because the decision is binding and non-appealable, the disgruntled party may challenge the validity of the arbitration clause in court, compounding an already complex resolution procedure.

Arbitration may look much like litigation, but it is still private and still within the control of the parties. Where expertise is important, an arbitrator with that expertise can be chosen. Arbitration is faster, less costly, and more private than litigation, but it also has disadvantages. There may be little certainty or predictability, as precedents are not binding and there is generally no right to appeal the decision. The process may, however, be reviewed by the courts, which have reserved to themselves the power to ensure that the process is fair. Animosity between the parties may actually increase, as the process is by nature adversarial. When disclosure of information is important, obtaining that information will not be as effective as with the discovery process in litigation.

### Case Summary 2.6

#### CAMVAP's Successful Arbitration

Miguel bought a new vehicle from a dealership in town, purchasing straight off the showroom floor. He was pleased with it until the CD player stopped working, as did the clock and the interior lights. He took the car back to the dealership, which agreed to have the car repaired, even going to the extent of replacing the

---

58. *Arbitration Act, 1991,* S.O. 1991, c. 17, *supra* note 56, s. 50.

*Margin notes:*

**Decision cannot be appealed but process may be reviewed by court**

**Third party makes a decision that is binding**

**Arbitration is private**

stereo. In fact, the service department spent hours, at no charge to Miguel, trying to find the problem in the electrical system. After each visit, things would work normally in the car for a short while, but inevitably some quirky new electrical problem would arise, bringing Miguel back to the shop every week or so for months. The service people could not locate the source of the problem. Finally, Miguel was fed up with the inconvenience of all this and demanded a new car, adamant that he would not pay another cent for it. By this time, the dealership was certain that Miguel was tampering with the car and that he was, in effect, creating his own problems. Their good relationship had deteriorated to the extent that there was a shouting match every time Miguel came into the dealership. Fortunately, the manager of the dealership became involved. He suggested that Miguel apply to the CAMVAP (the Canadian Motor Vehicle Arbitration Plan)[59] to have his case heard. Miguel, recognizing that he would be unlikely to get satisfaction any other way, booked an appointment with the arbitrator. In this instance, the manufacturer, the dealership, and the owner all had the opportunity to put forward their stories, and the arbitrator, experienced in the issues and complaints surrounding the purchase of new cars, was able to make a decision that was binding on all the parties.

## Variations on Arbitration

Often, the tools of mediation and arbitration will be brought together in a *mediation–arbitration process.* This involves the third party starting out as a mediator and, if it grows clear that the parties cannot reach a settlement even with the mediator's help, the mediator then becomes an arbitrator, making a decision that is binding on both parties. The advantage is that mediation is attempted in a non-adversarial atmosphere, preserving the good will and trust relationship between the parties. Still, the parties have the added pressure of knowing that if they fail to reach an agreement one will be imposed on them. Where a fast decision is needed, this approach can be very effective.

**Mediator may become an arbitrator**

*Private judging* is another variation of arbitration, but is much more formal in nature. The parties, in effect, hire a judge to hold a private trial—using formal rules of evidence, due process, precedent, and other legal requirements, but where the process and the outcomes are still private and confidential. This is just a very formal form of arbitration. In some jurisdictions in the United States, parties can hire a retired magistrate or judge to hold a private trial. Where such a process is authorized by statute it takes on the same characteristics as a trial, with

**Private judges may be hired**

## Reducing **Risk** 2.6

ADR services are now being offered online. Such services can be very helpful in attempting to mediate between corporations and their customers, when information, services, or products do not meet expectations or where customers have not fulfilled their obligations. In addition, such intermediaries may serve to set standards, monitor compliance, and warn potential customers where problems exist. As there is little regulation controlling ADR generally, it is likely that there will be even less in the electronic environment. Businesspeople should ensure that the services are being offered by qualified professionals and be aware that they may have little recourse if things go wrong.

---

59. For more information on CAMVAP, see online: **http://camvap.ca**, and Peter Portlock, "Fair, Fast, Free, Friendly, and Final," *Law Now* (April/May 1997) 19.

the hired judge having the same power and authority as a regular judge. In these situations, the decision has the status of a court decision and can be enforced using the power of the court. There is also a right of appeal.

As the courts have become more congested, with corresponding increases in delay and costs, they too have resorted to their own methods of reducing the caseload. Some provinces have informal *judicial dispute resolution (JDR)* processes, such as judicial mediation and mini-trials. Outside the courts, private alternative dispute resolution is becoming much more commonplace and acceptable. We can expect it to play a greater role in the future.

# Summary

## The courts

- Procedural rules govern structure and function, which may vary with jurisdiction.
- Open to the public, with some exceptions.
- Both criminal and civil functions at trial and appellate levels.
- All but lower-level provincial court judges are appointed by federal government.

### Provincial courts
- Handle less serious criminal offences; civil matters under a set amount; custody and maintenance in family divisions; youth offenders.

### Superior courts
- Handle serious criminal offences; civil matters with unlimited monetary jurisdiction; divorce.

### Appellate courts
- Deal with appeals of law from trial courts; usually have three judges; do not rehear the facts; usually hold final hearing for most criminal and civil matters.

### Federal courts
- Tax Court hears cases involving federal tax matters.
- Federal Court hears disputes within federal jurisdiction and appeals from some administrative tribunals.
- Federal Court of Appeal hears appeals from Federal Court, Tax Court, and some administrative tribunals.

### Supreme Court of Canada
- Highest-level appeal court.
- Deals primarily with Constitutional and Charter matters, as well as cases of national importance.

## Process of civil litigation

### Pre-trial
- Plaintiff files writ of summons (if required) and statement of claim.
- Defendant responds with appearance (if required) and statement of defence.
- Discovery of documents and questioning of parties by opposing counsel.

- Payment into court or offer of settlement to encourage reasonable demands and offers.
- Purpose—to bring information to light and encourage settlement.

Trial
- Examination of witnesses and presentation of evidence.

Judgment
- Jury decides questions of fact.
- Judge decides questions of law.
- Some legal costs usually paid by loser.

Remedies
- Damages—general, special, punitive.
- Accounting, injunction, specific performance, declaration.

Enforcement
- Examination in aid of execution
- Seizure of property.
- Garnishment.

Limitation periods
- Set by statute.

## Alternative dispute resolution (ADR)

- Recent trend to avoid costs and delays associated with litigation.

Advantages
- Control, timeliness, productivity, cost, privacy, good will, flexibility.

Disadvantages
- Unpredictable, no precedents set, cannot deal with complex legal problems.
- Must be voluntary, must have a balance of powers between the parties.
- Parties must cooperate to ensure agreement and resolution.

Methods
- Negotiation—direct discussion between parties.
- Mediation—neutral third party facilitates discussion.
- Arbitration—neutral expert makes a binding decision.

## QUESTIONS

1. Describe the court hierarchy in Canada, including provincial and federal courts.

2. Distinguish between questions of law and questions of fact, and explain why this distinction is significant.

3. Who appoints provincial superior court judges? Provincial court judges?

4. What are the pleadings used to commence an action in the superior trial court in your jurisdiction?

5. How does the discovery process take place, and what is its significance in civil litigation?

6. Explain how a payment into court can affect the judgment award made by the court to the plaintiff.

7. Describe the recent initiatives taken in your jurisdiction to "speed up" the litigation process.

8. Explain the trial process.

9. Compare party–party costs to solicitor–client costs. To whom are these costs generally awarded?

10. Distinguish among the various remedies available to a successful plaintiff in a civil action.

11. Explain what an examination in aid of execution is and explain its value in the collection process.

12. How can a judgment be enforced against a debtor who is trying to avoid payment?

13. Explain the value of an injunction as a pre-judgment remedy. Discuss other pre-judgment remedies available to aid in the collection of debt.

14. What is a limitation period, and what effect can it have on the right of parties to litigate a matter in dispute?

15. List and describe the principal advantages of alternative dispute resolution.

16. Distinguish between negotiation and mediation.

17. While a mediated settlement is not binding on the parties, it brings with it certain benefits. What are they?

18. What are the essential differences between mediation and arbitration?

19. How are arbitration and litigation similar?

20. What are the disadvantages of having matters resolved outside the courts?

---

## CASES

### 1. *T. v. T.*, [2003] O.J. No.132.

A husband and wife were involved in matrimonial litigation. The husband asked the Court for an order that he and his wife be identified only by initials, and that the court documents be sealed. The husband said that the wife's allegations were malicious and false, and that embarrassing sexual matters were in issue. He also argued that his wife and children from his second and third marriages would be hurt by publication. Should there be an open trial, or should the court documents remain sealed? Explain your reasoning.

### 2. *Royal Trust Corp. of Canada v. Dunn* (1991), 6 O.R. (3d) 468 (Gen. Div.).

Royal Trust loaned just over $200 000 to the four defendants, taking security in the form of a mortgage for the loan. The loan was defaulted upon, and an action was commenced against them. The lawyers acting for Royal Trust served a copy of the statement of claim on the lawyer who had acted for the defendants when they had purchased the property, and that lawyer, in turn, forwarded it to the defendant he had dealt with. None of the defendants responded to the statement of claim, and so Royal Trust obtained a default judgment against them. In this action, the defendants are applying to have the judgment set aside, claiming improper service. Explain the nature of their complaint and the likely outcome.

### 3. *Ferme Gérald Laplante & Fils Ltée. v. Grenville Patron Mutual Fire Insurance Co.* (2002), 61 O.R. (3d) 481 (C.A.).

A fire on a farm caused much damage to property, including livestock. The insurer made an initial payment to the insured, but some aspects of his claim became very contentious, such as the applicability of co-insurance for some of the property, and compensation for the injured livestock, the loss on the sale of the remaining cattle, and the loss of business earnings. The jury decided all of these issues in favour of the insured. Because the insurer had refused to pay the amounts claimed in respect of these issues and had delayed in paying other parts of the claim, the jury awarded punitive damages of $750 000. The insurer appealed to the Court of Appeal. Should the appellate court set aside the punitive damages award? Why or why not? Justify your conclusions.

### 4. *Automatic Systems Inc. v. Bracknell Corp.* (1994), 18 O.R. (3d) 257 (C.A.).

An American corporation (Automatic Systems Inc.) entered into a contract with an Ontario corporation to do electrical work on an Ontario construction project involving the assembly line of an automotive manufacturing plant. The work was subcontracted to Bracknell Corp. This subcontract provided that the agreement was to be subject to Missouri law and that any disputes arising under the contract were to be settled by arbitration in Missouri. When disputes arose that were not resolved, Bracknell filed a construction lien against the property, as permitted under Ontario law. This application was brought by Automatic Systems Inc. to have that lien set aside and to force the dispute to be resolved by arbitration. Explain any arguments that might be presented by the parties and the likely outcome.

### 5. *Her Majesty the Queen in right of Alberta v. Advantico Internet Solutions Inc.*, BCICAC File No. DCA-689 CIRA, online: Canadian Internet Registration Authority

http://www.cira.ca/en/dpr-decisions/00012-albertagovernment-en.pdf.

Advantico registered the domain name **albertagovernment.ca** on November 9, 2000. (It also registered the domain name **ontariogovernment.ca**.) Advantico used the domain name in connection with a pornographic website that attracted internet users intending to contact the Alberta government. Advantico does not produce any goods, and does not provide any services, for which the words "Alberta government" are displayed. What legal process can the government of Alberta use to get the domain name transferred to it? (Hint: Check out the Canadian Internet Registration Authority.)

# 3

# Government Regulation and the Environment

## CHAPTER HIGHLIGHTS

- Source and nature of government powers
- Function and purpose of administrative tribunals
- Role of the courts in reviewing administrative decisions
- Remedies available when administrative bodies abuse their powers
- Legislative restrictions on judicial review of administrative decisions
- Legal issues relating to the protection of the environment
- Competing interests of economic growth and environmental protection
- Resolving conflicts in environmental law

It should be evident to students that not all disputes can or should be heard by the courts. In fact, the most likely forum where businesspeople will face disputes will be before administrative tribunals. One of the characteristics of our society is the ever-expanding role of government, especially where business activities are concerned. Government, through its statutory power, creates agencies to oversee the implementation and enforcement of the statutes that are passed. In the process, government agents are authorized to create regulations that have a wide-reaching impact on businesspeople. When government officials overstep the authority granted to them under the statute, or otherwise abuse their powers, individuals have some recourse against unfair treatment. Our rights before such tribunals, and the role of the courts in resolving such disputes, are the first concerns of this chapter. We conclude the chapter by demonstrating how judge-made, statutory, and regulatory laws work together to facilitate the functioning of business and to preserve societal interests and standards in the area of environmental law. In the process, we will see how the various dispute resolution processes discussed in this chapter and in Chapter 2 complement and balance each other in this controversial and politically conflict-ridden area.

## Case Summary 3.1

### WasThere a Reasonable Apprehension of Bias? *Ahumada v. Canada (Minister of Citizenship and Immigration)*[1]

W, employee of CIC, seconded to CRDD,
where she sits as a member of panel on A's refugee claim

CIC → CRDD

employees appear in front of CRDD on refugee claims, such as that made by A

panel members make decisions on refugee claims, such as that made by A

W will return to CIC—will she be rewarded because "proper" decision was made by panel on A's refugee claim?

Mr. Ahumada applied for refugee status in Canada. The Convention Refugee Determination Division of the Immigration and Refugee Board (CRDD) dismissed his claim. Ms. Workun was a member of the panel of the CRDD that made the decision. She was an employee of Citizenship and Immigration Canada (CIC), where she worked as an enforcement officer. During her appointment to the CRDD, she was on a temporary leave of absence from CIC. The Federal Court, Trial Division, quashed the CRDD's decision, and remitted the matter to a different constituted panel. The Trial Division held that, as Ms. Workun was sitting as a member of the CRDD, a tribunal she appeared before on behalf of the CIC, there was a reasonable apprehension of bias.

The Federal Court of Appeal dismissed the government's appeal. The Court stated that the test for bias in an independent adjudicative tribunal, such as the CRDD, is "whether a reasonable person, who is informed of the facts, viewing the matter realistically and practically … would think it more likely than not that the tribunal was biased." The Court held that a reasonable apprehension of bias arose because a panel member in Ms. Workun's position might believe that when she returned to her duties with CIC she would be rewarded or punished, depending on whether her decisions had conformed to CIC's view. To eliminate this potential bias, CIC enforcement employees appointed to the CRDD must relinquish their CIC employment.

Many activities are scrutinized and controlled, either by government regulators and administrators or by professional and business organizations that, while private, are created by statute. These bodies have considerable power, but it must be exercised fairly; otherwise, the decision can be challenged in court. A reasonable apprehension of bias on the part of the decision maker may cause the courts to declare the process invalid. This does not necessarily mean that the complainant escapes all consequences or penalties attendant to his conduct. Often, the courts order a new hearing to be held if there were procedural defects in the first hearing. So, while the right to challenge such abuse might be available, it is not always wise to do so. This portion of the chapter discusses the role of government, its regulatory agencies, and the rights of people who deal with them.

1. [2001] 3 F.C. 605 (C.A.).

# Regulatory Role of Government

The commercial and industrial progress of the past century has been matched by the growth of government agencies to regulate it. In the last few decades, the size of government has expanded at an astonishing rate, intruding into the lives of its citizens in an unprecedented way. There has recently been some relief through deregulation, but businesses still face a daunting variety of stringent government restrictions and regulations. While in most cases the intrusions are beneficial, and the decisions of administrators justifiable, government officials sometimes abuse their positions, or go beyond their authority, when they make decisions that affect individuals or businesses.

**Government consists of legislative branch, judicial branch, and executive branch**

Government is divided into three different functions: legislative, judicial, and executive. While the **legislative branch** is supreme in Canada, its powers have been limited in two significant ways. First, the *Constitution Act (1867)* divides power between the federal and provincial governments, thus limiting the power of each to its assigned area. Second, the *Charter of Rights and Freedoms* places specific limits on what Parliament and the provincial legislatures can do.

There is little difficulty in distinguishing the **judicial branch** of government (the courts) from the rest of government activity. However, the legislative branch and the executive branch have become somewhat blurred in Canada. Parliament and the provincial legislatures are the principal law-making bodies. From those assemblies are drawn the prime minister, premiers, and cabinet ministers who are, in turn, responsible for the various ministries and departments that perform the work of government. This is the **executive branch** of government. In Canada, the theoretical head of the executive branch is the Queen, and so this aspect of government is often referred to as the Crown.

**Executive branch also known as the Crown**

**Executive branch creates and enforces regulations**

People's dealings with government are usually with *civil servants*, or the people who make up the bureaucracy of the executive branch. The executive branch is divided into categories on the basis of primary function: for example, service agencies, such as law enforcement, education, health, and welfare; administrative departments, which include revenue, taxation, and the internal management of government systems; and regulatory bodies, concerned with such matters as the environment, product safety, employment, and human rights. When a legislative body creates a statute that needs to be enforced, the statute will normally provide for the establishment of a department and for the regulations that will control the affairs of that department. Such regulations stipulate how the terms of the statute will be implemented and enforced, and how complaints will be dealt with.

**Must follow recognized standards of justice**

Administrators of the statutes thus have decision-making powers that can profoundly affect the people with whom they have dealings. In exercising these powers, they must act not only in accordance with the enabling statute, but also according to the standards of justice that have been recognized in our democratic tradition. So, while the administrators have been given considerable discretionary powers, and while they need not follow all the rules found in the judicial system (such as the rules of evidence) when making decisions, they must, however, act within the terms of the legislation that empowers them, adhere to certain basic procedural fairness requirements, and not abuse their powers. If they do not satisfy these requirements, their decisions may be overturned by the courts.

The Government of Canada exercises its power and control over businesses and individuals in many ways. The power may be exercised directly through government departments and their bureaucrats, or indirectly through Crown corporations (such as the Canadian Broadcasting Corporation) or independent agencies (such as the Canadian Radio-television and Telecommunications Commission or the National Energy Board). The methods used to wield this power can take several forms. Often, control is exercised directly through rules that are enforced with various kinds of penalties. This means of achieving compliance is supplemented by other less direct methods, such as economic incentives and other forms of political persuasion, including public education. One of the main functions of government, and the most significant aspect of its power, is the distribution of government funds through grants, loans, investments, and various types of joint initiatives. It is also common for governments to influence how businesses operate, through advertising, educational programs, and public awareness campaigns.

**Compliance achieved through rule enforcement, economic incentives, and education**

The following discussion is primarily concerned with the rules and controls created under the various statutes and imposed on businesses and individuals by administrative bodies and agencies. The administrator may be implementing government policy, choosing among applicants when distributing government funds, granting licences and permits, or determining when there has been an infringement of the regulations. There are as many different ways that government exerts control over business as there are statutes and regulations, and it is not possible to examine them all. Rather, we will concentrate on what can be done when these government activities collide with our basic rights and interests, and then look at the impact of the regulatory system on environmental law as an example.

# Administrative Law

## Regulators

The regulation of business is conducted through many government institutions, including ministries, departments, boards, commissions, agencies, tribunals, and individual bureaucrats at the federal, provincial, and municipal levels. Government departments, such as Transport Canada or Health Canada, administer programs, while other departments, such as the Office of Consumer Affairs and Environment Canada, are primarily regulators whose responsibility is to ensure that private individuals and organizations conform to statutory regulations. Often, the functions of government departments overlap—as in transportation and environment when they are concerned with the transport of hazardous products. Crown agencies or Crown corporations have regulatory responsibilities assigned to them under the Act that created them. They have been granted more political autonomy to provide some distance between the decisions they make and the government. The CRTC operating under the terms of the *Broadcasting Act* is an example of such a commission.

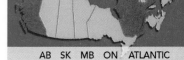

AB   SK   MB   ON   ATLANTIC

### Case Summary 3.2

**Can a Cabinet Minister Change His Mind?** *Comeau's Sea Foods Ltd. v. Canada (Minister of Fisheries and Oceans)*[2]

The Minister of Fisheries and Oceans advised the plaintiff (and other fishermen) that he had authorized the issue of offshore lobster licences. The Minister specifically allocated the allowable annual fishing catch for each of the fishermen. The Department of Fisheries and Oceans then asked each of them to submit fishing

2. [1997] 1 S.C.R. 12.

plans for the balance of the current season. The plaintiff provided all of the required information, and then incurred $500 000 in expenses in converting a fishing vessel. Some time later, the Minister announced that the licences would not be issued, pending a study of the relevant issues. The Supreme Court held that the Minister was not acting *ultra vires* (or beyond his legal authority) in revoking the authorization to issue licences he had previously given. The legislation gives the Minister "absolute discretion" to either issue, or authorize to issue, fishing licences. The only restriction on this discretion is the requirement of natural justice. The Minister must base his decision on relevant considerations, avoid arbitrariness, and act in good faith. An authorization to issue a licence does not confer an irrevocable legal right to a licence. Until the licence is actually issued, the Minister can reconsider his original decision to authorize the licence.

**Standards set for regulators**

Whether government administrators are merely implementing government policy (such as a clerk granting a building permit or business licence), or acting as a referee or judge (such as a labour relations board adjudicating a labour dispute), there are certain standards they must maintain. When acting as judges or referees, government decision makers are often referred to as **administrative tribunals** (whether the decisions are made by a committee, a commission, a tribunal, or an individual). The area of law that describes an individual's rights before such a tribunal is called *administrative law*. The administrator's authority is granted by statute.

## Advantages of Administrative Tribunals

**Administrative decision makers have special expertise**

Keeping in mind that one of the purposes of these administrative bodies is to keep matters out of the courts, it is important to note some functional advantages. Administrative decision makers are appointed to their positions because they have expertise in the area. They are often career public servants who, through their continuity of service, acquire a detailed knowledge of the terms and goals of the statute, as well as the programs and activities of their departments. They often have considerable discretionary power to allow for decisions that can serve the interests of both the department and the complainant. In most cases they are not bound by precedent, and so each case can be judged on its merits. Tribunals can hear a matter and make a decision promptly, overcoming the delay and expense often associated with court hearings. While a tribunal's job is to enforce the regulations, the possibility that a court will review the process by which its decision was made constrains it to act within the jurisdiction of the statute and the limits prescribed by the court.

To determine whether the decision of a civil servant or administrative tribunal can be challenged or reviewed by a court, reference should be made to two basic principles that govern the actions of decision makers. First, the decision must have been made within the authority of the official or board (*intra vires*). Second, the process involved and the conduct of the decision maker must have been proper. As a general rule, the merits of the decision itself are not questioned, as would be the case in an appeal. It is not the function of the court to revisit the decision; rather, the court is to supervise the process. For this reason, **When powers are abused, judicial review available** the process is called **judicial review** rather than an appeal. It is only where a decision is completely unreasonable that the court will overturn the decision.

The courts recognize that administrative tribunals have special expertise in the matters being considered and that their decisions should not be interfered with lightly. The Supreme Court of Canada has established a standard to determine when the decision of a tribunal can be challenged; as long as the administrative decision maker has acted within the authority granted, and any discretion has been exercised in a fair and honest way so that the decision can be said to be reasonable, the decision will stand.[3] This general reluctance on the part of the courts to interfere with the decisions of properly functioning administrative tribunals should be kept in mind while reading the following discussion.

## The Authority of the Decision Maker

A fundamental aspect of the constitutional tradition we inherited from Britain is the **rule of law.** The rule of law holds that, even given parliamentary supremacy, neither Parliament nor any government official representing Parliament can act arbitrarily. They cannot rely on their status to justify their actions, but must be able to point to some authorizing statute or regulation. When a government official or board cannot point to some valid statute that authorized their conduct or decision, the decision can be challenged as *ultra vires* (or beyond their power), and set aside. The courts and the executive branch are also bound by the rule of law, and even when they have been given discretionary power that discretion cannot be exercised arbitrarily. Such discretionary power must be exercised within a framework of rules based on fairness, equality, and justice.

**Government agents must act within existing law**

### Statutory Authority

The first step in challenging an administrative tribunal, then, is to examine the statutory authority and determine if the tribunal's conduct or actions were authorized under it. This statutory authority may be found not only in the statute itself, but also in the regulations passed under that statute. While Parliament and the provincial legislative assemblies create law primarily through legislation, the resulting statutes often give government institutions (such as workers' compensation boards, human rights commissions, and labour relations boards) the power to make further rules under that legislation, called **regulations.** These regulations have the same force as the statute under which they were created. When an administrative tribunal makes a decision, it must be authorized by the statute or regulation in question. Even when the decision is within the authority granted by the regulation, the validity of the regulation itself can be questioned. If that regulation has not been properly passed, or exceeds the scope of the statute authorizing it, the regulation is *ultra vires* (without authority) and cannot support the action of the decision maker. When the decision or conduct is unauthorized, the courts will have no hesitation in overturning it.

**Does administrative tribunal have authority?**

### Case Summary 3.3

**When Is a Plebiscite Not Binding?** *Oil Sands Hotel (1975) Ltd. v. Alberta (Gaming & Liquor Commission)*[4]

Video lottery terminals (VLTs) were introduced into Alberta, on a test basis, in 1991. Retailers operate VLTs pursuant to VLT Retailer Agreements ("the Agreements") with the Alberta Gaming and Liquor Commission ("the Commission").

---

3. *Canada (Director of Investigation and Research) v. Southam Inc.*, [1997] 1 S.C.R. 748.

4. (1999), 241 A.R. 45 (Q.B.).

Numerous concerns, including some about the addictiveness of this form of gambling, caused public pressure for the removal of VLTs to mount. The provincial cabinet issued a press release, stating that the Alberta government would honour the results of any community plebiscite favouring the removal of VLTs from the community. Plebiscites were conducted in 36 municipalities; five of them had a majority of voters in favour of removal of VLTs. Notices purporting to cancel the Agreements were delivered to retailers in these communities. Those retailers brought an application for judicial review of the process.

The Commission was found to be exercising statutory powers, and such exercise is reviewable by the courts. The sole basis for terminating the Agreements was a direction from the provincial government to honour the results of the plebiscites. But there was not a provision in the *Gaming and Liquor Act* authorizing the cabinet, or any minister, to give binding directions to the Commission; nor was there a provision that allowed the Commission to delegate its decision-making powers to any other body, not even to voters. The Commission thus acted outside its jurisdiction in allowing others to exercise the discretion conferred upon it by statute. By responding to the plebiscite, and to the pressure from the provincial politicians, the Commission acted upon irrelevant considerations. There was not any evidence that the Commission considered the enabling legislation, or genuinely addressed the issues before it. Termination of the Agreements was thus done in a manner not authorized by the legislation. The terminations were declared invalid, as the Commission had failed to act within the terms of the enabling statute.

## Statutory Interpretation

**Rules of statutory interpretation**

When determining whether a regulation has been properly imposed under the statute in question, or whether any other aspect of the statute is being properly enforced, the courts will apply accepted rules of statutory interpretation. These rules have been developed from three basic principles. First, if a provision of the statute is clear and unambiguous, and conveys a certain meaning that is not inconsistent with other sections of the statute, the court is obligated to apply the

• plain meaning

plain or literal meaning. If the statute is ambiguous, either because the provisions are inconsistent with other sections of the legislation or because the wording is capable of more than one meaning, the courts may apply either the golden rule

• golden rule

or the mischief rule. The **golden rule** means that a reasonable interpretation based on common sense will be used, and that the literal meaning of the statute will be departed from only as far as necessary to overcome the ambiguity or

• mischief rule

inconsistency. The **mischief rule** means that the courts will try to give effect to the specific purpose for which the statute was enacted. For example, when a statute has been passed to cure some defect or injustice in common law, or in some other statute, the court can identify the defect or injustice and, in face of the ambiguity, interpret the statute in such a way as to give the best effect to the original intent of the legislation. Thus, if there were a problem of interpretation with the federal *Youth Criminal Justice Act*, the application of the mischief rule would require that any ambiguity be interpreted to give effect to the intention of the Act; that is, to give the youth involved the same kind of rights and protection given to adults. Today, these rules are rolled into one basic principle; the words of a statute should be read in their ordinary grammatical sense, unless it is clear from the overall statute that they were intended to have a different meaning, and then the words should be read in such a way as to be in harmony with the objective and other provisions of the statute.

## Case Summary 3.4

### How Should a Statute Be Interpreted? *Chieu v. Canada (Minister of Citizenship and Immigration)*[5]

Mr. Chieu was born in Cambodia. He moved to Vietnam, where he married a Vietnamese citizen and had a son. He applied for permanent residency in Canada, but stated in his application that he was single, with no dependents. After arriving in Canada and becoming a permanent resident, he applied to sponsor his wife and child to come to Canada. He was ordered removed from Canada, on the grounds that he had become a permanent resident on the basis of a misrepresentation. His appeal to the Immigration and Refugee Board was dismissed, and that decision was upheld by the Federal Court, Trial Division, and the Federal Court of Appeal. Both Courts held that it was correct to refuse to consider potential foreign hardship when reviewing the removal order.

The Supreme Court of Canada allowed Chieu's appeal. The key issue was the meaning of the phrase "having regard to all the circumstances of the case" from the *Immigration Act*. The Court used the modern approach to statutory interpretation to conclude that the phrase allows for the consideration of potential foreign hardship when reviewing a removal order. The Court quoted with approval—as it has in many cases—the following statement from E. A. Driedger in *Construction of Statutes*:

> Today there is only one principle or approach, namely, the words of an Act are to be read in their entire context and in their grammatical and ordinary sense harmoniously with the scheme of the Act, the object of the Act, and the intention of Parliament.

The Court therefore set aside the judgment of the Court of Appeal and returned the matter to the Board for another hearing, at which the potential hardship in the likely country of removal had to be considered.

Another rule of statutory interpretation available to the courts states that a judge is not obligated to follow a statute, unless it clearly and unambiguously overrules the common law provision. This is referred to as **strict interpretation** of the statute. Other specific rules have been developed to assist the courts in interpreting statutes. These rules range from principles of grammatical construction to rules favouring one interpretation over another in different situations. The courts may also turn to similar statutes (both within and outside the legislative jurisdiction involved), to the official translations of statutes, or to other publications such as dictionaries and academic articles.

**Statutes strictly interpreted**

Each jurisdiction in Canada has passed legislation setting out general principles and specific rules judges must follow when determining the meaning of statutes or regulations. These rules are called **interpretation statutes.**[6]

In addition, most statutes begin with a definition section that sets out specific meanings that must be applied to words used throughout that particular statute.

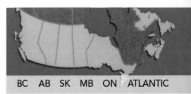

BC   AB   SK   MB   ON   ATLANTIC

It is beyond the scope of this chapter to discuss statutory interpretation in any greater detail. However, it is apparent that when faced with disputes over the

---

5. [2002] 1 S.C.R. 84.

6. See, for example, *Interpretation Act,* R.S.C. 1985, c. I-21.

meaning of statutory provisions the courts have a cohesive framework of rules and guidelines to help them determine the appropriate interpretation. With respect to administrative matters, the interpretation eventually settled on by the court may affect whether the particular regulation in question was valid, whether the conduct complained of violated a particular statute, or whether the particular regulatory body or government agency had the power to make the decision or impose the control it did. Once this has been determined, the question remains whether or not the statute itself was validly passed pursuant to the division of powers as set out in the *Constitution Act (1867)*.

## Jurisdiction

As mentioned in Chapter 1, the powers of government are divided between the federal and provincial levels of government as set out primarily in sections 91 and 92, respectively, of the *Constitution Act (1867)*. When the statute empowering the administrator to act has been passed by a level of government that does not have the power to do so under this division of powers, the courts will find the statute to be *ultra vires,* and therefore void. The conduct of the decision maker acting under the void statute will also be *ultra vires.*

**Statutes must be passed by appropriate level of government**

For example, if a city council passed a bylaw prohibiting the sale of adult videos within the city boundaries and, on the strength of that bylaw, the relevant city department denied a business a licence to operate, the business could challenge that decision. Neither the province nor a city deriving its authority from the province can pass such a bylaw, as it encroaches on the federal government's criminal law powers. Since the bylaw would be invalid, any decision made under its authority would also be invalid, and the courts would, upon application, declare the decision *ultra vires* and therefore void.

**Regulations must comply with *Charter***

In the same way, a statute or regulation must be consistent with the provisions of the *Charter of Rights and Freedoms*, also discussed in Chapter 1. A statute that had the effect of discriminating on the basis of gender, religion, or ethnic origin, or that denied a person the right to a hearing (where life, liberty, and security of the person were involved), or that restricted freedom of the press or religion could be challenged. A decision made under such a statute would also be invalid.

### Case Summary 3.5

#### Did the Tribunal Have Jurisdiction? *BCE Nexxia Inc. v. Canada (Commissioner of Corrections)*[7]

The Correction Services of Canada (CSC) selected BCE Nexxia Inc. (BCE) to be the supplier of telephone services to inmates in Canadian prisons. The service included provisions for the control and monitoring of inmate telephone calls by CSC. Telus Integrated Communications Inc. (Telus) filed a complaint with the Canadian International Trade Tribunal (CITT), arguing that BCE's proposal to provide the telephone services did not satisfy the Request for Proposals issued by CSC. CSC and BCE objected to the CITT's jurisdiction to enquire into the matter. The CITT denied their motion, finding it had jurisdiction to consider and decide the Telus complaint. CSC and BCE appealed this decision.

Chapter Five of the Agreement on International Trade required a procurement value of $100 000 for the CITT to have jurisdiction over a contract. The

7. [2001] F.C.J. No. 1955 (C.A.).

CITT found that the contract had a procurement value greater than $100 000. The Court held that a procurement value required a financial commitment. Here, however, BCE was going to be remunerated for providing the telephone services through tolls and charges that would be paid by the prisoners. As there was no financial commitment from CSC, and therefore no procurement value, the CITT did not have jurisdiction. Its decision was quashed by the Court. This case shows not only that an enabling statute must be *intra vires*, and in compliance with the *Charter of Rights and Freedoms*, but also that the administrative tribunal must have been given jurisdiction by the legislation over the specific issues in question or any decision by the tribunal will be overturned on judicial review.

## Proper Process

Once it has been established that the decision maker has acted within the authority given under a valid statute or regulation, the question remains whether that authority was exercised in a proper way. Historically, the obligation of the administrator to act in a procedurally fair manner varied to a great extent depending on the function performed. The decision maker might be acting as a judge adjudicating disputes, or simply acting as an administrator implementing government policy. The distinction is less important today. Even when the decision maker is acting as an administrator, there is an obligation to maintain at least a minimum standard of **procedural fairness.** The courts are much more likely to find an obligation on the decision maker to act fairly when the issues being dealt with are important, when the decision maker's function is to decide among competing parties or interests, or when the remedies or penalties that can be imposed will have a significant impact on the parties. (These minimum standards of fairness have been imposed on the cabinet and the ministers of the Crown as well, although it should be noted that such obligations are often modified by statute.) What constitutes fairness in these situations is determined by the *rules of natural justice*; the minimum requirements of justice or procedural fairness are set out below. It should be noted that some of the provinces also have statutes that set out common procedural standards.[8]

**Administrator must act fairly**

# Rules of Natural Justice

### Case Summary 3.6

### Was There a Breach of Natural Justice? *Mikkelsen v. University of Saskatchewan*[9]

Ms. Mikkelsen's first-year law school examination results were below the law school's minimum requirements. The Board of Examiners of the College of Law decided that she was not entitled to be promoted to second year, and she was asked to discontinue her studies. She was also asked to advise the College of "any special circumstances" that may have affected her performance. Ms. Mikkelsen did so, citing medical, personal, and financial reasons. The Board of Examiners concluded that this explanation did not change its decision. Ms. Mikkelsen asked

---

8. See, for example, *Administrative Procedures Act*, R.S.A. 2000, c. A-3; *Statutory Powers Procedure Act*, R.S.O. (1990), c. S.22; and *An Act Respecting Administrative Justice*, R.S.Q., c. J-3.

9. (2000), 191 Sask. R. 53 (Q.B.).

for a meeting with the Dean to explain her situation. The Dean advised that Ms. Mikkelsen had to appeal to her based on non-academic factors. Ms. Mikkelsen provided written submissions, but the Dean confirmed that there were no grounds to alter the Board's original decision. Ms. Mikkelsen appealed to the Bylaws Committee, which concluded that the matter involved "substantive academic judgment," that the Board of Student Appeals had no jurisdiction over such matters, and that she was therefore not entitled to a hearing, or to any further appeal within the University.

Ms. Mikkelsen then appealed to the courts. She claimed that the University had breached the rules of natural justice by denying her an oral hearing, and by not providing her with a copy of the written response of the Dean to her application to the Bylaws Committee for an appeal to be heard. Although the Court ruled that there was no requirement for an oral hearing, it did state that the minimum standards of procedural fairness required that Mikkelsen be provided with a copy of the Dean's response to the Bylaws Committee, and that she have an opportunity to correct or contradict anything unfavourable to her position. Without such an opportunity, any injustice could continue under the guise of "substantive academic judgment." Such a breach of natural justice would normally result in the matter being sent back to the administrative tribunal for another hearing. But, in this case, the University had permitted Ms. Mikkelsen to re-enroll in first-year law, and she had expended time and money in continuing her classes. The Court therefore quashed the decision of the Bylaws Committee, and reinstated Ms. Mikkelsen in the first year of the law-school program.

The Supreme Court of Canada recently stated[10] that:

> The duty of procedural fairness is flexible and variable and depends on an appreciation of the context of the particular statute and the rights affected. The purpose of the participatory rights contained within it is to ensure that administrative decisions are made using a fair and open procedure, appropriate to the decision being made and its statutory, institutional and social context, with an opportunity for those affected to put forward their views and evidence fully and have them considered by the decision-maker.

**Statutes may modify duty of procedural fairness**

The first step in determining whether there has been procedural fairness is to see whether any procedural requirements set out in the statute governing the area have been complied with. Such statutory procedural requirements must conform to the *Charter of Rights and Freedoms*—in particular with section 7, which states that everyone has the right to "life, liberty, and security of the person," and that such right cannot be taken away, except "in accordance with the principles of fundamental justice." The **principles of fundamental justice** have been taken to mean the same thing as procedural fairness and natural justice.

### Fair Hearing

The most fundamental requirement of the rules of natural justice is that the party being affected by the decision of an administrator has an opportunity to a fair hearing. What constitutes a fair hearing will vary from situation to situation, but

---

10. *Baker v. Canada (Minister of Citizenship and Immigration)*, [1999] 2 S.C.R. 817.

essentially the person being affected by the decision must have been notified that a decision is to be made and must have been given an opportunity to put his side forward. The courts have held that a fair hearing has not taken place when proper notice of the hearing was not given, or when the person was not informed of the nature of the complaint or given the information needed to present his case. There cannot be a fair hearing without notice and an opportunity to prepare a defence. In the above case, Ms. Mikkelsen was successful in her application because she did not have sufficient opportunity to present her case, as she was not allowed to review the Dean's response on the issue of "substantive academic judgment."

**Notice must be given and all information must be disclosed**

## Case Summary 3.7

### Was There a Fair Hearing? *Rochon v. Board of Education of Spirit River School District No. 47*[11]

At a public meeting, the Superintendent made comments critical of members of the School Board. Immediately after the meeting, the Chairman of the Board distributed a memo giving notice of a special meeting to be held three days later. The Superintendent was not involved in calling the meeting or in setting the agenda. He did hear rumours that his employment would be terminated at the special meeting. The special meeting was initially conducted in public, and then continued *in camera*. After a couple of hours, the Superintendent was asked to appear, but he advised that he would not under the circumstances, and left. In his absence, the Board passed a resolution terminating his contract.

The Superintendent was not provided notice that termination of his contract was on the agenda. Without notice, the Superintendent did not have an opportunity to prepare, or to consult with legal counsel. His dismissal was discussed without him being present. This failure to provide proper notice, and a proper opportunity to be heard, caused the Court to set aside the Board's decision to terminate the Superintendent's contract.

A fair hearing requires that all of the evidence that forms the basis of the decision be disclosed to the individual being affected by it. The individual must be given an opportunity to cross-examine witnesses who present material testimony, or to refute any written declarations. Similarly, it is essential to a fair hearing that the individual be given an opportunity to present arguments and supporting evidence.

A fair hearing may extend to the right to demand an adjournment in certain circumstances. But there is not a requirement that the decision maker follow the strict rules of evidence, or even that the person affected have a right to counsel, although legal representation is a right if the proceedings might result in criminal charges. There is no general obligation on the decision maker to give reasons for the judgment, but many statutes do impose a duty on the decision maker to give reasons, and often require that these reasons be put in writing.[12]

**No obligation to follow rules of evidence or allow counsel**

The test is *reasonableness,* and an unreasonable imposition on the time of an administrator will not be tolerated. In some situations, the opportunity to present a case by letter is enough to satisfy the requirement of a fair hearing. This illustrates that the applications of the rules of natural justice or procedural

---

11. (1994), 149 A.R. 106 (C.A.).

12. See, for example, *Administrative Procedures Act, supra* note 8, s. 7.

fairness involve a considerable degree of flexibility. No set rules can be stated, since what is required will be a reflection of what constitutes fairness in any given circumstance.

## Case Summary 3.8

### What Is "Fair"? *Gerle Gold Ltd. v. Golden Rule Resources Ltd.*[13]

Gerle and SouthernEra applied for judicial review of the assistant deputy minister's (ADM) decision regarding the ownership of a mining claim. Both corporations filed notices of protest against a claim recorded in the name of Warner. Warner provided the ADM with a statutory declaration that he was holding the claim on behalf of Golden. This was inconsistent with a prior statement. The statutory declaration was given substantial weight by the ADM in determining the owner of the claim. Gerle and SouthernEra requested the opportunity to cross-examine Warner, but the ADM denied the request. The application for judicial review relied on several grounds, including the display by the ADM of a reasonable apprehension of bias, an improper refusal of the request to cross-examine Warner, and a failure by the ADM to give adequate reasons for the decision.

The Federal Court, Trial Division allowed the application, and set aside the ADM's decision. While the ADM was not disqualified by a reasonable apprehension of bias, his refusal to permit a cross-examination was a breach of the duty of fairness. The Court also held that the ADM erred in law by failing to provide adequate reasons for his decision.

The Federal Court of Appeal allowed the appeal, in part. The ADM's decision was set aside, but the matter was remitted for a new hearing. The Court held that the ADM did not err in the exercise of his discretion when he denied the cross-examination. His reasons for decision were, however, inadequate to meet the statutory obligation. This case shows that the rules of natural justice are indeed flexible, and that what is viewed as "fair" will depend upon the facts of the case.

## Heard by Decision Maker

**Decision must be made by persons hearing evidence**

**Decision maker must hear all evidence**

Another requirement of the rules of natural justice is that the decision must be made by the persons hearing the evidence. If a board of inquiry is convened requiring five people to participate in the decision and something happens to one of them after the commencement of the hearing, that person cannot be replaced by another because the new person would not have heard all the evidence presented. Similarly, the board of inquiry cannot proceed and make the decision with only four people, because the statute requires five. It is permissible for the decision maker to use staff services to gather and summarize the evidence, but the decision must be made only by those who have heard all the evidence.

## Case Summary 3.9

### Did the Decision Makers Hear All of the Evidence? *Doyle v. Canada (Restrictive Trade Practices Commission)*[14]

Pursuant to the *Canada Business Corporations Act*, the Restrictive Trades Practices Commission had an Investigator examine the affairs of Javelin International Ltd.

13. (1999), 2 F.C. 630 (T.D.), varied, [2001] 1 F.C. 647 (C.A.).

14. [1985] 1 F.C. 362 (C.A.), leave to appeal to S.C.C. refused (1985), 21 D.L.R. (4th) 366 n (S.C.C.).

After such an investigation, the Commission held a hearing in which the Investigator presented evidence of what she had found, while the investigated party was given an opportunity to respond. During the Javelin hearing, three members of the Commission sat and listened to the proceedings. At various times the members stepped out, always leaving two members present (two members were required for a quorum). The Commission found evidence of fraud and made recommendations to the Minister. Mr. Doyle, a principal of Javelin, brought this application to have the findings of the Commission set aside. The Court agreed. People who had not heard all the evidence had participated in the decision, resulting in an unfair hearing.

## Impartiality

A significant requirement of the rules of natural justice is that the decision be made impartially and in good faith. If it can be shown that the decision maker is biased, the decision will be overturned. Because it is so difficult to establish bias, the courts have developed the principle that a reasonable likelihood of bias is enough to invalidate the decision. The *Ahumada* case at the beginning of this chapter provides an example of a court quashing a tribunal's decision because of a reasonable apprehension of bias.

**Decision maker must be free of bias**

Bias is assumed when the matter being decided involves a relative, friend, or business acquaintance of the decision maker. Similarly, if there has been an exhibition of bad feelings or hostility between the decision maker and the individual being affected by the decision, there is a real likelihood of bias and the decision can be successfully challenged. Where it can be shown that the decision maker has an interest in the matter being decided, or has already decided the matter, that person will be disqualified from the decision-making process. A monetary interest in the subject matter affected by the decision will be grounds for challenge, and the size of such an interest will not be relevant.

**Case Summary 3.10**

### Is It Necessary to Prove That There Was Actual Bias? *Bennett v. British Columbia (Superintendent of Brokers)*[15]

BB, former premier, and HD, president of forestry company, charged with insider trading  Hearing → Decision of panel, including DD, president of another forestry company  Judicial Review → Court of Appeal overturns decision because of reasonable apprehension of bias, as DD's company may benefit if HD convicted

Bill Bennett, former Premier of British Columbia, was charged with insider trading, a violation of the *Securities Act*. One of the people accused with him, Herb Doman, was the President of a forestry company. Under the legislation,

15. (1993), 109 D.L.R. (4th) 717 (B.C.C.A.) There was a subsequent application to have certain other members of the panel disqualified, also on the grounds of reasonable apprehension of bias. This application was dismissed: (1994), 40 Admin. L.R. (2d) 283 (B.C.C.A.), leave to appeal to S.C.C. refused, [1994] S.C.C.A. No. 52.

Mr. Bennett and Mr. Doman had the right to a hearing before a Panel of Commissioners. During the hearing, an objection was heard that David Divine, one of three Commissioners, should not be sitting on the Panel. He also was a director of a forestry company. The Court of Appeal held that there was a reasonable apprehension of bias and overturned the decision of the Panel. If Mr. Doman were convicted, he would be prohibited from managing his company. This would deprive his company of his expertise, giving an advantage to other forestry companies, including Mr. Devine's. This created a reasonable apprehension of bias. Note that it was not necessary to actually show that Mr. Devine was influenced by this consideration, only that there was an appearance to a reasonable person that this was likely.

**Bias may be permitted by statute**

Decision-making bodies are sometimes structured to incorporate a bias. For example, those appointed to labour relations boards and arbitration panels are usually appointed as representatives from labour and management. Often, a panel of three arbitrators is struck, each side appointing one of the arbitrators who together then choose a third. The principle involved is that the bias represented by one side will be balanced by the bias of the other, and the third arbitrator chosen by both will mediate between them. This principle emphasizes the point that the rules of natural justice are guidelines only. The courts retain a considerable amount of flexibility in the exercise of their supervisory jurisdiction as they ensure that the procedures involved are fair to all parties.

### Case Summary 3.11

**Does an Administrative Tribunal Have to Be Independent of the Government?** *Ocean Port Hotel v. British Columbia (General Manager, Liquor Control and Licensing Branch)*[16]

A senior inspector with the Liquor Control and Licensing Branch ("the Branch") concluded that Ocean Port had committed infractions of the relevant legislation. He suspended its liquor licence for two days. Ocean Port appealed to the Liquor Appeal Board, which confirmed the penalty. On further appeal, the Court of Appeal set aside the Board's decision, holding that it lacked the necessary guarantees of independence required of administrative tribunals that impose penalties. The Court ruled that as the Board members were hired "at the pleasure" of the government, they were not sufficiently independent.

## Reducing **Risk** 3.1

It is vital that businesspeople remember that challenging government regulators and administrators should be done only as a last resort. As with all litigation, an administrative proceeding can be a frustrating, costly, and often fruitless exercise that should be avoided if at all possible. Further, this is a specialized field in which the costs incurred may be even higher than the expense of litigation. The complainant must deal with government officials who have access to large funds and who may be more than willing to spend those funds to save themselves the embarrassment of being found in the wrong.

16. [2001] 2 S.C.R. 781.

The Supreme Court of Canada allowed the Branch to appeal. The Court stated that the degree of independence required of an administrative tribunal was determined by its enabling statute. The Court stressed that administrative tribunals, unlike courts, are created for the purpose of implementing government policy. They therefore are not protected by the independence requirements of the *Charter of Rights and Freedoms*. Tribunals are not required to be judicially independent, like courts. This means that as long as the intention of the legislation is clear and within the power of the legislature, then the tribunals need not be independent. They must implement the stated government policy, and in doing so they are not in breach of the rules of natural justice.

This illustrates a fundamental distinction between administrative tribunals and courts. Courts must possess guarantees of judicial independence. Judges must be impartial and be insulated from external influence, including the executive branch of government. But the purpose of administrative tribunals is to implement government policy, and the degree of independence of the tribunal can be determined by the government.

# Judicial Review

Many statutes establishing administrative tribunals provide for appeals of their decisions to another level of decision maker. This may be a board, a commissioner, a director, or the responsible minister. In some instances, the appeal can even go to the courts. Judicial review must be distinguished from this appeal process. **Appeal** is the process whereby the decision of an inferior court or tribunal is reconsidered at a higher level. Generally, an appeal focuses on whether an error of law was committed. Judicial review involves the superior court's inherent right to supervise the judicial process. Whether an appeal is provided for, and whether there are other courses of action open to the person affected by the decision, the courts retain the right to supervise and oversee the administration of justice. They will correct the action of a decision maker who acts improperly. In judicial review, the concern of the court is with the decision-making process itself and not with the merits of decisions.

**Judicial review—inherent right of courts**

As a rule, the courts require that all other remedies be exhausted before they exercise their supervisory capacity in the form of judicial review. If an appeal is available under the statute or regulations, that appeal process must be finished before the courts will become involved. The following is a summary of the situations in which a person affected by the decision of an administrative tribunal will usually be successful in going to the courts for relief.[17]

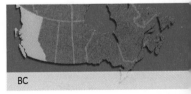

BC

**1.** When the decision maker does not have authority to make the decision, or has stepped outside of his authority in some way, that decision can be successfully challenged in the courts. In determining whether the decision maker has the required authority, the courts must look not only to the contents of the statute or regulations, but also to the constitutional validity of the statute itself. This requires reference to the *Charter of Rights and Freedoms* and the *Constitution Act (1867)*. If the statute is valid, the decision can still be

17. For a discussion of the procedures the courts must follow when conducting judicial reviews, see below under the heading "Modification by Statute."

**Authority of decision maker may be reviewed**

challenged on the grounds that the administrator was not functioning within the **authority** granted under the statute. For example, if a school board is required by statute to review a dismissal application but, because of the inconvenience of meeting over the summer, it appoints a committee of the board to hear the complaint, the decision of that committee may be invalid. The school board must first have the statutory power to delegate its authority to a committee.

**Must function within prescribed jurisdiction**

Another error enabling the courts to intervene occurs when the decision maker makes an initial incorrect decision as to whether the matter in dispute falls under its jurisdiction. For example, a labour relations board may be given the authority by statute to hear disputes between employees and employers. If it decides that a dispute between independent fishers and the fish-packing corporations they do business with falls within its jurisdiction, this primary jurisdictional determination (that an employer–employee relationship exists) can be successfully challenged in the courts. Another type of jurisdictional error occurs when a decision-making body rehears a matter after it has made a final decision. Usually, statutes will empower such a body to make a decision in the first place, but not authorize it to rehear the matter. The second hearing is therefore outside the jurisdiction of the decision maker and void. Note that this differs from when a second hearing is held after the first has been declared invalid because of some procedural defect. That is not a rehearing because, in law, the first hearing, being void, never took place.

**Process must be fair**

**2.** The decision-making process itself is subject to the scrutiny of the court. There is a requirement of **procedural fairness**, as discussed above. This requirement must be satisfied whenever a decision is made that has an adverse impact on a party.

**3.** If the decision maker is functioning within the proper jurisdiction and the process is procedurally fair, the courts are generally reluctant to interfere with the decision. But if a decision incorporates a remedy that is beyond the decision maker's power to grant, it will be reviewable on the grounds of jurisdiction. For example, under labour legislation, an arbitrator may be given the authority to determine whether an employee was properly dismissed. If that arbitrator were to impose some consequence, such as a suspension from employment for a number of weeks, rather than simply deciding whether the dismissal was justified, the arbitrator would be assuming authority he does not have, and his decision would then be invalid.

**Jurisdiction includes power to grant specific remedy**

**Must be some evidence**

**4.** Under rare circumstances, the court may find that there was not sufficient legal evidence for the administrator to reach a particular decision. The legal standard requires that there be at least some evidence to justify the conclusion reached by the decision maker.

**Abuse of discretionary power**

**5.** The courts have been willing to overturn a decision when the decision maker has committed an **abuse of power**. If in the exercise of his power (including discretionary power) a decision maker acts dishonestly, out of malice, or with fraudulent intent, his decision is reviewable on the basis of abuse of power. The case of *Roncarelli v. Duplessis*[18] is a classic example involving an abuse of power by a minister of the Crown that was reviewable

---

18. [1959] S.C.R. 121.

by the courts. In that case, the plaintiff, a restaurant owner in Montreal, supported some Jehovah's Witnesses facing criminal charges by paying their legal expenses. The Premier of Quebec exerted his influence to have the plaintiff's liquor licence cancelled. This act was clearly outside the jurisdiction he had as Premier, and was an abuse of his power. The Court ordered the Premier to pay compensation to the plaintiff.

The decision maker must consider all relevant matters and must not make a decision for an improper purpose. The exercise of any discretion must be a genuine exercise. For example, if a decision maker with discretionary power merely follows the direction of a superior, that is an abuse of such power and is reviewable by the courts.

**6.** Finally, the courts are willing to interfere with any decision that involves an **error of law** that is incorporated into the record of the hearing. The record consists of the decision, the reasons for it, and any documents involved in the process of reaching the decision. A transcript of the proceedings can also be included as part of the record. The supervising judicial body cannot tolerate such an error of law on the record, and the decision will be overturned whenever such an error is substantial enough to affect the decision. An error of law must be distinguished from an **error of fact.** The decision maker is generally empowered to decide questions of fact and those decisions will not be interfered with. But when there is an incorrect declaration as to the law, this is of concern to the superior court and will not be tolerated. The error of law may be in misconstruing common law or statutes, or may be a procedural error, such as the refusal to hear evidence or hearing evidence that ought to have been excluded. The court will not usually interfere with the decision merely because it does not like the decision or would have come to a different one itself.

**Error of law on record**

## Case Summary 3.12

### What Is the Standard of Review? *Dr. Q v. College of Physicians and Surgeons of British Columbia*[19]

A patient of Dr. Q alleged that their relationship had become sexual. Q denied the allegations. The Inquiry Committee of the College of Physicians and Surgeons accepted the patient's evidence and found Q guilty of infamous conduct. The Council of the College therefore suspended him from the practice of medicine for 18 months. On appeal, the British Columbia Supreme Court ("the Reviewing Court") disagreed with the Committee's findings as to credibility, allowed the appeal, and set aside the finding of infamous conduct. The Court of Appeal dismissed the College's appeal.

The Supreme Court of Canada allowed the College's appeal, and reinstated the Committee's decision. The Court stated that the Reviewing Court applied the wrong standard of review. In a judicial review, a court must apply the "pragmatic and functional approach," which includes applying a series of factors to discern the standard of review. The possible standards are *standard of correctness* (an exacting review by the court); *reasonableness simpliciter* (involves significant searching or testing by the court); and *patent unreasonableness* (left to the near-exclusive

---

19. 2003 S.C.C. 19.

determination of the administrative tribunal). The factors to be considered in determining the standard of review are:

1. The presence or absence of a privative clause or statutory right of appeal.

2. The expertise of the tribunal relative to that of the reviewing court.

3. The purposes of the legislation.

4. The nature of the question—law, fact, or mixed law and fact.

The overall aim of this approach is to determine the intent of the legislation. In this case, the Supreme Court of Canada decided that the appropriate standard of review was reasonableness simpliciter. Applying this standard, the Court found that the Committee's decision was reasonable and therefore should not have been overturned by the Reviewing Court.

## Methods of Judicial Review

### Prerogative Writs

**An order to release a person improperly detained**

The courts have traditionally used prerogative writs in exercising their supervisory power over administrative tribunals. These are ancient remedies traceable to the prerogative power of the Crown. Five prerogative writs are in use today, the best known of which is the writ of **habeas corpus**, a court order to the custodial authority to present before the court a person being kept in custody. *Habeas corpus* is used whenever there is concern over whether a person is being improperly detained. While this remedy is primarily used in criminal matters, it is also used in immigration and child custody cases, and when people have been institutionalized for mental health reasons.

**Certiorari overrules a decision**

**Prohibition prevents a decision from being made**

The other prerogative writs—*certiorari*, prohibition, *mandamus*, and *quo warranto*—play a significant role as the courts exercise their supervisory jurisdiction over administrative tribunals. **Certiorari** renders the decision of the inferior body as having no legal effect and, thus, null and void. The granting of an application for *certiorari* quashes a tribunal's decision and eliminates any impact that decision might have. **Prohibition** is similar to *certiorari*, but while *certiorari* overturns a particular decision, prohibition prevents the decision from being made. For *certiorari* to apply, a decision must have been made that can be challenged. Prohibition is used to prevent tribunals from using their power to make a decision in an unfair or otherwise inappropriate procedure. It can be extremely effective in stopping an unfair or abusive process at an early stage.

**Mandamus forces decision**

*Mandamus* has quite a different application. When an individual is dealing with an administrative tribunal, delay in reaching a decision can be every bit as devastating as an improper decision or an abuse of procedure. *Mandamus* can force the administrator to perform his duty and make the decision. It should be noted that administrators sometimes have the discretion to act or not; in such circumstances, *mandamus* cannot be used. But when the administrator has a duty to decide, usually imposed by statute, *mandamus* can be used to force a decision, although the decision made may not be the decision the party prefers. But at least a decision has been made, and then other means can be used to challenge it if appropriate. In the rare case in which there is only one decision the decision maker can legally reach, *mandamus* can be used to compel that decision. This was the situation in the *Trinity Western* case discussed below; once the Court ruled that the discriminatory practices were irrelevant, there was only one decision the British Columbia College of Teachers could make.

*Quo warranto* is used to challenge the right of a person to hold public office, be it created by the Crown or by statute. Because the courts generally refuse to grant this remedy if other procedures are provided by statute that will attain the same end, this remedy is not frequently sought.

*Quo warranto* **prevents exercise of unlawful authority**

## Case Summary 3.13

### Was *Mandamus* Justified? *Trinity Western University v. British Columbia College of Teachers*[20]

Trinity Western University (TWU) established a teacher training program, offering education degrees upon completion of four years at TWU and a fifth year at Simon Fraser University (SFU). TWU applied to the British Columbia College of Teachers (BCCT) for permission to assume full responsibility for the program. This reflected TWU's desire to have the full program reflect its Christian philosophy. The BCCT refused the application because it was contrary to the public interest to approve a teacher education program based on discriminatory practices. This concern related to TWU's requirement that all of its students had to sign a document indicating they would refrain from homosexual behaviour. TWU applied for judicial review.

The B.C. Supreme Court found that it was not within the BCCT's jurisdiction to consider whether the program follows discriminatory practices under the public-interest component of the legislation, and that there was no reasonable foundation to support the BCCT's decision with regard to discrimination. The Court granted an order in the nature of *mandamus,* allowing approval of TWU's proposed program. Both the Court of Appeal and the Supreme Court of Canada found that the BCCT had acted within its jurisdiction, but affirmed the trial judge's decision on the basis that there was no reasonable foundation for the BCCT's finding of discrimination. There was not any evidence indicating that graduates would treat homosexuals unfairly or disrespectfully. The order of *mandamus* was justified because the only reason for the denial of certification was the consideration of discriminatory practices—an irrelevant consideration.

## Declaration

There are many situations in which seeking an order in the nature of *certiorari, mandamus,* or prohibition is ineffective. These remedies are available only when a duty to act fairly is not met; they do not provide remedies when the impact of the decision has already been felt. For example, if Telsa owns property and builds a home on it that Adolfo, the city engineer, believes does not comply with the zoning regulations, and Adolfo then orders and supervises the demolition of the house, it would be little comfort to Telsa to go to court, obtain an order of *certiorari,* and have Adolfo's decision quashed. The damage has already been done, and a court order nullifying the decision will not undo it.

To deal with situations in which there is no other appropriate action, the court has developed the concept of the *declaration*. The court reserves the right to declare the law, assess damages, and grant compensation, in almost all situations.

**Court can make declaration**

20. [2001] 1 S.C.R. 772.

A declaration is an effective tool to assist the court in exercising its supervisory jurisdiction over administrators. The eminent English jurist Lord Denning went so far as to say, "I know of no limit to the power of the court to grant a declaration, except such limit as it may in its discretion impose upon itself."[21]

## Injunction

**Injunction prevents doing of specified act**

Another remedy available to the courts to help them in their supervisory jurisdiction is the injunction. An injunction is simply an order by the court to a party to stop breaking the law or otherwise interfering with another's rights. In the example above, an appropriate remedy for Telsa (after the decision to demolish was made, but before the demolition took place) would be an injunction, to prevent the implementation of the decision.

An injunction is somewhat limited in its application. In fact, there are many situations in which an injunction is completely inappropriate, such as when the damage has already taken place. In addition, there are limitations concerning whom an injunction can be obtained against. In many cases, the Crown and officers of the Crown are immune to the effect of an injunction.[22]

### Modification by Statute

Judicial review was often complicated in administrative law proceedings by technical requirements that parties had to overcome when seeking a prerogative writ, or a declaration or an injunction. Because of this, some jurisdictions passed statutes incorporating these methods of judicial review into a consolidated and simplified procedure.[23] Other jurisdictions have simply made reforms through changes in civil procedure rules.[24]

It must be emphasized that one of the dominant elements present in the common law provisions has been carried over by these various enactments; that is, the discretionary power of the judges. The courts always reserved the right to refuse to grant a prerogative writ, or a declaration or an injunction, whenever it would be inappropriate to do so. This exercise of pure discretionary power has been retained in all jurisdictions.

**Procedural requirements modified by statute**

It should also be remembered that several provinces have legislation setting out the procedures to be used by administrative tribunals.[25]

## Privative Clauses

Historically, the courts have been reluctant to give up their power. With the creation of administrative tribunals, the legislators have included, in the statutes, clauses that specifically prohibit review by the courts of the tribunal's decision.

---

21. *Barnard v. National Dock Labour Board,* [1953] 2 Q.B. 18 at 41 (C.A.).

22. See, for example, *Proceedings Against the Crown Act,* R.S.A. 2000, c. P-25, s. 17.

23. See, for example, *Judicial Review Procedure Act,* R.S.B.C. 1996, c. 241, and *Judicial Review Procedure Act,* R.S.O. 1990, c. J-1. The *Federal Court Act,* R.S.C. 1985, c. F-7, ss. 18, 18.1–18.5, 28, gives the Federal Court and the Federal Court of Appeal jurisdiction to issue prerogative writs, or declarations or injunctions, in applications for judicial review of proceedings of federal administrative tribunals.

24. See, for example, Alberta, *Rules of Court,* Parts 56.1 and 60, and Saskatchewan, *Queen's Bench Rules,* Part 52.

25. See *supra* note 8.

Because of the principle of parliamentary supremacy, one would expect these privative clauses to effectively keep the courts from interfering with such administrative decisions. The courts, however, must interpret such statutes and determine what they mean, and in the process the judges often find ways to avoid the operation of privative clauses. It is important not to take privative clauses at face value. They may appear to clearly prevent the court from interfering, but the actual effect may be quite different. A typical example of a privative clause, taken from the current *Ontario Labour Relations Act*, is:

> No decision, order, direction, declaration, or ruling of the Board shall be questioned or reviewed in any court, and no order shall be made or process entered, or proceeding taken in any court, whether by way of injunction, declaratory judgment, *certiorari, mandamus*, prohibition, *quo warranto*, or otherwise, to question, review, prohibit or restrain the Board or any of its proceedings.[26]

The intent of this provision is obvious, but the courts interpret it to apply only when the Board is acting within its jurisdiction. Thus, the original question as to whether or not the administrator has jurisdiction is still open to review. In fact, the way the courts have interpreted this type of privative clause varies with circumstances. If the courts wish to review a decision, they will often find a way to do so, despite the presence of a privative clause.

**Privative clauses attempt to prevent judicial review**

**Courts resist operation of privative clauses**

## Case Summary 3.14

### Will a Privative Clause Prevent Judicial Review?
### *Syncrude Canada Ltd. v. Michetti*[27]

An employee of Syncrude died. After a joint investigation by the Workers' Compensation Board and the Occupational Health and Safety Branch, it was determined that the employee died of an electric shock received while on the job. This resulted in an increased assessment in workers' compensation premiums to be paid by Syncrude. Syncrude appealed the decision to the Appeals Commission, without success. Syncrude applied for judicial review, ending up at the Court of Appeal. Syncrude's complaint was that a staff physician of the Workers' Compensation Board, who was also an adviser to the Commission, made the report with respect to the cause of death. When the physician testified before the Commission, Syncrude was not permitted to cross-examine him, or to introduce any further evidence. Its hands were effectively tied, even though under the statute the appeal was to provide an opportunity for the parties to be heard and to submit new or additional evidence. The Commission also refused to let Syncrude keep any record of the process, and eventually destroyed its own notes. In the Judge's words, "The whole course of conduct recited above is unfair, in every sense of the word, and deeply unfair. It was not a real hearing, but a mere simulacrum. If carefully analyzed, it will be seen to violate most of the traditional rules of natural justice."

---

26. S.O. 1995, c. 1, Sched. A, s. 116.

27. (1994), 162 A.R. 16 (C.A.).

A major argument against review by the Court was the presence of a very strong privative clause that prohibited review of the Commission's decisions by a court. The Judge had no difficulty overcoming this provision, for several reasons. First, when the Commission did not permit Syncrude to submit further evidence as required by the statute, it had declined jurisdiction (failed to act as it was required). Second, by its failure to follow the rules of natural justice, including its refusal to allow Syncrude an opportunity to be heard and to cross-examine the witnesses, the Commission exceeded its jurisdiction. Finally, the Court held that the decision was, in the circumstances, patently unreasonable and unfair. The decision of the Commission was quashed and a new hearing ordered. It must be stressed that the courts will not lightly intrude on a decision made by such an administrative tribunal, but in the face of such abuses the presence of a privative clause will not deter such judicial review.

In addition to privative clauses that directly prohibit judicial review, legislators have embodied in statutes other clauses that indirectly have the same effect. Legislative provisions that assign the right to review specific questions of law or other matters to a minister or other administrator can exclude the courts from this function. Other clauses try to define the nature of the power exercised as discretionary, by using subjective wording such as: "The director may," "Where the administrator is satisfied," "Where it appears to be," or "Where in the opinion of." When discretionary power is assigned in a subjective way, judicial review becomes more difficult. Subjective assignments of power are, therefore, quite effective in keeping the courts from reviewing a decision.

**Privative clauses subject to the *Charter***

The effect of privative clauses must also be viewed as subject to the operation of the *Charter of Rights and Freedoms*. The *Charter* guarantees the right to fundamental justice when a person's life, liberty, or security is at stake. If these rights are interfered with by an administrative tribunal, the decision can be reviewed in the courts regardless of the existence of a privative clause.

Even when there is not a privative clause present, the courts must be very cautious when intervening in the area given to an administrative tribunal. Usually, there is good reason to give this decision-making function to a tribunal rather than to a court. The tribunal is usually more efficient and quicker in dealing with a particular kind of problem. It is possible to tailor the procedures involved to the types of disputes and parties involved, and the decision maker usually has particular expertise not found in a court. For these and other reasons, shifting the decision-making power from the courts to such administrative bodies may be both prudent and efficient. When legislators give authority to administrators, the courts must be cautious in interfering and usually do so only when a decision appears unreasonable. As stated by the Supreme Court of Canada, "…even where there is no privative clause … the concept of the specialization of duties requires that deference be shown to decisions of specialized tribunals which fall squarely within the tribunal's expertise."[28]

## Other Remedies

**Contract and tort remedies may be available**

The powers discussed in this section are largely extraordinary, available when administrators abuse their power or act incorrectly when making decisions that affect the rights of individuals. In addition to the special remedies discussed, the normal rights that arise when an individual has been injured by the acts of

---

28. *Pezim v. British Columbia (Superintendent of Brokers),* [1994] 2 S.C.R. 557.

another may be available. For example, if a contract is breached, all the rights relating to breach of contract are applicable, even when one of the parties is the government or a Crown corporation. Similarly, if the actions of the decision maker involve the commission of a tort, such as negligence, defamation, trespass, or even assault and false imprisonment, the injured individual has the right to pursue tort remedies against the administrator. We will examine these remedies in more detail in the following chapters.

However, there are some limitations to the availability of remedies under these headings. Until recently, an individual had no power to sue the Crown, on the premise that since the government was the source of the law, it was not subject to it and therefore could not be sued in its own courts. All jurisdictions in Canada have passed legislation making it possible to sue the government and to pursue judgment for breach of contract, in tort, and so on.[29]

Most jurisdictions have, however, retained some of the Crown's former immunity, so it is almost impossible to get an injunction against the Crown or an officer of the Crown.[30] Similarly, the property of the Crown will not generally be available to satisfy judgment. Once a judgment has been obtained, the good faith of the government agency has to be relied on to satisfy that judgment. Seizure and garnishment cannot be used to ensure payment.[31] This restriction does not apply to Crown corporations.

It should also be noted, as a matter of common law, that when an administrator exercises a statutory power properly it will not give rise to tort action, even if damage to an individual results from it. Some jurisdictions have extended this protection by statute. New Brunswick's *Protection of Persons Acting Under Statute Act*[32] is an example, giving blanket protection against liability to persons acting pursuant to an enactment. The effect of such legislative protections may be to exclude a right of action in any given case, and businesspeople should be aware of any such legislation.

**Enforcement of judgment may be difficult**

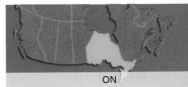

ON

## You Can't Fight City Hall

When a person is adversely affected by the decision of an administrative tribunal, she should consider some of the following factors before initiating any action. First, she should carefully determine whether there is any benefit to the action. When a tribunal has made a decision that is disliked, even when there is some ground to challenge that decision, it may be of no use to do so. For example, when the tribunal has made a decision but had failed to provide proper notice, it may be possible to have the decision overturned, but to what end? If the tribunal simply holds another hearing and reaches the same decision, making sure that everything is done correctly, it would be just a waste of time and money. There has to be some realizable objective that can be accomplished by the challenge, and creating a delay is usually not good enough. When a person proceeds in such an action as a matter of principle, the question usually asked is, just how much principle can she afford?

The second major concern, then, is cost. Government agencies usually have considerable funds available to fight any challenge to their actions or authority, and they may be willing to use all the options at their disposal to resist such a challenge.

**Challenging administrative decisions may be**

• futile

• costly

29. See, for example, *Proceedings Against the Crown Act, supra* note 22.

30. *Ibid.,* s. 17.

31. *Ibid.,* s. 25.

32. R.S.N.B. 1973, c. P-20.

The matter might be much more important than this particular case; the danger of setting a precedent may drive the tribunal to focus all of its efforts on defeating the challenge. The costs of such an action as a result will usually be considerable.

• lengthy

A criticism that has been levelled against the tribunal process—in particular against human rights commissions—is that often lengthy delays are involved. The third factor that must be considered is time. This includes not just the time it will take before a decision is made, but also the amount of time a party must spend on the matter.

These factors should be taken into consideration whenever a person pursues judicial review, and many a justified complaint is abandoned because of the cost and time required. This helps to explain why the alternatives to court action discussed in Chapter 2 are becoming much more attractive. Even government agencies that have a specific mandate, such as protecting the environment or ensuring fair competition, are willing to look to alternatives to the mandated enforcement process and litigation. Alternative dispute resolution, such as mediation and negotiation, should be explored before directly challenging the validity of government decisions in court.

**ADR may provide better resolution**

**Political pressure may be most effective**

It should also be remembered that the principles discussed above apply only when a person's rights or interests have been directly affected by a government decision maker. But the government often wields its power, and implements its policies, in more indirect ways, through various government initiatives, joint ventures, financing projects, government grants, and public relations mechanisms. In these situations, the only effective method of responding is usually a political one, rather than litigation. A political response where public pressure—or even internal pressure, such as by talking to a superior—is brought to bear may be much more effective than turning to the courts.

# Regulating the Environment

One of the characteristics of our modern society is the ever-expanding role of government within it. This involvement is even more extensive when business activities are concerned. The first part of this chapter was concerned with government regulation of business generally. The rest of the chapter provides an overview of the impact of law and government regulation on the environment. The environmental statutes, government departments, and enforcement bodies that businesses have to deal with illustrate the expanding regulatory environment within which businesses must function. We will also look at what happens when interactions between regulatory bodies and business come into conflict.

**Case Summary 3.15**

**Should There Be Fines and Jail Terms for Environmental Violations?**[33]

| Aqua-Tech operates hazardous waste site | → | Ministry of Environment lays 125 charges | → | Conviction of:<br>1) Corporation—fined $720 000<br>2) Plant manager—fined $40 000 and sentenced to 6 months in jail<br>3) President—fined $193 000 and sentenced to 6 months in jail<br>4) Director—fined $100 000 and sentenced to 4 months in jail |
|---|---|---|---|---|

33. Ontario Ministry of the Environment, News Release, June 9 and August 4, 2000.

Aqua-Tech Blue Inc. operated a liquid industrial and hazardous waste site. The Ontario Ministry of the Environment laid 125 charges under the *Ontario Water Resources Act* and the *Environmental Protection Act* against Aqua-Tech, two numbered corporations, and four individuals. The charges were related to illegal handling, storage, and disposal of waste, as well as to the furnishing of false information to government officials. The charges were laid after oil was found in sewers near the site.

The operating manager of Aqua-Tech pleaded guilty to four offences relating to illegal hazardous waste discharges into the Don River. He was sentenced to 90 days in jail. At trial, the president of the corporation was convicted on 12 counts, and received a six-month jail term and fines totalling $193 000. The plant manager was also convicted on 12 counts and sent to jail for six months. His fine was $40 000. A director was convicted on 13 counts, and received a four-month jail sentence and fines totalling $100 000. Aqua-Tech was convicted on 17 counts and fined a total of $720 000. One of the other corporations was convicted on one count and fined $50 000.

Laws to protect the environment are significant and are an important consideration in calculating the cost of doing business. As can be seen from this example, directors, officers, and even employees of a corporation must carefully consider the risks and the potential costs associated with their positions. An individual, for example, may refuse to serve on the board of directors of a corporation when doing so may expose her to personal civil and criminal liability. A corporation should carefully assess the risk of future environmental liability, and purchase the appropriate type and amount of insurance coverage.

# Protecting the Environment

Our society and the natural world are interdependent in a way that historically has not been recognized in either our economic system or our laws. The production of wealth is the underlying objective of the business world (which the economic system facilitates), and wealth is produced, to a large extent, through the consumption of natural resources. In the wake of economic progress, forests are cleared, fish stocks are depleted, mineral, oil, and gas reserves are exhausted, and great scars are left on the Earth in the process. Species of animal life are decimated, as they are either directly consumed or their environment is destroyed around them. The byproducts of all this, in the form of waste materials, are discharged into the atmosphere, into the seas and onto the lands, further degrading the environment. Industries such as mining, fishing, forestry, farming, construction, transportation, and manufacturing have all greatly contributed to Canada's environmental problems.

The economic structures that form the basis of business and industry have traditionally not factored in these environmental costs. The range of problems contributing to the environmental crises is vast. From nuclear disasters to automobile emissions, from the disposal of chemical wastes to domestic sewage, and from the depletion of the ozone layer to the depletion of the

**Business has great impact on the environment**

Reducing pollution is a significant cost of doing business.

soil—all have serious consequences for the environment. We have been forced to consider the depletion of the environment as one of the important factors in the economic equation.

The law has been even slower than the economic system to react to these modern realities; it has been only in the last few decades that our legislators have considered it necessary to create statutes to introduce some balance into the system. In the 1970s and 1980s there was a rash of statutory enactments to try to remedy the problems. With those statutes came government departments and agencies to administer and promote compliance with the regulations. A product of public pressure and general concern for the environment, the legislation has sometimes failed to ensure the necessary balance between the production of wealth and the preservation of the environment. Most of the statutes were remedial in nature and became increasingly stringent as the extent of the damage that had already been done to the environment was realized. The goal of the original legislation was to bring polluters into compliance. Governments sought to achieve that by restricting certain practices and imposing harsh penalties. This process created new problems, as the economic cost of compliance began to discourage—and even destroy—industries, particularly those based on harvesting natural resources. Over the past decade, there has been a realization that the primary mandate of legislative action should be investigation, education, and negotiation so that government and industry can work together to resolve common problems. The courts, administrative tribunals, and alternative dispute resolution methods all have important roles to play in achieving the essential balance.

**Statutes designed to protect environment have had varying degrees of success**

## Common Law

**Common law protections**

• riparian rights

The common law has always had some provisions that relate to the preservation of the environment. These generally take the form of individual rights associated with a person's right to property. **Riparian rights** give people living near rivers and streams the right to have the water come to them in undiminished quantity and quality, subject to limited domestic usage such as washing, drinking, and normal sewage disposal. These rights are, however, fragile. The government commonly overrides them by issuing permits allowing for the withdrawal of large quantities of water for irrigation or other uses, or for the discharge of waste into those rivers and streams.

BC

• nuisance

• negligence
• trespass

The law of torts is the subject of the following chapter. Tort law has been used, with some significant limitations, to control environmental damage. When a person's use of his property interferes with his neighbour's use of his property (through the escape of noise, fumes, or other substances), the tort of "private nuisance" gives that neighbour the right to sue for compensation and to put a stop to the offending conduct. The torts of negligence and trespass can also be used to enforce a person's right not to be interfered with in this way by others (including municipal, provincial, and federal government agencies, which are to some extent liable for their wrongful conduct in tort law.[34]

---

34. But see *Pearson v. Inco,* [2002] O.T.C. 515 (Ont. Sup. Ct. J.), currently under appeal, which states that while a government body exercising statutory powers may have a general duty to the public, it does not have private law duties to individuals. The Court found no cause of action against the Crown for failure to prosecute under an environmental statute, as the discretionary exercise of such a statutory power "cannot give rise to a claim in negligence by a particular individual due to the fact that no duty arises." See also Barry Spiegel, "Class action bites the dust," *The Lawyers Weekly,* 22:18 (13 September 2002) at 8.

Although tort law and the other common law remedies are important, the necessity of personal involvement in obtaining such remedies is a significant disadvantage. An individual must bear the costs of litigation and, as a prerequisite, must show that he personally suffered damage from the offending conduct. Some modern statutes give individuals the right to sue in tort under the statute and receive private compensation for personal loss, but this still requires the personal involvement and commitment of that individual to the litigation process. One of the main advantages of the modern approach of statutory control and regulation is that a government agency is specifically charged to enforce the legislative framework. Such agencies can use various methods to ensure compliance, before applying sanctions and penalties. These methods include education, cooperation, and negotiation.

**Plaintiff must suffer personal injury and be involved and incur costs**

### Case Summary 3.16

#### Is There a Right to Use Water? *Steadman v. Erickson Gold Mining Corp.*[35]

Steadman had a spring on his property feeding a small reservoir from which he took water, mainly for domestic use. The Erickson Gold Mining Corporation built a road on the adjacent property and, in the process, silted the water supply. Even after some corrective action was taken, the water remained unusable, and Steadman had to truck water in. He sued for nuisance. The Court said that, although the Crown owned the water, Steadman had a right to the use of it; Erickson's conduct amounted to a nuisance, and it was liable for its interference. This is an example of common law control of environmental interference. Steadman's right to use the water is a riparian right, and his remedy in nuisance illustrates the effectiveness of this common law tort action.

## Statutory Law

### Case Summary 3.17

#### What Happens If You Ignore an Enviromental Order? *R. v. Consolidated Maybrun Mines Ltd.*[36]

Consolidated owned a copper–gold mine in northwestern Ontario. Employees of the Ministry of the Environment inspected the site about 10 years after its shutdown and discovered that the mine site had been abandoned. It had been vandalized, windows were broken, chemicals were strewn about, the mine shaft had filled with water, and oils contaminated with PCBs had leaked from several transformers.

Ministry officials wrote to Consolidated asking it to correct the situation, but it did not do anything. The Ministry's director then served notice on Consolidated that an order would be issued requiring it to take specific steps to clean up the property. Consolidated was given 15 days to make written submissions to the Ministry before the order would be issued. Consolidated responded that the order was "ridiculous" and blamed the government for the problems. The

---

35. (1987), 43 D.L.R. (4th) 712 (B.C.S.C); aff'd (1989), 56 D.L.R. (4th) 577 (B.C.C.A).

36. (1996), 28 O.R. (3d) 161 (C.A.); aff'd [1998] 1 S.C.R. 706.

Director then issued the order. He also informed Consolidated that it had the right to appeal the order by making written submissions, again within 15 days.

No appeal was made, and the order was generally ignored. The Ministry stepped in, took the necessary steps to clean up the site, and laid charges against Consolidated, and the individual who was its "guiding mind," for failing to comply with the order. This was an offence under the *Environmental Protection Act.*

The case was quite complex, but it is sufficient to note that the accused responded to the charges by saying that the Director's order was unreasonable, which was why Consolidated did not comply. At the trial, the accused were allowed to argue as to whether the order was reasonable.

On appeal, the Court held that whether the order was reasonable was irrelevant, and that Consolidated was required to respond to it. Other methods had been available to deal with the merits of the order; Consolidated could have appealed and challenged the order, in effect gaining a new hearing. Consolidated did not take advantage of this option, but simply ignored the order. It was the failure of Consolidated to respond to the order that resulted in the charges, and the accused were convicted.

**Common law ineffective against polluters**

Common law (and the civil law in Quebec) is basically ineffectual in providing any kind of general environmental protection. Because of this, most effective environmental law is embodied in federal and provincial statutes. Such legislation not only prohibits polluting activities, but also provides for government enforcement whether or not individuals have been harmed.

## Jurisdiction

**Environment a shared responsibility between federal and provincial governments**

Both federal and provincial governments have powers to make law with respect to the environment as they exercise their assigned responsibilities primarily under sections 91 and 92 of the *Constitution Act (1867)*. Historically, municipalities have had a limited role in environmental regulation. Recent case law and statutory amendments suggest, however, that municipal governments will become increasingly active in this area.[37]

### Reducing **Risk** 3.2

The *Consolidated* case is instructive because it illustrates not only the statutory liability of businesspeople and their corporations for long-forgotten operations, such as an old mine, but also the power given to government officials by environmental legislation such as the *Environmental Protection Act*. Orders given by such officials should not be ignored, or treated lightly, for their impact can be profound. Prompt action must be taken in response to such orders. It is important to take advantage of all of the remedies within the structure of the regulatory body involved—in the *Consolidated* case, the original right to respond with written submissions and, once the order was given, the right to appeal. It was Consolidated's lack of willingness to treat these matters seriously, and its resulting failure to take advantage of the available options, that ultimately led to the convictions.

37. See Michael Bowman and Michael Millar, "Municipal Role in Regulating the Environment Likely to Increase," *The Lawyers Weekly,* 22:17 (6 September 2002) at 16.

## Case Summary 3.18

### Who Has Jurisdiction Over Environmental Matters? *R. v. Hydro-Québec*[38]

This dispute arose over allegations that Hydro-Québec dumped PCBs into a river at a higher rate than allowed under the appropriate regulations. It was charged with violating an order under the *Canadian Environmental Protection Act.* Hydro-Québec entered a plea of not guilty. It claimed that the provisions relied on were not within the authority of the federal government, since environmental protection did not fall under the responsibilities assigned to the federal government under section 91 of the *Constitution Act (1867).* The charges were dismissed at trial, and appeals to the Quebec Superior Court and Court of Appeal were also dismissed. The matter was further appealed in the Supreme Court of Canada.

The Court agreed that the environment had not been specifically assigned to the federal government, but went on to observe that it had not been given to either level, federal *or* provincial. "It is a diffuse subject that cuts across many different areas of constitutional responsibility."[39]

If a provision in pith and substance falls within the parameters of a power assigned to the body (be it Parliament or a provincial legislature) that enacted the legislation, then it is constitutionally valid.

The problem then was to decide whether the *Canadian Environmental Protection Act* fell under any other existing federal responsibility, such as criminal law. It was found that the protection of the environment through the regulation of toxic substances was a legitimate public interest that needed to be protected and was therefore a proper use of the criminal law power. The legislation was valid and proper and, so, the matter was sent back to the original court for trial.

The case is important because it establishes that the federal government has authority to make legislation with respect to the environment and enforce it as a valid exercise of the criminal law power. This is true even when the legislation does not relate to subjects given specifically to the federal government under section 91. The case also illustrates that there can be overlapping jurisdictions on environmental matters. Similar provincial legislation could also have been valid, but on different grounds.

Forests, minerals, air, and water are all local matters and under the jurisdiction of provincial governments. But when activities involving such resources become interprovincial or international in scope, or when they take place on federal lands or in coastal waters, the federal government then has jurisdiction. The federal government can enact environmental protection legislation under its criminal law power, as evidenced by the *Hydro-Québec* case discussed in Case Summary 3.18. It can also exercise a considerable amount of indirect control by requiring that provincial environmental projects satisfy federal standards to qualify for federal funding.

Often, both federal and provincial regulatory authorities become involved when businesses initiate projects and activities that have significant environmental implications. These businesses must receive permits and licences, and submit to environmental laws, from both levels of government. Businesses engaged in

---

38. [1997] 3 S.C.R. 213.

39. *Ibid.,* at 286.

smaller projects that are local in nature may have to deal only with provincial and municipal laws. There is, however, growing cooperation among the three levels of government that will, hopefully, lead to the harmonization of legislation that will enable businesspeople to deal with only one level of bureaucracy.[40]

**Businesses may face federal, provincial, and municipal laws**

But this level of coordination has not yet been reached, and there are therefore laws at the federal, provincial, and municipal levels with respect to environmental regulation with which businesses must comply.

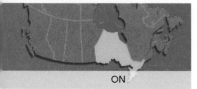

ON

## Penalties

The criminal prosecution model has largely been incorporated into the environmental area, including the imposition of fines and even imprisonment for violations. While it is much debated whether this approach is appropriate when offenders often have not acted intentionally or maliciously, recent trends include the increase of the penalties that can be imposed for violations of environmental laws and the expansion of the categories of individuals and corporations who face such liability. These trends are illustrated by the *Aqua-Tech* case discussed in Case Summary 3.15, in which directors, officers, and employees of the corporate offender were also convicted, receiving significant fines and jail sentences. A review of news releases from the Ontario Ministry of the Environment confirms the trends. The Ministry announced that environmental fines increased by 118 percent, and that investigators had laid 23 percent more charges, in the first half of 2001.[41]

**Penalties and enforcement increasing**

The Ministry also confirmed the longest prison term ever given for an environmental offence in Ontario: 18 months for an individual convicted of causing a discharge of cyanide into a creek, resulting in a large fish kill.[42] Another news release confirmed that Shell Canada Products Limited was convicted along with one of its contractors when the contractor allowed products to be illegally discharged, forcing the evacuation of a nearby daycare centre.[43]

Ontario recently increased the penalties for environmental offences under the *Environmental Protection Act,* relevant in the *Aqua-Tech* and *Consolidated* cases discussed above. Individuals convicted could face penalties of up to $6 million, and imprisonment for up to five years, while corporations could be fined up to $10 million.[44] The *Canadian Environmental Protection Act, 1999,* allows for fines of up to $1 million per day and imprisonment for up to five years for those convicted of environmental offences.[45]

---

40. In 1998, the Canadian Council of Ministers of the Environment (CCME), with the exception of Quebec, signed the Canada-wide Accord on Environmental Harmonization. Under the accord, each government retains its existing powers, but will attempt to use them in a coordinated manner to achieve enhanced environmental results. A Standards Sub-Agreement attempts to facilitate environmental results by encouraging joint development and execution of agreed-to plans of action. Principles are set out for the implementation of "Canada-Wide Standards" relating to environmental matters. These standards do not have any legal force, as the federal and provincial governments have retained their legislative discretion. It remains to be seen whether the Accord will eliminate duplication and streamline environmental regulation, making compliance clearer and easier. See the CCME website **http://www.ccme.ca/index.html**.

41. Ontario Ministry of the Environment, News Release, 31 August 2001.

42. Ontario Ministry of the Environment, News Release, 10 December 2001.

43. Ontario Ministry of the Environment, News Release, 16 January 2003.

44. R.S.O. 1990, c. E19, s. 187.

45. S.C. 1999, c. 33, Part 10. See discussion below.

Businesspeople should be aware of these trends, as they confirm that penalties for environmental offences are significant, that there is more enforcement of environmental laws, and that the list of those potentially facing liability is lengthy.

# Federal Legislation

The federal government exercises its power over the environment both directly and indirectly. As mentioned above, it has the power to make law with respect to the environment under the *Constitution Act (1867)* in matters that have an international or interprovincial scope, in matters that take place on federal land or coastal waters, and in those areas that have been determined to have been assigned to the federal government, such as the fisheries, military areas, airports, and air transportation. The federal government exercises an indirect control over the environment when it provides funding to the provinces to help pay for their environmental programs. The federal government can stipulate how the funds will be used and, to some degree, control the extent of the environmental legislation in place in the provinces. When the federal government finances a project under provincial jurisdiction, it can require compliance with federal as well as provincial regulations.

**Federal regulations control provincial areas through funding conditions**

## Canadian Environmental Protection Act[46]

Environmental legislation is intended to control environmental deterioration. Such legislation regulates things such as the transport and disposal of waste, the use and transportation of hazardous materials, the cleanup of contaminated sites, the treatment of sewage, and the disposal of byproducts from manufacturing, mining, and other activities. Environmental statutes also control specific locations by limiting industrial, commercial, and residential uses. They control contamination of the air, land, and water. Even noise and odour are controlled by such statutes. Essentially, environmental laws are designed to ensure that the natural state of the environment is retained as much as reasonably possible and that pollution in all its forms is kept to a minimum.

**Environmental laws to maintain natural state**

This is accomplished in several ways. The legislation usually provides for the creation of a ministry, charged with establishing standardized codes for the use of natural resources and the elimination of waste products or any other kind of activity that might degrade the environment. The ministry employees then enforce the standards through inspection, investigation, holding hearings, and levying fines and other penalties.

**Government departments set and enforce standards**

Typically, government ministries concerned with the environment are divided into several departments. One department requires that permits be obtained before engaging in an activity that causes pollution and provides those permits, setting appropriate limits and controls. Another department is responsible for research and development designed to establish standards and identify possible future threats to the environment. A third department is devoted to prevention, education, achieving compliance, investigation of violations, and prosecutions.

---

46. *Ibid.*

**Major federal environmental act**

The *Canadian Environmental Protection Act* (CEPA 1999) is the principal federal statute dealing with the environment. This is a comprehensive statute meant to prevent pollution, provide for research and development, investigate and measure pollution levels, and monitor industry. It has become a model for other levels of government to follow. Its preamble states that it is "An Act respecting pollution prevention and the protection of the environment and human health in order to contribute to sustainable development." It imposes significant duties on the federal government regarding the environment, defined as "the components of the Earth, including air, land, water, all layers of the atmosphere, all organic and inorganic matter and living organisms, and the interacting natural systems that include these components." The discussion below summarizes relevant provisions of CEPA 1999.

**Many obligations of federal government**

A national advisory committee must be appointed by the federal government to provide advice on environmental matters. This advice must be based on the "precautionary principle." The federal government may negotiate agreements with provincial governments or aboriginal people with respect to the administration of CEPA 1999. Agreements may also be made with the provinces regarding equivalent provisions. Under these agreements, the federal government may agree that federal regulations do not apply when there are equivalent provincial laws in place.

The federal government must keep an environmental registry containing notices and other published documents relevant to CEPA 1999. "Whistleblower" provisions protect those who provide information relating to the commission of environmental offences. An individual may request an investigation of environmental offences and, if dissatisfied with the government's response, can apply for an "environmental protection action." A court may grant a declaration, or any other order (except for damages), to prevent environmental offences. The defence of *due diligence* is available to the party alleged to have committed the environmental offence.

The federal government must maintain a system for monitoring environmental quality, and conduct research relating to specified environmental matters. It must formulate plans for pollution prevention and publishing relevant information. A person may be required to provide information to the government on environmental matters. The government must issue environmental quality objectives, guidelines, and codes of practice.

The government may require a person to prepare a pollution prevention plan for toxic substances. It must publish, and keep current, a list of toxic substances (such as asbestos, lead, mercury, and PCBs), and may pass regulations dealing with the control of such substances. Information relating to toxic substances must be reported to the government, including releases into the environment. The government may order remedial measures with respect to breaches of the law relating to toxic substances. "Living organisms" may be added to the list of toxic substances.

**Several environmental issues dealt with**

CEPA 1999 contains provisions relating to nutrients; the disposal of substances at sea; the production, importation, and selling of fuels; vehicle emissions; engines and equipment; international air and water pollution; and the movement of hazardous waste and recyclable material.

CEPA 1999 also deals with environmental emergencies. This includes accidental releases of prescribed substances into the environment. A person may be required to prepare an environmental emergency plan regarding environmental emergencies.

# Enforcement

Part 10 of CEPA 1999 sets out the enforcement provisions of the legislation. Government enforcement officers may enter and inspect any place (a warrant is needed before a private dwelling-place may be entered) if there are reasonable grounds to believe that it contains substances, fuels, vehicles, or equipment to which the statute applies, or records or documents relevant to administration of the statute. If the court is satisfied that there has been a contravention of the statute, it may issue a warrant entitling an enforcement officer to search a place and make a seizure of any relevant evidence. A search and seizure can even be done without a warrant in certain circumstances (for example, to avoid the loss of evidence, or to prevent danger to human life or to the environment). If the person is convicted of an environmental offence, the seized assets may be forfeited to the federal government.

**Inspections, searches, and seizures possible**

Based on such an inspection or search, an enforcement officer may issue an *environmental protection compliance order* (EPCO) with respect to any contravention of the statute. An EPCO can put an immediate stop to a violation (acting as a "stop order"), or prevent a violation from occurring. This ability to handle offences quickly is especially useful in emergency situations. In most cases, the enforcement officer must give a notice of intent to issue an EPCO, and allow the offender an opportunity to make representations. If the EPCO is not followed, then an enforcement officer may take the measures specified in the EPCO at the expense of the offender. An EPCO is subject to review by a review officer, whose decision may be appealed to the Federal Court. Failure to comply with an EPCO is an offence under the legislation.

**EPCOs can be issued**

As noted above, significant penalties are set out for those convicted of committing environmental offences. Officers, directors, and agents of corporations who "directed, assented to, acquiesced in, or participated in the commission of the offence" may be convicted whether or not the corporation has been prosecuted or convicted. The defence of due diligence is available, except for offences involving providing false or misleading information to enforcement officers; obstructing or hindering enforcement officers; or knowingly providing any person with false or misleading information or filing a false or misleading document.

**Individuals may be charged**

When someone has been convicted of an environmental offence, the court not only may impose the appropriate penalties under the statute, but also may make any other relevant order. The offender may be fined an amount equal to the benefit or advantage he gained as a result of the commission of the offence. Other possible orders may prohibit the illegal activity; direct the offender to take remedial or preventive action; direct the preparation and implementation of a pollution prevention plan, an environmental emergency plan, or an environmental management system; direct the conduct of an environmental audit; direct the offender to publish the facts relating to the conviction; direct the posting of a bond to ensure compliance of the order; direct the offender to compensate the government for any remedial or preventative action it took; direct the offender to perform community service; or direct the offender to pay for relevant environmental research, the costs of work done by environmental or health groups, or scholarships for students enrolled in environmental studies. The court may even order the offender to comply with any other reasonable condition it considers appropriate and just in the circumstances to secure the offender's good conduct and to prevent the offender from committing other environmental offences.

**Many orders possible**

**EPAMs can be negotiated**

*Environmental protection alternative measures* (EPAM) may be used in certain cases as an alternative to court prosecution. An EPAM is a negotiated agreement designed to restore the offender to compliance with the legislation. The government may, for example, propose an EPAM to an offender who had a good compliance history prior to the alleged violations. The person must accept responsibility for the commission of the offences; charges will be dismissed if the person complies with the agreement. This would enable the offender to avoid the costs and time inherent in judicial proceedings, as well as the stigma of a conviction. All EPAMs must be filed with the court and be included in the environmental registry.

**Ticket offences a non-criminal alternative**

The federal cabinet may designate offences under CEPA 1999 as "ticket offences." An enforcement officer may complete a ticket for a violation of such an offence and deliver it to the alleged offender. The offender may plead guilty and simply pay a prescribed fine. If the offender does not plead as required, then the court will enter a conviction and impose the fine. This approach allows for the use of administrative monetary penalties, and is a non-criminal alternative to the criminal prosecution model. Sanctions resulting from administrative, rather than judicial, proceedings are generally expected to be less costly and more expeditious. This administrative approach may, however, have the effect of overcoming the due diligence defence, thereby re-imposing strict liability.

### Case Summary 3.19

**Who Has the Burden of Proof for Strict Liability Offences?**
**R. v. Glenshiel Towing Co.**[47]

A tugboat was tied up to a dock at False Creek. It sank, and oil leaked into the water. The ship and the company that owned it were charged, under the *Canadian Shipping Act,* with discharging a pollutant. The ship sank accidentally, and the provincial court trial judge found the accused not guilty. That verdict was upheld on appeal to the Supreme Court of B.C.

The Court of Appeal, however, allowed the appeal from the acquittal. The Court quoted from the Supreme Court of Canada decision in *R. v. City of Sault Ste. Marie,*[48] which stated that there are three types of offences:

**1.** True criminal offences, for which intent to commit the offence must be proven;

**2.** Strict liability offences, for which the defence of due diligence is available to the accused to overcome the presumption of guilt arising from proof of the culpable act; and

**3.** Absolute liability offences, for which the defence of due diligence is not available to the accused to overcome the presumption of guilt.[49]

47. (2001), 90 B.C.L.R. (3d) 289 (C.A.), leave to appeal to S.C.C. refused, [2001] S.C.C.A. No. 464.

48. [1978] 2 S.C.R. 1299.

49. This type of offence is rare, as courts are reluctant to punish someone if there is no evidence of negligence; see *Reference re Section 94(2) of the Motor Vehicle Act, R.S.B.C. 1979, c. 288,* [1985] 2 S.C.R. 486, at 584.

The relevant offence in this case was a strict liability offence. The legislation stated that a ship that discharged a pollutant into water was guilty of an offence. While the prosecution had to prove that the accused committed the offence beyond a reasonable doubt, it did not have to prove negligence. Instead, the accused had to prove that, on a balance of probabilities, reasonable care had been taken to prevent the discharge of the oil. This illustrates the defence of due diligence.

## Due Diligence

Corporations may be required to refrain from future activities that threaten the environment. They may also face prosecution for past violations of environmental laws. As these laws will often allow for the lifting of the corporate veil, officers and directors may be personally liable for the offences committed by the corporation they manage and direct.

Most environmental offences are strict liability offences. As the *Glenschiel* case shows, this means that once the prosecution proves that the prohibited act occurred, the accused can avoid liability only by proving that there was due diligence. A corporation, and its directors and officers, should therefore ensure that all reasonable steps are taken to satisfy the requirements of relevant environmental legislation. Obviously, the extent of **due diligence** that is required will vary depending on the circumstances. Given the trends of increasing penalties for environmental offences, more enforcement of the environmental laws, and a growing list of those facing liability under those laws, it would appear prudent for directors and officers to take a conservative approach in determining the extent of due diligence to be exercised. The probability of a conviction will, of course, be reduced significantly if a pattern of environmental responsibility can be established.

**Need due diligence to avoid liability**

One practical step that can be taken in this regard is a compliance audit. This can be used by a corporation to periodically examine its policies and procedures to determine whether they are in compliance with the legislation. This is essential in an age when the law is constantly changing and technology is constantly improving. If a corporation is charged with an offence, it may be difficult to convince a court that there was due diligence if an environmental audit had not been completed recently, and if appropriate steps to ensure legislative compliance, and to minimize the risk of environmental damage, had not been taken.

## Reducing **Risk** 3.3

A receiver, or a trustee in bankruptcy, of a corporation—or even its creditors, such as mortgagees and landlords—can be held responsible for the costs of cleaning up polluted property. It is uncertain how far this responsibility would, or should, go in a particular case. It does seem clear, for example, that secured creditors who realize their security by taking possession of the property will probably assume responsibility for cleaning it up. Lenders may therefore choose not to exercise their security in the face of a default. It is now incumbent on lenders, investors, and potential purchasers of property or a business to make a careful examination to determine any environmental risks before they become involved. This may require an environmental *site audit,* to determine contamination problems associated with a business or site before entering into a transaction.

### Case Summary 3.20

#### Do Environmental Costs Take Priority Over the Claims of Secured Creditors? *Panamericana de Bienes y Servicos S.A. v. Northern Badger Oil and Gas Ltd.*[50]

Panamericana lends money and takes a debenture ➤ Badger defaults on loan ➤ Receiver–manager appointed and Badger placed in bankruptcy ➤ ERCB orders receiver–manager to seal wells

Receiver–manager sells wells that had belonged to Badger ➤ Court of Appeal rules that cost of sealing wells takes priority over rights of Panamericana

This case was the first in Canada to find that the costs of an environmental cleanup take priority over a secured party's claim in the distribution of assets of an insolvent party. Badger defaulted on its debenture to Panamericana, which obtained a court order appointing a receiver–manager. Subsequently, Badger was placed in bankruptcy. The receiver–manager found buyers for all but five of Badger's oil and gas wells. Before the proceeds of the sales were paid to Panamericana, the Energy Resources Conservation Board (ERCB) ordered the receiver–manager to "abandon," or seal, the five wells. The trial Judge treated this cleanup expense as just another liability of the debtor that ranked behind that of the debenture-holder. This meant that the proceeds could be paid to Panamericana, without first attending to the cleanup.

The Court of Appeal, however, found that the receiver–manager, by carrying on the debtor's business, had an obligation to do so according to the general law of the province, which required oil and gas wells to be sealed. When the ERCB ordered abandonment, the receiver–manager had a duty to comply, even though doing so would reduce the amount of the payout to the creditor, the debenture-holder.

This case underscores the importance of a financier examining potential risks, including environmental cleanup costs, prior to lending money secured by property. A failure to do so may result in that "security" ultimately being a liability.

## Other Federal Statutes

**Many other federal environmental acts**

CEPA 1999 is supplemented by several other federal statutes, each governing particular environmental matters. The *Transportation of Dangerous Goods Act 1992*[51] controls the transporting of dangerous goods between provinces or internationally. The *Fisheries Act*[52] attempts to protect fish habitat. It prohibits the discharge of any "deleterious" substance into waterways, lakes, and oceans, and does not allow "any work or undertaking that results in the harmful alteration, disruption or destruction of fish habitat."

---

50. (1991), 117 A.R. 44 (C.A.), leave to appeal to S.C.C. refused, [1991] S.C.C.A. No. 497.

51. 1 S.C. 1992, c. 34.

52. R.S.C. 1985, c. F-14.

## Case Summary 3.21

### Does Environmental Law Apply to Municipalities?
### *R. v. Richmond (Township)*[53]

The Township of Richmond was charged with a violation of the *Fisheries Act* for discharging a pollutant into a river. The Act provided that "no person shall deposit or permit to be deposited any deleterious substance or cause any such deleterious substance to enter any such water." At the trial, the charge was dismissed on the basis that the judge did not have jurisdiction because the township did not qualify as a "person" under the Act. The Court of Appeal referred to the *Interpretation Act*, which states that "person" includes a corporation. The Court found that even though Richmond was a unique kind of corporation, it was indeed a corporation and that the Act therefore applied to it. The Chief Justice stated, "I think it is only common sense that Parliament, in providing for the protection of waters from pollution, intended that that should apply to all persons in Canada and could not, unless there was some specific language, exclude a municipal corporation."

This case illustrates just how extensive the provisions of the *Fisheries Act* are and that it applies even to municipalities. It also shows that a corporation is a "person" in the eyes of the law, a matter that will be discussed later in the text.

The *Canada Shipping Act*[54] deals with matters such as the handling, shipping, and discharge of pollutants, as well as oil-pollution incidents. The *Arctic Waters Pollution Prevention Act*[55] is an attempt to preserve the relatively pristine conditions found in the North and to avoid the kind of disasters (such as oil spills) that have happened in other areas. Other examples of federal environmental legislation include the *Navigable Waters Protection Act*,[56] the *Nuclear Fuel Waste Act*,[57] the *Hazardous Products Act*,[58] and the *Canada Wildlife Act*.[59] The most recent development was the proclamation into law, on 5 June 2003, of the *Species at Risk Act*.[60] It is designed to facilitate conservation and protection of Canada's biological diversity.

## The Environmental Assessment Process

A trend in Canadian legislation at both the federal and provincial levels is to impose an environmental assessment review process on those wishing to undertake a potentially hazardous project. (This applies both to new projects and to modifications of existing projects.) The objective is to require the parties proposing the project to file, with a designated government agency, a report that highlights the project's potential impact on the environment, including any health

**Environmental assessments often required**

---

53. (1983), 4 D.L.R. (4th) 189 (B.C.C.A.).

54. R.S.C. 1985, c. S-9.

55. R.S.C. 1985, c. A-12.

56. R.S.C. 1985, c. N-22.

57. S.C. 2002, c. 23.

58. R.S.C. 1985, c. H-3.

59. R.S.C. 1985, c. W-9.

60. S.C. 2002, c. 29.

risks. The government authority studies this report, and seeks public input, maybe even holding a public hearing to air all the various points of view. The authority then decides whether to give its permission for the activity, to withhold it, or to grant the permit with conditions. Environmental assessment reviews were initially limited to public activities, but now environmental impact studies are generally required for private industrial and resource-based projects as well. Producing such reports has significantly increased the cost of doing business. Such reports are now required not only for large projects, such as steel plants, pulp mills, and hydroelectric dams, but also for smaller types of business activities that use specific types of chemicals or otherwise threaten the environment.

**Purposes of Act**

The *Canadian Environmental Assessment Act*[61] (CEAA) replaced non-legislated cabinet guidelines and imposed significant reporting obligations on businesses dealing with the federal government. The proclaimed purposes of the CEAA are the following:[62]

**1.** To ensure projects are carefully considered so that they do not cause significant adverse environmental effects.

**2.** To promote sustainable development and thus a healthy environment and a healthy economy.

**3.** To ensure federal authorities carry out their responsibilities in a coordinated manner, to eliminate unnecessary duplication in the environmental assessment process.

**4.** To promote cooperation and coordination between federal and provincial governments with respect to environmental assessment processes.

**5.** To promote communication and cooperation between federal authorities and aboriginal people with respect to environmental assessment processes.

**6.** To ensure that projects carried out in Canada or on federal lands do not cause significant adverse environmental effects to other lands.

**7.** To ensure opportunities for timely and meaningful public participation throughout the environmental assessment process.

**Types of assessments**

The CEAA requires an environmental assessment for any project for which the federal government holds decision-making authority—whether as issuer of permits and licences, financier, proponent of the project, or land administrator (where the government plans to dispose of an interest in those lands to further the project). All such projects are to receive an appropriate degree of environmental assessment, the degree depending largely on the scale and complexity of the project. The four types of environmental assessments include *screening, comprehensive study, mediation,* and *panel review*. The vast majority of all projects are assessed using the first two methods.

A *screening* documents the environmental effects of a proposed project and determines the need to eliminate or minimize these harmful effects, to modify the plans for the project, or to require further assessments through either mediation or a panel review. Small-scale, routine projects are typically screened. At any stage of a screening, the Minister of the Environment may call a public review by a mediator or panel. Large-scale, environmentally sensitive projects, as identified

61. S.C. 1992, c. 37.

62. *Ibid.,* s. 4.

by the *Comprehensive Study List Regulation*,[63] usually undergo a more intensive assessment called a *comprehensive study.*

*Mediation* is a voluntary process in which an impartial mediator appointed by the Minister helps interested parties resolve issues surrounding a project. This process is best reserved for situations where the parties are few and a consensus is possible. *Panel reviews* offer large numbers of groups and individuals with different points of view a chance to present information and express concerns. Panels can compel the attendance of witnesses and the disclosure of information.

Consideration of alternative means of carrying out the project, as well as the project's purpose and effects on the sustainability of renewable resources, is also mandated. Responsible authorities must address the need for a follow-up program to verify the accuracy of the environmental assessment and determine the effectiveness of any measures adopted to mitigate adverse environmental impact.

**Follow-up programs ensure mitigation measures**

To ensure public access and involvement, a registry (accessible through the internet) is established to make available all information collected or submitted relative to the environmental review process for the various projects. The CEAA also established the Canadian Environmental Assessment Agency, which advises and assists the Minister by administering and promoting the environmental assessment process, encouraging research, promoting uniformity throughout Canada, and ensuring an opportunity for public input. In the process, the Agency provides administrative support, training, and information. The CEAA is an attempt to establish a comprehensive process for protecting the environment. To prevent possible overlaps or confusion with the environmental assessment processes of a province, the federal environment minister may negotiate a harmonized environmental procedure that provides for joint panel reviews with that province. The Agency has concluded bilateral arrangements with Manitoba, Saskatchewan, Alberta, and British Columbia.

**Public access to reports on internet**

**Joint reviews with provinces**

There has been a great deal of criticism concerning the considerable burden that complying with environmental assessment laws imposes on businesses. A zero-tolerance policy has required businesses that impact the environment even in only a minor way to embark on a lengthy and complicated process with little tangible benefit but great cost. In an effort to alleviate this burden on industry, the federal government recently amended the CEAA.[64]

Some of the amendments were designed to streamline the process, reducing and in some cases eliminating altogether the assessment requirements. A screening report may sometimes be used instead of a comprehensive study of a project, if the screening demonstrates that a project is not likely to cause significant adverse environmental effects. The list of projects that are exempt from an assessment because they do not have significant effects on the environment has been expanded. Cabinet has been given the power to exempt from environmental assessment minor projects below a set cost threshold. If a project is subject to an assessment through a comprehensive study, it cannot be referred to a review panel or mediator at a later date. It remains to be seen whether these changes to the CEAA will provide sufficient relief to commercial interests or are a significant step backward in the war against environmental contamination.

**Amendments attempt to improve assessment process**

63. S.O.R./94-638.

64. S.C. 2003, c. 9.

## Provincial Legislation

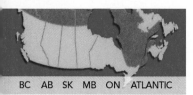

BC  AB  SK  MB  ON  ATLANTIC

**Every province has unique environmental laws**

All of the provinces have some form of legislation dealing with environmental issues within provincial jurisdiction. This legislation varies from province to province. Like the federal government, each of the provinces has one general environmental statute, supplemented by issue-specific legislation. Examples of general environmental statutes include British Columbia's *Environment Management Act*,[65] Alberta's *Environmental Protection and Enhancement Act*,[66] Ontario's *Environment Protection Act*,[67] and Nova Scotia's *Environment Act*.[68]

**Which are often changed after an environmental disaster**

While the specific environmental legislation varies from province to province, one common aspect is that politicians in every jurisdiction appear to be very sensitive to public opinion with respect to environmental matters. If an environmental disaster occurs, the relevant legislation may be changed as a result of the public outcry. A recent example involves the tragedy that occurred in Walkerton, Ontario in the spring of 2000. The town's water supply was contaminated with *E. coli*. Hundreds of people became sick, and seven of them died. After much public outcry and intensive lobbying by various groups, the government conducted a public inquiry. This inquiry culminated in a set of recommendations designed to protect drinking water from its source to the tap. Based on these recommendations, the Ontario government passed the *Safe Drinking Water Act, 2002*.[69] This legislation includes a number of important measures to protect the consumers of drinking water. While it remains to be seen whether this legislation will be successful in achieving a satisfactory level of protection, the example does illustrate how environmental legislation can be amended after an environmental catastrophe.

## The Economy versus the Environment

**Environmental regulation and costs unpopular with businesses**

The tendency of government toward increasing interference in business activities in relation to the environment appears to some to be an unwarranted and unfair intrusion. Whenever the economy worsens and costs increase, some businesses have difficulty surviving as profitable enterprises. Pressing bottom-line concerns are bound to affect the perception of environmental issues. The increased attention that government is paying to the environment may be justified, but the imposition of more government regulation is not popular in business circles. It is usually in this regulatory arena that the clash between government bureaucrats, businesses, and individuals takes place.

The ongoing dispute between the environmental movement and various industries is forcing a reassessment of how government should deal with these matters; businesspeople not only must concern themselves with a costly and interfering regulatory environment, but also must contend with uncertainty and flux. Government regulatory officials impose standards, establish environmental screening processes, and often require reports when a new project is undertaken. An involved process of public hearings and submissions may be required before a licence or permit is granted. Once the project is underway, inspectors may meas-

65. R.S.B.C. 1996, c. 118.

66. R.S.A. 2000, c. E-12.

67. *Supra* note 44.

68. S.N.S. 1994–95, c. 1.

69. S.O. 2002, c. 32.

ure compliance; for industries that are considered dangerous, such inspections may become routine.

Businesses must consider the costs of complying with environmental standards, as well as the costs of prosecution when offences do take place. Even if a site was previously contaminated, modern legislation may require that it be cleaned up by—or at the expense of—the polluter or current owner and that compensation be paid to injured parties. These statutes may apply even when no regulations were in place at the time the pollution occurred, or if the standards in place were lower than they should have been.

Businesses must recognize that they are subject to inspection and prosecution when their day-to-day activities pose a risk to the environment. It is crucial that any business plan contain provisions for compliance to current and projected regulations. In order to protect directors, officers, and the corporation itself, strategies must be developed so that the reasonable conduct required to establish due diligence is built into the business operation.

The controversy extends to whether development ought to take place at all—whether the forests ought to be cut down; rivers ought to be dammed; plants ought to be built. The recurring examples of environmental activists risking jail terms to stop logging in sensitive areas, or strapping themselves to oil drilling rigs, illustrate that the problem is more fundamental than waste disposal and pollution. The impact of these disputes can have a profound effect on businesses to the point of raising the question of whether they will be able to carry on business at all.

For example, when a company applied to develop a copper mine in the Tatshenshini wilderness area, the outcry and pressure were so great that the British Columbia government stepped in, declared the area a provincial park, and put an end to the project. The Oldman River hydroelectric project in Alberta ran into many obstacles, most hinging on environmental concerns. The fixed-link bridge between Prince Edward Island and the mainland ran into similar difficulties. The Kemano Completion Project in British Columbia was stopped because of concerns about the fish habitat in the Fraser and Nechako river systems. Fast ferries ran into difficulty because the wake they created destroyed shorelines. Even when a government has given approval for a project, protesters may continue their activities: the provincial government gave permission to log in the Clayoquot Sound area on the west coast of Vancouver Island, but environmental protestors (arrests were in the hundreds) put great pressure on the government to backtrack from its decision.

An important aspect of these protests is the involvement of private groups, such as Greenpeace, the Sierra Club of Canada, the World Wildlife Fund, and the Sierra Legal Defence Fund, positioning themselves against the government and businesses. These groups not only provide a vehicle for promoting the position of their members but also play an important role in intervening in litigation or providing the financial support for those involved. To further complicate matters, recent court decisions and treaty negotiations with respect to Native rights bring one more group into the equation that must be satisfied before projects can be advanced.[70]

Another factor involves international treaties entered into by the federal government. Once a treaty is in effect, it will be implemented by the federal and provincial governments, in accordance with the constitutional division of responsibilities. A recent example is the Kyoto Protocol, which sets targets and

**Businesses must consider costs of environmental compliance**

**Due diligence and self-regulation necessary**

**International commitments must be considered**

70. See *R. v. Bernard* (2003), 230 D.L.R. (4th) 57 (N.B.C.A.), leave to appeal to S.C.C. requested, where the Court ruled that natives have the right to cut trees for commercial purposes on all Crown land in the province.

timetables for the reduction of emission of greenhouse gases. There has been much public debate as to the cost of Canada's commitment to the Protocol, not only to the national and the provincial economies but also to specific industries.

As the population continues to grow, and with it the consumption of resources and the production of goods, the pressure on the environment will increase. Government is the only body that can mediate conflicting interests. It has managed to create a greater public awareness and interest in environmental issues. It has legislated and otherwise encouraged solutions that address the major problems. A spirit of cooperation, consultation, and compromise will allow for the development and maintenance of workable programs and policies that satisfy the needs of everyone.

**Negotiation and mediation preferred alternatives**

This discussion with respect to environmental law illustrates just one of the areas in which business must deal with government, and shows the extensive regulatory environment within which businesses today must function. Although a businessperson has some right to resist the improper use of government power, individuals and businesses are usually at a disadvantage, not having access to unlimited resources. Confrontation should thus be avoided if at all possible. Usually, the controls imposed are necessary. In these circumstances, negotiation is more appropriate than resistance, and collaborative mediated solutions will be more advantageous to all when compared to dealing with disputes in the courts. Businesspeople and environmental activists alike should explore this avenue first and exercise great caution before turning to the courts for relief.

# Summary

### Government agents

- Derive their power from statutes.
- Powers consist of the right to create, apply, and enforce regulations that accomplish the goals of the legislation.

### Administrative tribunals

- Enforce policies and resolve disputes when individuals or corporations challenge the law.
- Act within the jurisdiction granted by the enabling statute.
- Comply with the *Charter of Rights and Freedoms.*
- Have a duty to maintain a minimum standard of procedural fairness.
- Must follow the rules of natural justice.
  - Fair hearing with adequate notice.
  - Decision made by person who heard the evidence.
  - Process must be free of bias.

### Courts

- Review administrative decisions when the administrative tribunal did not have jurisdiction or did not follow the rules of natural justice.
- Can apply sanctions by way of prerogative writs including *habeas corpus, certiorari, mandamus, quo warranto,* and prohibition.
- Can make a declaration or order an injunction.

### Privative clauses

- Statutory terms that attempt to prevent judicial review, which often are resisted by the courts.

### Environmental protection

- Statutes designed to protect the environment are examples of government regulation and the administrative process.
- Common laws such as riparian rights and the torts of nuisance and negligence may be useful in some cases.
- Both federal and provincial governments have jurisdiction over the environment.
- Goals of statute law are to prohibit environmental offences, assess damage of proposed projects, levy fines and penalties for violations, educate the public, and encourage good environmental practices.
- Resolving environmental conflicts by negotiation and incentives generally is more effective than imposing administrative decisions and judicial remedies.

## QUESTIONS

1. Identify and describe the three different functions of government. Explain how the concept of parliamentary supremacy affects how the three functions interrelate.
2. Describe the principle of the rule of law. Explain how it affects the exercise of government power.
3. What is meant by the term *ultra vires,* and how does it relate to federal and provincial legislation?
4. What is the golden rule? The mischief rule? Under what circumstances can the courts apply these rules of statutory interpretation?
5. What is an administrative tribunal?
6. What obligations are placed on an adjudicative decision maker, even if not included in the legislation under which she is acting?
7. What three main elements constitute the rules of natural justice? Under what circumstances must a decision maker follow these rules of natural justice?
8. What requirements must be met for a person to receive a fair hearing?
9. Under what circumstances will judicial review be available?
10. Discuss the possible standards of a judicial review.
11. Distinguish between *certiorari*, prohibition, *mandamus*, and a declaration.
12. What is a privative clause? How do courts usually react to them?
13. Give examples of three different types of privative clauses.
14. What are some of the disadvantages of having a dispute resolved before an administrative tribunal?
15. What common law provisions protect the environment? Why was it necessary to pass federal and provincial legislation?
16. What are the trends relevant to the incorporation of the criminal prosecution model into the environmental area?
17. Discuss the terms *EPCO, EPAM,* and *ticket offences* as they are used in the *Canadian Environmental Protection Act.*

18. What type of offence are most environmental offences? What defence is available to someone charged with such an offence?

19. What is the purpose of an environmental assessment? Describe the four types of environmental assessments.

20. How would you recommend that businesses deal with environmental issues and regulations?

---

## CASES

### 1. *Black v. Canada (Prime Minister) (2001), 54 O.R. (3d) 215 (C.A.).*

Mr. Black, a Canadian citizen, was nominated for appointment by the Queen as a peer. The nomination was accepted and recommended by the British government. Mr. Black later obtained English citizenship. Prime Minister Chrétien intervened to block the peerage. He asserted that he had a legal right to block the nomination because of a resolution passed by the Canadian House of Commons in 1919, requesting the king to refrain from conferring titles on his Canadian subjects.

Mr. Black's appointment as a peer was deferred. He commenced an action against the Prime Minister for abuse of power, misfeasance in public office, and negligence. Should his action succeed? Be sure to consider the "Crown prerogative" in your answer. When does the prerogative exist? Can the Prime Minister exercise the prerogative?

### 2. *Blencoe v. British Columbia (Human Rights Commission), [2000] 2 S.C.R. 307.*

Blencoe, a minister in the British Columbia government, was accused by an assistant of sexual harassment in March 1995. He was removed from Cabinet and dismissed from the NDP caucus. Similar complaints were then made to the Human Rights Commission by two other women, in July and August 1995. Hearings were scheduled for March 1998. Blencoe applied for judicial review, requesting that the complaints be stayed on the basis that the Commission had lost jurisdiction due to unreasonable delay causing serious prejudice. He claimed that some prospective witnesses had died, and that the memories of others may have faded.

Should Blencoe's application succeed? Does section 7 of the *Charter of Rights and Freedoms,* guaranteeing security of the person, apply? Does the right to be tried within a reasonable time apply to non-criminal matters?

### 3. *Abbott v. Pelican Lake First Nation, [2003] F.C.J. No. 577 (T.D.).*

The Pelican Lake Indian Band decided to change its procedure for electing a band council. It held a referendum, but a majority did not approve of the change. Despite this, and despite the fact that the Minister's consent had not been granted, the Band proceeded with an election for band council under the new procedure. The Federal Court set aside the results of this election.

The members of the Band then selected five members of an appeal board. One member resigned before the next election. After the election, the applicants appealed to the appeal board, claiming that the election should be overturned because of legislative violations and corruption. The four remaining members of the appeal board, along with the chief electoral officer and the deputy returning officer, met and decided that the election was fair and binding. The applicants applied for judicial review of the appeal board's decision. Should their application succeed? Note that the legislation states that meetings of the appeal board require five impartial members to be present. What if the chief electoral officer and the deputy returning officer were not impartial observers?

### 4. 114957 Canada Ltée (Spraytech, Société d'arrosage) v. Hudson (Town), [2001] 2 S.C.R. 241.

Spraytech and Chemlawn used pesticides in the course of their business activities. The Town of Hudson passed a bylaw that restricted the use of pesticides within its borders to essential situations where the use was not for purely aesthetic reasons. Spraytech and Chemlawn were charged with using pesticides in violation of the bylaw. They sought a declaration that the bylaw was *ultra vires* the town's authority, or inoperative by virtue of conflict with federal or provincial legislation. Should the Supreme Court of Canada make such a declaration? Note that provincial legislation empowered municipalities to make bylaws to secure "peace, order, good government, health and general welfare." Furthermore, the federal and provincial environmental legislation appeared to envision the enactment of complementary municipal bylaws.

### 5. R. v. Safety-Kleen Canada Inc. (1997), 32 O.R. (3d) 493 (C.A.).

The business of collecting, transporting, and re-refining waste oil is closely regulated. Manifests must be filled out by the generator of the waste, as well as the transporter and the receiver of it. Cochrane picked up oily waste from a Petro-Canada facility, along with the proper manifest. His truck broke down and he contacted a representative of Safety-Kleen. The oil was transferred from Cochrane's truck to Safety-Kleen's truck. The transfer required verbal permission from the Ministry, as well as the completion of a new manifest. Although an attempt was made to contact the Ministry, the necessary authorization was not given. False information was provided on the original manifest. The Safety-Kleen truck was stopped by a Ministry official as soon as it went on the highway.

Charges were laid for failing to comply with the regulations and for providing false information. What types of offences are these? Should Safety-Kleen be held responsible for the offences committed by its employee? Is the defence of due diligence relevant here?

### 6. Bank of Montreal v. Lundrigans Ltd. (1996), 146 Nfld. & P.E.I.R. 252 (Nfld. C.A.).

Lundrigans operated a series of businesses, including interests in "road construction, civil engineering construction, building supply sales, mixed and pre-cast concrete production and sales, gypsum wallboard production, and sales and residential, commercial, and industrial real estate development." It was having financial difficulties and could not meet its obligations to the Bank of Montreal. The Bank wished to appoint a receiver, but the receiver insisted that a clause be included in the court order stating that the receiver would not be personally liable for any environmental liability incurred. The Government of Canada and the Government of Newfoundland objected to such a clause, on the grounds that it would infringe upon existing federal and provincial environmental legislation.

Discuss whether creditors, and receivers appointed by them, should be responsible for environmental damage and cleanup costs, and the extent of any such liability. In your answer, consider whether a receiver ought to be responsible for the continuing environmental problems that arise while it operates the business as a going concern in order to preserve its value.

# The Fundamentals

**B**efore dealing with the specialized legal relations and transactions that are the major focus of this text, it is necessary to understand the basic concepts and principles upon which they are built. These fundamentals are covered in Chapters 4 to 8. Chapter 4 is an examination of tort law, the basis of liability imposed on professional and businesspeople for their wrongful conduct that causes injury to others. Chapters 5 to 8 examine the law of contract, including the requirements for a valid contract, problems that can arise between contracting parties, and how a contractual relationship ends. Most of the transactions and relationships discussed in the rest of the text are specialized forms of contracts with their own unique rules.

# Torts and Professional Liability

## CHAPTER HIGHLIGHTS

- Torts defined and categorized
- Intentional torts
  - Assault, battery, trespass, private nuisance, defamation, invasion of privacy
- Distinguishing between careless and negligent conduct
- **A** Duty of care and when the duty is owed
- **B**reach of the Standard of Care and how it is determined
- **C**ausation—physical and legal
- **D**amage—case law indicates the types recognized as compensable
- Defences to tort actions
- Negligence—business concerns
- Product liability
- Professional liability
- Tort law—implications for businesspeople

The law of torts involves private disputes decided in the civil courts. When one person harms another, either intentionally or carelessly, a tort has been committed and an action can be brought seeking compensation for injuries suffered from the person who committed the wrong. In this chapter, we discuss the distinctions between intentional and negligent torts, the defences that the person being sued may raise, and the conditions that must be met for the plaintiff to be awarded compensation.

# Introduction

### Case Summary 4.1

**Childproof Your Premises or Pay:** *Qulette v. Daon Dev. Corp.*[1]

The plaintiff, a five-year-old girl, and her 10-year-old sister were in Sunridge Mall, on their way to meet their 17-year-old sister at the Food Fair. While the 10-year-old was momentarily distracted, the five-year-old grasped the moving handrail of a free-standing escalator. She began to ride up along the exterior glass wall of that escalator, calling for help. When she reached the top, her progress was impeded by a wall and as she could not climb over it, the five-year-old fell 17 feet to a brick floor below, fracturing her skull. An action was brought against the defendant occupier of the premises pursuant to the *Occupiers' Liability Act*. The Court found that the infant plaintiff was a visitor, as defined by the Act and, as such, was owed the "common duty of care" described as "a duty to take such care as in all the circumstances of the case is reasonable to see that the visitor will be reasonably safe." In light of the danger posed by having a free-standing escalator located in a mall frequented by children, the Court found that the defendant's failure to obstruct unauthorized use with some sort of barrier constituted negligence. Further, the risk of children falling was foreseeable. The accident was caused not by a lack of supervision but by the condition of the escalator. Claims of contributory negligence on the part of the plaintiff, her mother, or her sisters were all dismissed.

The case raises some interesting questions. Who should bear responsibility if a young child is harmed? Is there a duty to childproof places that are frequented by children? Who should be watching the child? What factors affect liability?

When people engage in commercial activities, conflicting interests or simple interactions can sometimes lead to the commission of *torts*. It is difficult to find a wholly satisfactory definition for torts because of the different kinds of acts that may be considered tortious. Some general principles, however, do apply. A **tort** is committed when one person causes injury to another, harming their person, property, or reputation. The right to sue for compensation arises when the injurious conduct falls below a minimum social standard. A tort is a social or civil wrong that is remedied by a right to sue for compensation. The approach we use in this text is to look at different categories of torts (because different rules sometimes apply), and though this is convenient it can be somewhat misleading in that only some kinds of torts are dealt with. The court may find that a tort has been committed that does not conveniently fit into the identified categories. From a business perspective, it might be better to approach tort as one basic principle of law that provides remedies where wrongful conduct is involved.

*A tort is a civil or social wrong*

**Crimes** must be distinguished from torts. Harmful conduct that is so serious that it poses a threat to society generally is said to be criminal in nature. The prosecution for such acts is done by the state in a criminal court where the goal is to punish the wrongdoer, not to compensate the victim. A tort is considered a private matter where the victim of the injurious conduct sues the person responsible

*Crimes are wrongs that affect society as a whole*

---

1. (1998), 58 Alta. L.R. (2d) 261 (Q.B.).

for the injury. With many crimes, the victim has the right to sue for tort, even if the prosecution results in an acquittal. Thus, wrongful conduct is often both a crime and a tort. Most of the torts discussed in this chapter have a *Criminal Code* counterpart. The O.J. Simpson trial in the United States is a good example: although a jury acquitted Simpson of murder, he was found liable in a subsequent civil action for the tort of causing wrongful death and had to compensate the relatives of the victims. It is much easier to successfully sue for tort, because the standard of proof is based on a "balance of probabilities." In a criminal action, the standard is "beyond a reasonable doubt," a much higher standard than required in a civil action.

**Torts differ from actions based on breach of contract**

A tort must also be distinguished from a **breach of contract.** An act that breaches a contract may not be inherently wrong, but the contractual relationship makes the violation of its terms unacceptable. A tort, on the other hand, is inherently wrongful conduct that falls below a minimal social standard. When the victim sues, the court imposes the standard and determines who should bear the loss for the injuries suffered and also the amount that will adequately compensate the victim.

**Torts may involve intentional or inadvertent conduct**

There are two major categories of tortious activity: *intentional* (or deliberate) acts and *unintentional* (or careless) negligent acts. Businesspeople can find themselves liable over both intentional and unintentional torts, but the latter is by far the most important area of tort law for businesspeople and professionals to understand. One important difference between deliberate torts and negligence is in the remedies that the courts are willing to grant to the injured party. When the interference has been intentional, the courts may be persuaded to grant punitive damages in addition to the more common general and special damages. **General damages** compensate for estimated future losses, including both future pecuniary losses (such as loss of earning capacity) and non-pecuniary losses (such as pain and suffering). **Special damages** are awarded to cover actual expenses and calculable pre-trial losses. **Punitive or exemplary damages** are designed to punish the wrongdoer and do not relate to the injury suffered. To avoid excessive awards, the Supreme Court of Canada has placed an upper limit that can be awarded to compensate for pain and suffering and loss of enjoyment of life of approximately $272 000.[2] Occasionally, the court will also order the return of property or grant an injunction to stop some offending activity.

**Employer may be vicariously liable for employees' torts**

It is important for businesspeople to keep the concept of **vicarious liability** in mind while studying tort law. An employer can be held liable for the tortious act an employee commits while at work. This liability is limited to torts committed while carrying out employment duties. The employer will not be vicariously liable when the employee is off doing his or her own thing during working hours. The importance of vicarious liability in the business world cannot be overemphasized. A detailed examination of the master/servant (employer/employee) relationship and vicarious liability can be found in Chapter 11. Several provinces have imposed vicarious liability by statute on the owners of motor vehicles, making them liable for damage and injury caused by the people they allow to drive their cars.

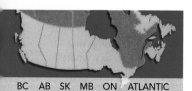

BC   AB   SK   MB   ON   ATLANTIC

2. The Supreme Court of Canada established a cap of $100 000 for non-pecuniary damages for personal-injury actions in the 1978 "trilogy": *Andrews v. Grand & Toy Alberta Ltd.,* [1978] 2 S.C.R. 229; *Thornton v. Prince George School District No. 57,* [1978] 2 S.C.R. 267; *Arnold v. Teno,* [1978] 2 S.C.R. 287. Due to inflation, the amount is approximately $272 000 (as of 2002).

## Reducing **Risk** 4.1

Perhaps the most valuable thing to gain from the study of tort law—or for that matter any of the rules discussed in this text—is the habit of mind that anticipates and avoids legal problems. This is called *risk avoidance* or *risk management*. Businesspeople have a responsibility to manage their legal affairs in the same way they manage the production, marketing, and distribution of their products. Too often, managers wait for something to go wrong, then put the matter into the hands of a lawyer and wait for the results of a lawsuit. Managing risk responsibly means avoiding the problem in the first place. As you learn about torts and other aspects of the law, you might observe the conditions and practices that pose a danger to the public, customers, suppliers, or employees, and decide how they should be corrected. This might be as simple as checking the creditworthiness of customers, keeping a record of e-mails, putting a warning sticker on a plate-glass window, or lighting a dark stairwell. Businesspeople should adopt an attitude of risk avoidance to reduce exposure to costly and time-consuming legal actions.

# Intentional Torts

## Assault and Battery

### Case Summary 4.2

#### Bouncers Beware! *Bruce v. Coliseum Management Ltd.*[3]

Jeffery Bruce was a 22-year-old college student at the time that he went with a friend to a local nightclub. While there, after consuming a moderate amount of beer, he and his friend got into a friendly tussle. Unfortunately, the doorman in the club saw this as a fight and ordered the two off the premises. The friend left quietly, but Mr. Bruce put up a struggle. He verbally abused the bouncer, swore, and resisted eviction. Finally, he was forced out onto a second-storey balcony, and after continued resistance the bouncer pushed him in the chest causing him to fall backward down the stairs. Mr. Bruce broke his kneecap, causing serious pain and suffering. The Court found that even in the face of the provocation the doorman had used excessive force. While the provocation did not justify the excessive use of force, it did mitigate the damages awarded, which were considerable. Mr. Bruce was awarded $50 000 special damages and, on appeal, a further $40 000 general damages. The award was reduced by 30 percent because of the provocation.

This case shows how careful commercial establishments must be in whom they hire and how the staff are trained. In the face of this kind of provocation, keeping one's composure would be extremely difficult—and still, the employee and (because of the principle of vicarious liability) the business were *both* responsible for the excessive force used. Do employees always realize that what they do on the job might lead to personal liability? Or do some believe that if it's "part of the job" only the boss will be liable? Bouncers beware!

Assault and battery (or **trespass to person**) involve the intentional physical interference with another person. These torts are a concern to businesses whose employees serve the public. An action that makes a person think they are about to be struck is an **assault.** If someone fakes a punch, points a gun, or picks up a stone to threaten another person, an assault has been committed. A **battery** takes place when someone is in actual physical contact with another person. Since

**Intentional physical interference**

**Fear of contact—assault**

**Actual contact—battery**

---

3. (1998), 165 D.L.R. (4th) 472 (B.C.C.A.).

battery almost invariably involves an assault, the term "assault" is often used to refer to both assault and battery. Assault and battery are actionable, even where there is no injury; "the least touching of another in anger is battery."[4] The purpose of the tort of trespass to the person is to recognize the right of each person to control her body and who touches it. Damages are awarded when this right is violated.

The test to determine whether an assault has taken place is to look to the victim and ask if she was fearful or anticipated unwanted physical contact. If the defendant's conduct would cause a reasonable person to feel threatened with imminent harm, it constitutes an assault. The contact might be anything from a physical blow, to unwanted medical treatment, to a kiss. The motive or good will of the person attacking is not relevant. The words are taken into consideration as well as the gestures and actions. The action of a person walking toward another can be an assault when accompanied by threatening words, whereas the words "How nice to see you again" remove the threat.

**Intent to harm not required**

## Defences

There are several defences that can be raised to an assault or battery claim. Normally, doctors escape liability for their actions when operating on or otherwise treating patients through the principle of **consent.** Essentially, a person who expressly or impliedly consents to conduct that would otherwise constitute an assault or battery loses the right to sue. This is the reason why injured boxers cannot sue their opponents.

**Consent is a defence**

It is important to remember, however, that the level of interference cannot exceed the consent. Excessive violence in a hockey game or other sporting activity will constitute a battery despite the consent. Excessive violence may also constitute a crime, as Marty McSorley discovered when he was charged and subsequently convicted of assault with a weapon for a vicious slash to the head of Donald Brashear in an NHL game.[5] Also, the consent must be *informed consent;* people must know what they are consenting to. People may refuse or give only limited consent to medical treatment. Followers of a certain religion, for example, refuse blood transfusions.[6] If this is made clear to a doctor and he administers the refused treatment anyway, even where the patient would die without it, he can be sued for the battery he has committed.[7]

The issue of **self-defence** can also be raised to counteract an assault and battery accusation. The law entitles people who are being attacked to use necessary force to defend themselves. The test is reasonable force. An attack is not a licence to respond with unrestrained violence. Of course, the experience of the person being attacked will be taken into account in determining what is reasonable. Thus, a boxer is held to a higher standard than an ordinary person not accus-

**Reasonable force to defend permitted**

---

4. *Cole v. Turner* (1704), 6 Mod. 149, 87 E.R. 907.

5. *R. v. McSorley,* [2000] B.C.J. No. 1994 (B.C. Prov. Ct.).

6. See *Malette v. Shulman* (1990), 67 D.L.R. (4th) 321 (Ont. C.A.), where the physician administered a blood transfusion, which likely saved the patient's life, and yet the plaintiff successfully sued for battery. The plaintiff had a card in her purse stating that, as a Jehovah's Witness, she refused consent to receive any blood products.

7. This right may not extend to others within their care. When for religious reasons parents refuse treatment needed to save the lives of their children, the courts are often willing to interfere by taking custody of the children away from the parents and ordering treatment.

tomed to such violence. When ejecting an unruly patron, the same principle applies. If a patron refuses to leave when asked, he becomes a trespasser, and reasonable force can be used to eject him. But as seen in the *Bruce* case in Case Summary 4.2, use of excessive force may result in the occupier of the premises being held liable.

**Reasonable force permitted to eject trespasser**

The importance of careful training of employees with respect to how to interact with customers and the public cannot be overemphasized. When faced with shoplifting, fraud, and other improper conduct employees must know what they can and cannot do in order to protect the business from the possibility of devastating lawsuits. The courts may be somewhat sympathetic to the plight of businesses when faced with the considerable losses caused by shoplifting, fraud, and other wrongs committed by customers, but they have to protect the rights of people who have done nothing wrong from assault, intimidation, or improper restraint. The damages awarded are based not only on what the employee has done, but also the plaintiff's status in the community and any injury they might have suffered. This can all be out of proportion to any loss suffered by the business by the alleged wrongdoing. For example, in the *Osz* case, a 16-year-old struck a city bus with a snowball, splattering the defendant driver with snow. The driver stopped the bus, confronted the teen, hit him twice in the face breaking his nose and then kicked the plaintiff. In addition to suffering a painful and debilitating injury, the plaintiff suffered the embarrassment and indignity of being throttled in the presence of his friends. He was awarded general, special, and punitive damages exceeding $10 000, for which sum the City of Calgary, as the driver's employer, was vicariously liable. Quite a price to pay for losing one's cool![8]

## Trespass to Land

Trespass to land involves going onto another person's property without having either the lawful right or the owner's permission to do so. Such a trespass is an actionable wrong, even when no damage or injury takes place and even if the intruder does not know she is trespassing. Ignorance of the location of the property line is no excuse. Only if the intruder had no control of where she was would there be a defence. Thus, if she was struck by a car and thrown on the property, there would be no trespass. But if she was running away and went on the property to escape a threat, it is still a trespass and she would be responsible for any damage caused. Trespass can also take place indirectly. When a person throws some item on another's property, a trespass has taken place.

**On land without authority**

**Trespass can be indirect**

People acting in an official capacity, such as postal workers, meter readers, municipal inspectors, and the police, have the right to come on private property and are not trespassing. In shopping malls and other premises where the public is welcome there is an implied right to be there, even where the visitor has not come to shop. Permission is also implied when visitors have been allowed on the property over time without steps being taken to remove them. If such visitors become unruly or dangerous to other patrons, they can be asked to leave. If they refuse, they become trespassers, and reasonable force can be used to eject them.

8. *Osz v. Calgary (City of ) and Mahar* (1987), 56 Alta. L.R. (2d) 435 (Q.B.).

### Case Summary 4.3

**Trespassers Present without Lawful Right:** *Costello v. Calgary (City)*[9]

The Costellos owned a property on which a 10-unit motel was situated. They applied for a development permit seeking to build a 40-unit motel on that site, but the application approval was delayed because the city wanted to expropriate the land for a roadway interchange. The subject lands were expropriated in 1972 and leased to a third party. The Costellos opposed the expropriation, and in 1983 the Supreme Court of Canada ruled the expropriation illegal and invalid. The Costellos then commenced an action for trespass against the city.

The trial Judge found the city liable and awarded damages. (The subsequent appeal was dismissed, and leave to appeal to the SCC was refused.) The Court held that a trespass occurs if an authority takes possession of land pursuant to an expropriation that is subsequently determined to be invalid. The fact that the city did not intend to commit the tort was not a defence. Neither mistaken belief of fact or lawful authority nor the absence of fault operates as a defence in the trespass context.

The trial Judge correctly assessed damages on the basis that the Costellos would have developed a 40-unit motel on the property. Damages were calculated to place the Costellos in the position they would have enjoyed had the city not committed the wrong. Damages of $572 265 were awarded to reflect the profits the Costellos would have earned from the proposed 40-unit motel. Additionally, $518 295 in interest plus solicitor–client costs were awarded. The case emphasizes the care that parties must exercise before taking possession of or entering another's property.

*Occupiers' Liability Act*

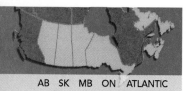

AB   SK   MB   ON   ATLANTIC

**Injunction available to remedy continuing trespass**

Trespassers who cause damage while on private property bear responsibility for any injury or loss caused. This is the case whether injury was foreseeable or not. A trespasser who is injured while on the property generally has no claim against the occupier. Provincial occupiers' liability legislation requires only that the occupier of property not wilfully or recklessly cause harm to a trespasser or someone on the property for a criminal purpose. A greater duty is owed, however, to minors who trespass. If it is foreseeable that minors who trespass may be harmed, a duty may arise to take reasonable steps to ensure reasonable safety. Check the appropriate provincial statutes to determine the exact nature of the duties owed.

Trespass can also involve a permanent incursion onto the property of another. This is referred to as a **continuing trespass** and can take the form of a building or other structure that encroaches on the property of another. Where multi-storeyed buildings are involved, the costs of correcting the problem can be enormous.

## False Imprisonment

**Restraint without lawful excuse—false imprisonment**

**False imprisonment,** including false arrest, occurs when people are intentionally restrained against their will and the person doing the restraining has no lawful authority to do so. This may be in the form of complete imprisonment, where the person is held in a cell or room, or may take the form of an arrest. In either case,

---

9. (1995), 163 A.R. 241 (Q.B.), varied (1997), 209 A.R. 1 (C.A.), leave to appeal refused, [1997] S.C.C.A. No. 566.

the person's liberty to go where he pleases must be totally restrained. Even a person who submits to authority or threat can be considered imprisoned, since in his mind he has been restrained. The second requirement is that the restraint be unlawful. When a security guard arrests someone found shoplifting, there has been no false imprisonment. Generally, a private person has the power to make an arrest, but only when she finds someone in the process of committing a crime, such as shoplifting.

**Submission to authority can constitute imprisonment**

A citizen's powers of arrest are set out in section 494 of the *Criminal Code*:[10]

**494. (1)** Any one may arrest without warrant
- (*a*) a person whom he finds committing an indictable offence; or
- (*b*) a person who, on reasonable grounds, he believes
  - **(i)** has committed a criminal offence, and
  - **(ii)** is escaping from and freshly pursued by persons who have lawful authority to arrest that person.

**(2)** Any one who is
- (*a*) the owner or a person in lawful possession of property, or
- (*b*) a person authorized by the owner or by a person in lawful possession of property, may arrest without warrant a person whom he finds committing a criminal offence on or in relation to that property.

**(3)** Any one other than a peace officer who arrests a person without warrant shall forthwith deliver the person to a peace officer.

## Case Summary 4.4

### Arrest and Be Sued: *Bahner v. Marwest Hotel Co.*[11]

This case is typical of the kind of problems faced by restaurants, hotels, bars, and retail stores. The defendant, Mr. Bahner, was unfamiliar with the provincial liquor laws. He ordered and obtained a bottle of wine shortly before 11:30 p.m. When Mr. Bahner discovered just before midnight that he had to consume the wine in only the few minutes remaining, he left it and refused to pay for it. He paid for the meal but not the wine. When he attempted to leave, he was detained by the manager and a security guard until the police arrived. Mr. Bahner was arrested and spent the night in jail. The court held that he had been falsely imprisoned twice, once at the restaurant and once by the police. Although there was a way to escape at the restaurant, he had submitted to the authority of the security guard. The Judge said, "The plaintiff, commanded by the security officer to stay and prevented by the officer from leaving by the ordinary exit, behaved with admirable restraint in making no forcible attempt to pass the security officer. After what the officer had said and done, he could reasonably expect to be restrained by force if he tried to leave by any exit, and he was not required to make an attempt to run away."[12] The Court also found that the imprisonment was without authority. There was no right to arrest here because no criminal act had taken place. There was a dispute as to whether the wine should be paid for, and if the proprietor wanted to he could have sued for breach of contract. Only where it is clear that a patron is trying to sneak out without paying can he be restrained.

10. R.S.C. 1985 c. C-46, s. 494.

11. (1969), 6 D.L.R. (3d) 322 (B.C.S.C.); aff'd (1970), 12 D.L.R. (3d) 646 (B.C.C.A.).

12. *Ibid.* at 325–26.

Because these facts were known to the police when they arrested Mr. Bahner, their action constituted a second false arrest, which was also actionable. Although police have broader powers of arrest, because they knew the facts they could not show that they had "reasonable and probable grounds" to suppose a crime had been committed.

Normally, in a tort action the courts will order only compensatory damages to be paid. Here, the Court went further and awarded the victim punitive damages, something done infrequently but appropriate where the courts seek to discourage the perpetrator from doing the same thing again. The legal costs and judgment overwhelmed the few dollars that would have been lost had the employees not detained the customer. So, how will you train your employees to act?

**Punitive damages may be available for false imprisonment**

A charge of false imprisonment is a significant risk for any business involved in serving the public. This risk is great when, either because of store policy or inexperienced staff, customers are detained whenever they are suspected of wrongdoing. It may be well for managers to discourage their employees from apprehending shoplifters, since the potential loss from goods stolen is far outweighed by the danger of losing a false-imprisonment action. If the customer has not in fact stolen any goods, there is no justification for holding him. Case Summary 4.5 demonstrates the difficulties a retail store or other business may encounter should its security guards be overzealous.

### Case Summary 4.5

**Keep Your Cool!** *Chopra v. Eaton (T.) Co.*[13]

The plaintiff, Mr. Chopra, attended at Eaton's seeking a refund. An argument ensued. Mr. Frauenfeld (from security) told Chopra that he would have to leave; Frauenfeld took Chopra's elbow and started to escort him out of the store. Chopra protested, but did not create a disturbance. Near the doors, Chopra pushed Frauenfeld away, presumably wishing to go through the doors unassisted. Frauenfeld reacted quickly and violently, putting Chopra into a headlock. Chopra's glasses were knocked off and his lip was cut; he was handcuffed, detained in the security office, and subjected to racial slurs. Chopra asked to leave, asked to call his wife, and asked Frauenfeld to call the police; all of these requests were refused. After Chopra had been detained for four hours or more, the police arrived and charged Chopra with assaulting Frauenfeld and causing a disturbance. Chopra was subsequently acquitted of both charges.

Chopra's complaint to the Alberta Human Rights Commission and his civil action against Eaton's were both successful. The Court awarded damages totalling $38 000 as against Frauenfeld and vicariously against Eaton's.

The Court found that once Chopra was told he would have to leave the store, he did not resist. Thus, Chopra never became a trespasser against whom reasonable force could be justified. But Chopra did push Frauenfeld, which constituted an assault, albeit a nominal one, contrary to section 265 of the *Criminal Code*. This offence gave lawful authority to the initial arrest and detention. (The *Criminal Code* authorizes private citizens to arrest individuals found committing a criminal offence.) But the failure to deliver the party arrested to the police forthwith transformed an initially lawful imprisonment into an unlawful one. In addition, the

---

13. (1999), 240 A.R. 201 (Q.B.).

amount of force used by Frauenfeld in restraining Chopra was excessive, constituting an unjustified battery against Chopra. Since the arrest was made while Frauenfeld was acting within the scope of his employment, Eaton's was held vicariously liable for the damages awarded.

What instructions should businesses give to their security personnel in light of the tort of false imprisonment?

# Private Nuisance

The tort of **private nuisance** is committed when an individual or business uses property in such a way that it interferes with a neighbour's use or enjoyment of their property. Such interference is usually ongoing and continuous. When a commercial building, such as a mill, is built near a residential neighbourhood, and the resulting odour and noise interfere with the neighbours' enjoyment of their yards, it is appropriate for them to sue for nuisance. Such an action is possible only where the property is being used in an unusual or unreasonable way, and the problem caused is a direct consequence of this unusual activity. A person living in an industrial section of a city cannot complain when a factory begins operating in the neighbourhood and emits noise, smoke, and dust. Nor could the residents of a rural area complain about the normal odours associated with farming.

**Private nuisance—use of property interferes with neighbour**

Normally, the properties would need to be in close proximity for private nuisance to apply and for a nuisance action to be brought. However, in an Alberta case a telephone was used to harass a resident on the other side of the city, interfering with the enjoyment of their property. The court found this to be a private nuisance, even though the two parties were kilometres apart.[14] It is quite likely that we will see similar nuisance cases in the future arising from abuses of fax transmissions and other forms of electronic communications.

**Private nuisance at a distance**

### Case Summary 4.6

#### Nuisance May Take Many Forms: *Banfai v. Formula Fun Centre Inc.;*[15] *Schneider v. Royal Wayne Motel Ltd.*[16]

Typically, nuisance is equated with noxious substances invading property. In the *Banfai* case, the plaintiff operated a motel adjacent to some lands that Ontario Hydro had leased to the defendants, who operated an amusement business that consisted of a racecourse for scaled-down versions of Grand Prix racing cars. The noise from the motors and screeching tires as the cars raced around the track was constant during the summer season from 11:00 a.m. until 11:00 p.m. The Court found that this constituted a nuisance and awarded damages to the plaintiff and granted an injunction. The Court deemed that this was an unusual use of the property. Both the noise and the air pollution generated from the activity were out of keeping with what was normally expected in the area.

But even golf balls can constitute a nuisance. In the *Schneider* case, the plaintiffs complained that during the golf season their properties were bombarded by so many golf balls that they had to resort to wearing hard hats when out in their yards. Stray golf balls broke their windows and dented their cars, and on some

---

14. *Motherwell v. Motherwell* (1976), 73 D.L.R. (3d) 62 (Alta C.A.).

15. (1984), 19 D.L.R. (4th) 683 (Ont. H.C.).

16. (1995), 164 A.R. 68 (Prov. Ct.).

occasions golfers would even want to hit their balls from where they lay on the plaintiffs' properties. The interference with the use and enjoyment of the plaintiffs' yards was both serious and substantial. Relevant to the assessment of damages was the fact that the golf course had taken steps to alleviate the nuisance by reconfiguring the golf course. Damages were still awarded because although the nuisance was lessened, it nonetheless continued.

For a private nuisance to be actionable, the consequences must be reasonably foreseeable to the defendant. Reasonable foreseeability is discussed in the section on Negligence. Because nuisance often involves offending substances, it is one of the few common law tools that can be used to enforce environmental protection. For example, in the *Pyke* case,[17] the plaintiff's complaint stemmed from odours emanating from the composting phase of the defendant's mushroom farm. The Court considered the proximity of the neighbours and the fact that the plaintiffs were there first. The degree and intensity of the disturbance exceeded that of a "normal farm practice" and thus damages exceeding $260 000 were awarded.

## Defamation

### Case Summary 4.7

**CBC Painfully Discovers Innuendo Is Actionable:** *Myers v. Canadian Broadcasting Corp.;*[18] *Leenen v. Canadian Broadcasting Corp.*[19]

In an episode of *Fifth Estate*, the CBC interviewed Dr. Myers on his views about a certain heart medication; Myers had conducted a study on behalf of Bayer concerning the drug. The broadcast clips from the interview distorted Myers' statements and conveyed the impression that Myers promoted the interests of pharmaceutical companies over the interests of patients. The innuendo suggested that Myers was dishonest, recommending medication he knew to be harmful.

The CBC tried to establish the defences of fair comment and qualified privilege, without success. The Court determined that the distortion of Myers' words invited viewers to make false inferences. The defence of qualified privilege failed because there was no duty on CBC to communicate the information. The defence of fair comment failed when the trial Judge found malice based on the CBC's decision not to include reference to other doctors who concurred with Myers. $200 000 in general damages plus $150 000 in aggravated damages were awarded by the trial and appeal courts, respectively.

Even greater damages ($950 000) were awarded against the CBC in the *Leenen* case. Again through innuendo, the CBC called into question the plaintiff doctor's honesty, integrity, and credibility as a research scientist. Malice defeated the defences of qualified privilege and fair comment as the court found the CBC had invented or misstated the facts.

Professionals guard their reputations carefully, so what precautions should be exercised where comments critical of their competence, performance, or integrity are expressed?

17. *Pyke v. TRI GRO Enterprises Ltd.* (2001), 55 O.R. (3d) 257 (Ont. C.A.), leave to appeal to S.C.C. refused, [2001] S.C.C.A. No. 493.

18. (2001), 54 O.R. (3d) 626 (C.A.), leave to appeal to S.C.C. refused, [2001] S.C.C.A. No. 433.

19. (2001), 54 O.R. (3d) 612 (C.A.), leave to appeal to S.C.C. refused, [2001] S.C.C.A. No. 432.

**Defamation** is a published false statement that is to a person's detriment. It is a primary concern for businesses involved in media communications, but all commercial enterprises face some risk over defamation, even if it is only from a carelessly worded letter of reference. For the statement to be an actionable defamation, it must be derogatory, false, published, and refer to the plaintiff. If the false statement causes people to avoid or shun someone, it is derogatory. In the *Youssoupoff* case, Lord Justice Scrutton said that a statement was defamatory if it was "a false statement about a man to his discredit."[20] A complimentary statement about a person, even if it is false, is not defamation. Thus, if a manager were to say of an employee that he was the best worker in the plant, it would not be defamation even if false. Once the plaintiff establishes that the derogatory statement was made, he need not prove it was false. This is assumed, and it is up to the defendant to prove the truth if he can. If the statement can be shown to be true, it is an absolute defence to a defamation action.[21]

For a statement to be actionable, it must be clear that it refers to the person suing. Thus, a general negative reference to a group, such as the faculty or student body of a university, will not qualify. It is not possible to defame a dead person; however, it is possible to defame a corporation, which is a person in the eyes of the law, and it is possible to defame a product. (See the discussion of product defamation or trade slander under Injurious Falsehood, p. 176.)

Further, the false statement must be published. In this sense, "to publish" means that the statement had to be communicated to a third party. Publication could have occurred in a newspaper, in the broadcast media, on the internet, or simply by word of mouth. It is sufficient publication if just one other person hears or reads the defamatory statement.

Another important factor to consider is that statements often contain **innuendo,** which is an implied or hidden meaning. A statement may appear perfectly innocent on the surface, but when combined with other information it may take on a different meaning. It is no excuse to say that the person making the statement thought it was true or did not know of the special facts that created the innuendo. Such a mistake is no defence, and the offending party can be held liable for the defamatory remark. (The CBC cases discussed in Case Summary 4.7 illustrate that suggested inferences can be actionable.)

**Detrimental false statement**

**Statement must be published**

**Innuendo**

**Mistake no excuse**

## Libel and Slander

Defamation can be either **libel,** which is *written* defamation, or **slander,** which is *spoken* defamation. The significance of finding a defamatory remark to be libellous rather than slanderous is that libel is easier to prove because there is no requirement to show that special damages have been sustained. Libel is seen to be more deliberate, more premeditated, and also more permanent than slander, thus causing more harm. However, modern means of mass communication give slander a potentially huge audience, so the rationale for distinguishing between libel and slander is breaking down. In fact, this distinction has been eliminated by legislation in some provinces.

While defamation is primarily governed by common law, most provinces have passed statutes modifying those common law provisions in light of the needs of a

BC

**Libel written/slander spoken**

---

20. *Youssoupoff v. Metro-Goldwyn-Mayer Pictures Ltd.* (1934), 50 T.L.R. 581 at 584 (C.A.).

21. *Elliott v. Freisen et al.* (1982), 136 D.L.R. (3d) 281 (Ont. H.C.); aff'd (1984), 6 D.L.R. (4th) 388 (Ont. C.A.); leave to appeal refused (1984), 6 D.L.R. (4th) 388 n (S.C.C.).

modern society. Should defamation by the media occur, for example, legislation may reduce the damages plaintiffs can claim where material was published in good faith. If the publisher shows that the damage was done by mistake or misapprehension of the facts, and a full apology or retraction has been made, damages may be restricted to special damages.[22]

**Apology reduces damages**

These statutes will need even more modification to take into account the new problems associated with defamation on the internet. It is often difficult to trace the original source of defamation in an internet message because it can be so easily copied and transferred by intermediate parties. Nevertheless, the injury caused by such transmission of defamatory information can be extensive. Another problem is that in a traditional communication environment there is usually a broadcaster or publisher that can be held responsible for the damaging words, but in online communication there is often no intermediary who checks and authorizes material, nor is there any clear way of determining just how far a message has been spread.

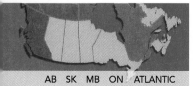

AB   SK   MB   ON   ATLANTIC

## Case Summary 4.8

### The Courts Address Internet Defamation: *Reichmann v. Berlin*[23]

The internet provides direct and inexpensive access to a massive audience and with it the opportunity to defame. Who should be held liable for defamatory statements broadcast via the internet, the originator alone or the service provider as well? In the *Reichmann* case, defamatory statements published on the internet repeatedly asserted that Reichmann interfered with an estate by knowingly cheating an innocent man out of a multi-million-dollar inheritance. The statements were published over a 3½-year period, using seven different websites. General damages of $200 000 were awarded against the originators and service providers jointly, but a further $50 000 in aggravated damages and $50 000 in punitive damages were awarded as against each of the originators—whose motives were malicious and who had tried to extort funds from the plaintiffs.

The courts are also prepared to order a service provider to disclose the identity of an originator once a *prima facie* case against the unknown originator is disclosed, as was the case in *Irwin Toy Ltd. v. Doe*.[24]

Should the internet be subject to defamation laws? Since the information is disseminated on a worldwide basis, which country's laws should apply? What do you think?

## Defences

Once it has been established that a defamatory statement has been made, several defences are available to the defendant. **Truth,** also called the **defence of justification,** is an absolute defence. But even when a statement is technically true, it can still be derogatory if it contains an innuendo or is capable of being interpreted as referring to another person about whom the statement is false.

**Truth is an absolute defence**

The second defence is called **absolute privilege.** Anything discussed as part of parliamentary debate on the floor of the legislature, Parliament, or in govern-

**Absolute privilege**

22. See, for example, Alberta's *Defamation Act*, R.S.A. 2000, c. D-7, s. 16, or New Brunswick's *Defamation Act*, S.N.B. c. D-5, s. 17.

23. [2002] O.J. No. 2732 (Sup. Ct. J.).

24. [2002] O.J. No. 331 (Sup. Ct. J.).

ment committees and statements made in a trial cannot give rise to a defamation action, no matter how malicious, scandalous, or derogatory they are. The rationale for this defence is that there are certain forums where, for the good of society, people should be able to exercise freedom of expression without fear of being sued. For example, even statements made to an investigator in the context of a *Human Rights Act* investigation are privileged.[25]

**Qualified privilege, requires duty**

The most significant defence for businesspeople is called **qualified privilege.** When a statement is made pursuant to a duty or special interest, there is no action for defamation so long as the statement was made honestly, without malice, and circulated only to those having a right to know. A manager reporting to a superior about the performance of a worker or members of a professional organization discussing the performance of an officer of that organization would be instances protected by qualified privilege. When a manager sends a defamatory email specifically to one interested party or a limited group of interested addressees there can still be qualified privilege if the other requirements are met. But if the same message were sent to a website, the publication would likely be too broad and the defence of qualified privilege would be lost. Thus, in *Egerton v. Finucan,* a community college professor's claim for wrongful dismissal was complicated by the fact that his supervisor sent a highly critical performance evaluation to all the professors in the institution via email. The court found that the plaintiff had grounds for a defamation suit against his superior.[26]

**Fair comment**

A further defence available in the field of defamation is the defence of **fair comment.** When people put their work before the public, as with movies, plays, artwork, books, and the like, they invite public criticism and run the risk that the opinions expressed may not be complimentary. Even when these opinions amount to a vicious attack and may be unreasonable, they cannot sue for defamation. The defence raised here is fair comment. Public figures are also open to such criticism. To successfully use this defence, the critic or editorial writer must be able to show that what was said was a matter of opinion, drawn from true facts that were before the public, and was not motivated by malice or some ulterior motive. A food critic expressing a negative opinion of a restaurant[27] and a theatre critic attacking a play or movie are examples of fair comment. The same defence should apply where a play, photograph, or musical performance is put on the internet and made available to a wide audience.

**Significant damages available**

In those situations where legislation does not specifically restrict damages payable, the damages for defamation can be substantial. The courts not only will compensate the victim for actual losses as well as for a damaged reputation, but will go further, awarding damages to rehabilitate the victim's reputation. For this reason, the Supreme Court of Canada upheld a decision to award a Crown prosecutor defamed by a church $1.6 million in damages, far in excess of what would be awarded for general damages in a normal tort action.[28] Justice Cory stated that, unlike for non-pecuniary losses in personal injury cases, in defamation there is no cap on general damages.

25. *Ayangma v. NAV Canada* (2001), 197 Nfld. & P.E.I.R. 83 (P.E.I.S.C. (A.D.)), leave to appeal to S.C.C. refused, [2001] S.C.C.A. No. 76.

26. *Egerton v. Finucan,* [1995] O.J. No. 1653 (Gen. Div.).

27. See Case 4 at the end of this chapter. *Sara's Pyrohy Hut v. Brooker* is an example where fair comment was successfully raised.

28. *Hill v. Church of Scientology of Toronto,* [1995] 2 S.C.R. 1130.

## Successfully Establishing a Tort Claim

When a plaintiff commences a tort action, he bears the burden of establishing each of the required elements or *ingredients* of that tort. Failure to prove an ingredient should result in the action being dismissed. See Table 4.1 for a simplified list of ingredients for the intentional torts examined thus far.

## Privacy

The laws relating to intentional torts generally protect people who are harmed by another's deliberate actions, and the courts have been willing to expand common law to include new technologies, even when the method of committing the tort was not in existence when the common law principle was established.[29] We can expect that the general body of tort law will also be expanded to include new forms of wrongs committed over the internet.

**Privacy protection found only in statutes**

Breach of privacy is imperfectly protected by the common law. In the past, the courts were reluctant to recognize an express common law privacy right. Often, other torts have been used to grant a remedy in privacy cases. However, there has been an increasing tendency among lower-court judges to award damages for "invasion of privacy." Some provinces have elected to enact privacy legislation that creates a statutory tort or cause of action.[30] These statutes enable claimants to sue if, for example, their likeness or voice is used without their consent. Remedies ranging from damages to injunctions and accounting for profits may be awarded. Often, consent of the claimant operates as a defence.

What about concerns regarding the privacy of one's health information? A host of provincial statutes now restrict access to private information, including health records, but the protection will vary from province to province.

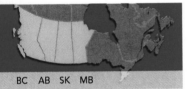

BC    AB    SK    MB

### Table 4.1 How to Bake a Tort: Ingredients List

| | |
|---|---|
| Assault | 1) Deliberate threat creating fear of imminent harm<br>2) No consent |
| Battery | 1) Deliberate physical interference (contact) with one's body<br>2) No consent |
| Trespass to land | 1) Deliberate interference with property<br>2) No consent/permission/lawful right to be there |
| False imprisonment | 1) Deliberate restraint<br>2) No lawful authority |
| Private nuisance | 1) Unusual use of property<br>2) Interference caused to neighbour's enjoyment/use of property<br>3) Foreseeable consequences |
| Defamation | 1) False statements made<br>2) Derogatory to the plaintiff's reputation<br>3) Publication or communication to a third party |

---

29. See *Motherwell, supra* note 14.

30. See *Privacy Act*, R.S.B.C. 1996, c. 373; *The Privacy Act*, R.S.S. 1978, c. P-24; *The Privacy Act*, C.C.S.M. c. P125.

In the last decade, the number of consumer complaints has increased exponentially as a result of e-commerce. Governments have taken steps to help protect consumers but still face the seemingly insurmountable challenge of enforcing new regulations in light of the borderless nature of the internet. The challenge is to encourage retailers to regulate themselves, because if one country makes the rules too harsh businesses will simply set up elsewhere to avoid those rules. This is an area where international treaties may make an important contribution.

One way that violation of privacy is manifested occurs when private information that is exchanged in a commercial transaction over the internet is then used again without consent or sold to another company for another purpose. The new *Personal Information Protection and Electronic Documents Act*[31] regulates the collection and use of personal information, requiring organizations to account for their activities, identify the purposes for which the information is being collected, inform and get the consent of the individuals involved, and limit the use, disclosure, and retention of the information. They would have to ensure the accuracy of the information, protect it with security safeguards, and be open about their policies and practices relating to the management of the information. The Act requires that organizations make available to individuals, upon request, the nature of the information and how it is being used. It also outlines how an individual would proceed to have a complaint reviewed, and empowers a privacy commissioner appointed for the purpose to impose fines for violations.

The *Personal Information Protection and Electronic Documents Act* has attached as its central core—and has given statutory standing to—the Code of the Canadian Standards Association (CSA). The CSA code, entitled the "Model Code for the Protection of Personal Information," was approved as a national standard by the Standards Council of Canada and was published in 1996. It sets out 10 privacy protection principles. The Act applies to federal agencies initially, then after three years to provinces as well, unless the provinces have similar legislation already in place. A federal privacy commissioner will enforce the provisions of the Act. The European Community enacted legislation to protect privacy in this area some time ago, and the passage of this Act provides similar protection here, removing a major barrier that threatened to interfere with international business.

Another problem relating to privacy is the unauthorized interception of communications between individuals. While most sites where important information is transferred have encryption devices, determined hackers can break those codes. If the codes become too sophisticated, then governments that make use of this information in their surveillance activities cannot decode the information and so are reluctant to allow advanced encryption. This creates a serious dilemma.

Another topic of controversy related to the internet is the widespread use of *cookies,* which are embedded devices that track a user's internet activities and allow others to read private information about their internet browsing. The information may simply be used by the user's internet service provider to improve its service, but it may also be sold to retailers for marketing purposes or used to incriminate a person who has been downloading and inappropriately using sites. In addition, a relatively new issue is that the technology now exists for internet advertisers to insert links on competitors' websites that redirect web traffic to their own sites.

**Collection and use of private information**

**Internet poses new problems**

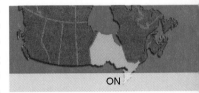

**Model Code**

**Limits on advanced encryption**

---

31. S.C. 2000, c. 5.

**Notice and consent**

The new Act will require that notice and consent, as well as disclosure as to how the information will be used, be given before private information can be collected. Individuals will also gain the right to check for accuracy of the information collected and to determine that the information is secure and not being used for other purposes. Again, the problem is enforcement. Studies have shown that voluntary privacy protection has been poor, with many businesses secretly collecting and using personal information. Secret surveillance of computer users is a major problem, especially in the work environment, where it seems that employers have the right to read employees' e-mails and monitor their internet use on their office computers.

# Negligence

To establish the tort of negligence, the plaintiff must prove each of the four required elements or *ingredients* of this tort. See Table 4.2, which succinctly sets out those ingredients and lists the *tests* used by the courts to determine whether these ingredients have in fact been proven.

### Case Summary 4.9

#### Contestants Having a "Blast": *Crocker v. Sundance Northwest Resorts Ltd.*[32]

Mr. Crocker and his friend went to Sundance Resorts, and one evening, at the bar after a day of skiing, they saw a video of an inner tube race that was part of an event called the Sundance Spring Carnival. The race was run on the regular ski slopes in a section where the moguls caused the tubes and the people on them to bounce around like "rag dolls." A videotape of the event showed the contestants "falling off these tubes, being bounced off, releasing their grip, chasing after the tubes," and generally having what was described by another contestant as a "blast." The event was put on by the defendants, the operators of the ski slope.

The plaintiff, Mr. Crocker, signed up for the race. In the process, he signed, without reading, a release absolving the ski slope operators of all responsibility

### Table 4.2 How to Bake a Tort: Negligence

| Ingredients | Tests used |
| --- | --- |
| A  A duty of care is owed to the plaintiff | 1. Foreseeable plaintiff test (reasonable foreseeability test)<br>2. Policy considerations—may negate existence of a duty |
| B  Breach of that duty; breach of the standard of care | Reasonable person test |
| C  Causation | 1. Physical: "but for" test<br>2. Legal: remoteness test |
| D  Damage | A type recognized by courts as compensable |

---

32. [1998] 1 S.C.R. 1186.

for any injuries he might suffer as a result of the race. Mr. Crocker and his friend, in a festive mood, went down the slope once, with only minor injury, and won their heat. By the second heat it was clear that Mr. Crocker had been drinking, and the manager of the facility suggested that he not go down the hill. In fact, Mr. Crocker not only had a couple of drinks at the bar, but also had been given two large swallows of brandy by the driver of a beer van. In the next race, Mr. Crocker fell off the tube and broke his neck, which rendered him a quadriplegic.

The Supreme Court had to decide whether Sundance should be responsible for Mr. Crocker's foolish conduct and, if so, to what extent. It had to determine just what nature of duty was owed by Sundance to Mr. Crocker and the other contestants. The Court determined that a clearly dangerous competition was established for commercial gain. There was a duty of care toward visibly intoxicated participants, who are obviously susceptible to more damage and more potential injury than sober persons. Sundance had an obligation to take all reasonable steps to keep Mr. Crocker from competing in his inebriated state. Although Mr. Crocker was told he should not proceed, Sundance failed to prevent him from competing. Furthermore, when his inner tube slid down the hill, Sundance provided him with another. This clearly breached Sundance's duty of care toward Mr. Crocker, and so negligence on the part of Sundance was established.

The trial Judge's conclusion with respect to contributory negligence was not challenged and thus not interfered with by the Supreme Court. The trial court had determined that Mr. Crocker had contributed to his loss through his own negligence. Under the statute in place in Ontario, the Court apportioned the blame assessing Mr. Crocker 25 percent responsible; damages were reduced accordingly.

The case illustrates the requirements of a duty of care and application of the reasonable person test in determining fulfillment of that duty. It also examines the defences of contributory negligence and voluntary assumption of risk. In this case, it was argued that Mr. Crocker put himself voluntarily into a position of danger and, in the process, assumed the risk. This would completely bar the negligence action on his part. The Court pointed out that the defence of voluntary assumption of risk has been restricted in recent times to such an extent that it had to be clear that Mr. Crocker not only assumed the physical risk, but also absolved Sundance of any legal responsibility for anything that happened. In fact, Mr. Crocker had signed a waiver to that effect, but the Court said it was meaningless because Sundance failed to draw its provisions to Mr. Crocker's attention, nor had Mr. Crocker read it. So what is an event organizer to do in order to eliminate its potential liability?

## Negligence: Its A, B, C, and D's

**Negligence** is by far the most important area of tort liability for businesspeople and professionals. It involves inadvertent or unintentional careless conduct causing injury or damage to another person or their property. The main problem for the court is to determine what standard of care was required of the defendant and whether there was a failure to meet that standard. The **reasonable person test** is used by the court in many areas of law to establish standards of socially acceptable behaviour. Faced with the problem of having to decide if certain conduct is socially acceptable, the judge or members of the jury simply ask themselves, "What would a reasonably prudent person, in possession of all the facts of the case, have done in this situation?"

**Negligence—careless conduct causing another injury**

**Reasonable person test establishes standard**

It is important to understand that the standard determined using the reasonable person test is not what would be expected of an average person. A reasonable person is expected to be particularly careful, a level of behaviour considerably better than average. On the other hand, the conduct is not required to be perfect. An analogy can be made to the concept of par in a golf game. A standard score, called *par*, is set for each hole on the course. If par for a particular hole is 3, the average golfer would likely score 4 or 5. On the other hand, 3 is not the best possible score. Rather, par is the score you would expect from a good golfer playing well. Similarly, the reasonable person test represents the standard of care expected from a prudent person who is being careful. To avoid liability for negligence, the standard of care is reasonableness and not perfection.[33]

## A: A Duty to Exercise Care Must Exist

**Reasonable foreseeability test establishes duty**

Negligence involves a failure on someone's part to live up to a duty to be careful to someone else. We do not have a duty to be careful to everyone. The court must determine whether a duty of care was owed by the defendant to the plaintiff. The court uses the **reasonable foreseeability test,** also called the *foreseeable plaintiff test*, to determine the existence of such a duty. If it were reasonably foreseeable that the conduct complained of would cause harm to the plaintiff, a duty to be careful exists. It seems almost self-evident today that we should act carefully toward people who we can see are put at risk by our behaviour,[34] but this was not always the case.

### Case Summary 4.10

#### "Neighbours" Are Owed a Duty of Care: *Donoghue v. Stevenson*[35]

The reasonable foreseeability test was developed in *Donoghue v. Stevenson*, one of the most significant cases of the 20th century. Two women went into a café, where one ordered a bottle of ginger beer for her friend, Mrs. Donoghue. After consuming some of it, Mrs. Donoghue discovered part of a decomposed snail at the bottom of her bottle. She became very ill as a result of drinking the contaminated beverage. In the process of suing, she discovered that she had some serious problems. She could not successfully sue the café that had supplied the ginger beer for breach of contract; she had no contract with the establishment, as her friend had made the purchase. Similarly, she could not successfully sue the café for negligence, since they had done nothing wrong, the ginger beer having been bottled in an opaque container and served to her in the bottle. Her only recourse was to sue the manufacturer for negligence in producing the product, but the bottler claimed they owed her no duty to be careful. The court had to determine whether a duty to be careful was owed by the manufacturer to the consumer of its product. In the process of finding that such a duty was owed, the House of Lords developed the reasonable foreseeability test. Lord Atkin, one of the judges in the

---

33. See *St. Anne (Litigation Guardian of) v. Hamilton (City)* (2001), 20 M.P.L.R. (3d) 290 (Ont. Sup. Ct. J.), where the Court held that daily screening of the infield was sufficient—further steps to remove goose excrement from the baseball diamond were not required as the standard of reasonable care had been satisfied.

34. But does a mother owe a duty of care to her unborn child? See *Preston v. Chow* (2002), 163 Man. R. (2d) 134 (C.A.), where the court determined that no such duty of care to a fetus existed. Thus, the mother could not be sued by the child for injuries sustained during pregnancy.

35. [1932] A.C. 562 (H.L.).

case, made the following classic statement when discussing how to determine to whom we owe a duty:

> The rule that you are to love your neighbour becomes in law, you must not injure your neighbour; and the lawyer's question 'Who is my neighbour?' receives a restricted reply. You must take reasonable care to avoid acts or omissions which you can reasonably foresee would be likely to injure your neighbour. Who, then, in law, is my neighbour? The answer seems to be—persons who are so closely and directly affected by my act that I ought reasonably to have them in contemplation as being so affected when I am directing my mind to the acts or omissions which are called in question.[36]

We owe a duty, then, to anyone whom we can reasonably anticipate might be harmed by our conduct. The reasonable foreseeability test has been further refined in the English *Anns* case.[37] The *Anns* case created a two-stage test for determining the existence of a duty of care. The first question to ask is whether there was a degree of neighbourhood or proximity between the parties such that if the person being sued had thought of it, he or she would have realized that his or her actions posed a risk of danger to the other. Essentially, this question restates the *Donoghue v. Stevenson* reasonable foreseeability test. The second set of questions probe deeper, providing for exceptions or modifications to the principal test. Was there any reason that the duty should not be imposed? Should the scope of the duty be reduced? Should the class to whom the duty is owed be limited, or should the damages be reduced? These questions allow the court to consider social policy rather than strict legal rules when looking at special situations and relationships. Essentially, the courts try to avoid situations where a defendant may be exposed to "liability in an indeterminate amount for an indeterminate time to an indeterminate class."[38] The English have abandoned the principles set out in the *Anns* case, but the Supreme Court of Canada has made it clear that it is good law in Canada.[39] In Canada, then, the existence of a duty of care is established by the reasonable foreseeability test set out in the *Donoghue v. Stevenson* case; however, for policy reasons, existence of a duty may be negated in accordance with the *Anns* precedent.

**Duty owed to anyone who could foreseeably be harmed**

**Scope of duty can be reduced where appropriate**

### Case Summary 4.11

**Negating the Duty of Care—Taxpayers Should Not Have to Pay: *Cooper v. Hobart*[40]**

This is a recent case where the Supreme Court of Canada applied the *Anns* case to determine whether a duty of care ought to exist. Cooper, one of more than 3000 investors who suffered a loss after advancing funds to a registered mortgage broker, brought a class action, suing the Registrar of Mortgage Brokers, a statutory regulator. The basis for the plaintiff's claim was that the Registrar was negli-

36. *Ibid.* at 580.

37. *Anns v. Merton, London Borough Council*, [1977] 2 All E.R. 492 (H.L.).

38. *Ultramares Corp. v. Touche* (1931), 174 N.E. 441 at 444 (N.Y.C.A.).

39. *Canadian National Railway Co. v. Norsk Pacific Steamship Co.,* [1992] 1 S.C.R. 1021.

40. [2001] 3 S.C.R. 537.

gent in that it was aware of serious violations of the B.C. *Mortgage Brokers Act* committed by the broker since August 1996, and it should have acted earlier than October 1997 to suspend the broker's licence and notify investors of the investigation.

The issue was whether a duty of care was owed by the Registrar to the investors. Under the Act, the Registrar's duties were owed to the public as a whole. Even though it may have been reasonably foreseeable that losses to investors could result if the Registrar were careless in carrying out his duties, there was insufficient proximity between the Registrar and investors to found a duty of care. The Supreme Court further held that even if a *prima facie* duty were established, it would have been negated for overriding policy reasons. Imposing a duty would have effectively created an insurance scheme for investors, at great cost to the taxpaying public. This result, on policy grounds, was unacceptable to the Court. This leads one to ask whether rejection of a duty of care on the basis of "policy grounds" injects uncertainty into the law. Does this undermine the predictability of case law? What do you think?

In most negligence cases, the existence of a duty is obvious and the court need not deal with the problem at length. Still, it is a required element in a negligence action and is important in those cases where the existence of a duty of care is brought into question.

### Misfeasance and Nonfeasance

**Unacceptable action— misfeasance**

**Failure to act—nonfeasance**

**Usually no duty where nonfeasance**

**Once started, a person must give reasonable care**

When discussing duty of care, it is also important to note that the law imposes a duty on people to carry out their activities carefully so as to not cause harm to others. This involves misfeasance or wrongful conduct. But the courts are very reluctant to provide a remedy in a case of nonfeasance (when a person fails to do something), unless it can be established that a particular relationship existed, such as in the case of a swimmer and a lifeguard, or a child and a guardian. People who see a child drowning have no duty in tort law to rescue that child, unless they happen to be lifeguards. Doctors have no legal duty to come to the aid of an accident victim when they pass a car crash. But once someone does start to help, they have an obligation to continue to do so in a reasonable way. When someone attempts to repair a car a friend has no legal duty to help, but if he does he is responsible for any damage caused by his carelessness. These rules discourage people from coming to the aid of others. In an attempt to alleviate such harsh consequences, some jurisdictions have introduced legislation either creating a duty to assist or at least protecting rescuers from liability for injuries arising out of their rescue efforts.

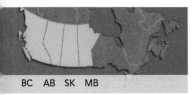

BC   AB   SK   MB

## B: Breach of the Standard of Care

**Reasonable person test determines standard of care**

The existence of a duty to be careful is usually apparent. Normally, the main problem for the court is to determine just how careful the defendant should have been. Did the defendant breach the standard of conduct demanded in this situation? Here, the **reasonable person test** is used to determine what level of care should have been exercised. The court asks what a reasonable person would have done in the same circumstances. If the conduct of the defendant is found to have fallen below this standard, he is negligent and liable for any injury or loss resulting. What is reasonable conduct will vary with the circumstances. For example, the court will take into account the risk of loss.

In *Blyth v. Birmingham Water Works, Co.*,[41] the plaintiff's home was flooded when a water main serving a fireplug froze and burst during a severe winter cold spell. The court rejected the plaintiff's claim that the water works company was negligent for not having placed the pipes deeper. The great costs of doing so would not have been reasonably justified considering the risk, this being the coldest winter in 50 years. The judge in the case said, "Negligence is the omission to do something which a reasonable man, guided upon those considerations which ordinarily regulate the conduct of human affairs, would do, or doing something which a prudent and reasonable man would not do."[42]

Similarly, a person driving a truck or car must be more careful than a person driving a hay wagon because of the increased risk of significant injury. A teacher must exercise greater vigilance in supervising students engaged in risky gymnastics exercises, especially if students are unfamiliar with the equipment.[43] Expense or costs will also be taken into consideration in determining the required standard of care. It may be possible to design and build an automobile that would suffer minimal damage in a high-speed accident, but the costs involved would be prohibitive. No one could afford such a car; therefore, it would be unreasonable to hold a manufacturer to such a standard. But here, care must be taken because saving money will not excuse the production of a defective or dangerous product. A balance must be struck.

**Risk of injury affects standard, as does cost**

What constitutes reasonable behaviour will also vary with the expertise of the person being sued. A doctor is expected to function, at least as far as medical matters are concerned, at a higher level than a non-medical person, and so is held to a higher standard. The test asks: Was the person's conduct up to the standard expected of a reasonable person in the same circumstances? Did he or she conduct himself or herself as a reasonable doctor, reasonable lawyer, reasonable accountant, reasonable plumber, or reasonable driver? This has special implications for professionals and other experts as the standard is not lowered due to inexperience; the novice is required to perform at the same standard as the reasonably prudent practitioner. Note also that the standard does not diminish in the case of an elderly person.[44]

**Standard depends on expertise**

The opposite is true when children are involved. The courts recognize that a 13-year-old cannot be expected to act at the same level of responsibility as an adult. Children are liable for their torts, but the standard required of them is the level of conduct that would be expected of a reasonable child of the same age. Thus, a small child playing with matches may not be liable for a resulting fire, whereas a teenager doing the same thing could very likely be held responsible. At this point, attention usually turns to the parents. Although many people do not realize it, parents are not, as a general rule, vicariously liable for the torts committed by their children. In the absence of a statute to the contrary (and these are

**Liability varies with age**

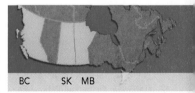

BC    SK   MB

---

41. (1856), 156 E.R. 1047 (Ex. Ct).

42. *Ibid.*, p. 1049.

43. See *MacCabe v. Westlock Roman Catholic Separate School District No. 110*: reversed in part (2001), 293 A.R. 41 (C.A.), where liability was imposed partly on the teacher for failing to adequately supervise a gym class at which the student was rendered quadriplegic.

44. See *McKee (Guardian ad litem of) v. McCoy* (2001), 9 C.C.L.T. (3d) 294 (B.C.S.C.), where the standard of care applicable for a driver was that of an ordinary driver, not that of a person whose capacities are reduced by age.

becoming much more common[45]) parents are liable only if it can be established that they were negligent in their own right by failing to properly train, control, or supervise their children.

### Case Summary 4.12

**Parents Not Liable for Torts Committed by Their Children:**
***D.C.B. v. Zellers Inc.**[46]*

A child was caught shoplifting in the defendant's store. The store, through its lawyers, sent a letter to the child's mother demanding payment to compensate it for the losses and threatening to start a civil action against her if she did not pay. The amount demanded was more than the amount stolen; the store justified this by suggesting the claim was designed to offset the cost of security people the store was forced to employ. The mother paid the money, but after receiving legal advice she brought this small claims action, demanding its return. She was successful. The Judge found that parents ought not to be held liable for torts of their children. Unless some personal liability on the part of the mother could be shown, such as negligence, there was no liability and no right to demand payment from her.

It is not always necessary for the plaintiff to show that the defendant was careless. This can sometimes be implied from the surrounding circumstances. For example, if a piano were to fall into the street from a fourth-floor apartment, injuring a passerby, those facts by themselves seem to say more eloquently than anyone could that the people who were handling the piano were careless in the way they moved it. From the evidence of the falling piano, the court can conclude that the handlers were negligent.

This type of situation used to be dealt with under a special provision of the law of negligence called ***res ipsa loquitur*** ("the thing speaks for itself"), but the Supreme Court of Canada has said that it is better approached as matter of circumstantial evidence.[47] The new approach is somewhat more flexible, but the effect is similar. The Court can find that the circumstantial evidence establishes a ***prima facie*** (**"on the face of it"**) **case** and then turn to the defendants to produce evidence that they were not negligent. Without such evidence from the defendants, the plaintiff will be successful.[48]

## C and D: Causation and Damages

**Damage or injury must be present**

Unlike intentional torts, which may be actionable even without any specific damage, negligence requires that some sort of loss to person or property be suffered. When a customer slips and falls on a wet floor in a store but suffers no injury there is no right to sue, even though the store employees have been careless.

---

45. See, for example, Manitoba's *Parental Responsibility Act,* S.M. 1996, c. 61, C.C.S.M. c. P8.

46. (1996), 111 Man. R. (2d) 198 (Q.B.).

47. *Fontaine v. British Columbia (Official Administrator),* [1998] 1 S.C.R. 424.

48. See *Jordan v. Power,* [2002] A.J. No. 1080 (Q.B.), which held: (i) in discharging the plaintiff's primary burden of proving negligence, circumstantial evidence can be used with or without direct evidence; (ii) to avoid liability, the defendant need only neutralize or negative the inference of negligence, with evidence explaining the occurrence of injury without the defendant's negligence.

However, if the customer breaks a leg, this would be a tangible, physical injury, which would provide grounds for an action.

In the past, there had to be some actual physical damage or injury for the person to successfully sue for negligence. Today, the courts are willing to provide a remedy even in cases of pure economic loss or where the negligence has caused a recognized mental disorder, such as depression. Parents have even successfully sued physicians for the "wrongful birth" of their child. Where a physician fails to advise parents of a potential genetic defect and the pregnancy is allowed to continue, the cost of raising a child born with severe defects has been awarded.[49]

## Case Summary 4.13

### No Pain, No Gain: *Joslyn & Olsen Contracting Ltd. v. Bouey*[50]

The school division hired the architects who originally designed the school to design an addition to the building. The plaintiff, an excavating contractor, successfully bid on the excavating and earth-hauling work, basing its tender on the architectural plans. The architects had made a mistake—their drawings erroneously set the level of the floor line nine inches too high. The error was discovered when the plaintiff noticed it was hauling away far more earth than anticipated.

The architects were sued by both the plaintiff excavating company and by the school division. Liability to the contractor was established, as the architects' negligence caused the contractor extra work valued at $6761.22. But as to the school division, had the architects not erred, the level of the floor would have been correctly stated from the outset and the excavating contractor would have added an extra sum for excavating the greater amount of earth. In other words, but for the architect's error the end result would have been the same. The school division would, in any event, have to pay for removal of this earth to attain a floor level even with that in the existing school building. Accordingly, as no damage or added expense or loss was shown, the Court found the architects were not liable to the school district. Only nominal damages were awarded. This case illustrates the very important principle that in order for an action in negligence to succeed, it must be demonstrated that the conduct complained of actually caused a loss or injury.

## "But For" Test: Physical Causation

For negligence to apply, not only must there be damage, but also that damage must be a direct result of the careless conduct. If the operator of a motor vehicle knowingly drives at night without tail lights, the driver can be said to be careless. However, if the vehicle is involved in a head-on collision, the driver of the other car could not rely on the first driver's failure to have tail lights to support a negligence action. The test usually applied in such situations is called the **"but for" test.** The plaintiff must prove to the court's satisfaction that but for the conduct complained of, no injury would have resulted. In this illustration, the plaintiff cannot say that but for a failure to have properly functioning tail lights, no collision would have occurred.

**Conduct must be cause of injury**

The "but for" test is the general test for causation. Where this test is unworkable, as where multiple causes bring about a single harm, the courts will look for material causation. If the defendant is part of the cause of an injury, the

---

49. *Zhang v. Kan*, [2003] B.C.J. No. 164 (B.C.S.C.).

50. (1976), 2 A.R. 18 (C.A.).

defendant may be liable even though his act alone was insufficient to cause the injury. For example, the Red Cross was found negligent in employing certain donor screening procedures. Even though others, such as the blood donors, may have been part of the cause of the injury, the Red Cross was held liable because the Court found that its carelessness was a material cause of injury to the recipients of tainted blood.[51]

### Remoteness Test—Legal Causation

Once the plaintiff has established that the defendant owed a duty to be careful to the plaintiff, that the defendant's conduct fell below the standard of care required in the situation, and that the conduct complained of caused some injury or loss to the plaintiff, negligence is established. Problems sometimes arise, however, when the connection between the conduct complained of and the injury seems tenuous or where the nature of the injury suffered is unusual or unexpected. For example, if a careless driver were to damage a power pole causing an interruption of power to a business resulting in considerable economic loss, should the driver be held responsible for such an unexpected result? The suggestion is that the connection between the conduct complained of and the actual damage suffered is too remote. In Canada today, our courts will impose liability only when the defendant could have reasonably anticipated the general nature of the injury or damage suffered. Liability is avoided if the injury is too remote, or too unforeseeable. As Justice Dickson in *The Queen v. Coté* explained it: "It is not necessary that one foresee the precise concatenation of events; it is enough to fix liability if one can foresee in a general way the class or character of injury which occurred."[52]

The "remoteness" test is often confused with the test to determine whether a duty of care exists, since both are based on reasonable foreseeability. However, with duty the test is used to determine whether **danger to the plaintiff** should have been anticipated, whereas with remoteness it is the **type of injury** itself that must have been foreseen. It is likely that the problem of remoteness is also dealt with by applying the second half of the *Anns* test, which asks: Was there any reason that the duty should not be imposed? Should the scope of the duty be reduced? Should the class to whom the duty is owed be limited, or should the damages be reduced? In addressing these issues the courts will determine whether the injuries or damages suffered were too remote.

Although the application of these principles may be confusing, there is one area of certainty: where the *nature* but not the extent of a personal injury was reasonably foreseeable, the rule is simply that *we take our victims as we find them*. If a person has a weak heart or a tendency to a particular disease or physical condition, we cannot avoid responsibility by claiming that we could not reasonably be expected to foresee the special condition. If a person experiences greater injury from our conduct than would be expected because of a unique physical condition, there is nonetheless a responsibility to compensate for all consequences of the injury. This principle is often referred to as the **thin skull** rule.

In the case of *Smith v. Leech Brain & Co.,*[53] the defendant's employee was hurt when he was struck on the lip by a drop of molten metal. Because of a precancer-

*Margin notes:*

**Problem of remoteness**

*Anns* **case applied to determine existence of duty**

**We take our victims as we find them**

---

51. *Walker Estate v. York-Finch General Hospital,* [2001] 1 S.C.R. 647.

52. [1976] 1 S.C.R. 595 at 604.

53. [1961] 3 All E.R. 1159 (Q.B.).

ous condition existing in the employee, this burn developed into cancer, which eventually killed him. Although this consequence of the injury was in no way reasonably foreseeable, the employer was held liable for the death of the employee because the original accident was caused by the employer's negligence and physical injury itself was foreseeable.

But we must be careful in applying the principle. If the aggravated injury was inevitable and the conduct of the defendant simply determined the timing, the defendant will not be responsible for the additional loss. If a worker has one eye and loses the other in an accident, the damage is much more devastating than the loss of a single eye. Under the thin skull rule, the defendant will be responsible for the greater damages resulting from the total blindness. But if that one-eyed worker had a deteriorating condition in his remaining eye that would have eventually caused its loss, the defendant's conduct is not responsible for the worker's blindness; the deteriorating condition is, and the worker will receive considerably less compensation. This has been dubbed the **crumbling skull rule,** and must be used in conjunction with the thin skull rule.[54] When the Court applies the crumbling skull rule, it recognizes the pre-existing frailties and the award of damages aims at restoring the plaintiff to that (original) position.[55]

**Not responsible for inevitable loss**

## Contributory Negligence

Historically, when a defendant could show that the plaintiff was also careless, contributing to his own loss, it was a complete bar to recovery. This was an all-or-nothing result and was clearly unfair. For example, if the defendant driver fails to stop at a light and the plaintiff driver fails to notice the car coming into his path because he is adjusting his radio, he will not be able to recover for any injuries suffered in the accident. In this case, it is clear that the plaintiff driver was being careless by not being fully aware of what was happening on the road; this conduct at least contributed to the accident and would completely bar him from recovery of damages. Because this approach is rather harsh, it was somewhat modified by the **last clear chance doctrine,** which made the person who had the last opportunity to avoid the accident responsible. This was still an unfair all-or-nothing approach, and legislation was enacted to alleviate the problem.

The *Negligence Act* in Ontario[56] is one example; it abandons the all-or-nothing approach and permits the court to apportion responsibility between the two parties. Compensation must be paid in proportion to that assigned responsibility. (Each province will have its own legislation and students should consult the statute enacted in their jurisdiction to determine how contributory negligence is dealt with there.) In the example above, the defendant driver was at fault for driving through the stoplight, and the plaintiff driver contributed to the accident through lack of attention. The courts in Ontario would apportion liability and require each to bear a percentage of the responsibility for the losses suffered.

**Act allows apportionment of responsibility**

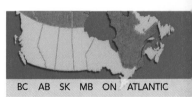

BC   AB   SK   MB   ON   ATLANTIC

54. *Athey v. Leonati,* [1996] 3 S.C.R. 458.

55. For example, see *Whitfield v. Calhoun* (1999), 242 A.R. 201 (Q.B.), where the plaintiff developed anti-social, paranoid, and schizoid behaviour and depression as a result of a motor vehicle collision. His pre-existing personality traits contributed to these psychological problems and the reduced damages reflected this original pre-disposition.

56. R.S.O. 1990, c. N.1.

## Reducing **Risk** 4.2

Can an investor or business simply rely on investment advice given by others? Can that investor later sue if the advice were negligently prepared? It cannot be overemphasized that, in business, people are expected to have a certain amount of business acumen. They should seek the advice of professionals and not simply trust the information they receive from others. When investors are less than vigilant, they may find themselves responsible for at least a portion of their own losses.

## Voluntary Assumption of Risk

**The law will not assist volunteers**

A plaintiff in a negligence action may also lose the right to receive compensation where he has voluntarily assumed the risk. The principle being applied is that the law does not assist a volunteer or one who consents (*volenti non fit injuria*). If a person knowingly gets into a car with a driver who is obviously intoxicated, should he be able to sue if injured? Historically, the answer would be no; the plaintiff who voluntarily assumed the risk would be completely barred from recovery. Today, the principle is much more restrictive. To escape liability, the defendant must show not only that the plaintiff voluntarily put himself in danger, but also that he did so in such a way as to clearly absolve the defendant of responsibility. If a person puts himself in harm's way like this, assuming both physical and legal responsibility, he is completely barred from recovering any damages. It is difficult, however, to establish this waiver of legal responsibility, and so only rarely will a claim of voluntary assumption of risk be successful.

**But assumption of legal risk must be clear**

The courts now usually deal with such foolhardy behaviour under the heading of **contributory negligence,** and this, in turn, permits the courts to apportion the loss between the parties—a much more satisfactory result. This was done in the *Crocker v. Sundance* case in Case Summary 4.9: the court rejected voluntary assumption of risk and found contributory negligence instead.

Some jurisdictions have included provisions in their occupiers' liability acts absolving responsibility where the visitor has voluntarily assumed the risk. Although the legislation does not say it, the Supreme Court of Canada has interpreted this in the same restrictive way, and so this provision will absolve the occupier of responsibility only where it is clear that the visitor has assumed the legal risk as well as the physical risk.[57] This will happen in only the rarest of circumstances.

What about a rescuer? If the rescuer gets hurt, can it be said that she voluntarily assumed the risk? A mother who is injured when she jumps in front of a train to save her child can hold the railway responsible for failing to have proper barriers. If the rescuer is injured, the author of the danger cannot escape liability by claiming the rescuer voluntarily assumed the risk. If the potential danger was reasonably foreseeable, so was the potential need for a rescue. The person who caused the danger must pay compensation to both the victim and the injured rescuer.[58] Similarly, the principle of *volenti* does not apply to work-related accidents, even if the work being performed is inherently dangerous.

## Special Situations

**Occupiers owe special duty**

The court deals with some special situations in unique ways. In common law, people who occupy property have a special obligation to people who are injured on

---

57. *Waldick v. Malcolm*, [1991] 2 S.C.R. 456.

58. *Videan v. British Transport Commission*, [1963] 2 All E.R. 860 (C.A.).

their property. Note that this obligation rests on the occupier, not the owner; thus, where the property is leased, the duty falls on the tenant, not the landlord. The obligation to look out for the welfare of visitors varies with their status. A person coming on a property for a business purpose is referred to as an *invitee*. A person on the property with permission but for a non-business purpose is a *licensee*, and a person there without permission is a *trespasser*. At common law, the occupier has to act more carefully toward the invitee. They are required to take reasonable steps to protect invitees from unusual dangers. This may extend to putting up a fence around an elevator shaft or providing a hard hat. The duty toward licensees is less, requiring the occupier only to take reasonable steps to warn of hidden dangers on the property; here, a sign would suffice. The only duty to a trespasser is not to wilfully or recklessly cause him harm.

These different standards have caused problems, especially where children are involved. Most provinces enacted legislation in the form of occupiers' liability acts, which eliminated the distinction between invitees and licensees, imposing just one standard of care for "visitors" and their property while on the premises of others. (Note, however, that rules vary from province to province, so reference to the provincial supplements to this text is recommended.)

As for trespassers, the legislation usually retains the common law minimal obligation not to wilfully or recklessly cause the trespasser injury, but again the specific statute should be consulted. This minimal duty also applies to those visitors who have voluntarily assumed the risks of being there. But for trespassers who are children, the duty of care may well equate that extended to visitors.

**Invitee/licensee distinction may no longer be important**

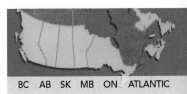

BC  AB  SK  MB  ON  ATLANTIC

## Case Summary 4.14

### Legislation Demands Extra Precaution: *Houle v. Calgary (City)*[59]

This case involved an abandoned supermarket in a suburban area of Calgary. Located in the parking lot of that supermarket was an electrical transformer surrounded by a 10-foot fence. Sean Houle, an eight-year-old child, managed to climb up a power pole over the fence. He was seriously burned when he came into contact with a live power wire and his arm had to be amputated. While there was some dispute about who was responsible for the property, the court held that because the City of Calgary had built the enclosure and had the only keys to it, the city was responsible for it as the "occupier." The Court of Appeal then applied Alberta's *Occupiers' Liability Act* to the situation and found that Sean was a child trespasser under the Act. This was a residential neighbourhood with lots of children, and the city should have known that the parking lot had become a children's playground. In addition, the electrical power represented a substantial danger to the children. The Court applied section 13 of the Act: "the occupier owes a duty to that child to take such care as in all the circumstances of the case is reasonable to see that the child will be reasonably safe from that danger." The city clearly failed in this duty and was, therefore, liable for the child's injuries. The Court stated that the danger could have been eliminated by simply placing the pole inside the fence. People must take care to ensure that the property they are responsible for is safe for all those using it. This applies to businesses as well as to occupiers of private residences.

59. (1985), 60 A.R. 366 (C.A.), leave to appeal to S.C.C. refused (1985), 63 A.R. 79 n.

**Special duties of innkeepers**

An even more onerous duty is imposed on occupiers when an inn or hotel is involved. At common law, innkeepers owe a duty to their guests to provide protection from the wrongful acts of others, even when the innkeeper or servant is not at fault. This is a much higher duty than normal, and it is only when the damage or loss to a guest's property is caused by that guest's own negligence that the innkeeper is relieved of responsibility. Most provinces have reduced the common law liability of innkeepers through legislation so that they are liable only where they or their employees are negligent. It is important to note, however, that their liability is reduced only where they have carefully complied with the statute by placing notices at designated locations. (Refer to the appropriate provincial supplement to review the specific legislation and note how it is applied.)

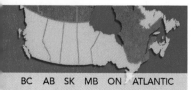

BC   AB   SK   MB   ON   ATLANTIC

A special problem arises when alcohol is served. The courts are willing to hold commercial dispensers of alcoholic beverages at least partially responsible when a patron becomes intoxicated and is injured, as the Supreme Court of Canada made clear in the *Crocker* case in Case Summary 4.9. Following this trend, we can expect companies, and even individual hosts, to be liable when private parties or gatherings lead to similar results.

**Case Summary 4.15**

### Serving Alcohol to Drivers Can Lead to Liability: *Jacobsen v. Nike Canada Ltd.*[60]

Mr. Jacobsen was an employee of Nike Canada and was working for them setting up a display at a trade show in the B.C. Place Stadium. Because of the nature of the job, he was required to work for a long period of time. The employer, through its representative, supplied the workers with food and considerable amounts of beer, which they were allowed to drink while on the job. At 11:30 p.m., they finished working. Mr. Jacobsen, along with some of the other employees, went to two clubs where they consumed more beer. The plaintiff consumed about 10 beers while working and more at the clubs. Driving home that night, he was involved in a serious single-vehicle accident that left him a quadriplegic.

There was no question that the employer owed a duty of care to its employee, having put him in this position. The problem was the nature of that duty and whether the duty had been breached. The Court held that the employer should have known that he would likely drive home drunk and had a duty to ensure that he did not. The employer had required him to drive his car that day, and the employer's agent had supplied the beer. Nike was in breach of its duty to provide a safe place of work. "I find that Nike failed to meet the standard of care required of an employer by providing alcohol in the workplace in the circumstances in which it did so on September 6, 1991, not monitoring the plaintiff's consumption and taking no steps to ensure the plaintiff did not drive while impaired."[61] Even though Mr. Jacobsen had consumed more alcohol at other establishments later, Nike had breached its duty and was held liable for his injuries.

How careful do employers have to be toward their employees? This case indicates the direction the law is moving. Liability is being imposed on those who provide alcohol to their customers and guests. Note, however, that Mr. Jacobsen was found to be contributorily negligent and bore responsibility for 25 percent of his own injuries.

---

60. (1996), 133 D.L.R. (4th) 377 (B.C.S.C.).

61. *Ibid.* at 388.

## Legislation

Although the reasonable person standard discussed in the context of negligence is extremely important, there are many situations where this has been changed by statute. Examples are the occupiers' liability acts and innkeepers' acts discussed above. The motor vehicle acts of the provinces also create special categories of duty that make people responsible for the condition of their car even if they were not aware of a defect. As a general rule, however, these statutes do not create new categories of tort unless they specifically say so. Thus, human rights acts and privacy legislation may impose new obligations on people, but violations of these obligations do not amount to a tort unless the act says they do. Some jurisdictions have also changed tort law with respect to automobile collisions. Because of the devastating losses and injuries associated with this area, many provinces have turned to compulsory insurance schemes. Some jurisdictions have gone further, instituting "no fault" programs by which people are treated the same and compensated for their injuries whether they were at fault or not. Others rely on compulsory insurance as the main method of distributing loss among all the driving public. Whichever method is employed, it is generally agreed that it is necessary to ensure that, as much as possible, all users of the road are covered.

**Modifications imposed by statute**

**The trend away from fault**

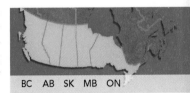

BC  AB  SK  MB  ON

## Negligent Misstatement

Until recently, liability for negligence was thought to be limited to **conduct** that fell below an acceptable standard of care. In 1963, the House of Lords in the United Kingdom indicated its willingness to expand this liability to **careless words** causing economic loss.[62]

**Negligent words causing economic loss actionable**

The Supreme Court of Canada adopted a similar approach in the case of *Haig v. Bamford*.[63] An accounting firm negligently prepared financial statements for a company, knowing that the statements would be used to encourage investors. Mr. Haig purchased a number of shares but found the company to be considerably less profitable than the incorrect financial statements had led him to believe. As a result, he suffered a financial loss.

There was no direct relationship between Mr. Haig and the negligent firm. The accounting firm was negligent in the performance of its services to the company; at that time Mr. Haig was just a potential investor. Previously, the imposition of liability depended on the negligent conduct causing *physical* injury or damage. Here, there was no physical contact and/or loss. Mr. Haig lost money when he relied on the financial statement.

**Negligent words may create liability**

This case is significant because for the first time in Canada liability for the tort of negligence was extended to **pure economic loss caused by negligent words** spoken by experts. As a result, such experts may find themselves responsible not only to their immediate clients, but also to others who suffer loss because of their careless statements. This has had a considerable impact on all those claiming professional expertise. The liability of professionals and other experts will be discussed as a special topic below.

---

62. *Hedley Byrne & Co. v. Heller's Partners Ltd.,* [1963] 2 All E.R. 575 (H.L.).

63. [1977] 1 S.C.R. 466.

## Strict Liability

As mentioned above, the commission of a tort involves wrongful conduct. This requires fault, and in a negligence action that fault usually takes the form of conduct falling below the standard of a reasonable person in the circumstances. It must be noted, however, that there are some situations where the courts will impose liability even when the defendant has acted completely reasonably.

**Liability even when conduct was reasonable**

The case of *Rylands v. Fletcher*[64] established a rule applicable in such instances. The defendant had built a reservoir on his property, but under the surface there was a shaft from a coal mine leading to his neighbour's property. The water escaped, flooding his neighbour's mine. Rylands was in no way negligent, having no knowledge of the underground shaft. His conduct was well within what would have been expected of a reasonable person. Still, the court held him liable for the damage. The principle applied was that if a person brings something inherently dangerous, such as stored water or explosives, onto his property and it escapes, the occupier is liable for any damage. The House of Lords supported Justice Blackburn's earlier decision, which said, "The true rule of law is that the person who, for his own purposes, brings on his land and collects and keeps there anything likely to do mischief if it escapes, must keep it at his peril; and if he does not do so, is *prima facie* answerable for all the damage which is the natural consequence of its escape."[65] The House of Lords, incidentally, focused more on the non-natural use of the land, rather than on the introduction of something inherently dangerous onto the land.

**When dangerous things escape**

It must be noted that strict liability will not be imposed unless the use of the property is unusual. Today, electricity and plumbing are part of normal operations for modern buildings, and damage caused by these conveniences will normally not support a claim of strict liability. To succeed in such situations, nuisance or negligence must be established.

**Must be unusual use of property**

### Case Summary 4.16

#### Strict Liability for Dangerous Substances: *Ira-Berg Ltd. v. Skrow's Produce Ltd. (1971)*[66]

The tenant, Skrow's Produce, owned a truck that had propane tanks built into it. One of the tanks leaked when the truck was parked in front of the plaintiff's place of business during a sale. The fire department ordered evacuation of the premises until the gas dissipated, causing considerable loss of business. The plaintiffs sued under the principle of strict liability. The Court agreed that storing propane on the truck was a dangerous and unusual use of property and applied the precedent from *Rylands v. Fletcher.* The Court also found that the defendant had caused a nuisance and that the case was actionable on that basis as well. At the time that the truck was parked alongside the store, the driver knew it was discharging propane. That made it an abnormal use.

A form of strict liability—that is, liability without fault—is also imposed on employers when they are held liable for torts committed by employees during the course of their employment. This is referred to as **vicarious liability.** The

**Vicarious liability of employer**

---

64. (1868), L.R. 3 H.L. 330.

65. *Ibid.* at 339–40.

66. (1990), 76 D.L.R. (4th) 431 (Ont. Gen. Div.).

employer is without fault and yet is held liable for the wrongful acts of employees. This is justified by the fact that the employer profits by the employees' conduct, and therefore ought to bear responsibility. This will be covered in Chapter 11 under "Liability of Employer."

Only in these rare circumstances will liability be imposed strictly. But there are other situations where the standard imposed is extremely high. Negligence is normally determined by finding that there was a failure to live up to the standard of a reasonable person. Where dangerous products, processes, or animals are involved, the standard of care required is very high because the risk of injury is great. The obligations of persons in control in such situations approach strict liability. Food handlers, for example, find themselves in this unenviable position.

# Product Liability

**Case Summary 4.17**

### Defective Designs with Explosive Consequences:
### *Nicholson v. John Deere Ltd.*[67]

The Nicholsons purchased a second-hand riding lawnmower manufactured by John Deere Ltd. Before using the mower one day, Mrs. Nicholson opened the hood to fill up the gas tank. She took off the cap, placed it on the tank, and started to pour in the gas. She had to stop to retrieve the gas cap when it rolled off the tank. She again placed it on the hood and continued to pour gas into the tank. The cap rolled away again; this time it hit the battery and caused a spark that ignited the gasoline fumes. As the fire started, she spontaneously dropped the gasoline can she was holding, spilling the gas. The resulting fire destroyed both the garage and her home. Mrs. Nicholson sued the manufacturer for compensation for the losses she had suffered. The Court found that the design was defective and that the manufacturer was aware of the problem, since there had been several incidents and lawsuits over this and the previous models. In fact, John Deere recognized the danger associated with its product and had manufactured a battery-covered safety kit to solve the problem. It also took steps to warn the users of its mower of the danger and of the availability of the safety kit. There was a decal on the gas tank warning of the danger of spark. There were several warnings of the danger in the operating manual, and John Deere had a program in place whereby its dealers and agents were encouraged to tell customers about the safety kit and have it installed.

The Nicholsons did not receive a manual with their used mower and were not aware of this safety kit, which had not been installed on their mower. When they had it serviced, the dealer did not tell them of the safety kit. The court held that these efforts on the part of John Deere were inadequate. The manufacturer should have taken much more positive action to make sure the defects were corrected. In addition, the dealer, who failed to tell the Nicholsons about the danger and the safety kit, was also liable for negligence. This case is interesting in that it shows the great responsibility placed on a manufacturer when such a defective and dangerous product is produced. Once it had been established that the

67. (1986), 58 O.R. (2d) 53 (H.C.J.), varied (1989), 68 O.R. 191 (C.A.).

design was defective and dangerous, it was very difficult, if not impossible, for the manufacturer to show that it was not negligent, despite its stringent efforts to correct the situation. Is this fair? What do you think?

Injury and loss are often caused indirectly. When products are manufactured, those products are sometimes dangerous because of their inherent nature, such as chemicals or explosives, or because they are defective. The American approach to product liability is somewhat different from that in Canada. In the United States, by statute and case law, a much greater responsibility has been imposed on manufacturers. Injured consumers are required only to demonstrate that a defect in the product caused the injury. There is no need to establish negligence by demonstrating a failure to live up to a standard of care. Liability is based on either contract, where the principle of **privity** has been abandoned, or strict liability. In either case, once the defect and injury have been established, liability falls on the producer of the product.

This **strict liability** approach to product liability has not yet been adopted in most provinces in Canada. Here, it is not enough to show that the defective product caused injury. In this country, it is still necessary for a plaintiff to establish negligence. It is necessary not only to establish that there was a duty to be careful, but also that there was a failure to live up to that duty. Either the manufacturer, or an employee, must be shown to have been negligent or careless. *Donoghue v. Stevenson*, discussed in Case Summary 4.10, had a significant impact on product liability in tort law. Historically, because there were usually several intervening steps or intervening parties between the manufacturer and the ultimate consumer of a product, it was thought that the manufacturer owed no duty of care to the ultimate consumer. This case established that if a product were designed in such a way as to get into the hands of the consumer without intervening inspection or modification, a duty of care did exist. Now, as we deal with more complicated manufactured goods, there is even less likelihood that a problem will be disclosed by intermediate inspection. As a result, today it is much more difficult for a manufacturer to deny the existence of a duty of care. This duty, along with evidence of a breach of that duty, will impose liability on the producer of the product.

A particularly difficult problem in product liability cases is to show that someone was "careless" in the manufacturing process. In Canada, the courts are willing to draw, from the circumstantial evidence of the injury or loss, a conclusion that someone must have been negligent, leaving it to the defendant to then produce evidence to the contrary. As discussed above, this **"circumstantial evidence"** method replaces the *res ipsa loquitur* approach used in the past and also seems more appropriate for product liability cases.[68]

The manufacturer may find itself in a no-win situation. On the one hand, where policies and procedures are in place such that if followed no injury could happen, then they must not have been followed if injury did occur. On the other hand, if policies and procedures were followed and still injury occurred, this suggests the policies were not adequate. Either way, negligence is established. Once the court has drawn the inference of negligence from the circumstances of the injury, the manufacturer will have to show that it was not careless in order to

**Breach of duty must be shown for product liability**

**Breach of duty can be implied from circumstances**

68. *Fontaine, supra* note 47.

avoid liability. The figurative snail in the bottle will be enough for the court to draw an inference of negligence on the part of the defendant.

Where the products are inherently dangerous, as is the case with chemicals, explosives, tools, and pharmaceuticals, the requirements are a little different. The manufacturer must do all that he can to make the product as safe as reasonably possible given the risks, and to give appropriate warnings and instructions. In Canada, the defendant must still show negligence on the part of the manufacturer, but the focus is on whether the warnings and instructions are clear and whether everything reasonably possible has been done given the considerable risk. For example, there have been great strides made in making pharmaceutical products safe for children by sealing the products and providing child-proof caps. Power tools generally have a double switch mechanism or a locking device to prevent children or even adults from accidentally turning on the power. Where this has been done effectively, the manufacturer will likely escape liability. That is why such great care is now taken to place warnings on dangerous goods. To say that the misuse of a knife or table saw might result in injury seems self-evident. Warnings to that effect appear on such products nonetheless. Many warnings now appear on cigarette packages. Case Summary 4.18 examines the issue of whether cigarette manufacturers should take further steps to ensure their products are safe.

**Manufacturers must warn and act reasonably to make dangerous products safer**

## Case Summary 4.18

### Design Safer Cigarettes or Be Sued? *Ragoonan Estate v. Imperial Tobacco Canada Ltd.*[69]

The plaintiffs argued that cigarette manufacturers should be held liable to those injured when a smouldering cigarette, likely dropped into a sofa, caused a fire. That there was likely negligence on the part of the smoker was not disputed. However, others in the room were also injured and they were not negligent.

One of the issues was whether Imperial Tobacco was negligent in failing to design fire-resistant cigarettes when it was a known risk that an unattended cigarette could cause a fire. The court refused dismissal of the cause of action because the risk–utility theory of liability (for the defective design of a product) created a plausible theory in support of the cause of action. The first step is to determine whether the product is defective under ordinary use or, although non-defective, has a propensity to injure. (Smouldering, unattended cigarettes constitute a risk of fire—this fact is well known.) The second step is in assessing the manufacturer's knowledge of the dangerousness of the product. If the value of the product outweighs the propensity to injure, then the third step is an assessment of the reasonableness of the warning to consumers. Fourth is the determination of causation and damages.

The interesting argument put forward by the plaintiffs was that "Whether, notwithstanding the notoriety of the risks of misuse, manufacturers have deliberately designed the product in such a way as to cause misuse. It is arguable that, by enhancing the addictive features of the product, they encourage obsessive use that leads to people smoking when they are weary or unwell and likely to fall asleep." What do you think? Should cigarette manufacturers be liable if an addictive product they've produced—one that they know has caused several fires—is not "fire resistant" but rather continues to smoulder while unattended?

69. (2000), 51 O.R. (3d) 132 (Ont. Sup. Ct. J.).

**Liability for breach may be set out in contract for sale or statute**

It must be emphasized that liability for damage or injury caused by products is not always based on negligence. When a **contract** exists between the injured party and the seller, and the product is defective or dangerous or otherwise causes injury or damage, that seller may be liable for breach of contract. Implied in contracts for the sale of goods is a promise or warranty that the goods will be fit and defect-free. Damages for breach of the contract may thus be awarded even when there is no fault on the part of the seller. In the case of *Donoghue v. Stevenson* described in Case Summary 4.10, had Mrs. Donoghue been the one to purchase the ginger beer instead of her friend she could have sued the café for breach of contract, because the product was not fit to consume. But because she was not the purchaser, she had no action against the seller. Some provinces have removed this privity of contract restriction in product liability cases, thus imposing a contractual duty on the manufacturer, the wholesaler, and the seller to protect the ultimate consumer even when no fault is involved. For a more complete discussion of contractual product liability, refer "Consumer Protection Legislation" in Chapter 9.

Finally, it should also be noted that it is becoming increasingly rare, especially when a civil jury is involved, for the manufacturer not to be found liable when its product causes injury. It remains to be seen whether this reflects a rising standard, a move toward adopting strict liability, or a decision to place the liability on the party likely to have insurance.

# Liability of Professionals and Other Experts

**Professional liability and insurance costs important aspects of business**

For business students who are planning to enter professions or who intend to do consulting work, the subject of **professional liability** may be one of the most important covered in this text. Experts are simply people who hold themselves out to have some specialized knowledge or skill not generally available. Professionals are usually experts who belong to professional organizations and practise in a specific area of service. The definition is obviously imprecise and, for the purposes of this discussion, should be viewed as expansive rather than restrictive. Whether we are talking of medical malpractice or the responsibilities of accountants, litigation over the quality of their work by disgruntled clients has become an important aspect of their practice. Not only have the occurrences of such malpractice actions increased dramatically in recent years, so too have the damages awarded by the courts. Today, an important consideration for any professional is the amount of **liability insurance** they must retain at a very high cost. The liability of professionals may be founded in contract law or based on fiduciary duty, but the recent expansion of liability has been in the area of tort law, specifically negligence. Professionals must also adhere to the rules and standards set by their governing bodies. Failure to comply with the rules, or complaints from unhappy clients, may result in disciplinary action with the potential consequence of losing the right to practice.

**Liability must be based on contract, fiduciary duty or tort**

## Contract

**In past, contractual risk determined price**

In the past, the liability of accountants, bankers, lawyers, business consultants, and other professionals was based on the contract they had with their clients. Contracts will be discussed in the next chapters, but briefly, the parties could make whatever arrangement they wanted, either expanding or limiting their liability. In theory, the risk borne by the professional in each agreement would be reflected in the price agreed to. The contracts spell out exactly what is expected of the professional, setting out not only what is to be done but also limitations on what is expected. Such contracts may contain exemption clauses or disclaimers that limit the liability of the professional for any mistakes made and damages incurred. If the client does not like this arrangement, he can go elsewhere or insist that the clause be removed, usually resulting in a higher fee to be paid. The fee negotiated should reflect the risks and duties agreed to by the parties. The courts have always been reluctant to interfere in this bargaining process. In fact, there often is no written contract, and terms have to be implied from the relationship and the normal practices of the profession. Implicit in such contracts is that the professional perform the service requested with due diligence. Thus, the requirement to adhere to a **reasonable standard of performance,** which is the basis of tort liability, is incorporated into the contractual obligations as well. But it is important to remember that the presence of a disclaimer, waiver, or other limitation cannot be overcome by suing in tort instead.

**Tort standard implied in contract, but note disclaimer**

**Privity of contract** is also extremely important when exploring the limits of the liability of professionals. The contract is between the professional and the client, and outsiders would generally have no rights under the agreement. Thus, an accountant would have a contract with the company for which he prepares financial statements. If a mistake is made, the shareholders and investors would have no recourse against the accountant for damages suffered in contract law, only the company itself would. The court's willingness to expand tort liability beyond these immediate parties has had an important impact on the risks faced by accountants and other experts.

**Tort liability extends beyond parties to contract**

## Negligence

The expansion of tort liability has introduced considerable uncertainty into the area of professional liability. The standard of care expected of a professional is reasonably straightforward and will be discussed below. What has changed in recent times, expanding the liability of most experts far beyond what it has been, is just who can sue. Is an architect liable to a person injured in a collapsed building when errors are found in her designs? Is an accountant liable to shareholders or investors because of erroneous financial statements prepared for a specific client? The extension of liability to these third parties has greatly expanded the risks faced by professionals who provide these services. The discussion that follows will take a closer look at a professional's liability for negligence.

**Extension of liability to third parties**

### Standard of Care

The standard of care expected from an expert is a little different from that expected from a non-expert. The expert must live up to the standard of a reasonable person *in the circumstances*. There are two problems here: first, the level of skill they must have, and second, how they exercise that skill. Essentially, these people are required to have the skills and abilities that one would expect from an expert or professional in that field. If a person professes to be a medical doctor, he had better have the training and skills of a medical doctor. If he claims to be a specialist, such as a plastic surgeon, he must be able to demonstrate that he has gone through the specialized training required for that designation. The same

**Standard is that of a reasonable member of the profession**

applies to a chartered accountant or investment counsellor: they have to have the training and skills expected of someone in that profession. It will be no excuse for them to claim they are not familiar with that standard or theory if it can be shown to be part of the normal knowledge or skill expected of an expert in that field.

The accounting professions, for example, have established standards of practice for their members: GAAP (generally accepted accounting principles), and GAAS (generally accepted auditing standards). Where it can be shown that an accountant has failed to live up to these standards, that failure generally will be enough to establish negligence.

The second problem relates to how that skill is exercised. In assessing liability, the court determines what a reasonable person, possessed of the same skills and abilities as the defendant, would have done in the circumstances. For a doctor, the test is that of a reasonable doctor; for an accountant, a reasonable accountant; for a lawyer, a reasonable lawyer. It must be emphasized that a client or patient is not required to tolerate ineptitude on the part of professionals because of inexperience. It may be true that a doctor or mechanic in the first month of employment is more likely to make a mistake, but these people have represented themselves as proficient members of their profession. They must, therefore, live up to the level of competence one would expect of a normal member of their profession functioning in a reasonably prudent manner.

**Common practice may not measure up to reasonable standard**

It can be very helpful to the defendant to show that what he did was common practice among his colleagues. Such common practice in the profession is generally an indication of competent professional service. But this is not always the case. The test is that of a reasonable person, not an average person. Although one would hope that the average standard of practice in the skilled professions would coincide with the practice one would expect from a reasonable person, this is not always so. When it is obvious that the common practice is dangerous or careless, then such sloppy practice will not be tolerated. The court, in such circumstances, is not reluctant to declare that the common practice falls below the standard of a reasonable person and is, therefore, negligent. This principle has recently been reinforced by the Supreme Court of Canada in the *Waldick v. Malcolm* case, where Justice Iacobucci, quoting Linden, states: "Tort courts have not abdicated their responsibility to evaluate customs, for negligent conduct cannot be countenanced, even when a large group is continually guilty of it." In short, no amount of general community compliance will render negligent conduct "reasonable... in all the circumstances."[70] It is clear, however, that to find such negligence in the face of common practice in a profession would happen only in extraordinary circumstances.

### Case Summary 4.19

#### Not Enough to Follow GAAP: *Kripps v. Touche Ross*[71]

The British Columbia Court of Appeal held that even where accountants follow GAAP (*generally accepted accounting principles,* the standard used by the Canadian Institute of Chartered Accountants), they cannot be sure they are acting reasonably. In this case, the company involved raised funds from investors and then invested those funds in mortgages. In fact, more than $4 million of its mortgages (about one-third of the company's entire investment portfolio) were in default,

---

70. *Waldick v. Malcolm,* [1991] 2 S.C.R. 456 at 473.

71. [1997] 6 W.W.R. 421 (B.C.C.A.); leave to appeal to S.C.C. refused (1997), 102 B.C.A.C. 238 (note).

and this was not disclosed in the 1983 financial statements even though the auditors were aware of the situation. The Court held that the investors were misled by the accounting statements, and the accountants were held liable even though they had carefully followed GAAP. They did not disclose this information (that the mortgages were in default) because the GAAP rules then in place did not require such disclosure. The Court said, in effect, that the accountants could not hide behind the GAAP standards to escape liability.

## To Whom Is the Duty Owed? (The Problem with Words)

In the past, professionals and other experts faced liability to their clients only for shoddy work (based on contract law), and to their colleagues and clients on the basis of a breach of a fiduciary duty. Liability to strangers or third parties arose only where physical or bodily injuries were sustained. For example, experts such as architects and engineers, whose services produced physical structures that would cause injury if they failed, might be subject to liability to strangers. If those injured were not immediate parties and their loss (whether caused by physical acts or words) was purely economic, there was considerable reluctance on the part of the court to extend the professional's liability to them.

Today, accountants, bankers, lawyers, business consultants, and other professionals giving financial advice may be sued when their negligent words cause economic loss. As mentioned above under "Negligent Misstatement," it has been only in the past few years that courts have been willing to grant compensation for this kind of loss.

**Modern standards recognize economic loss caused by negligent words**

The case of *Haig v. Bamford*[72] was the first in this country where accountants were found liable to third-party investors for their negligence in preparing audited financial statements. As a result of this precedent, accountants and other experts now find themselves responsible not only to their immediate clients but also to others who suffer loss because of their careless statements.

Once the court decided to provide liability for economic loss caused by such negligent words, it then had to decide just how far this liability would extend. Should the same test be used to determine the existence of duty as when physical conduct was involved? As you will recall, with conduct causing injury the test to determine whether a duty existed came from the case of *Donoghue v. Stevenson* (see Case Summary 4.10). A duty to be careful was owed to anyone one could reasonably foresee as being harmed by one's conduct. Should careless words be treated the same as careless conduct, or should a narrower test to determine duty be adopted? Many argue vigorously that the reasonable foreseeability test is much too broad for determining liability when mere words are involved and only economic damage has been suffered. They argue that words are much more volatile and that the adoption of the reasonable foreseeability test would expose professionals and other experts to considerably greater liability than would be appropriate.

**Liability may extend beyond immediate parties**

In fact, the judges in the *Haig* case stopped short of adopting the reasonable foreseeability test but said that a duty of care was owed only when the person making the misleading statement knew it was to be used by an individual or a limited class of people. There have been several subsequent cases involving negligent misrepresentation. Currently, the courts are asking whether the plaintiff's reliance on these representations was reasonable, especially where the

72. [1977] 1 S.C.R. 466.

defendants may have tried to eliminate or reduce their liability by using dis-claimers or exculpatory words. To determine if there was "reasonable reliance," courts may ask whether:

**(1)** The defendant had a direct or indirect financial interest in the transaction in respect of which the representation was made.

**(2)** The defendant was a professional or someone who possessed a special skill, judgment, or knowledge.

**(3)** The advice or information was provided in the course of the defendant's business.

**(4)** The information or advice was given deliberately, and not on a social occasion.

**(5)** The information or advice was given in response to a specific enquiry or request.

These indicia have been accepted as helping to distinguish those situations where reliance on a statement is reasonable from those when it is not.[73] For example, in the *Micron* case, Micron brought a misrepresentation action against the promoters of a large construction project and the bank funding the project. The plaintiff claimed the defendants had falsely misrepresented that the promoters had the funds to complete the project. They did not. The bank had even sent Micron a letter of reference, leading it to believe that the project was on strong financial footing. The letter contained a disclaimer. The court applied the five indicia detailed above; since the first four were present, the court concluded that there was "reasonable reliance" on the statements by the plaintiff, establishing that a duty of care did exist in these circumstances.

**Duty determined by reasonable forseeability**

The *Hercules* case[74] illustrates a slightly different approach to establishing the existence of a duty of care. There, the shareholders of a company relied on incorrect financial statements to make further investments in that company. The shareholders were clearly a group that the accountants could expect to rely on the statements, and so, using the *Haig* case, a duty was owed. But these financial statements were prepared not to encourage further investment but to evaluate the capabilities of the management team at the shareholders' meeting. Should accountants' liability extend beyond the purpose for which the statements are prepared? Applying the *Anns* case, the Supreme Court of Canada found there was a *prima facie* duty owed by the accountants. But, applying the second part of the test developed in the *Anns* case, the Court also decided that the duty of the accountants should impose liability only for the purpose for which the financial statements were prepared, in this case to evaluate management and not to be used by shareholders for investment decisions. The accountants, therefore, escaped liability.

**but**

**Scope of duty may be reduced where appropriate**

It seems clear that the *Anns* case remains important in Canadian law, allowing the courts to apply social policy to limit duty and liability where it seems appropriate to do so. From the point of view of a professional or any other person professing expertise, it is vital to understand that a duty to be careful exists not only to their clients but also to others who may be affected by the advice or service

**Tort liability of professionals extends beyond clients**

---

73. See *Micron Construction Ltd. v. Hongkong Bank of Canada* (2000), 184 D.L.R. (4th) 75 (B.C.C.A.), leave to appeal refused, [2000] S.C.C.A. No. 193, where these five indicia were applied.

74. *Hercules Management Ltd. v. Ernst & Young*, [1997] 2 S.C.R. 165.

## Reducing **Risk** 4.3

It has been suggested that risk avoidance is the most appropriate course for businesspeople to reduce the likelihood of being sued. Professionals should examine not only the condition of their premises, tools, cars, and other physical objects used in the course of business, but also the habits and practices that may give rise to a complaint. Medical professionals, such as doctors, nurses, podiatrists, chiropractors, and the like, run some risk of being sued in the torts of battery and negligence. Since the nature of their practice depends on physical contact with their clients and patients, securing consent is a vital component of risk management. If the nature of the contact is more invasive, as in performing surgery, the consent must be fully informed. Detailed explanations of the procedure, the risks attached, and the alternatives available must all be given to secure an informed consent. Problems may also arise when physical injury is caused by an error in judgment or a mistake in practice. People involved in sports, education, training, and recreational activities face such a risk. The main thing to remember is that the standard of care demanded of such experts is that of the reasonable person operating in similar circumstances.

they give. This liability may result from careless conduct or careless words. With any luck, at least from the professional's perspective, that duty may be reduced or restricted by the application of the second test set out in the *Anns* case.

Finally, it should be emphasized that in order to succeed in any negligent action, the plaintiff must show that the negligent conduct (or words) *caused* the loss. If the professional can show that the negligent words were not relied on, that the investment or action involved would have taken place in any case, there is no liability. Also, the liability of the defendant will be reduced by any contributory negligence that might be present on the part of the plaintiff.

For many business professionals, the risk of being held liable for *physical* injury is small because of the lack of any physical contact. When dealing with irate clients or colleagues, however, a confrontation might result in physical injury, exposing the professional to liability for battery. Obviously, such confrontations should be avoided. Furthermore, great care should be taken to ensure that premises are safe for the public, clients, and employees. The best method of risk avoidance is to carefully inspect the premises and examine the practices of the business, anticipating what might go wrong and taking steps to correct the problems.

**Practices should be adapted to avoid risk**

When false or inaccurate information is unintentionally conveyed by an expert (who should have known better), and a client suffers economic loss because they relied on that information, this constitutes negligent misrepresentation for which a professional can be held liable. Professionals are expected to be experts in their areas and should be certain that the information they provide is truthful and accurate. Even disclaimers will not protect the professional from liability if the court determines that he or she should have been aware of the fault. **Deceit** occurs when misleading words are said knowingly or without belief in their truth, and the person committing such **fraudulent misrepresentation** is liable for any damages suffered by someone relying on those words. Because the tort was committed intentionally, punitive damages might also be awarded by the courts. Often, professional liability insurance will provide coverage for negligent misrepresentation, but not for fraud. The deceitful professional will thus be personally responsible for damages in cases of deceit.

ON

## Fiduciary Duty and Breach of Trust

When a person places **trust** in a professional, the professional has a fiduciary obligation to act in the client's best interests. In the past, it was thought that this duty arose in only narrow circumstances where the fiduciary was in a position of power

**Fiduciary duty extended**

**Loyalty and good faith required**

**Information must not be disclosed**

to make decisions affecting the client and where the client was peculiarly vulnerable or at the mercy of the fiduciary. However, the Supreme Court in *Hodgkinson v. Simms* (Case Summary 4.20) seems to have extended this duty to any situation where one person advises another and reliance is placed on that advice. This is, in effect, a relationship built on the trust placed in the professional by the client, and when this is the case the duties on the fiduciary are significant. A fiduciary duty requires loyalty and good faith. It also requires the fiduciary to avoid any situation where her self-interest conflicts with that duty. It demands that one acts in the best interests of the person to whom the duty is owed. Any opportunity to acquire property or some other business interest or benefit that arises as a result of that relationship belongs to the client. Even when taking advantage of the opportunity will not harm the client, the fiduciary cannot do it. Any information coming to the fiduciary because of his or her position must remain confidential and not be disclosed. Nor can the fiduciary use such information for her own benefit. Fiduciaries must always put the interests of their clients ahead of their own.

### Case Summary 4.20

#### Conflict of Interest: *Hodgkinson v. Simms*[75]

Perhaps the most difficult and common violation of a fiduciary duty is the conflict of interest. This case is a classic example, where an accountant advised a client to invest in a real estate development while also acting for the developers. Such a conflict would require the accountant to at least disclose his role in the development to the investors. The defendant's failure to disclose his financial interest in the investment to those putting their trust in him was a breach of fiduciary duty that resulted in a judgment against him for more than $350 000.

**Fiduciary duty owed by directors and officers to company**

**Trust funds**

People acting as agents sometimes have the opportunity to take a commission from both the seller and the buyer. This may constitute a breach of fiduciary duty. Real estate agents, travel and insurance agents, professionals giving advice, and bankers and financial planners are all likely to find themselves in a fiduciary relationship. Even within organizations, **fiduciary duty** is common. Directors, officers, and managers owe a fiduciary duty to the company. Any situation where a person puts their affairs in the hands of a trusted adviser or employee can give rise to a fiduciary duty. Generally, ordinary employees are not fiduciaries but may inherit such an obligation, depending on the function they assume. Even where no fiduciary duty exists, specific aspects of it, such as the obligation to keep information confidential, may rest on the employees.

Often, funds from transactions or property are left in the hands of professionals for periods of time. Real estate agents, accountants, lawyers, and financial planners, for example, often find themselves in possession of large amounts of their clients' money. Any misuse of such property or funds is actionable as a breach of trust. Struggling professionals may be tempted to borrow from such funds, with every intention of paying the money back. No matter how sincere the intention this is a very serious violation, and the professional not only is liable for any loss but also is subject to disciplinary action within his professional organization. Criminal penalties may also be imposed.

75. [1994] 3 S.C.R. 377.

The fiduciary duty goes far beyond the avoidance of negligence and can be the greatest potential risk to a business if it is not taken seriously. The subject of fiduciary duty will be discussed again in the chapters devoted to employment, agency, and business organizations.

## Insurance

Professionals find themselves in the position where it is vitally important to have **liability insurance** (sometimes called "errors and omissions" insurance). The premiums associated with such insurance can be a significant cost of carrying on business and some may be tempted to avoid the cost.

**Insurance reduces risk**

Insurance is required for professionals practising in limited liability partnerships (see Chapter 13 for more details). Lawyers and accountants may require insurance as a condition of practice. Law societies often arrange for coverage for their members, and a lawyer cannot practise without it. Problems often arise as to the type of coverage acquired. Insurers will cover **negligence** on the part of the insured but often will not cover **fraud** or **breach of trust.** This can cause great difficulties when a person is held responsible for the frauds committed by his or her partner. The type of policy might also be important. Some policies cover only claims that have been made during the period of coverage. If the coverage is allowed to lapse and claims are then made, even if for events that happened during the period of coverage, the insurer will likely not be required to pay.

**Professionals often require insurance**

The courts have recently been stricter in their interpretation of the insurer's obligations. With the increased risk caused by the expansion of liability to third parties for negligent words and for economic loss, it is not surprising that the premiums have been rising at an accelerated rate.

A service typically provided by the insurer is to arrange for legal representation for the insured professional when litigation does arise. This is normally done to ensure that the interests of the insurance company are protected along with those of the insured, since the insurer will have to pay if liability is established. Because of the significant costs of litigation, malpractice actions involving professionals require the commitment of significant resources, even if the professional wins. It has been suggested that professional malpractice is an ideal area to be handled by the mechanisms for alternative dispute resolution discussed in Chapter 2. (Insurance will be covered as a general topic in Chapter 12.)

**Problems have increased significantly**

## Professional Disciplinary Bodies

Many professionals are members of and are regulated by self-governing professional bodies. Examples are the Law Society, the Medical Association, the Teachers' Association, and the various accounting organizations. Most of these bodies are created under provincial legislation that gives them varying degrees of control over the practice, as well as the individuals offering that kind of service. The highest degree of control, as found in such organizations as the Law Society or Medical Association, is the licensing function. No one can carry on the activities associated with the practice of law or medicine without being a member in good standing of the relevant association. The accounting bodies have somewhat less control, being able to restrict, for example, who can call themselves a chartered accountant (CA) or a certified general accountant (CGA) but not people who offer accounting services yet do not claim to have a professional designation. Some organizations are completely voluntary and have no authority over their

**Some professional bodies exercise significant control**

members. Practising professionals should determine just how important it is to belong to an organization and the kind of power that body has over them.

**Power of suspension**

All of these organizations, even the voluntary ones, have the power to determine who can join them. They also have the power to suspend or expel members, if the situation warrants. Where membership in the organization determines a person's right to practise, as is the case with the Law Society, suspension or expulsion can destroy that person's career and poses a greater threat than a malpractice lawsuit. The professional bodies set standards of conduct, both as to ethical practice and relating to quality of practice. They also typically set educational qualifications and continuing training requirements that must be met in order to maintain membership.

When these bodies find a problem, either as the result of a complaint against a member or through their own auditing process, a disciplinary process may be initiated. Since these are self-governing bodies, the actual process will vary. These bodies are administrative tribunals, so whether they acquire their power through government statute or regulation they must adhere to the rules of procedural fairness (as described in Chapter 3) or their decision will be subject to judicial review.

**Must act fairly or decision can be challenged**

Basically, what is needed is a fair hearing. This requires clear notice to the member of when and where the hearing is to be held and notice as to the nature of the complaint and the charge that must be answered. There must also be sufficient time provided for the member to prepare that answer.

At the hearing, certain requirements must be met. The member must be given a chance to face his accusers, if that is necessary to determine the matter. He must be given the opportunity to hear all the evidence against him and answer it. He must be able to put his side forward. The decision makers must be bias-free, must hear all the evidence presented, and must base their decision only on that evidence. Usually, the member has the right to be represented by counsel, although this is not always the case. Any statutory provisions must be adhered to. Where internal procedural practices have been established, they also must be adhered to. Where legislation is involved, the statute must be in compliance with the *Charter of Rights and Freedoms,* and the process and decision of the disciplinary body must not violate any human rights legislation in place in that jurisdiction. Finally, the penalty itself must be within the power of the disciplinary body to administer. Should hearings before these bodies fall short of these requirements, the disciplined member may have the right to have the decision overturned.

**Charter may apply**

**Compliance with human rights statutes**

**Penalties, suspension, expulsion**

The penalties that can be imposed by these tribunals are limited usually to suspension or expulsion from the professional organization, possibly with upgrading requirements or some other qualification such as supervision by a colleague before practice can be resumed. Suspension or expulsion can be devastating to the practitioner, much more significant than a large damage award in a malpractice action. To the public, however, this is often seen as just a minor penalty. It is a difficult part of the governing body's responsibilities to balance these different perceptions of the severity of the penalties imposed. Professionals cannot incorporate to shield themselves from personal liability. At best, they may be permitted to form professional corporations (PCs) or practise through limited liability partnerships (LLPs). But shareholders and partners in such organizations are still exposed to personal liability to varying degrees.

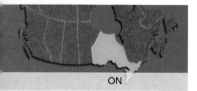

ON

The governing bodies may also find themselves the object of a professional malpractice action. It is their function to ensure that a certain level of competency and ethical practice is maintained among the members. If someone is cheated or hurt by the incompetence of a member of that society, she may turn to the society itself, claiming that it has failed in its duty to protect the public from the wrongdoer.

### Case Summary 4.21

#### *Schilling v. Certified General Accountant Association of British Columbia*[76]

In this case, a member of the Certified General Accountants Association was under disciplinary review for misconduct when he resigned from the organization. Prior to this time, the plaintiffs had placed their entire life savings in his care. About a year after his resignation as a CGA he absconded with these funds, leaving the plaintiffs with nothing. They sued the CGA Association, claiming that the body had failed to protect the public (and themselves specifically) by failing to provide notification of the resignation and that the accountant was no longer a member in good standing. The plaintiffs claimed as well that the Association had failed do anything to ensure that he was no longer presenting himself as a CGA. The Court agreed, and the CGA Association had to reimburse the plaintiffs for their losses. The decision, however, was overturned. The appellate court held that no duty of care was owed to the plaintiffs, for it was not foreseeable that they would rely on the CGA certification in deciding whether to entrust their money to this "investment adviser."

Note, however, that other professional societies do go further toward protecting the public. The Law Society of Alberta, for example, requires its members to contribute financially to an Assurance Fund. Then, if one of its members misappropriates a client's funds, that client can seek reimbursement for his pecuniary loss out of that fund. In the *Petrashuyk* case, where a lawyer had absconded with monies entrusted to him by his client (his mother!), the client sought and eventually obtained reimbursement from the Assurance Fund.[77]

In addition to establishing licensing, certification, training, and disciplinary standards, these organizations also arrange for malpractice insurance for their members. Another significant role played by these organizations lies in public education. For example, Law Societies hold "law for laypeople" seminars to promote public awareness of the law and educate the public on various legal matters. Of course, all this costs money, and belonging to these professional organizations typically requires the payment of significant annual fees.

## Other Business Torts

People involved in business activities can find themselves faced with tortious liability for their conduct in all the categories of torts discussed in this chapter. Businesses that deal directly with the public, especially in the service industries such as restaurants, hotels, and retailers, may find their employees becoming involved in altercations with customers in the course of their work. Such altercations can result in actions against the business on the basis of vicarious liability for

**Intentional torts important in some businesses**

---

76. [1995] 2 W.W.R. 115 (B.C.S.C.); reversed on appeal, [1996] 7 W.W.R. 268 (B.C.C.A.); leave to appeal refused, [1996] S.C.C.A. No. 397.

77. *Petrashuyk v. Law Society of Alberta* (1983), 50 A.R. 386 (Q.B.), rev'd (1984), 58 A.R. 94 (C.A.), rev'd, [1988] 2 S.C.R. 385.

assault and battery, negligence, trespass, and even false imprisonment. When business premises visited by customers or the public are involved, there can be actions for negligence based on occupiers' liability.

**Negligence more common**

Much more likely, depending on the nature of the business, are actions for negligence for injury or damage caused by improper performance of the service supplied or the product sold. As discussed above, even if only careless words are involved and the business is restricted to giving advice and opinions, there can now be liability to both clients and third parties who suffer financially from relying on those words. Those providing consulting services to businesses and private individuals, such as bankers, accountants, auditors, lawyers, financial advisers, engineers, and architects, are only a few of the professionals who find themselves increasingly vulnerable to damage actions for both tort and breach of contract. If information disseminated is false and causes damage to someone's reputation, the business can be sued for defamation.

In addition to the torts already discussed in this chapter, there are other unique ones that can be important to businesses: inducing breach of contract; deceit; conversion; passing off; and defamation with respect to a product, called **injurious falsehood.** Most of these are associated with unfair or overaggressive competition.

**Inducing breach of contract actionable**

**Inducing breach of contract** usually involves an employer persuading an employee of another business to leave that employment and work for him or her. This practice is common when that employee has special knowledge about trade secrets or customer lists or has a special relationship with customers enabling him or her to bring them to the new job. If the employee is contractually committed to stay in that position of employment for a period of time or not to disclose the secret information, he will breach that contractual obligation if he does so. For the other employer to persuade the employee to commit such a breach, usually with financial incentives, violates a duty not to intervene in that relationship. As a result, the new employer may face the tort action of inducing breach of contract. For the victim to sue for inducing breach of contract, he must be able to establish that there was a contract that was breached and that the person being sued knew about the contract and intentionally induced the breach. The victim likely has the right to sue the employee for breach, but it is often preferable to sue the other employer because they tend to have "deeper pockets" (the funds to make the action worthwhile), whereas suing the employee is likely not worth the effort.

This type of tort can also be committed when one business induces another to breach contractual relations with someone else, as when a supplier is persuaded to abandon one customer in favour of another or a customer is persuaded to breach its contract with a competing supplier. An interesting application of this tort is to sue a director of a corporation for inducing the corporation to breach a contract it had with the plaintiff.

### Case Summary 4.22

#### From One Pocket to Another: *369413 Alberta Ltd. v. Pocklington*[78]

When Gainers, a corporation beset with financial difficulties, breached its agreement with the Province of Alberta, Alberta opted to sue the corporation's director, Peter Pocklington. Alberta claimed that Pocklington "induced" the breach by

---

78. (2000), 271 A.R. 280 (C.A.).

signing a director's resolution transferring certain shares owned by Gainers (valued in the millions) to his own company, Pocklington Holdings Ltd., for $100. Gainers had earlier agreed not to sell or dispose of its assets without the prior written consent of Alberta. Pocklington (the infamous owner of the Edmonton Oilers hockey franchise) was the sole director of Gainers. One day before Alberta gave notice of its intention to exercise its rights under its security agreements Pocklington signed the resolution, thus inducing a breach of Gainers' promise not to dispose of the shares. The Court awarded the province $4.7 million in damages as against Pocklington. Certainly, the province may have sued Gainers for breach of contract, but suing the party that induced the breach may have resulted in a judgment against the party with "deeper pockets."

A related problem exists when one business intentionally interferes with the operation of a competitor. When this is done through ordinary competition there is no complaint, but sometimes that competition becomes unfair. Examples of unfair competition are one business seeking confidential information from the employees of another; intimidation to discourage someone from opening a business in an area or to sell a particular product at a lower price; or even where one restaurant sends employees to the door of another to redirect customers to the first. These are all examples of improper interference in business. Most of these kinds of problems are dealt with by the federal *Competition Act,*[79] and this will be discussed in Chapter 9.

The tort of **deceit** involves the fraudulent and intentional misleading of another person, causing damage. This is where one person lies to another, causing loss. It is an intentional tort and one of the few situations where the court will entertain an application for punitive damages. An award of punitive damages is an order that one party pay money to the other, not to compensate the victim but to punish the wrongdoer and to discourage that kind of conduct. The case of *Derry v. Peek*[80] established that deceit did not require actual knowledge that what was stated was incorrect. It was enough that the person making the statement did not believe it to be true. This is a common wrong committed in business and will be dealt with in Chapter 7 under "Fraudulent Misrepresentation."

**Fraud or deceit actionable**

**Conversion** involves one person intentionally appropriating the goods of another person for her own purposes. Theft of goods, in addition to being a crime, is also actionable under the tort of conversion. Conversion also takes place when someone sells or otherwise wrongfully disposes of goods belonging to someone else, or when a person acquires possession of goods through deceit and the goods are damaged or destroyed to the extent that they are no longer of any value to the rightful owner. In such circumstances the courts will usually award damages as a remedy, the person converting the goods in effect being forced to purchase them. The courts also have the power to order the return of the goods if that is a more appropriate remedy. Of course, any direct intentional interference causing damage to the goods of another is a **trespass to chattels,** and other remedies may be available as a result. When someone "keys" the paint on a new car or kicks the door in, they have committed trespass to chattels and are liable to pay compensation and possibly punitive damages to the victim.

**Conversion actionable**

79. R.S.C. 1985, c. C-34.

80. (1889), 14 App. Cas. 337 at 374 (H.L.).

**Passing off actionable**

A **passing-off action** is appropriate when a business or product is presented to the public in such a way as to lead the public to believe that the product is being provided by another. When imitation Rolex watches are sold as the real thing, or when a restaurant adopts the golden arches logo leading the public to believe it is part of the McDonald's chain when it is not, the tort of passing off has been committed. The court can award damages in these circumstances, but an injunction or an order that the offending product be delivered to the plaintiff for destruction may be a more appropriate remedy. This will be discussed in more detail in Chapter 16 under "Intellectual Property."

**Injurious falsehood actionable**

The tort of **injurious falsehood** will also be discussed in Chapter 16. This tort takes place when one person attacks the reputation of another's product or business. When a person spreads a false rumour that the wine manufactured by a competitor is adulterated with some other substance, or that his business is about to become bankrupt, she has committed an injurious falsehood. Although this tort is often called **trade slander** or **product defamation,** it must be distinguished from the tort of defamation that involves injury to the personal reputation of the injured party. Injurious falsehood deals with the reputation and value of a person's property. It may reflect negatively on the quality of the product, or it may relate to title. When a person falsely claims that the seller does not own what he is selling or that the product is in violation of patent or copyright, he has uttered an actionable injurious falsehood.

### Case Summary 4.23

#### Unfounded Accusations Can Be Costly: Procor Ltd. v. U.S.W.A.[81]

Procor Ltd., a manufacturer that exports much of its product to the United States, was involved in a serious and difficult labour dispute with its employees. In the air of hostility created by the labour dispute, members of the union accused the company of customs fraud, saying that it was exporting Japanese products into the United States (marked as products made in Canada) without disclosing the fact. This caused an intensive and disruptive investigation into the operations of the company, even stopping production for a time. In addition, there was considerable negative publicity. The investigation exonerated the company, showing the union members to be wrong and the accusations to be unfounded. Procor Ltd. then sued the union and the members who had made the accusations for injurious falsehood. These defendants had made statements that they knew, or should have known, to be false to customs agents, thus instigating the investigation.

In addition to the presence of a false statement made to a party causing damage, it is also necessary to establish malice to succeed in an injurious falsehood action. *Malice* is usually described as a dishonest or improper motive. While the Judge did not find that they lied outright, he did find that the union officials were "willfully blind to the truth" when they made these false statements to the customs officials. That was enough to establish malice. In addition, their motive was not to act as good citizens but to further their labour dispute and vent their frustrations and hostility toward the company. This was an improper purpose supporting the finding of malice. The Judge also found that the defendants had participated in a conspiracy to accomplish these goals and were, as a result, liable

81. (1989), 65 D.L.R. (4th) 287 (Ont. H.C.J.).

to pay $100 000 general damages and a further $100 000 punitive damages. In a society like ours, we have to be careful about what we say about others. This case is an example of the difficulties that a few misplaced words can cause.

A particular problem that arises in business is the issue of **privacy.** Invasion of a person's privacy may take the form of a physical intrusion, surveillance, misuse of an image or name, or access to information. Businesses often use information that people would like to keep private. They sometimes use images or likenesses to promote products without permission. In common law, there is no tort of invasion of privacy, but several provinces have made interfering with a person's privacy a tort.[82] Others, including the federal government,[83] have passed statutes restricting the use of private information with penalties limited to those set out in the statute. The federal government has appointed a privacy commissioner to enforce its statute. Even where there is no privacy tort, the action complained of may qualify as another kind of tort. For example, where a business uses a person's image, name, or likeness to promote its product without permission, there is an innuendo communicated that the person has endorsed the product. That is a false statement and is actionable as defamation.

Businesses are often tempted to extract private information from their employees or even to use surveillance techniques to obtain information about them. Telephones and electronic mail are sometimes monitored. Medical information, political or religious affiliations, treatment for alcohol- or drug-related problems, even mental conditions, all may be of considerable interest. Surveillance for detecting theft and monitoring other security concerns is also common. This is dangerous territory, as it may violate statutory rights to privacy in place in that jurisdiction. It may also be a violation of human rights legislation, depending on the kind of information being sought and the methods used to obtain it.

Finally, it must be noted that particular problems arise through the use of the internet. Because the internet is uncontrolled, people can say whatever they want. All sorts of salacious, mischievous, defamatory, and obscene material appears on the internet every day. Confidential information may be involved. Defamation and injurious falsehood may take place. Privacy may be invaded. Fraud and negligent misrepresentations may be made. What can the victim do? The person who made the offending comment is liable for what they say, but often this is a useless remedy because either the wrongdoer has no money or it is not possible to determine who is responsible. Can the online service provider, the people who operate the internet server, or the operators of the particular website or chat room be sued for allowing their facilities to be used in this way? Arguably, the people who have direct control will have some responsibility, but the larger service providers, such as AOL Time Warner Inc., may be treated more like a telephone company that does not have direct responsibility for the calls, unless it has been asked to intervene. These questions have yet to be clarified in Canadian law.

**Protection of privacy legislated**

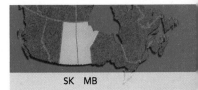

SK   MB

**Privacy and the internet**

---

82. Note that B.C., Saskatchewan, Manitoba, and Newfoundland and Labrador have such legislation.

83. *Privacy Act,* R.S.C. 1985, c. P-21.

**Case Summary 4.24**

**Torts in Cyberspace: *Braintech, Inc. v. Kostiuk*[84]**

A case heard in British Columbia helps to clarify some of the problems regarding jurisdiction in internet-related disputes. In this case, a Vancouver firm sued a Vancouver investor for defamation over comments he made about the company in a chat room at Silicon Investor. The lawsuit was filed in a Texas court (even though both litigants were in Vancouver, and there was no active presence of the plaintiff in Texas) primarily because the court in that jurisdiction has a reputation for making huge damage awards. The defendant did not defend himself, believing that the court had no jurisdiction in the case. The plaintiff was awarded US$300 000 in damages. When the successful plaintiff took the judgment to the British Columbia court to have it enforced, the defendant argued that the Texas court had no jurisdiction in the matter and was not the appropriate forum to hear the case. He lost at the trial level but that decision was reversed on appeal.

It was argued that the case should have been heard where there was a "real and substantial connection" to the matter in dispute. Because of the nature of the internet, the only connection with Texas was that a Texas resident could have logged on to an out-of-state internet site and read the alleged libel. But that was true of any location in any country, and to allow any location to have such jurisdiction would have a "crippling effect" on the internet and freedom of expression. The danger is having several different parallel actions going on at the same time. The action should be brought according to American law in a jurisdiction where there was a "real and substantial presence," or according to Canadian law if that was the jurisdiction having a "real and substantial connection" to the case. The jurisdiction demonstrating that connection was British Columbia and not Texas. The Supreme Court of Canada refused leave to appeal. The decision is important because it spells out under what conditions a given jurisdiction can rule on an internet dispute and, by extension, which set of laws ought to apply to cyberspace behaviour.

Note, however, that the use of the internet here was passive. An active use of the internet occurs where the parties are using the internet to communicate, negotiating and engaging in commercial activities. In such circumstances, do you think the legal outcome ought to be different? Could several jurisdictions then have a "real and substantial" connection to the case?

# Summary

## Tort law

- Protects people from intentional or careless interference with their person, property, or reputation.
- Aims at compensating the victim.

84. (1999), 171 D.L.R. (4th) 46 (B.C.C.A.); leave to appeal to S.C.C. refused, [1999] S.C.C.A. No. 236.

## Intentional torts

- Assault and battery—defences are consent or self-defence (reasonable force).
- Trespass—temporary or permanent intrusion on someone else's property.
- False imprisonment—restraint of a person by someone without authority.
- Defamation—a false, published statement that discredits a person.
  - Libel is written defamation; slander is spoken.
  - Defences—absolute privilege, qualified privilege, truth, and fair comment.

## Negligence

- Inadvertent conduct falling below an acceptable standard of behaviour.
- Plaintiff must establish:
  - **A** duty of care was owed—using reasonable foreseeability test;
  - **B**reach of duty—by conduct falling below the level expected from a reasonable person;
  - **C**ausation—"but for" test establishes physical link; remoteness test used to determine if the injury or damage was unforeseeable;
  - **D**amage—must show that material damage resulted from the conduct.
- Defences to negligence
  - If there is contributory negligence, courts may apportion the losses.
  - If the plaintiff voluntarily assumed the risk, the defendant has a complete defence.

## Product liability

- Based on negligence.
- Manufacturers owe a duty to consumers of their products.

## Professional liability

- Also usually based on negligence.
- Professionals may be liable for:
  - false or inaccurate information that causes economic loss
  - breach of fiduciary duty or of contractual obligations

## Other business torts

- inducing breach of contract.
- deceit.
- conversion.
- passing off.
- injurious falsehood.

---

## QUESTIONS

1. Explain what is meant by the statement "A tort is a civil wrong."

2. How do the courts usually determine what standard people must meet to avoid being declared negligent?

3. Distinguish between assault and battery.

4. How do doctors avoid liability for the tort of battery when operating on or otherwise treating patients?

5. What limitations are there on the right of self-defence when people are defending themselves against an attack?

6. Describe the situations in which battery may be justified.

7. What are the necessary elements that must be present for a person to be classified as a trespasser?

8. What may the proprietor of a business do when faced with an unruly patron?

9. Imprisonment can take the form of confinement, arrest, or submission to authority. Explain.

10. What must be established to sue successfully for false imprisonment?

11. Distinguish between libel and slander and explain the significance of the distinction.

12. Define the terms "innuendo" and "qualified privilege."

13. List and explain what a plaintiff must establish to succeed in a negligence action.

14. What remedies are available when a tort is committed intentionally that may not be available when the conduct is unintentional?

15. What test do courts use to determine whether the defendant owed to the plaintiff a duty to be careful?

16. What problem earlier faced in product liability cases was overcome by the decision made in *Donoghue v. Stevenson*?

17. Distinguish between misfeasance and nonfeasance and explain the significance of the difference in tort law.

18. Explain how the test used to determine the standard of care required from professionals is different from the test used to determine the standard of care required generally.

19. Explain how the standard of care that an occupier must exercise to a person using the property has changed in recent years.

20. How does the "but for" test help to satisfy the requirements of causation?

21. Explain how the effect of contributory negligence has been modified in recent years.

22. Why is the case of *Haig v. Bamford* considered important in the recent development of tort law?

23. Identify the legal principles related to professional liability established by the British *Anns* case.

24. Discuss the tort implications of making false claims against another person or company.

25. Privacy concerns are becoming more problematic in the technological age. What tort principles protect the rights of individuals in this area?

26. Consider the problems related to jurisdiction where the internet is the means of communicating a defamatory message.

## CASES

### 1. *Edwards v. Tracy Starr's Shows (Edmonton) Ltd.*, (1987), 61 Alta. L.R. (2d) 233 (C.A.)

In this case, a man and his friend went to a nightclub for dinner and a few drinks and to see the show. Toward the end of their visit, both men went to the washroom. When they returned, the plaintiff tripped over a step that protruded into the aisle from the stage, fell, and was seriously injured. It is likely that had he been watching where he was going, he would have seen the step and avoided it, though there was some dispute about the lighting. The judge in this case said that the plaintiff was distracted by an exotic dancer on the stage and that was why he fell. Explain the liability of the nightclub in these circumstances and any defences they might have. Would your answer be different in a jurisdiction with no occupiers' liability act?

### 2. *Kovacs v. Ontario Jockey Club*, (1995), 126 D.L.R. (4th) 576 (Ont. (Gen. Div.)).

Mr. Kovacs tried to use a credit voucher that he had obtained from one racetrack at another, both owned and operated by the Ontario Jockey Club. Because of some misunderstanding, he was identified as a person who had committed a fraud on the racetrack. He was approached by two security guards and was asked to go to the office to discuss the matter. Mr. Kovacs felt that he had no choice, and he accompanied them. The matter was straightened out in about 20 minutes, and he went on his way. Mr. Kovacs sued for false imprisonment. What is the likely outcome?

### 3. *Conrad v. Snair*, (1995), 142 N.S.R. (2d) 224 (N.S.C.A.).

Mr. Snow operated and owned a 10-metre sailboat, which he had built by hand and which he moored along with several other boats in Echo Bay. Mr. Snair was visiting his former girlfriend Ms. Conrad, who owned property in Echo Bay, in his 4.6-metre Boston Whaler runabout. Mr. Snow's vessel was already in the bay when Mr. Snair arrived. Dinner was served overlooking the bay containing the various boats, and later that night Mr. Snair took Ms. Conrad in the Boston Whaler over to the yacht club, in the process of which he had to pass by Mr. Snow's boat. Shortly after midnight, on returning from the yacht club, Mr. Snair operated his boat at high speed and collided with Mr. Snow's sailboat. Ms. Conrad suffered severe brain damage. The Canadian collision regulations require that sailboats moored in this fashion hang a white light from the mast; Mr. Snow had failed to post such a light. Several other vessels in the bay had also failed to post such lights, and it seemed to be the practice in that area not to bother. Ms. Conrad sued Mr. Snair as well as Mr. Snow for negligence. Explain who would be held responsible for the accident.

### 4. *Sara's Pyrohy Hut v. Brooker* (1993), 141 A.R. 42 (C.A.).

A freelance restaurant reviewer's review of the plaintiff restaurant was broadcast on radio. In his conversation with the radio host, the reviewer described his meal as bland, overpriced, and inferior to a meal that one could expect to receive at a Ukrainian friend's home. A number of problems with the service and the food were mentioned. The reviewer also commented that after a visit, a customer might conclude that the co-owner's dog, "Sara" (the restaurant's namesake), had been in the kitchen. No apology was made by the reviewer in response to the co-owner's complaint. The restaurant sued the reviewer, the radio host, and the CBC network for damages for defamation. At issue was whether the defence of fair comment applied, for the court found the comments were capable of conveying a defamatory meaning to reasonable people. Discuss the probable outcome.

### 5. *Dixon v. Deacon Morgan McEwan Easson* (1989), 62 D.L.R. (4th) 175 (B.C.S.C.).

Mr. Dixon was an investor who chose to invest $1.2 million in National Business Systems when the share price was $12.89 per share. These shares went up in price somewhat, but before he could sell the Securities Commission suspended trading. When trading resumed, the shares sold at about $3. Dixon had invested on the strength of financial statements, including one marked "Consolidated Statements of Income and Retained Earnings (Audited)," which had been audited by the defendants. In fact, these statements were based on fraudulent information supplied by the management of National Business Systems to indicate annual profits of $14 million, when the company had in fact lost $33 million. There is no question that the accounting firms involved in the audit were negligent for not detecting the inaccuracy. Mr. Dixon sued the accounting firm for negligence. Nothing on the document indicated who the auditors were, and the statements had been prepared without the auditors knowing that they would be used by an investor, such as Mr. Dixon. Did the auditors owe a duty to Mr. Dixon to be careful? If the auditors had known that the statements were being prepared to attract investors, would this affect your answer?

# Formation of Contracts

## CHAPTER HIGHLIGHTS

- The requirements of a valid contract
- Offer and acceptance—the necessary conditions
- Consideration—essential ingredient in a valid contract
- The principles of promissory estoppel and *quantum meruit*
- When a contract requires a seal

Along with torts, the second area of private law affecting businesspeople—and by far the most important—is the law of contracts. The world of commerce and most business relationships are based on contracts. In this and the following three chapters, we will discuss how a contract is formed, various factors that affect those contracts, and how they can come to an end. This chapter introduces the first two of the five essential elements necessary for valid contracts, and the other three will be discussed in the following chapter.

# The Contractual Relationship

**Exchange of promises enforceable in court**

Knowledge of contract law is vital to all businesspeople because most commercial transactions have contracts at their base. A **contract** is a voluntary exchange of promises, creating obligations that if defaulted on can be enforced and remedied by the courts.

It is important to understand that when drawing up a contract people create and define their own rules and obligations, as opposed to other areas of the law, such as torts, where the rules and obligations are imposed on them. A valid contract creates a situation that enables parties to the contract to predict with some certainty their future relationship because each party knows that the courts will hold them to their agreement. Although the courts will enforce a valid contract after it has been created, what the parties agree to in the first place is generally unrestricted, creating an environment often referred to as *freedom of contract*. People can enter into almost any kind of contractual agreement they want to, as long as the contract meets the common law requirements that will be discussed in this and the following chapters. Although the law of contracts is found primarily in the common law or case law, there are a number of specialized areas where legislation has been enacted that modifies, restricts, or replaces these common law principles, sometimes interfering with this freedom to contract. Examples include the sale of goods, consumer protection, employment, partnerships, corporations, and real property, which will be the subjects of later chapters.

When we study contract law, the focus is on the problems, and there is a danger of concluding that most contracts go bad. In fact, most contractual agreements are honoured or resolved to the mutual satisfaction of the parties. The courts become involved only when a conflict arises. The law has been shaped by the courts' resolution of those disputes.

## Ingredients of a Contract

Not all agreements are contracts. To qualify as a valid contract, an agreement must meet certain basic qualifications. They are:

**1. Consensus**. Parties to a contract must reach a mutual agreement to commit themselves to a certain transaction. They are assumed to approach the agreement from equal bargaining positions, free to enter it as they choose. The process by which this agreement is reached usually involves an offer and an acceptance, although consensus can be inferred.

**2. Consideration**. There must be a commitment on the part of both parties to do something or to abstain from doing something. The consideration is the price each is willing to pay to participate in the contract.

**3. Capacity**. Parties to a contract must be legally capable of understanding and entering into the bargain. Limitations in contracting capacity have been placed on infants, insane or intoxicated persons, aliens, and, in some instances, Native peoples and corporations.

**4. Legality**. The object and consideration involved in the agreement must be legal and not against public policy.

**5. Intention**. Both parties must be serious when striking the bargain, and both must intend that legally enforceable obligations will result from it.

It should be noted here that although the general rule is that an agreement reached verbally between parties is every bit as binding as a written one, legislation has been passed requiring that certain types of contracts be supported by evidence *in writing* before they can be enforced in the courts. For convenience, this limited requirement of writing will also be discussed along with the five essential ingredients of contract.

## Terms and Definitions

Before addressing these elements of a contract in more detail, it is necessary to outline some basic terminology used in the discussion of contractual obligations.

### Formal and Simple Contracts

A formal contract is one that is sealed. Traditionally, a seal involved making an impression in sealing wax. A modern seal normally consists of a paper wafer affixed to a document by the party to be bound, but any mark or impression will do. Simple contracts, sometimes called **parol contracts,** may be verbal or written but are not under seal.

## Express and Implied Contracts

An **express contract** is one in which the parties have expressly stated their agreement, either verbally or in writing. An **implied contract** is inferred from the conduct of the parties. When people deposit coins in vending machines, it can be inferred that they intend to create a contractual relationship, and thus an implied contract is in force. Portions of an express contract may also be implied.

**Contracts may be inferred**

## Valid, Void, and Voidable Contracts

A **valid contract** is one that is legally binding on both parties. A **void contract** does not qualify as a legally binding contract because of some missing ingredient. If the parties to a void contract thought they were bound and followed the agreement, the courts would try to put the parties back to their original positions. A **voidable contract** does exist and has legal effect, but one of the parties has the option to end the contract. This distinction between void and voidable can have important implications for outsiders to the contract who have acquired an interest in the subject matter. If the original contract is void the goods must be returned, but if it is only voidable, the outsider has acquired good title and can keep the goods.

**A void contract is no contract**

**A voidable contract is valid but one party has the right to escape**

## Unenforceable and Illegal Contracts

An example of an **unenforceable contract** is one that is required to be in writing under the *Statute of Frauds* and is not. It may be good and valid in all other respects, but the courts will not help either party to force the other to perform such a contract. As well, once it has been performed, the courts will not help either party get out of it.

**Court won't enforce unenforceable contract**

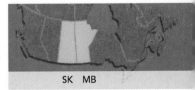

SK   MB

An **illegal contract** is one that involves the performance of an unlawful act. It is void, and the parties to such an agreement cannot be required to perform it. If the contract has been performed or partially performed, the court, because of the moral taint, normally will not assist either party to undo it by returning them to their original positions, as would usually be the case in a void contract. For example, when a deposit has been paid, the court will not order its return, nor will it require property to be returned, even when one of the parties has been enriched at the other's expense. Of course, the courts will help a person who is innocent of any wrongdoing even when the contract is illegal.

**Illegal contract is void**

The status of these two types of agreements, then, is quite different. The unenforceable contract is valid, and the illegal contract is void. The two are handled in a similar fashion by the courts; however, the courts are more sympathetic where an unenforceable contract is involved and are more likely to help the parties when disputes arise than is the case with an illegal contract.

## Bilateral and Unilateral Contracts

A **bilateral contract** is one in which both parties make commitments and assume obligations. There is no exchange of promises in a **unilateral contract.** This type of contract comes into effect when one party actually performs what has been requested by the other as the subject matter of the contract. A reward is an example of a unilateral contract. It is not until the lost item is returned that the offer is accepted and the contract created. Thus, a bilateral contract involves an exchange of promises, whereas a unilateral contract involves a promise followed by an act.

**Unilateral contract performance is acceptance**

# Consensus

The essence of a contract is, at least in theory, the *meeting of the minds* of the contracting parties. The two parties must have a common will in relation to the subject matter of their negotiations, and they must have reached an agreement. They must share an understanding of the bargain struck and be willing to commit themselves to the terms of that contract.

**Agreement reached—bargain struck**

In practice, however, it is not necessary that both parties fully understand or even have read all the terms of the contract. Few people thoroughly read the major contracts they enter into, such as insurance policies, leases, and loans, and of those who do, few fully understand the specific meaning of the documents. The law does not recognize the excuse that one of the contracting parties did not read the contract or that he or she did not understand it.

**Terms must be clear and unambiguous**

The only requirement is that the terms of the agreement must be clear and unambiguous and that both parties had an opportunity to know of them. It is only when the terms themselves can be taken more than one way that the court may decide that there has been no consensus and thus no contract. Case Summary 5.1 illustrates the problems with vague or ambiguous wording in a contract.

## Case Summary 5.1

### Effect of a Vague Interim Agreement: *McIntyre v. Pietrobon*[1]

Mr. and Mrs. McIntyre decided to purchase a house being offered for sale by the Pietrobons. They signed an interim agreement and paid a deposit of $10 000. The interim agreement contained a standard provision, which stated, "Subject to purchaser obtaining satisfactory personal financing." The McIntyres did not obtain financing; they did not even try. They simply changed their minds and wanted their $10 000 deposit back. The Pietrobons would not return the money because they claimed that the McIntyres had breached their contract and had forfeited their right to it. The McIntyres sued. The Judge held that since the clause was so vague there was no agreement, and ordered the return of the money.

People in the real estate business and other commercial activities must be well versed in the law and must be very careful when drawing up these contracts, making sure that all terms are clear and concise.

Obviously, mistakes happen, and some very complex rules, which we will discuss later, have been developed to handle them. Nevertheless, contract law is based on the assumption that the culmination of the bargaining process occurs when one party states its position in the form of an offer in the expectation that the other party, through acceptance, will make a similar commitment to be bound by the terms of that offer. It should be stressed that a valid offer and an acceptance are not always obvious, and yet, from the conduct of the parties or other factors, it is clear that the parties have a mutual understanding between them. In such circumstances, the courts are willing to imply the existence of a contract, and no evidence of a specific identifiable offer and acceptance is required.

---

1. (1987), 15 B.C.L.R. (2d) 350 (B.C.S.C.).

# Offer

The **offer** must contain all the terms to be included in the contract; all that is required of the other party is to give its consent or denial. The offer is a tentative promise on the part of one party to do whatever is set out, providing that the other party consents to do what is requested in return. When a sales person offers to sell a car to a customer for $5000, the offer is a tentative promise by the seller to deliver the car contingent on the customer's willingness to pay the $5000. The process of making an offer is the communication of a willingness to be bound by the terms and conditions stated in that offer.

**Offer—tentative promise**

This aspect of the offer can be confusing to those involved in commercial activities. People often have documents placed before them and are asked to sign "the contract" (for example, in transactions such as insurance or leases). In fact, at that stage the document is merely an offer. Only after it is accepted and signed can it be said to be the "contract," and even then it is probably only the written evidence of the contractual relationship between the parties. The offer must contain all significant terms of the proposed contract. The parties, the subject matter of the contract, any price to be paid, as well as any other important terms should all be stated in the offer.

**Offer—must include all important terms**

The courts do have the power to imply into contracts many of the insignificant terms the parties may not have considered, such as time of delivery, time of payment, and so on. Such terms must be incidental to the central agreement but consistent with the apparent intention of the parties. Courts will often turn to the common practice of the trade or industry to help them imply such terms. When goods are sold, the *Sale of Goods Act* sets out the terms to be implied when missing in the contract of sale. The sale of goods is a major topic discussed in Chapter 9. As mentioned, it is possible for the courts to infer the entire contract from the conduct of the parties, but if it is clear that important terms have been left out or are to be negotiated later, there is no contract.

**Some terms can be inferred**

## Case Summary 5.2

### An Agreement to Enter into a Contract Is Not Good Enough: *Bawitko Investments Ltd. v. Kernels Popcorn Ltd.*[2]

Kernels Popcorn Ltd. sold popcorn products in a number of specialty stores franchised in Canada and the United States. Anthony Passander, who represented Bawitko Investments Limited, negotiated with Kernels to open such a franchise at a particular location in Ontario. After some negotiation the parties shook hands, and the representative for Kernels said, "You've got a deal." But then the parties could not agree on what was to be included in the written contract, and Kernels pulled out. Passander sued to enforce the original oral agreement. While it is possible to have an enforceable oral agreement that will be formalized and put into writing, the Judge found that that did not happen here. The parties never did reach an agreement. The Judge stated that

> [W]hen the original contract is incomplete because essential provisions intended to govern the contractual relationship have not been settled or agreed upon; or the contract is too general or uncertain to be valid in itself and is dependent on the making of a formal contract; or the understanding or intention of the parties, even if there

---

2. (1991), 79 D.L.R. (4th) 97 (Ont. C.A.).

is no uncertainty as to the terms of their agreement, is that their legal obligations are to be deferred until a formal contract has been approved and executed, the original or preliminary agreement cannot constitute an enforceable contract. In other words, in such circumstances, the "contract to make a contract" is not a contract at all.

Do you think that this is a fair result from Bawitko's perspective? What about the expectations created?

**Interim agreement binding**

It must be emphasized that the parties can make it clear that they intend to put the agreement into a more formal document later and still be bound in contract so long as all of the important terms have been agreed upon. An **interim agreement** (agreement of purchase and sale) in a real estate transaction is an example of such a contract that is binding even though a more formal document will follow. A letter of intent will also be binding if all requirements are met. If a person does not want to be bound by such a letter, she should clearly state that in the document. The common practice of a particular industry will also affect just what constitutes a contract and at what stage it is considered binding.

**Contract not binding until condition satisfied**

It should also be noted that **subject-to clauses** often raise the same concerns. An offer may include a term making the contract conditional on some future event. A person may offer to purchase a house "subject to" the sale of their house. These types of provisions are not necessarily uncertain or ambiguous, unless the subject-to clause itself is uncertain, as would be the case if the sale were made "subject to my satisfaction," as in the *McIntyre v. Pietrobon* case discussed in Case Summary 5.1. If the terms of the offer are clear and nothing is left to be negotiated or agreed upon, the parties are bound to perform as agreed once the subject-to term has been satisfied.

**Note exception for service**

Some types of contractual relationships, often referred to as **quasi-contracts,** must be viewed as exceptions to the rule that important terms must be clear. These contracts involve requests for goods and services and will be discussed below along with *quantum meruit* under the heading "Request for Services."

### Invitation to Treat

An offer is usually made to an individual or to a group of people, but it is also possible to make an offer to the world at large, such as a notice offering a reward for information or the return of a lost item. Most newspaper, radio, television, and internet advertisements, however, are just **invitations to treat.** They are simply invitations to potential customers to engage in the process of negotiation, and as part of the prenegotiation process they have no legal effect. The typical process to create a contract is illustrated in Figure 5.1.

**Invitation not an offer**

It is sometimes difficult to distinguish between an offer and an invitation to treat. A newspaper ad stating "Automobile tires for sale, two for the price of one," is not an offer at all. The ad is meant to encourage the reader to visit the store and then make an offer to purchase some tires. Catalogues and personal ads in

**Figure 5.1 Typical Process to Create a Contract**

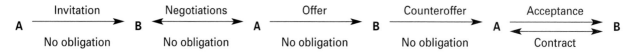

the classified section of a newspaper are also invitations to treat. According to the famous English case *Pharmaceutical Society of Great Britain v. Boots Cash Chemists (Southern), Ltd.,*[3] goods displayed on the shelves of self-service stores are also mere invitations to treat, even though the price of the items may be clearly marked.

With the display of such goods being merely an invitation, a customer might be tempted to switch the prices on items displayed for sale in a store. To do so, however, is a crime.[4] The reasoning is that the customer is only being *invited* to make an offer to purchase at the price displayed.

**Goods displayed on a shelf an invitation only**

## Offer by Conduct

A customer in a self-serve store brings the goods to be purchased to a cashier and places the goods and money on the counter. This is an offer implied by conduct. When a person hails a cab by the gesture of raising a hand and calling "Taxi!" this constitutes an offer. An auctioneer's comment, "Do I hear $50?" is merely an invitation to the customer to make an offer. When a person in the audience raises a hand or makes some other acceptable gesture, that is the offer, and the auctioneer is free to accept or reject it. A further question, "Do I hear $60?" is an invitation for more offers. The statement "Sold!" is an acceptance of the customer's offer. These are also examples of offers by conduct.

**Offer may be implied by conduct**

## Communication of an Offer

You can accept only an offer that has been made to you as an individual, to you as a member of a group, or to the world at large. You can't accept an offer made to someone else no matter how you learn about it. Also, you can accept only an offer you know about. If someone returns a lost item unaware that a reward has been offered, they have no claim to the reward because the offer has not been communicated.

**Only person(s) to whom the offer is made can accept**

**Offer must be communicated**

Even where two offers cross in the mail with both parties of the same mind there is no contract. If one party sent a letter offering to sell, and the other in another letter sent at the same time offered to buy a particular car for $500 there would be no contract. Neither could be an acceptance since neither party was aware of the other's offer.

It is also important to note that for an agreement to be binding all important terms must be disclosed to the offeree. In contracts with customers, merchants will often include exemption clauses that favour their own position or limit their liability. There are usually signs disclaiming responsibility for theft or damage to cars or contents posted in parking lots. Tickets to athletic events or for the use of sporting facilities will often include terms disclaiming responsibility for injury, damages, or loss of personal property by theft. In both cases, the term is binding only when it has been reasonably brought to the attention of the patron at the time the contract is made. The sign in the parking lot must be placed in a well-lit location where the driver will see it before or at the time the contract is made; this is usually at the cashier's booth or vending machine, along with other strategic locations on the lot. When the clause is on the back of a ticket, there must be a reference on the front of the ticket drawing the patron's attention to the back for it to be binding, and the ticket must be given at the time the contract is made, not afterward. When a business regularly depends on such exemption clauses in its

**Important terms must be disclosed**

3. [1953] 1 All E.R. 482 (C.A.); aff'g, [1952] 2 All E.R. 456 (Q.B.).

4. Obtaining goods by false pretences, *Criminal Code*, R.S.C. 1985, c. C-46, s. 364.

## Reducing **Risk** 5.1

Whether terms are set out in signs or included in written agreements, it is vital that any that are at all unusual be reasonably brought to the attention of the other party, especially if they limit the liability of one party. It is no longer good enough for the term to appear in small print in a document, or to put it on a receipt so that it can be seen only after the contract has been created. It is likely that those terms will simply not be considered part of the agreement and therefore not binding on the other party.

contracts it is vital, especially where consumer transactions with the public are involved, that it takes care to draw the customer's attention to this provision at the time the contract is created. Even so, these clauses may be ineffective because of consumer protection legislation; this topic will be discussed in Chapter 9.

Exemption clauses are more commonly found in written contracts. When people sign contracts they are generally taken to have read the entire document. Even then, where an exemption clause is unusually restrictive the court may hold that there was a requirement to specifically bring the clause to the attention of the other contracting party and that the obligation was not met. Even when the clause *was* brought to the attention of the other party, if the merchant's failure to perform amounts to a fundamental breach he or she still may not be able to rely on the exemption clause for protection. The topic of fundamental breach will be discussed in Chapter 8.

## The End of an Offer

### Case Summary 5.3

**An Offer Can't Be Accepted after You Know the Offeror Has Changed His Mind: *Dickinson v. Dodds*[5]**

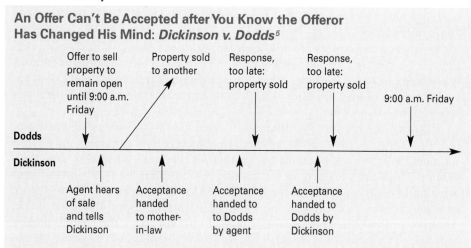

*Dickinson v. Dodds,* an old case from the latter part of the 19th century, remains one of the best cases to illustrate how offer and acceptance work. Mr. Dodds made an offer to sell certain property to Mr. Dickinson for £800, stating: "This offer to be left over until Friday, 9:00 a.m." Before the expiration of that deadline, Mr. Dickinson learned through his agent that Mr. Dodds had been trying to sell or had sold the property to someone else.

5. (1876), 2 Ch. D. 463 (C.A.).

He quickly went to Mr. Dodds' home and left a written acceptance with Dodds' mother-in-law. The next morning, Mr. Dickinson and the agent went down to the train station to intercept Mr. Dodds as he arrived in town. The agent found him first and handed him a written acceptance. Mr. Dodds replied that it was too late and that he had already sold the property. This scenario was repeated a few minutes later when Mr. Dickinson intercepted Mr. Dodds, with the same response—all before the stated deadline.

This case illustrates that an offer is only a tentative commitment. Even though Dodds promised to hold the offer open, he was not obligated to do so. He could change his mind and sell it to someone else, but he had to let the other party know he had changed his mind. In this case Dodds was extremely lucky, because although he didn't tell Dickinson directly that he had changed his mind Dickinson found out indirectly and couldn't accept an offer he knew was no longer available. Had Dickinson not found out about the sale, the acceptance would have been valid and Dodds would have been bound in contract to sell the property to two different purchasers. Do you think that Dodds should have been bound by his promise to hold the offer open? Should a sale to someone else automatically end the offer?

For the acceptance of an offer to be effective, the offer must be in force at the time of the acceptance. There are several ways for an offer to come to an end before acceptance.

**Offer ends**

**1. End of a specified time**. The offer will end at the time stated. Note that the offeror is still free to revoke the offer before this time expires, unless an option has been purchased. Option agreements will be discussed below.

• when specified

**2. The expiration of a reasonable time.** If no time is specified the offer will end at the end of a reasonable time; thus, an offer to sell a ship would likely last longer than an offer to sell a load of ripe peaches.

• at a reasonable time

**3. Death or insanity of offeror.** The offer will end even if the offeree is unaware of the death or insanity.

• at death or insanity of offeror

**4. Revocation of offer.** The offeror may revoke an offer any time before acceptance, but the revocation must be communicated to the offeree to be effective. When letters are used, the revocation is effective only when received. Until that time, an offeree can still accept the offer. The offeror should take care not to contract with another or even make an offer to do so until he is sure that the message that he has changed his mind has gotten through to the offeree. While it is possible for the revocation to be communicated indirectly, as in *Dickinson v. Dodds* discussed above, reliance on such a method would be foolish in the extreme. Dodds was extremely lucky in that case.

• when revoked

**Revocation must be communicated**

**5. Rejection and counteroffer**. During the bargaining process, several different proposals may be put forward, rejected, and then followed by counterproposals. Each counteroffer or rejection ends the offer before it. For example, when a car is offered for sale for $5000 and the customer replies "I'll give you $4500," a counteroffer has been made and the original offer comes to an end. If the seller rejects the counteroffer, it is too late for the purchaser to reconsider and accept the original offer; it no longer exists. Under such circumstances, an attempt to accept the original $5000 offer constitutes a new offer, which the seller is free to accept or reject.

**Rejection or counteroffer also ends offer**

**Request for information is not a counteroffer**

Note that a simple request for information or clarification, such as an inquiry as to whether the sale of a car includes the stereo, does not constitute a counteroffer or a rejection and does not end the offer. On the other hand, a counteroffer that is worded like a question will end the offer (such as "Will you take $4500?").

The existence of an offer can be affected by other factors as well. For example, the offer will be ended if the activity contemplated by the contracting parties becomes illegal before acceptance, or if the goods forming the subject matter of the contract are destroyed without the parties being aware of it.

## Offers That Cannot Be Revoked

Often, businesspeople find the uncertainty associated with the offeror's right to revoke any time prior to the point of acceptance very inconvenient, especially when they are arranging their business affairs in order to take advantage of the offer.

**Where option exists, offer cannot be revoked**

For example, when assembling land a land developer will get offers from several sellers but will not accept any of them until sure that all properties can be obtained. The seller's right to revoke is inconsistent with this process, and so the developer will acquire an option on each property. This is a separate subsidiary contract with separate consideration given to the offeror in exchange for a commitment to keep the offer open for a specific length of time. The developer now has the certainty necessary to accomplish his goal. Such arrangements are quite common and found in all areas of finance and business. Options can also be put under seal; the use of the seal will be discussed later under "Consideration."

A similar problem exists when dealing with *tenders,* the normal practice in the construction industry. A purchaser puts out a request for bids in order to get the best possible price on a required product or service. The request for bids is an invitation to treat, and the submitted bid is the offer. The problem is that normally there would be nothing to stop the offeror from withdrawing his offer if he realizes he has made a mistake, or upon seeing the other bids realizes his is too low. The Supreme Court of Canada has decided that in some circumstances such tendered bids cannot be revoked. Where the original request for tenders made it clear that bids would be considered only where the offeror agreed that the offer could not be withdrawn once submitted a subsidiary contract exists, and the offer then cannot be revoked. As above, the problem is also avoided when the tendered bid is made under seal.

**Subsidiary contracts may be implied**

It is likely that the same principle will apply in any situation where a unilateral contract is involved and performance of the act requested has started. Thus, if an employer promises to give her business to an employee if he stays until she retires, the acceptance is made simply by the employee staying on. With such an implied subsidiary contract, the employer could not wait until just before her retirement and then revoke the offer.

### Case Summary 5.4

**Request for Tenders Established Contract: *M.J.B. Enterprises Ltd. v. Defence Construction* (1951) Ltd.**[6]

This case deals with tenders in the construction industry. Defence Construction invited tenders for the construction of a water-distribution project. That invitation for tenders specified certain conditions that the bid had to meet, but also

---

6. (1999), 170 D.L.R. (4th) 577 (S.C.C.).

stated that the "lowest or any tender shall not necessarily be accepted." The plaintiff complained when the accepted bid did not meet the conditions while its own did. This case went to the Supreme Court of Canada, which held that there was a subsidiary contract relating to the tendering process that had been breached. There was an implied term that the bids had to meet the specified conditions. While Defence Construction was not bound to accept the lowest or any other tender, it was required to choose one that met those specified conditions. Had the process been properly followed, the plaintiff's bid would have been accepted. Thus, the subsidiary contract had been breached and the plaintiff was awarded almost $400 000 in damages. Note that in a similar case where specified qualifications were not met there was no breach. This advertisement contained the clause "This is an invitation for proposals and not a tender call." Since it was an invitation and not a call for tenders there was no subsidiary contract.[7]

## Standard Form Contract

This process of negotiation culminating in offer and acceptance is based on the presumption that both parties are in an equal bargaining position and that a fair bargain will be reached. In actual fact, most large businesses do not negotiate with their customers. Rather, they present a contract with fixed terms, which the customer is invited to accept (a passenger purchasing an airline ticket is an example). These are called **standard form contracts** and contain one-sided terms favouring the business. The exemption clauses discussed above that attempt to limit the liability of the business are examples of such one-sided terms.

*Bargaining difficult with standard form contract*

To correct the imbalance and alleviate some of the unfairness, *consumer protection legislation* controlling the worst abuses has been enacted in most jurisdictions (consumer protection is covered in Chapter 9). When the courts deal with these exemption clauses they interpret them strictly so that any ambiguity is read in favour of the disadvantaged party. Thus, a business that includes in its contracts terms disclaiming responsibility for "damage" to goods left on the premises would still be held responsible for goods that were stolen. Even where the exemption clause is clear, the courts are showing a willingness to set them aside on the basis of fairness and good faith.

*Statutes and attitude of court mitigate this*

## Acceptance

At the heart of contract law are the concepts of consensus and mutual commitment. The manifestation of an intention to commit on the part of the offeror is found in the offer; the offeree's intention to commit is found in the acceptance. The contract is formed, and the parties are bound by it at the point of acceptance. The key to understanding acceptance is that the commitment must be total. If a condition or qualification is put on the acceptance it then becomes a counteroffer, not an acceptance. If a salesperson offers to sell a car and a trailer to a customer for $5000 and $3000, respectively, and the response is "I accept, provided you include new tires," that response is a counteroffer. Nor is it possible to accept only part of an offer. In this example the purchaser cannot say, "I accept your offer, but I want only the car." For an acceptance to be valid, it must be an all-or-nothing proposition.

*Acceptance must be complete and unconditional*

7. *Mellco Developments Ltd. v. Portage la Prairie (City)* (2002), 222 D.L.R. (4th) 67 (Man. C.A.).

A serious problem can arise where customers and suppliers exchange order forms. Sometimes, instead of filling in the supplier's order form the customer simply sends his or her own, which may include different terms. This is not an acceptance but a counteroffer, and if the supplier simply sends the product in response they have accepted and are bound by the new terms but often do not realize the difference. Such a mistake is easily made, and care should be taken to watch for such substituted forms.

Even a clear acceptance cannot correct an incomplete offer. When the wording of an offer is unclear, the courts will interpret the agreement to find the most reasonable construction but will not go so far as to strike a bargain on behalf of the parties. As mentioned, there is no such thing as a contract to enter into a contract.

### Case Summary 5.5

#### An Incomplete Offer Can't Be Accepted: *Halifax (County) v. Giles*[8]

In 1963, John and Hazel Giles conveyed certain property to Halifax County to be used for a fire hall. The deed contained a covenant that if the property were no longer used as a fire hall at any time over the next 50 years, the Gileses or their heirs would have "first right or option to purchase" the property. The property's use as a fire hall ended in 1987, and at that time the Gileses' sole heir demanded the property be sold to him. When negotiations failed the dispute was taken to court, but when the Judge examined the original deed he found that the option provision was void since no price or method to determine a price had been set out. The offer was incomplete and as a result could not be accepted. No matter how definite the acceptance, it will not overcome the defect of an incomplete or otherwise defective offer.

## Communication of Acceptance

**Offer may be accepted by conduct, where specified**

Usually, acceptance of an agreement is accomplished by communicating it to the offeror. However, it is possible for an offer to be accepted by conduct. If the offeror has indicated particular conduct to specify acceptance, the offeree must comply with that stipulation for it to be effective. Or acceptance may be inferred from conduct as when, for example, a purchaser leaves a deposit on a car he has purchased.

### Case Summary 5.6

#### Communication of Acceptance May Be Indirect: *Lanca Contracting Ltd. v. Brant (County) Board of Education*[9]

In this case the president of Lanca Contracting was present when the Board of Education passed a resolution to accept Lanca's tender for the construction of a new school building. The members of the board were aware of his presence, and several members of the board, as well as the board's architect and controller, spoke at the meeting in terms that implied that the plaintiff was going to be building the school. Two days later, the board rescinded its resolution and awarded the contract to someone else. The Court decided that despite the requirement that a formal contract be entered into later there was sufficient notice of acceptance given to the plaintiff and a binding contract resulted. The board was liable for its breach.

8. (1994), 111 D.L.R. (4th) 614 (N.S.C.A.).

9. (1986), 26 D.L.R. (4th) 708 (Ont. C.A.).

A **unilateral contract** is accepted by performance of the act specified in the offer. If a prize were offered for the first human-powered flight across the English Channel, acceptance would be by making the flight. Starting the flight would not qualify; only the completion of the cross-Channel flight would constitute effective acceptance of the offer. But what if the offeror tried to revoke his offer when the flight was only partially performed? In theory the offer can be revoked any time before acceptance. As discussed above, a Canadian court would likely follow the American example and find a subsidiary contract requiring that once the performance starts the offer cannot be revoked. In any case where acceptance is by conduct there is no requirement to communicate the acceptance to the offeror, although there may still be a need to notify the offeror that the required conduct has taken place where this is not self-evident.

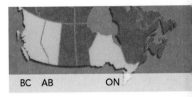

**Unilateral contract accepted by completion of performance**

Merchandisers often send unsolicited goods to people along with an invoice stating that if the goods are not returned within a specified time, the customer will have purchased them. But silence, as a general rule, does not constitute acceptance. When goods are supplied in this way, you can normally ignore them. Just put them away. If you use the goods, you are receiving a benefit and have accepted the offer. This is another example of an unacceptable practice curbed by consumer protection legislation in many jurisdictions.

**Unsolicited offer not accepted by silence**

An important exception to silence not being an acceptance is where there is an ongoing business relationship between the parties. It is quite common for a supplier to send materials used by a business on a regular basis with the understanding that they will continue to be sent unless the supplier is informed otherwise. A relationship of trust has developed, and the purchaser now has a duty to inform the supplier when he changes his mind. When a person joins a book-of-the-month club or similar scheme a similar duty is created, and return of the book (or CD, or DVD) is likely required to escape obligation. But these clubs often continue to send products where there has been no request or even after they have been told to stop. There is now consumer protection legislation in place in most jurisdictions to prevent this kind of abuse.

**But silence can be acceptance where prior dealings**

Where acceptance is not by conduct, the general rule is that the contract is formed when and where the offeror learns of the acceptance. If a supplier of lumber products in Halifax makes an offer to a customer in Winnipeg and the offeree accepts over the telephone, the contract comes into existence in Halifax, where the offeror hears the acceptance. Where the contract is formed can be an important factor in determining what court has jurisdiction and the law of which jurisdiction will apply to the contract.

**Acceptance is effective when and where communicated**

## The Postbox Rule

### Case Summary 5.7

#### Should the Postbox Rule Be Extended? *The Queen et al. v. Commercial Credit Corp. Ltd.*[10]

This case dealt with whether a creditor had lost its priority by failing to properly register a security as required by Nova Scotia law. If the contract were formed within the province the creditor would lose any claim to the assets because of the failure to register; if it were formed outside the province the creditor would still have a claim. The original offer had, in fact, been made by Commercial Credit

---

10. (1983), 4 D.L.R. (4th) 314; (N.S.S.C.[A.D.]).

Ltd. residing in Nova Scotia and sent by courier to the offeree outside the province. This offer was then accepted and the acceptance returned, also by courier. The court held that this communication was akin to using the mail and so the postbox rule applied, making the acceptance effective where sent, which was outside the province. Referring to the finance company, the Judge said that "They were the ones that chose the method of communication, and having done so on behalf of both parties, the mailbox doctrine was brought into play. Its extension to a courier service was sound in principle and, in my opinion, the contracts were therefore made outside of Nova Scotia when their acceptances were sent back to Commercial Credit." This is one of the few cases where the postbox rule has been extended beyond communication by mail or telegram, and it remains to be seen whether it will be followed in other jurisdictions in Canada. Is there any justification to extend the postbox rule to other forms of communication? Should it even be in effect today?

Difficulties arise when parties deal with each other over long distances using non-instant forms of communication. Because neither party can be absolutely sure of the other's state of mind at a given time, there can be no certainty of the contract's status. The **postbox rule** was developed to solve this problem. When use of the mail is reasonable, an acceptance is effective when and where it is deposited in the mailbox. This is a clear exception to the general rule discussed above, where an acceptance is not effective until the offeror learns of it. Figure 5.2 illustrates how the postbox rule works.

**Mailed acceptance effective when and where dropped in postbox**

One problem—determining the point of consensus—is solved, but another is created. For a period of time, while the letter of acceptance is still in the mail, the offeror is bound in contract but unaware of that fact. Note that the offeror can stipulate a different means of communication *to avoid this problem*. When use of the mail is inappropriate or another method of acceptance was specified by the offeror the acceptance will be effective only when received.

**Only applies where response by mail appropriate**

Response by mail when an offer is sent by mail is normally reasonable. The problem arises when a different means of communication is used to make the offer and acceptance is then by mail. This is illustrated in *Henthorne v. Fraser*.[11] Mr. Henthorne was handed an offer in the defendant's office, which was to remain open for 14 days. He took the offer home to think about it and, after several days,

## Figure 5.2 Postbox Rule

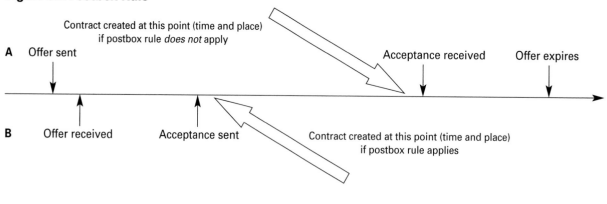

11. [1892] 2 Ch. 27 (Eng. Ch. D.).

posted a letter of acceptance. In the meantime, the defendant, Mr. Fraser, sold the property to another party and wrote a letter to Henthorne revoking the offer. The two letters crossed in the mail and the court decided that even though the offer had been handed to Henthorne, use of the post for acceptance was reasonable and therefore the acceptance was effective when sent. Note that the letter of revocation was not effective until Henthorne received it.

The question also must be asked whether the postbox rule applies to any other form of communication. The postbox rule has been extended to include telegrams but not to instantaneous forms of communication, such as telex or fax.

**Postbox rule extended to telegrams**

### Case Summary 5.8

**Limitation of the Postbox Rule:** *Entores Ltd. v. Miles Far East Corp.*[12]

In this case, an American company contracted with a British company through a Dutch subsidiary for the purchase of electronic components. The British company wanted to sue the American company in England, but the British court would have jurisdiction only if the contract came into existence in the United Kingdom. It was argued that since the Dutch company made the acceptance by telex (similar to a modern fax machine), applying the postbox rule the contract came into existence where the acceptance originated, in Holland. The Court rejected this argument. The Court found that because telex was instantaneous, like the telephone, there was no need to extend the postbox rule exception to this kind of communication. Therefore, the general rule applied and the acceptance was effective in the United Kingdom, where it was received. The contract, therefore, came into existence in the United Kingdom, and the court there had jurisdiction.

This case illustrates the operation of the postbox rule and its limitations. There is some question whether there is any justification for the postbox rule in this day of modern high-tech communication. What do you think?

Today, it is becoming much more common to use electronic means of communication, such as electronic mail and fax, rather than the postal service, and the question arises whether the postbox rule will be extended to these methods of doing business. Since these new electronic communications are instantaneous or near-instantaneous, it is not likely that the postbox rule will be extended to them. This conclusion is confirmed at least with respect to communication by fax in *Eastern Power Limited v. Azienda Comunale Energia and Ambiente*,[13] where the Ontario Court of Appeal found that an acceptance sent by fax was effective only when it was received by the offeror. There is also a U.S. case indicating that an acceptance by e-mail will not be effective until read by the offeree, which likely indicates the direction our courts will go.[14]

---

12. [1955] 2 All E.R. 493 (C.A.).

13. (1999), 178 D.L.R. (4th) 409 (Ont. C.A.); leave to appeal to S.C.C. refused (June 22, 2000) Doc. 27595.

14. *Corinthian Pharmaceutical Systems Inc. v. Lederle Laboratories* (1989), 724 F. Supp. 605 (S.D. Ind.).

## Reducing **Risk** 5.2

People often make the mistake of thinking that if they make an offer to sell to several people and then sell it to one of them it automatically ends their offers to the others. But you normally have to notify those others that you have sold the item to revoke the offer. If you fail to do so you face the risk of someone else accepting and being bound to sell the same item to two different people. To avoid the problem of being bound in contract without knowing it, the offeree should be careful to specify the method of acceptance and clearly state in the offer that it will not be considered accepted until the acceptance is actually received and in the hands of the offeree. Of course, when a long-term business relationship is involved this may not be a problem.

It should be noted that there are still significant advantages to using the mail. The use of the mail involves the exchange of a permanent tangible record of the transaction and its terms. Electronic communication, such as email, may be convenient, but it suffers from a lack of permanency or certainty. These records can be lost with the crash of a system or simply altered in an undetectable way, making written records and communications through the mail still—and likely to remain—an attractive option as a common aspect of future business transactions.

**The postbox rule will also determine where a contract is formed**

As mentioned above, where a contract is formed can also help determine what law applies or whether a court has jurisdiction, and that can also be determined by the postbox rule. In the *Entores* case the British court had jurisdiction because the postbox rule did not apply to an acceptance by telex and the contract was made in England. In the *Commercial Credit Corp.* case the transaction was not subject to Nova Scotia law because the postbox rule did apply to a couriered acceptance and the contract was made outside the province.

**Postbox rule does not apply to revocation**

It must be stressed that the postbox rule is an exception to the requirement that an acceptance must be communicated to be effective. It does not apply to the offer or to a revocation of that offer. In the *Henthorne v. Fraser* case discussed above the postbox rule was applied only to the letter of acceptance and not to the letter of revocation, which had to be received before it could have any effect on the transaction.

## Consideration

Central to contract law is the *bargaining process,* in which people trade promises for promises and all parties derive some benefit from the deal. That benefit, essential to the existence of a contract, is called **consideration** and is defined as the price one commits to pay for the promise of another. Consideration is not restricted to the exchange of money. A bargain may involve the exchange of anything the parties think is of value. For example, where Brown purchases a computer from Ace Computers Ltd. for $2000, there is valid consideration on both sides. The promise to deliver the computer is valid consideration, as is the promise to pay $2000. Note that before the parties actually exchange the computer for the cash they are still bound in contract, because the consideration given is the exchange of commitments or promises and not the actual money or goods. If one of the parties fails to honour that commitment, the other can successfully sue for breach of contract.

**Consideration—the price one is willing to pay for a promise**

**Consideration—not necessarily money**

Because it is sometimes difficult to determine the value a person is getting from a deal, it is often better to look at what the parties are giving or paying. For example, if a public-spirited business agrees to pay someone to clean up a public park, the commitment is still binding, even though it might have been made out of a sense of civic responsibility and may result in no actual benefit to the business. Both sides have exchanged promises or commitments. Normally, the promise to make a charitable donation is not enforceable because it is a one-sided promise or gift, but when the charity makes a commitment in return—such as a promise to name a building after the donor or to use the money in a certain way—it has made a commitment, and both parties will be bound.

Similarly, the contract is just as binding if the consideration involved is a commitment not to do something as opposed to a promise to do something. For example, if a business promises to pay its employees $500 to quit smoking, such an arrangement is a valid, binding contract. The consideration on the one side is the promise to pay $500, and the consideration on the other side is the promise to refrain from doing something the party has a legal right to do (that is, smoke). Consideration is a benefit or a detriment flowing between the parties to an agreement as the result of a bargain being struck (see Figure 5.3).

**Consideration can be benefit or detriment**

If the agreement is one-sided and only one of the parties is getting anything from the deal, it is called a **gratuitous promise** or a gift, and the courts will not enforce it. It may well be that such gratuitous promises ought to be honoured from an ethical point of view, but there is no legal obligation to do so. Once the gift has been given, however, the courts will not assist the giver in getting it back. Also, when services are performed gratuitously, there is still an obligation to do a proper job. If through the negligence of the person performing the gratuitous service damage or injury results, he or she can be sued in tort. For example, if a skilled carpenter out of the goodness of his heart helps his neighbour repair a roof and because of his negligence the roof leaks and causes damage to furniture and belongings, the neighbour can sue in tort for compensation.

**Courts will not enforce one-sided agreement**

## Case Summary 5.9

### Consideration for Promissory Note Was Rearranging Obligations: *Bank of Nova Scotia v. Hallgarth*[15]

A woman was indebted to the Bank of Nova Scotia, and in the process of the renewal and rearrangement of those debts her husband signed a promissory note to the bank. Before that time, there was no indebtedness on his part. Eventually, the husband and wife separated, and upon the wife's default the bank came after the husband for payment on the promissory note. The husband claimed that he had received no consideration in exchange for his promise to be responsible for his wife's pre-existing debts. The Court found that because pursuant to the husband's signing the promissory note the bank had given up its rights or claims under the old arrangement, which would not have happened without the husband's promise, consideration did exist. The bank had made a commitment in exchange for the husband's promise.

## Figure 5.3 Consideration Involves the Exchange of Promises or Commitments

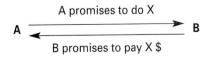

15. (1986), 32 D.L.R. (4th) 158 (B.C.C.A.).

## Adequacy of Consideration

### Case Summary 5.10

**Both Sides Must Make Commitments:** *Gilbert Steel Ltd. v. University Construction Ltd.*[16]

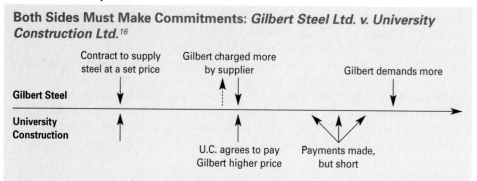

Gilbert Steel had supplied construction steel to University Construction on a number of their projects. For one particular project, they had a contract for a specified amount of steel to be provided at a set price and of set quality. But Gilbert Steel's costs for the steel increased, and they requested that University Construction agree to pay a higher price for the steel supplied for that project.

The steel was delivered, but the payments made were never enough to cover the increased price. When Gilbert demanded payment University refused to pay the higher amount, claiming they didn't get anything in return for their promise to pay more. They had agreed to pay more but Gilbert's position hadn't changed; they still had the same obligation to deliver steel that they had under the original agreement. Such a one-sided agreement was not a binding contract. In order for a contract to exist, there must be an exchange of promises or commitments between the parties—a one-sided agreement is not enforceable.

The lawyers for Gilbert Steel argued that University received consideration in that Gilbert promised to give University Construction a "good price" on a subsequent project. The Court found that this promise was not specific enough and that there was no commitment involved. Gilbert also argued that because University did not have to pay for 60 days when the price went up they were getting more free credit, but the Judge also rejected that argument. There was no bargain struck. Only one side made a commitment, and so there was no obligation to pay the higher price even though there was a promise to do so. (Note that Gilbert also argued there was a promissory estoppel in this case, which was also rejected by the Court. This aspect to the case will be discussed below.)

Consideration need not be fair. The court will not interfere with the bargain struck even where it is a bad deal for one of the parties. If a person agrees to sell someone a brand-new Cadillac for $100, this becomes a valid, binding contract. When businesses deal with each other the value of a particular deal to the parties is not always apparent, and the wisdom of the courts not reviewing the fairness of the consideration is clear. But when businesses deal with consumers, the courts are much more concerned with fairness and are much more willing to rescue consumers who have been taken advantage of by merchants. This power to intervene is now usually found in statute, but the courts themselves have developed

**The courts will not bargain for the parties**

---

16. (1976), 67 D.L.R. (3d) 606 (Ont. C.A.).

such concepts as *unconscionability, fraud,* or *mistake* (to be discussed below), which give them power to review these transactions. The courts will also examine the fairness of consideration when insanity, drunkenness, or undue influence may have affected the transaction.

Although the consideration paid does not need to be fair, it must have some legal value. The promise of "love and affection" is not good enough, nor is a promise to stop "bothering" your father.[17] Whatever the parties have bargained for must have some material value for the courts to enforce the bargain.

In addition, the parties must agree to a specific consideration or price. Suppose someone agrees to exchange a car for another's promise to "do some work around the house." Such a promise would not be enforceable because the work to be done is not specified. This was the problem in the *Gilbert Steel* case discussed in Case Summary 5.10, where Gilbert promised to give University a "good price" on future projects. This problem becomes acute whenever a monetary consideration is involved. It is not sufficient to promise to give "some money" as payment for the promise of another. Such a commitment must refer to a specific or calculable amount of money. When the parties agree to pay the "market value" of an item, or where some other objective method or formula for pricing a product at some time in the future is used, the consideration is calculable and is thus sufficiently specific to be binding, thus overcoming the problem. Even then, great care must be taken to make sure the price at that time will be clear.[18]

**Inadequate consideration may indicate fraud, insanity, etc.**

**Consideration**

## Case Summary 5.11

### Continued Employment Not Consideration without Notification: *Watson v. Moore Corp.*[19]

Ms. Watson was hired by Moore Corporation Ltd. in 1968, and after 25 years was terminated with only 20 weeks' notice. After working there for several years, she had been required to sign a document stating that if her employment was terminated she would be entitled only to one week's notice more than the statutory minimum, which in 1993 was 18 weeks under the *Employment Standards Act.* The problem for the Court to determine was whether she was entitled to 18 months' notice, which would have been reasonable notice under the common law, or whether she was required to take the much-reduced notice she had agreed to in her employment contract. When that agreement was made, what consideration did Moore give in order to persuade Ms. Watson to give up her common law right to reasonable notice? Was her continued employment sufficient consideration? The trial Judge said yes, but on appeal it was determined that continued employment would constitute consideration only if she had been informed that she would be dismissed if she failed to sign, and there was no evidence to that effect. As a result, she was entitled to the higher standard of notice as required by common law, in this case 18 months' notice. There was a strong dissenting opinion arguing that the continued employment was good consideration and there was no need to inform her of that. What do you think?

17. *White v. Bluett* (1953), 23 L.J. Ex. 36 (C.E.).
18. *Folley v. Classique Coaches* (1934), 2 K.B. 1 (C.A.).
19. (1996), 134 D.L.R. (4th) 252 (B.C.C.A.).

## Existing Duty

Sometimes people enter agreements to do what they are already legally obligated to do. This raises a problem concerning the adequacy of consideration. For example, Olsen agreed to paint Chang's house for $1500 and then when the painting was three-quarters finished demanded $500 more to finish the job on time. Even if Chang agreed, there would be no binding obligation because Chang got nothing in exchange for the promise to pay more. Olsen was obligated to finish painting the house before the promise to pay the extra $500 was made, and after the promise the obligation remained the same. Olsen's legal position did not change; therefore, there was no consideration. These types of problems often arise in the construction industry, where unforeseen factors may increase the costs significantly, as in the *Gilbert Steel* case discussed in Case Summary 5.10. This is just one more reason for the parties to take great care to predict all costs that are likely to arise and to build into their agreement provisions for resolving conflicts over these unexpected eventualities.

When a duty to act exists but that duty is owed to a third party, a promise to do the same thing for someone else is enforceable. In the situation above, if Chang's tenant Adams promised to pay Olsen the extra $500 to ensure the job was finished on time, that agreement would be binding. Before Adams' promise to pay the extra $500, Olsen was legally obligated to Chang to finish painting the house. After the promise to Adams, Olsen is now legally obligated to Adams as well as to Chang to paint the house. Olsen's legal position has changed because Olsen now runs the risk of having to pay Adams' damages as well as Chang's if the contract is breached. There is a valid consideration here, and the contract is binding.

Where a public duty is involved a demand for further compensation will not be tolerated. A police officer, firefighter, or other public servant can't demand more money to do her job. A firefighter cannot arrive at a blaze and extract a promise from the victim to pay an extra $500 to put out the fire. Such a contract would be against public policy and unenforceable. However, paying police personnel in their off-duty hours to provide security at a rock concert or celebration is valid, because they are on their own time and not otherwise obligated to help.

## Past Consideration

There are situations where there is no consideration even though it appears to be present. One of these is when the consideration was given in the past; that is, the bargain is struck after the price agreed on has been paid. An employer's promise to pay a bonus in recognition of good work already performed by the employee would not be binding: the work has already been done. Although it may appear that both parties have given something (the employer the promised bonus and the employee the good work), such a promise is not enforceable. The key to this problem is in the timing. When the promise to pay the bonus was made, the work had already been performed, so where is the bargain? In fact, the employee is in exactly the same legal position before the promise as afterward. Thus, it is often said, "Past consideration is no consideration."

## Paying Less to Satisfy a Debt

A creditor will often agree to take less in full satisfaction of a debt, and this also raises problems with respect to consideration. A creditor who agrees after a $5000 debt is due to take $3000 from the debtor as full payment has received no consideration for the reduction in that claim. In fact, the reduction of the debt is gratuitous. Previously, it was quite clear under common law that such a one-sided promise was not binding and the debtor could still sue for the remaining $2000. Even when the partial payment was actually taken, the creditor could then turn around and sue for the remainder.[20]

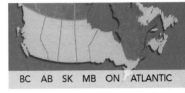

BC  AB  SK  MB  ON  ATLANTIC

But as a practical business matter, in many situations such an arrangement to take less is beneficial to the creditor as well as the debtor. The creditor might otherwise have to sue to recover and get nothing. Many jurisdictions have passed legislation providing that when a creditor has agreed to take less in full satisfaction of a debt and has actually received the money the creditor is bound and cannot sue for the difference.[21]

Where the creditor has agreed to take less but the money has not yet been paid the creditor is still free to change his or her mind and insist on the entire amount being paid. Of course, when the debtor has agreed to pay the lesser amount early, or to do something in addition to the payment such as pay a higher rate of interest, there is consideration on both sides to support the new arrangement, and the creditor is bound by the promise to take less.

## Settlement Out of Court

When the parties to a dispute settle the matter outside of court there is also valid consideration on both sides. When a litigant learns later that he would likely have won it may look like there is no consideration, but in fact both parties have given up their right to have the court determine the matter, and so there is consideration on both sides. As a result, the release signed in such situations is a binding contract.

**Consideration not a factor in out-of-court settlements**

## Illegal Consideration

There are some policy restrictions on what constitutes good consideration. For example, where illegal drugs are sold the agreement is void because the consideration is illegal. Contracts between businesses to interfere with free competition and unduly restrain trade may also be invalid due to illegality.

**Illegal or impossible consideration is no consideration**

In addition, for consideration to be valid it must be possible to perform the consideration promised. An agreement to change lead into gold for a cash payment would also be void due to the impossibility of performance (at least at this time).

## Reducing **Risk** 5.3

The old adage that you cannot get something for nothing has been enshrined in the law of contract in the form of the requirement of consideration. In all contracts, except those under seal, there must be a bargain where both parties make some commitment to each other. The lack of such consideration is often difficult to see, especially in business deals where pre-existing obligations are being modified. In such circumstances we have to be especially vigilant in our dealings to ensure that the deals made are legally binding and not simply one-sided gratuitous arrangements that can be ignored by the other party.

20. *Foakes v. Beer* (1884), 9 App. Cas. 605 (H.L.).

21. *Law and Equity Act*, R.S.B.C. (1996) 253, s. 43.

## Request for Services

Where services are requested from providers, such as lawyers or mechanics, the parties often do not agree on a specific price before the service is performed. When you ask a plumber to fix a leak in your kitchen or a mechanic to fix your car, often you are not given a firm price for the service. In these circumstances, the courts will impose an obligation to pay a reasonable price. This is an application of the principle of **quantum meruit,** sometimes called a quasi-contract. *Quantum meruit* means "as much as is deserved," and the courts use this principle to impose an obligation to pay a reasonable price when services are requested. The courts will also use *quantum meruit* to determine what should be paid when a person providing the services is not allowed to finish by a breaching party. For example, when a person has agreed to paint a house and before the job is finished and payment is due the other party refuses to allow completion the courts use the *quantum meruit* principle and require the breaching party to pay a reasonable price for the benefit he has received. The same is not true if the breaching party is the one seeking payment. In the example above, if the painter were the one who refused to finish the job, he could not demand partial payment for what had been done. The requirement to pay a reasonable price when no specific price has been agreed upon has also been applied to the sale of goods by provincial statute.

## Promissory Estoppel

Another exception to the rule that a promise is enforceable only if consideration is present is on the basis of the principle of **promissory estoppel,** sometimes referred to as *equitable estoppel*. The more common or ordinary use of the term *estoppel* involves statements of fact, and will be discussed in Chapter 11. Promissory estoppel, in contrast, deals with a person making a promise or a commitment to do something in the future. As we have discussed, an exchange of such promises or commitments constitutes consideration, and the result is a binding contract.

But where the promise is one-sided such a one-sided or gratuitous promise is normally not enforceable. Figure 5.4 illustrates how promissory estoppel works.

But sometimes the promisee incurs expenses or other obligations in anticipation of the promise being performed that otherwise could be avoided. In the presence of such reliance, unique remedies have been developed to compensate for significant loss. In the United States when such reliance is placed on a gratuitous promise and injury results it is possible to sue for compensation, but in the United Kingdom and Canada such an unfulfilled promise can be used only as a defence to an action initiated by the person who made the promise.

**Figure 5.4 Promissory Estoppel**

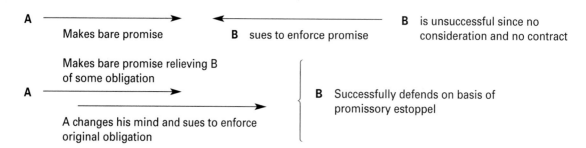

In London, England, just before the Second World War, High Trees House, Ltd. leased an apartment building from Central London Property Trust, Ltd. under a 99-year lease, with the intention of renting out the individual flats in the building.[22]

The two parties agreed to a set yearly rent of £2500. Because of the outbreak of the war, it soon became apparent that High Trees would not be able to rent out all the flats, and so in 1942 the property owners agreed to lower the yearly rent to £1250. After the war, they changed their minds and demanded payment of the entire rent, including back rent for the portion that had not been paid since 1942. They argued that the promise to take less rent was one-sided and, as a gratuitous promise, was not binding on them. The court agreed that for the period after the war High Trees had to again pay the full rent, but as far as the back rent was concerned the property owners were bound by their promise to take the lower amount. The key to understanding why is to realize that High Trees was not suing to enforce the promise; rather, the property owners were suing for the higher amount *in spite of* their promise. High Trees was using the plaintiff's promise as a defence to the plaintiff's claim.[23] Thus, in Canada and the United Kingdom, the principle of promissory estoppel is remedial in nature. In *Combe v. Combe*, Lord Denning made it clear that "it does not create new causes of action where none existed before," and Lord Asquith, in his concurring judgment, said that promissory estoppel could be used only as "a shield but not as a sword."[24]

Canada has followed the English example, limiting the use of promissory estoppel to a defence—which is why in the case of Gilbert Steel the argument of promissory estoppel failed. In that case, Gilbert Steel argued that because University Construction promised to pay more and Gilbert Steel relied on the promise it created an "estoppel" and University should be required to pay the higher amount. But Gilbert was not using the promise as a defence here; it was suing claiming payment on the basis of that promise. Since they were using the promise as a sword instead of a shield, they failed. Note that had University made the higher payments and sued Gilbert to get them back, then promissory estoppel may have been available to Gilbert as a defence.

In fact, in almost every case where promissory estoppel has been successfully used as a defence there was an existing legal relationship, usually contractual, that was modified by the promise. The promisor was attempting to enforce the original terms of the agreement, ignoring the relied-upon promise to alter the terms. The disappointed promisee then was using the promise as a shield or defence to the action. To raise this defence successfully, the victim must also demonstrate reliance on the promise and suffer an injury as a result of that reliance. This was another reason why the promissory estoppel argument raised in the Gilbert Steel case failed. True, they delivered the steel as required, but they were required to do this under the original contract in any case. They did only what they were required to do under the agreement; they didn't take on any extra obligation or incur any extra expense that could have otherwise been avoided.

**Promissory estoppel can only be used as a defence**

**There must also be reliance placed on the promise.**

22. *Central London Property Trust Ltd. v. High Trees House, Ltd.,* [1947] 130 (K.B.).

23. [1951] 1 All E.R. 767 at 769 (C.A.).

24. *Ibid.* at 772.

**Case Summary 5.12**

**Promissory Estoppel Used by a Government Agency:**
*Re Toronto College Street Centre Ltd. and City of Toronto et al.*[25]

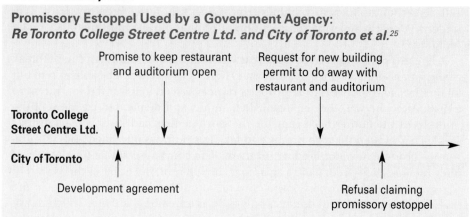

The use of promissory estoppel is not limited to contract. An example of the use of promissory estoppel in a non-contract case involved the owner of a building that was recognized as an important heritage site. The owners had been allowed to develop the building but had promised the city to retain a restaurant and auditorium on the seventh floor. When this proved uneconomical, the owners applied for a building permit to change the use of the seventh floor to rental units. The permit was refused, and that decision was challenged by way of judicial review of administrative action, as discussed in Chapter 3. The Court based its decision partly on promissory estoppel. The owners of the building had promised to maintain the seventh floor as a restaurant and auditorium, and the city had refused to grant a permit to do otherwise. The owners were estopped by their promise. Note that the promise of the owners of the property was being used as a defence by the city and that it was clear that the city had relied on the promise when allowing them to do other things with the building. The case is interesting in that it involves the enforcement of the doctrine in a non-contract situation and to the benefit of a government entity rather than an individual.

Do you think we would do better to adopt the American approach and allow an action for compensation whenever someone relies on a gratuitous promise to their detriment?

## Sealed Documents

The last major exception to the requirement of consideration is the use of the seal. Seals were originally made by placing melted wax on a document and impressing a signet ring in it, thus lending authenticity or authority to the document. When the parties went to so much trouble to indicate they were serious, they were bound by their commitment. This practice—which predates modern contract law—has been retained; thus, when a seal is used it is not necessary to show consideration for a contract to be binding. Today, instead of a wax impression the seal normally takes the form of a paper wafer, although almost any form

**Sealed documents do not require consideration**

25. (1986), 31 D.L.R. (4th) 402 (Ont. C.A.).

of marking on the document that the parties have identified as a seal can be used. These types of contracts are now considered formal contracts or deeds, and the court will not entertain any suggestion that the promise contained in the document is not supported by consideration. Although it is not necessary to look for consideration when a seal is present, the existence of the seal does not do away with the other requirements of a valid contract.

In general, there must be some form of valid consideration in the form of a benefit or detriment flowing between the parties for a court to enforce a promise. Only when the document embodying the agreement is sealed, or on those rare occasions when the promise of the promisor is being raised as a defence by the promisee will the court not require consideration to be established.

# Summary

## Contract

- A contract is an exchange of promises or commitments enforceable in court.
- There are five essential ingredients of a contract: consensus, consideration, capacity, legality, and intention.

## Consensus

- Offer—a tentative promise by the offeror contingent upon an acceptance by the offeree
  - All the essential terms of the contract must be contained in the offer
  - Non-essential terms will be implied
  - The offer will end at a specified time, but it may be revoked earlier simply by notice to the offeree, unless an option agreement has been entered into
  - In the absence of a specified time limit, the offer will lapse after a reasonable time
  - A counteroffer, rejection, or the death or insanity of the offeror will also cause an offer to lapse
- Acceptance—an indication of a willingness to be bound
  - Must be communicated
  - Postbox rule—an acceptance by mail (where reasonable) is effective when and where it is dropped in the mailbox

## Consideration

- The price paid for the promise of another
- Both contracting parties must have experienced some benefit
- Gratuitous promises are not enforceable
- Must be both specific and legal
- Past consideration is no consideration
- Promissory or equitable estoppel—a one-sided promise is generally not enforceable, but the promise may be used as a defence
- *Quantum meruit*—when there is a request for services with no agreement as to the amount, a reasonable price must be paid under this principle
- Seal—when there is a seal, consideration is not necessary

QUESTIONS

1. What is meant by "freedom of contract"? Explain the impact of this principle on the development of contract law.

2. List and explain the elements that must be present for an agreement to qualify as a contract.

3. At what stage in the process of forming a contract are the terms of the contract clearly set out?

4. Explain what is meant by an implied term in a contract.

5. What circumstances might prompt a court to imply terms into a contract?

6. Distinguish between an offer and an invitation to treat.

7. List and explain the various ways an offer can come to an end.

8. What is the effect of the offeror stating in an offer that the offer will remain open for acceptance until a specific date?

9. Give examples of offers that cannot be revoked and explain why.

10. What risks are faced when a person offers to sell certain goods to A and then sells them to B? How can this problem be avoided?

11. What qualities must an acceptance demonstrate to be effective?

12. Explain how a unilateral offer is accepted.

13. Explain the effect of the postbox rule on the principles governing acceptance.

14. Discuss the role the postbox rule plays when modern communication methods are used.

15. How do the courts determine when the postbox rule should be applied?

16. Define consideration and explain what is meant by the term "the exchange of consideration."

17. What difficulty might be faced by a person who has already agreed to do a specific job and then extracts a promise of more pay from the other party?

18. Explain why a contract dispute settled out of court is considered binding even though one party would have obtained more if the action had been taken to court.

19. Explain a person's obligation regarding payment when he or she has requested a service without specifying a particular fee.

20. Describe what is meant by promissory estoppel and the circumstances in which it will arise in contract disputes.

21. How does the presence of a seal affect the requirement that consideration must be present in a contract?

22. Explain under what circumstances a person who fails to properly perform a gratuitous promise can be held legally liable for that failure.

------------------------------------------------------------

# CASES

## 1. *Regina v. Dawood,* [1976] 1 W.W.R. 262 (Alta. C.A).

Mrs. Dawood had been shopping in a department store and came to a display rack containing children's jumpers and blouses. On some of the hangers, the jumpers and blouses were combined to make an outfit on sale for a single price, while some of the hangers contained individually priced jumpers and blouses. Mrs. Dawood took a blouse from one of the two-piece outfits and put it on its own hanger with a jumper from one of the individual hangers and took the outfit she had made to the cash register. She had removed any indication of price from the blouse so that the clerk was led to believe that the price from the jumper was the price for the whole outfit. The cashier charged her the lower price, which she paid. It is important to note that there was no attempt to hide the blouse in any way but the effect was that she paid for only the jumper. Mrs. Dawood was subsequently charged with theft, and the problem for the Court was to determine if a crime had taken place. Discuss.

## 2. *Data Wiz Information Systems Inc. v. Q.W. Page Associates Inc.* (1995), 20 B.L.R. (2d) 1 (Ont. Gen. Div.).

Both the plaintiff and the defendant were in the software development business. The defendant manufactured accounting software, and the plaintiff, Data Wiz, developed a data-based information system and sold it through a telemarketing scheme. Data Wiz wanted the exclusive distributorship rights to sell the defendant's accounting software in the United Kingdom and entered into negotiations with the defendant to that effect. These negotiations resulted in a memorandum of understanding and an international distribution agreement being executed by both parties. However, an important provision of the contract, namely, the discount that the distributor was to get, was left blank. There was some delay in obtaining the financing, and the defendant refused to go ahead until the financing was in place, insisting on some significant changes to the memorandum of understanding. What arguments could the defendant bring forth to escape liability under the contract? How could these be countered by the plaintiff?

## 3. *McCunn Estate v. Canadian Imperial Bank of Commerce* (2001-02-15), ONCA C32521 (Ont. C.A.).

The deceased had a line of credit with the bank with insurance coverage that was to end at age 70. The bank automatically deducted the premiums from her account every month. Unfortunately, after she turned 70 it simply continued to do so. The deceased was not aware of this and the bank obviously made these deductions in error. When she died more than a year later the estate claimed that the insurance coverage had continued or been renewed and was in effect when she passed away. They refused to pay the amount owing on the line of credit, claiming continued insurance coverage. This claim was based on the continuing deduction of the insurance premiums from her account. The Court had to decide whether a new contract had been created giving her the additional coverage. Explain what arguments could be raised by both sides and the likely outcome.

## 4. *Calgary v. Northern Construction Ltd.,* [1985] 2 W.W.R. 426, (Alta. C.A.).

The City of Calgary advertised for tenders for a construction project. One of the terms of the advertisement was that once submitted the bid could not be revoked. Northern

Construction submitted the low bid on the job. They then examined their bid and realized they had made an error in their calculations. They showed these documents to the City's representatives, who agreed that they had made an error. Northern Construction then requested that they be released from their bid. The City, however, would not release them from the bid and accepted it as the winning one. Since Northern Construction refused to honour the contract, the City was forced to go with the second-lowest bid, and they sued. Explain the legal arguments available to each side and the likely outcome of the action.

### 5. *Eastern Power Ltd. v. Azienda Communale Energia and Ambiente* (1999), 178 D.L.R. (4th) 409 (Ont. C.A.).

An Italian company and an Ontario company were both in the power generation business and were negotiating the terms of a cooperation agreement. Finally, the Ontario company sent a fax to the Italian company accepting their offer and a contract resulted. Subsequently, a dispute arose and the Italian firm terminated the relationship. The Ontario company submitted an invoice for their services and brought an action in Ontario to enforce the claim. The Court had to decide whether the appropriate jurisdiction in which to bring the action was Italy or Ontario. Indicate the likely outcomes and the factors on which the decision would be based.

### 6. *Francis v. Canadian Imperial Bank of Commerce* (1994), 120 D.L.R. (4th) 393 (Ont. C.A.).

After several interviews with the bank, Mr. Francis was offered a position of employment in a letter dated June 9, 1978. He responded on June 15 accepting the offer, by which he was to start work on July 4. When he showed up for work, he was presented with a number of documents that required his signature, including one entitled "Employment Agreement," which he signed along with the others. One of the terms of that employment agreement was that if he should ever be terminated, he was entitled to only three months' notice. After working for the bank for a number of years his employment was terminated with only three months' notice, and he sued for wrongful dismissal. There was no finding in these circumstances that Mr. Francis had done anything wrong, and so the Court assessed that under normal circumstances he would be entitled to 12 months' notice or pay in lieu of notice upon termination, given the length of service and surrounding circumstances. Discuss the arguments available to Mr. Francis to support his claim for the higher amount of notice and the arguments available to the bank in response.

### 7. *Re 6781427 Holdings and Alma Mater Society of U.B.C.* (1987), 44 D.L.R. (4th) 257 (B.C.C.A.).

The holding company in this case leased an area from the Alma Mater Society in the Student Union Building, where it operated a cookie shop with a three-year lease containing an option to renew. The renewal provision of the lease required that notice of renewal be given to the landlord in writing before midnight, July 31, 1986. In fact, the holding company approached the general manager of the Alma Mater Society to see if they could expand the area that they were using. The manager could not give a response right away but said he would probably know by September.

When September came, the manager said he would not know until December. As a result, the holding company missed the July 31 deadline while waiting for a response to their request. In September, the Alma Mater Society ordered it to vacate the premises. Explain the arguments available to each party to explain its position.

# Formation of Contracts (Continued)

## CHAPTER HIGHLIGHTS

- Capacity to contract
- Illegal contracts and contracts against public policy
- Intention to contract
- Forms of a contract
- The requirement of writing

In addition to consensus and consideration (discussed in the previous chapter), contracting parties must have the capacity to contract, the contract must be legal, and both parties must have intended that legal consequences would follow from their agreement—all of which will be discussed in this chapter. Although it is always a good idea to put a contract in writing, the general principle is that an oral contract is as binding as a written one. There are several situations, however, where contracts are required by statute to be evidenced in writing and these will also be discussed in this chapter.

# Capacity

Our lawmakers have always recognized that some people are more vulnerable than others and thus require special protection. Over the years, several categories of people have been protected by having their freedom to enter into contracts limited, or in some cases eliminated completely.

## Minors/Infants

**Age of majority varies with provinces**

The age of majority was 21 at common law but has been reduced by statute to 18 or 19 depending on the province. The general principle is that persons under the age of majority, called *infants* or *minors*, are not bound by their agreements but the adults with whom they contract are bound. The courts try to balance protecting the minor against the objective of not imposing undue hardship on the adult. It is important to distinguish between the actual incapacity of a child who is incapable of understanding what is happening and the artificial incapacity imposed on a youth who is a functioning member of society. Most problems arise when dealing with young people who are approaching the age of majority. The test is objective. When an adult deals with a customer who is a minor, it makes no difference that the adult was under the impression the other party was an adult, or even that the youth clearly understood the terms of the contract. The only question is whether the person was under the statutory age of majority at the time the contract was created. As a general rule, whenever a minor enters into a contract with an adult the adult is bound by the contract, but the minor can escape.

**Minors not bound by contracts, but adults are**

For example, where a car dealership offers to sell a car for $2500 to a minor who accepts the offer, the dealership will be bound by the contract. The young person who has not yet taken delivery of the car would be free to go through with the deal or not. If the youth takes delivery of the car and then chooses not to pay for it, he would have to return the car but could not be forced to pay or otherwise go through with the contract, even if he wrecks the car.

In most provinces these principles are based on English and Canadian case law. British Columbia, however, has a unique *Infants Act* that declares such contracts to be unenforceable against the infant. The distinction is not as important as it may at first appear. In B.C. the courts will not assist someone to enforce a contract against an infant, but if that infant has performed the courts will not assist the infant to get out of it, since the unenforceable contract is valid. Unenforceable contracts are discussed below under the requirement of writing.

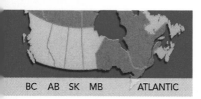

BC   AB   SK   MB          ATLANTIC

## Necessaries and Beneficial Contracts of Service

**Minors bound by contracts for necessaries**

Except in British Columbia, minors are bound by contracts for the acquisition of necessaries and for contracts of service that benefit the infant. **Necessaries** are things required to function in society, such as food, clothing, lodging, and transportation. What constitutes a necessary will vary with the particular needs of an infant and his or her status. If the young person is purchasing clothing and already has a sufficient supply, that clothing is not a necessary.

Where a minor is married or living on their own, what constitutes a necessary will be broader than would be the case if they were single and dependent on their parents. The courts have held that medical, dental, and legal services, along with toiletries, uniforms, and even a house can be necessaries in different situations, but it is unlikely that they will find that a car qualifies, since other alternative forms of transportation are generally available. Even when the subject of the contract is determined to be a necessary it does not guarantee that the merchant will get paid full price, as the infant is only obligated to pay a reasonable price for such necessaries.

**Minors must repay money borrowed and used for necessaries**

When an infant borrows money to buy necessaries, there is an obligation to repay the debt only if the funds advanced are actually used for necessaries. For this reason, a creditor cannot recover money loaned to an infant to pay for school tuition if it is used instead for gambling. Government student loans are exceptions because they are supported by legislation requiring repayment regardless of what the money is used for and regardless of the age of the borrower.

**Minors bound by contracts of service which substantially benefit them**

Contracts of employment, apprenticeship, or service are binding if it can be demonstrated that, taken as a whole, the contract is for the benefit of the infant. If it becomes apparent that the infant is being taken advantage of or the contract is not in the infant's best interests, the infant will not be bound. Today, these kinds of relationships are usually controlled by legislation.

**Note B.C. exception**

Note that in the British Columbia statute, all contracts, including necessaries and beneficial contracts of service, are unenforceable against an infant. Only student loans and other contracts made specifically enforceable by statute will be binding on infants in that province.[1]

## On Becoming an Adult

A minor can lose the right to avoid a contract by ratifying it upon becoming an adult. The process of ratification breathes new life into old agreements, making them binding. For example, if an infant agrees to pay $5000 for an automobile in a series of instalments, the infant cannot be forced to pay. If, however, on coming of age another instalment is paid or a written statement is made indicating that he or she intends to be bound, the contract is now binding. This ratification is normally in writing but can also be implied. (In some provinces, written ratification is required by statute.)

**Infant can ratify contract at age of majority**

### Case Summary 6.1

#### What Amounts to Ratification? *Bayview Credit Union Ltd. v. Daigle*[2]

Daigle was a minor when he borrowed a considerable sum from the Bayview Credit Union using his motorcycle as security. He stopped making payments and hid the motorcycle while still a minor. After turning 19 he disclosed the location of the motorcycle to the manager of the credit union. It was repossessed and sold, leaving more than $4100 still owing. Bayview sued Daigle, claiming his disclosure of the location of the motorcycle when he was an adult amounted to ratification of the contract, making it enforceable against him. The Court held that Daigle was not liable. His action was not ratification but merely assisting the credit union in realizing their security. The Judge commented, "Surely the acts of the defendant here, in co-operating as he did to the benefit of the plaintiff, should not place him in a worse position than a person who would refuse cooperation to reduce the plaintiff's loss." The case illustrates the danger of businesspeople dealing with minors as if they were adults. Do you think that an infant should lose the protection of a minor when, whether out of ignorance or a sense of obligation, he chooses to continue to pay or acknowledges a debt after becoming an adult?

Although these principles may seem reasonably straightforward, their application has created a good deal of confusion. To appreciate the reasons for this confusion, it is necessary to think of the contractual relationship progressing through prescribed stages. At the first stage, when the parties have entered into the agreement but the infant has not yet obtained any benefit from it and has not yet paid, the infant can get out of the agreement. This is an **executory contract.** If the

## Reducing **Risk** 6.1

Merchants run a great risk when they deal with even mature youth as if they were adults. Contracts cannot be enforced against them, and, while security can be taken in goods, as Case Summary 6.1 illustrates even that may not be much protection when the goods used as security are destroyed or otherwise made unavailable. In such circumstances a personal guarantee by parents may be the wisest course. Secured transactions will be discussed in Chapter 10.

---

1. *Infants Act*, R.S.B.C. 1996, c. 223.

2. (1983), 3 D.L.R. (4th) 95 (N.B.Q.B.).

infant has received the goods but has not yet paid for them, he or she is not necessarily bound by the agreement. This is a **partially executed contract**. When the goods are in the infant's possession, the infant will be required to return them or pay for them, and upon return is entitled to the return of any money already paid. If the infant has passed those goods on to a third party or the goods have been destroyed, the merchant will not be entitled to repayment, nor can the merchant insist that the party to whom the goods have been given return them.

Conflict may arise when the contract has been **executed**. Can minors change their minds once they have obtained the benefit under the contract and insist on the return of their money? In Canadian law, the conclusion seems to be that minors are bound by the agreement unless it can be demonstrated that what was received was of no value at all. An infant can insist that payment be returned if there is total failure of consideration where the infant gained nothing from the deal.

**Where contract bestows no benefit, infant can escape even executed contract**

## Parents' Liability

**Parents not responsible for infant's contracts**

There is a popular misconception that liability will rest with the parents if a child fails to pay a debt. As a general rule, parents are not responsible for the torts of their children, nor are they responsible for their contractual obligations in the absence of specific legislation creating such a responsibility. If an infant enters into a contract, it is that infant's responsibility alone. The adult contracting with the infant cannot turn to the parents if the infant does not live up to the contract.

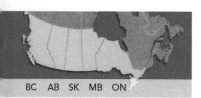

BC   AB   SK   MB   ON

**Parents may be responsible where there is agency, guarantee, or where goods are necessaries**

Many jurisdictions have passed legislation making parents liable for the torts, contracts, and even criminal activities of their children, often in specific situations such as school-related activities. But in the absence of such legislation, there must be something more involved for the parents to be liable for their children's contracts. Parents can be liable where the infant is acting as an agent having the appropriate authority to bind the parent in contract (agency will be discussed in a subsequent chapter). Parents will also be bound if they guarantee the infant's obligation at the time the contract is entered into. A **guarantee** is a written commitment whereby the guarantor agrees to pay the debt if the debtor does not. Since the very purpose of the guarantee is to encourage the merchant to go through with the contract, these guarantees have been held to be binding on the parents in Canadian law. Also, because parents are responsible to provide for their minor children, they can be held responsible by the merchant for contracts entered into by their children for necessaries.

## Infants' Liability for Torts

**Infant may be liable in tort**

**Adults cannot avoid protection given to minors by suing in tort**

**Except where tort arises independent of contract**

Often, a merchant will try to get around the protection given to a minor in contract law by suing in tort instead. Sometimes the act that constitutes the breach of contract will also qualify as negligence or some other tort as discussed in Chapter 4. It is a basic tenet of tort law that an infant is as liable as an adult for torts committed, although the standard of behaviour expected may differ. But the courts will not allow adults to change to a tort action just to get around the incapacity problem in contract law. If the infant used the subject matter of the contract in a way that would be expected under the contract, then the adult must sue in contract, not tort, and live with protection given to the infant.

On the other hand, if the infant used the subject matter of the contract in a way that was not contemplated in the contract, carelessly causing injury or damage to those goods, the adult would be able to sue for negligence and the youth would not be protected by the defense of infancy. For example, if an infant rents a two-wheel-drive automobile and then damages it while off-roading, the merchant would be able to sue the infant for negligence because the use to which the automobile was put was outside what was anticipated in the contract.

However, if the infant had an accident while driving the rented automobile on the highway the adult could not sue for tort, even if the infant were clearly negligent, because that activity would be just what would be expected when a car is rented. In short, the adult cannot circumvent the protection afforded to the infant in contract law by suing for tort instead. Nor are the parents responsible, since parents are not liable for the torts of their children unless they can be said to have been negligent in their own right or where there is a statute in place imposing such liability.

Special problems arise when dealing with the internet. The law with respect to capacity will be determined by the jurisdiction where the contract is created, which often is not clear. Also, there is no way for online merchants to know the personal characteristics of the parties with whom they are dealing. These unique challenges arising from advances in technology and communications will be discussed in the final chapter of this text.

## Insanity and Drunkenness

### Case Summary 6.2

#### Age Alone Will Not Establish Insanity: *Hardman v. Falk*[3]

Nora Falk and her sister, Ethel Swenson, lived with their 87-year-old mother on her farm located on Annacis Island in the Fraser River. They negotiated to give the plaintiff one dollar for an option to purchase the property at a price higher than its market value. After reaching agreement they revealed that their mother actually owned the property and so the deal was explained to the mother, who nodded her understanding. They then explained that she was too old and feeble to sign, and they assisted her to mark the document with an X beside her name.

When the sisters realized the agency was assembling land for the Annacis Island Industrial Estates, they claimed that the option agreement was void because of the mother's insanity and refused to go through with the sale as agreed. The court found that although the aged mother's mind was gone the option agreement was still binding on her. The plaintiffs were not in a position where they knew or ought to have known of the mother's insanity. Age, by itself, does not prompt a person to enquire as to that person's mental capacity, and the dollar paid for the option was not unreasonably low since the actual price to be paid was higher than the property was worth. This case illustrates that for a contract to be void because of insanity not only must the person be insane, but also the other contracting party must be shown to have known or ought to have known of the insanity.

The law extends its protection to those incapacitated because of insanity in a way similar to the protection given to minors, and as with minors the insane or intoxicated person is also required to pay a reasonable price for necessaries. To

3. [1955] 3 D.L.R. 129 (B.C.C.A.); aff'd, [1955] 1 D.L.R. 432 (B.C.S.C.).

qualify for this protection, it must be shown that the insane person could not understand the nature of the act being performed. For example, if a man thinks that he is Napoleon and that he is selling his horse when, in fact, he is selling his car, he would be declared insane because he does not understand the nature of the transaction. To escape contractual liability on the basis of insanity, the insane person or a representative must prove not only insanity but also that the person he or she was dealing with knew or ought to have known of the incapacity. This is the point illustrated in the case discussed above.

Once a person has been committed to a psychiatric institution or declared incompetent by a court, all contracts entered into are considered void and are not binding on either party. A trustee is appointed to handle their affairs. To understand the precise rights and obligations of such patients and the care and use of the patient's property, the appropriate provincial legislation should be carefully examined.

People who lose their ability to reason through intoxication, whether from alcohol or drugs, are treated in the same way as the insane. And, like insanity, for the contract to be voided the person must have been so intoxicated that they didn't know what they were doing and the other person must have known or ought to have known of the incapacity. The person trying to escape a contract on the basis of drunkenness must also be able to show that, on reaching sobriety, the contract was repudiated. An intoxicated person who purchases shares is not permitted, on becoming sober, to wait and see whether the stocks go up or down before repudiating the contract. Hesitation to repudiate makes the contract binding. This requirement of **repudiation** also applies to insane people who regain their sanity. A person who is of weakened intellect, or otherwise vulnerable but not insane, is still to some extent protected. Unconscionable transactions, the legal principle providing this protection, will be discussed below.

**Insanity applies if person did not understand and if other party knew or ought to have known of incapacity**

**Provincial legislation applies to people committed to institutions**

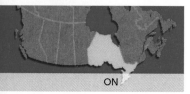

ON

**Drunkenness treated like insanity**

**Must repudiate upon becoming sober**

## Others of Limited Capacity

Limited companies have their capacity to contract determined by the legislation under which they are incorporated. In some jurisdictions, companies can limit their capacity to contract by so stating in their incorporating documents. Otherwise, all companies incorporated under these general statutes have "all the power of a natural person" to contract. Even in those jurisdictions where the capacity of a corporation can be limited, people dealing with those companies are affected by that limitation only if they have notice of it.

**Corporate capacity—usually no longer a problem**

### Case Summary 6.3

**Failure to Incorporate Results in No Capacity: *Teskey v. Grzelak*[4]**

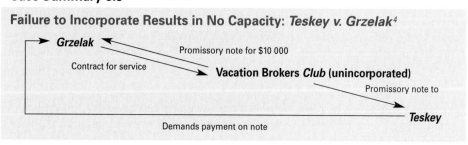

4. (2000), as reported in *Lawyers Weekly* Vol. 20 (2000), (Ont. S.C.).

Grzelak entered an agreement to become a member of a vacation brokers club and pursuant to the contract submitted a promissory note for $10 000 made out to the club. The club then negotiated that note on to Teskey, who brought this action to enforce it when Grzelak defaulted on the note. In fact, the vacation brokers club was a nonentity: it was not incorporated and did not exist from a legal point of view. The Court held that since the club did not exist it did not have the capacity to contract. Because there was no contract between Grzelak and the vacation club, the promissory note made pursuant to it was invalid and not enforceable. While today a corporation has the capacity to contract, here there was no corporation at all. This case serves as a reminder that we all have to be careful in the assumptions we make when dealing with others.

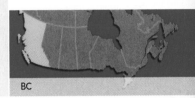

BC

Other corporate bodies are created by special legislation. These include some private companies, Crown corporations, and other government bodies that have been created to accomplish a particular government purpose. The Canadian National Railway, Canada Post, Petro-Canada, Air Canada, and Canada Mortgage and Housing Corporation are some examples. The capacity of these entities depends on the legislation creating them, and their power to contract is often limited by that legislation. If they have not been given the capacity to enter into a particular type of contract, that agreement will be void. Outsiders dealing with that corporation or government body would be well advised to determine ahead of time the validity of any such dealings. This is especially true when the contract involved is unusual in some way.

**Capacity of government bodies and Crown corporations limited by legislation**

### Case Summary 6.4

#### When a City Lacks Capacity: *Pacific National Investments Ltd. v. Victoria (City)*[5]

In this case a developer thought it had a deal with the City of Victoria not to rezone several lots it was developing. When the property was "downzoned," the developer sued. At trial the City was held in breach of an implied contract. On appeal to the Supreme Court of Canada, the Court decided that upon examination of the *Municipal Act,* as well as the history and tradition surrounding that statute, the City did not have the power to bind itself in this way. In other words, the City did not have the capacity to agree to the terms claimed in the contract. This case illustrates how important it is to determine the power of incorporated bodies before dealing with them.

## Reducing **Risk** 6.2

Since Crown corporations or government bodies acting under statutory authority will have their power to contract limited by that legislation, people dealing with them should determine that those dealings are within their statutory power before proceeding. If they do not and the deal goes bad, the contract will be void—usually leaving the businessperson to suffer the loss.

---

5. (2000), 193 D.L.R. (4th) 385 (S.C.C.).

**Capacity of enemy aliens limited in times of war**

Dealing with aliens and representatives of foreign governments also gives rise to capacity issues. When at war, any contract with a resident of an enemy country is void if detrimental to Canada. If not detrimental the contract is merely suspended for the duration of the hostilities. Note that the government normally passes special legislation covering this area whenever hostilities break out.

**Contracts with foreign governments may or may not be enforceable**

Even in times of peace, contracts with foreign governments or their representatives were traditionally thought to be unenforceable because of that government's sovereign immunity. The principle is that the sovereignty of the foreign government would be lost if subjected to the jurisdiction of our courts. This provision was particularly important when dealing with matters of state that were of diplomatic importance. However, since foreign governments are now more frequently involved in simple commercial enterprises that have nothing to do with matters of state, the courts have been willing to treat them as any other party to commercial transactions. These principles are now embodied in legislation.[6] Representatives of foreign governments, such as ambassadors and their families, have traditionally been immune from prosecution in our criminal courts and continue to be. In a civil matter, a court will not issue a writ against such a person, and their property is immune from seizure. Of course, these representatives can waive this immunity, if they wish, but anyone dealing with people who have diplomatic immunity ought to be aware of the protection they have been given.

**Trade unions have capacity to contract for union activities**

A problem also arises with respect to the capacity of trade unions. While they are not incorporated as such, it is likely safe to conclude that they at least have the capacity to enter into contracts that relate to their trade union activities.

*Undischarged bankrupts* also have their capacity to contract limited. An undischarged bankrupt is a person who has made an assignment in bankruptcy or been forced into bankruptcy through a receiving order obtained by a creditor. Simply being unable to pay debts as they become due is not enough. Bankruptcy will be discussed in Chapter 10.

**Status Indians still protected under *Indian Act***

Finally, the capacity of Native people living on reserves (Status Indians) is still limited to some extent by the *Indian Act*.[7] Although they may seem discriminatory, these provisions remain because they are viewed as protections exempted from the operation of the *Charter of Rights and Freedoms* by section 35, which recognizes and affirms existing aboriginal and treaty rights.

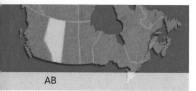

AB

---

## Reducing **Risk** 6.3

As a general rule, the capacity to enter into contracts is not a problem facing most businesspeople. Still, in those few situations listed, it is vital to be aware of the problem and alert to the possibility that the law may protect the person being dealt with, especially where merchants are dealing with underage customers. As a practical matter, the diffi-culty is usually avoided where cash is involved and no credit is extended to the underage customer. The problem of capacity may come up in the other types of transactions as well, and the businessperson should be aware of the potential for difficulties so that steps can be taken to avoid the problem.

---

6. *State Immunity Act*, R.S.C., 1985, c. S-18.

7. *Indian Act*, R.S.C. 1985, c. I-5.

# Legality

The objectives of an agreement must be legal and not contrary to public interest for the agreement to qualify as a binding contract. If the terms, consideration, or objectives of the agreement are immoral, prohibited by statute, or determined to be against public policy, the validity of the whole contract or the specific term may be challenged. Agreements to commit crimes are obviously invalid, but there are other types of transactions that, while not specifically prohibited in law, are considered immoral or contrary to public interest and also not binding on the parties. The consequences of such "illegality" depend on the nature of the defect and the moral taint involved. The courts have taken several different approaches when faced with these problems.

**Response of the court varies with nature of violation**

## Illegal and Prohibited Contracts

Contracts to commit illegal acts are not only void but also illegal. The distinction is important because when faced with a void contract the court will restore the parties to their original position, ordering them to return any deposits advanced and property that had been transferred. When a contract is **illegal,** it involves unacceptable or immoral conduct. Under such circumstances the contract is still void, but the courts will not assist the parties by restoring them to their original position unless one of them is innocent of any wrongdoing. An illegal contract usually involves the commission of some prohibited conduct, such as the sale of a controlled substance or the commission of some violent or antisocial act. The conduct may be identified as wrongful and specifically prohibited by the *Criminal Code* or some other statute, or it may simply be inconsistent with the provisions of such a statute. Common law actually goes further and labels some types of immoral conduct as unacceptable and against public policy, and, even though they are not crimes or violations of statute, when people attempt to create bargains in such circumstances they are treated as illegal contracts (prostitution is one example).

**Illegal contracts—courts will not assist parties**

Where the contract involves clear moral wrongdoing, it is illegal. But many federal and provincial statutes are more regulatory in nature. These statutes often contain provisions declaring any agreement in violation to be void or to incur specific consequences. The courts then will apply those statutorily mandated outcomes.

**Statute may set out consequences**

However, these statutes often are silent as to what will happen in the event of a violation. When there is a violation that involves no moral wrongdoing the courts simply treat the contract as void but not illegal. If the unacceptable term can be separated from the main agreement, only that part will be void. In circumstances where it is clear that the purpose of the contract is to generate income and the violation is more one of procedure than of substance the courts may actually enforce the contract, allowing the parties to correct the procedural defect. Case Summary 6.5 illustrates this point.

### Case Summary 6.5

#### Valid Contract Despite Failure to Register: *Agasi v. Wai*[8]

Mr. Agasi did renovation work on Mrs. Wai's home, and sued for $15 000 still owing. Mrs. Wai claimed that the contract was not legally enforceable because Mr. Agasi had failed to obtain the required municipal licence.

---

8. (2000), 4 C.L.R. (3d) 101 (Ont. Sup. Ct.).

The Court held that in this case the contract was legally enforceable. The bylaw provided for a range of fines for failure to obtain the appropriate licence; there was no indication in the bylaw that it was intended to interfere in the contractual relations between the parties. While the purpose of the bylaw may have been to protect consumers from unqualified service providers, that was not the situation in this case as the defendant had carefully checked out the *bona fides* of the plaintiff and there was no question about his qualifications or the quality of the work done. The Court, however, did reduce the claim by $5000, which represented cost overruns not agreed to by Mrs. Wai.

## Examples

The following is a list of some of the types of contracts that have been determined to be illegal and against public policy.

**1. Contracts to commit a crime or a tort.** For example, if Mullins offers Nowak $100 to falsely claim that Abercromby did a poor job of repairing his house it would be defamation, and the contract to pay Nowak to defame Abercromby would be illegal.

**2. Contracts involving immoral acts.** For example, although prostitution is not illegal in Canada, a prostitute could not expect the courts to enforce a bargain made with a client because the act is considered immoral.

**3. Contracts that interfere with government or obstruct justice.** If the effect of the contract is to interfere with the judicial process, it is against public policy. An agreement that encourages criminal activity by providing to pay a person a salary when he gets caught and is in jail would involve such an obstruction of justice. Bribing public officials or selling defence secrets would interfere with government and also would be prohibited.

### Case Summary 6.6

**An Agreement Made to Avoid Prosecution Is Void:**
*Re Royal Bank of Canada v. Newell*[9]

In this case, a woman forged her husband's signature on 40 cheques totalling more than $58 000. He tried to protect her from prosecution by signing a letter prepared by the bank agreeing to assume "all liability and responsibility" for the forged cheques. The Court found that this was "...an agreement to stifle a criminal prosecution which is an illegal contract and unenforceable." Because the contract was illegal, his agreement to accept responsibility for the cheques was void and he was entitled to his money back. A merchant may find such an arrangement very attractive, but it smacks of blackmail and interferes with and covers up a criminal act avoiding proper prosecution.

What do you think? Should the parties be free to make their own arrangements in these circumstances?

**4. Contracts that promote litigation.** An agreement whereby one person, to satisfy some ulterior motive, pays another to sue a third would be void as promoting litigation. An exception is the lawyer's contingency fee. In this

9. (1997), 147 D.L.R. (4th) 268 (N.S.C.A.).

arrangement, the lawyer agrees to proceed with an action without payment, in return for a share of the judgment (often amounting to 30 or 40 percent). This agreement appears to be permissible because it does not promote litigation but serves to make the courts more accessible to those who normally could not afford to proceed.

**Contingency fee arrangements permissible because they make courts accessible**

**5. Contracts that are bets and wagers.** Historically, the courts would not enforce most contracts related to gambling activities. Now this area is covered by statute, and the rules vary from province to province. These statutory provisions are designed primarily to limit and regulate gambling activities, and the courts will enforce only contracts where the activities have statutory approval or are licensed.

Insurance is like a wager. A person owning property pays for insurance against the destruction or loss of the property. If the property is destroyed, the insurer compensates the owner for the loss. This requirement of loss is called an **insurable interest** and must be present for the insurance to be valid. Insurance will be discussed in Chapter 12.

**Insurance contract is valid where there is an insurable interest**

Contracts for the sale of shares have the same difficulty. If the contract merely requires the parties to pay each other the difference if the share price goes up or down, it is void as a wager. To avoid this problem, the contract must provide that the share will actually change hands. Commodities traded in a similar fashion suffer the same problem.

**6. Contracts that unduly restrain trade.** When a business is sold, the parties often include a clause prohibiting the seller from opening another business in competition. If such a provision is reasonable and necessary to protect the interests of the parties it is enforceable, but if the provision is unreasonably restrictive or against public interest that provision of the contract is void. For example, Beaudoin purchases a barbershop from Ahmed for $50 000. A considerable portion of the purchase price may be for the customer relations established by Ahmed. This is called *good will*. If Ahmed then opens another barbershop next door, it would destroy the goodwill aspect of the contract. It would be reasonable for the buyer to include a provision in the contract prohibiting the seller from carrying on a similar business for a specified time (for example, three years) and within a specified geographical area (for example, five kilometres). If the time and distance restrictions agreed to are not excessive, this would be classed as a reasonable restraint of trade and the contract would be valid.

**Restrictive covenants must be reasonable**

## Case Summary 6.7

### "Sham" Fails to Get Around Contract Restrictions: *Misasiv v. Guzzo*[10]

When Mr. Guzzo sold his retail fruit market, he signed a written agreement that included the term that for a period of five years he would not become involved in a similar business within five miles of the one he sold. Within a year of the sale, a similar business was opened up by Mr. Guzzo's son within the prohibited five-mile radius. The purchasers suspected that it was really Mr. Guzzo's new business and sued for breach of the non-competition clause in the purchase agreement. The question was whether the non-competition clause was valid, since it was an attempt to limit competition. The Judge decided that the clause was valid, that

10. (1984), 78 C.P.R. (2d) 70 (Ont. H.C.).

the arrangement for the new business was no more than a "sham," and that Mr. Guzzo himself was at least indirectly involved in it in violation of the non-competition covenant. The plaintiff was awarded damages of $20 000.

Where a restriction is excessive and is deemed to be an unreasonable restraint of trade, normally only that provision will be void and the rest of the agreement will be enforceable. The effect would be that the purchase price and all other terms of the agreement would be the same, but the seller would have no restrictions at all and would be free to open a similar business anywhere. In the example above, if the provision in the contract for the purchase of the barbershop prohibited Ahmed from opening another shop anywhere in Canada or imposed an unreasonably long period of time, such as 10 years, this provision of the agreement would likely be void. Ahmed would then be free to open a new barbershop wherever he wanted. Thus, great care must be taken to avoid the purchaser's normal inclination to make the restriction on competition as broad as possible, drafting a clause that goes no further than necessary to protect those interests.

### Case Summary 6.8

#### A Too-Broad Restrictive Convenant Frees an Accountant to Compete: *Bassman v. Deloitte, Haskins, and Sells of Canada*[11]

Mr. Bassman was a partner in an accounting firm who left to work for a competitor. A term of the partnership agreement prohibited him from doing business

with anyone who was a client or had been a client of the firm within a five-year period preceding his separation. When the former partners sued, the Court had to determine whether this clause was an undue restraint on competition. Did it go too far? The clause was held to be invalid as it prohibited doing work for former clients. Since these people had already left it didn't harm the partnership for Mr. Bassman to do business with them. The provision was, therefore, an unreasonable restraint of trade and void. This case illustrates the dilemma: Why not simply determine whether what was done amounted to unreasonable competition, rather than give the restricted party complete freedom to compete because of a poorly drafted restrictive covenant?

Provincial statutes regulate gambling activities such as video lottery terminals.

An employer will often impose a similar restrictive covenant requiring employees to promise not to compete during or after their employment. Although the same test of reasonableness is used, the courts are much more reluctant to find such restrictive covenants valid. It is only where the employee is in a unique position to harm the company (for example, by having special access to customers or secret information) that these provisions will be enforced. This will be discussed in more detail in Chapter 11.

---

11. (1984), 4 D.L.R. (4th) 558 (Ont. H.C.).

**7. Contracts between businesses to fix prices or otherwise reduce competition.** These are controlled by the federal *Competition Act.*[12] This statute specifically prohibits agreements that have the "undue" restriction of competition as their primary purpose or objective:

> 45.(1) Everyone who conspires, combines, agrees, or arranges with another person.... (c) to prevent or lessen, unduly, competition in the production, manufacture, purchase, barter, sale, storage, rental, transportation, or supply of a product, or in the price of insurance upon persons or property, or (d) to otherwise restrain or injure competition unduly, is guilty of an indictable offence and is liable to imprisonment for five years or to a fine not exceeding ten million dollars or both.

Thus, if two merchants agreed not to sell a particular commodity below a certain price, or not to open up branches that would compete with each other in specified communities, and they were the only ones selling the products in that community, such agreements would likely be void. Such a conspiracy may be punishable as a criminal act. This is another example of a contract in restraint of trade. The *Competition Act* prohibits a number of other unacceptable business practices, which will be discussed in Chapter 9.

The list above describes some of the categories restricted by statute or held to be against public policy. This list is neither complete nor exhaustive, and it may well be that new types of activities made possible by changing technology could also be controlled by statute or declared as being against public policy in the future. Special care should be directed to activities on the internet. Gambling and pornography account for a large portion of internet use; the validity of the activity depends on the jurisdiction involved, which often is not clear at all. Several jurisdictions have passed or will soon enact statutes controlling these activities, and great care should be taken by both businesses and consumers who become involved to determine the legality of that involvement.

## Reducing Risk 6.4

There is a great temptation for a purchaser of a business or an employer to protect herself from competition. Purchasers of a business and employers are particularly vulnerable to unreasonable competition and can include terms in their contracts that restrict that competition, but those clauses must not go too far. There is a tendency for the person who is advantaged by such a clause to make it much broader than is necessary to prevent unfair competition. But such clauses must be reasonable in the circumstances and must not be against the public interest. They must go no further than is necessary to prevent unfair competition. They should have a geographical limit and a time limit to their operation. A clause restricting competition within a 500-kilometre radius when 50 kilometres would be sufficient is void. So would a clause with a five-year restriction when one year would be enough. Great care should be exercised in drawing these non-competition clauses, and legal advice should be obtained to make sure that the resulting clause would be enforceable.

---

12. *Competition Act,* R.S.C. 1985, c. C-34.

# Intention

Not all agreements are contracts. Often people enter into arrangements or undertakings never intending that legal consequences will flow from them. If a person invited a friend over for dinner and the friend failed to show up for some reason, the delinquent guest would probably be quite surprised if the would-be host were to sue for breach of contract. The law requires that the parties must have intended that legal obligations and rights would flow from their agreement for it to be a binding contract. Since neither the host nor the guest intended to create a legal obligation, the host's legal action would fail.

**Parties must have intended legal consequences from agreements**

When determining intention, the courts do not look to the state of mind of the person making the promise. Rather, they look to the reasonable expectations of the promisee. The test is objective. Would a reasonable person have thought that the person making the promise was serious and that the agreement was legally binding? If so, it is not going to help the person making the promise to say he was only kidding.

**Courts will enforce reasonable expectations**

## Case Summary 6.9

### When Friends Fall Out Over Money: *Osorio et al. v. Cardona*[13]

Osorio and Cardona went to the horse races together and bought tickets on the Sweep Six (betting on six races where they had to predict all six winners). After the third race they discovered that both their tickets were still in the running to win, and they made an agreement that if either of them won they would split the winnings. Cardona went on to win $735 403, but refused to honour the deal. Because of the odds involved Osorio was entitled to $147 000, but Cardona refused to pay, offering Osorio $60 000 or nothing. Osorio took the $60 000 and then sued for the remainder. The Court decided that there was an intention to be bound and a valid contract: the fact that they adjusted the split to reflect the odds indicated they were serious. Cardona had always acted toward Osorio in a way that led Osorio to believe that he was serious and that he intended the agreement to be in force. Note that because there were threats involved, the agreement to take $60 000 was held to be unconscionable and not binding as a settlement. Osorio was able to collect the other $87 000.

This case illustrates not only the requirement of intention but also that the test whereby the Court seeks to enforce the reasonable expectations of the parties is objective. But was the result just and fair? What do you think?

The following situations illustrate instances in which this problem arises and indicate the courts' probable responses.

**Courts will enforce stated intention**

**1. Stated intention of the parties.** If the parties clearly state that they do not wish to be legally bound by their agreement or that the agreement is not to be enforceable in any court, that instruction will be honoured. Such a statement must be embodied in the terms of the contract and be very clear as to the intention. Often in commercial relationships the parties will have arrangements that are convenient but where they don't want to be bound legally. Sometimes the parties are in pre–contract negotiations and are not yet ready

---

13. (1984), 15 D.L.R. (4th) 619 (B.C.S.C.).

to be bound. So-called "letters of intention" are examples of such communications that clearly carry no legal obligations.

**2. Commercial relations.** If the relationship between the contracting parties is primarily commercial in nature, the courts will presume that the parties intended to be legally bound by their agreement. The contract will be binding on them in the absence of any evidence or clear instructions to the contrary.

*Courts will presume intention in commercial transactions*

**3. Domestic and social relations.** When an agreement is between members of a family or friends involved in domestic (non-business) activities, there is a presumption that the parties do not intend legal consequences to flow from the agreement. If members of a family informally agree to make payments to each other, such as a child agreeing to pay room and board or parents to pay an allowance, the courts would assume that there is no intention to be legally bound and would not enforce the agreement. However, if the parties had gone to the trouble of having a lawyer draw up a formal contract, then the court would be satisfied that the parties did intend that legal consequences would flow from their agreement and would enforce the contract. The presumption of no intention would be rebutted.

*Courts will presume no intention in domestic and social relations*

**4. Social and business relations.** Problems arise when the relationship involved is a mixture of social and commercial relations, such as when people jointly enter a contest and dispute over the distribution of the prize. This problem could become more prevalent in Canada with the proliferation of lotteries with large prizes. In such cases, the court must treat each situation on its individual merits. In fact, the courts turn to the reasonable person test to determine whether it is reasonable for the parties trying to enforce the agreement to think that a legally binding contract had been created.

*Reasonable person test applies where social and business relations mix*

**5. Exaggerated claims.** Merchants often exaggerate the qualities of their products in advertisements or as they talk to customers, claiming their product to be "the biggest" or "the best." To some extent, this enthusiasm is expected and is not taken seriously by the public or the courts. The problem is where to draw the line, and the courts again apply the reasonable person test to determine whether in the circumstances the customer should have taken the exaggerated claim seriously. Note, however, that even where the exaggeration is obvious it may still be prohibited by statute as misleading advertising or an unfair trade practice. Such consumer protection legislation will be discussed in Chapter 9.

*Reasonable person test also applies when dealing with exaggerated claims*

## Case Summary 6.9

### Are Manufacturers and Retailers Permitted to Exaggerate?
*Carlill v. Carbolic Smoke Ball Company*[14]

In this case, the defendants manufactured a product that they claimed would protect users from influenza. They offered £100 to anyone who used their product as prescribed and still contracted influenza, and stated in an advertisement that £1000 had been deposited in the Alliance Bank, Regent Street, which showed their sincerity in the matter.

Mrs. Carlill used the product, got influenza, and claimed the money; however, the company reneged, stating that the advertisement was an advertising puff that

14. [1893] 1 Q.B. 256 (C.A.).

merely indicated some enthusiasm for the product and was not meant to be taken seriously by the public. The Court held that depositing money to back up the claim had taken it out of the category of an advertising puff. It was determined that a reasonable person would have thought the advertisement was serious, so the offer was valid. There was intention, and Mrs. Carlill's use of the product and contracting the illness were appropriate forms of acceptance; thus, there was a valid contract.

Misleading advertising has become a much greater problem and is now controlled by legislation that will be discussed in Chapter 9.

## Form of the Contract

We have established that the essential ingredients of contracts are consensus, consideration, capacity, legality, and intention (as summarized in Table 6.1 on p. 230). Historically, the form of the contract was also very important. Promises were enforceable because they were contained in sealed documents, called *deeds*. Today, there is no general rule that a contract must take a certain form, although deeds are still required in some jurisdictions to transfer land. Contracts may be in writing, they may be under seal, or they may simply be verbal or even implied from the conduct of the parties.

People are often surprised to find out that most verbal agreements have the same legal status as written ones, as long as they meet the requirements described in this and the previous chapters.

**Verbal contracts binding but writing advised**

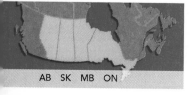

The importance of the written document is practical, not theoretical. It is always a good idea to put the terms of an agreement in writing so that if a dispute arises there is something permanent that establishes the terms to which the parties agreed. In the absence of such a document, it is surprising how differently even well-intentioned people remember the terms of their agreement. If the dispute between the parties does end in litigation, the parties will be in a better position to prove their case if they can produce written evidence to support their claim. We can also expect changes to these requirements as we move away from a paper-based economy to an electronic one.

## Where Writing Is Required

**Writing required to enforce some contracts**

**Statute of Frauds requires writing for enforcement in courts**

In some limited circumstances, a contract is required by statute to be evidenced in writing for it to be enforceable. These requirements for writing are found primarily in the *Statute of Frauds*, but other statutes have similar requirements.

The first statute of frauds was enacted in England in the 17th century, and adopted with some variation by the Canadian provinces. The statute requires that certain types of contracts be evidenced in writing to be enforceable. But the statute has been criticized as causing as much abuse as it was intended to prevent. As a result many important changes have been made to the *Statute of Frauds*, with Manitoba and British Columbia repealing the statute altogether. British Columbia retains some of its provisions in its *Law and Equity Act*.[15]

---

15. R.S.B.C. 1996, c. 253, s. 59.

## Case Summary 6.11

### Writing Still Needed in Manitoba: *Megill-Stephenson Co. v. Woo*[16]

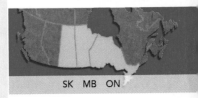

SK  MB  ON

Two parties were negotiating by telephone, and at the conclusion of their conversation a deal was struck for the purchase of a parcel of land. However, before any documents were drawn up the vendor changed his mind, and the purchaser sued. The court held that despite the fact that the *Statute of Frauds* had been repealed in that province, there was the usual expectation of the parties that the contract dealing with the sale of land would not be effective until put into writing; therefore, that expectation was honoured and the Court refused to enforce the agreement.

Note that the Court first had to find that a deal had been struck, and it can be argued that by this decision the vendor was allowed to take advantage of the purchaser for his own profit. What do you think?

The following is a discussion of the types of contracts generally included under the *Statute of Frauds* in Canada. The actual wording varies among provinces.

**1. Contracts not to be performed within one year.** When the terms of the agreement make it impossible to perform the contract within one full year from the time the contract is entered into, there must be evidence in writing for it to be enforceable. For example, if Sasaki Explosives Ltd. agrees in March 2003 to provide a fireworks display at the July 1 celebrations in Halifax in the summer of 2004, that contract must be evidenced by writing to be enforceable. Failure to have evidence in writing will make it no less a contract, but the courts will refuse to enforce it. British Columbia and Ontario have eliminated the requirement of writing in this area. Note that even where it is impossible for one party to complete performance within the year, written evidence is not required where it is clear in the contract that the other is expected to perform within that year.

**When contract cannot be performed in one year**

**2. Land dealings.** Any contract that affects a party's interest in land must be evidenced in writing to be enforceable. It is often difficult to determine just what types of contracts affect interest or ownership in land and what types do not. Any sale of land (or part of it, such as the creation of a joint tenancy in land) must be evidenced in writing. Any creation of an easement or right of way or estate, such as a life estate, is also covered by the *Statute of Frauds*. But contracts for services to the land that do not affect the interest to the land itself are not covered. For example, if a carpenter agrees to build a house, such an agreement may affect the value of the land but not the interest in the land itself and so need not be evidenced in writing to be enforceable. This provision of the *Statute of Frauds* has also been modified in some jurisdictions. In British Columbia and Ontario, a lease for three years or less is exempt from the legislation, but longer leases are treated just like any other interest in land and must be evidenced in writing to be enforceable.

**When an interest in land is involved**

**3. Guarantees and indemnities.** When money lenders are not satisfied with the creditworthiness of a debtor, they may insist that someone else sign as well. This means that the creditor wants another person to add his or her

16. (1989), 59 D.L.R. (4th) 146 (Man.C.A.).

**When guarantee is involved**

credit to the transaction and assume responsibility for the repayment of the debt. The arrangement can be in the form of a guarantee or an indemnity. If the third party incurs a secondary liability for the debt, it is called a **guarantee**. The guarantor promises that if the debtor fails to pay the debt he or she will assume the responsibility and pay. Note that in this type of transaction the obligation is secondary or contingent; there is no obligation on the guarantor until the debtor actually fails to pay the debt.

An **indemnity** describes a relationship in which the third party assumes a primary obligation for the repayment of the debt or other obligation along with the debtor. As a result both owe the debt, and the creditor can look to either for repayment. When a third party says, "I'll see that you get paid," there is an assumption of a primary obligation, and the promise is an indemnity. The distinction between the two is important because in most provinces the *Statute of Frauds* requires that a guarantee be in writing but not an indemnity. If the court classifies the nature of the third-party agreement as an indemnity, there is no requirement of writing. The distinction can be vital when a person has made only a verbal commitment to pay the outstanding loan to the debtor. In British Columbia, the *Law and Equity Act* requires that both indemnities and guarantees be evidenced in writing to be enforceable. In some jurisdictions, this requirement of writing extends to promises to be responsible for the torts (miscarriages) of others as well.

**When goods sold over specific value**

**4. Others.** The original *Statute of Frauds* required that whenever the purchase price of goods sold exceeded a specified minimum, there had to be evidence in writing for the sale to be enforceable. This provision has been included in the *Sale of Goods Act* in many jurisdictions in Canada but is not a requirement in British Columbia, although B.C.'s *Consumer Protection Act* requires contracts entered into with direct sellers (door-to-door sales) to be in writing when they are over a certain value.

It is usually sufficient evidence in writing if a receipt or sales slip has been given or if delivery of the goods has been accepted. The definition of goods and the sale of goods generally will be discussed in Chapter 9. Parliament and the provincial legislatures have passed many statutes that require the transaction itself to be in writing to be valid. Some examples are the *Bills of Exchange Act*, insurance legislation, consumer protection legislation, some of the legislation dealing with employment relations, and the carriage of goods and passengers. In many jurisdictions the *Statute of Frauds* also requires the promises of executors (to be responsible personally for the debts of an estate) and promises made in consideration of marriage to be in writing to be enforceable.

## What Constitutes Evidence in Writing

**Writing must contain all essential terms**

Note that it is not the whole agreement that must be in writing to satisfy the *Statute of Frauds*, only that there be evidence in writing supporting the essential terms of the agreement. The essential terms are normally an indication of the parties, the subject mater of the contract and the consideration to be paid. But other terms may become essential depending on the nature of the contract. This evidence can take the form of the actual agreement itself or simply a receipt or note and can even come into existence after the creation of the contract referring to it. The writing can be a single document or a collection of documents, which taken together provide the required evidence. The documents must also be signed, but only by the person denying the existence of the contract.

• and may arise after agreement
• and be signed by party to be charged but need not be in the same document

Note that important adaptations have been necessitated because of changing technology. As electronic records and communications become the norm and paper plays less of a role, these traditional requirements of writing and signatures are becoming obsolete. One solution is to give digital records and electronic signatures the status of written documents, and legislation to allow this is now either in place or in progress. However, this leads to other challenges. The problems brought about by computers and electronic communications will be discussed in Chapter 16.

## Effect of the Statute of Frauds

It is vital to remember that if a contract is not in writing this does not make it void under the *Statute of Frauds*; it is merely unenforceable. This means that the contract is still binding on the parties, but the courts will not assist them to enforce it. If the parties have already performed, or if there is some other remedy available that does not require the court's involvement, the contract will still be binding even in the absence of evidence in writing. The courts will not assist a person who has performed to get out of a contract. Nor will the court order the return of money even when there is no evidence in writing of the contract. In effect, the party did only what was required under the contract. Similarly, when there is a lien (a right to seize property) or when there is a right to set off a debt against the obligations established within the contract, the parties themselves may be in a position to enforce it without the help of the courts. In that sense, such a contract is binding, even though there is no evidence in writing.

**Contract still valid even where no writing, just unenforceable**

### Case Summary 6.12

**Part Performance Satisfies Statute: *Hill v. Nova Scotia (Attorney General)*[17]**

**Effect of Statute of Fraud**

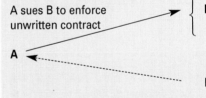

A sues B to enforce unwritten contract → B  Contract is valid but unenforceable; B can't be forced to perform.

A ←

B  But if B performs he can't change his mind to get $ back, since contract is valid.

In this case, land was expropriated to build a highway. But the Crown agreed to allow the owner of the land to move people, livestock, and equipment across the highway, and a government department even helped by producing fencing and ramps to accomplish it. This arrangement continued for 27 years. The result was that the owner of the property acquired a right of way across the highway that was an equitable interest across the property. The Court held that even though the *Statute of Frauds* required evidence in writing, this was not a necessity here because the 27 years of crossing the highway with the help of the government constituted part performance.

17. (1997), 142 D.L.R. (4th) 230 (S.C.C.).

## Part Performance

**When part performance consistent with contract, writing not required**

The court will waive the requirement of writing if the parties can produce evidence to show that a contract dealing with an interest in land has been partially performed. There are some important limitations to this principle. The part performance must be evidence of the existence of the contract and consistent only with the existence of the contract. The payment of money owed under the contract will not usually be acceptable as proof of part performance because the payment of money is consistent with any number of different obligations. In British Columbia, by statute, the payment of a deposit is sufficient part performance with respect to land transactions to make such a contract enforceable.[18] A good example of acceptable part performance when land has been sold is the start of construction. The permission to enter onto the land and start building is consistent with the sale of the land, and so the courts will accept the part performance as sufficient evidence to support the contract. Table 6.1 summarizes the elements required to make a contract legally binding.

### Table 6.1 Summary of Contract Formation

| | | |
|---|---|---|
| No consensus | Contract void | But must pay for requested services |
| No consideration | Contract void | But note promissory estoppel, gift, and seal |
| No capacity | Contract voidable | But infants can enforce contracts with adults |
| | | But infants bound by necessaries and beneficial contracts of service |
| | Contract void | But insane must show the others knew of insanity |
| No intention | Contract void | Note presumptions |
| Illegal | Contract void | But depends on statute |
| No writing | Valid | But note *Statute of Frauds* exceptions |

## Reducing Risk 6.5

Although there are only a few situations where evidence in writing is required, from a practical business point of view such contractual arrangements should always be put into writing (or, as technology develops, some other permanent form). Even people with the best of intentions will remember things differently as time passes. It is vital, therefore, to have a permanent memorandum that can be referred to later so that the terms are certain and the good will between the parties is retained. Where relations have broken down, there is nothing better than a written document to resolve a dispute that arises over a soured business transaction. Chances are that the existence of the document by itself may prevent litigation, and if it does not at least there is evidence as to what the parties agreed to that can be used in the action. And so, while in law it may be true that an oral contract is as binding as a written one, it is poor practice indeed to rely on such oral arrangements in business.

18. *Law and Equity Act*, R.S.B.C. 1996, c. 253, s. 59 (4).

# Summary

In order to be able to create a binding agreement the parties to a contract must meet other conditions in addition to the consensus and consideration discussed in the previous chapter. The first has to do with the legal capacity of the parties; the second is their legality; and the third is that the parties must have an intention to be bound. The *Statute of Frauds* and other statutes in most jurisdictions require that some contracts also be evidenced in writing.

## Capacity

### Minors
- Contracts with minors in most provinces are not binding on them, except for contracts for necessaries and beneficial contracts of service.
- In British Columbia, by statute, all contracts with minors are unenforceable, except those that are specifically made enforceable by legislation, such as government student loans

### Insanity and drunkenness
- A contract will be rendered invalid only when the person was so incapacitated as to not know what he or she was doing and the other contracting party knew or ought to have known of that incapacity

### Other
- Corporations, enemy aliens in times of war, trade unions, government agencies, bankrupts, and Status Indians on reserves have their capacity to enter into contracts limited to some extent

## Legality
- Contracts that are illegal or against public policy may also be invalid or unenforceable
- Agreements to commit crimes or immoral acts, agreements that interfere with government or obstruct justice, agreements that promote litigation, and in some circumstances bets or wagers may be held to be illegal or against public policy
- Contracts that unduly restrain trade, such as price fixing, are generally prohibited, but contracts in which one party agrees not to carry on business in competition with another are valid, if they can be shown to be reasonable in terms of the interests of the parties and the public

## Intention
- Both parties must intend to be legally bound by their agreement
- In family and other social relationships, there is a presumption of no intention, but this can be challenged by evidence that shows an intent to be bound. In commercial relationships, intention is presumed
- In unusual situations, the reasonable person test is used to determine intention

## The requirement of writing
- Contracts dealing with interests in land, contracts that will not be performed within one year, and contracts involving guarantees are examples of contracts that, under the *Statute of Frauds*, must be evidenced in writing to be enforceable
- The *Statute* has been repealed or modified in many jurisdictions
- When part performance is established, such agreements are enforceable

## QUESTIONS

1. Explain the circumstances in which an infant may escape liability for a contract and the circumstances in which an infant is bound by a contract.

2. What is the significance of an infant's contract being designated as a beneficial contract of service?

3. What is the responsibility of parents for the actions of their infant children in both tort and contract law?

4. What are the rights and obligations of the parties involved when an infant makes a contract with an adult for non-necessaries?

5. Explain the circumstances in which an infant can be sued for tort even though a contract between the parties is involved.

6. What must an insane or drunk person establish to escape liability under a contract?

7. Explain four other situations where businesspeople must be careful that those they deal with have the capacity to contract.

8. Explain what care businesspeople must exercise when entering into contracts with Crown corporations or government bodies.

9. Describe how the courts treat a contract to commit a crime.

10. Give five examples of contracts deemed by the courts to be against public policy and describe the effect of such a designation.

11. Are all contracts that restrain trade unlawful? Explain.

12. Explain how the courts' treatment of domestic agreements differs from their response to commercial transactions when the question of intention arises.

13. Describe tests the courts will use in determining whether the parties were serious when they enter agreements.

14. What is the significance of a written document in contractual relations?

15. Explain why some people have suggested that the *Statute of Frauds* has led to more frauds than it has prevented.

16. Give examples of the types of contracts currently included under the *Statute of Frauds*.

17. What must be evidenced in writing to satisfy the requirements of the *Statute of Frauds*?

18. Under what circumstances will a contract falling under the jurisdiction of the *Statute of Frauds* be enforceable even though it is not evidenced by writing?

## CASES

**1. *Re Collins* Lawyers Weekly, (1991) Vol. 11, No 26 (B.C.S.C.).**
Mrs. Collins was divorced from a famous rock star and living in Vancouver with his two children. As part of the divorce, she received a substantial payment along with a sup-

port payment for each child. She persuaded Mr. Collins to purchase a large house in the city, which he did, but he arranged that the house be held in trust for the two minor children. Mrs. Collins became concerned about her financial position and persuaded the two children to transfer the title of the house to her. At the time of the trial, the oldest child who had reached the age of majority confirmed the sale, but the youngest child was still underage. Evidence was presented that this contract was for the benefit of the children, giving the children the security they needed until they reached the age of 25 years. Evidence indicated that the minor child had received independent legal advice, and a psychiatrist testified that it was truly the desire of the child to make sure the mother had financial security. Explain the arguments that support the transfer of the house and the arguments against it.

### 2. *Lenson v. Lenson* (1987), 44 D.L.R. (4th) 1 (S.C.C.).

The father owned a farm in Saskatchewan and his son, the plaintiff, lived on that farm with his wife. For a number of years, they had a crop-sharing arrangement, which was essentially a lease on the property paid for by the son sharing the crop with his father. This arrangement had been going on for some time, when the son alleged they had entered into an oral agreement whereby he would buy the farm for $100 000 and be given the land immediately around the farmhouse as a gift. According to the son's testimony, he and his wife gave up several opportunities to buy surrounding property and made considerable improvements on the land in question, but eventually there was a falling out between the parties and the father denied that any agreement existed. Explain what difficulties the son will face in trying to establish his claim to the land and how those difficulties can be overcome.

### 3. *Ouston et al. v. Zurowski et al.* (1985), 18 D.L.R. (4th) 563 (B.C.C.A.).

A number of plaintiffs including Ouston were persuaded to invest in a scheme run by the defendant, "Kulnan Investment Corp.," which was a pyramid investment scheme. Such a scheme is similar to a chain letter, where one person higher on the chain makes money on the basis of others being persuaded to join the chain for a fee. The idea is that the person joining the chain will get higher in that chain as others join and make a considerable amount of money on those they recruit. The problem with such schemes is that the people who are last to join lose all their money.

The plaintiffs testified that they were told when they were brought into the scheme by Zurowski that if the board should stop, Zurowski would make sure they got their money back; that is, if the pyramid scheme failed, he would reimburse the defendants. The scheme did fail because of local publicity that discouraged any further meetings and the attraction of any further investors. Pyramid schemes are illegal under the *Criminal Code*. In this action, Ouston and the other plaintiffs seek to have their money returned. Explain what arguments they can put forward to support this request and the likely attitude of the court in granting remedies. How would your answer be affected if there were not *Criminal Code* prohibition?

### 4. *Canadian American Finance Corp. v. King* (1989), 60 D.L.R. (4th) 293 (B.C.C.A.).

The Canadian American Finance Corporation markets a registered scholarship savings plan for profit. King was employed to market the plan as director of agencies. King set up a separate company to market the plan. The agreement between the Canadian American Finance Corporation and King included a non-competition clause that said that once the relationship was terminated, King could not enter into competition with the corporation for a period of two years in Canada or Bermuda. King eventually quit and went to work for a rival company in Alberta and British Columbia. Comment on the arguments available to both parties as to the validity of this non-competition clause.

### 5. *Transport North American Express Inc. v. New Solutions Financial Corp.* (2002), 214 D.L.R. (4th) 44 (Ont. C.A.).

Note that this case has been appealed to the S.C.C.

A borrower agreed to pay 4 percent interest per month as well as a 30-percent royalty payment and other fees on borrowed money. This was an effective interest rate of 60.1 percent annually. The *Criminal Code* declares anything over 60 percent to be a criminal rate of interest. It was clear that neither party intended to violate or understood that they were violating the *Criminal Code,* and so the creditor asked the court to adjust the amounts to be paid for royalties, interest, and bonuses so that there would be no criminality. What should the Court do in these circumstances? What will the outcome be with respect to the obligations of the parties?

### 6. *Professional Institute of the Public Service of Canada v. Canada (Attorney General)* (2002), 222 D.L.R. (4th) 438 (Ont. C.A.).

The federal government passed legislation allowing it to "deal with" the surpluses in government pension plans, and the validity of this action was challenged by a certified trade union and an incorporated employee organization. The federal government in turn brought an application challenging the status of these bodies to sue or be sued. In effect, they claimed that they didn't have the capacity to appear in court and challenge the legislation. The employee organization was an incorporated non-profit society and the trade union was a certified trade union under the *Public Service Staff Relations Act.* What arguments could be advanced by the parties to support their positions?

How would it affect your answer to know that the federal *Rights of Labour Act* stated that a trade union could not be a party to an action unless it had status "irrespective to of this act or the *Labour Relations Act*"?

### 7. *Bursey v. Bursey* (1995), 533 A.P.R. 291 (Nfld. C.A.).

This case involves the enforcement of a separation agreement between husband and wife. The husband operated a business and the wife was an employee. To avoid paying retail sales tax they brought in a considerable amount of equipment from outside the province. When they separated, a term of the separation agreement required the wife to pay half of the evaded sales tax if the husband were eventually required to pay. The scheme failed and the husband was required to pay some $54 000 in unpaid provincial sales tax. This action is brought by him to enforce the separation agreement and recover half of those funds from his former wife. Should the wife have to pay?

# Factors Affecting the Contractual Relationship

## CHAPTER HIGHLIGHTS

- The nature and effect of a mistake in a contract
- Misrepresentation and its consequences on a contract
- The implications of duress and undue influence
- The rules governing privity and assignment

The two previous chapters examined the process of forming contracts. This chapter will discuss the extent of the responsibilities and obligations of the original parties to an agreement, what happens when the parties disagree as to the nature and effect of the contract, and how those obligations are affected when an innocent third party or a stranger to the contract becomes involved.

# Mistake

In limited circumstances, the courts will provide a remedy where one or both of the parties have made a mistake with respect to a contract. This is especially true when it is clear that because of the mistake the parties have failed to reach a consensus and there is no complete agreement between them. It must be made clear at the outset that the court will not interfere when the parties have simply made a bad bargain: this is an error in judgment and the person who made it must live with it.

**Misunderstanding that destroys consensus results in void contract**

Reviewable mistakes in contract involve a person's mind being at odds with the terms, surrounding circumstances, or other factors relating to the contract. Such a mistake can relate to the terms of the contract, including the identity of the parties. It can relate to an assumption upon which the contract is based, whether as to a matter of fact, some future event, or the law surrounding the contract. And it can also concern an expected result or consequence of the agreement. The mistake can be made by only one of the parties or by both. Where both parties are making a mistake, it can be a *shared mistake,* where both are making the same mistake, or it can be a *misunderstanding,* where each party has a different idea as to the meaning of the terms of the contract. This is a complex and difficult area of contract law to understand. It will help to keep in mind that the guiding principle seems to be that the courts will try to do what is necessary to give effect to the reasonable expectations of the parties.

**Mistake must be part of agreement, not just affect agreement**

**Courts will try to give effect to the reasonable expectations of the parties**

When the mistake relates to the terms of the agreement itself, such as the identity of the parties or the subject matter of the agreement, the courts are more willing to provide a remedy. The courts also will not interfere with contractual obligations unless the demonstrated mistake is significant or material with respect to the agreement. If a person ordering a new car is delivered one that is a slightly different colour than the one he had in mind when he chose it, that will not be enough to allow him to avoid the contract. Finally, where the mistake is caused by the negligence of one of the parties that party will normally be held responsible for the error.

It should also be noted that if the mistake is one about the facts involved, the court will be more likely to provide a remedy than if the mistake is based on an interpretation of the law or its effect. Still, where one party stands to make a wind-fall at the expense of the other the courts will likely review the transaction whether the mistake is one of law or of fact. For example, when one party receives a payment they are not entitled to because the other has misunderstood their legal obligation the court will likely order those funds returned on the basis of **unjust enrichment.**

The area of mistake in contract law is very confusing, and it has not been uncommon over the years for the courts to reverse or modify their position. The discussion below is an attempt to summarize the important aspects of the law in this area. The approach taken concentrates on three different ways that a mistake can be made. It should be remembered that if a contract is found to be *void* it is not a contract at all; if it is *voidable* the contract does exist, but one of the parties has the option of getting out of it. When an innocent third party has acquired goods that are the subject of a voidable contract, that party gets to keep the goods, but if the contract was void—that is, there never was a contract—the person who sold the goods to the third party never had title to them, and those goods must be returned to the original owner.

## Shared Mistake

A **shared mistake** occurs when the two parties are in complete agreement but they have both made the same mistake regarding some aspect of the contract (see Figure 7.1). The courts will review the transaction only where the mistake relates to some fundamental aspect of the subject matter of the contract. The most common example of such a shared mistake resulting in a void contract is where the subject matter of the contract no longer exists at the time the contract is made. Thus, where the parties enter into an agreement for the sale and purchase of the cargo of a ship, without knowing that the ship and cargo were destroyed the night before, the contract is void because of the shared mistake. The courts have also found a contract void because of a shared mistake when, unknown to the parties, the property being sold was already owned by the purchaser. In both these instances, the parties have together made the same significant mistake with respect to a factual aspect of the agreement that has destroyed the basis of the contract. As a result, the contract is void for lack of consensus.

**Mistake must be serious**

**Careless party responsible when mistake is result of negligence**

**The courts are less likely to remedy a mistake in law**

**Fundamental shared mistake about subject matter—void**

### Figure 7.1

Mind of party one ———————➤◄——————— Mind of party two

(Both parties are of the same mind, making the same mistake.)

When the shared mistake relates only to the value of what they are dealing with, it normally will not affect the enforceability of the contract. For example, if both vendor and purchaser think that they are dealing with an ordinary violin when, in fact, they are dealing with a rare and valuable Stradivarius, the contract would be binding nevertheless.

## Rectification

If the written document does not reflect the common intention of the parties to the contract, the courts are willing to correct or rectify the document. For example, if two parties had agreed to the sale of land for $500 000 and a clerical error made the document read $50 000, the court would add the missing zero and require the parties to perform the corrected agreement. The courts will do this only where it is clear that both understood what they were agreeing to and what was written was different from that understanding. If in the above example both parties intended to write $50 000 on the basis of a shared error about how much land was included, the court will not rectify this, as they both intended to put down that amount in the written document. The fact that it was based on an error will not support rectification, although it may be grounds for setting the contract aside on the basis of a shared mistake about a fundamental aspect of the subject matter. It is important to remember that the courts are not rewriting the agreement during rectification. They are simply correcting a written document so that it corresponds to the demonstrated intention of the two parties. Rectification of the contract may be available as a remedy in other situations as well, such as where one person makes a mistake caused by the fraud of the other party.

**Courts will correct an improperly recorded agreement**

### Case Summary 7.1

#### The Case of the Million-Dollar Comma: *AMJ Campbell v. Kord Products Inc.*[1]

This case involved AMJ Campbell selling the assets of a subsidiary (KPL) to the defendant, Kord. The transaction included the sale of a significant inventory of plant containers with the value determined by calculating the "average sales price" over the prior eight months. This was to be calculated "net of taxes, freight rebates and discounts," but the solicitors for Kord changed that by inserting a comma between the words *freight* and *rebates*. This change was made, along with some others, to the final contract by AMJ Campbell. Before the change only freight rebates would be deducted from the average price, but with the insertion of the comma all of the freight costs as well as any rebates would also be deducted. This resulted in a saving to Kord of more than $759 000 (hence the million-dollar comma).

AMJ Campbell, claiming mistake, asked the Court to rectify the contract by removing the comma. The Court refused, saying that for rectification to take place it had to be clear that both parties had intended the document to read the other way. Here the solicitors for Kord had intentionally inserted the comma and intended that any freight costs be deducted from the purchase price. Only AMJ Campbell had made a mistake by agreeing to the change—and that is not good enough for rectification. This case is helpful in showing the limited power of the Court to rectify and the restricted situations where rectification can be used.

1. [2003] O.J. No. 329 (Ont. S.C.J).

## Misunderstanding

A different type of mistake occurs when the parties have a misunderstanding about the terms of the agreement itself and neither party is aware of the other's different understanding (see Figure 7.2). When one party to an agreement thinks that the agreement is to do something else, the courts will usually apply the reasonable person test to determine which interpretation of the contract is more reasonable. The court will then adopt the more reasonable position as the correct interpretation of the contract. This point is discussed below in more detail under the heading "Rules of Interpretation." Only if the error is a serious one and the court cannot choose between the two positions because both are equally reasonable will the contract be declared void.

**Court will enforce reasonable interpretation**

**Where equally reasonable and serious—void**

The case of *Raffels v. Wichelhaus*[2] is a good example of such a dilemma. In this case, the contract concerned a cargo being transported on a ship called the *Peerless*. It happened that there were two ships by this name, both leaving the same port but at different times. The seller intended one of these two ships, and the purchaser had in mind the other. There was no way of applying the reasonable person test to this case, and since the disagreement was fundamental there was no consensus between the parties and the contract was void.

### Case Summary 7.2

**Meaning of "Sale" Clarified: *Leading Investments Ltd. v. New Forest Investments Ltd.*[3]**

A real estate agent obtained an offer with a deposit from a purchaser. This was accepted and constituted a sale, which, according to the exclusive listing agreement, entitled the agent to a commission. When the deal fell through the agent who was holding the deposit refused to deliver it to the vendor, claiming he was entitled to a commission because a sale had taken place. The dispute made it to the Supreme Court of Canada, which decided after looking at the practice in the industry and the various contracts involved that the completion of a contract of sale was not enough; the sale itself had to go through. The agent was not entitled to a commission even though the vendor could keep the deposit as compensation. Here "sale" meant one that actually went through, not one that collapsed. This case illustrates what factors the courts will look at when determining what the terms of a contract actually mean.

### Figure 7.2

Mind of party one ⟶

⟵ Mind of party two

(Both parties have a different understanding of contract. They are of different minds.)

---

2. (1864), 2 H. & C. 906, 159 E.R. 375 (E.D.).

3. [1986] 1 S.C.R. 70; application for reconsideration refused (sub. nom. *H.W. Liebig Co. v. Leading Investments Ltd.*) (1986), 18 O.A.C. 80 (S.C.C.).

# One-Sided Mistake

## Case Summary 7.3

### Unilateral Mistake Leads to Rescission of Contract: *Moss v. Chin*[4]

Mrs. Moss was left unconscious after being struck by a car driven by Mr. Chin. Her representative, the public trustee, started a legal action and negotiated with the driver's insurer, ICBC. ICBC made an offer to settle, but Mrs. Moss died before it was accepted. The public trustee accepted the offer on her behalf without informing ICBC of her death. When ICBC found out what happened it applied to have the settlement set aside.

This was a unilateral mistake on the part of ICBC and normally it would not affect the rights of the other parties. But in this situation, rather than ICBC misleading themselves, the public trustee deliberately set out to make sure ICBC did not discover a mistake and the Court had the power to interfere. The Court ordered that the contract be rescinded. This case shows that even when a unilateral mistake is made, under some limited circumstances there may be a rescission of the contract.

A one-sided or **unilateral mistake** takes place where only one of the parties to the contract is making a mistake with respect to the contract (see Figure 7.3). This was the situation in *Moss v. Chin* in Case Summary 7.3. As a general rule, there is no recourse for a person who makes such a one-sided mistake. Thus, when the manager of a business buys a computer by name and model thinking it will do a specific job, and it turns out that it does not have the required capacity, a mistake has been made by the purchaser but there will likely be no remedy. This is a one-sided mistake, and if there were no reliance placed on the salesperson and no misrepresentation or misleading information supplied in the documentation and brochures there will be no remedy. In effect, the purchaser has misled himself, and the principle of *caveat emptor* ("Let the buyer beware") applies. It should be noted, however, that when the offeror makes an obvious error in relation to his or her offer, the purchaser will not be allowed to take advantage of this obvious error and snap up the offer. Thus, if the merchant selling the computer misquoted it agreeing to sell it at $25 instead of the $2500 normal price, the purchaser would not be able to ignore such an obvious error and "snap it up" at the bargain price. When a one-sided mistake takes place, the person making the mistake usually has a remedy only when he or she has been misled, and then the normal course of action is to claim for misrepresentation with its associated remedies.

**One-sided mistake—"Let the buyer beware"**

There are some situations, however, where the one-sided mistake is so fundamental as to destroy consensus between the parties. This may be important to

## Figure 7.3

Mind of party one

(Where only one party is making a mistake)

---

4. (1994), 120 D.L.R. (4th) 406 (B.C.S.C.).

establish even where misrepresentation is involved, since the contract would then be void providing even broader remedies. If goods that had been resold to an innocent third party were involved, the remedy of rescission for misrepresentation would not be available. However, if a mistake sufficient to destroy consensus had taken place, the contract would be void, allowing recovery of the goods involved even from an innocent purchaser.

For consensus to be destroyed, the one-sided mistake must be profound. Such a one-sided mistake can occur when there is incorrect identification of one of the parties to a contract. If the person claiming that a mistake has taken place actually thought the deal was with someone else and can demonstrate that identity was an important aspect of the agreement, the court can declare the contract to be void. However, if the error was only about some attribute of the other party, such as their wealth, this will not affect the existence of the contract. They have to have thought they were dealing with another person, not just that the person they were dealing with was wealthy.

**If mistake goes to identity—void contract**

For example, if a vendor thought that jewellery was being sold on credit to Ms. Paré, a wealthy movie star, and in fact the Ms. Paré the merchant was dealing with was a waitress and not associated with the movie industry at all, the contract would be binding and title would go to the purchaser. He knew he was dealing with a specific woman, Ms. Paré, but was mistaken in terms of one of her attributes: her wealth. If the jewellery is resold, the ultimate purchaser would acquire good title. Of course, the seller would still have recourse against Ms. Paré if she did not pay for the jewellery. But if the seller thought that the purchaser was Ms. Paré, a wealthy and well-known movie star, and in fact the purchaser was Ms. Capozzi, someone with similar appearance but who was a waitress, a mistake has been made about the identity of the person with whom the seller is dealing and there would be no contract. In this case, the mistake is not as to the woman's attributes but as to her very identity. He thinks he is actually dealing with someone else entirely, and there is no contract. Under these circumstances, if the goods have been resold to an innocent third party the jeweller can recover them since the original contract was void and he still has title.[5]

## Non Est Factum

Where one of the parties is unaware of the nature of the document being signed, the courts will, in rare circumstances, declare the agreement to be void on the basis of *non est factum* ("It is not my act"). If a person were led to believe he was guaranteeing a note and was, in fact, signing a mortgage agreement on his home, he could argue that there was no consensus between the parties and no contract. This might be a valid defence even against an innocent third party who had acquired rights under the agreement. For this defence to succeed and the contract to be void, it must be shown that the mistake about the document went to the very nature of that document rather than merely to its terms. In this example, if the mistake went only to the rates, with the mortgagee thinking he was to pay 10 percent interest when the document actually required 15 percent, he would still be bound, the mistake going to some aspect of the document and not the document itself. Today, negligence, such as failure to read the document before signing, can defeat the defence of *non est factum* and as a result successful claims of *non est factum* are quite rare.

**If mistake goes to nature of document signed—void**

**• but not where negligence present**

---

5. *Cundy v. Lindsay* (1878), 3 App. Cas. 459 (H.L.).

## Case Summary 7.4

### *Non Est Factum* Not Available for Pension Waiver: *Deraps v. Coia et al.*[6]

Mr. Deraps was a labourer who had paid into a pension fund for 20 years when he discovered he had lung cancer. He spoke to his union representative, Mr. Hickey, about a disability pension. Mr. Hickey explained to Mr. and Mrs. Deraps that they would receive a higher pension if she signed a waiver of spousal benefits. Mrs. Deraps signed the waiver; within a year, Mr. Deraps died. Mrs. Deraps claimed that when she signed the waiver she didn't understand that when her husband died she would be left with nothing. She applied to the Court to have the waiver declared void on the basis of *non est factum.* The Trial Court held in her favour, but this ruling was overturned on appeal. The effect of the waiver was clear and it had been explained to her "in as simple terms possible." Also, she read and wrote English and the document she signed was not fundamentally different from what she thought she was signing. In addition, the fact that she did not bother to read the document before signing disqualified her from claiming *non est factum.* In the end the Ontario Court of Appeal did decide in her favour, but on the basis of negligent misrepresentation. Mr. and Mrs. Deraps were dependent on Mr. Hickey, who had a duty to supply all material information. His failure to do so was just as misleading as a positive misstatement. Damages were awarded on the basis of what Mrs. Deraps would have received had she not signed the waiver.

This case shows how difficult it now is to succeed in claims for *non est factum.* Fortunately for Mrs. Deraps she was able to succeed on other grounds. Some critics might think that this case shows that we have gone too far in limiting the application of *non est factum.* What do you think?

## Rules of Interpretation

The test to determine whether a mistake has taken place is objective. The courts are not concerned with what the parties thought they were agreeing to but rather with what the parties should have been aware of and expected when they made the agreement. In such instances, the courts use the reasonable person test. Instead of declaring the contract void because one of the parties has made a mistake about the meaning of a term, the courts will look at the wording to determine what a reasonable person would have understood the term to mean. Only in those rare circumstances in which there is no reasonable interpretation of the agreement, or the positions taken by the two parties are equally reasonable, will the courts declare the contract to be void.[7]

**Reasonable person test applies when there is a misunderstanding**

Whenever there is a dispute involving the meaning of a specific term, the courts have a choice of applying the literal meaning of the term or adopting a more liberal approach by trying to determine the parties' intent. Usually, the courts will apply the literal meaning of the wording chosen by the parties if there is no ambiguity. If the term is ambiguous, the court will look at what was behind the agreement and apply the most reasonable meaning of the term to the contract.

**Courts apply literal meaning to specific wording**

**Ambiguous wording interpreted liberally**

---

6. (1999), 173 D.L.R. (4th) 717 (Ont. C. Gen. Div.); rev'd on other grounds (1999), 179 D.L.R. (4th) 168 (C.A.).

7. *Raffels v. Wichelhaus* (1864), 2 H. & C. 906, 159 E.R. 375 (E.D.).

Determining the literal meaning of the words is not as simple as it might first appear. Even dictionaries often have several different meanings for particular words. Determining the intention of the parties may also be difficult because of the conflicting positions taken by the parties to the dispute. The court will often look at how the terms are normally used in the particular industry involved. The court will also look at past dealings between the parties as well as their dealings at the time the contract was formed to determine what they intended by the words they used. The key to the court's approach to such ambiguous terms in an agreement is to choose the most reasonable interpretation. Another rule courts use in these situations is the **parol evidence rule.** Where the terms used in an agreement are clear and unambiguous, the courts will not allow other outside evidence to be introduced to show a different meaning was intended: "What you see is what you get." If you state in your agreement that the contract is for the sale of a "1994 Chrysler automobile," you cannot later try to introduce evidence that a Chrysler sailboat was intended. Of course, if the contract only referred to a "1994 Chrysler" it is ambiguous, and evidence then could be introduced to show that a car or a sailboat was intended.

Several exceptions to the parol evidence rule have developed over the years. The courts will override the parol evidence rule when the evidence to be introduced is of a **fraud** or some other problem associated with the formation of the contract, such as duress or undue influence. Other exceptions include evidence of a **condition precedent** (a condition that has to be met before the obligations set out in the contract are in force); evidence of a **collateral contract** (a separate contractual obligation that can stand alone, independent of the written one); evidence of a subsequent agreement entered into by the parties after the written one; or the absence of an intention that all of the contract would be embodied in the written document. When the evidence contradicting the terms of the agreement falls into one of these categories, the court can be persuaded to hear it, despite the parol evidence rule.

The courts are also willing to imply terms into an agreement when necessary. It does not occur to most contracting parties to provide terms in their agreement for every possible eventuality, and the courts are willing to supply these missing terms. Where the parties agree to the purchase of a car, for example, they might not specify the time of delivery or when the price is to be paid. The courts will imply what is reasonable in the circumstances, likely that delivery must take place within a reasonable time determined by the nature of the goods, and that the price is to be paid upon delivery. What is reasonable will often be determined by looking at past dealings between the parties or the normal practices and traditions found within that specific industry or trade. Some terms may be implied automatically by statute. The *Sale of Goods Act* has set down in rule form the terms that are implied in a contract for the sale of goods when the parties have not addressed them. As well, some consumer protection legislation imposes terms in contracts whether or not the parties have agreed to them. The courts have also been known to impose contract terms on the parties and modify obligations, using the principle of fairness[8] and unconscionability discussed below.

**Courts will not permit outside evidence to contradict clear wording**

**Exceptions to the parole evidence rule**

**Courts will imply terms, where appropriate**

AB

**Statutes may imply terms into contract**

8. *Cooper v. Phibbs* (1867), L.R. 2 H.L. 149 (H.L.).

## Reducing **Risk** 7.1

The interpretation of contracts is one of the areas in business where the greatest confrontation takes place and where businesspeople would be wise to review their practices. There may be great value in establishing the trust associated with a deal made on a handshake, but this examination of mistake and misrepresentation shows the downside. Even the most sincere businessperson can forget just what they have agreed to, or two parties may recall the terms quite differently even when they had the same understanding of the terms of the agreement in the first place. And that does not even consider the instances of wilful blindness and convenient memory loss. Putting an agreement into some permanent form, such as writing, is only the first step. Great care should be taken to ensure that the words used are clear and unambiguous so that there can be no question later of what has been agreed upon. This type of approach will usually contribute to the good will between businesspeople rather than threaten it. Conflict is reduced and confidence increased on the basis of good business practices.

### Case Summary 7.5

**Terms Are Sometimes Implied into Contracts:**
*Rapatax (1987) Inc. v. Cantax Corp. Ltd.*[9]

Two parties entered into a joint-venture agreement for the development of computer software with no provision for termination. One of the parties terminated without notice, causing significant damage to the other, who sued. The court held that termination by either party on reasonable notice should be implied into the contract. The party terminating should have given reasonable notice, and damages were ordered accordingly. This case illustrates at a very basic level that sometimes provisions must be implied into contracts for them to make sense.

# Misrepresentation

In pre-contract negotiations people often say things that are designed to persuade the other party to make the deal but that never become part of the contract. When these statements are false, misleading the other party and inducing them to enter into the contract, an actionable misrepresentation has taken place. **Misrepresentation** is a false statement of fact that persuades someone to enter into a contract. The false statement can be made fraudulently, when the person making the statement knew it was false; negligently, when the person should have known the statement was false; or completely innocently, when the misrepresentation is made without fault.

*Misrepresentation is a misleading statement that induces a contract*

### Case Summary 7.6

**Misrepresentation Gives Rise to *Non Est Factum*:**
*Edelweiss Credit Union v. Beck*[10]

Mr. Beck was sued for $26 000 by the Edelweiss Credit Union for failure to repay a personal loan. The problem was that throughout the arrangements for the transaction the vice-president of the Credit Union had repeatedly referred to the document as a "guarantee" rather than a "personal loan." The difference is significant, because under a personal loan Beck owed the money directly to the credit union,

---

9. (1997), 145 D.L.R. (4th) 419 (Alta. C.A.).

10. (1991-06-13), B.C.S.C. F882657 (B.C.S.C.).

whereas with a guarantee the obligation is only contingent: no money is owed until the primary debtor defaults. The court held that this negligent misrepresentation had misled Beck and his lawyer as to the nature of the documents. The fact that Mr. Beck was a sophisticated businessperson and that his lawyer was present didn't take away from the fact that he had been misled as to the contents of the documents. Since they were entitled to rely on the vice-president and had been misled, their failure to read the document did not amount to carelessness. In this case, because the misrepresentation had caused a fundamental mistake as to the very nature of the document there was no contract at all on the basis *of non est factum.*

## Allegation of Fact

**Misrepresentation must be fact, not opinion or promise**

The statement that forms the basis of the misrepresentation must be an allegation of fact. Only statements made about the current state of things that prove to be incorrect can be considered misrepresentation. "This car has a new motor" is a statement of fact. "I will have the car safety inspected when it comes due next year" is not a statement of fact, but a promise to do something in the future. A promise to do something in the future will qualify as a misrepresentation only when it can be clearly shown that person making the promise had no intention of honouring that promise at the time it was made. Such promises of future conduct have to be enforced under general contract law, and the buyer should take care to ensure that this commitment is included as a term of the contract. Where the misleading statement being complained of was an expression of opinion rather than fact, it too is not actionable, unless the person making the statement was an expert. When a person declares that the car he is selling is a "good car" or a "good deal" he is entitled to have that opinion, and the statement is not actionable if the car later breaks down. But if a mechanic makes the same statement, and it proves false, it can be actionable as misrepresentation because he is an expert.

**Opinion by expert may be misrepresentation**

## Silence or Non-disclosure

### Case Summary 7.7

**Representation and Reliance Required for Fraud: *Hoy v. Lozanovski*[11]**

Mr. Hoy sued for fraudulent misrepresentation when the house he purchased from Mr. and Mrs. Lozanovski proved to be infested with termites and had to be renovated at a cost of $25 000. Hoy was seeking damages, but the judge held that there was no fraud since the Lozanovskis did not know of the termites when they sold the house. Also, they had remained silent and so no representation had been made. Finally, since Mr. Hoy had had the house inspected, he had not relied on any representations from them. To obtain damages, Mr. Hoy had to demonstrate fraud and that he had relied on their representation. In this case, not only was there no fraud and no reliance, but also there was no representation at all. When we make a mistake or mislead ourselves there is normally no remedy.

**Silence not misrepresentation, unless there is duty to disclose**

For a misrepresentation to take place, there also must be some positive misleading form of communication. Silence or non-disclosure by itself is not usually

11. (1987), as reported in *Lawyers Weekly*, April 3, 1987 (Ont. D.C.).

actionable. There are, however, some special situations where the person contracting is required to disclose certain information. For example, insurance contracts require the parties acquiring insurance to disclose a great deal of personal information that affects the policy. People who apply for life insurance are required to disclose if they have had heart attacks or other medical problems. The sale of new shares involves a similar obligation of disclosure to an investor in a prospectus. If the terms require that the parties disclose all information to each other as a condition of the agreement, the contract can be rescinded if they fail to do so. Professionals also have an obligation to disclose certain information at their disposal that might affect the actions of their clients. These are often referred to as **utmost good faith** contracts. This requirement of good faith is being expanded, and it is now much more common for the courts to find that a misrepresentation has taken place where one party withholds information from the other.

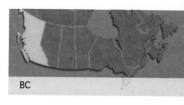

BC

Where a person actively attempts to hide information that would be important to the other contracting party, this also might qualify as misrepresentation. A person anxious to sell a car might be tempted to hide a noisy transmission by using a heavier grade of oil, and such an act might well invite a claim of misrepresentation. It is not necessary that the statement be written or verbal; misrepresentation can occur even if the method of communicating it is a gesture, such as a nod of the head.

**Partial disclosure may be misrepresentation**

Misrepresentation is normally available only as a cause of action when an actual representation has been made. When individuals mislead themselves, *caveat emptor* applies, and there is no cause for complaint. It is for this reason that in Case Summary 7.7 the action against the vendors of the property infested by termites failed. Mr. Hoy, the purchaser, went to considerable trouble to inspect the property and so, in effect, misled himself about its condition. The vendors had made no representation in relation to it.

**Misrepresentation must have misled the victim**

## False Statement

It is necessary to demonstrate not only that the misleading comment qualifies as an allegation of fact, but also that the statement is incorrect and untrue. Even when a person technically tells the truth but withholds information that would have created an entirely different impression, this can amount to misrepresentation. For example, if a used car salesperson tells a potential purchaser that the transmission of a particular car has just been replaced but fails to say it was replaced with a used transmission, this partial truth can be misrepresentation if it leads the purchaser to believe a new or rebuilt transmission was installed.

## Statement Must Be Inducement

A victim of misrepresentation must show that he or she was induced into entering a contract by a false statement. If the victim knew that the statement was false and entered into the agreement anyway, either because he or she did not believe the statement or believed that the statement did not make any difference, the misrepresen-

A salesperson who hides faults in a used car may be guilty of misrepresentation.

tation is not actionable. Similarly, if the person thought the statement was true but would have entered into the contract even if he or she had known it was false, there is no misrepresentation. The false statement must affect the outcome of the agreement, and the victim must have been misled into doing something that he or she otherwise would not have done for there to be an actionable misrepresentation. In Case Summary 7.7, even if the court had found that the Lozanovskis had made a misleading statement it likely would not have qualified as an actionable misrepresentation because the purchaser did not rely on it. We know this because Mr. Hoy was careful to have the house inspected before it was purchased.

### Case Summary 7.8

**False Information Induces Purchase of Bar:** *Papaioannou et al. v. 370684 Ontario Ltd. et al.*[12]

When Mr. Papaioannou discovered the bar he had purchased catered to a gay clientele, he surrendered possession of it back to the sellers and brought this action to recover the deposit and for other compensation. He claimed he had been negligently or fraudulently misled as to the nature of the business and with respect to its gross sales. The judge found that since Mr. Papaioannou had visited the bar before purchase he must have known of the nature of the business, but did find that the profitability had been overstated and this false statement had induced Mr. Papaioannou to purchase the business. This fraudulent misrepresentation allowed the plaintiff to rescind the contract and obtain damages in the amount of $100 822. It is not enough that the statements are false; to be actionable misrepresentation it must also be demonstrated that the statements persuaded the victim to enter the contract.

## As a Term of the Contract

**Breach of contract action may be appropriate if misleading term in contract**

The law of misrepresentation discussed here applies where the misleading statement induced or persuaded the victim to enter into a contract. These special remedies are needed because the misleading statement usually does not become a term of the agreement itself. If the misleading statement complained of has become a term of the agreement, the normal rules of breach of contract apply, providing much broader remedies that are easier to obtain. If Osterman agreed to sell Nasser a used Toyota automobile, which in the contract was described as a 1995 Camry with a rebuilt transmission, Nasser could sue for breach of contract if the car turned out to be a 1993 Camry and the transmission was used, not rebuilt. But if Osterman bought a particular property because the vendor Nasser said that the municipal council had voted to build a new highway nearby, it would be a rare contract that would include such a provision as a term of the agreement. Because the statement is an inducement to buy, not a term of the contract, the victim must rely on the rules of misrepresentation to obtain a remedy. The remedies available will depend on whether the statement was made inadvertently, fraudulently, or negligently.

Even so, the courts today are more open to the suggestion that such representations have become terms of the contract. Even statements in advertisements now can be taken to be part of the contract. Many provinces in their consumer

---

12. (1986), as reported in *Lawyers Weekly*, Full Text Order No. 634-009 (Ont. Dist. Crt.).

protection legislation not only have provisions controlling misleading and deceptive trade practices but also state that the representations of salespeople are specifically made part of the contract. The topic of consumer protection legislation will be discussed in Chapter 9.

## Innocent Misrepresentation

An **innocent misrepresentation** is a false statement made honestly and without carelessness by a person who believes it to be true. Where a heavy-duty equipment supplier sells a truck claiming it can haul five tonnes of gravel but its actual capacity is only three tonnes this is misrepresentation, even where the seller believed what he was saying was true. If the person making the misrepresentation is in no way at fault, the misrepresentation is innocent, and the remedies are limited. The only recourse available to the victim is to ask for the equitable remedy of rescission. As soon as the victim realizes what has happened, he or she can either choose to ignore the misrepresentation and affirm the contract or rescind the contract.

**Innocent misrepresentation —remedy is rescission**

### Rescission

**Rescission** attempts to return both parties to their original positions; the subject matter of the contract must be returned to the original owner, and any monies paid under the contract must also be returned. The courts will also require the party who is returning the subject matter of the contract to return any benefit derived from the property while it was in his or her possession. Similarly, a person can be compensated for any expenses incurred. Damages are not available as a remedy, because both parties are innocent. Although rescission is an important remedy, because it is equitable, it is quite restricted in its application. Rescission is not available in the following situations:

**Property returned along with monetary benefit minus expenses**

**Rescission not available**

1. **Affirmation**. Victims of misrepresentation who have affirmed the contract are bound by the affirmation and cannot later insist on rescission. Thus, where a person uses the proceeds of a contract knowing of the misrepresentation, he has affirmed the contract.

• if contract affirmed

2. **Impossible to restore**. The remedy of rescission is not available if the parties cannot be returned to their original positions because the subject matter of the contract has been destroyed or damaged. Since neither party is at fault, with innocent misrepresentation the court will not impose a burden on either one of them but will simply deny a remedy.

• restoration impossible

3. **Third-party involvement**. Rescission will not be granted if it will adversely affect the position of a third party. When the subject matter of the contract has been resold by the purchaser to a third party who has no knowledge of the misrepresentation and otherwise comes to the transaction with "clean hands," the courts will not interfere with that person's possession and title to the goods.

• or it will affect third party

4. **Failure on the part of the victim**. Where the victim comes without clean hands, rescission will not be available. Where the victim has also misled or cheated, rescission will be denied. Where the victim has caused unreasonable delay, rescission will be denied. These principles apply to all equitable remedies, and these will be discussed in the next chapter.

**An equitable remedy with restrictions**

Note, as discussed above, that in those few situations where the misrepresentation causes the victim to make a fundamental mistake about the nature of the contract, the agreement may be void because of the failure to reach a consensus. When this happens there is no contract and the victim can recover money or goods supplied even despite the effect on third parties or the presence of affirmation.

## Fraudulent Misrepresentation

If a misrepresentation of fact is intentional and induces another person to enter into a contract, the victim of the fraud can sue for damages under the tort of deceit in addition to or instead of the contractual remedy of rescission. According to the decision in *Derry v. Peek*,[13] fraud is established when the false statement was made "(1) knowingly, (2) without belief in its truth, or (3) recklessly careless, whether it be true or false."[14] There have been some difficulties over the years in interpreting just what these words mean, but essentially it is fraud if it can be demonstrated that the person who made the false statement does not honestly believe it to be true. The persons making the statement cannot avoid responsibility by claiming they did not know for sure that what they said was false, or because they did not bother to find out the truth. Fraud exists even if the victim of the misrepresentation could have found out the truth easily but relied instead on the statement of the defendant.

When a person innocently makes a false statement and later discovers the mistake, he or she must without delay inform the other person of the misrepresentation. Failure to do so will turn an innocent misrepresentation into a fraud. If during the process of negotiating the terms of a contract a person makes a statement that was true but later becomes false because of changing circumstances, she must correct the statement upon finding out the truth.

Once it has been established that the false statement was intentional and thus fraudulent, the courts can award rescission or damages:

1. **Rescission or avoidance**. The victim of fraudulent misrepresentation retains the right to have the parties to the contract returned to their original positions and to be reimbursed for any out-of-pocket expenses.

2. **Damages for deceit**. The victim of fraudulent misrepresentation can seek monetary compensation as well as rescission for any loss incurred as a result of the fraud. Since the damages are awarded for the tort of deceit, the courts try to put the victim in the position he or she would have been in had the contract not been entered into. Note that to obtain damages there is no obligation to return property, nor is the court attempting to return both parties to their original positions, as with rescission. Rather, the courts require financial compensation to be paid to the victim by the person at fault. A victim of fraud can seek damages even where rescission is not available. The victim does not lose the right to demand monetary compensation by affirming the contract or where the goods have been resold to a third party. On rare occasions, the victim of a fraudulent misrepresentation can seek *punitive damages*; that is, damages intended to punish the wrongdoer rather than compensate the victim.

---

13. (1889), 14 App. Cas. 337 (H.L.).

14. *Ibid.* at 374.

The major problem with fraudulent misrepresentation is the need to establish that the person being sued knowingly misled the victim. This is often difficult to do and is not necessary if only rescission is sought. If rescission will suffice as a remedy, the person suing will commonly claim only innocent misrepresentation even where fraud is apparent.

## Negligent Misrepresentation

An important recent development in tort law is the granting of the remedy of damages for negligent misrepresentation (sometimes called *negligent misstatement,* as discussed in Chapter 4). Today, if it can be shown that the parties should have known what they said was false, even though they honestly believed it was true, the remedies of damages as well as rescission will be available. Even when the negligent statement becomes a term of the contract or arises out of a contractual relationship, the plaintiff may have a choice about whether to sue in contract or sue in tort for negligence. The Supreme Court of Canada made it clear that such "concurrent liability" may exist, subject to limitations that may be included in the contract. Thus, the plaintiff cannot circumvent the protection provided in an exemption clause by suing in tort instead.[15]

**Damages for negligence may be available in cases of misrepresentation**

Damages are available as a remedy where the misrepresentation has become a term of the contract that is breached, where the misrepresentation is fraudulent, and where there is negligence.[16] Thus, it appears that only when the misrepresentation is truly innocent and without fault is the victim restricted to the remedy of rescission.

# Duress and Undue Influence

When people are forced or pressured to enter into contracts against their will by threats of violence or imprisonment, the contract can be challenged on the basis of duress. Today, duress includes not only threats of violence and imprisonment but also threats of criminal prosecution and threats to disclose embarrassing or scandalous information.

**Duress involves threats of violence or imprisonment— contract voidable**

In Canada, duress also includes threats to a person's goods or property. If O'Rourke threatened to vandalize Tong's store unless Tong agreed to purchase his vegetables from O'Rourke, this would qualify as duress and Tong would have recourse against O'Rourke. To succeed, it is necessary to show that the threat was the main inducement for entering into the agreement.

### Case Summary 7.9

#### Son's Threats Amount to Duress: *Byle v. Byle*[17]

A family's plan to develop land led to serious conflict, with one son threatening physical harm to a sibling. Fearing that threat, the parents conveyed some land and gave other advantages to that son. The Trial Court found the transactions void on the basis of duress but the Court of Appeal reversed this decision, finding the contract to be only voidable. A void contract is no contract and nothing can

15. *Central Trust Co. v. Rafuse et al.* (1986), 31 D.L.R. (4th) 481 (S.C.C.).

16. *Beaufort Realties v. Chomedey Aluminum Co.* (1981), 116 D.L.R. (3d) 193 (N.B.C.A.).

17. (1990), 65 D.L.R. (4th) 641 (B.C.C.A.).

save it, but a voidable contract could be revived later by affirmation and be binding on the parties. In this case the difference was not important, for although the parents continued to perform after the threat was passed they were not aware of their right to rescind and so could not be said to have affirmed the contract. This case also points out the fact that when duress is involved, the force or threat does not have to be directed at the other party in the contract; it can be directed at some other person.

**Economic advantage not enough**

Even though the threat of loss of employment and other financial losses can amount to economic duress and be actionable, it is important not to mistake the normal predicaments in which we all find ourselves for improper pressure or duress. If a person has no choice except to use a particular taxi because it is the only one on the street, or has to deal with the only airline or telephone company that services a particular area, these accepted conditions of the marketplace do not amount to duress. Likewise, where a person has to pay a high rate of interest because no one else will loan money at a lower rate it is not duress. Even the threat of suing when the person doing so has a legitimate right to sue is not duress. Rather, it is the legitimate exercise of the rights of that person.

**Voidable contracts cannot affect third parties**

Note that duress only causes a contract to be voidable. Thus, a third party's position cannot be jeopardized if the victim of duress seeks a remedy. If someone is forced to sell a gold watch by threat of violence and the watch is then resold to an innocent third party, the watch cannot be retrieved. Because a voidable contract is still a contract, the title has passed on to the third party. Had the watch been stolen from the original owner and then sold to an innocent third party, the original owner would not have given up title to the watch and could, therefore, retrieve it.

## Undue Influence

The types of pressure brought to bear upon people are often more subtle than those described by duress. When pressure from a dominant, trusted person makes it impossible to bargain freely, it is regarded as **undue influence,** and the resulting contract is also voidable.

**Undue influence involves undue pressures—contract voidable**

In the case of *Allcard v. Skinner,*[18] a woman entered a religious order and gave it all her property. The court determined that there had been undue influence when the gift was given, even though there was clear evidence that there had been no overt attempt on the part of the religious order to influence this woman. The court would have set the gift aside, except that she had affirmed it after leaving the relationship.

### Case Summary 7.10

**Undue Influence Presumed: *Rochdale Credit Union Ltd. v. Barney*[19]**

Mr. Barney was a friend and client of John Farlow, a solicitor, and he reluctantly guaranteed Farlow's loan from Rochdale Credit Union for $50 000. Mr. Farlow died, and the credit union demanded payment from Mr. Barney. The Ontario Court of Appeal found undue influence on the part of Mr. Farlow in persuading his client to guarantee the loan, and because Farlow represented both parties the

---

18. (1887), 36 Ch.D. 145 (C.A.).

19. (1984), 14 D.L.R. (4th) 116 (Ont. C.A.); leave to appeal refused (1985), 8 O.A.C. 320 (S.C.C.).

credit union was also responsible for that undue influence. Mr. Barney did not have to pay the debt. The relationship of solicitor/client leads to a presumption of undue influence. Note as well how the credit union was also affected by that presumption.

Is it a just outcome that the credit union was also responsible in this case? Would it be better if undue influence in these situations had to be proven? What do you think?

The court may find undue influence in the following situations:

**1. Presumption based on a special relationship**. In certain categories of relationships the courts will presume the presence of undue influence, and if the presumption is not rebutted the contract will be set aside. Some examples of such relationships are:

*Undue influence presumed in certain relationships*

- Parents or guardians contracting with infant children
- Professionals such as doctors or lawyers contracting with their clients
- Religious adviser contracting with parishioner (as in *Allcard v. Skinner*, discussed above)
- Trustee contracting with beneficiary

Note that in contracts between parents and adult children and between spouses, undue influence is not automatically presumed but may be established upon consideration of special circumstances.

**2. Presumption based on unique circumstances**. If the relationship involved does not fall into one of the protected classes listed above, there still can be a presumption of undue influence on the basis of unique circumstances. The courts then attempt to determine whether one person was in a position to dominate the will of another, in which case the court may still presume undue influence where it is just and reasonable to do so. A husband or a wife signing a guarantee for the indebtedness of their spouse might constitute such a situation. If the court makes that presumption, it falls on the party trying to enforce the contract to show that there was no domination or unfair advantage taken of the other party.

*Undue pressure from circumstances*

**3. Undue influence determined from facts**. In the absence of a relationship that gives rise to the presumption, it is still possible for a victim to produce actual evidence to satisfy the court that undue influence was, in fact, exerted and that there was coercion. This can be difficult to prove, since the victim must show that a relationship of trust developed because of the relationship between the contracting parties and that that trust was abused. When it can be shown that the person trying to enforce the contract took advantage of the fact that he or she was being relied on for advice, the courts may find that there was undue influence.

*Where undue influence must be proven*

## Case Summary 7.11

### No Undue Influence on Wife: *Bank of Montreal v. Duguid*[20]

Mrs. Duguid was a real estate agent and guaranteed a loan made with the Bank of Montreal by her husband, a school principal, to be invested in real estate.

---

20. (2000), 185 D.L.R. (4th) 458 (Ont. C.A.).

Although the bank was concerned about the wisdom of the investment, it did not send Mrs. Duguid to get independent legal advice. The question is whether there is an automatic presumption of undue influence when one spouse guarantees a loan for the other. The court held that that might be the case in a marriage where one partner is unaware of and not involved in financial decisions, but in this case the wife was a sophisticated real estate agent who knew what she was doing, and so there is no such presumption of undue influence. For the presumption to arise there has to be a close relationship; the guarantor has to be vulnerable and the bank has to know of that vulnerability.

Even when undue influence has been established, the contract will be binding if the person trying to enforce the contract can show that the undue influence was overcome and that the victim either affirmed the contract, which was the situation in the *Allcard* case, or did nothing to rescind it after escaping the relationship. The courts may also refuse a remedy if the person trying to escape the contract is not altogether innocent of wrongdoing.

Of course, if the party accused of undue influence can convince the court that in fact there was no such influence, any presumption is rebutted and the contract is binding. It is advisable, therefore, for contracting parties who are concerned about this problem to ensure that the other party get independent legal advice before entering into an agreement. This is especially true for professionals who are contracting with clients for matters outside that professional relationship.

**Independent legal advice desirable, but contract must be fair**

When it can be demonstrated that the potential victim followed independent legal advice, it is very likely that the courts will enforce the agreement. It must be stressed that the terms of the agreement must be reasonable in such circumstances. The courts will resist enforcing a contract that conveys great advantage to one of the parties, whether or not independent legal advice has been taken.

## Unconscionable Transactions

The concept of unconscionable transactions has received a greater acceptance by the courts in recent years. This is an equitable doctrine that permits the court to set aside a contract in which one party has been taken advantage of because of such factors as desperation caused by poverty and intellectual impairment that falls short of incapacity. To escape from such a contract, it must be shown that the bargaining positions of the parties were unequal, that one party dominated and took advantage of the other, and that the consideration involved was grossly unfair.

**Case Summary 7.12**

### Insurance Settlement Set Aside Because of Unconscionablility: *Woods v. Hubley*[21]

Mrs. Woods suffered back and neck pain resulting from a car accident caused by the negligent driving of Michael Hubley. A week before her spinal surgery she was offered a $3500 settlement by the insurance adjuster, "take it or leave it." She took the money, but when her condition got worse she applied to the Court to

---

21. (1995), 130 D.L.R. (4th) 119 (C.A.); leave to appeal refused (1996), 136 D.L.R. (4th) vii (note) (S.C.C.).

have the settlement set aside. She was awarded more at trial, but the amount was reduced to $150 000 on appeal.

Mrs. Woods had been taken advantage of and the original settlement was set aside on the basis of unconscionability. The insurance adjuster had deceived and misled her and "...effectively dissuaded her from seeking the services of a lawyer, thereby taking advantage of her ignorance and her need." A transaction can be set aside as unconscionable where the evidence shows that (1) that there is an inequality in the bargaining positions of the parties arising out of ignorance, need, or distress of the weaker party; (2) the stronger party has consciously used the position of power to achieve an advantage; and (3) the agreement reached is substantially unfair to the weaker party. The presence of these elements in this case warranted setting aside of the settlement agreement. The courts today are showing an increased willingness to find a transaction unconscionable where it is unfair or prejudicial to one of the parties.

In fact, the courts are showing a willingness to expand this concept and apply it in situations where they believe an injustice has been done or where the results of the agreement are simply unfair, as was the case in *Woods v. Hubley*. It must be remembered that simple economic advantage will not qualify. If a person having limited assets cannot get a loan from anyone else and must pay 20 percent interest, that in itself will not make the contract unconscionable. There must be evidence that the debtor was taken advantage of because of some problem, such as lack of sophistication, age, or desperation, and then it must be shown that the resulting deal was not reasonable. If the 20-percent interest charged was reasonable given the risk, the contract is not unconscionable.

There is some overlap in the principles of unconscionable transactions and undue influence. Although legislation has been passed in most common law provinces prohibiting unconscionable transactions, in most instances the statutory provisions are limited to loan transactions. The recent acceptance of this equitable doctrine developed by the courts makes the defence of unconscionability available even when the contracts in question do not involve the loan of money. Of course, like other equitable remedies where there is undue influence or unconscionability, the court will not grant a remedy where a third party is negatively affected or where the victim also has unclean hands.

**Both common law and statute**

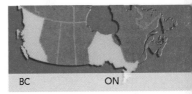

BC          ON

## Case Summary 7.13

### When Is Legal Advice Independent? *Bertolo v. Bank of Montreal*[22]

When Mr. Bertolo borrowed money from the Bank of Montreal to open a restaurant, he needed his mother to mortgage her home as added security. The mother was not fluent in English and didn't really understand what was going on other than that she was helping her son, so the bank sent her to obtain independent legal advice. They referred her to the bank's lawyer, who was also Mr. Bertolo's lawyer, and he had his partner advise her of her legal position. There was no actual evidence of just what advice she did receive, but before leaving the Bank's lawyer assured her that she should not worry and that all would be fine. The bank manager later gave her similar assurances.

---

22. (1986), 33 D.L.R. (4th) 610 (Ont. C.A.).

The Court held that both the lawyer for the bank and his partner were in a conflict of interest position and as a result the advice given was not independent. They should have known better. The manager knew they had to provide Mr. Bertolo's mother with independent legal advice, and their failure to do so caused the mortgage to be set aside on the basis of it being unconscionable. This was a failure on the part of the lawyers as well as the bank manager. When dealing with such vulnerable people every effort must be taken to ensure that there is no undue influence, that they are not being taken advantage of, and that they receive proper independent legal advice.

# Privity of Contract and Assignment

## Privity

**Contract only affects parties to it**

When two parties enter into a contract, they create a world of law unto themselves. Contracting is a bargaining process, and only those participating in the bargain can be affected by it. It is a fundamental principle of contract law that the parties to a contract do not have the power to impose benefits or obligations on third parties or outsiders who are not parties to the contract. The contracting parties have created a private agreement, and outsiders to it can neither enforce it nor be bound to perform its terms. This principle is called **privity of contract.**

The case of *Donoghue v. Stevenson*[23] referred to in Case Summary 4.10 illustrates the application of the privity principle. In that case, a woman bought her friend a bottle of ginger beer, which contained a decomposed snail. The victim, who consumed the contaminated drink, could not sue the owner of the café for breach of contract because she was not the person who bought it. There was no contract between them. Under normal circumstances, merchants can be sued by the purchaser for breach of contract for selling faulty products, even though they are unaware of the problem. But if as here there is no contract, the victim can normally sue only the manufacturer in tort for negligence.

## Exceptions

**Original party to contract can enforce it where benefit to be bestowed on outsider**

There are several exceptions and apparent exceptions to the operation of the privity rule. First, it must be emphasized that while a third party designated to receive a benefit cannot enforce the contract, the original parties still have the right to insist on performance. Thus, if Aguilar, who operates a landscaping com-

## Reducing **Risk** 7.2

Businesspeople—especially professionals in service industries, such as lawyers, bankers, and accountants—should be careful when dealing with their clients to avoid situations where an accusation of undue influence or unconscionability can arise. Business arrangements other than those related to the profession should be avoided, and even those related to the profession should be guarded so that conflicts of interest do not arise. When in doubt, the transaction should be avoided or care should be taken to ensure that the client obtains independent legal advice. The problem is that if the deal goes well no one will complain, but if a loss occurs the client may have grounds to seek compensation from the professional for any losses suffered.

23. [1932] A.C. 562 (H.L.).

pany, contracts with Balzer to mow Carriere's lawn, Carriere cannot enforce the agreement but Balzer certainly can. The court may provide either damages or money compensation calculated on the basis of what it would cost to have somebody else mow the lawn.

Where land is involved, the rights of the parties are said to run with the land. If a person leases a suite in a house and the owner sells the house, the new owner must honour the lease, even though the lessee was not a party to the contract of sale.

When an agent acts on behalf of a principal in contracting with a third party, the actions of that agent are binding on the principal. When a clerk in a store sells a magazine to a customer, the storeowner is bound. This may seem inconsistent with privity, but in fact the contract is between the storeowner and the customer; the clerk is merely acting as a go-between. Agency will be discussed in detail in a subsequent chapter.

The concept of the **trust** is a little more complicated. This involves one person transferring their property to a second person obligated to use it to the benefit of a third. This is often done in estate planning, the beneficiaries being the family of the person creating the trust. In order for this to work, the third-party beneficiary must be able to enforce the contract between the original parties. Since the person creating the trust is often dead and unable to enforce the original contract, it would be an affront to allow the trustee to ignore the obligations set out in the agreement and take the benefits for himself. The Courts of Chancery developed the equitable principle of the trust to overcome this problem, and the beneficiary now can enforce the terms of the original trust agreement even though he is not a party to it.

Insurance is handled in a similar fashion, the beneficiary of an insurance contract having the power to enforce it after the death of the insured. Sometimes, when a contract bestows a benefit on a third party, the courts will infer a trust, even though parties did not specifically create one. This is called a **constructive trust** and provides an important method for the third party to obtain the benefit promised.

Finally, when the parties to contract agree to substitute someone new for one of the original parties, there is also no problem with privity so long as all three parties agree to the change. This is called a **novation**. If Jones has a contract to provide janitorial services to a college and he sells his business to Brown, there is no problem with Brown taking over that service contract, provided the college agrees. A new contract has been substituted for the old one, and no privity problem arises since all parties have agreed to the change. In fact, there are signs that the doctrine of privity may be breaking down.

Contracting parties often protect themselves from contract and tort liability by including exemption clauses in contracts that limit that liability. In the case of *London Drugs Ltd. v. Kuehne & Nagel International Ltd.*,[24] Kuehn & Nagel contracted to store a large and valuable transformer for London Drugs. The contract between them limited Kuehne & Nagel's liability for damage to only $40. Unfortunately, two employees were careless in their handling of the transformer causing significant damage, and London Drugs sued. However, instead of suing Kuehne & Nagel for breach of contract, they sued the employees in tort for

24. [1993] 1 W.W.R. 1 (S.C.C.).

negligence. By doing this they thought to avoid the protection of the exemption clause limiting any claim to $40, the theory being that the employees were not privy to the contract and therefore not protected by it. The Supreme Court, however, found that the protection of the exemption clause extended to the employees, even though they were not party to the contract. The departure of the Supreme Court from the privity rule in this case may indicate a willingness to do so in other circumstances as well.

### Case Summary 7.14

**Privity Prevents Payment of Commission: *Winners Development Ltd. v. Goddard and Smith International Realty Inc.*[25]**

*Winners Development Ltd.*

List property with

Pays over only $37 177
Keeping $12 823

**Remax Realty** —— Property advertised through ——> **multiple listing**

*Goddard and Smith International Realty Inc.*

$50 000          Finds purchaser and collects $50 000 deposit

**Purchaser**

Winners Development Ltd. listed property for sale with Remax Realty, which advertised the property in the multiple listing service. Goddard and Smith, another real estate firm, saw the advertisement and procured a buyer for the property. When the deal fell through Goddard and Smith insisted on withholding $12 823 of the $50 000 deposit they were holding as their commission on the sale. Winners Development Ltd. sued for the entire amount.

The Court held that there was no privity of contract between the vendors and the defendants, who eventually sold the property. Goddard and Smith had to pay over the deposit to Winners. If they could look to anyone for compensation, it would be to Remax for a commission. This demonstrates the operation of privity and also shows how it might lead to an injustice. It could be argued that the rule was used to cheat the defendants out of a fair payment for the contribution they made to the sale. What do you think?

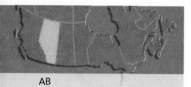

AB

Another area where the rule of privity of contract may be weakening is in the field of product liability. In *Donoghue v. Stevenson*,[26] the consumer of the ginger beer could not sue the merchant because she was not the one who purchased it and there was no contract between them. Some provinces have passed legislation allowing the consumer of such products where the defective product causes injury to sue the seller in contract law, even when the injured person is not the purchaser and not party to the contract. The courts have also extended the right to sue in contract law in product liability cases by finding collateral contracts cre-

---

25. [1992] 6 W.W.R. 102 (B.C.S.C. Apr. 14/92).

26. [1932] A.C. 562 (H.L.).

ated by advertising brochures, giving the purchaser a right to seek redress in contract law past the retailer back to the manufacturer. These topics will be discussed in Chapter 9 under "Consumer Protection Legislation."

## Assignment

Just as a person buying goods under a contract is then free to resell them, so can a person entitled to receive a benefit under a contract transfer that benefit to a third party (see Figure 7.4). This is called the **assignment of contractual rights,** and the benefit transferred is known as a **chose in action.** While the practice of transferring such rights was originally not permitted because of privity, it is now an essential aspect of doing business. The principle is that a person who has acquired a right or a benefit under a contract has the right to assign that benefit to another. Where Jung does carpentry work for Simons and is owed money for those services, Jung is free to assign (sell) that claim to Green. Jung is referred to as the *assignor,* a party to the original contract, and Green as the *assignee,* a stranger to it. It is common for a business to assign their accounts receivable (money they are owed by their customers) outright to obtain immediate cash or to make a conditional assignment to a creditor to secure a loan.

**Contracting parties can assign rights**

The ability to make such assignments has become a vital component in our commercial world. There are, however, some important qualifications to keep in mind. First, only the benefit can be assigned, not an obligation. In the example above, if Jung has done poor work or failed to do the job Jung is still obligated to Simons, despite the assignment. Jung cannot say that it is no longer his problem, as he has assigned the contract to Green. Jung has assigned only the benefits, not the obligations.

**Only benefits can be assigned**

Of course, if Green tried to collect those benefits (the money owed) in face of the defaulted contract, he would fail. While it is true that the assignment of the benefits of the contract between Jung and Simons was valid, Green can be in no better position to collect that benefit than was Jung, and Jung has no claim since he has defaulted; Jung cannot sell something he doesn't have. The principle is that an assignee is "subject to the equities" between the original parties, meaning that the assignee can be in no better position than was the assignor. Jung transferred only what claim he had against Simons to Green, and that claim was tainted. If the debtor, then, has a good defence against the assignor, he also has a good defence against the assignee.

**Assignee in no better position than assignor**

## Figure 7.4 Assignment

(Obligated to provide payment or other contractual benefit)

**Original party** ——————————————————→ **Original party** (Creditor and assignor)
(usually a debtor)

| Benefit assigned (sold)

↓

**Stranger** (Assignee)

### Case Summary 7.15

**The Vulnerability of an Assignee: *First City Capital Ltd. v. Petrosar Ltd.*[27]**

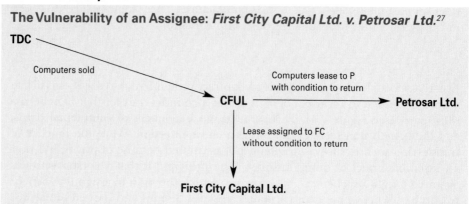

TDC graphics was to supply specialized computers to Petrosar Limited. For financing purposes TDC graphics sold the computers to Casselman Financial Underwriters Limited (CFUL), which in turn leased them to Petrosar. An important term of the agreement gave Petrosar the right to terminate the lease at the end of one year and either return the computers or purchase them for "the residual amount left owing." This was not set out in the lease agreement itself (it was contained in a purchase order and a schedule attached to the lease), but was found by the Court to be an essential part of the lease agreement. When CFUL assigned this lease agreement to First City Capital Ltd. they failed to inform them of Petrosar's right to terminate at the end of the first year.

At the end of one year Petrosar opted to purchase the computers, but when a price couldn't be agreed on Petrosar simply stopped paying and put the computers in storage. First City sued, and the main problem for the Court was to determine whether First City was bound by Petrosar's right to purchase or to terminate. The Court held that as assignees they could be in no better position than the person who assigned the lease to them. Whether they knew of the provision or not, they took it "subject to the equities." What First City got was only what CFUL had to give, and that was a lease subject to this right to purchase or terminate. First City's failure to convey Petrosar the computers for that amount, as agreed, entitled Petrosar to stop paying. This case illustrates how an assignee gets only what the assignor has to give. It also shows how careful we have to be in arranging these kinds of transactions.

**Contractual obligations can be performed by others**

Although only the benefits can be assigned, that does not mean the original party to the contract always has to be the one to perform. Often, it is understood that the actual work or service involved will be performed by an employee or subcontractor. This is called **vicarious performance.** The point is that the original party to the contract remains responsible for the work no matter who does it. But in many cases, the service must be performed by the person so contracting. If a famous artist agreed to paint a portrait, it is likely that the customer would not be satisfied if the actual painting were subcontracted to another.

Because of the restrictions of privity, it was left to the courts of chancery to develop an "equitable" method to enforce assignments. This involved the assignee bringing an action against the original contracting party through the assignor and is referred to as "joining" the assignor in the action. Joining can be a cumbersome process, and it has since been modified by statute. If the assignment meets certain qualifications, it qualifies as a **statutory assignment** and the assignee can enforce the claim directly without involving the assignor. In the example above, in the past Green would have had to bring an action in Jung's name to collect funds owing under the contract by Simons. But today, if the assignment qualifies as a statutory assignment, Green can simply sue Simons for the money directly.

The qualifications that have to be met to establish a statutory assignment are as follows: first, the assignment must be absolute, meaning that it must be both unconditional and complete. The full amount owed must be assigned without any strings attached. Second, the assignment must be in writing, signed by the assignor. And third, the original party obligated to pay must be notified in writing of the assignment. Only when all these requirements are met will the assignee be able to sue directly; otherwise, he still must join the assignor in any attempt at collection.

**Qualifications for statutory assignment**

Some things cannot be assigned, such as the right to collect support payments or the right to sue another in a tort action. Certain statutes, such as the *Workers' Compensation Act* (in some jurisdictions), prohibit the assignment of provided benefits. Note, however, that although the right to sue cannot be assigned, there is no such restriction on the assignment of the proceeds from such a lawsuit once awarded.

**Some things cannot be assigned**

Sometimes, an assignor may be tempted to assign the same claim to two assignees. This, of course, is fraud, and the victim has the right to seek redress from the assignor. Often, however, that assignor has fled or has no funds. The original debtor against whom the assignment is made is obligated to pay only once, and one of the two assignees will be out of luck. In such circumstances, it is the first assignee to give the debtor notice of the assignment who will collect. The other assignee will be left to seek remedies against the assignor, which may be worthless. It is, therefore, vital in business to take such assignments with care and then to immediately notify the debtor. It is only when the debtor makes the mistake of ignoring such notice and paying either the wrong assignee or insisting on paying the original assignor that they may have to pay twice.

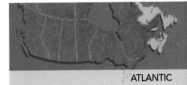

ATLANTIC

**Debtor must pay first who gives notice of assignment**

The principles discussed so far relate to voluntary assignments. There are some circumstances in which the assignment of rights can take place involuntarily. For example, rights and obligations are automatically transferred to the administrator or executor of the estate when a person dies. This representative steps into the deceased's shoes and is not restricted by the privity of contract rule, unless the terms of the contract require personal performance by the deceased. The second situation of **involuntary assignment** is when a party to a contract goes

**Involuntary assignment in cases of death and bankruptcy**

---

## Reducing **Risk** 7.3

Businesspeople should never ignore a notice of assignment and continue paying the original party. There is no problem so long as the payment is passed on, but you cannot be sure that this will be done. Also, businesspeople often assume that once they have assigned the debt they no longer have anything to do with the transaction. If a product has been sold and the financing arrangements have been assigned to a finance company, the merchant vendor is still responsible with respect to the performance of the product. If it is defective or dangerous, causing injury or loss, it is the vendor that is responsible, not the finance company. You can assign only the benefits, not your obligations under such a contract.

bankrupt. Under bankruptcy legislation, the bankrupt's assets are transferred to a trustee, called the *receiver*, who will then distribute them to pay the creditors as much as possible. Bankruptcy will be discussed in Chapter 10.

## Negotiable Instruments

Another exception to the privity of contract rule recognizes the commercial realities of modern business. As commerce developed it became necessary to devise a method to freely exchange and pass on claims for debt that had been incurred in the process of business. When these claims met certain qualifications, they were defined as **negotiable instruments,** and through them unique rights were bestowed on the parties. Cheques, promissory notes, and bills of exchange (commonly called drafts) are examples of negotiable instruments. While the use of cheques as a method of paying in personal or consumer transactions has significantly decreased as credit and debit cards gain popularity, cheques are still an important method of transferring funds in business. Promissory notes retain their popularity where credit is involved because of the unique advantages they bestow.

These rights will be discussed in more detail in Chapter 9. Briefly, a negotiable instrument can be freely passed from one person to another, conveying with it all the rights associated with the original agreement between the parties, and no notice of the transfer is required. This flexibility is completely inconsistent with the doctrine of privity of contract and the law of assignment discussed above. The most significant innovation of negotiable instruments was that better rights or claims than those held by the initial parties could be passed on. As discussed under "Assignment," it is clear that even when it is possible to assign contractual rights, the assignee can be in no better position than was the assignor. Thus, if a defence such as deceit or breach of contract was available against the original party to the contract (the assignor), it was available against the assignee as well. This is not the case with negotiable instruments. When you give a cheque or promissory note to someone who is cheating you, if that instrument gets into the hands of an innocent third party who satisfies the qualifications to be a "holder in due course" you can be required to pay despite the existence of the fraud.

# Summary

### Mistake

- Must go to the nature of the agreement or the existence of the subject matter, not just to the effect of the agreement when performed

| Types | Remedy |
|---|---|
| Both parties making a common error | If serious there is no contract |
| An error in recording the terms | Can be corrected by rectification |
| A misunderstanding between the parties | Most reasonable interpretation of the contract |
| A one-sided mistake | *Caveat emptor* applies unless the mistake is so fundamental as to destroy consensus or there is fraud |

## Misrepresentation

- A false statement that induces a person to enter a contract

| Types | Remedy |
|---|---|
| Innocent misrepresentation | The remedy is rescission |
| Fraudulent misrepresentation | The victim may sue for damages for the tort of deceit and/or rescission |
| Negligence | Damages and/or rescission |

## Duress or undue influence

- Contract is voidable if made under duress or undue influence
- Unconscionability may cause the court to set aside or modify a contract

## Privity of contract

- Only the original parties to the contract are bound. Any benefit going to a third party must be enforced by the original party to the agreement
- The *trust* is a true exception to the privity rule because the beneficiary can enforce it even though he or she is not a party to the original agreement
- Other exceptions include real estate transactions, insurance, and employees

## Assignment

- Only the benefits, not the obligations, in a contract can be sold (assigned) to a third party, and those benefits must be enforced through the original contracting party, the assignor
- Only when it qualifies as a statutory assignment can the assignee enforce the assigned rights directly
- Negotiable instruments also may be enforced by third parties without notification to the original drawer of the instrument, sometimes conveying better rights than existed between the original parties

---

## QUESTIONS

1. Distinguish between a mistake about the effect of a contract and a mistake about its nature. Explain the significance of this distinction.

2. Distinguish among shared mistakes, misunderstandings, and one-sided mistakes.

3. What approach will the courts usually take when the mistake involves disagreement about the meaning of the contract?

4. How will the courts respond to ambiguous wording in a contract?

5. Explain the parol evidence rule.

6. What must a party to a contract show to obtain rectification of a document?

7. When will a misunderstanding as to the terms of a contract cause that contract to be void?

8. Under what circumstances would a person raise a claim of *non est factum*? What restrictions are there on its availability?

9. Explain what is meant by *caveat emptor*. What is this principle's significance in relation to a one-sided mistake?

10. What happens when a misrepresentation becomes a term of the contract?

11. What is the distinction among fraudulent, negligent, and innocent misrepresentation? Why is the distinction important?

12. Under what circumstances can silence or a statement of opinion become misrepresentation?

13. What factors may affect the availability of the remedy of rescission?

14. Describe the relationship between misrepresentation and mistake.

15. What is the significance of determining whether a contract is voidable rather than void?

16. Distinguish among duress, undue influence, and unconscionability and give examples of each.

17. What is meant by privity of contract?

18. Explain what is meant by the term "novation."

19. Explain the relationship of the privity principle to land transactions, agency, trusts, assignment, and the position of employees.

20. What qualifications must be realized before there can be a statutory assignment?

21. What limitations are placed on the rights and obligations of the assignee when a contract is assigned?

22. What is meant by "the assignee takes subject to the equities"? When is it appropriate to determine these equities?

23. What is the significance of a negotiable instrument in terms of the rights conveyed to third parties?

---

## CASES

### 1. *Corporate Properties Ltd. v. Manufacturers Life Insurance Co.* (1989), 63 D.L.R. (4th) 703 (Ont. C.A.).

In this case, Bloor West leased property from Manulife and, in turn, sublet that property to Corporate Properties Ltd. The arrangement was that Bloor West would pay Manulife a certain set percentage of the gross revenues earned from the property. Corporate Properties, which initially owned Bloor West but eventually sold their interest through refinancing, had agreed to a different calculation for paying rent to Bloor West. But Corporate Properties, instead of paying their rent to Bloor West, paid it directly to Manulife. Instead of basing the rental payment on what Bloor West earned from the property, they based it on what they earned from the property, which was considerably more—thus, from their perspective, creating an overpayment for a considerable period of time. When they discovered this in 1983, they demanded repayment of the overages paid. While the matter was in dispute, they, under protest, made further payments for the period 1984 to 1986.

The ambiguity is whether the term "gross annual income" refers to that received by Bloor West or the income from the properties obtained by Corporate Properties. Certainly, Corporate Properties treated it for years as if it referred to their gross income from the properties. Explain how the courts would approach this problem, the arguments available to all the parties, and whether Manulife will have to repay these overpayments.

## 2. *Hayward v. Mellick* (1984), 5 D.L.R. (4th) 740 (Ont. C.A.).

Mellick had 94 acres of land that he wanted to sell. In the process of negotiations with Hayward, he represented to Hayward that the farm had approximately 65 acres of workable farmland. Relying on this representation, Hayward purchased the farm and later learned that the farm had only 51.7 workable acres. In fact, Mellick had never measured the farm, and it was only his own personal belief that it had 65 workable acres, but he never told Hayward that he was not sure. Hayward sued for compensation. Discuss the legal position of the parties. How would your answer be affected by the knowledge that the written contract included an exemption clause that stated, "It is agreed that there is no representation, warranty, collateral agreement, or condition affecting this agreement or the real property or supported hereby other than as expressed herein, in writing"?

## 3. *Hi-Tech Group Inc. v. Sears Canada Inc.* (2001), 52 O.R. (3d) 97 (Ont. C.A.).

Hi-Tech had a contract with Sears to operate a consumer club for them. The contract was for a one-year period starting in May 1994 and provided that the contract would "...automatically renew for successive terms of one year, subject to termination by either party upon 120 days prior written notice." On February 21, 1996, Sears gave notice to end the relationship effective the end of June of that year. Hi-Tech sued, claiming among other things that they had not been given proper notice of the termination of the contract. They claimed that the termination should have been given 120 days before the anniversary date of the contract and this had not been done. Sears claimed that the term allowed them to terminate anytime providing they gave 120 days notice. Explain how a court would deal with this problem and the likely outcome.

## 4. *Pettit v. Foster Wheeler Ltd.*, [1950] 2 D.L.R. 42 (Ont. H.C.).

Roderick Ashley Ltd. was supplying materials for Foster Wheeler Ltd. at a project at the University of Alberta in Edmonton. Mr. Pettit had supplied financing worth $14 000 to Roderick Ashley Ltd. Pursuant to that agreement, Pettit took an assignment of all accounts of Roderick Ashley. Notice of this assignment was given to Foster Wheeler Ltd., which was told to make all payments to Mr. Johnston, Pettit's lawyer, who would hold the money in trust for him. Some payments were made, but on December 27 the Bank of Nova Scotia sent a letter to Foster Wheeler Ltd. stating that it had received a general assignment of book debts of Roderick Ashley as collateral security for a debt and that any payments to be made to Roderick Ashley should now be paid to the Bank of Nova Scotia. Accordingly, Foster Wheeler Ltd. immediately paid the $7345 outstanding to the Bank of Nova Scotia instead of paying to Pettit and Johnston. Pettit and Johnston then sued Foster Wheeler Ltd. for this amount, claiming that it should have been paid to them. Explain the likely outcome.

## 5. *Re Royal Bank of Canada and Gill et al.* (1988), 47 D.L.R. (4th) 466 (B.C.C.A.).

The younger Mr. Gill was fluent in English and a sophisticated businessman who had worked in a credit union for a number of years as well as managing his father's berry farm. To take advantage of a business opportunity, he arranged with the Royal Bank to borrow $87 000. During the negotiations, it became clear that he could get a more favourable rate of interest if his father guaranteed the loan. In fact, the son had done a considerable amount of banking on behalf of his father, who was also a customer of the same bank. The elder Mr. Gill could not read, write, or speak English and relied on his son in all his business dealings. The documents were prepared, and the son brought his father to the bank to sign. At no time did he explain to his father that he was signing a personal guarantee, and the evidence is clear that the father had no idea what he was signing other than that it was a document associated with a loan transaction. Mr. Gill, Sr., had implicit faith in his son's handling of his business affairs. Mr. Gill, Jr., on the other hand, was so excited about the deal that he apparently never explained the nature of the documents to his father. It is clear in this situation that at no time was there any misrepresentation to the father or the son on the part of the bank. When the loan was defaulted, the bank turned to the father for payment. Explain the arguments of the father and the bank as to whether Mr. Gill, Sr., should be held responsible for this debt and the likely outcome.

### 6. *Stott v. Merrit Investment Corp.* (1988), 48 D.L.R. (4th) 288, (Ont. C.A.).

Stott was a sales representative working in the securities business for the defendant. He was approached by a customer who wanted to start an account to speculate in gold futures, a very risky business. The account was started and some successes were achieved, but then the market reversed itself and the customer lost heavily. The customer ended up indebted to the company for $66 000. Stott was called into his supervisor's office and asked to sign an agreement stating that Stott would be fully responsible for that amount if the customer could not pay. Stott observed that he should have legal advice and was told, "You are probably right, but if you don't sign it won't go well with you at this firm, and it would be very difficult for you to find employment in the industry." Stott signed the document and continued to work for Merrit. Deductions were taken off his income for this debt over the employment period. Several months later, he said that he had received legal advice and offered to settle the debt for 25 percent of the outstanding amount.

Some time later, he left and obtained other employment; he refused any further responsibility and sued Merrit for the amount that had been deducted from his income to pay this debt. Merrit countersued for the amount still outstanding. What are the legal arguments to support each position? Would your answer be different if you were to learn that it was the practice in the industry to hold sales representatives responsible to some extent for such bad accounts?

### 7. *Kassian v. Hill* (2002-02-06) 202 ABQB 106 (Alta Q.B.).

Mrs. Kassian was injured in an automobile accident, and two days later the insurance adjuster persuaded her to sign a waiver of any claim for bodily injury in exchange for a $2000 settlement. She didn't read the document before signing. Note that prior to the accident she was taking Prozac and Ativan as treatment for depression and distress but she couldn't recall whether she was taking the medication at the time she signed the waiver. She didn't cash the cheque, and upon getting legal advice she brought this action for damages for the accident. The insurance company relied on the waiver, but she asked that the waiver be set aside on the basis of either *non est factum* or unconscionability. Explain the factors the Court would consider and the likely outcome of the action. How would it affect your answer to know that Mrs. Kassian had a good education, that she had been in a similar accident in the past and had signed a similar waiver, and that the judge found the amount of the settlement was reasonable given her injuries?

# The End of the Contractual Relationship

Contracts can come to an end or be discharged by performance, breach, agreement between the parties to end or modify, and frustration. This chapter will examine each of these, and ends with a discussion of remedies for breach of contract.

# Performance

Contractual obligations are discharged and a contract is ended when both parties have satisfactorily completed their obligations under the contract. With most bilateral contracts one party completes their side before the other is required to perform. When I order a new car, the dealer produces the car and then I am obligated to pay. If the car is not delivered I have no obligation. It becomes vitally important, then, to determine whether one party has properly performed their side in order to determine whether the other party is obligated to perform in turn. The question that must be asked is, Will anything short of exact performance satisfy the requirement?

In fact, there are two situations where something short of exact performance of the contract will still be considered proper performance. Contracts usually consist of major terms called **conditions** and minor terms called **warranties.** When the failure to perform involves only a warranty or a minor term, that party will have performed their side of the agreement. The other party will be required to perform subject to a claim for compensation for whatever loss was caused by the breach of warranty. Thus, if the new car is delivered without fog lights as requested, a minor term or warranty has been breached but I will still be required to take delivery and pay for the car minus the cost of the fog lights.

**Where warranty breached, contract still considered performed**

When a **condition** or major term of the contract is breached, the contract is normally considered discharged and the other party is relieved of performing their obligations under it. But when the condition is breached in some minor inconsequential way, the court will usually treat it like a breach of warranty, requiring the other party to perform subject to a claim for the loss caused by the shortfall. This is called **substantial performance**. For example, if a farmer is required to deliver 2000 kg of potatoes and delivers only 1987 kg the contract would be considered substantially performed. The farmer would be discharged from further performance and the purchaser would have to pay for the potatoes that were delivered. Of course, exact performance will be required where only exact performance will do. If a contract with a driller requires a producing well and 25 dry holes are produced, there has been no substantial performance and there is no obligation to pay.

**Contract discharged when contract substantially performed**

**But some contracts must be performed exactly**

### Case Summary 8.1

**Minor Breach Will Not Discharge Contract:** *Sail Labrador Ltd. v. Navimar Corp.*[1]

Sail Labrador Ltd. leased a ship from Navimar Corp. Ltd. with an option to purchase, but only if every payment was properly made. The contract required cash, but the parties agreed to payment through a series of post-dated cheques. One cheque was dishonoured because of a bank error, and despite immediate correction the owner took the position that the option was no longer available because of this failure.

The Supreme Court of Canada decided that the owners had assumed this kind of risk when they agreed to take post-dated cheques. Since the error was inconsequential and immediately corrected, the contract had been substantially performed and the option was still available. This case illustrates not only the nature of an option but also the doctrine of substantial performance. Here the contract was properly performed except for some minor variation and the owners then had to honour their contractual obligations.

## Tender

The general rule in common law is that when a person has tendered performance of a contract it counts as if the contract had been performed. This means that if a person is ready, willing, and able to perform a contractual obligation and attempts to do so, but the other party refuses to accept it or prevents it, the first party is taken to have completed its obligation and the other party is then required to perform. If they fail to do so then they are in breach, not the party who has tendered performance.

**Tender of performance ends obligation**

Where goods and services are involved and tender of performance is refused, the tendering party has no further obligation and can sue immediately. If Chan's Renovation Service contracted with Smith to install new gutters on his house, and when Chan shows up to do the job on the specified day he is refused entrance, he has discharged his obligation and can sue. It is no excuse for Smith to claim that the work was not done.

1. [1999] S.C.R. 265 (S.C.C.).

The effect of tendering proper payment of debt is different. It does not extinguish the debt but simply relieves the debtor of the normal obligation to seek out the creditor to make payment. Once proper payment has been tendered and refused the debtor can just wait for the creditor to collect the debt. Any costs associated with that process will then be borne by the creditor.

Proper payment of a debt requires legal tender. Cheques, even certified cheques, are acceptable only when the parties have agreed to allow cheques to be used to pay debts. This may be an actual agreement between the parties, or it may be implied from accepted business practice.

If there is any question about the acceptable form of payment, it is advisable to present cash and then only the exact amount in proper legal tender. Under the *Currency Act*[2] creditors can refuse to take more than a limited amount in coins as set out below.

> **Where debt owed and money refused—money still owed, but creditor bears expense**

| When paying by coins of this denomination | No more than this need be taken |
|---|---|
| $2 | $40 |
| $1 | $25 |
| 10, 25, 50 cents | $10 |
| 5 cents | $5 |
| 1 cent | 25 cents |

There is no limit on what qualifies as legal tender when paper money is offered, as long as official Canadian bank notes are used. To avoid problems, especially as we move toward a cashless society, the parties should specify the appropriate method of payment in their agreement.

> **Payment must be in legal tender**

When not specified in the contract the tendering of performance must be done at a reasonable time and place. Usually, this means during normal business hours at a person's place of business. Thus, if Jones has a contract to deliver five tonnes of ripe tomatoes to Sharif by July 10, Jones would be expected to make that delivery to Sharif's packing house rather than to his home or office. The delivery should also take place during the usual working day. Sharif would not be obligated to accept delivery at 6:00 p.m. on Saturday, unless such a time was permitted in the contract.

> **Delivery must be as specified or at a reasonable time and place**

When the parties do specify a time for performance in the contract the court will have to determine whether it is an important term or not. Where the parties specify or the court determines that "time is of the essence," it must be strictly adhered to. Even just a few seconds can make a difference.

This was the case in *Smith Bros. & Wilson (B.C.) Ltd. v. British Columbia Hydro and Power Authority*,[3] where a bid was submitted for a job just a few minutes after the time specified in the tender for the bidding to close. Even a bid tendered that close in time could not be considered.

Even when the contract has been properly performed by both parties, there may be some continuing obligations. For example, where a product is sold and the purchase price has been paid, title has transferred to the purchaser. Even then, if the product is dangerous or fails to meet the specifications of the agreement, the purchaser can turn back to the seller and seek compensation for the breach.

> **Some obligations continue after discharge**

---

2. *Currency Act*, R.S.C. 1985, c. C-52.

3. (1997-02-24) B.C.S.C. C970590 (B.C.S.C.).

# Breach

Breach of contract involves the failure of the breaching party to properly perform its contractual obligations. Such a breach can take place in two ways: (1) by improper or incomplete performance of the obligations set out in the agreement, and (2) by refusal to perform. Refusal, also called repudiation, will be discussed below.

### Case Summary 8.2

**When Is a Breach Enough to Discharge a Contract?**
***968703 Ontario Limited v. Vernon***[4]

Vernon contracted with an auctioneer to sell the equipment located at his gravel pit. The proceeds were to be deposited in a joint bank account and then split between the parties in specified proportions. But when the auctioneer refused to deposit the first $100 000 as required, Vernon refused to allow him back on the property to complete the sale. Shortly before the trial but after the auctioneer ignored an interlocutory injunction the funds were finally put into a joint account. The auctioneer had also sold the equipment below market value to related companies, breaching his fiduciary duty. The lower court found in favour of Vernon but this decision was reversed by the Divisional Court. Finally, the Ontario Court of Appeal found that failure to initially deposit the funds in the joint bank account or to quickly do so when ordered by a court was a significant breach, as was the auctioneer's breach of fiduciary duty. Vernon's refusal to continue performance was justified, and the auctioneer was entitled to nothing.

It is often difficult to determine just how serious a breach must be to discharge a contract. In this case, although the auctioneer had brought in $100 000 in sales and expected to bring in more, they got nothing because of their breach and had to pay Vernon's costs in the action as well. Do you think that this is an appropriate result?

## Conditions and Warranties

Terms essential to the substantial performance of a contract are called **conditions**. Terms that are minor, insignificant, or peripheral to the central obligation of the contract are called **warranties**. A breach of warranty will not relieve the other party of the obligation to fulfill his or her side of the agreement. The victim of such a breach of warranty has the right to sue the other party for whatever it costs to overcome the deficiency in performance but still must perform his or her part of the agreement. However, when a condition or important term is breached so that the victim of the breach is deprived of the major benefit of the contract the other party can usually treat his or her obligation as ended and sue for breach of contract. It must be stressed that the breach of condition must be a serious impairment of the performance of the contract. A minor breach of even an important term will not generally allow the victim of the breach to discharge the contract. This problem often arises when goods are to be delivered in instalments. When one is missed that usually will not be enough to discharge the agreement even though it is the breach of an important term.

---

4. (2002-02-20) ONCA C36260 (Ont. C.A.).

Although the breach of a condition will normally allow the victim of the breach to treat the contract as discharged, they can treat the contract as still binding if they choose. Also, if the non-breaching party has received some significant benefit under the agreement, they lose the right to discharge and must perform their obligations subject to a claim for compensation for the breach.

It may be tempting for one party to breach a condition of the contract and relieve themselves of any further obligation to perform. But the breaching party can't choose to breach thus escaping further obligations. It takes both parties to end a contract. If Beaman provided a sculpture of a moose instead of the flying geese agreed to for the foyer of Singh's new office building in Regina, this would normally be a breach of a condition, and Singh would not have to pay. However, if Singh liked the moose sculpture he could keep it, but he would have to pay for it—albeit at a reduced value. Thus, a breach of condition in a contract that has been accepted by the other party is treated as a breach of warranty.

**Where breach accepted— performance required**

What is important to one person might seem unimportant to another. Therefore, terms can be designated as either conditions or warranties in the agreement. Normally, when a person orders a new car the particular shade of red ordered would be a minor term, and if a car of a slightly different shade were delivered the purchaser would still have to take it. But where the exact shade is important to the purchaser, which might be the case where it is used as a trademark for a business, they can designate the required shade to be a condition and refuse to take the car if a car of any other shade of red is delivered. Similarly, the person supplying goods or services will often designate a term that would normally be a condition as a warranty in the agreement. The *Sale of Goods Act* states that in transactions governed by the Act the court has the option of treating a term as a condition although it is specified as a warranty in the contract.[5]

**Act allows specified warranty to be treated as a condition**

## Exemption Clauses

Exemption clauses are an attempt by a party to significantly limit or eliminate their liability under an agreement. The courts will generally enforce exemption clauses because the object of contract law is to carry out whatever the parties have freely bargained to do. But they do so reluctantly, especially where the parties are not in an equal bargaining position. If there is any ambiguity in the terms of the exemption clause, the narrow or restrictive meaning will be used.

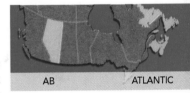

**Exemption clauses attempt to limit liability**

If a restaurant has a sign above the cloakroom stating, "Not responsible for lost or stolen clothing," bringing this term to the customer's attention would make it part of the contract for care of the goods, or *bailment*. If clothes left were damaged by fire or water the proprietor would not be protected, as that kind of loss was not specified on the sign. Similarly, if a briefcase were stolen, the exemption clause would not apply because it was not clothing that was stolen.

Exemption clauses are intricate and involved because the people who draft them try to cover all possible eventualities, knowing that the courts will take a restrictive approach in their interpretation. They usually form a part of the written document, but they could be included in a sign or notice. In any case, the terms cannot be unilaterally imposed and must be brought to the attention of the customer at the time the contract is made. If the clause is on the back of the ticket or receipt, there must be a reference on the front directing the holder to read

**Exemption clauses strictly interpreted**

**Must be brought to attention of party at time of contract**

5. *Sale of Goods Act*, R.S.B.C. 1996, c. 410, s. 15.

the back. Where a sign limiting liability is involved, as at a car park or bus depot, it must be in clear view so that a reasonable person would notice it when entering the premises or undertaking a contractual obligation. Even when the exemption clause is part of a written contract, if it is in any way unique or unusual it must be brought to the attention of the other contracting party. If it is buried in other insignificant writing, or so small it cannot be read, it is doubtful that it will have any legal effect.

When goods or services are sold in consumer transactions, these exemption clauses are usually embodied in terms referred to as "limited warranties." The term is misleading and causes confusion, since these are major terms of the contract or conditions, not minor ones. The courts are likely to be much more sympathetic to the plight of a customer in a consumer transaction who has not read the exemption clause than to the more sophisticated parties in a business transaction. It is important to note that under the *Sale of Goods Act* or other consumer protection legislation, the sellers' rights to restrict their obligations in such sales may be extremely limited. Consumer protection and the sale of goods will be discussed in Chapter 9.

AB

**Effect of legislation**

### Case Summary 8.3

**Exemption Clause Strictly Interpreted:** *Meditek Laboratory Services Ltd. v. Purolator Courier Ltd.*[6]

A Purolator employee delivered an expensive medical machine meant for Meditek to the wrong address. To make matters worse, the delivery sheets showing where the goods were delivered had been falsified and the goods could not be traced. After a long delay the goods were found, but Meditek had in the meantime obtained a replacement machine. They refused delivery and sued Purolator for damages. Purolator relied on an exemption clause in the contract limiting its liability "whether or not from negligence or gross negligence." But the act of the employee in falsifying the documents had been wilful, not negligent, and the Court found that Purolator was not protected by the clause. Such exemption clauses are strictly interpreted against the breaching party, and although this one covered even gross negligence it did not cover wilful or fraudulent conduct.

## Fundamental Breach

Contracting parties often try to limit their liability as much as possible, and sometimes they try to contract out of all obligations and responsibilities. The courts will enforce an exemption clause that protects even in face of such a **fundamental breach** because of the parties' freedom to contract, but it must be absolutely clear that they understood the exemption clause to cover such a basic failure to perform for it to provide protection. In most cases it is unlikely that one party would knowingly exempt the other from such basic obligations, and so the courts usually have no difficulty finding that such an exemption clause, even a carefully worded one, does not apply. This is called the **construction approach** to fundamental breach. It is important to remember, however, that the Supreme Court of Canada, in *Hunter Engineering*,[7] has made it clear that a properly worded

---

6. (1995), 125 D.L.R. (4th) 738 (Man. C.A.).

7. *Hunter Engineering Co. v. Syncrude Canada Ltd.,* [1989] 1 S.C.R. 426; see also *Beaufort Realties v. Chomedey Aluminum Co. Ltd.,* [1980] 2 S.C.R. 718.

## Reducing **Risk** 8.1

In business dealings, people often think that they are bound only by the narrowest interpretation of the words they have used in their contract. In fact, the courts often take a more expansive view, even implying obligations that may not be stated. Such a commonly implied obligation is the duty to act in good faith toward the other contracting party. The significance of such a finding is illustrated in Case Summary 8.4.

exemption clause can overcome even a fundamental breach—especially where sophisticated businesspeople are involved on both sides. The Ontario Court of Appeal has taken the position that they will not enforce such exemption clauses where, given the fundamental breach, it would be unconscionable, unfair, or unreasonable to do so.[8]

**Exemption clauses usually ineffective in cases of fundamental breach**

### Case Summary 8.4

**Doctors Had a Duty of Good Faith to Medical Lab:** *MDS Health Group Ltd. v. King Street Medical Arts Centre*[9]

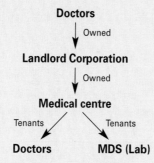

A group of Ontario doctors owned a building and leased a portion of it to the MDS Group to set up a medical lab. During the term of the lease the landlords demanded that the lab pay a much higher rent. When MDS refused, the doctors in retaliation boycotted the lab, setting up one room in the building as a collection point for samples going to another lab and encouraging their patients not to use the MDS services. This effectively destroyed the lab's business and they sued. The Court held that the doctors were breaching an implied obligation to act in good faith and an injunction was granted stopping the practice. Do you think this was just, or has the Court effectively rewritten the contract?

## Repudiation

Repudiation occurs when one of the parties to a contract indicates to the other "an intimation or an intention to abandon and altogether to refuse performance of the contract."[10] Repudiation that takes place after performance is due is just one more way that a contract can be breached, but if this refusal occurs before performance is due it is called **anticipatory breach** and is treated somewhat dif-

**Repudiation is refusal to perform**

---

8. *Fraser Jewellers (1982) Ltd. v. Dominion Electric Protection Co.* (1997), 148 D.L.R. (4th) 496 (Ont. C.A.).

9. (1994), 12 D.L.R. (2d) 209 (Ont. Gen. Div.).

10. Comment of Lord Coleridge, C.J. in *Freeth v. Burr* (1874), L.R. 9 C.P. 208 (Crt. C. P.).

ferently. In the face of such an anticipatory breach, the victim has a choice. The courts allow the victim to immediately treat the contract as breached, to sue or otherwise make different arrangements, and to refuse to go through with any further performance on their part. Alternatively, the victim of the repudiation can ignore the breach, demand performance, and continue to perform their side of the agreement. If the repudiating party still fails to perform, the innocent party can then sue for breach of contract, and the party repudiating will be held responsible for damages incurred even after the repudiation. If the choice is made to discharge the contract, the repudiation must relate to an important term of the contract and be a clear refusal to perform, not just a disagreement as to the nature of the contractual obligations.

**Victim is discharged and can sue if repudiation occurs before due date—or demand performance and wait**

**Victim is bound by choice**

Once made, the choice is binding. This can have serious consequences, and if the victim chooses to insist on performance and then in turn cannot perform they are then in breach themselves, as happened in the *Vanderwal* case discussed in Case Summary 8.5.

### Case Summary 8.5

**Bound by Choice When Faced with Anticipatory Breach:**
*Vanderwal v. Anderson*[11]

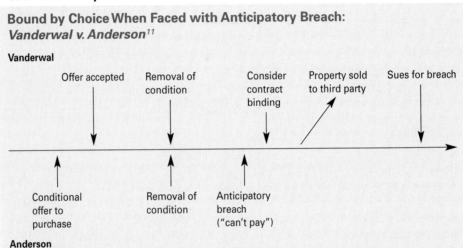

Anderson agreed to purchase property from Vanderwal conditional on the purchaser selling her house, but this condition was removed. Her obligation to purchase was unconditional when she explained to the vendor through her lawyer that she didn't understand what she had done and didn't have the money to complete the transaction. She asked that the condition be reinstated and the time extended. The vendor refused, insisting that the contract was binding on her unconditionally. The vendor then sold the property to another purchaser and sued Mrs. Anderson for breach. The appeal court found that the purchaser's claim of insufficient funds and plea for an extension amounted to an anticipatory breach. The vendors had a choice to ignore the breach and insist on performance or treat the contract as discharged. By their later insisting that the contract was binding unconditionally they made their choice to reject the repudiation and insist on performance. When they sold the property they abandoned the contract—so they were in breach, and not the purchaser.

---

11. (1999), as reported in *Lawyers Weekly,* Vol. 19 (1999) (Ont. Div. Ct.).

This case illustrates the nature of anticipatory breach. You have a right to demand performance or to sue for breach, but if you do demand performance, you had better be prepared to perform your side of the agreement.

When repudiation in the form of an anticipatory breach does take place, the innocent party also runs the risk of being affected by changing circumstances. In the case of *Avery v. Bowden*,[12] the defendant chartered the plaintiff's ship and agreed to supply it with a cargo at the Russian port of Odessa. However, when the ship arrived, because of the strained relations between the United Kingdom and Russia at the time the defendant refused to supply a cargo and insisted that the boat leave. The captain stayed in port hoping that the supplier would change his mind. Before the expiration of the specified time for the cargo to be delivered the Crimean War broke out, making it impossible to go through with the contract whether the parties wanted to or not. The owner of the ship sued for breach of contract.

**Changing circumstances may affect repudiation**

Although the court agreed that the plaintiff would have had the right to treat the contract as discharged by breach once the defendant had clearly indicated that he was not going to go through with the agreement, the defendant had chosen not to acknowledge the repudiation. Therefore, the contract had not been breached. Since the time specified for performance had not yet expired when the war broke out, the contract was discharged by *frustration,* not by breach. Frustration will be discussed later in the chapter.

Repudiation can be expressed or implied from the conduct of the parties. Where the goods to be sold are sold to someone else, such repudiation will be implied. Also, repudiation may be implied from the failure to properly perform a term of the agreement. For example, where there is an ongoing obligation and one part is breached, such as the failure to deliver an important instalment, repudiation may be implied. Missing just one delivery will normally not be serious enough, but where that failure is delivery of the first instalment or of several instalments it may be serious enough to cast doubt on the proper performance of the rest of the agreement. Thus, if Chan agreed to deliver ten loads of gravel to Singh's building site and failed to deliver the first two on the specified days, that might well be considered a repudiation of the contract and Singh could look for another source. See Table 8.1 for a summary of the results of a failure to perform.

**Repudiation may be implied from conduct**

## Table 8.1 Result of Failure to Perform

| | | | |
|---|---|---|---|
| Breach of minor term | | Other party must perform but can seek damages | |
| Repudiation | major refusal | victim chooses to perform | contract binding on both |
| | | victim chooses to discharge | contract ends but victim can seek damages |
| Breach of major term | major failure | other party can be discharged | |
| | minor failure | substantial performance | other party must perform but can seek damages |

12. (1855), 5 E. & B. 714; aff'd (1856), 6 E. & B. 953 (Ex. Ct).

# Discharge by Agreement

**Contracts can be modified
or ended by agreement**

Just as the parties to a contract can agree to the creation of contractual obligations between them, they can also agree to end or modify those obligations. When an old contract is ended that contract is **discharged by agreement,** whether or not a new one is substituted. Whether the old agreement is being ended or simply modified, the basic principle is that all of the ingredients necessary to form a binding contract must be present, including consideration and consensus.

### Case Summary 8.6

#### Must Be Consideration to Support Change: *Gregorio v. Intrans-Corp.*[13]

Gregorio ordered a truck from Intrans conditional upon financing, which was arranged on July 3, 1984, removing the only condition on the sale and creating a binding contract. When the truck was delivered on August 2, Gregorio was required to sign a one-year limited warranty that excluded all other implied warranties and other liability for consequential damages for failure to perform.

The truck turned out to be a lemon, and when the company couldn't fix it in 1987 Gregorio sued to get his money back. The company claimed to be protected by the limited warranty, but the Court held that this was a modification of the original May 12 agreement and since Greforio had received no consideration for the change he was not bound by it. The statutory protections set out in the *Sale of Goods Act* still applied to the purchase, and Gregorio was entitled to his money back as the truck was defective. (The *Sale of Goods Act* will be discussed in Chapter 9.) A contract can be modified by agreement, but it is vitally important that all the elements be present. In this case, consideration was missing and Gregorio was not affected by the changes.

**Must have consideration**

When the parties together are merely altering the terms of an existing agreement before either has performed there is usually no problem with consensus or consideration. Since neither has yet performed they have mutually released each other from their legal obligations and there is consideration on both sides. Sometimes such changes benefit only one of the parties and when this happens the agreement to modify is one-sided and will be void unless supported by some added consideration or made under seal. This was the reason the limited warranty provision agreed to later did not bind Gregorio in *Gregorio v. Intrans-Corp.* Even when the change is entirely one-sided, the person being relieved of their obligation may be able to raise the defence of promissory estoppel if sued under the original agreement. Such one-sided discharge or modification of contractual obligations is primarily where the principle of promissory estoppel arises, as was discussed in Chapter 5.

When the agreement is to end an existing contract the principle is the same. So long as both parties have yet to perform their obligations and mutually release each other from the agreement, the contract is effectively discharged. There is consideration and consensus on both sides. But where one party has completed their obligations under the old contract before the agreement to discharge, there would be no consideration and the old contract would still be binding on the

---

13. (1994), 115 D.L.R. (4th) 200 (Ont. C.A.); additional reasons (1994), 15 B.L.R. (2d) 109 (note) (Ont. C.A.).

parties. In this case the parties must put the agreement to discharge under seal or the party benefiting must agree to do something extra to support the discharge. This is called **accord and satisfaction**; the accord refers to the agreement to end the old contract and the satisfaction is the extra consideration to be supplied by the party benefiting from the discharge. For example, if Newcombe were renovating his house and paid Aiello in advance to paint it there would be a problem with consideration if he allowed Aiello to abandon the contract to take advantage of an opportunity in another country. But if Aiello were to agree to do something extra, such as paint Newcombe's fence instead, there would be a new agreement (an accord) with added consideration (satisfaction), and the new arrangement would be binding.

**Accord and satisfaction overcomes consideration problem**

Sometimes the old contract is discharged by agreement and a new contract is substituted for it. This is often mistaken for a simple modification of the old contract, but when a major term of the agreement is being changed the transaction will more likely be viewed as a discharge and substitution rather than a modification. The difference can be important since it may affect whether various terms from the old agreement, such as exemption and penalty clauses, are carried over to the new one.

When the new agreement involves a new party being substituted for one of the original parties to the agreement, it is called a **novation**. It must be emphasized that whether the contract is being discharged or where the terms of the agreement or the parties to it are being changed, there must be complete agreement among all the parties before the new agreement becomes binding. It may be tempting to cancel a deal when a better one comes along, but if there is a binding contract it must be honoured even when the job has yet to been started. One person cannot impose these changes on the other.

**Novation involves new party but all must agree to the change**

**Must have consensus**

### Case Summary 8.7

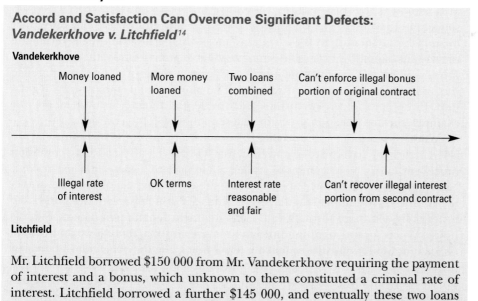

## Accord and Satisfaction Can Overcome Significant Defects: *Vandekerkhove v. Litchfield*[14]

**Vandekerkhove**

| Money loaned | More money loaned | Two loans combined | Can't enforce illegal bonus portion of original contract |

| Illegal rate of interest | OK terms | Interest rate reasonable and fair | Can't recover illegal interest portion from second contract |

**Litchfield**

Mr. Litchfield borrowed $150 000 from Mr. Vandekerkhove requiring the payment of interest and a bonus, which unknown to them constituted a criminal rate of interest. Litchfield borrowed a further $145 000, and eventually these two loans plus the unpaid interest were consolidated into one loan for $318 250 at 12.5 per-

---

14. (1995), 121 D.L.R. (4th) 571 (B.C.C.A.); leave to appeal to S.C.C. refused (1995).

cent interest secured by a mortgage on Litchfield's house. Vandekerkhove tried to enforce the original bonus but couldn't because it was part of an illegal contract. This prompted Litchfield to bring this action to recover $23 250 of the consolidated loan since it represented the unpaid interest portion of that illegal contract. The trial Judge agreed, but on appeal the Court held that since the parties had renegotiated in good faith not being aware of the illegality, the new agreement was binding on them. There was an exchange of consideration on both sides supporting the modification, and the new interest rate was fair and reasonable.

This is an example of the principle of accord and satisfaction with consideration on both sides supporting a renegotiated contract. It also shows a court's more lenient attitude toward illegal contracts where both of the parties are innocent or act in good faith.

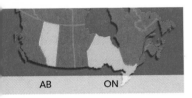

**Partial payment of debt acceptable, if actually taken**

As explained in Chapter 5, a problem arises where a creditor agrees to take less than is owed in full satisfaction of a debt. So long as the payment is made before the due date there is consideration, but where it is made after there is no consideration to support the reduced payment and the full debt is still owing.[15] This result is unacceptable from a business point of view, since most creditors would prefer such partial payment to nothing and the debtors would not likely pay if they couldn't be certain of discharge. As a result, several provinces, including Ontario and British Columbia, have passed statutes making such partial payments binding if the funds have actually changed hands. Nothing forces the creditor to accept the lesser amount, but if it is taken as payment in full satisfaction of the debt the creditor must be satisfied with it.

## Contractual Terms

Most contracts, by their nature, will end upon proper performance. However, sometimes they involve an ongoing relationship, with no provision to bring that relationship to an end. In these circumstances, the parties can usually terminate the contract simply by giving the other reasonable notice. Often, the contract will provide for its own termination, usually by specifying a particular period of notice that must be given, and that provision will be binding subject to contrary legislation. In employment relationships and residential tenancy arrangements, for example, such termination provisions must comply with the governing statutes.

**Contract may provide for its own discharge**

**Condition precedent**

**Conditions subsequent**

When the contract itself specifies that some event or requirement must be satisfied before the parties are bound by it, this is properly referred to as a **condition precedent** but is more commonly called a **"subject to" clause**. For example, if Nishi were to agree to buy Fafard's house, subject to the sale of her own house, the contract is conditional on that event. Thus, if Nishi fails to sell her house, she is not obligated to go through with any agreement for the purchase of Fafard's house. When such a condition precedent is not satisfied, there is no contractual obligation. **Conditions subsequent** are terms that bring the obligations of the parties to an end upon some event or condition taking place. Whereas conditions precedent determine when the obligations between the parties begin, conditions subsequent determine when they end. For example, if Agar agreed to pay Nguyen $400 per month for janitorial services "until Nguyen ceases to be a full-time student," this term is a condition subsequent. Agar will be obligated to pay only until Nguyen finishes school.

15. *Foakes v. Beer.* (1884), 9 App. Cas. 605 (H.L.).

Sometimes the contract anticipates some catastrophic event, such as a riot, invasion, earthquake, or flood, that will interfere with the performance of the contract. This is referred to as a *force majeure* **clause**. Such terms might provide for discharge but might also set out the consequences, such as which party will bear the risk of loss. When such catastrophic events take place and are not anticipated in the contract they will likely cause the contract to be discharged by frustration, as discussed below.

Of course, when such terms are not included in the contract the parties can always agree to end, modify, or substitute obligations with a new agreement, as discussed above. Contracts can also end by operation of law, as would be the case when one of the parties dies or becomes insane or bankrupt. Bankruptcy will be discussed in Chapter 10.

# Frustration

Sometimes some unexpected event out of the control of the parties makes the performance of the contract impossible. For example, where a construction firm agrees to repair a bridge but the bridge is destroyed in a storm before they can perform, performance has become impossible. In such circumstances, the contract is considered discharged through frustration. **Frustration** occurs when some unforeseen, outside event out of the control of either party interferes with the performance of the contract, making the basic object of the agreement unobtainable.

**Frustrating event may end contract**

It is easy to understand frustration when performance of the contract is made impossible, such as when a person agrees to paint a house that is destroyed in a fire before the job can be performed. The difficulty arises because the courts have expanded the principle to also cover situations where the foundation of the contract is destroyed. Performance may still be technically possible, but the whole nature of the relationship has changed, making performance something essentially different from what the parties anticipated.

In the case of *Krell v. Henry*,[16] the parties agreed to the rental of an apartment to view the coronation parade of Edward VII. A small deposit was paid at the time the contract was entered into, but the coronation parade was cancelled before the balance was paid because of the King's sudden illness. It was still possible to occupy the flat, but to require the tenant to do so with no coronation parade to watch would be something essentially different from what the parties had in mind when they entered into the contract. Although performance of the contract was possible in a literal sense, it was no longer possible to obtain the purpose or object of the contract itself. Thus, the contract was discharged through frustration.

The destruction of a building may lead to frustration of a contract for janitorial services.

## Case Summary 8.8

**Contract Is Frustrated Even Though Performance Still Possible: *KBK No. 138 Ventures Ltd. v. Canada Safeway Ltd.*[17]**

Canada Safeway sold property to KBK, both parties under the impression that it was zoned for high-density development. But when the city rezoned the property

16. [1903] 2 K.B. 740 (C.A.).

17. (2000), 185 D.L.R. (4th) 650 (B.C.C.A.).

to a much lower density this destroyed KBK's plans for redevelopment, and they demanded the return of the $150 000 deposit paid, claiming frustration. Safeway argued that the essential nature of the contract was for the purchase of the property and that remained intact, but the court found frustration and ordered the return of the deposit. In this case the whole substance of the contract had been radically altered by the unanticipated intervention of the city in rezoning the property. The change struck at the root of the contract, fundamentally changing its nature and thus frustrating it. Did this application frustration lead to a just result?

**Shared mistake not the same as frustration**

Care should be taken not to confuse frustration with *shared mistake*, discussed in the preceding chapter. With shared mistake, there is no contract because the subject matter had been destroyed before the contract was entered into. Frustration deals with situations where the problems arise after the formation of the contract. If a ship that is the subject of a contract is destroyed before the contract is made, the parties are making a mistake assuming the ship to still be as expected. But if the ship is destroyed after the contract is made, the contract is discharged through frustration.

**Circumstances constituting frustration**

Frustration commonly arises in the following circumstances:

**1.** Performance of a contract becomes impossible because the subject matter of the agreement is destroyed or is otherwise unusable. Contracts may be frustrated when a person who has agreed to supply personal services becomes ill or dies, or when the specific article that formed the object of the contract is destroyed before the agreement can be performed.

In the case of *Taylor v. Caldwell*,[18] there was an agreement between the parties to rent out a music hall. The hall burned down six days before the performance was to take place. The court held that the contract was discharged through frustration.

**2.** An event that forms the basis of a contract fails to take place. An example is the cancellation of the coronation parade in *Krell v. Henry* cited earlier.

**3.** Acts of the government interfere with performance. Government policy can interfere with the performance of a contract in several different ways. A contract with someone in another country may become unlawful or impossible to perform because of a declaration of war; contracts involving the manufacture and production of particular drugs or foodstuffs may become illegal by statute. A contract may anticipate the acquisition of a licence or permit that the government does not grant. Note as well that all levels of government have the power to expropriate the property that may form the basis of a contract. The above is not intended to be a complete list, but most of the frustrating events that do take place fall into one of these three categories.

## Circumstances Not Constituting Frustration

**Self-induced frustration** involves one of the parties causing—or, if it is within his control, failing to prevent—the frustrating event. It may appear to be frustration, but self-induced frustration is simply treated as a breach of contract. For example, if Moser has a contract to build an apartment building for Wu but the city refuses

**Self-induced frustration is breach**

---

18. (1863), 3 B. & S. 826 (Q.B.).

to grant Moser a building permit, we would expect the contract to be frustrated. However, if the building permit is refused because Moser failed to submit the appropriate plans as required by city bylaw, the frustration is self-induced. Moser is responsible for the misfortune and the refusal of the city to grant a permit will not provide an excuse for Moser's failure to perform the contract.

Also, the contract itself may state what is to happen in the event of such an occurrence often indicating which party would bear the risk. Such terms, called *force majeure* clauses, will prevail and frustration will not apply even where performance has become impossible. It is only when the event is an unforeseen interference, not caused by either party and not covered by the contract, that the courts are willing to find frustration.

**Must be unanticipated to be frustration**

Finally, the contract is not frustrated if the unforeseen outside event only makes the performance of the contract more costly or more difficult.

**Increase in costs is not frustration**

In the case of *Tsakiroglou Co. v. Noblee & Thorl G.m.b.H*,[19] delivery of a cargo from a port in the Sudan on the east coast of Africa to Germany became more onerous when the Suez War closed the canal. The seller claimed that the contract was frustrated. The court, however, found the seller liable for breach, holding that although it was more difficult and costly to ship the cargo around Africa the essential nature of the contract remained intact and frustration did not apply. Note that the result would likely have been different had they specified delivery through the Suez Canal, since using that route was now impossible.

**Increased difficulty is not frustration**

Similarly, if a farmer agrees to sell 50 boxes of Golden Delicious apples to a buyer and then his crop is destroyed by hail, this is not frustration unless the terms of the contract specifically stated that the apples were to come from his trees. The source of the apples was not a term of the contract, and the farmer can simply obtain them from another farmer or on the open market and thus fulfill his contractual obligation, albeit at a higher cost.

### Case Summary 8.9

**Frustration Requires More Than an Inability to Pay:**
*Korol v. Sask. Federation of Police Officers*[20]

Koral was an ex-police officer and was offered a job to manage the collective bargaining activities of a nonprofit society made up of seven municipal police forces. But his employment was terminated when these bodies withdrew their support and funding. When Korol sued the society they claimed frustration, having no work for him and no funds. The court found in favour of Korol, holding that that the federation's inability to pay did not frustrate the contract. Lack of financial ability alone will not establish frustration.

To find frustration performance must be impossible or the foundation or purpose of the contract must be fundamentally or radically changed. Lack of profits or funding will not frustrate a contract.

## Effect of Frustration

The major problem associated with frustration is to determine who shall suffer the loss when the contract is discharged. Under common law, the general principle was, "Let the loss lie where it falls." In other words, the party who had done

**Let loss lie where it falls under common law**

19. [1962] A.C. 93 (H.L.).

20. [2000] 11 W.W.R. 364 (Sask. Q.B.).

work or provided services before the frustrating event would bear the loss and could not seek compensation from the other party. Similarly, money already paid was lost. Note, however, that where payment was due before the frustrating event that payment still had to be paid. This is illustrated by *Chandler v. Webster*,[21] a case that also involved the rental of a flat to view King Edward VII's coronation parade. But in this case the entire rent of just over £141 was due and payable in advance, but only £100 had actually been paid. Because the principle was that the loss should lie where it fell when a contract was frustrated, the tenant could not get his money back. In addition, because the sum not yet paid was owed before the frustrating event, that sum had to be paid as well.

**Problems with deposits**

This position was considered unsatisfactory and the House of Lords made a significant change in the *Fibrosa* case,[22] which required the return of a deposit paid by a Polish company to a British manufacturer after the outbreak of war frustrated their contract. Because the Polish company had received no benefit, it was entitled to the return of its deposit. This represents the common law position today but still leads to some unsatisfactory results. The whole deposit or nothing has to be returned, depending on whether any benefit was received.

Where a benefit has been obtained by one party prior to the frustrating event, legislation in most jurisdictions in the form of the *Frustrated Contracts Act* now permits the court to order that party to pay the other for it.

**Legislation allows deposits to be split**

Where a deposit has been paid, the legislation usually allows the court to take into consideration the costs that have been incurred in preparation to perform the contract, whether or not the other party has received a benefit. The court can now apportion that deposit on the basis of the costs incurred and the benefits received (see Table 8.2). In British Columbia and the Yukon, such costs can be apportioned between the parties whether or not a deposit is involved.

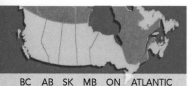

BC  AB  SK  MB  ON  ATLANTIC

Other statutes also modify the common law application of the frustration principle. In common law, frustration does not apply to leases, but most jurisdictions have clearly stated that in residential leases frustration will apply. British Columbia extends the application of frustration to commercial leases as well. When goods are being sold, the *Sale of Goods Act* provides that if the goods, through no fault of the parties, perish before the risk passes to the purchaser, the contract is voided. The effect is that the contract is not binding on the purchaser, and any moneys paid have to be returned.

### Table 8.2 Effect of Frustrated Contracts Act

| Frustrated contract | No deposit | –discharge |
|---|---|---|
| | With deposit | –used to pay for benefit & discharge |
| | | –split to cover expenses & discharge |
| | | –otherwise returned & discharge |

21. [1904] 1 KB 493 (C.A.).

22. *Fibrosa Spolka Akeyjna v. Fairbairn Lawson Combe Barbouk Ltd.*, [1943] A.C. 32 (H.L.).

## Case Summary 8.10

**Reimbursement for Expenses Where Contract Frustrated:**
***Can-Truck Transportation Ltd. v. Fenton's Auto Paint Shop Ltd.***[23]

The plaintiff's truck was sent to the defendant for repairs after an accident. Repairs worth some $28 000 were completed when a fire destroyed both the shop and the truck, thus frustrating the repair contract. The *Ontario Frustrated Contracts Act* provided that when funds were paid (as with a deposit) or were payable before the frustrating event took place, they could be used to reimburse for expenses incurred. The court found that payment for repairs was payable prior to the fire and still had to be paid to reimburse the company for the expenses they incurred in repairing the vehicle even though it had been destroyed.

# Remedies for Breach of Contract

At the outset, note that several examples of remedies provided to the parties involved in contractual disputes have already been discussed. These remedies deal with problems with the formation of a contract and consist of restoring the parties to original position, interpreting or correcting the terms, or compensating a victim who has been misled or pressured into the contract. The following discussion looks at remedies where a party has failed to properly perform their obligations under the contract.

## Damages

The most common remedy for a breach of contract is an order that the breaching party pay damages. **Damages** are amounts of money assessed by the court and designed to compensate victims for their losses. The object is to put the victim, as near as monetary compensation can, into the position he or she would have been in had the contract been properly performed. Thus, in contract law damages look forward, whereas damages awarded in a tort action look backward and try to put the victim in the position he would have been in had the tort never taken place. For example, if a person bought defective paint from a supplier that blistered when put on the walls, necessitating repainting, the court would not only award the cost of the paint as damage but also take into consideration the amount it would cost for a painter to scrape the blistered paint off and repaint the house. The courts will then order the vendor to pay a sum sufficient to put

*Damages in contract law designed to compensate*

*Victim of breach compensated as if contract had been properly performed*

## Reducing **Risk** 8.2

It must be emphasized that the following remedies are obtained though the litigation process and, as such, represent a failure not a victory. Disputes are much better resolved through negotiation or even with the help of third parties, as with mediation and arbitration. Suing should be viewed as a last resort and the remedies that follow as a poor consolation.

---

23. (1993), 101 D.L.R. (4th) 562 (Ont. C.A.).

the purchaser in the position he or she would have been in if the paint had not been defective.

**Damages awarded may be special, general, or punitive**

When the damages awarded are to cover specific costs and expenses they are called **special damages**, but when the funds awarded are an estimate of what has been lost or what will be lost they are called **general damages**. The calculation of damages may be based on the shortfall from what was expected from proper performance, but sometimes damages are designed to cover what has been lost because reliance was placed on the performance of the contract. Only in very rare circumstances involving particularly vexatious conduct will courts award **punitive damages** for breach of contract. Punitive damages are intended to punish the offending party rather than compensate the injured and may result in a considerably higher award as a result.

### Case Summary 8.11

**Damages to Look Forward, Not Backward:**
***Ed Learn Ford Sales Ltd. v. Giovannone*[24]**

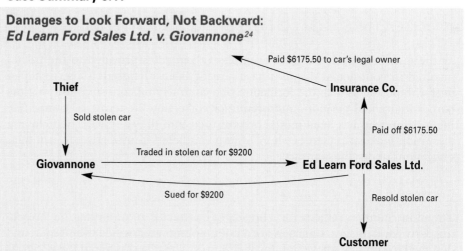

Giovannone traded his Lincoln car in for a truck at Ed Learn Ford Sales Ltd., and the car was resold before they discovered it had been stolen before Giovannone acquired it. The dealer paid $6175.50 to the insurance company to cover what had been paid on the original loss, and sued Giovannone for the $9200 trade-in allowance. But the Court awarded the dealer only the $6175.50 paid to the insurance company. The Judge quoted from *Wertheim v. Chicoutimi Pulp Co.*: "…it is the general intention of the law that, in giving damages for breach of contract, the party complaining should, so far as it can be done by money, be placed in the same position as he would have been in if the contract had been performed."[25] Damages for breach of contract are designed to put the victim where he would be had the contract been properly performed. But in this case it can be argued that Giovannone benefited unfairly since he was allowed $9200 for the car, not $6175.50. What do you think?

24. (1990), 74 D.L.R. (4th) 761 (Ont. Gen. Div.).

25. [1911] A.C. 301 at 307 (P.C.).

# Limitations on Recoverable Damages

Although damages are designed to compensate a person for injuries suffered, not all losses are recoverable. Remoteness and mitigation are two limitations on the recoverability of damages. As well, the parties are free to place terms in the contract itself limiting the damages recoverable or specifying other courses of action in the event of breach.

## Remoteness

The important case of *Hadley v. Baxendale*[26] involved the shipping of a broken crankshaft from a steam engine to be used as a pattern for the manufacture of a new one. The shipper was asked to send it quickly but failed to do so. Unknown to the shipper, the plaintiff's entire plant was shut down while waiting for the crankshaft.

This caused great expense to the plaintiff, who sued the shipper for lost profits. The shipper claimed that he could not be responsible for the unusual damage because he had no knowledge of it. The court used the reasonable person test to determine the extent of the shipper's responsibility for damages and held that the shipper was responsible only for the usual damages that could be expected if the contract were breached and therefore should not be responsible for the plaintiff's lost profits.

The principle that has developed from this and other cases is essentially that a breaching party is responsible only for those damages that, at the time the contract was entered into, seem a likely outcome if the contract were breached. Thus, the breaching party is responsible not only for the normally expected damages that flow from a breach but also for any unusual damages resulting from special circumstances that were communicated to him or her at the time of the contract. In short, the breaching party is responsible in contract law for any damages that can be reasonably foreseen at the time the contract is entered into.

One area where the problem of remoteness often arises is in a claim for damages to compensate for lost profits. Applying this principle, the breaching party will be responsible only for the loss of ordinary profits that could have been expected given his knowledge of the business. In *Horne v. Midland Ry*[27] the defendants were one day late in the delivery of a shipment of shoes, causing the merchant to lose an opportunity to sell the shoes at an exceptionally high price. The shipper knew only that the merchant would have to take the shoes back if they were late, not that an exceptional profit would be lost. The defendants were not responsible for the unusually high lost profit since they were not aware of those special circumstances, and such a loss was not reasonably foreseeable.

When a contract is breached, damages are awarded in order to compensate for economic losses. Courts have only recently shown a willingness to award monetary compensation for mental distress. These situations are generally limited to cases where some non-monetary benefit was the subject matter of the contract, such as a disrupted vacation or cruise.[28]

---

26. (1854), 156 E.R. 145 (Ex. Ct).

27. (1873), L.R. 8 C.P. 131 (C.P.).

28. *Jarvis v. Swan Tours Ltd.*, [1973] Q. B. 233 (C.A.).

## Reducing **Risk** 8.3

Businesspeople are sometimes tempted to do nothing when they are the victims of a breach, allowing damages to accumulate on the assumption that they are the responsibility of—and therefore will be paid by—the breaching party. This is bad practice for several reasons, not the least of which is that it may be very difficult and prohibitively expensive to collect compensation from that other party. More importantly for our purposes, the victim of the breach has a responsibility to mitigate the damages, meaning they must do what they can to keep those damages as low as possible. For example, if computers that were purchased to keep inventory and financial records proved to be not up to the task, the supplier may have breached the contract but the business cannot simply stand by allowing huge losses. It must take steps to upgrade, replace, or repair those computers to minimize the loss. Even where the seller has given assurance they can do the job, when it becomes obvious that they cannot an effort should be made to mitigate the losses. Note that reasonable costs associated with mitigation can be recovered from the breaching party.

## Mitigation

**Victims must mitigate their losses**

Victims of breach are required to mitigate their losses; that is, to keep them as low as is reasonably possible. The failure to mitigate is a common problem in wrongful-dismissal actions. A person who has been wrongfully dismissed has a right to sue but must make a reasonable effort to find other employment. Damages in such actions are based on the difference between how much notice the employee should have been given as opposed to how much they actually received. If the employer can show that the dismissed employee failed to look for another job, the damages will be reduced by the amount he should have earned during that notice period. He should have mitigated by trying to find other employment.

Note also that the obligation to mitigate means simply that the victim of the breach must take all reasonable steps to minimize losses suffered. That person is not required to take personal risks or to incur unreasonable expense in the process.

### Contractual Limitations

It is possible for a contract to set out the consequences in the event of breach. Such terms may require mediation or arbitration to resolve disputes. Where instalments are involved a breach may trigger an **acceleration clause**, which makes the entire outstanding debt due and payable immediately. It is more common, however, for contracts to contain a term specifying the amount of damages to be paid in the event of a breach, or limiting the compensation to be paid to a specific amount.

**Remedies set out in contract**

### Case Summary 8.12

**Limitation of the Damages Payable Set Out in Contract:**
*Elite Bailiff Services Ltd. v. British Columbia*[29]

In this case the B.C. government sent out a request for tenders, which establishes a contract with those responding with respect to the tendering process that is independent of the contract created when one of the tenders is eventually accepted. Here, after the tenders were submitted the government changed the rules, imposing new considerations that were then used to evaluate the tenders presented. When another tender was selected, the plaintiff sued, claiming the change of conditions made the selection unfair and thus violated the terms of the

---

29. (2003), 223 D.L.R. (4th) 39 (B.C.C.A.).

selection contract. The Court found that the selection contract had been breached, but refused to award damages for lost profits since the government's request for tenders contained a clause limiting damages to "an amount equivalent to the reasonable costs incurred by the proponent in preparing its proposal." The Court held that this excluded any claim for lost profits and was a valid term of the agreement.

This case illustrates the use of contractual terms to significantly reduce the amount payable when a contract is breached. There is considerable controversy surrounding the use of these exemption clauses, and while courts often are reluctant to enforce them in this case the B.C. government was clearly successful in its use.

When the contract specifies the damages to be paid, they are called **liquidated damages**, and the courts will normally enforce such terms once liability has been determined. Where the amount is actually prepaid with the provision that the funds are to be forfeited in the event of a breach, it is called a **deposit**. For example, the vendor of an automobile will usually require the buyer to pay a substantial deposit when ordering to secure the purchase. If the purchaser fails to go through with the deal when the car arrives, the vendor can retain the deposit.

**Liquidated damages are specified in contract**

It is important to distinguish between deposits and down payments. **Deposits** are to be forfeited in the event of a breach, whereas a **down payment** is just the first payment and may have to be returned. Of course, from a practical point of view, when the victim of the breach has the down payment in hand, it may be used as a lever to force performance. But if it comes to trial, the court will order its return, usually setting off the actual damages to be paid against the down payment. As a rule it does not matter what the term is called, but it is the provision requiring the forfeiture of the prepayment that will cause the court to treat it as a deposit.

**Deposit is forfeited—down payment is not**

The temptation to take a large deposit entails significant risk. To qualify as liquidated damages, a deposit must be an honest attempt by the parties to estimate the damages that would be suffered if the contract were breached. Too large a prepayment becomes an unreasonable penalty rather than liquidated damages and must be returned. A $1000 deposit on a new car might be fair in view of the cost of advertising, the time lost, the extra interest payments, and so on. But a $10 000 deposit on a $15 000 car is no longer an attempt to compensate for possible loss or injury but becomes an attempt to punish the breaching party for failure to go through with the contract. Such a penalty clause, being excessive, is unconscionable and void. Such a penalty would have to be returned subject to an action to establish the actual loss. Thus, demanding too large a deposit defeats itself.

**Deposit must be reasonable**

Even when no prepayment is involved, a liquidated damages clause is held to the same standard and may be challenged if the amount involved is exorbitant and the object is to unreasonably punish rather than to compensate.

## Case Summary 8.13

### Liquidated Damages Must Be Reasonable: *Meunier v. Cloutier* [30]

When Cloutier returned to Timmins with his wife and purchased a hotel only a block away from the one he had sold to Meunier four years earlier, he was in violation of a non-competition clause prohibiting him from participating in the hotel

---

30. (1984), 9 D.L.R. (4th) 486 (Ont. H.C.).

business in Timmins for five years. The original contract required him to pay $50 000 for such a breach as liquidated damages, and Meunier brought this action to recover that amount. The Court determined the clause was not a penalty and that the amount, time, and geographical area were all reasonable from the point of view of when it was made. Nor was the public interest offended. But the Court, following the Supreme Court of Canada in *H.F. Clarke Ltd. v. Thermidaire Corp. Ltd.*,[31] held that when such a lump sum was involved the amount had to be "reasonable in the circumstances." They determined that given the minor nature of the breach and no evidence that the plaintiff suffered any damage, requiring Cloutier to pay the $50 000 in these circumstances would be unconscionable. Therefore the non-competition clause was a penalty and unenforceable.

While predetermined damages are acceptable, unreasonable penalties clauses are not. Note that in this case, the non-competition clause was valid; it was the damages portion of that provision that was unacceptable.

## Equitable Remedies

The following are examples of remedies that have been developed by the Courts of Chancery to deal with special situations in which the ordinary remedy of damages would not be adequate. Note that these remedies are discretionary and will be granted only when the judge thinks it right and fair to do so.

### Specific Performance

Specific performance occurs when the court orders the defaulting party to live up to the terms of the contract. Where a development company acquires a number of options on properties to build a new shopping mall and one property owner refuses to go through with the deal, it would be appropriate to obtain a court order for specific performance, ordering that property owner to transfer the property at the agreed-upon price. But if the same developer ordered a number of new trucks from a dealer who then refused to deliver them, specific performance would not be appropriate as equivalent vehicles could be obtained elsewhere. The appropriate remedy would be damages, and they would be assessed on the basis of the extra cost of getting the vehicles from another dealer. Only if the trucks were unique and not available from some other source might specific performance be available.

**Courts will not force performance of contracts for personal services**

The courts will not order the defaulting party to perform a contract that requires personal service. If our developer were to contract with a famous performer to sing at a concert celebrating the opening of the shopping mall and the performer then refused to perform, finding a more lucrative engagement elsewhere, the court would not order specific performance and require the performer to sing in these circumstances. Similarly, the courts will not award specific performance as a remedy in any situation that would require close supervision to ensure that the contract is properly performed. Nor will specific performance be available where it would hurt a third party.

On the theory that all land is unique, the courts in the past have been willing to award specific performance whenever the parties to the purchase of land breached their contract. The Supreme Court of Canada has indicated, however,

---

31. [1976] 1 S.C.R. 319 (S.C.C.).

that now contracts dealing with the purchase of land will be treated like any other contract, limiting the availability of specific performance to those situations where damages are inappropriate.[32]

## Injunction

Specific performance involves a court order to do something (to perform the contract), whereas an injunction usually involves an order to refrain from some offensive conduct. In our example above, the court would not order the performer to fulfill the contract by singing at the concert but may well order her not to breach the agreement by performing somewhere else. The injunction is not limited to breach of contract; it may be available in any situation in which wrongful conduct is involved.

In rare circumstances, the courts may issue a mandatory injunction when a person does something to violate a contractual term and thereby creates an ongoing problem. Striking workers involved in an illegal work stoppage are often ordered to stop breaching their contract and return to work. Another example might involve our developer above if he were to place a sign above his shopping centre that exceeds the permitted height limit set out in a restrictive covenant or a municipal bylaw. He would likely be ordered to remove the sign or reduce it to the permitted height. Such mandatory injunctions are not common.

As with specific performance, there are many instances in which the courts will refuse to issue an injunction. The courts are reluctant to order an injunction that would make it impossible for the person defaulting on the contractual agreement to earn a living. A court might well enforce by injunction a term requiring an employee not to work for a competitor for three years upon leaving, but would not enforce a term preventing that employee from working for anyone for three years. Similarly, the courts will not issue an injunction when damages provide a sufficient remedy. An injunction is designed not to punish someone for breaching a contract, but to prevent further injury. An injunction will also not be awarded where it will cause harm to a third party.

An injunction is sometimes ordered even before there has been a trial on the issues. If an employee leaves and works for a competitor, it is important to get an injunction right away and sort out the merits of the dispute later. This is called an **interlocutory injunction** and is issued by the court when some ongoing injury will increase the damage done to the person seeking the interlocutory injunction; making waiting for the trial to determine the matter an unacceptable alternative.

## Accounting

It is often difficult for the victim of the breach to determine just what kind of injuries he or she has suffered, especially when the offending party has taken advantage of some opportunities or rights belonging to the victim. This can happen when there is a fiduciary relationship between the contracting parties; that is, a relationship in which the person breaching the contract has a duty to act in the best interests of the other party. In these circumstances, the court can order that the defaulting party disclose all financial dealings and records so that the injured party can determine what he or she is entitled to claim. In some circumstances the court will then order the offending party to pay over all or a portion of the profits

> **Courts may order breaching conduct to stop**

> • but not where a person can no longer earn a living

> • but not where damages are more appropriate

> • but not where it would hurt a third party

> **Interlocutory injunction issued before the trial**

> **Court may order accounting and require profits to be paid over**

---

32. *Semelhago v. Paramadevan*, [1996] 2 S.C.R. 415 (S.C.C.).

made from the wrongful conduct to the injured party. So the court, instead of awarding damages on the basis of what has been lost by the victim, awards damages on the basis of what has been wrongfully obtained by the breaching party.

## Quantum Meruit

**Court may order payment for part performance**

In some situations, the contract is breached when only part of the work has been done and before the amount agreed to in the contract is due and payable to the injured party. In these circumstances the courts have the power to award compensation for the value of work that has been done on the basis of *quantum meruit*. This is the same principle as discussed in Chapter 5 that allowed the supplier of a service to collect a reasonable fee, even when no price had been agreed upon. Note that only the victim of the breach can claim compensation on the basis of *quantum meruit*. The courts are extremely reluctant to grant any compensation for the breaching party's partial performance of the agreement, unless the contractual obligations have been substantially performed. Sometimes partial payment is payable before completion, and in that case, even the breaching party can collect.

If a contractor has agreed to build a house with payment due upon completion of the job and refuses to continue after completing half, he will not be successful in claiming compensation for what he has done. He should finish the job. But if he has finished half the project and the owner of the property with whom he has contracted refuses to let him continue, the contractor, being the innocent party, will be able to claim compensation for the work that has been done under the principle of *quantum meruit*. Only where the contract called for partial payments at different stages of completion will the breaching party be able to collect for those payments due before the breach.

**Undue delay**

Some general requirements must be met before the courts will grant an equitable remedy. If there has been **laches,** an undue delay on the part of the person seeking the equitable remedy, the courts can refuse to grant the remedy. The plaintiff will still be able to pursue any common law remedy, such as damages without penalty for delay, provided the action is brought within the limitation period in place, as discussed in Chapter 2. The courts can also refuse to award an equitable remedy in any situation in which it would cause undue hardship to the parties or to some other person or would be inappropriate for any other reason. A person seeking equity must come to the court with clean hands, meaning the remedy will be denied when the person seeking the equitable remedy is also guilty of some wrongdoing. These requirements apply to all equitable remedies.

**Hardship**

**Clean hands**

### Case Summary 8.14

**Equitable Remedies Are Not Always Available:**
*Island Properties Ltd. v. Entertainment Enterprises Ltd. et al.*[33]

Entertainment Enterprises Limited and Denis Galway made arrangements to sell property through one real estate agent and then made similar arrangements with another. Two different purchasers acting though the two different agents accepted the offer to sell. The Court found that both were valid and that the property had been sold to both purchasers. The property was transferred to Pegasus and Island Property, which had accepted first, sued for specific performance.

---

33. (1986), 26 D.L.R. (4th) 347 (Nfld. C.A.)

At trial, the Judge ordered that the property be returned by Pegasus and transferred to Island Properties. But the appeal court ordered that the property be returned to Pegasus. Pegasus was a completely innocent third party, and an equitable remedy cannot be given where it will cause harm to such an innocent party. Because the property had been conveyed to the innocent Pegasus, it could not be taken back. This case dramatically illustrates the limitations placed on such equitable remedies. Island Properties was limited to a remedy of damages for breach.

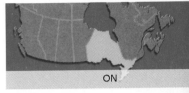

Another factor that may affect the right of the victim of a breach of contract to obtain any remedy is the limitations legislation, discussed in Chapter 2. The limitation periods outlined in these statutes apply to any action brought to court including contract claims, with the result that once the limitation period has expired none of the remedies discussed in this chapter will be available to the victim of the breach.

**Time limits**

Finally, it should be noted that when a judgment or an equitable remedy has been awarded and a defendant refuses to comply, the defendant may be held in contempt of court and can be jailed for contempt, although this is extremely unlikely. The remedies to enforce a judgment, outlined generally in Chapter 2, are available to the victim of a breach of contract as well.

**Contempt**

# Summary

### Contracts
- Can come to an end through performance, breach, agreement, or frustration

### Performance
- When properly tendered but refused, contract may be discharged
- When money is still owed, the creditor must bear the cost of its collection

### Breach
- The victim may treat the contract as discharged and sue
- Breached warranty—contract is still binding but the victim can sue for damages
- Anticipatory breach—victim can treat the contract as discharged immediately or wait for performance but is bound by choice

### Agreement
- Contract provides for its own end
- Condition precedent, condition subsequent, liquidated damages

### Frustration
- Performance impossible or fundamentally changed
- Monies advanced may be apportioned to compensate for expenses or losses incurred
- Self-induced frustration is breach of contract

### Remedies
- Damages paid to compensate the victim
- Damages limited to what was reasonably foreseeable
- Damages must be reduced or mitigated by victim

- Liquidated damages set out in contract must be reasonable
- Deposit cannot be a penalty
- Specific performance requires the breaching party to fulfill agreement
- Injunction—a court order to stop conduct that breaches the contract
- Accounting and *quantum meruit* also available

---

## QUESTIONS

1. Describe the various ways in which a contractual relationship can come to an end.

2. Under what circumstances would a breaching party who had partially performed the terms of the contract be entitled to receive part payment?

3. Describe the differences between a condition and a warranty. What is the significance of the distinction?

4. How may the victim of the breach of a condition lose the right to not fulfill her side of the contract?

5. What constitutes adequate tender of performance?

6. What recourse is available to one party to a contract when performance is made impossible by the other party's conduct?

7. What options are available to the victim of an anticipatory breach? Explain the advantages, disadvantages, and risks associated with these options.

8. How do the courts approach an exemption clause in a contract?

9. What is meant by fundamental breach, and how does the court deal with the problem?

10. What two factors required for the formation of a contract are most likely to be absent when a claim that a contract was discharged or modified by agreement is challenged in court?

11. Explain what happens when a creditor agrees to take less than is owed to settle a debt.

12. Distinguish between contractual terms that are conditions precedent and those that are conditions subsequent.

13. Define frustration. List three ways in which frustration can take place.

14. What is the significance of a court's determination that a contract was frustrated through the fault of one of the parties?

15. Explain how the *Fibrosa* case and subsequent statute law have modified the previously accepted common law rule on the obligations of the parties in the face of a frustrating event.

16. Distinguish between a deposit and a down payment. What is the significance of this distinction?

17. What must be the demonstrated intention of the parties for money paid under a term of a contract to be categorized as a deposit?

18. Explain what limitations on the recovery of damages were developed from the case of *Hadley v. Baxendale*.

19. Describe what is meant by mitigation. Explain how the obligation to mitigate damages limits the ability of the victim of a breach to obtain damages.

20. Distinguish between specific performance and injunction. Explain the restrictions on their availability.

- - - - - - - - - - - - - - - - - - - - - - - - - - - - - - - - - - - - - - - - - - - - - - - - -

## CASES

### 1. *Sumpter v. Hedges*, [1898] 1 Q.B. 673 (C.A.).

The plaintiff agreed to erect certain buildings for the defendant for a lump-sum payment to be made upon completion. The plaintiff failed to finish the work and asked for reimbursement for the amount he had done. The defendant refused. The plaintiff then sued for payment for the work he had done. What factors would the court need to determine before they decided the case? Explain the likely outcome.

### 2. *Betker v. Williams* (1991), 86 D.L.R. (4th) 395 (B.C.C.A.).

Mrs. Williams owned property in Cranbrook and listed the property for sale with Mr. Klinkhammer, a real estate agent. It was advertised as a residential lot in the local newspaper, with a clear indication that a house could be built on it. Mr. Betker bought the property after specifically asking Mr. Klinkhammer if it would be appropriate for a solar home and receiving a positive reply. Four years after the sale, they discovered that a house could not be built on the property because it was too small for a septic tank and had no access to the city sewer line.

It turned out that neither Mrs. Williams nor the real estate agents were aware of this problem. The Betkers brought an action against the agents and Mrs. Williams. There was a term in the agreement stating that there were no representations other than those contained on the written agreement itself, but this provision had not been specifically brought to the attention of the purchasers. Explain the arguments available to both parties and the appropriate remedies that might be sought.

### 3. *Bell v. St. Thomas University* (1992), 97 D.L.R. (4th) 370 (N.B.Q.B.).

Bell was enrolled at the defendant university in a four-year program leading to a bachelor of social work degree. The program required the successful completion of a field practice course called Social Work 410. He took this course but failed it in 1987. The university calendar contained a provision about the repeating of courses that stated, "Students may without special permission register for a course already taken in order to meet a prerequisite or other degree requirement or in order to improve their grade." But in this case, before allowing Bell to repeat Social Work 410, the department required him to fulfill certain conditions. He made several attempts to comply, but these attempts were rejected and he was not permitted to retake the course.

Explain what options were available to Mr. Bell in these circumstances. Would your answer be different if you understood that the course required Mr. Bell to interact with the community, including people at risk, and that his failing grade, and the terms and conditions imposed, related to making sure that no damage was done to the people he was dealing with?

### 4. *Capital Quality Homes, Ltd. v. Colwym Construction Ltd.* (1975), 61 D.L.R. (3d) 385 (Ont. C.A.).

The plaintiff paid a $13 980 deposit to the defendant for some undeveloped land in Windsor, Ontario. The agreement involved the conveyance of 26 separate building lots, and the defendant was required to deliver 26 individual deeds of conveyance, one for each building lot. After the contract was entered into by the parties but before it was executed, legislation was passed bringing planning consent for the land in question under the control of a designated committee. The parties disagreed about who bore the obligation to get the required consents.

At the closing date, the defendant was unable to deliver the individual deeds required, even though the plaintiff was ready to pay the required funds. It should be noted that this change of law took place only 33 days before the closing date for the transfer of the property, and it is questionable whether it was possible to obtain the required consent in time.

The plaintiff sued for the return of the $13 980 deposit paid. Explain the likely outcome. Would your answer be affected if the reason consent was not obtained was that the defendant had made no effort to obtain the required consents?

### 5. *Rinn v. Parent Seeds Ltd.* (2001), 156 Man. R. (2d) 191 (Man. C.A.).

Rinn had a contract to supply a quantity of black and white beans to Parent Seeds Ltd. Unfortunately, Rinn's crop was damaged by frost and he couldn't deliver the beans from his farm. He then made arrangements to obtain the beans from another source and Parent accepted the alternative white beans supplies not knowing Rinn didn't grow them. Parent refused to take delivery of the black beans, claiming that the contract had been frustrated. Explain the arguments that could be advanced by both parties.

How would it affect your answer to learn that the contract required the delivery of specific black beans grown by Rinn with seed supplied by Parent?

### 6. *Computer Workshops v. Banner Capital Market Brokers* (1988), 50 D.L.R. (4th) 118 (Ont. H.C.).

Banner, the defendant in this action, was in the brokerage industry and was developing a computer software network to handle his business. The plaintiff, Computer Workshops Ltd., entered into an agreement with Banner to provide him with the necessary hardware and software equipment to do the job. After 25 of the 100 computers agreed to were delivered, Banner discovered that Computer Workshops was negotiating with Banner's competition to provide them with a similar system with similar capabilities. Banner learned that in those discussions, certain confidential information that he had given to Computer Workshops had been disclosed to their competitor. Banner refused to take the rest of the computers.

Computer Workshops sued for breach. Explain the arguments on both sides and any defence that might be available to Banner in these circumstances.

### 7. *Ferme Gérald Laplante & Fils Ltée v. Grenville Patron Mutual Fire Insurance Co.* (2002), 217 D.L.R. (4th) 34 (Ont. C.A.).

The plaintiff had a fire on his farm and made a claim on his fire insurance. The insurance company paid $1.17 million but disputed a further claim for $700 000. The farmer was forced to sue and after much delay was eventually awarded not only $500 000 of that claim but also a further $750 000 in punitive damages. The award of punitive damages was appealed to the Ontario Court of Appeal. Explain what factors should be taken into consideration in awarding punitive damages and whether punitive damages were appropriate in this case given the facts as stated.

## PART 3

# Commercial Transactions

The world of commerce involves myriad individual transactions which, taken together, create markets that establish the economic structure of our society. Whether these transactions are associated with complex commercial activities or simple purchases, they are all controlled by an involved set of rules embodied in both common law and legislation. This section examines that complex body of rules. Chapter 9 examines the *Sale of Goods Act*, negotiable instruments, and various statutes in place intended to protect the consumer. Chapter 10 looks at secured transactions and the legislation controlling activities involving the use of personal property as security and the other means used by creditors to ensure that they get paid first by a debtor. This chapter also covers the law related to bankruptcy and insolvency.

# CHAPTER
# 9

# Sales and Consumer Protection

## CHAPTER HIGHLIGHTS

- *Sale of Goods Act*
- Negotiable instruments
- Consumer protection legislation
- *Competition Act*

The preceding four chapters were devoted to a general examination of the law of contracts as developed primarily by the courts and embodied in case law. There are, however, several important areas where legislation has been enacted that profoundly affects the contractual relationship. This chapter is devoted to an examination of sale of goods legislation, negotiable instruments, and various consumer protection provisions. It should be noted that the topics covered in this chapter and the one following fall primarily within provincial jurisdiction, resulting in various statutes with considerable provincial variation. This causes some confusion when looking at the different, sometimes conflicting, provisions in different provinces. In the United States this is overcome to a large extent by each state adopting the unified commercial code, resulting in only minor state variations. Many advocate for the adoption of a similar approach in Canada.

# The Sale of Goods

## The *Sale of Goods Act*

**Sale of Goods Act implies terms into contract**

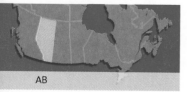

AB

The *Sale of Goods Act* is another example of the summation and codification by the British Parliament of the case law in place in the 19th century. This statute was adopted with only minor variations by every common law province in Canada.

The primary purpose of the Act is to imply the terms that the parties to sale-of-goods transactions often leave out. For example, the parties may not specify a date for payment or time of delivery, and the Act will imply the missing terms into the contract. Note that the Act provides only missing terms, and so the stated intention of the parties will override the provisions of the Act. Note as well that the *Sale of Goods Act* applies not only to retail and consumer transactions but also to all situations where goods are bought and sold, even significant commercial transactions involving large machinery such as railway locomotives or earth-moving equipment.

It must be emphasized that the normal contract rules apply to sale of goods transactions except where overridden by the *Sale of Goods Act*. Thus, offer and acceptance, as well as consideration, capacity, legality, and intention, must be present for the contract to be formed. Also, the rules with respect to mistake, misrepresentation, privity, and breach apply to the contract.

**All other contract rules must be complied with**

## Goods and Services

Property can be divided into real and personal property. Real property consists of land and things permanently attached to the land, such as buildings. Personal property can be divided into tangible movable property such as books, computers, and vehicles (called **chattels** or **goods**), and intangible property, such as a claim or right, including contracts for services, negotiable instruments, and stocks and bonds (referred to as a **chose in action**). The subject of property will be discussed in Chapter 15. The *Sale of Goods Act* deals only with the sale of goods and is not concerned with transactions involving real property or intangibles such as service agreements.

**Act applies only to sale of goods**

Transactions involving both goods and services can pose a problem. When an artist paints a portrait, the client gets a physical item, the portrait, but the main component of the transaction is the service provided and so the *Sale of Goods Act* will not apply. Of course, if the client were to then resell the portrait, the Act would apply. When the goods and services component can be separated, as when parts are used to repair a car, the *Sale of Goods Act* will apply to the goods portion of that contract. Note as well that when only services are involved the court may still be willing to imply terms, such as the requirement of a certain level of quality, even though the *Sale of Goods Act* does not apply.

### Case Summary 9.1

**Restaurant Liable for Selling Contaminated Food:**
***Gee v. White Spot Ltd. and Pan et al. v. White Spot Ltd.*** [1]

In July 1985, Mr. Gee suffered botulism poisoning from food obtained at the White Spot restaurant. He sued, and the Judge decided that since the primary purpose of the transaction was to obtain the food, a chattel, the service component being incidental, the *Sale of Goods Act* applied to the purchase. Section 18(b) of the Act required the goods to be of merchantable quality, meaning that they had to be fit for their normal purpose; in this case, fit for human consumption. Section 18(a) required that when the skill of the seller is relied on, and it is in the normal course of the business to supply the goods, those goods have to be fit for the purpose for which they are purchased. The Judge found that the goods failed these tests and Mr. Gee was successful in his action, the contract of purchase having been breached.

## Transfer of Goods

The *Sale of Goods Act* applies only when it can be demonstrated that the parties intended that the actual possession and property of the goods would transfer to the buyer.

**Goods must be transferred**

---

1. (1986), 32 D.L.R. (4th) 238 (B.C.S.C.).

When goods are used to secure a loan with no intention that they actually be transferred, the *Sale of Goods Act* will not apply even though a **bill of sale** may have been used to create the credit relationship. However, when the goods used as security actually do change hands, as in a conditional sale, the Act will apply. These secured transactions will be discussed in the following chapter.

### Monetary Consideration

**Act does not apply to barter**

It is also necessary that the sale involve the actual payment of some money. The Act will not apply to traded goods unless some money is also exchanged.

### Requirement of Writing

**Some provinces require evidence in writing**

Despite the trend to move away from the *Statute of Frauds*, some provinces still require in their *Sale of Goods Acts* that goods sold over a specified amount (varying from $30 to $50 depending on the province) must be evidenced in writing or partly performed for the contract to be enforceable. Giving something in earnest (anything of value) will also make the contract binding. Other provinces, including British Columbia, Ontario, and Manitoba, have eliminated any writing requirement in sale of goods transactions, although B.C., in its *Consumer Protection Act*, still requires that there be a written contract for direct sales of consumer goods over a certain value.

**Distinction between sale and agreement to sell**

**Normally risk follows title**

## Title and Risk

When the title (the property interest in the goods) does not transfer immediately upon the sale agreement being concluded, it is called an **agreement to sell**. The *Sale of Goods Act* also applies to this future transfer of goods. Determining who has title at any given time is important because under the *Sale of Goods Act* whoever has the title bears the risk of damage or destruction to the goods, unless the parties have agreed otherwise.

Four common methods are sometimes used to override this provision of the Act.

**1. C.I.F. contracts (cost, insurance, and freight).** In this type of contract it doesn't matter when title transfers, because one of the parties has been designated as being responsible for paying the costs involved in the shipping of those goods as well as arranging insurance, in the process assuming the risk if anything goes wrong.

**2. F.O.B. contracts (free on board).** With F.O.B. contracts, the parties have agreed that the seller will bear the risk until a specified point in the transport process. For example, if the goods are to be delivered F.O.B. the loading dock at the seller's place of business, the buyer assumes the risk at that point.

**3. C.O.D. contracts (cash on delivery).** This type of contract entitles the seller to maintain the proprietary rights or title as well as control over the possession of those goods until they are delivered to the buyer's premises and paid for. The risk stays with the seller until delivery at the specified location is complete.

**4. Bill of lading.** Bills of lading are also often used by the seller to maintain control over the goods during shipment. A **bill of lading** is a document given by the transporter or carrier of the goods to the shipper as a form of receipt. The seller can maintain control (and the risk) with respect to those goods by naming themselves as the party entitled to receive delivery of the goods at their destination.

## Reducing **Risk 9.1**

There are many opportunities to exercise control over the various legal aspects of business transactions, such as who bears the risk and when title transfers. While there have been many restrictions imposed when consumers are involved it is still important to understand what options you can exercise to reduce the risk you face in both consumer and commercial transactions.

## Transfer of Title

Who has title not only can determine who bears the risk but also may affect what remedies are available in the event of a breach. The rules for determining who has title as found in the *Sale of Goods Act* are set out below.[2]

**Remedy may depend on who has title**

**Rules for determining title**

### Rule 1

> Where there is an unconditional contract for the sale of specific goods in a deliverable state the property in the goods passes to the buyer when the contract is made, and it is immaterial whether the time of payment or the time of delivery or both are postponed.

**Title transfers immediately**

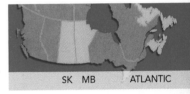

If the goods are identified and nothing more has to be done to them, the purchaser gets title at the point of contracting to purchase. Thus, if Lynch pointed to a television set in Amann's store and said "I'll give you $300 for that one," title would transfer as soon as his offer was accepted even though he might take delivery and pay at a later date.

### Rule 2

> Where there is a contract for the sale of specific goods and the seller is bound to do something to the goods for the purpose of putting them into a deliverable state, the property does not pass until such thing is done and the buyer has notice thereof.

**Notice required if something needed to put goods into deliverable state**

If some repair has to be done on the television set in the above example, title and risk would pass to the buyer only after the repair was done and after the purchaser was notified the goods were ready. If there were a fire at Amann's store before the notice, the loss would be the merchant's.

**Notice required if repairs are needed**

### Rule 3

> Where there is a contract for the sale of specific goods in a deliverable state, but the seller is bound to weigh, measure, test, or do some other act or thing with reference to the goods for the purpose of ascertaining the price, the property does not pass until the act or thing is done and the buyer has notice thereof.

**Notice required if testing is required**

If Schmidt bought a truckload of potatoes from Naslund, title would not pass until they had been weighed to determine price and Schmidt had been notified.

---

2. These provisions are taken from section 21 of the *Sale of Goods Act*. References to the Act throughout this chapter refer to the *Sale of Goods Act*, R.S.O. 1990, c. S.1. Every province has a similar act, although the wording of the provisions may vary.

## Rule 4

> When goods are delivered to the buyer on approval or on "sale or return" or other similar terms, the property in them passes to the buyer:
>
> (a) when he signifies his approval or acceptance to the seller or does any other act adopting the transaction,
>
> (b) if he does not signify his approval or acceptance to the seller but retains the goods without giving notice of rejection, then if a time has been fixed for the return of the goods on the expiration of that time, and if no time has been fixed on the expiration of a reasonable time and what is a reasonable time is a question of fact.

**Title passes when approval by acceptance is signified or reasonable time has passed**

This rule covers situations in which goods are taken by the buyer to test for a trial period before deciding to keep them. In our earlier example, if Amann had allowed Lynch to take the television set home and try it for four days, title and risk would not transfer to Lynch until the expiration of those four days, unless Lynch notified Amann before that time that he was happy with the goods. Title would pass earlier if Lynch resold the TV or built it into the wall of his den.

## Rule 5

> (a) When there is a contract for the sale of unascertained or future goods by description, and goods of that description and in a deliverable state are unconditionally appropriated to the contract, either by the seller with the assent of the buyer, or by the buyer with the assent of the seller, the property in the goods thereupon passes to the buyer and such assent may be express or implied and may be given either before or after the appropriation is made.
>
> (b) Where pursuant to the contract the seller delivers the goods to the buyer or to a carrier or other bailee (whether named by the buyer or not) for the purpose of transmission to the buyer and does not reserve the right to disposal, he shall be deemed to have unconditionally appropriated the goods to the contract.

The goods covered by Rule 5 are those that have not been manufactured at the time the contract was entered into or that exist but have not yet been separated out and identified as the particular goods to be used in a given transaction. Normally, in the example above, Lynch would not be given the particular television set on display but would be given one like it from storage. Rule 5 would apply because no specific goods have yet been appropriated to the contract at the time of the sale. Rule 5 also applies when a person orders something that has not yet been manufactured, such as an order for a new car.

**When goods are not manufactured or identifiable as goods in question, unconditional appropriation and assent needed**

Only when the goods have been manufactured or separated out and unconditionally committed to the buyer with the buyer's assent does title pass. While notice to the buyer that the goods are ready may be the most common method of satisfying the assent or approval provision, assent is often implied from the circumstances. Thus, if a person were to leave her car with a dealer for the installation of a new stereo cassette player, she will be taken to have assented to the selection of the stereo when it is installed, since she left her car there for that purpose.

It must always be remembered that the parties can specify a contrary intention in the contract, overriding these rules with respect to title and risk. Great care should be used in examining the terms of the contract to determine whether this has been done.

## Case Summary 9.2

### Does the *Sale of Goods Act* Apply to Prefabricated Buildings?
### *Re Royal Bank of Canada and Saskatchewan Telecommunications*[3]

Tritec was in the process of building several prefabricated buildings for Saskatchewan Telecommunications when the Royal Bank put Tritec into receivership and seized the unfinished buildings. The Court decided that because the buildings were portable they were chattels rather than real property, and the *Sale of Goods Act* applied. Since this was an agreement for sale Rule 5 determined that title would transfer only after the buildings were completed and unconditionally appropriated to the contract. This had not yet happened, and so Tritec still had title to the trailers giving the Royal Bank first claim on the buildings.

Who has title is important to determine not only who bears the risk but also who has first claim to the goods in the event of default or bankruptcy.

## Rights and Obligations of the Parties

The *Sale of Goods Act* implies both conditions and warranties into the contract. The difference is important. An implied warranty is a minor term, and its breach does not discharge the victim from the rest of their contractual obligations, whereas the breach of an implied condition allows the victim to treat the contract as ended. But a breach of a condition does not always bring a contract to an end. The victim of a breach of a condition has the option to ignore it or treat it as a breach of warranty. The victim of a breach may also lose the right to have a contract discharged by a breach of condition by accepting the goods. In our example above of the television set purchased from Amann by Lynch, Lynch would lose the right to return the goods if he had resold them or built the television into his living room. It should also be noted that the parties are free to designate a term as a condition or warranty, but the court retains the right to make the final determination.

**Conditions and warranties under *Sale of Goods Act***

**Acceptance causes victims of breach to lose right of discharge**

## Title

The *Sale of Goods Act* implies several terms into sales agreements that cover a seller's right to sell goods to a buyer. Section 13(a) of the Ontario *Sale of Goods Act* makes it a condition that the seller has the right to sell the goods or will have the right at the time title is to be transferred. Thus, Amann breaches a condition of the contract if he cannot deliver good title at delivery, and Lynch would be free from any further obligation under the contract.

Section 13(b) requires that the seller provide quiet possession of the goods as a warranty of the contract. This means that the goods must be delivered in such a condition that they can be used and enjoyed by the buyer in the way they were intended, free from any interference. If the television set sold to Lynch operated only on 220 volts it would be useless to him, interfering with his right to quiet enjoyment.

**Seller must convey good title**

**• and quiet possession**

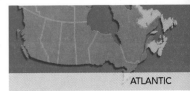

ATLANTIC

---

3. (1985), 20 D.L.R. (4th) 415 (Sask. C.A.).

**• and goods free from charge or encumbrance**

Section 13(c) of the Act specifies that it shall be an implied warranty of the contract that the goods shall be free from any charge or encumbrance that has not been disclosed to the buyer. Such **liens** give the lien holder (a secured creditor) the right to retake the goods if not paid. The presence of such a lien without telling the purchaser would be a breach of warranty under section 13(c) of the Act. Secured transactions will be discussed in the next chapter.

## Description

**Goods must match description**

Goods sold on the internet, by catalogue, by mail order, or other forms of distance shopping, usually with a picture and accompanying text, are being sold by description. Section 14 of the Ontario *Sale of Goods Act* provides that when goods are sold by description there will be an implied condition that the goods delivered must match that description. If Afsari ordered a camera pictured as a Nikon F100 on the internet and what was delivered was a Nikon 80, there has been a breach of the implied condition that the goods match the description.

### Case Summary 9.3

**Tableware Didn't Match Description:** *Coast Hotels Ltd. v. Royal Doulton Canada Ltd.*[4]

Coast Hotels ordered a specific pattern of tableware from Royal Doulton Canada. Only the early deliveries had the Royal Doulton stamp on the bottom, and Coast Hotels sued. The Court held that section 17 of the B.C. *Sale of Goods Act* applied, which implied a condition into the contract that the goods must match the description; the later deliveries failed to satisfy this condition. The contract was breached and the damages awarded were based on what was a reasonable cost to replace the nonconforming tableware with tableware of equivalent quality.

**Most sales of manufactured goods are by description**

**Goods bought must match the description or picture provided**

In fact, today the sale of any manufactured good is a sale by description, one item being indistinguishable from another of the same model. When we buy we are relying on the manufacturer's description, whether that description is found on the box, a specification sheet, a brochure, a catalogue, or the internet, and all goods delivered must match that description.

## Fitness and Quality

### Case Summary 9.4

**Suppliers of Defective Gears Fail to Protect Themselves:** *Hunter Engineering Co. v. Syncrude Canada Ltd.*[5]

---

4. (2000), 76 B.C.L.R. (3d) 341, 6 B.L.R. (3d) 44 (B.C.S.C).

5. [1989] 1 S.C.R. 426 (S.C.C.).

Syncrude operated large conveyor belts as part of its tar sands extraction project and ordered a number of gearboxes for the system from two different companies. Both companies, Hunter Engineering and Allis Chalmers, obtained the gears from the same manufacturer, and after several gears failed it was determined that all would have to be replaced. Syncrude sued both companies, and both claimed they were protected by clauses in their contracts limiting their responsibility to a specific period of time that had expired. Although the *Sale of Goods Act* applied requiring the goods to be fit for their intended purpose, the Court had to determine whether the exemption clauses contained in the contracts overrode the operation of the Act.

The Hunter Engineering contract did have a clause limiting their liability, but they had failed to include a clause exempting the operation of the *Sale of Goods Act* provisions, which, still being in force, imposed liability on them. The Allis Chalmers contract specifically excluded all statutory warranties or conditions, and so there was no liability. It was also argued that if the breach were fundamental, this exemption clause could not stand. But the Supreme Court of Canada held that even in the face of such a fundamental breach, it was still possible for the parties to exempt themselves from liability, as Allis Chalmers had effectively done in this instance. Fundamental breach is discussed in more detail in Chapter 8.

The *Sale of Goods Act* applies to both small and large transactions, whether they are commercial or consumer in nature. But the parties can contract out of its provisions, if they wish, and even the principle of fundamental breach can be overcome by a very careful and specifically worded exemption clause. Many argue that there is a great difference between business and consumer transactions and that the same rules should not be applied to both. They also argue that merchants should not be able to override provisions that obviously are meant to protect the consumer. What do you think?

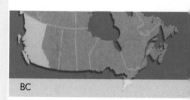

BC

**Goods must be of merchantable quality**

**Goods must be suitable for purpose of purchase when sales person relied upon**

A very important provision requires as a condition that when goods are sold by description they must be of merchantable quality (section 15 of the Ontario Act). This means that the goods must be free of any defect that would have persuaded the purchaser not to buy them at the agreed-upon price if the purchaser had known of the defect at the outset. If a sample has been inspected, the defect must not have been readily apparent upon examination. Because of the broader approach taken today as to what constitutes goods sold by description, this provision has become much more important, covering virtually all sales of mass-produced goods.

Sometimes a purchaser with a particular need will rely on a seller's recommendation as to what product to use. In these circumstances there is an implied condition that the goods will be reasonably fit for that purpose. This applies not only when the goods are being used for some unique purpose, but also when they are being used normally. This is the section applicable to the *Hunter* case discussed in Case Summary 9.4.

Goods bought online must match the description or picture provided.

This protection does not apply when the goods are purchased by trade name in such a way that it is clear that the skill of the seller is not being relied on,[6] or where it is not in the normal course of their business to supply.

If Florio were to buy a particular kind of paint from McGregor's paint company after asking if it were suitable for concrete and later found that the paint peeled, Florio would be able to sue McGregor for compensation because of the breach of the implied condition that the goods would be reasonably suitable for their intended purpose. However, if he bought it by trade name, disregarding any recommendations from the sales staff, he would have only himself to blame.

**Goods must be durable in B.C.**

In British Columbia this protection has been extended to leased goods and a provision has been added that the goods be "durable for a reasonable period of time."[7] While these provisions do not relieve the purchaser of the obligation to be cautious, they do provide for a certain minimum level of protection and quality.

### Case Summary 9.5

**Product Liability Where the Buyer Relies on a Manufacturer's or Retailer's Instructions: *Caners v. Eli Lilly Canada Inc.*[8]**

Eli Lilly Canada sold an herbicide to the Caners, which was ineffective in the two years they used it. Eli Lilly claimed that the Caners did not follow the instructions properly, but the Court found that the instructions provided were imprecise. This was a breach of the *Sale of Goods Act*'s implied warranty as to fitness and quality. The Appeal Court also found that contributory negligence did not apply in a sale of goods action.

Many argue that people don't take enough responsibility for themselves. Have we shifted too much of this responsibility to merchants and manufacturers?

## Sample

The Act uses a similar approach for the purchase of goods after examining a sample. There is an implied condition that the bulk of the goods must match the sample provided and be free of any hidden defects. For example, if the load of bricks Tsang bought from Cashin after first inspecting a sample brick looked fine, but in fact had not been baked properly and disintegrated after being used in Tsang's building, the bricks would be of unmerchantable quality, a breach of an implied condition of the contract.

**Goods must match sample and be free of hidden defects**

It is in these areas related to fitness and quality that manufactures and retailers usually try to override the provisions of the Act. They do this in "warranties" that include exemption clauses attempting to limit their liability. If such clauses are carefully worded, they can override these provisions unless prohibited by statute. In the *Hunter* case discussed in Case Summary 9.4, the exemption clause was effective with respect to Allis Chalmers but not with respect to Hunter, which had failed to exclude the implied conditions of the statute. Most jurisdictions in Canada have enacted legislation prohibiting the seller from excluding or limiting these provisions relating to fitness and quality in consumer sales transactions. In B.C., this prohibition is found in the *Sale of Goods Act*. Elsewhere, it is included

**Parties free to contract out**

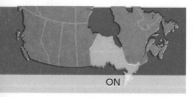

ON

---

6. *Baldry v. Marshall,* [1925] 1 K.B. 260 (C.A.).

7. *Sale of Goods Act*, R.S.B.C. 1996 c. 410, s. 18(c).

8. (1996), 134 D.L.R. (4th) 730 (Man. C.A.).

along with a specific list of the warranties in the consumer protection acts of the respective provinces. Consumer protection legislation will be discussed below.

## Other Implied Terms

There are several other terms that are implied by the *Sale of Goods Act* unless otherwise specified by the parties. Where no price is stated, a reasonable price must be paid for goods. Delivery must take place within a reasonable time, and payment is due upon delivery. The time of payment will be treated as a warranty, but whether the time of delivery will be treated as a condition or a warranty will be implied from the conduct of the parties. When bulk goods, such as grains, lumber, and ore, are involved, if significantly too little or too much is delivered the buyer is free to either reject the goods or keep them and pay for them at the contracted rate. The provisions affecting delivery, place, time, and quantity of the goods are usually made conditions by the parties.

**Where price omitted— reasonable price**

**Time, payment, and place for delivery implied terms**

### Case Summary 9.6

**Performance Required within a Reasonable Time:**
***Dansway International Transport Ltd. v. Lesway and Sons Ltd.***[9]

Dansway International Transport Ltd. bought two trailers from Lesway and Sons Ltd., paying a $2000 deposit on the $100 000 purchase price on July 16, 1998. Nothing had been said as to the time of delivery or whether the time for delivery and payment were important. The purchaser claimed they had said that payment had to wait for an insurance settlement, but the seller said they thought that the deal was to go through within one week. The seller claimed they sent notification of termination on July 29, 1998, but the purchaser denied receiving it and continued arranging financing. On August 27 the purchaser tried to complete the deal but Lesway told them of the termination and returned their deposit.

Dansway sued, and the Judge determined that since neither party had either stated that time was important or specified a time for performance there was an implied term that performance had to be within a reasonable time. What constituted a reasonable time depended on the circumstances, and in this case would be one month. In any case, the party wishing to terminate had to serve notice on the other that performance was required or the contract would be considered at an end. Since this wasn't done the sellers were in breach of the contract and damages were awarded accordingly.

## Remedies on Default

When the buyer defaults, the seller has an unpaid seller's lien against the goods, giving the seller the right to retain the goods until appropriate payment has been made even though title may have transferred.

Similarly, when the goods are en route to the buyer, upon default the seller has the right to intercept them and retake possession from the transporter, so long as the goods have not yet reached the buyer. This is referred to as the seller's right of *stoppage in transitu.*

Recent changes in the *Bankruptcy and Insolvency Act* also allow a supplier of goods to recover those goods even after they are delivered to the purchaser if,

**Unpaid seller's lien and *stoppage in transitu***

**Seller protected in case of bankruptcy**

within 30 days of delivery, the debtor has become bankrupt or a receiver has been appointed—and, of course, provided the debtor or trustee still has them. This gives the seller priority over the bankrupt's other creditors.

When the seller exercises this power to retake the goods sold, and after appropriate notice the seller remains unpaid, the goods can be sold to recover the loss. When perishable goods are involved such notice of resale is not required.

**Seller can sue for price in cases of default or refusal of delivery once title has passed**

In the event of a breach, the seller retains all the normal breach of contract remedies that were discussed in Chapter 8. And in some special circumstances where the sale of goods is involved, the seller may be able to sue for the entire purchase price rather than just damages in the event of a breach. For example, when title has transferred and payment is in default, the buyer is in effect refusing to take his own goods. But the seller must be careful and do nothing inconsistent with his continued willingness to perform. If he tries to sell the goods to someone else, for example, he will no longer be able to sue for the whole price, just for what he has lost on the sale. These losses will normally include the costs involved in restocking and resale, and where the goods are resold at a lower price that loss will be included as well. The seller also has an obligation to mitigate losses, which usually requires the seller to take steps to resell the goods immediately. When a deposit is involved, the seller can keep the deposit. This is not the case where the pre-payment is a down payment only. In fact, it may well not be worth the effort if it is not possible to sue for the actual price of the goods.

**Purchaser's remedies those of contract law**

The remedies available to the buyer if the seller defaults are those of general contract law. Where misrepresentation is involved, the purchaser may be able to rescind the contract or seek damages when there has been fraud or negligence. Where a condition of the contract is breached, the buyer may refuse to perform or demand return of any money paid; but if only a warranty is breached, the buyer must go through with the deal, subject to a right for damages. If title has passed, the purchaser may lose his right to discharge the contract in the event of a breach of condition. The damages usually are determined by what it costs to bring the goods up to the specifications in the original contract or their reduction in value because of the breach. But when there are additional injuries suffered because of the delay in obtaining the goods or the defect involved, the buyer will be able to claim them as well.

**Extent of damages depends on circumstances**

Where defective goods have caused physical injury or damage to other property, those damages are also recoverable providing they were reasonably within the contemplation of the parties at the time the contract was entered into. Thus, someone who suffers food poisoning because of poor-quality food at a restaurant can seek compensation for their injuries under the *Sale of Goods Act* provisions, and those damages can be substantial. When unique goods are involved, the

## Reducing **Risk** 9.2

Businesspeople should always be aware of the operation of the *Sale of Goods Act*, especially the provisions related to fitness and quality. Even in large commercial transactions, it is important to specify the nature and limits of the obligations of the parties where the sales of goods are involved to avoid unwanted terms from being implied into the contract. This is true even where heavy-duty machinery is involved, as was the case in the *Hunter Engineering* case discussed in Case Summary 9.4, where the failure of one supplier to exclude the operation of the *Sale of Goods Act* made them responsible for substantial damages. Such unexpected and unplanned-for responsibility can have devastating results not anticipated in the price charged. And so, whether buyer or seller, it is important to keep in mind that the *Sale of Goods Act* applies in any circumstances where goods are being transferred for money.

buyer may also be able to claim a remedy of specific performance and force the seller to go through with the sale rather than pay damages in compensation.

Finally, it should be mentioned that most provinces have enacted an international *Sale of Goods Act*. The federal government is a signatory to a United Nations convention along with many other nations, and the provincial legislation is intended to implement that international treaty. A great deal of trading today is done in the international arena, and these statutes are intended to bring the same kind of structure and certainty to import and export dealings as the *Sale of Goods Act* provides domestically.

# Negotiable Instruments

Negotiable instruments are often associated with the sale of goods and services and other forms of commercial transactions. They take many different forms but are primarily *cheques, bills of exchange* (sometimes called drafts), and *promissory notes* as set out in the federal *Bills of Exchange Act*.[10] The most familiar form of negotiable instruments is the **cheque** (see Figure 9.1), which is an order made by the drawer to his bank to pay funds to a third party called the *payee*; these funds must be paid as soon as the cheque is presented for payment (on demand).

A **bill of exchange** or draft (see Figure 9.2) is similar to a cheque but with two important differences. Here also there are three parties involved, and the *drawer* orders the *drawee* to pay the *payee* a certain sum of money. But with the bill of exchange the drawee need not be a bank, and the instrument may be made payable at some future time. (A cheque is defined as a "bill of exchange drawn on a bank, payable on demand.")

Much more common today than the bill of exchange is the cheque. With these kinds of instruments the drawer retains the power to countermand even after he has given the cheque or bill of exchange to the payee. To overcome this problem the payee will often take the instrument directly to the drawee to deter-

**Negotiable instruments are controlled by federal statute. They include**
- Cheques
- Bills of exchange

**Figure 9.1 Cheque**

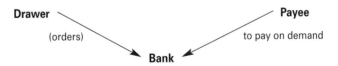

The drawee physically hands the cheque to the payee, who later presents it to the bank.

**Figure 9.2 Bills of Exchange**

Physically, the drawer hands the instrument to the payee, who then presents it to the drawee for payment or acceptance.

---

10. R.S.C. 1985, c. B-4.

### Figure 9.3 Promissory Note

**Maker** ————————————————————————→ **Payee**

(Promises to pay a certain sum on a future date or on demand)

The maker hands the note to the payee, who later presents it to the maker for payment.

mine if they will honour it. If the drawee "accepts" the instrument a direct obligation is created on the drawer to pay the payee ensuring payment. Having a cheque certified has a similar result.

• Promissory notes

A **promissory note** (see Figure 9.3) involves only two parties. The *maker* promises to pay a certain sum to the *payee* at a specified future date or on demand; because of their nature, promissory notes are always associated with a creditor–debtor relationship.

Cheques are used primarily as a convenient means of transferring funds, and to a considerable extent their use has been replaced by tools associated with electronic banking including debit and credit cards. Cheques are still common, however, and students should be familiar with their unique qualities. Often sellers will require payment by **certified cheque,** where payment is in effect guaranteed by the bank. Another common practice when goods are bought on credit is to give the creditor a series of post-dated cheques that are subsequently deposited on the appropriate dates. Negotiable instruments are also regularly used to bolster secured transactions, which will be discussed in the following chapter.

### Case Summary 9.7

#### A Certified Cheque Is Like Cash: *Centrac Inc. v. Canadian Imperial Bank of Commerce*[11]

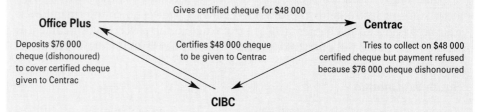

Gives certified cheque for $48 000

**Office Plus** ————————————————————→ **Centrac**

Deposits $76 000 cheque (dishonoured) to cover certified cheque given to Centrac

Certifies $48 000 cheque to be given to Centrac

Tries to collect on $48 000 certified cheque but payment refused because $76 000 cheque dishonoured

**CIBC**

Office Plus Interiors paid for office furniture purchased from Centrac with a $48 000 certified cheque. The CIBC had certified that cheque on the strength of the deposit of another cheque for $76 000 to the account Office Plus held at that bank. When CIBC learned that the $76 000 cheque would not be honoured, they phoned Centrac informing them that they had stopped payment on the $48 000 cheque. The cheque was dishonoured when Centrac presented it for payment, and Centrac sued CIBC. When the bank had certified the cheque, it was considered equivalent to cash. "Once certification was made, any attempt made by the bank to avoid payment was too late." The bank could not hide behind their failure to check the validity of the $76 000 cheque. They had committed to honour the certified cheque, and were required to do so.

11. (1994), 120 D.L.R. (4th) 765 (Ont. C.A.).

## Reducing **Risk** 9.3

Negotiable instruments can be very dangerous to those who make and endorse them, and great care should be taken in their use. People often think that if they write a cheque and something goes wrong they can simply stop payment. This is often not possible, since once that cheque gets into the hands of an innocent third party—even if it is the payee's bank—you will likely have to honour the instrument. The same holds true with respect to the liability of the endorser.

The most unique feature of negotiable instruments also makes their use particularly attractive when used with secured transactions. When a negotiable instrument such as a promissory note or cheque is transferred (negotiated) to some innocent third party, they can enforce that instrument despite any difficulties that arise under the original transaction (short of forgery or alteration of the instrument). This characteristic is important to the free transferability of negotiable instruments, which is their essential characteristic. As was discussed in Chapter 7, when a benefit under a contract is assigned the assignee can be in no better position than the person assigning that right. Thus any defence that the original contracting party has against the person assigning those contractual rights can also be used against the assignee. Whether the negotiable instrument is used as a method of enhancing a secured transaction or as a convenient method of payment, it is important to remember that when a negotiable instrument is signed and gets into the hands of an innocent third party—called a **holder in due course**—the signee almost certainly will be required to honour it.

**Stop payment order may not protect drawer**

To qualify as a holder in due course the person receiving the negotiable instrument, whether it is a cheque or a promissory note, must be innocent in that they had no knowledge of the problems with the original transaction and there is no indication of alteration or irregularity on the instrument itself. Consideration must have been given for the instrument by someone during the process, and they must otherwise receive the instrument in good faith. For the instrument to be negotiable it must meet several requirements, including that it be an unconditional promise to pay a specific amount at some future date or on demand.

**Holder in due course can enforce N.I. independent of problems**

Another important feature of negotiable instruments also comes from the need for free transferability. As the instruments transfer from holder to holder others not party to the original instrument will be required to sign or endorse the back of the instrument. There are several different forms of endorsement, but the usual purpose is for the endorser to add their credit to the instrument. This means that if it is not honoured when presented for collection the holder can then turn to the endorser for payment providing they have given proper notice of dishonour to that endorser immediately after payment was refused.

**Endorser can be liable for payment**

# Consumer Protection Legislation

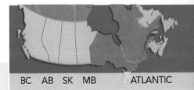

BC   AB   SK   MB          ATLANTIC

### Case Summary 9.8

#### Honest Expression of Opinion Is Actionable: *Rushak v. Henneken*[12]

Mrs. Rushak purchased a beautiful German sports car after being assured by Mr. Henneken, the salesperson and owner of the car lot, that it was a "good vehicle … the best in Vancouver." Mr. Henneken had cautioned her to have it checked out

12. (1991), 84 D.L.R. (4th) 87 (B.C.C.A.).

by a Mercedes dealer. She took it to a mechanic, who found only minor rust but also told her to have it checked out by a Mercedes dealer.

Mrs. Rushak failed to follow that advice, and unfortunately it turned out that the car had serious rust and mechanical problems. She sued Mr. Henneken for compensation. Mr. Henneken had acted honestly and encouraged her to have the vehicle inspected by a Mercedes dealership, and so there was no complaint in common law or under the *Sale of Goods Act*. But Mr. Henneken's comments about the quality of the vehicle were misleading statements that were violations of the *Trade Practices Act* and therefore actionable.

The Judge in this case said, "While it used to be said that what is described in general terms as 'puffery' on the part of the salesman does not give rise to legal consequences, I am not satisfied that the same can necessarily be said today, in light of the provisions of the *Trade Practices Act*; 'puffery' cannot, in my view, excuse the giving of an unqualified opinion as to quality when the supplier has factual knowledge indicating that the opinion may, in an important respect, very well be wrong."

Have we gone too far in protecting consumers?

Another major area where legislation has an impact on contractual relations is in consumer transactions. **Consumer transactions** involve goods or services purchased by individuals for personal use and not for resale or for business purposes.

**Consumer transaction involves purchases for personal consumption rather than business use**

These consumer protection statutes impose standards and responsibilities on manufacturers and suppliers of goods and services. They control the use and disclosure of information and advertising. They control the safety and quality of the goods sold. And they control unethical or otherwise unacceptable business practices. The rest of this chapter will examine these areas and consider the regulatory bodies created to enforce these statutes. There are both federal and provincial statutes involved, with considerable variety among provincial jurisdictions.

**Statutes prevent abuse**

Although there has been some limited form of consumer protection in our law for centuries, modern statutes have significantly expanded and modified the law in this area. Until recently, the common contractual themes of *caveat emptor* and freedom of contract dominated consumer transactions. But because of the vulnerability of consumers to abuse and their weakening bargaining position given modern business practices, limits have been placed on those principles. Note that Canada has established consumer protection guidelines for internet transactions; they are located online at the Office of Consumer Affairs Canada website: **http://strategis.ic.gc.ca/epic/internet/inoca-bc.nsf/vwGeneratedInterE/ca01863e.html**.

## Responsibility for Goods

When products are defective, causing injury or loss, consumers have recourse in either contract or negligence. As we learned in Chapter 4 the problem with suing in negligence is that there must be a failure on the defendant's part to live up to a demonstrated standard of care. This carelessness is often difficult to prove, and normally only the manufacturer can be sued since the wholesalers and retailers don't deal with or even inspect the prepackaged goods they sell. An action based on contract law is much simpler, since the consumer need only show that the product delivered was defective and caused loss or injury. But then, because of the principle of privity, any action for breach of contract is limited to the actual purchaser suing the merchant that sold the defective product. Also, the terms of the actual contracts involved usually include exemption clauses that attempt to significantly limit the responsibilities of the sellers. There are several examples of statutes that overcome these problems.

The sections of the *Sale of Goods Act* requiring the delivery of good title, that goods correspond to the description and sample, and that the goods supplied be fit and of merchantable quality have one serious drawback. In commercial transactions, these can be overridden by properly drafted exemption clauses. Most provinces in Canada have now enacted legislation removing the right to override these provisions in consumer transactions. Some do this in their *Sale of Goods Acts,* while others provide similar protection in separate statutes. Some jurisdictions require these goods to be "durable," and some have also extended the protection to leased goods.

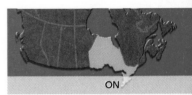

Manufacturers usually include a "warranty" with their products stating the extent of their responsibility for fitness and quality. These are in fact exemption clauses that attempt to limit the responsibility of the manufacturer and retailer for the product. With these changes in legislation, merchants can no longer rely on such exemption clauses to relieve themselves of the obligation to deliver quality goods to the consumer. Purchasers can now sue for breach of contract and receive significant compensation for their losses when products are unfit, even after the expiration of a stated warranty period. This also may apply to online consumer transactions depending on the legislation in place in the particular jurisdiction.

If Joyce bought a new vehicle for family use from Ace Chrysler and the engine seized three days after the expiration of the three-year warranty period, Ace would not be allowed to claim that the stated warranty had expired and refuse to fix it. The three-year/60 000-km warranty is an exemption clause and is void in a consumer transaction. The vehicle must be of merchantable quality. Since most people would expect a transmission in a modern car to last longer than three years, it is likely that Ace would be required to stand by its product and make or pay for the repairs in these circumstances.

As mentioned, there are several advantages to sue in contract—as is the case when proceeding under the *Sale of Goods Act*—rather than tort, not the least of which is not having to prove that the defendants failed in their duty of care. And, like negligence, the damages awarded in breach of contract cases can go far beyond a refund of the purchase price, as was the case in *Gee v. White Spot* discussed earlier. But a significant obstacle to suing in contract is often the principle of privity, where only the parties to an agreement can sue for breach.

Some provinces have extended the requirements of fitness and quality discussed above to anyone the seller could reasonably foresee might use the product. Others have eliminated privity as a defence where warranties of fitness are implied through their consumer protection statutes. The result in those jurisdictions is that anyone injured or suffering a loss because of the defective product can sue the seller or manufacturer, whether they are the purchaser or not.

## Case Summary 9.9

### Defective Bottle Cap Causes Injury: *Morse v. Cott Beverages West Ltd.*[13]

Mrs. Morse sustained a serious eye injury when she used a nutcracker to remove a difficult bottle cap, which exploded in the process. She sued, relying on Saskatchewan's *Consumer Products Warranties Act,* claiming that the manufacturer's

---

13. (2001), S.K.Q.B. 550 (Sask. Q.B.).

poor quality control caused the accident. The company's own records showed that on the day the bottle was manufactured more than half of the bottles produced required a pressure greater than that recommended. The Judge therefore concluded that the caps were defective, because they were too tight, and awarded damages to Mrs. Morse. The award included punitive damages because the company, given its own test results, had wilfully jeopardized the safety of the public by distributing a dangerous product. Note that the Act imposes contractual obligations with respect to fitness and quality, eliminating the need to prove negligence. It also removes the barrier of privity of contract, allowing the consumer to sue the manufacturer in contract.

• and by the courts

The right to sue for breach is extended by these statutes beyond the original parties to the contract, making the seller liable even when there is no indication of fault on their part. The courts have also shown a willingness to get around the privity problem. In the case of *Murray v. Sperry Rand Corp.*,[14] the manufacturer was found liable to the consumer in contract, even though the purchase was made from a retailer. Because false claims were included in the advertising brochures produced by the manufacturer, the court found that there was a subsidiary or collateral contract between manufacturer and purchaser that allowed the consumer to sue the manufacturer directly in contract. This is consistent with the tendency of the courts to abandon the privity principle.

It should be mentioned, however, that although exemption clauses in warranties will not protect the seller in consumer transactions, they might still be effective in limiting the liability of the manufacturer depending on the nature of the contract and the legislation in place in the particular jurisdiction in question. See the *Kelly v. Mack Canada* case discussed in Case Summary 9.10.

**Case Summary 9.10**

**Seller and Manufacturer Responsible for Goods Sold:**
**Kelly v. Mack Canada Inc. et al.[15]**

After receiving assurance that it would do a particular job, Mr. Kelly purchased a used truck from Maughans, a Mack dealership; when the truck proved inadequate, he took it back and traded it for a new Mack truck that also proved defective and had to be returned. He sued both the dealer and the manufacturer. Although Mr. Kelly had not dealt directly with the manufacturer, the Judge found that the manufacturer's warranty created a separate supplemental contract between Mr. Kelly and the manufacturer. Since that contract provided for only

Reducing **Risk** 9.4

Most salespeople don't understand the merchant's liability beyond the manufacturer's limited warranty included with the product sold. But it is vital for the merchant to understand their potential exposure for defective products, especially as consumers become more aware of their rights and become more aggressive in enforcing them.

14. (1979), 23 O.R. (2d) 456 (Ont. H.C.).

15. (1988), 53 D.L.R. (4th) 476 (Ont. C.A.).

the repair or replacement of the truck and not for its return, the manufacturer had no liability to Mr. Kelly. The dealer, however, was bound by the provisions of the *Sale of Goods Act* and, since the breach was "fundamental," any exemption clause could not be relied upon and the implied condition with respect to quality applied to the transaction. The dealer not only had to take the truck back, but also had to pay Mr. Kelly considerable compensation. Note that normally in commercial transactions exemption clauses would override the *Sale of Goods Act*, but here the Court found that the breach was "fundamental" and not protected by the exemption clauses.

Because the manufacturer's contract with Kelly was held to be supplemental they escaped the liability normally imposed by the *Sale of Goods Act*. Where the problem is caused by the manufacturer, why shouldn't they face the same liability as the retailer? Should the purchaser be entitled to less protection just because he is using the vehicle professionally? What do you think?

Some useful products, by their very nature, are hazardous. The obligation of the manufacturer and seller of such products is to make them as safe as possible, warn the potential user of the dangers, and provide information on their proper use. An injured consumer can sue in contract or negligence when these steps are not followed. Except where the danger is obvious, a warning incorporated into the product label must alert the consumer to the hazards associated with the product. If the warning is inadequate, the manufacturer and seller are liable for the injuries that result. Even where the dangers are obvious, as with a sharp knife, the practice is growing for manufacturers to include such a warning, out of an abundance of caution. Federal legislation dealing with the merchandising of dangerous products will be covered later in this chapter.

**Duty to warn when product hazardous**

## Unacceptable Business Practices

### False or Exaggerated Claims

Another area of unacceptable abuse involving consumer transactions is where the seller or their representative makes misleading or false statements to persuade people to buy a product. Under common law, these statements normally do not form part of the contract and generally are dismissed as mere advertising puffs, leaving the purchaser with little recourse. Further, contracts of sale often contain clauses stating that there are no other representations other than those contained in the written document, making any false or misleading claims by salespeople not actionable unless they are actually included in the contract itself.

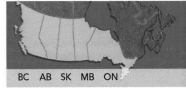

BC  AB  SK  MB  ON

Today these statements are controlled by statute, with most provinces incorporating them into the contract and making any attempt to override them void. As a result, when a salesperson makes a false or exaggerated claim, or one is included in an advertisement, they become terms of the contract and are actionable as breaches if they prove incorrect or are not honoured. If Mrs. Holberg, the purchaser of a used car from Affleck's Fine Car Co., was informed by the salesperson that the car had been driven only to church on Sundays, that statement would, under these provisions, be incorporated into the contract even if it were not contained in the written document. If Mrs. Holberg could convince the court that a false statement had been made, she could sue for breach of contract when the statement proved false. The actual statutes used to accomplish this vary considerably from province to province.

**Legislation incorporates misleading statements into contract**

## Case Summary 9.11

### Sales Scheme Prohibited: *Motor Vehicle Manufacturers' Assn. v. Ontario (Ministry of Consumer and Commercial Relations)*[16]

The Motor Vehicle Manufacturers' Association (representing the Canadian divisions of Ford, Chrysler, and GM) set up a promotion whereby purchasers could choose between buying a car at a certain price with a favourable rate of interest or paying a lower price for cash. The choices were clear in all advertising and other promotional material, and there was no attempt to mislead or hide anything. There was, therefore, no violation of the *Business Practices Act.*

But under section 24 of Ontario's *Consumer Protection Act*, the MVMA was required to disclose the true cost of borrowing. The Court held that the interest rate quoted should have been based on the lower cash price, to show what was really being paid to finance the purchase. This would increase the declared interest rate considerably, and so that provision of the *Consumer Protection Act* was violated.

This was not an attempt to cheat the customers, and there was no fraud or dishonesty. Still, the true cost of borrowing was not disclosed and the association had violated the Act. Again, have we gone too far?

**Unfair practices identified in statute**

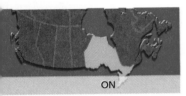

ON

**Government bodies have been given significant powers**

Typically, this type of statute lists several different kinds of misleading and deceptive statements deemed unfair practices. In addition to the penalties imposed by governments for violations, the consumer is given the right to have the contract rescinded or to sue for damages. Any attempt to override these provisions or to declare in a contract that there are no other representations other than what appears on the written document will be void, leaving the purchaser free to sue.

This is true even when the parties involved have been relatively innocent, as in the *Rushak* case discussed above. No one in that case faulted Mr. Henneken's honesty, but the statements he made still qualified as a deceptive practice and he was required to pay damages to Mrs. Rushak.

The government department involved is also given considerable powers to investigate complaints and to deal with complaints against offending merchandisers, including the powers to impose fines, to suspend licences, and, in some provinces, even to pursue a civil action on behalf of the consumer.

Perhaps the most effective provisions controlling misleading advertising and other deceptive business practices are contained in the federal *Competition Act,* which will be discussed below. The common law provisions concerning false and misleading claims in consumer transactions have been considerably strengthened by these statutory provisions.

## Case Summary 9.12

### B.C. Act Controls Frauds against U.S. Residents: *Director of Trade Practices v. Ideal Credit Referral Services Ltd. et al.*[17]

Ideal Credit was a B.C. company directing misleading advertising to customers in the United States. They claimed they would loan even to those with a bad credit rating. The advertising included such phrases as "Good or Bad Credit!"

---

16. (1988), 49 D.L.R. (4th) 592 (Ont. H.C.).

17. (1997), 145 D.L.R. (4th) 20 (B.C.C.A.).

"Bankruptcies O.K.!" and "Guaranteed Results!" The customers had to pay a non-refundable $300 "processing fee." Ideal did a $15 credit check, refused the application, and kept the rest of the $300. The director of trade practices applied for a declaration that this was a "deceptive or unconscionable act" and for an injunction. But Ideal claimed that since their customers were in the U.S., the B.C. Act did not apply. The Appeal Court held that the Act prohibited deceptive and misleading practices that take place in British Columbia no matter where the victim was, and that the Act was meant to control unethical business practices within the province.

Is this an extraterritorial application of provincial law? Should the provisions of the statute be limited to the protection of B.C. residents? Is this too much of an interference into the operation of a free-market system?

## Unconscionable Transactions

Consumers sometimes are taken advantage of because of some vulnerability, such as desperation, poverty, lack of sophistication, or intellectual weakness. Legislation has been enacted to prevent unscrupulous merchants from taking advantage of such vulnerable individuals, either in special acts (e.g. *Unconscionable Transactions Relief Act)* or included in other statutes.

**Unconscionable transactions or unfair bargains controlled**

### Case Summary 9.13

#### Aged Homeowner Protected from Unscrupulous Salesperson: Dominion Home Improvements Ltd. v. Knuude[18]

A door-to-door salesperson using extremely high-pressure tactics persuaded Mrs. Knuude, an 80-year-old homeowner, to purchase a number of home improvements that she didn't need. Mrs. Knuude signed a $300 cheque as a deposit but stopped payment on it immediately after the salesman left.

The next day, workers from the company came to do the work and she insisted they leave. This brought back the sales representative, who, by devious means, persuaded her to reinstate the contract. The work was done. She again refused to pay, and the company sued for the money owed under the contract.

The Judge determined that the contract was not binding on her as it was fraudulent, unconscionable, and did not conform to the requirements set out in the provincial consumer protection act. It is this kind of unscrupulous business practice that has led to the increase in consumer protection legislation. Some people think, however, that such legislation has gone too far and that consumers ought to assume more of the responsibility for their own mistakes. What do you think?

In some provinces these statutes are restricted to situations involving the borrowing of money. For the transaction to be found unconscionable when money is loaned, the actual cost of borrowing must be excessive in the circumstances. If the risk justifies the high rate of interest, even where the consumer was of weak intellect or in desperate straits, it is not an unconscionable transaction. When such unconscionability is demonstrated the courts can set the contract aside, modify its terms, or order the return of money paid.

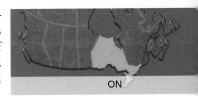

ON

---

18. (1986), 20 C.L.R. 192 (Ont. Dist. Ct.).

**Some statutes do not limit unconscionability to loan transactions**

In several other provinces the statutes go further, extending the concept of unconscionability beyond loan transactions to also cover unacceptable business practices. In these provinces, the courts can look at such factors as physical infirmity, illiteracy, inability to understand the language of an agreement, undue influence, a price that grossly exceeds the value of the goods, and the lack of reasonable benefit to the consumer as factors in establishing unconscionability. Remedies such as rescission, damages, and punitive damages are available, and in some provinces the government agency may assist in or even initiate an action on behalf of the consumer.

**Common law developments**

In addition to these legislative provisions, the common law doctrine of unconscionability in contract law, as discussed in Chapter 7, has become much more accepted and can also be applied in these consumer situations. In Case Summary 9.13, Mrs. Knuude was able to escape her contractual obligations because she was taken advantage of and unreasonably pressured by the sales representative. The key to understanding unconscionability is to find that there is an inequality of bargaining power. According to Lord Denning this inequality exists when a person "who, without independent advice, enters into a contract upon terms that are very unfair… when his bargaining power is grievously impaired by reason of his own needs or desires, or [ignorance]… coupled with undue influences or pressures brought to bear on him…."[19] This was certainly the situation with Mrs. Knuude; however, in the case that follows the terms of the agreement were not unreasonable and so, although there was pressure and desperation, there was no unconscionability.

### Case Summary 9.14

**High Rate of Interest Charged Desperate Businesswoman Not Unconscionable: *McHugh v. Forbes*[20]**

In serious financial difficulty with her business, Gwen Forbes borrowed money on several occasions from Mr. McHugh. These debts were consolidated under one promissory note with a high rate of interest (28–36%). Mr. McHugh had threatened to go to Forbes' husband if she didn't sign the note. She defaulted, and when sued asked for relief under the *Unconscionable Transactions Relief Act*. The Court found that it was not unconscionable for the creditor to seek payment from another source, the husband. The Court also held that although the rate of interest charged was high, it was not excessive or unreasonable given the risk.

Although the interest rate charged may have been reasonable from the creditor's point of view, it was still extremely high, taking advantage of the debtor's desperate circumstances. The attempt to seek payment from the husband may also have been reasonable from the creditor's point of view, but it was still a threat that went beyond the business relationship and from her perspective was nothing less than blackmail. Should this type of intimidation and exploitation be allowed?

## Controlled Business Practices

Consumer protection legislation also places controls on several specific kinds of business activities. All provinces restrict **door-to-door** or **direct sales**. The main

**Door-to-door sales controlled**

---

19. *Lloyd's Bank Ltd. v. Bundy*, [1975] Q.B. 326 (C.A.).

20. (1991), 83 D.L.R. (4th) 184 (Ont. C.A.).

method of doing this is by imposing a **cooling-off period**, which allows purchasers a given period of time, in most provinces up to 10 days, to change their minds and rescind the contract. Some jurisdictions also require certain disclosure of information, that the contract be in writing, and an extended cooling-off period when these contracts require performance at some future date.

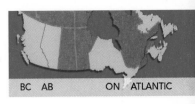

Other types of potentially abusive business activities that are prohibited or controlled in various jurisdictions are the sale of food plans, unsolicited goods and services or credit cards, discounted income tax returns, training courses, and prearranged funeral services; inappropriate debt collection activities; and referral selling. **Referral selling** involves a purchaser supplying a seller with a list of friends or acquaintances, and when sales are made to those people the purchaser is given a benefit such as a portion off the purchase price.

**Other activities controlled including referral selling**

## Methods of Control

Controlling these unacceptable activities through legislation is accomplished by several methods. One effective method involves requiring that the people supplying these goods and services be licensed, which gives the government additional control, allowing suspension or revocation of the licence and even the imposition of fines or imprisonment in the event of abusive behaviour. In addition to the power to investigate and seize records and impose penalties for violations, these government bodies often are given the power to initiate actions on behalf of the victimized consumer, or to help them start their own action.

**Several methods used to control abusive activity**

## Loan Transactions

Along with the unconscionable transactions legislation discussed above, every province has enacted legislation requiring that the true cost of borrowing be disclosed, thus prohibiting excessive rates of interest and costs in loan transactions. The federal *Interest Act* has similar requirements. The *Criminal Code* also prohibits the charging of excessive rates of interest.

**True cost of borrowing must be disclosed**

These provisions prevent the practice of hiding excessive interest rates in the payment of a bonus or through some other form of subterfuge. For example, Abrams borrows money at a rate of 10 percent on a $20 000 loan but also agrees to pay a $5000 bonus. Abrams walks out of the office with $20 000, but when the time comes to repay the money he discovers that the 10-percent interest quoted was on the $25 000 now owing, not the $20 000 that was borrowed. These statutes are designed to have all this information fully disclosed to the borrower at the outset. They usually prohibit misleading information in advertisements about the cost of borrowing, require cost of borrowing to be stated in a standard format, and require moneylenders to be registered, which makes them subject to suspension by the governing body for misbehaviour or incompetence.

Legislation is also in place controlling credit-reporting agencies. While providing a valuable service to the lender, these businesses sometimes cause great harm to the borrower through carelessness or indifference. It varies with the jurisdiction, but these statutes usually require such bodies to be registered, limit the type of information that can be disclosed, make it an offence to knowingly include false information, give the individual the right to inspect the file and to correct or remove erroneous information, and, in some jurisdictions, prohibit the agency from making any report to the creditor without the written permission of the borrower.

**Credit reporting practices controlled**

**Case Summary 9.15**

**Excessive Interest Charges Prohibited:** *Milani v. Banks*[21]

Mrs. Banks arranged to get a short-term loan from Mrs. Milani. She was to borrow $32 000 but repay $35 000 one month later, and pay interest on the $35 000 at 18 percent. Neither party intended to break the law, but with the bonus this amounted to an annual rate of interest of 250 percent, which violated section 347 of the *Criminal Code*. The Court also found that the 18-percent interest charged was, by itself, unconscionable. As a result, Mrs. Banks was required to repay only the $32 000 she actually received, and the interest payable on that amount was established at the rate normally charged litigants on money due, called the "prejudgment interest rate." Had the parties been aware they were breaking the law, they would have been subject to criminal penalties.

## Debt-Collection Processes

**Abusive debt collection practices controlled**

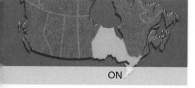

ON

Unpaid creditors often turn to debt-collection agencies to assist in the collection process. The actual debts owed are usually assigned to these agencies for a fee. The practices used by such agencies are sometimes abusive, and legislation has been enacted to control their activities. Common law remedies for abusive debt collection practices, such as defamation, assault and battery, trespass, and even false imprisonment, are usually ineffective. The legislation enacted requires these agencies to be licensed, adding the threat of a suspended or revoked licence in the event of infractions. These statutes set out specific unacceptable collection practices, such as excessive phone calls, calls at unreasonable hours, collect calls, threats of legal action with no foundation, issuing letters of collection that resemble official court documents, making deceptive or misleading statements, communicating with employers, friends, or relatives, and putting pressure on innocent relatives to pay the debt.

Some provinces require that debt-collection agencies use only previously approved form letters in their demands for payment. In British Columbia, any practice that involves the use of "undue, excessive, or unreasonable pressures on debtors or any member of his family or household or his employer" is prohibited.[22] The punishment for parties engaged in such activities may range from the loss of their licence to prosecution and a fine, and some provinces give debtors the right to civil action for any damages suffered because of the abusive practices.

The threat of criminal prosecution to pressure a debtor to pay is a violation of the *Criminal Code* and can result in prosecution against the person making the threat.

## Reducing **Risk** 9.5

It is important for businesspeople dealing with the public to keep up with statutory changes in this field. The enforcement sections have become stronger, and abusive practices that may have gone unchallenged in the past are much more likely to result in bad publicity, censure, fines, or even the loss of a business licence.

21. (1992), 98 D.L.R. (4th) 104 (Ont. C. Gen. Div.).

22. *Debt Collection Act*, R.S.B.C. 1996, c. 92, s. 14(1).

## Consumer Service Bodies

In most jurisdictions government departments have been empowered to implement and enforce these consumer protection statutes. The authority given to such departments usually includes the right to hear and investigate complaints, seize records, search premises, suspend licences, impose fines or some other corrective action, and initiate civil actions on behalf of the consumer.

**Government agencies enforce statutes**

In some jurisdictions, these bodies have become clearinghouses of consumer information, with a mandate to collect and disseminate that information to the public. Consumer bureaus can collect information on dangerous products, consumer business scams, or unacceptable practices. They may get involved in advertising to educate the consumer.

**Government agencies educate and publicize**

Private organizations, such as the Better Business Bureau, are also designed to be clearinghouses for such information. It must be remembered, however, that the Bureau is supported and sustained by the business community and, thus, has a vested interest in serving that community. The theory is that it is in the best interests of the business community to maintain high standards by weeding out disreputable businesses. The Better Business Bureau and similar organizations serve that function for members of the business community who join them. Specialized bodies have also been set up to deal with disputes in unique industries. In particular there are several organizations that are available to arbitrate disputes arising from the sale and repair of automobiles in Canada; the Canadian Motor Vehicle Arbitration Plan (CAMVAP) is a prime example.

**Private agencies also provide helpful information and services**

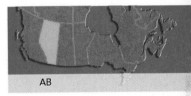

AB

## Federal Legislation

Although the most dramatic developments in consumer protection legislation have taken place provincially in recent years, there are some significant and effective federal statutes as well. The Department of Consumer and Corporate Affairs was established under the *Department of Consumer and Corporate Affairs Act* with a mandate to enforce legislation and provide service to consumers. The Act establishes that the department is to be concerned with consumer affairs and the restraint of trade and bankruptcy, as well as to provide systems to educate and protect consumers. The department has established extensive research facilities to identify unsafe products. It has also become active in consumer matters at the local level, hearing and investigating complaints and communicating with consumers and merchants.

**Federal department enforces statutes, educates and protects consumers**

### The *Competition Act*

One of the most important federal acts related to the protection of consumers is the *Competition Act*.[23] The act is primarily intended to prevent business activities that interfere with the operation of the free-market system, and so it indirectly protects the public from unfair pricing.

***Competition Act* controls abuses in free market**

A competition tribunal has been set up to enforce the provisions of the *Competition Act*. The tribunal functions much like a court, with prosecution of violations and the imposition of significant penalties. Courts also have the power to levy fines and imprisonments for many offences under the Act.

---

23. *Competition Act*, R.S. 1985, c. C-34 (as consolidated).

**Mergers controlled**

One of the main purposes of the *Competition Act* is to control mergers. Mergers are no longer treated as inherently bad; the tribunal just reviews them to determine whether they will have the effect of substantially limiting or lessening competition. **Horizontal mergers** take place when one competitor buys out another. The tribunal must weigh different factors and will tolerate some lessening of competition if it is justified by the efficiency gained. **Vertical mergers** involve the merger of a supplier and retailer, the danger being that the supplier will squeeze out the competition by favouring their own retailer, as explained below. **Conglomerate mergers** involve companies not in direct competition. The tribunal will look to determine if the overall effect is to unduly limit competition.

**Abusive trade practices prohibited**

The *Competition Act* has specific provisions prohibiting certain anti-competitive, abusive trade practices. This Act seeks to prevent one company that is dominant in a particular market from using its position to impose anti-competitive forces in that market. For example, suppose a dominant company in a market has a sale or uses loss leaders in such a way as to drive its competitors out of business. This is known as predatory pricing, which is prohibited.

Other, more indirect activities that have a similar effect are also prohibited. For example, the *vertical price squeeze* involves a vertically integrated supplier raising prices so that other retailers purchasing from them have to sell the goods at a higher price, thus reducing their profit margin. This price increase affects the supplier's own retail operation as well; however, its profit is made at the wholesale level at the expense of the retail level. A similar prohibited practice involves a newly vertically integrated company that refuses to supply other retailers as it has in the past in order to enhance the competitive position of its own retail operation. A third variation occurs where one of the related companies is a railroad or other transportation company and manipulates freight prices to give an advantage to its own retail operation at the expense of the competition.

**Undue restriction of competition prohibited**

The Act also contains provisions restricting agreements between merchants that unduly restrict competition. Thus, if two merchants agree not to sell specific goods in the other's area and they are the only source of those goods, this would likely violate this portion of the Act. In the *Clarke Transport* case discussed in Case Summary 9.16, their non-competition agreement was not in violation of the Act because there was no evidence that the arrangement in question had any impact on the overall market situation.

### Case Summary 9.16

**Conspiracy to Fix Prices Not a Violation: *Regina v. Clarke Transport Canada Inc.* (and four other corporations)** [24]

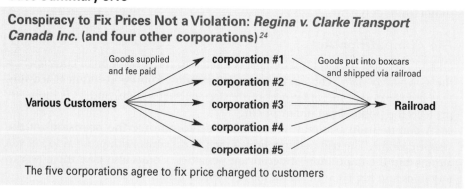

The five corporations agree to fix price charged to customers

---

24. (1995), 130 D.L.R. (4th) 500 (Ont. Gen. Div.).

The five corporations were involved in providing pool car freight-forwarding services. They paid a set price per boxcar and charged their customers a fee based on the weight of the commodities they wanted shipped. Representatives of these five corporations got together and agreed not to undercut each other's prices, exchanging the necessary documentation and pricing information required to accomplish this. They were charged with conspiring to unduly limit competition in the marketplace in violation of the *Competition Act*. This was a clear case of price maintenance, but the Court found that there were other alternatives, such as trucking services and intra-modal rail services (involving the shipping of trailers on flatcars). When the Court defined the market on this broader scale, the Crown had failed to show that the conspiracy resulted in *unduly* limiting competition, and a verdict of not guilty followed.

The primary purpose of the *Competition Act* is to ensure the proper operation of the free-market system. To accomplish that purpose provisions are included that prohibit any attempt to unduly restrain competition. The key here is "unduly." As a result, it is clear that not all agreements restricting competition will be illegal or in violation of the Act. Should all attempts to lessen competition be prohibited, or just those that are successful?

Other examples of prohibited activities are bid rigging (a group of bidders agreeing ahead of time who will be the low bidder); blacklisting someone in professional sports; agreements among banks controlling interest rates; and suppliers discriminating between customers with rebates and special discounts for only some.

The *Competition Act* also prohibits unacceptable practices affecting the consumer directly. False or misleading advertising in any form is prohibited, as is double-ticketing, which means that more than one price ticket is displayed on an item (goods must be sold at the lowest price). The Act also prohibits bait-and-switch advertising, where customers are enticed into a store by unreasonably low advertised prices and, when the goods are not available, are switched to higher-priced items. The act also controls referral selling schemes, pyramid selling schemes, and selling for higher prices than advertised, and requires that when promotional contests are involved the chances of winning be clearly stated.

**Misleading advertising and abusive sales tactics prohibited**

Previously, one of the most common complaints about both federal and provincial consumer legislation was that it was toothless. Ineffectual enforcement provisions often made it more profitable to break the law than to follow it. Many provincial consumer protection statutes have been significantly strengthened through increased maximum fines and the introduction of other methods of enforcement, such as allowing consumers to sue in their own right for violation of the legislation. The provisions of the *Competition Act* have also been enhanced. Jail sentences of up to five years and significant fines—up to $10 million for some offences—strengthen the Act. Other provisions allow consumers the right to sue offending parties directly for damages suffered due to misleading or deceptive sales practices.

**Effective penalties available**

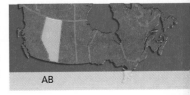

AB

## Other Federal Legislation

In addition to the *Competition Act* there are several other federal statutes that have a consumer protection aspect to them. The *Weights and Measures Act,*[25] the

---

25. R.S.C. 1985, c. W-6.

*Consumer Packaging and Labelling Act,*[26] and the *Textile Labelling Act*[27] are intended to force proper disclosure of information and thus help consumers make comparisons among products. The provisions added to the *Bills of Exchange Act*[28] requiring certain instruments to be marked "consumer purchase" (discussed in Chapter 10) are an example of consumer protection provisions being added to a statute that has a broader general objective.

**Food and Drugs Act carries strict penalties**

There are several statutes at both the federal and provincial levels that are designed to protect the consumer from dangerous products. The federal *Food and Drugs Act*[29] is intended primarily to control the sale of food, drugs, and cosmetics unfit for consumption or use. The legislation also prohibits misleading or deceptive claims associated with the sale, labelling, and advertising of these products. Several categories of drugs are created. *Unsafe drugs,* such as thalidomide, are prohibited from sale in Canada. Certain *dangerous drugs* that are useful are allowed to be sold under controlled conditions, and the Act makes it an offence to traffic in certain *controlled drugs,* such as amphetamines and steroids. Strong and effective enforcement provisions are included.

**Hazardous products controlled**

Another federal act, the *Hazardous Products Act,*[30] similarly controls the manufacture, import, and sale of products that are inherently dangerous. Some particularly dangerous products, such as inflammable clothing or dangerous toys, are prohibited from sale in Canada, while the sale of other potentially dangerous products is allowed provided that they comply with the enacted regulations. Examples of the latter are such products as cradles, cribs, carpets, kettles, toys, and pacifiers. The Act also contains important inspection, analysis, and enforcement provisions. Some hazardous products are covered by their own legislation, such as the *Explosives Act,*[31] the *Pest Control Products Act,*[32] and the *Motor Vehicle Safety Act.*[33]

Of course, consumers injured by dangerous products retain their common law right to seek compensation from the seller or manufacturer. This may be done in the form of a contract action (usually under the fitness and quality provision under the *Sale of Goods Act* or consumer protection legislation) or it can be done in tort, suing for negligence as illustrated by the *Donoghue v. Stevenson* case

## Reducing **Risk** 9.6

For businesspeople, it is important to understand that the operation of the consumer protection legislation has shifted the balance and now puts the merchant in a more vulnerable position and the consumers in a position that is much more favourable. The old principle of *caveat emptor*—which required the consumer of products or services to be careful in their dealings—has substantially gone by the board, with the responsibility shifting to the merchant to be careful when things go wrong. The only hesitation in coming to this conclusion is the criticism that even though these consumer protection statutes *seem* strong, they often are ineffective because of poor enforcement. Still, merchants must be aware that the nature of their responsibility has changed, becoming much more onerous in the process.

26. R.S.C. 1985, c. C-38.

27. R.S.C. 1985, c. T-10.

28. R.S.C. 1985, c. B-4.

29. R.S.C. 1985, c. F-27.

30. R.S.C. 1985, c. H-3.

31. R.S.C. 1985, c. E-17.

32. R.S.C. 1985, c. P-9.

33. S.C. 1993, c. C-16.

discussed in Case Summary 4.10. In that case the plaintiff consumed a ginger beer purchased for her by her friend that was contaminated by a decomposed snail, and she sued the manufacturer for negligence.

# Summary

## Sale of Goods Act
- Implies certain terms of a contract unless the parties have agreed otherwise
- Applies only when goods are being sold
- Except where there is agreement otherwise, risk follows title, and the Act supplies five rules to determine when title is transferred
- Seller must convey good title and quiet possession
- Goods must be free of any lien or charge and be of merchantable quality
- Goods must match the sample or description
- In the event of a default, where the goods are not yet in the hands of the purchaser the seller has an unpaid seller's lien and has the right of *stoppage in transitu*

## Negotiable instruments
- Negotiable instruments are cheques, bills of exchange, and promissory notes
- They are freely transferable without notice to the maker/drawer
- Holders in due course may be in a better position to enforce than the original parties
- An endorser is liable on default by the original drawer/maker only if property notified of default

## Consumer protection
- Various provincial statutes require that goods be of acceptable quality
- A number of other statutes are in place to protect consumers, including consumer protection acts, trade practices acts, and unconscionable transactions acts
- These statutes control unacceptable business practices, such as misrepresentation and other forms of misleading advertising; unconscionable transactions (that is, when a merchant takes advantage of a weak-willed or otherwise unequal customer); and specific activities, such as door-to-door and referral selling
- Moneylenders are required to disclose the true cost of borrowing to their customers
- Abusive debt collection practices are restricted
- The federal *Competition Act* controls inappropriate practices
- The federal *Hazardous Products Act* controls and restricts dangerous products
- Many other federal statutes protect customers

## QUESTIONS

1. Explain the purpose of the *Sale of Goods Act* in relation to the obligations of the parties to a sale-of-goods transaction.

2. What three qualifications must be met before the *Sale of Goods Act* applies to a transaction?

3. What is the distinction between a sale and an agreement to sell? What is the significance of that distinction?

4. When does the risk transfer to the buyer in a sale-of-goods transaction? Explain the exceptions to this general rule.

5. Indicate when title transfers in the following situations:

   a. When the contract for sale is unconditional and the goods involved are in a deliverable state at the time the purchase is made

   b. When the subject of the contract involves specific goods to which the seller is obligated to do something, such as repair, clean, or modify, to get them into a deliverable state

   c. When the contract for sale involves specific, identified goods, which must be weighed or measured before being given to the buyer

   d. When the goods are delivered to the buyer on approval

   e. When goods purchased by description have not been selected, separated out, or manufactured at the time the sales contract is entered into

6. The *Sale of Goods Act* imposes terms relating to goods matching samples or descriptions and meeting standards of fitness, quality, and title. Explain the nature of these implied terms and their effect on the parties. Indicate which terms are conditions and which are warranties. Explain the significance of the distinction.

7. Explain what merchantable quality means.

8. Explain the effect of an exemption clause included in a contract that is inconsistent with the terms set out in the *Sale of Goods Act*.

9. Explain the rights of the seller when the buyer of goods

   a. becomes insolvent;

   b. defaults on the contract of sale while the goods are still in the hands of the seller;

   c. defaults after the goods have been given to a third party to deliver but before they are received by the buyer; or

   d. Where the purchaser becomes bankrupt after the goods have been delivered.

10. Explain why a seller of goods might be less likely to sue for damages than for price.

11. Under what circumstances may a buyer refuse delivery of goods?

12. The *Sale of Goods Act* in each province implies certain terms into contracts of sale relating to the fitness and quality of the product. What are the approaches used in your jurisdiction to make these provisions mandatory in consumer transactions?

13. How does the concept of privity of contract limit the effectiveness of many consumer protection provisions? How have some jurisdictions overcome this problem?

14. Distinguish among a cheque, a bill of exchange, and a promissory note.

15  Explain how the position of a holder in due course compares to the position of an assignee of contractual rights.

16. Explain the nature of an endorsement and its significance on a negotiable instrument.

17. What common law provisions are available to protect consumers from unscrupulous business practices? Describe the limitations inherent in these provisions and the steps that have been taken to overcome these limitations.

18. Explain the object of the *Unconscionable Transactions Relief Act* and the limitations to its application. In your answer, discuss significant variations among provinces.

19. What statutory provisions have been introduced throughout Canada to control door-to-door selling, referral selling, and other potentially abusive practices?

20. Describe the methods outlined in federal and provincial consumer protection statutes to control businesses with a tendency to abusive practices. Discuss the effectiveness of these tactics.

21. What services are provided to consumers through organizations set up by the federal and provincial governments? Discuss whether these services are adequate.

22. Describe the practices controlled by the *Competition Act* and explain how that control is accomplished.

-------------------------------------------------------------------

## CASES

### 1. *Lasby v. Royal City Chrysler Plymouth* (1987), 37 D.L.R. (4th) 243 (Ont. Div. Crt.).

Mrs. Lasby, after considerable dealing with the defendants through their salesperson, Mr. MacDonald, decided on Mr. MacDonald's recommendation to purchase a Dodge 600. She had been given the impression that the car had a big engine and that it was executive-driven. After getting it home, she found out the engine had four cylinders, not six as she thought, but did not do anything about this since she was assured by Mr. MacDonald that it was the largest four-cylinder engine made. A few months later, when she was having it serviced, Mrs. Lasby mentioned to her mechanic that it had the big engine. He told her that it had, in fact, the smaller engine and that there was a much bigger engine than hers. She asked Royal City for her money back, but the dealership refused to either return her money or take the car back.

Under these circumstances, explain Mrs. Lasby's options. What would be the appropriate remedy? How would your answer be affected by learning that by the time of the trial the car was 22 months older and had been driven a further 40 000 kilometres?

### 2. *Harry v. Kreutziger* (1979), 95 D.L.R. (3d.) 231 (B.C.C.A.).

Harry was a Native Canadian with a grade-five education, a hearing defect, and a retiring manner. He owned a fishing boat worth very little except for the fishing licence that went with it. With the licence, the boat was worth about $16 000. Kreutziger persuaded Harry to sell the boat and licence to him for $4500, saying that as a Native Canadian Harry would have little trouble getting another licence. Harry sued to have the contract set aside. What would be the nature of Harry's complaint against Kreutziger? What defences would be available to Kreutziger in response to Harry's action? Predict the outcome.

### 3. *W.W. Distributors & Co. v. Thorsteinson* (1960), 26 D.L.R. (2d) 365 (Man. C.A.).

A salesman and his manager approached a young engaged girl and her mother at their home one evening and, after using some very high-pressure sales tactics, sold them some cooking utensils. The mother was persuaded to sign the contract after being told that it was not really important. By so doing, the mother became a party to the agreement, even though it had been made clear to the salesman that her only involvement was to lend her daughter $50 toward the purchase. The daughter was led to believe that she was getting very good value for her money, but experts clearly established that the price was more than 75 percent over the maximum value of the goods involved. The next day, unable to contact the plaintiff, the mother stopped payment on the cheque. When this was discovered, the salesman went to her home and was informed that the mother and daughter were repudiating the agreement. The company immediately commenced an action to recover the purchase price and the various penalties and service charges built into the agreement.

Explain the arguments that could be raised on both sides and the likely outcome. What effect would it have on your answer to learn that the engaged girl was under the age of majority? What legislation provisions have been put into place in most jurisdictions to curb this type of abuse?

### 4. *Regina v. Birchcliff Lincoln Mercury Sales Ltd.* (1987), 43 D.L.R. (4th) 417 (Ont. C.A.).

Birchcliff operated a car dealership with a service centre, where a sign was posted stating "Customer labour charges are based on $38 per hour flat rate." The sign was there because Ford, the manufacturer, insisted that such notices be posted in clear sight at its dealerships.

In fact, a flat rate of $38 per hour was not charged for the services given; rather, for each job, reference was made to a standard industry guide that set out the number of hours the job ought to take, and the charges were based on that guide. Even if the time spent on a particular job was less than that set out in the standard guide, the amount stated in the guide was charged.

Explain the nature of the complaint in these circumstances and the likely consequences that Birchcliff would face.

### 5. *Sumner Sports Inc. v. Pavillon Chasse & Peche (440) Inc.* (1990), 72 D.L.R. (4th) 317 (Q.C.A.).

Sumner and Pavillon were in the business of selling hunting and fishing gear in their respective areas. They entered into an agreement that for a specific period of time Sumner would not retail specific products in or around the city of Laval but would sell their goods only to Pavillon, and that Pavillon would not sell their products in the lower St. Lawrence area or the City of Ottawa and sell only products purchased from Sumner. In effect, the two companies agreed not to carry on business in competition with each other. Pavillon violated this agreement, and Sumner sued. Pavillon claimed that the contract was illegal, being a violation of the *Combines Investigation Act* (which was repealed and replaced by the *Competition Act*) and therefore could not be enforced. Explain the arguments that can be raised by both parties supporting their positions and the likely outcome.

### 6. A. E. LePage Real Estate Services Ltd. v. Rattray Publications (1994), 120 D.L.R. (4th) 499 Ont. (C.A.).

In 1985, Rattray agreed to lease certain premises from A. E. LePage on Yonge Street in Toronto. Pursuant to that agreement, Rattray delivered a cheque to LePage for $20 825.89 as a deposit. It was drawn at a branch of the CIBC. A. E. LePage was acting for London Life, the owner of the property. The offer was taken by LePage to London Life for their signature. Rattray changed his mind and stopped payment on the cheque, but because of a mistake at the CIBC branch the stop-payment order was ignored when the cheque was brought in for certification by a representative of LePage. The "certified cheque" was subsequently deposited in LePage's trust account at the Toronto Dominion Bank, but when it was sent to the CIBC branch they refused to honour it.

Indicate the arguments on both sides of this case as to whether A. E. LePage should be able to require the bank to honour this cheque. Explain Rattray's position. Would your answer be any different if the cheque had been certified by Rattray in the first place and then presented to LePage?

# CHAPTER

# 10

# Priority of Creditors

## CHAPTER HIGHLIGHTS

- Securing debt—the methods and processes
- Security transactions—rights and obligations
- Guarantees
- Other forms of security
- Bankruptcy and insolvency

A considerable industry has developed around the practices of lending money and granting credit. This chapter will examine the various methods that have been developed to ensure that money owed is properly repaid and the legislation that has been created to control such transactions. Federal bankruptcy and insolvency legislation will also be examined. Other than this federal statute, creditors' rights are generally a matter of provincial jurisdiction, and the common principles embodied in these statutes will be the primary area of concentration in this chapter.

# Methods of Securing Debt

**Security helps assure creditor of repayment**

When a debtor borrows money, the creditor is at risk if the debtor cannot repay. Usually, the debtor is required to take steps to reduce this risk by doing something to ensure that the creditor will be paid first before other creditors, even in the event of insolvency. Several methods have been developed to satisfy this requirement. When the parties are successful in creating a priority system of one creditor over the others, the party with priority is said to be a **secured creditor.**

## Personal Property

**Real property includes land and buildings**

**Personal property can be used as security**

Both real and personal properties have been used to create security. **Real property** includes land and any buildings or items, called **fixtures**, that are attached to the land. **Mortgages** are the common method of using real property as security and will be discussed in Chapter 15. Non-real property is called *personal property,* and such **personalty** is also used extensively to secure debt. Personal property can be divided into **chattels,** which are tangible, movable things, and intangible rights called **choses in action**, which are legally enforceable claims. A cheque, or a promissory note, is an example of such a chose in action, the paper merely representing an obligation that can be legally enforced. Although a chose in action is often used to secure debt, it is much more common to take real property or chattels as security.

Most people are familiar with the **pledge** (or **pawn**), in which a creditor (or pawnbroker) holds an item such as a watch or a ring until repayment. The debtor still owns the goods, and the pawnbroker gets the right to sell them only if there is a default.

But in most circumstances the debtor needs the use of the goods used as security. When you buy a new car on credit the whole idea is that you have the use of it while you are paying it off. In such circumstances the security of the creditor is the right to retake the car and sell it if the debtor fails to pay. In the past the creditor retained the title to the goods used as security while the debtor had possession. In the event of default the creditor would simply take possession of goods based on this title. Under modern legislation the creditor usually does not actually have title, but the effect is the same, giving the creditor first claim to the goods in the event of default. Note that default may occur not only where a regular payment is missed but also because of a failure to meet some other obligations, such as letting insurance coverage lapse or something else that increases the risk or threatens the value of the assets used as security.

*Personal property security involves right to take possession upon default*

## The Traditional Approach

Historically, conditional sales agreements, chattel mortgages, and the assignment of accounts receivable were the common methods of using personal property as security. A conditional sale takes place in a two-staged process. First, possession of the goods is given to the purchaser and the seller, who is also the creditor, retains the title as security. After the final payment is made, title to the goods is also conveyed. It should be noted that the *Sale of Goods Act* applies to this type of transaction even though the sale takes place over a protracted period of time.

*Conditional seller retains title until last payment*

### Case Summary 10.1

#### Supplier and Trustee Claim Lumber: *Goodfellow Inc. v. Heather Building Supplies Ltd.*[1]

Goodfellow Inc. supplied lumber to Heather Building Supplies Ltd. that was to remain the property of the seller until payment in full was received. When Heather Building Supplies failed to pay, Goodfellow Inc. obtained a court order and had the lumber seized by the sheriff. But before it could be delivered Heather became bankrupt, and the trustee claimed the lumber for the other creditors. The Court held that since Goodfellow Inc. had not properly registered the secured transaction as required under the *Conditional Sales Act* they lost their claim to the goods.

The seller retaining title until payment is received is the definition of a conditional sale, and failure to register such a secured interest will cause them to lose their priority against other interested parties. In this case the other interested party was a trustee in bankruptcy, which will be a major topic to be discussed later in this chapter.

---

1. (1996), 141 D.L.R. (4th) 282 (N.S.C.A.).

**Chattel mortgage**
• title to goods transferred to secure loan

A chattel mortgage differs in that the creditor is not the seller of the goods. Typically the debtor approaches a bank to borrow money and, to secure the loan, is asked to transfer the title of some good such as a car or a boat to the creditor as "collateral security." But throughout the duration of the loan transaction chattel mortgages, like conditional sales, involve the creditor having title to the goods as security while the debtor has possession. When the last payment is made, title is returned to the debtor. Even though a **bill of sale** is often used to create the security, since no actual sale is contemplated the *Sale of Goods Act* does not apply to a chattel mortgage transaction.

**Accounts receivable can be used as security for a loan**

The assignment of book accounts involves using a chose in action as security rather than goods. The creditor is given the right to collect money owed to the debtor's business in the event of a default. Often, a business will have few tangible assets but will have considerable funds owed to it for goods or services provided to customers, and these claims are called **accounts receivable**. If the debtor defaults, the unpaid creditor has the right to intercept these accounts receivable and the loan is therefore secured.

**Leases** are also a common method of creating a secured relationship between creditor and debtor. When most people think of leases they are usually thinking of an *operating lease,* where the goods are simply rented to the lessee to use during the lease period and then returned. Today the *lease to purchase* arrangement is becoming much more common. Here the object is essentially a credit purchase, where the goods will eventually transfer to the lessee at the end of the lease term with the lease simply providing security. In both cases the title remains with the lessor while possession goes to the lessee, providing the lessor with security for the transactions. Where the manufacturer or regular supplier of those goods leases them to the lessee the transaction is much like a conditional sale, where the lessee retains significant claims against the supplier for the quality and fitness of the goods supplied. But where the goods are sold to a financial institution and then leased to the lessee the relationship is more like a chattel mortgage, with the relationship being only a financial arrangement. Here the lessee would have to go back to the original manufacturer or supplier with problems relating to the goods themselves, and this may be more difficult because of the lack of privity between them.

In the past, separate statutes with different provisions governed these various ways of using personal property as security. To further confuse things, when other forms of personal property were used as security—such as negotiable instruments, shares, or bonds—there was no legislation at all. Today, personal property security acts are in place in most jurisdictions and govern all situations where personal property is used as security.

### Case Summary 10.2

**What to Do When Two Creditors Claims Funds: *Redi-Mix Ltd. v. Hub Dairy & Barn Systems Ltd.*[2]**

Both the Toronto Dominion Bank and Redi-Mix had valid claims against Hub Dairy. Hub Dairy had made an assignment of their accounts receivable to the

---

2. (1987), 41 D.L.R. (4th) 360 (Sask. Q.B.).

bank to secure a loan, and Redi-Mix had obtained a judgment against Hub for $10 553.50. The bank properly registered the assignment under the *Personal Property Security Act*. Farm and Garden was a customer and was making regular payments to Hub Dairy to pay for services supplied after Hub's assignment to the TD Bank. Both creditors served notice on Farm and Garden, demanding that any future payments be made to them. Redi-Mix argued that the bank had lost any claim to the funds because it had not properly notified Farm and Garden or Redi-Mix of the assignment.

The Farm and Garden Centre wisely paid the money into court, which decided that once the assignment had been perfected through registration additional notice was not necessary. The Bank had a properly perfected secured interest and was entitled to the money. The case illustrates not only the role and nature of an assignment of accounts receivable but also the importance of registration perfecting a secured transaction under the *Personal Property Security Act*. It also demonstrates the wisdom of the decision made by Farm and Garden to pay the money into court rather than risking making a mistake by paying the wrong claimant and having to pay the money twice.

## The Personal Property Security Act

The ***Personal Property Security Act*** now used in all jurisdictions in Canada creates a unified approach toward the use of personal property as security. As a result, the Act is a little more complicated because it embodies one set of rules and a common approach to cover both tangible and intangible forms of personal property and the various ways that security can be taken. The secured transaction is still created by contract in the traditional form of conditional sales, chattel mortgages, and assignment of book accounts, but other vehicles such as leases can also be used depending on the property used as security. But now, the formal requirements and procedures for all these types of securities are the same. As well, the *Personal Property Security Act* allows other, less common forms of personal property, such as licences, shares, bonds, and even intellectual property such as copyright patents and trade marks, to be used as security and treated in a uniform way. The Act also provides for some or all of the assets of a particular debtor to be used as security, and provides rules to determine the ranking of various claims when other secured creditors have claims against those assets.

**Personal property security acts creates common process**

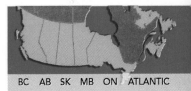

BC   AB   SK   MB   ON   ATLANTIC

The right to repossess the goods used as security even when they get into the hands of an innocent purchaser is the essential nature of a secured transaction. Thus, where Lee has purchased his car under a conditional sale agreement and defaults, the creditor must have the right to retake the car even if it has been resold or if Lee becomes bankrupt. In the past this was accomplished by the creditor retaining title to the goods and retaking them in the event of default. To protect an innocent third party who might be misled by the debtor having possession of the goods, the secured creditor was required to register his secured claim against the goods at the designated government agency. There, the would-be purchaser or a potential creditor also anticipating using those goods as security could search the title to the car or other item and would be forewarned of the prior claim of the secured creditor. Under the *Personal Property Security Act* the process is a little more involved but accomplishes the same purpose.

**Registration protects parties**

## Case Summary 10.3

### A Licence Can Be Used as Security: *Re Foster*[3]

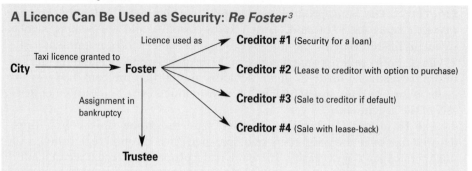

When Mr. Foster obtained his taxi licence for Mississauga there was a restriction on it prohibiting transfer for three years. During that three-year period, Mr. Foster used the licence as security in various forms for loans from four different creditors. Eleven days before the expiration of the three-year restriction, Mr. Foster made an assignment in bankruptcy; all four secured creditors claimed the taxi licence. The Court decided that although the licence was unique, it still was a valuable asset and therefore qualified as property that could be used to secure a loan under the *Personal Property Security Act*.

The Court then had to determine who was entitled to the licence. Only the first creditor properly registered the licence as required in the *Personal Property Security Act*. The second and third tried but failed to include Mr. Foster's middle initial on the registration form, which in Ontario was fatal to their claim. The fourth transaction was a sale of the licence to the creditor with a lease-back; the Court held that since this was a sale it did not have to be registered, although it would be subject to the properly registered security of the first creditor. Fortunately, the first and fourth creditors had already reached an agreement to that effect and the Court didn't have to make that decision. Even if the third and fourth creditors had properly registered, the outcome would have been the same since the first creditor perfected his security before the others.

This case illustrates not only the effect of the perfection of a security under the *Personal Property Security Act*, but also the flexibility of the statute allowing something as unique as a taxi licence to be used as security under the Act. It also demonstrates the unforgiving nature of the Act and how even minor mistakes can have dramatic effects on the validity of a claim, although the result may not have been the same in another jurisdiction. For example, in a recent B.C. case the name appearing on a financing statement was completely different from the actual name of the company appearing on the certificate of incorporation, but because the serial numbers of the vehicles involved were correctly registered the security had been properly perfected. Anyone searching using the serial number would not have been misled, and would have discovered the registered security interest.[4] Did this lead to a just result? Would someone dealing with a licence think to check the registry? Is this the sort of asset that ought to be caught by this legislation? What about the technical requirements of exact compliance—should it really matter whether the name is set out exactly?

3. (1992), 89 D.L.R. (4th) 555 (Ont. Gen. Div.).

4. *Gold Key Pontiac Buick (1984) Ltd. v. 464750 B.C. Ltd.* (2000), B.C.C.A. 435 (B.C.C.A.).

The method of creating a secured relationship under this statute is unique. There are three stages. First, the parties must enter into the contractual agreement; second, the secured interest must attach to the collateral that has been identified to provide the security; and third, the secured interest must be perfected.

**Attachment** takes place when the debtor receives some value under the contract. That is, if a person borrowing funds uses his car as collateral security for the loan, that security attaches to the car only when the bank makes the money available to the debtor pursuant to the agreement. Attachment gives the creditor a claim against the security in the event of default by the debtor normally consisting of a right to repossess if so stated in the contract. These contracts usually take the form of the more traditional conditional sale, chattel mortgage, or assignment of book accounts discussed above. But whether these traditional forms or other forms are used, it is important to remember that the obligations including the remedies must be set out in the contract. The purpose of the statute is to give effect to the contractual obligations entered into by the parties.

> **Security must attach to collateral**

> **Contract provisions prevail**

It is vital to understand that attachment gives the creditor rights against the actual debtor only in the event of a default. To protect the creditor's claim if the goods are sold or if another creditor becomes involved the secured transaction must be **perfected.**

> **Perfection required to prevail against outsiders**

This perfection can be accomplished in one of two ways. The first is by registering the security obligation at the appropriate government agency, as was done under the old system. This process has been simplified so that the actual contractual documents no longer have to be filed. Rather, a single form is used to provide notice of the security arrangement. There are some provincial variations, but in general this financing statement requires the complete name and address of the parties, and the type and description, including the serial number, of the security used and the date and time of registration. Where a motor vehicle is used as security, its year, make, model, and vehicle identification number must also be set out. In Ontario, when consumer goods are involved the financing statement must give the amount owed and the date of maturity of the agreement.

> **Perfection through registration**

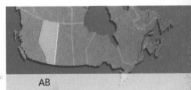

AB

## Case Summary 10.4

### Failure to Perfect Causes Loss of Security: *Re Telecom Leasing Canada (Re Giffen)*[5]

Telecom Leasing Canada (TLC) Ltd. leased a 1993 Saturn to the British Columbia Telephone Company, which in turn leased the car to their employee. During the term of the lease the employee made an assignment in bankruptcy, the car was repossessed and sold, and both the trustee and Telecom claimed the proceeds.

In a normal lease transaction the goods are returned at the end of the lease period. But here the employee had an option to purchase that gave her a proprietary interest in the car. On that basis the Supreme Court of Canada held that this was a secured transaction, which had to be properly registered under the *Personal Property Security Act*. Since Telecom had failed to do this, the trustee in bankruptcy kept the proceeds of the sale for the benefit of the other creditors. Note that it is the option to purchase that distinguishes this case from the *Foster* case described in Case Summary 10.3, where registration of the lease was not required. Today, several provinces have specified in their *Personal Property Security*

---

5. [1998] 1 S.C.R. 91 (S.C.C.).

*Acts* under what conditions such leases will create a secured transaction. This case clearly shows the broader reach of the *Personal Property Security Act,* redefining property and what can be used as security.

Should the option to purchase make this much difference? Should the trustee be in any better position than the person who has made the voluntary assignment in bankruptcy? Hasn't the value of the vehicle just been stripped away from the rightful owner? What do you think?

**Perfection through possession**

The second and less common way of perfecting a secured transaction is for the creditor to obtain physical possession of the collateral used. Whether possession or registration is used depends on the nature of the security. Where a promissory note or shares are involved there is no need for the debtor to keep them, and perfection by possession is appropriate. Note that the original note or certificate must be taken, not a photocopy. Where a physical item is involved, such as a car, a truck, or other type of equipment that is required for use by the debtor, registration is the more appropriate process. The purpose of registration is to ensure that others are alerted that the goods have been used as security and the debtor is not in a position to deal with them. Where perfection by possession is involved this is not necessary, since the goods are not in the possession of the debtor and third parties cannot be misled with respect to them.

**First to perfect usually prevails**

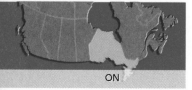

ON

If more than one secured interest is perfected by registering different financing agreements against the same collateral, the priority between those secured parties is generally determined by the date registration takes place. But this is not always the case. For example, sometimes a merchant will secure a loan by granting a security on all of their assets, including after-acquired assets. This can cause a problem if a creditor also claiming a secured interest in them has supplied those future acquired goods. The secured creditor selling those goods will have priority with respect to them providing that secured interest is registered within a specified time (10 days in Ontario). This is called a **purchase money security interest**, or PMSI, and will prevail over a general assignment of the merchant's assets if promptly registered.

Similarly, if a customer purchases goods from that merchant in the normal course of business they will normally be independent of any secured interest of the creditor. If you were to purchase a car from Ace Chevrolet, you would get good title even though the assets of the car dealership had been used to secure a general loan to operate the business. Since the creditor knows that the inventory will be sold in the normal course of business, an innocent purchaser will not be affected by that security.

## Reducing **Risk** 10.1

To protect a creditor's interest it is vitally important that a secured interest is properly perfected. Legislation in most jurisdictions has exacting requirements that must be carefully followed, including getting serial numbers and names exactly right. Sometimes errors can be corrected, but not after the interests of other parties become involved. Sometimes creditors actually register their interest first before advancing their credit, and although perfection actually takes place only when that credit is advanced (the point of attachment), it takes place immediately and there is no problem with intervening interests arising or subsequent errors taking place affecting the validity of the perfection.

## Case Summary 10.5

### Repossession after Default Does Not Perfect Security: *Re Bank of Nova Scotia and Royal Bank of Canada et al.*[6]

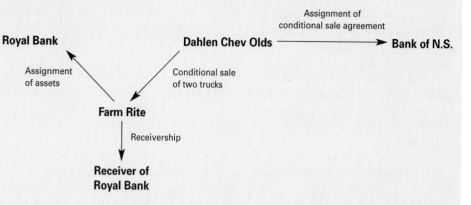

To secure a debt, Farm Rite Equipment Ltd. made an assignment of all its property, including after-acquired property, to the Royal Bank, which properly registered the security. A few years later, Dahlen Chev Olds Ltd. sold two trucks to Farm Rite secured by a conditional-sale agreement (not properly registered) that was then assigned to the Bank of Nova Scotia, which eventually did register the secured interest. Subsequently, a receiver acting for the Royal Bank took over the property of Farm Rite Ltd., including the trucks, sold them, and both the Royal Bank and the Bank of Nova Scotia claimed the proceeds.

The Royal Bank's problem was that the provincial statute required the registration of vehicles to include the serial number, which could not happen with a general assignment of property. Royal Bank argued that this was overcome because they had perfected their security by taking possession of the trucks. The Court rejected this argument, and even though the Bank of Nova Scotia's registration was greatly delayed it still perfected their secured claim and they had priority with respect to the proceeds of the sale. Perfection of a security by possession must take place at the time of the transaction in order to create the secured interest in the collateral. When a default has taken place, it is too late to repair any defects by taking possession of the property used as security at that stage. When there are such conflicting claims, they are not going to be settled by a race to see who can repossess the goods first.

What else could the Royal Bank have done? The effect is that the bank in this case gets priority over some future acquired property but not other property, even though they had done everything they could to secure their position. Is this result consistent with the philosophy behind the *Personal Property Security Act* and its objectives?

## Rights and Remedies upon Default

**Repossession**. In the event of a default by the debtor, the creditor has recourse as set out in the contract and as provided in the *Personal Property Security Act*. This normally involves taking possession of the goods and reselling them to recover

**All normal contract remedies available upon default**

---

6. (1987), 42 D.L.R. (4th) 636 (Sask. C.A.).

**Upon default, creditor can take possession and dispose of collateral**

**Court order and sheriff necessary when force required**

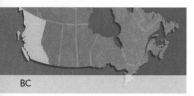

BC

**Creditor must take reasonable care of reposed collateral**

the amount owed. The creditor not only must comply with the contract, but also must not otherwise violate the law in the process. Normally, the creditor acts through an agent called a *bailiff*, who can come onto the property of the debtor and repossess the goods provided no force is used. No threats or violence can be used, and the bailiff is not permitted to force open windows or break down doors. When such measures are necessary the creditor must proceed by court order.

If Barbosa defaults on a loan to Wizinsky and Barbosa's car has been taken as security, Wizinsky would be able to tow the car away from Barbosa's open carport providing Barbosa didn't block the way. But if the car were in a locked garage, or if Barbosa blocked the way or had to be forcibly removed from the vehicle, towing would not be possible. In these circumstances, Wizinsky would obtain a court order and the sheriff or other appropriate judicial officer could then use whatever force was necessary to enforce the court order.

Note that some provinces will not permit repossession without a court order where consumer goods are involved and a significant amount has been paid off. Regardless of whether consumer or commercial goods are involved, once they have been repossessed the creditor must use "commercially reasonable" care to protect the goods and keep them in good repair. If the goods require repair to sell them, such "commercially reasonable" expenses will be added to the amount the debtor owes.

## Right to Redeem

**Debtor must be given notice and opportunity to redeem**

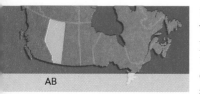

AB

Before resale can take place, interested parties (normally, other creditors) must be given a chance to redeem the goods by paying off any money owing. Notice must be given setting out a description of the goods and the amount owing, that the party receiving the notice has the right to redeem, and that failure to do so will result in the goods being sold. The notice should also declare, where appropriate, that the debtor will continue to be responsible for any shortfall between the amount owing plus costs and the amount realized from the sale. Sometimes only the missed payments plus expenses need be paid, but usually there is an acceleration clause requiring that the entire debt plus expenses be paid in order to redeem the goods. Many provinces prohibit such acceleration clauses.

## Resale

**Seized goods can be sold to satisfy debt**

After repossession and the expiration of the notice period, the goods are normally sold by private sale or public auction to satisfy the debt. Under the statute, the method chosen must be commercially reasonable.

### Case Summary 10.6

**Failure to Notify Causes Loss of Right to Sue for Shortfall:**
*Royal Bank of Canada v. J. Segreto Construction Ltd.*[7]

The Royal Bank seized from Segreto Construction certain construction equipment that had been used to secure a loan when they subsequently defaulted. The equipment was sold at public auction but did not bring in enough to cover what was owing. The bank sued Segreto for the shortfall, but had failed to notify the debtor of the sale as required by the Act. As a result, the bank was completely prohibited from claiming any shortfall from Segreto.

7. (1988), 47 D.L.R. (4th) 761 (Ont. C.A.).

Under the legislation the debtor must be given notice and time to recover the goods. This case illustrates how important it is to follow the designated procedures. The provisions of the statute are designed to protect both the rights of the debtor and the rights of the secured creditor. Should a creditor ever be able to sue for such a shortfall, or should they be limited to the remedy of repossession and resale?

Normally, if the proceeds from the sale do not cover the debt, additional costs, and interest, the debtor will have to make up the difference. Thus the debtor may not only lose his car or other security but also may still owe the creditor a considerable amount of money to pay for the shortfall. In several jurisdictions this right to sue for a deficit is lost as soon as the creditor chooses to repossess the goods. In some provinces this applies only where consumer goods are involved. For instance, in British Columbia, if Jones defaulted on a consumer car loan owing $15 000 and only $10 000 was realized from the sale of that car after repossession, the creditor would be out not only the $5000 shortfall on the loan but also any costs and interest incurred.

**Debtor may be liable for deficit**

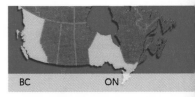

BC                    ON

Because this was a consumer loan in B.C., the creditor exhausted his remedies against Jones when he repossessed the car. Great care must be taken in these circumstances to balance the risks of suing and possibly getting nothing against repossessing the security and getting at least something toward the debt owed. The creditor can also lose the right to a deficiency by failing to properly look after the goods or failing to get a fair price because of an improvident sale, as happened in the *Segreto* case discussed in Case Summary 10.6.

**Creditor may lose the right to sue for deficit**

Note that in all jurisdictions where there is a surplus from the sale the debtor is entitled to that surplus. In the example above, if the car were sold for $20 000 and costs and interest brought the entire debt up to $17 000 Jones would be entitled to the $3000 surplus from the sale.

In some jurisdictions, instead of repossession and resale the creditor can retake the goods and simply keep them in full satisfaction of the debt. This ends any claim the debtor may have to a surplus and any claim the creditor may have to a deficiency. Notice must be given to all interested parties, and if someone files an objection the goods must be resold in the normal way.

**Option to retain the collateral**

These procedures may appear very cumbersome, and the legislation itself is very complex, but in actual practice it is quite straightforward and works quite well. Where a person borrows money from a credit union using a car as security, attachment takes place once the contract has been entered into and the moneys advanced. Perfection takes place when the credit union files the financing statement with the appropriate registry. A buyer or subsequent creditor interested in

## Reducing **Risk** 10.2

When a debtor defaults, creditors are often quick to seize property used as security. However, in some jurisdictions this might prevent the creditor from pursuing other more effective remedies. Even in those jurisdictions where it is possible to sue for a shortfall after the goods have been resold that right may be lost if the goods are not properly cared for and sold in a commercially reasonable manner. On the other hand, if the debtor defaults on this debt it is likely that any attempt to sue and seize other assets will be empty. These factors should all be carefully weighed before taking the serious step of repossession, including a consideration of whether the debtor can be rehabilitated and kept as a good customer. Just because you have the legal right to do something doesn't mean it is a good idea to do it.

the car would search the registry and, finding the registered security against the vehicle, would be forewarned to avoid any dealings with the car. If the car is purchased anyway and a default takes place the credit union can recover the vehicle even from the innocent third party. This is the essence of the creditor's security. Once there is a default, the credit union has the option of either pursuing its normal breach of contract remedies or taking possession of the vehicle and reselling it, but must follow the proper procedures in doing so.

# Guarantees

Another method creditors use to ensure the repayment of a debt is the guarantee. Where corporations are involved, the use of guarantees is very common as a means of circumventing the limited liability characteristic of incorporation, making the principals of a corporation directly responsible for loans and other obligations. In consumer transactions guarantees are used to make another more substantial debtor obligated to repay a loan or other debt. Guarantors ensure that the debt will be repaid even where the debtor defaults. Where Jones borrows $5000 from the bank with his mother as a guarantor and then fails to pay, the mother is responsible to repay that $5000 debt.

**Guarantor must pay when debtor defaults**

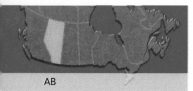

AB

A guarantee involves a secondary or conditional obligation that arises only in the event of a default. When a person agrees to be directly responsible for paying the debt of another, the obligation is not secondary but primary, with the debtors sharing the responsibility, and is referred to as an **indemnity.**

**Evidence in writing of guarantee required**

The distinction, although subtle, can be important. As discussed in Chapter 5, the *Statute of Frauds* requires that some agreements must be evidenced in writing to be enforceable. In most provinces only the guarantee must be evidenced in writing, but in British Columbia both indemnities and guarantees must be evidenced in writing.[8] In Alberta, personal guarantees must be notarized to be enforceable.

**Contractual requirements must be met for guarantor to be bound**

• including consideration

Since a guarantee is a separate contract, all of the elements of a contract must be present, including consensus (offer and acceptance) and consideration. Consensus is normally present, but consideration can sometimes be a problem. Because the creditor would not advance funds without the guarantee, the advancement of those funds amounts to consideration supporting the guarantee. Where the guarantee is given after default on a loan, the consideration is the creditor refraining from suing the debtor.

---

## Reducing **Risk** 10.3

People are often persuaded to sign guarantees thinking that it is just a formality and that no serious obligations are incurred since the primary debtor will pay the debt back. This is a dangerous position. Whether in business or in your personal affairs, you should never sign a guarantee without first carefully weighing the risks. The creditor is insisting on a guarantee because they don't have confidence that the debt will be repaid and want someone else to be responsible. You are adding your credit to the transaction and there is a good chance that you will be required to honour that commitment. Many bankruptcies are the result of people signing guarantees not realizing the risks they face.

---

8. *Bank of British Columbia v. Shank Investments et al.,* [1985] 1 W.W.R. 730 (Alta. Q.B.).

Where the guarantee is given after the funds are advanced there can be a serious problem. If Kotsalis borrows money from the Business Bank and the manager of the bank fails to obtain a guarantee as required by bank policy, he will be in trouble if tries to get it later. Since the funds have already been advanced there is no consideration to support the subsequent guarantee. To avoid any problem with consideration, these institutions usually require that all guarantees be placed under seal. As discussed in Chapter 5, when a seal is present consideration is conclusively presumed.

## Rights and Obligations of the Parties

The creditor has significant duties to protect the interests of the guarantor. At the outset, the creditor should make sure that the guarantor understands the full nature of the guarantee he or she is signing. Guarantors often escape their obligation by claiming misrepresentation, *non est factum,* or undue influence. When in doubt, the creditor should insist that the guarantor obtain independent legal advice.

**Case Summary 10.7**

### Guarantor Released Because of Change: *Reid et al. v. Royal Trust Corporation of Canada*[9]

Farries Enterprises gave Royal Trust a mortgage on certain property with Reid as guarantor on the loan. Farries then sold the property to a third party, who assumed the mortgage. The third party successfully persuaded Royal Trust to extend the loan for a year at higher interest, but eventually defaulted; once the property was sold, Royal Trust demanded payment of the shortfall from Reid as guarantor. But the nature of the agreement had been changed with the year extension and the higher interest, and the Court held that since this was done without Reid's consent he was no longer obligated on the guarantee.

Why should guarantors be treated with such deference when their involvement persuaded the creditor to loan money to the debtor? Why should the creditor be responsible to protect the interests of the guarantor? And if it is important for the creditor to protect the position of the guarantor, should we allow this to be changed by a one-sided exemption clause included in the guarantee agreement itself? What do you think?

The creditor should also avoid any subsequent dealings that may weaken the position of the guarantor. Any substantial change in the nature of the contract between the creditor and debtor without the guarantor's consent will relieve the guarantor of any obligation. If the creditor advances more funds, or even extends the terms of repayment at a higher interest rate without the consent of the guarantor, this will normally discharge the guarantee, as was the case in the Reid case. In any subsequent dealings with the debtor independent of the guarantor the creditor should at least include a statement reserving rights against the guarantor. The effect will be that the guarantor will continue to be bound by the original agreement. Note that a creditor simply deciding not to sue and giving the debtor more time to pay will not be a substantial change and will not discharge the guarantee.

**Creditors must not weaken the position of the guarantor**

**Significant changes may release guarantor**

**Creditor can reserve rights against guarantor**

9. (1985), 20 D.L.R. (4th) 223 (P.E.I. C.A.).

**Releasing security may release guarantor**

The guarantor is also released from obligation when other forms of security, such as chattel mortgages, are released. For example, if Kotsalis obtained a loan from the Business Bank, with the bank taking a guarantee from Bruno and a chattel mortgage against Kotsalis's car as security, such an arrangement would cease to be binding on Bruno if the bank subsequently allowed Kotsalis to sell the car without Bruno's consent. Similarly, Bruno would be released if the bank advanced Kotsalis more money or agreed to a change in the nature of the repayment terms without Bruno's consent.

**Withholding information may release guarantor**

The creditor simply withholding important information from the guarantor may also be enough to discharge the guarantee. This must be information of some substantial and unusual nature and not simply the normal kind of information that would pass between business associates. In the *Calderbank* case in Case Summary 10.8, the information that Mr. Calderbank, the driving force behind the company, intended to start another company in competition was of such a significant and unusual nature as to void the guarantee.

### Case Summary 10.8

**Bank Has a Duty to Disclose Information: *Toronto Dominion Bank v. Rooke et al.*[10]**

Mr. Calderbank was the driving force behind Skyhook Operations Ltd. and owned 50 percent of the company's shares. The other shareholders, Mr. Rodenbush and Mr. Rooke, had personally guaranteed significant indebtedness with the Toronto Dominion Bank. Calderbank went to the manager of the Toronto Dominion Bank and asked that Skyhook's line of credit be extended, explaining that Rodenbush and Rooke would be investing a further $20 000 each and would come in to sign a guarantee for the extended line of credit. He also told the manager that he would be starting another company to compete with Skyhook, cutting out Rodenbush and Rooke so that he could keep all of the profits himself. In effect, he told the bank manager that he intended to get his business "partners" to invest more money, thus taking on more liability, and that he intended to cheat them out of it.

When Mr. Rodenbush and Mr. Rooke came to the bank to sign the new guarantee the manager was careful not to tell them about Mr. Calderbank's plans, and this proved to be his undoing. Guarantors are particularly vulnerable and they must consent to any changes made in the debt relationship that would put them at greater risk. That consent must be informed consent, and the manager had a duty to tell Mr. Rodenbush and Mr. Rooke what Mr. Calderbank was doing to them. The manager's failure in this obligation amounted to misrepresentation. As a result, Rodenbush and Rooke were no longer bound by the guarantee when

---

10. (1983), 3 D.L.R. (4th) 716 (B.C.C.A.).

Skyhook subsequently went bankrupt. The personal guarantee is one of the important options available to creditors to increase their security, and will be discussed later in this chapter.

Because the basic obligations of the guarantor are determined by contract, they can be modified by contract as well. It is common for creditors to include provisions that attempt to exempt the creditor from the basic obligations discussed here, but like all exemption clauses the courts interpret them very carefully. It is becoming common practice for such transactions to contain a clause creating a **continuing guarantee**, allowing the creditor to continue to advance funds up to a pre-set limit without affecting the obligation of the guarantor to pay in the event of default. Often clauses are also included that allow the creditor to discharge and otherwise deal with security and to otherwise change the terms of the agreement, including changing terms of repayment and increasing interest rates. These clauses can be effective if carefully worded, significantly limiting the protection normally enjoyed by a guarantor.

### Case Summary 10.9

#### Failure to Register Security Releases Guarantor: *First City Capital Ltd. v. Hall*[11]

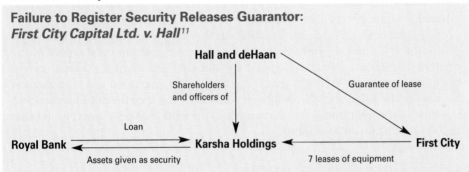

First City Capital leased word-processing equipment to Karsha Holdings, whose principals, Hall and deHaan, signed personal guarantees for the indebtedness. Karsha also owed money to the Royal Bank that was secured against the assets of the corporation. When Karsha Holdings defaulted, the Royal Bank was entitled to the word-processing equipment because First City had failed to register the security. First City turned to Hall on the personal guarantee for payment.

First City had an obligation to the guarantor to ensure that the security was perfected. Their failure to do so also relieved Hall of any liability on the guarantee. Note that the Court found that a provision in the contract stating that the guarantee would be enforceable ("notwithstanding that the lease or any other arrangements shall be void or voidable against the lessee... including... by reason... of... failure by any person to file any document or take any other action to make the lease... enforceable") did not apply since the failure to register did not make those leases void or voidable, just ineffective against third parties.

A similar case in Newfoundland had the opposite result. There, the bank also failed to perfect its security but the clause in the guarantee stated that the bank may "abstain from perfecting securities … as the bank sees fit." This term effectively covered the situation, and the guarantee remained binding despite the

11. (1993), 99 D.L.R. (4th) 435 (Ont. C.A.).

bank's failure to perfect.[12] Both cases illustrate not only the operation of the guarantee, but also the obligations placed on the creditor to preserve and protect the position of the guarantor doing nothing to weaken it. They also show that carefully worded provisions in the guarantee agreement may change that obligation, and how such provisions are strictly interpreted in favour of the guarantor.

This case raises the same question as the *Reid* case discussed in Case Summary 10.7. Why should the creditor have any obligation to the guarantor? They have guaranteed payment; why shouldn't the creditor be able to choose from whom they seek redress? And if the responsibility is justified, why should an exemption clause in a one-sided contract change that obligation?

**Guarantor assumes rights of creditor upon payment**

When a default occurs, the creditor is not required to demand payment from the debtor or to take steps to seize any other security before seeking payment from the guarantor unless this has been agreed to in the contract. A guarantor who pays the debt is **subrogated** to the rights of the creditor, which means, in effect, that the guarantor steps into the creditor's shoes. Any remedy or right available to the creditor after payment is assumed by the guarantor, including the right to seize a chattel used as security for the debt and to sue the debtor and take advantage of the proceedings available to assist in collecting the debt.

**Defences of debtor are available to guarantor**

Also, any defences that are available to the debtor are also available to the guarantor. If breach of contract, fraud, or misrepresentation on the part of the creditor has barred an action against the debtor it also bars an action against the guarantor. Note, however, that if the reason the guarantee was required was because of the infancy of the debtor or some other factor known to all parties at the time of the guarantee, the guarantor will normally not be allowed to use that as a defence against the creditor.

## Other Forms of Security

### The Bank Act[13]

This federal statute predates the passage of personal property security acts, and allows banks more flexibility in what they can take as security. Under the *Bank Act*, growing crops, inventories, and goods in the process of manufacture can be taken as security by the banks despite the fact that the nature of the goods has changed in the process. Because of the nature of this type of security it must be possible to sell them over the course of business without affecting the nature of the security, and sections 426 and 427 of the *Bank Act* allow this to happen.

**Anticipated crops can be used as security**

**As can goods in process of manufacture**

The *Bank Act* is still an important federal statute, but under the provincial personal property security acts other lenders now have similar flexibility. There is now more potential conflict between the *Bank Act* and provincial legislation. Under the Act securities must be registered with the Bank of Canada, creating duplication and further confusion. This confusion is compounded because the banks continue to use the normal types of secured transactions available to everyone, such as chattel mortgages, guarantees, real estate mortgages, assignment of debts, and so on.

---

12. *Bank of Montreal v. Mercer* (2000), 582 A.P.R. 88 (Nfld. T.D.).

13. S.C. 1991, c. 46.

## Floating Charges

Floating charges are used by creditors when dealing with corporations that must be free to purchase and sell the assets used as security without interference. When a corporation makes a bond or a debenture issue, it is often secured by such a floating charge.

A corporation's debt can take several forms, including a **bond** or **debenture**. In Canada, bonds are usually secured and in effect involve a mortgage of company assets, whereas debentures are usually unsecured. A bond or debenture issue normally involves more than one creditor, with a trustee looking after their interests. The series of bonds or debentures issued are commonly sold on the open market.

**Bonds and debentures**

The security granted often takes the form of a **floating charge** against the general assets of the corporation, including inventory machinery and the goods being produced. This allows the corporation to continue to deal with those goods, buying and selling in the normal course of business, unaffected by the floating charge. It is only upon default or some other specified event (such as the payment of unauthorized dividends, or the sale of a valuable asset) that the floating charge descends, attaches to the specific goods, and becomes a fixed charge. The advantage is that it does not interfere with the ongoing business and still provides a priority against unsecured general creditors.

Because the various personal property security acts now allow inventory and other changing assets to be used as security, the floating charge is of diminishing importance; however, it is still a common aspect of corporate financing.

## Builders' Liens

Builders' liens were created to overcome a problem in the construction industry. Normally, the suppliers of goods and services (such as electricians and plumbers, or merchants selling building supplies) dealt with a general contractor rather than directly with the owner of the building that was to be enhanced by their services. If they were not paid, their recourse was limited to the contractor. They had no claim against the owner or the building they worked on. Statutes in all provinces—variously called *Builders' Lien Acts, Mechanics' Lien Acts,* or, in Ontario, the *Construction Lien Act*—now give these suppliers of work and materials a claim for payment against the actual land and buildings enhanced by their services. Once the service is provided the worker or supplier can register a lien, giving them a claim against that property and putting considerable pressure on the owner to ensure they are paid. Under the acts the owner retains a percentage of what they would otherwise pay to the general contractor, called the **holdback**, which in most provinces is set at 10 percent. After a relatively short period within which any liens must be registered, the owner checks the registry and, if there are no liens, pays out the retained holdback to the general contractor.

**Suppliers of goods and services can file lien**

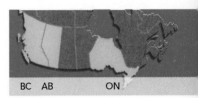

BC   AB            ON

**Holdback fulfills obligation**

If liens have been filed that amount is retained and made available to those lien claimants. The owner's obligation is normally limited to the amount of the holdback even where the total claimed in the liens exceeds that amount. In that case, the lien claimants will get a proportional share of the amount held back based on what they are owed.

This requirement of holdback applies to anyone paying down the line, and so the general contractor in turn must hold back from the payment to subcontractors to cover claims by their employees or suppliers of materials. The times, percentages, and amounts vary from jurisdiction to jurisdiction but the general

**All must hold back**

approach is the same, thus providing a form of security to those supplying work and material in this industry. In several provinces, similar liens are created by statute against property stored in a warehouse and for maintenance people working on vehicles, machinery, and other goods.

## Negotiable Instruments

**Negotiable instruments must be honoured in hands of holder in due course**

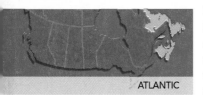

ATLANTIC

As discussed in Chapter 9, negotiable instruments in the form of cheques, bills of exchange, and promissory notes are often associated with secured transactions. **Cheques** were traditionally used as a convenient method of payment but have largely been replaced by debit cards, credit cards, and other forms of electronic banking. The common practice of giving a series of post-dated cheques to facilitate periodic payments continues. In whatever way cheques are used, it must always be remembered that once a cheque gets into the hands of an innocent third party—called a *holder in due course*—it will have to be honoured even if there was some problem with the original transaction (except in rare circumstances such as forgery).

### Case Summary 10.10

**Cheque Enforceable in Hands of Holder in Due Course:**
*578722 Ontario Inc. v. Dowma Ltd.*[14]

Dowma issued a cheque drawn on its bank to an employee, but when that employee failed to show up to work Dowma stopped payment on the cheque. In the meantime, the employee had negotiated the cheque to 578722 Ontario Inc. and been given cash for it. When the bank refused payment, 578722 commenced this action against Dowma and was successful. 578722 Ontario Inc. had received the cheque in good faith and given value for it before any notice of dishonour, and was therefore a holder in due course entitled to full payment. As a holder in due course the company was not affected by any personal defences that may have arisen between the employee and Dowma.

Cheques and other forms of negotiable instruments are dangerous to the drawer as they give an innocent third party (the holder in due course) who obtains the instrument better rights to be paid than the person who gave them the instrument.

Do you think it is a good idea that negotiable instruments should convey better rights to a holder than a simple assignment of contractual rights?

**Certified cheque includes commitment by bank**

A **certified cheque**, although not the same as cash, is extremely secure because the bank has made a commitment to honour the instrument. Once the cheque has been transferred to the payee, the bank will no longer honour an order to stop payment. Instead of certifying a cheque, many banks now issue a bank draft in the name of the payee to be given by the customer to the payee at the appropriate time.

**Bills of exchange** can also be used as instruments of credit because they can be made payable at some future date, and when they have been accepted payment is guaranteed by that drawee/acceptor; this provides a significant aspect of

14. Ontario Provincial Court, Feb. 16, 1988, as reported in *Lawyers Weekly* Vol. 7 (1988) (Ont P.C.).

## Reducing **Risk** 10.4

People often give cheques and sign promissory notes simply as one aspect of transactions they are involved in. If they think about the deal going sour at all, they assume they can either stop payment on the cheque or simply not pay the promissory note. But these negotiable instruments are much more dangerous than simple contractual obligations. If they are negotiated to a third party (as they are designed to be), and that innocent third party qualifies as a holder in due course, the instruments can be enforced despite problems with the original transaction. Never give someone a cheque or sign a promissory note without realizing that you could very likely be called on to pay it independent of the transaction for which it was given. Even the bank of the payee where the cheque is deposited can be a holder in due course and force you to pay despite any stop-payment order you may have given.

security to the transaction. Bills of exchange are not common in consumer dealings but are still used in sophisticated financial transactions.

In most credit transactions, debtors are required to sign **promissory notes** as part of the process. This may seem redundant given the commitment to repay in the primary contract, but remember that the promissory note provides a great deal of flexibility—making it much more attractive to third parties to whom the creditor may wish to assign the transaction. Merchants supplying goods or services on credit will often assign that transaction to a finance company. With the promissory note the finance company becomes a holder in due course able to enforce the promissory note independent of any problems that might arise from the original transaction or with the product sold.

> *Promissory notes often included in loan agreement*

Under a 1970 amendment to the *Bills of Exchange Act*, any negotiable instrument used to advance credit in a consumer transaction must be marked "consumer purchase." This is notice to any third party that the instrument does not convey the same rights as normal and that a holder in due course would in fact be subject to the same defences that the drawer would have against the original payee. Thus, most of the advantages of being a holder in due course are lost. This applies only to consumer transactions, however, and when negotiable instruments are used in normal business transactions the advantages of being a holder in due course would still hold true.

> *Advantages reduced in consumer transactions*

## Letters of Credit

Similar to negotiable instruments, the letter of credit is used in commercial relationships, especially in international trade. The **letter of credit** is a commitment by the importer's bank that the price stated will be paid upon presentation of appropriate documentation confirming delivery, thus giving assurance from the financial institution to the seller that they will be paid by their customer. This letter of credit is normally delivered to the exporter by the importer, who upon delivery of the goods submits the appropriate documentation (indicating shipment, insurance, customs declarations, etc.) to the importer's bank and receives payment. Sometimes, especially when the importer's bank is in a foreign country, the exporter will require that a bank they have confidence in, usually in their own country, become involved as a confirming bank. The two banks are in communication with each other, and both commit to honour the letter of credit upon receiving the appropriate documentation.

> *Letters of credit used in international trade*

> *Role of confirming bank*

The confirming bank plays a role similar to endorsing a negotiable instrument in that they add their commitment to honour the letter of credit. The exporter then simply submits to their bank the appropriate documents indicating performance and receives payment.

If Chan were exporting pianos from Hong Kong to Weiss in Canada, Weiss might ask the Royal Bank to generate a letter of credit to support this transaction and to satisfy Chan. The letter of credit would guarantee payment to Chan of a specific amount (for example, $200 000) upon production of documentation such as proof of insurance, a bill of lading, a customs declaration, an invoice, and possibly a certificate of inspection from some third party to indicate that the goods are as expected. The Royal Bank would give the letter of credit to Weiss for delivery to Chan, who would, upon shipping the goods, present the required documentation including the letter of credit and collect the money from the bank.

Chan also might involve his own bank, either in an advisory capacity where it assumes no liability or to guarantee payment as a confirming bank. If Chan were to use the Hong Kong Bank as the confirming bank he would so advise Weiss, who would in turn advise the Royal Bank of this when making arrangements for the letter of credit. The Royal Bank contacts the Hong Kong Bank directly, making arrangements for the **confirmed letter of credit**. The Hong Kong Bank then sends a confirmed letter of credit to Chan, who then ships the pianos. Chan then submits the appropriate documentation confirming delivery to his bank, and if after careful examination they are satisfied, the Hong Kong Bank will pay him the stated sum. These documents are then sent to the Royal Bank, which pays the Hong Kong Bank and appropriately debits the account of Weiss.

This may seem like a very complex process, but it is really quite simple in that the two traders choose banks that they trust to hold and transfer the funds. The effect is quite similar to that of a bank draft, but this process is often more convenient and more flexible.

**Also used in domestic transactions**

Letters of credit are primarily used in international trade, but they are very flexible and, because of this quality, it is not uncommon to find them being used in domestic business transactions as well. Letters of credit are also used in other ways—for example, to guarantee, in effect, that one party to a contract will properly perform. If there is a breach, the victim has recourse to the bank that has issued the letter of credit. This is referred to as a **standby letter of credit.**

## Other Related Legislation

### Bulk Sales

**Creditors protected when merchant sells bulk of business**

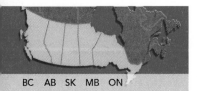

BC  AB  SK  MB  ON

Other legislation has been enacted to protect creditors against frauds committed by debtors. The Bulk Sales Acts in place in some provinces are designed to prevent merchants from selling all or almost all of their business's assets before a creditor can take action to stop them. Creditors expect a business to sell inventory in the normal course of operations, but when all or most of the inventory or other assets or equipment needed for the ongoing operation are sold this indicates that the merchant is going out of business, and the *Bulk Sales Act* operates in these circumstances to protect the creditors. This is done by requiring that the purchaser obtain a list of creditors, that they be notified of the sale, and that, if they wish, the proceeds be paid directly to them. In those provinces that still have a *Bulk Sales Act* great care must be taken to comply with its requirements. Otherwise, the purchaser could end up having to pay twice for those goods.

## Case Summary 10.11

### The Danger of Ignoring the *Bulk Sales Act*: National Trust Co. v. H&R Block Canada[15]

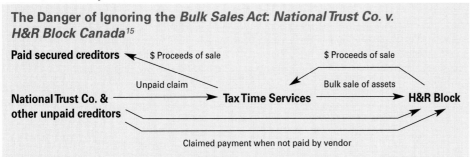

H&R Block purchased all of the assets of Tax Time Services for $800 000. This transaction was a sale in bulk and the parties should have complied with Ontario's *Bulk Sales Act*. Instead, the vendor Tax Time Services gave H&R Block a commitment to indemnify them for any loss caused by the failure to comply with the Act. Tax Time Services then used the money obtained from that sale to pay back two of its secured creditors, leaving other secured and unsecured creditors unpaid. National Trust was one of those unpaid creditors, having an unpaid judgment against Tax Time Services for more than $200 000. Tax Time Services was not able to pay the judgment and went out of business. National Trust claimed payment against H&R Block to the value of the assets purchased and the Court agreed, ordering that those funds be made available to pay the claims of all the unpaid creditors. In effect, H&R Block had to pay for the purchased stock twice because of the failure to comply with the *Bulk Sales Act*. Tax Time Services' promise to indemnify them for such a loss was worthless since they had gone out of business. This case illustrates the danger of ignoring the operation of the *Bulk Sales Act*. It is still in place in some provinces and, as can be seen in this case, still has teeth. It is very easy to overlook the provisions of the *Bulk Sales Act,* and very dangerous to do so. In this case H&R Block even tried to cover itself against this risk and was still caught by its operation.

## Landlord's Right to Distrain for Rent

When a tenant fails to pay rent on a leased property, an ancient common law right called *distress* is available to the landlord of commercial property. This gives the landlord the right to seize and hold the tenant's assets that are on the rented premises, eventually selling them to pay for the rent owed. There are several restrictions and procedural requirements that must be carefully adhered to, and it must be emphasized that this right is not available in residential tenancies. The nature of residential and commercial tenancies and the rights of the parties will be discussed further in Chapter 15.

## Fraudulent Transfers and Preferences

Sometimes, desperate debtors are tempted to hide property or otherwise protect it from the claims of creditors. Giving or selling property to a friend or relative to avoid the debt is a fraudulent transfer and the transaction is void. The creditor

**Fraudulent conveyance void**

15. (2001-10-26), O.N.C.A. c28654 (Ont. C.A.).

Businesspeople sometimes are so focused on a deal that they miss complying with related statutory requirements, which later comes back to haunt them. In those jurisdictions where there is a bulk sales statute in place businesspeople must take great care to comply with it whenever the sale of significant portions of a business's assets are involved. Failure to do so can result in paying twice. Similarly, whenever dealing with an insolvent debtor creditors must take care to comply with fraudulent conveyance, fraudulent preference, and other legislation that may affect the validity of that transaction.

**Fraudulent preference void**

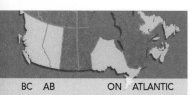

BC    AB              ON    ATLANTIC

can seek out the fraudulently transferred property and get it back from the purchaser. If it is a valid arm's-length sale at a fair price to an innocent third party, called a *bona fide* **purchaser for value**, the transaction is valid and cannot be reversed. Sometimes a debtor will seek an advantage by paying one creditor in preference to another. This is also a prohibited transaction, called a **fraudulent preference**, and can also be reversed.

Legislation embodying these provisions varies from province to province; the statutes are variously called *Fraudulent Conveyances Act, Fraudulent Preferences Act, Assignment and Preferences Act,* and *Fraudulent Creditors Act.* They are designed primarily to prevent debtors from unfairly making payments or transferring property in such a way as to keep it from the just claims of creditors. The Saskatchewan *Fraudulent Preferences Act* reads as follows:

> 3. … every gift, conveyance, assignment or transfer, delivery over, or payment of goods, chattels, or effects or of bills, bonds, notes, or securities or of shares, dividends, premiums, or bonus in a bank, company, or corporation, or of any other property real or personal, made by a person at a time when he is in insolvent circumstances or is unable to pay his debts in full or knows that he is on the eve of insolvency, with intent to defeat, hinder, delay, or prejudice his creditors or any one or more of them, is void as against the creditor or creditors injured, delayed or prejudiced.[16]

**Similar restriction in federal bankruptcy**

The federal *Bankruptcy and Insolvency Act* discussed below also has provisions prohibiting settlements (gifts of assets) and fraudulent preferences, and these provisions apply uniformly throughout Canada. The wording used in the federal statute is quite different than that found in the provincial statutes. Care should be taken to determine under which statute it would be more effective to proceed given the particular circumstances of the case.

# Bankruptcy

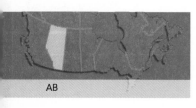

AB

As discussed above, debtors will often find themselves in a position where they cannot repay their debts. For that reason, at the outset of a relationship wise creditors take steps to ensure repayment, by arranging either to take an asset of the debtor's as security or to get someone else, such as a guarantor, to also be responsible for the debt. An unsecured creditor still has all of the normal remedies available when someone reneges on a legal obligation, including the right to

---

16. *Fraudulent Preferences Act*, R.S.S. 1978, c. F-21, s. 3.

proceed to a civil judgment and have the debtor's assets seized and sold to recover the judgment, or to garnishee bank accounts and other income as discussed in Chapter 2. Of course they must take second place to any secured creditor with respect to any asset against which they might claim.

Such action taken by an unsecured creditor in these circumstances is often a waste of time and money due to the number of creditors and claims outstanding and given the debtor's limited resources to pay. In the face of such a personal or business failure bankruptcy often becomes the only viable alternative for the debtor.

The *Bankruptcy and Insolvency Act*[17] is a federal statute that is uniformly applicable throughout Canada. Its purpose is not only to preserve as many of the debtor's assets as possible for the benefit of the creditors, but also to rehabilitate such debtors by forgiving the unpaid debt, thus removing an insurmountable burden and restoring them as productive members of society. Significant amendments have recently been made to introduce a further objective to help viable businesses survive restructuring and to facilitate consumers

in making arrangements with creditors and thus avoid actual bankruptcy. Other important amendments are anticipated. It should be noted that the *Bankruptcy and Insolvency Act* does not apply to banks, insurance companies, trust companies, loan companies, and railways. It should also be noted that farmers and fishers cannot be forced into bankruptcy, but they can make a voluntary assignment.

The government official in charge for all of Canada is the **Superintendent of Bankruptcy**. The superintendent in turn appoints official receivers in various bankruptcy districts throughout the country (there must be at least one in each province). The actual **trustees in bankruptcy** are licensed private professionals who, for a fee, assist the debtor in the bankruptcy process—administering the bankrupt's estate for the benefit of the creditors, filing various documents with the official receiver, and otherwise shepherding the bankruptcy through the process from initiation to discharge. They serve the same purpose when a proposal is involved and are called administrators when dealing with consumer proposals. Up to five inspectors may be

A growing number of businesses face bankruptcy.

appointed by the creditors to supervise the trustee and the process and to ensure that the creditors' interests are protected. The courts also become involved when a receiving order is requested and in other types of disputes that can arise. The superior trial court of each province and territory is designated as a bankruptcy court for the purposes of the Act. Although these are courts of the provinces or territories, they have a national jurisdiction when administering the *Bankruptcy and Insolvency Act* and related legislation because these are federal statutes.

People are often confused by the terms used to describe bankruptcy. **Insolvency** simply means that a person is unable to pay his or her debts as they become due. **Bankruptcy**, on the other hand, is the process by which a debtor's assets are transferred to a trustee in bankruptcy who then deals with them for the benefit of the creditors. When the debtor does the transfer voluntarily it is called

---

17. R.S.1985, c. B-3 (as consolidated).

an **assignment in bankruptcy**, but when it is forced on the debtor the bankruptcy is accomplished by a creditor obtaining a **receiving order** from the court.

## The Process

**Bankruptcy can be forced by receiving order**

With an involuntary bankruptcy, a creditor who is owed more than $1000 can petition the court to force the debtor into bankruptcy. In granting the petition the court makes a **receiving order** and this results in a statutory assignment of the debtor's assets to the trustee, ensuring that the assets will be preserved and distributed fairly so that the creditors will recover as much as possible of what they are owed. The relevant section is section 71(2):

> (2) On a receiving order being made or an assignment being filed with an official receiver, a bankrupt ceases to have any capacity to dispose of or otherwise deal with his property, which shall, subject to this act and to the rights of the secured creditors, forthwith pass to and vest in the trustee named in the receiving order or assignment....

To obtain a receiving order, the creditor must specify in the petition that the debtor owes more than $1000 in debt and has committed an act of bankruptcy. Significant acts of bankruptcy include the voluntary assignment of assets to a trustee in bankruptcy, fraudulent transfers of money or assets to keep them out of the hands of the trustee, a fraudulent preference given to one of the creditors, trying to leave the jurisdiction without paying debts, and general insolvency. Normally it is the failure to pay debts as they become due that is the specified act of bankruptcy stated in the petition. A sworn affidavit must also be filed verifying the facts alleged in the petition. If the debtor opposes the petition, as is often the case, a hearing before a judge will take place; if satisfied, the judge can issue a receiving order designating a trustee in bankruptcy (normally chosen by the creditors) to receive the assets of the bankrupt. Where unopposed, the hearing can be held before the **registrar** of the court. This is an involved process normally requiring the assistance of a lawyer. Caution should be exercised before embarking on this course. Great damage can be done to the business and reputation of the debtor, and if the application is refused the creditors may be liable to pay compensation for the losses incurred. See Figure 10.1 for an illustration of the receiving-order process.

**Bankruptcy can be voluntary by assignment**

When a **voluntary assignment** is involved the debtor must make an "assignment for the general benefit of his creditors" in the prescribed form. The debtor must also prepare a "statement of affairs" summarizing his property and listing all creditors including the amounts and nature of their claims (whether they be secured, preferred, or unsecured). These documents are filed with the official receiver, who then appoints a licensed trustee to receive the debtor's property and administer the estate. In practice, debtors will first seek out a trustee in bank-

## Figure 10.1 Receiving Order Process

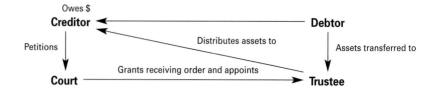

**Figure 10.2 Voluntary Assignment**

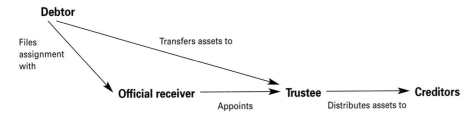

Debtor

Files assignment with

Transfers assets to

Official receiver ——→ Trustee ——→ Creditors

Appoints

Distributes assets to

ruptcy who will counsel them, advising of the various alternatives and, if appropriate, assisting them in the preparation of the documents and their filing with the official receiver. Where larger estates are involved, the debtor will usually also involve the services of a lawyer. The voluntary assignment process is illustrated in Figure 10.2.

It should be noted that not all of the debtor's property is transferred to the trustee. Exempt property may vary somewhat from province to province but includes basic clothing, furniture, appliances, and tools and other items used to earn a living up to a limited value. A vehicle (of limited value) and a personal residence where the debtor has a limited equity ($12 000 in Vancouver) may also be protected, depending on the jurisdiction. There may be other property that the trustee will not bother with that he considers of little value or more trouble than it is worth to liquidate.

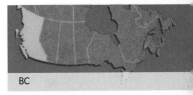

BC

The trustee holds the property in trust for the creditors and therefore owes them a duty to preserve those assets and get as much as reasonably possible for them. The bankrupt must cooperate with the trustee, disclosing all assets, documentation, tax receipts, and so on. Often a meeting of the creditors will take place and the debtor must attend, answering their questions and otherwise cooperating in the process. The creditors may ask to appoint up to five inspectors to supervise the process and look after their interests. The debtor may also be required to meet with and the answer questions directed at him by the official receiver.

**Trustee holds property in trust for creditors**

## Alternatives to Bankruptcy

Of course, the debtor should do all he can to avoid bankruptcy where possible; he will lose most of his property and will also find it difficult in the future to conduct business or to make personal credit purchases due to a poor credit rating. If a corporation is involved, it will not be discharged and will not survive. A personal bankruptcy will remain on an individual's credit record for about six years, and even after that it will be obvious to any credit grantor that there have been serious financial problems because of the lack of credit transactions during that six-year

Reducing **Risk** 10.6

Bankruptcy is a very serious and drastic step and both the creditors and the debtors should do all they can to avoid it. Often negotiation between the parties with a banker or other representative of the debtor acting as mediator will result in an acceptable alternative, where creditors get

more than they would normally get by forcing bankruptcy and a valued customer is preserved. If these informal steps fail and proposals are presented they should be treated seriously and bankruptcy used only as a last resort.

period. The first step for the debtor who is having problems should be to go to the creditors involved to try to make arrangements for paying back the debt. Creditors are usually quite responsive to reasonable arrangements for avoiding both commercial and personal bankruptcies. Often they will get much less if bankruptcy is forced, and there are many tangible and intangible advantages for the creditor to do all they can to keep their debtor as a functioning customer. Often, especially where significant credit card debt is involved, a bank or other institution will provide a loan sufficient to consolidate the various debts owed so there is only one creditor and a more manageable payment schedule, often at a lower rate of interest. Individual creditors will sometimes agree to take less to pay off the debt, realizing that they will be better off getting less than risking getting nothing by continuing to demand full payment and thus forcing bankruptcy.

**Debtors can make proposal and avoid bankruptcy**

**Division I proposals for corporation and commercial debtors**

If these informal negotiations fail, the *Bankruptcy and Insolvency Act* still provides for an alternative to bankruptcy. Two separate procedures are involved; both allow the debtor to reorganize her affairs and make proposals for partial payment that will satisfy her creditors sufficiently to avoid actual bankruptcy. **Division I proposals** usually involve commercial debtors in the form of corporations or individual debtors with significant claims against them (more than $75 000), and the process is started by filing a notice of intention to file a reorganization proposal with the official receiver. This is done with the help of a professional licensed to provide these services (the trustee). Within 10 days of filing the notice of intention a statement of projected cash flow must also be filed, followed within 30 days by the filing of the reorganization proposal itself (although this time limit may be extended). A meeting with the creditors is then held and the proposal is discussed. For the proposal to be approved, two-thirds by value and majority of the creditors by number must vote to accept it. Note that they may be divided into classes of creditors and then vote within that class. The court also must approve the proposal.

## Case Summary 10.12

### Proposal Abused: *Janodee Investments Ltd. v. Pellegrini*[18]

Pellegrini had two mortgages on his home, and when he defaulted on them the mortgagees/creditors proceeded to judgment and obtained an order to take possession of the house. Before the order could be enforced, Pellegrini served notice of intention to make a proposal under the *Bankruptcy Act*. Normally such a notice would result in a stay of proceedings delaying enforcement of the order, but in this case the Court held that Pellegrini was using the notice as a delaying tactic. He had no serious intention of reordering his affairs. No other secured creditors were involved, and the mortgagees would not be responsive to such a proposal in any case.

This case is instructive in that it shows not only the normal operation of a proposal but also how such a proposal can be abused. In this case the Court refused to order the stay, thus thwarting such abuse. The difficulty with the operation of such proposals—as well as the whole bankruptcy process—is that it interferes with the creditors' rights to proceed against the debtor and enforce full payment in a timely manner. The justification is that in the long run the creditors get more, and after discharge the bankrupt is able to carry on without overwhelming

18. (2001), 25 C.B.R. (4th) 47 (Ont. S.C.J).

debt. But in fact many creditors get very little or nothing and are barred from further proceedings after discharge. Do we worry too much about insolvent people and businesses at the expense of legitimate creditors?

If the creditors approve the proposal all are bound by it, including secured creditors who have given approval. If the creditors reject the proposal, the insolvent debtor is deemed to have made an assignment in bankruptcy from the day the notice of intention was filed, and normal bankruptcy procedures follow. These proposals are very flexible and may be anything from arranging to reduce the debt, to devising a new payment structure, to helping the creditors wind up the company. But note that a secured creditor must not lose his priority status by such a proposal and will retain the right to first payment up to the value of the asset used as security.

An important effect of starting this process by filing the notice of intention is that creditors, including secured creditors who have been included in the proposal process, are prevented from taking action against the debtor or the assets until the vote takes place about two months later, and this time may be extended. In effect, the insolvent debtor is protected from the creditors, and if the proposal is accepted that protection continues.

Consumer debtors with less than $75 000 in claims against them (excluding a mortgage on their home) are similarly protected when they make a consumer proposal under Division II of the Act. The insolvent debtor goes to a professional administrator, who examines the debtor's finances, prepares the proposal and any reports required, and provides counselling for the debtor. With the administrator's help, the insolvent debtor files a consumer proposal. This is a simpler process, and no actual meeting is required unless demanded by the creditors. The proposal must contain a commitment by the debtor to make a payment to the administrator at least once every three months, which is then distributed to the creditors. As long as the debtor lives up to the obligations in the proposal, acts honestly, and participates in the mandatory counselling required, action cannot be taken against him or her by unsecured creditors, public utilities, landlords, and so on. Even those supplying ongoing services, such as power, gas, and telephone, must continue supplying them. But if the debtor defaults, the proposal is annulled and the debtor may then face the normal bankruptcy procedures. Court approval of Division II proposals is not required.

In the case of each of these processes, if the proposal is accepted and then properly performed a certificate is issued and the debtor's obligation will be over with respect to those matters covered by the proposal or arrangement. There are some matters that cannot be included in such a proposal, just as some types of obligations cannot be discharged though bankruptcy, and these will be discussed below. If a secured debt was not included in the proposal that obligation remains and is not affected by the completed performance of the proposal or the certificate issued.

There is an alternative process available only to companies owing more than $5 million to restructure their affairs and avoid bankruptcy. This alternative is available under the *Companies' Creditors Arrangement Act*, a federal statute providing parallel protection to debtors with some advantages over the *Bankruptcy and Insolvency Act*. The attraction of this statute is in the protection given against creditors, which may provide more flexibility to the debtor company in its restructuring efforts providing more complete protection from any action by creditors,

**Consumer proposals available for people with debts less than $75 000**

**Large corporations can ask court for protection from creditors**

both secured and unsecured, for a longer period of time. A judge will often combine the flexibility provided under this Act with the power under section 47 of the *Bankruptcy and Insolvency Act* to appoint an interim receiver to supervise the restructuring process.

Commercial and consumer proposals under the *Bankruptcy and Insolvency Act* as well as arrangements under the *Companies' Creditors Arrangement Act* can avoid the bankruptcy process, but bankruptcy will normally follow if the creditors reject the proposals or the debtor defaults. Business students must be aware of bankruptcy and the alternatives to it from both a consumer and a commercial perspective. Consumer bankruptcies are much more numerous than commercial bankruptcies, and any business dealing with the public must factor this risk into its business considerations. Commercial bankruptcies may be less common than consumer bankruptcies but they generally involve much more money and have a greater impact on the businesses with which they are dealing. Even very high-profile businesses are facing bankruptcy or restructuring in these difficult economic times. A businessperson ignores these risks at their peril.

## Priority among Creditors

Once the trustee has been given the property of a bankrupt debtor, which is now referred to as the bankrupt's **estate**, he holds those assets in trust for the benefit of the creditors. The trustee has the right and responsibility to lease, repair, receive rents, or otherwise deal with those assets in order to preserve their value, and eventually to sell them and distribute the proceeds fairly to the creditors. The creditors must first establish the validity of their claim by filing a **proof of claim** with the trustee. This document sets out the nature of the debt, how much remains owing, and any claims the debtor might have in return. If this is rejected by the trustee the creditor cannot claim against the assets of the debtor, and so it often becomes a matter of dispute.

It should be noted that the *Bankruptcy and Insolvency Act* now allows a supplier of goods to demand the return of those goods upon learning of the bankruptcy, provided this is within 30 days of delivery of those goods and the debtor or trustee still has them. Even suppliers of goods that become commingled and lose their identity, such as crops, produce, and fish, have a prior claim. They become a secured creditor with respect to the value of those goods provided the products were delivered within 15 days preceding the bankruptcy and the claim filed within 30 days after.

Secured creditors retain their priority position, having a prior claim to at least the value of the asset used as security. Most creditors are prevented from taking any further independent action once the assignment or receiving order has been made. (Note that this doesn't affect prosecutions or matrimonial disputes, which continue.) A secured creditor, on the other hand, retains a right to repossess or otherwise proceed against the property used as security without waiting, unless the court orders otherwise. A secured creditor can choose to file a proof of claim for all of what they are owed, giving up any claim for security, and will be treated as an unsecured creditor for the entire amount. This tactic may be attractive where there is little value in the asset, where the asset is of such a nature that it would be difficult to sell, or where there are considerable resources in the estate. Otherwise, on the basis of a filed proof of claim, after they retake and sell the security they can claim against the estate for any shortfall, becoming a general creditor for that amount. Of course, the trustee has the same rights as the debtor

**Creditors must file proof of claim**

**Suppliers of goods can now reclaim those goods from bankrupt**

**Secured creditors have prior claim**

if there is sufficient value in the goods to simply pay off the secured creditor's claim, retaining those goods for the benefit of the other creditors. The trustee can also serve notice on the secured creditor, requiring them to place a value on those goods and deal with them on the basis of that value—or, if dissatisfied with the value given, require the assets to be sold by the creditor.

An important function of the trustee is to evaluate the creditors' various claims. If they are accepted as valid they will form part of the body of claims against the assets. Some claims of questionable legitimacy may be rejected. These creditors have the right to challenge that decision by making application to the bankruptcy court. Mediation is often employed to resolve these and other disputes.

**Trustee must evaluate claims of creditors**

After the secured creditors have received what they are entitled to, the trustee distributes the remaining assets, or the proceeds from the sales of those assets, to the other creditors. Next to be paid are preferred creditors as follows: funeral expenses; costs associated with the bankruptcy process; claims for arrears in wages for a limited amount and time period; municipal taxes; arrears in rent for a limited period; some direct costs incurred by creditors in the execution process; amounts owed for workers' compensation, employment insurance, and income tax that should have been deducted from salaries; and other claims of the Crown. Note that some claims of the Crown, such as the costs of cleaning up environmental contamination, have the status of secured claims against the property involved and must be paid first. General creditors, usually suppliers of goods and services, are paid only after these obligations have been met. If there is anything left the general creditors will receive a share on a pro rata basis (a share of the remaining estate determined by the percentage of overall claims their particular claim represents).

**Preferred creditors paid before general creditors**

## Case Summary 10.13

### Preferring One Creditor Prohibited: *Re Speedy Roofing Ltd.*[19]

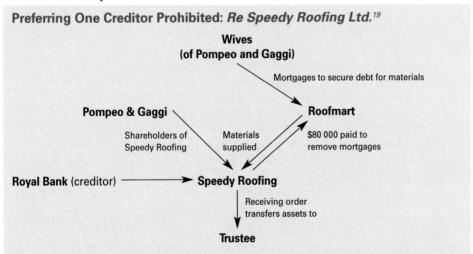

Roofmart supplied materials to Speedy Roofing, and after some time and increasing debt mortgages were given to Roofmart as security. The mortgages were on the homes of Mrs. Pompeo and Mrs. Gaggi, the wives of the principal shareholders of Speedy Roofing. Shortly before the Royal Bank, another creditor, forced them into bankruptcy, Speedy Roofing paid Roofmart $80 000 to discharge the

19. (1987), 45 D.L.R. (4th) 142 (Ont. S.C.).

mortgages. The Court must determine in this action whether that payment was a fraudulent preference and prohibited under the *Bankruptcy and Insolvency Act.* Since this payment was made within three months of the bankruptcy it amounted to a fraudulent preference and the court ordered Roofmart to repay the $80 000 to the trustee.

A debtor can't choose to pay one creditor over another or transfer property to others to escape the debt. Do you agree with this policy? If a debtor chooses to pay money owed, should other creditors be able to complain if a legitimate debt has been properly paid? Also, in this case the wives owned the houses and the payment removed the mortgages on them. In many jurisdictions, such residences are exempt from seizure and sale even if owned by the debtor. Should the application of the bankruptcy and insolvency process be the same in all jurisdictions? Should personal residences be exempt from seizure and sale? Should the debtor be able to choose creditors who will be paid and who will not be paid?

## Offences

As discussed above, debtors often attempt to keep their property out of the hands of creditors by transferring it to friends or relatives (called *settlements* in the Act), or they sometimes try to pay off one preferred creditor and not others. This happens in bankruptcy situations as well, and the trustee in bankruptcy can reverse these **fraudulent transfers and preferences.**

**Fraudulent transfers and preferences prohibited**

The relevant sections for the *Bankruptcy and Insolvency Act* are as follows:

> 91. (1) Any settlement of property made within the period beginning on the day that is one year before the date of the initial bankruptcy event in respect of the settlor and ending on the date that the settlor became bankrupt, both dates included, is void against the trustee.

> 95. (1) Every conveyance or transfer of property or charge thereon made, every payment made, every obligation incurred, and every judicial proceeding taken or suffered by any insolvent person in favour of any creditor or of any person in trust for any creditor with a view to giving that creditor a preference over the other creditors is, where it is made, incurred, taken, or suffered within the period beginning on the day that is three months before the date of the initial bankruptcy event and ending on the date the insolvent person became bankrupt, both dates included, deemed fraudulent and void as against the trustee in the bankruptcy.

**Settlements prohibited**

**Settlements** involve the transfer of assets where nominal or no consideration is involved. For these transactions the transfer is void if it took place within one year of bankruptcy, and that can be extended to up to five years if it can be proven that at the time of the settlement the bankrupt knew he was insolvent. A payment made in preference to one creditor over the others is likewise void, and the trustee can force the return of those funds so that they can be fairly distributed to all the creditors. This was the situation in the *Speedy Roofing* case discussed in Case Summary 10.13. There is a presumption that a payment was made to create a preference if it was made within three months of the bankruptcy. Such payments can be challenged even farther back if it can be shown that the debtor was doing it to avoid other creditors. As part of the bankruptcy process, the debtor is required to file an affidavit setting out all debt, creditors, and assets as well as a summary of all transactions that have taken place regarding these assets over the last year, or longer if so ordered. If they lie or otherwise try to hide assets or transactions they have made with respect to assets, they have committed a bankruptcy offence that carries serious consequences.

A bankrupt has an obligation to cooperate with the trustee by disclosing all relevant information and answering any relevant questions. The bankrupt can also be brought before the official receiver or the court, where they can be asked questions about how they got into financial trouble as well as questions regarding their debts, creditors, assets, and what they have done with them. In addition to settlements, fraudulent preferences, and fraudulent transfers, the *Bankruptcy and Insolvency Act* sets out several other bankruptcy offences: lying while under examination by the trustee in bankruptcy, hiding or concealing property, misleading or falsifying records, or otherwise trying to cheat the creditor.

**Bankrupt discloses information, cooperates, and answers questions**

Once the assets have been transferred to a trustee by voluntary assignment or through a receiving order, the debtor is an **undischarged bankrupt**. While in that state, if the bankrupt is involved in any transaction or borrows more than $500 she must disclose this status or face fine or imprisonment. Also, she cannot be a director of a corporation until discharged. She may also be restricted from carrying on some professions, such as acting as an auditor or an accountant, but this is controlled by the particular rules of the professional body in question.

**Limitations on undischarged bankrupts**

Once the process is completed and the creditors have received all they can from the assets, the bankrupt may apply to the court to be discharged. This application is automatic for an individual involved in his first bankruptcy. After nine months the discharge is also generally automatic for a first-time personal bankruptcy unless a creditor or the trustee opposes the discharge. Note that the discharge may be denied or have conditions set upon it.

**Discharge for first bankruptcy usually automatic**

## Case Summary 10.14

### Transferring House to Wife Prohibited: *Re Fancy*[20]

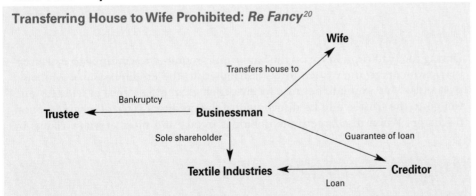

A successful businessman guaranteed the debts of his corporation, Textile Industries, making him personally responsible when it ran into financial difficulties. An ongoing action against him and the corporation eventually resulted in a judgment, causing it to fail, which in turn forced the businessman to claim personal bankruptcy. Shortly before the bankruptcy he transferred his interest in the matrimonial home to his wife and continued to live there with her. At the time of transfer it was clear that the matter would go to trial and that he was facing sub-

20. (1984), 8 D.L.R. (4th) 418 (Ont. S.C. Bktcy.).

stantial losses. The Court reversed the transfer, determining that the transfer of the house to the wife amounted to a prohibited settlement under the provisions of the *Bankruptcy and Insolvency Act*. A settlement occurs when a person transfers property to another in order to preserve some benefit for himself, which is exactly what happened in this case. The Court also found that the transfer was done to defeat or defraud the creditors and amounted to a fraudulent conveyance under the provincial *Fraudulent Conveyances Act*.

A lawyer became bankrupt because a business enterprise he was involved in failed. He maintained a very high lifestyle while going through the bankruptcy process and looked forward to a reasonable income after his discharge as well. He had made no payments to the trustee, and under the circumstances the judge ordered that he would not receive an unconditional discharge but would be required to pay back a significant amount to his creditors. The court has the discretion to place such conditions on the discharge of a bankrupt.[21]

**Discharge of bankrupt not always unconditional**

On the other hand, the same court dealt with another lawyer who was 53 years old when he ran into financial difficulties. He did all he could to repay his creditors, including significantly reducing his lifestyle. It was only after his honest efforts to repay failed, through no fault of his own, that he was forced to make an assignment in bankruptcy. Here the judge had no hesitation in finding that he was entitled to an unconditional discharge and a fresh start, even though his assets were not sufficient to pay back 50 cents on the dollar. In reaching this conclusion, the court considered his honesty, his struggle for nine years to pay back his creditors, and at his age his need to be free to prepare for his retirement so that he could support his wife and family.[22] These two cases illustrate the power of the bankruptcy court to place significant conditions on a discharge and the factors that might affect that decision.

## After Discharge

During the bankruptcy process the bankrupt is required to continue to make regular payments to the trustee to be distributed to the creditors (surplus-income payments). Any windfall they may receive, such as an inheritance or a lottery win, will go to the trustee and be distributed to the creditors. That all changes upon discharge. When discharged, the debtor is freed from most previous claims by

**Effect of discharge is to end most debts**

---

## Reducing **Risk** 10.7

Debtors sometimes use bankruptcy as a convenient method of avoiding paying their debts, and may in fact declare bankruptcy several times. This is an abuse of the process, and merchants and other creditors must be ever-vigilant to avoid doing business with such people. Use of credit checks can be a great help even where goods or services are being supplied. On the other hand, debtors who are tempted to abuse the process should realize that as a rule they may find it very difficult to preserve their assets by hiding them or transferring them to friends or relatives, and that any attempt to do so is an offence that may result in prison or a refusal by the court to grant an unconditional discharge. When faced with such abuses, with the debtor failing to cooperate with officials or trying to hide assets or otherwise abuse the process, the courts generally will not grant the discharge requested.

---

21. *Re McAfee* (1988), 49 D.L.R. (4th) 401 (B.C.C.A.).

22. *Re Irwin* (1994), 112 D.L.R. (4th) 164 (B.C.C.A.).

creditors and is in a position to start over. Any assets subsequently obtained by the discharged bankrupts are theirs to do with as they wish, and unpaid creditors cannot claim against them. By statute, some obligations do survive the discharge, such as family maintenance payments and outstanding fines. Student loans are also still payable for 10 years, although there is considerable controversy over this provision.

Debtors who commit bankruptcy offences as set out above will normally not be discharged and are liable to be imprisoned. The court will also be reluctant to unconditionally discharge bankrupts who have paid creditors less than 50 cents on the dollar. Under such circumstances, the court can put conditions or restrictions on the bankrupt, such as requiring that they make additional payments to the creditors, thus granting only a conditional discharge. In the Supreme Court of Canada, Justice Estey commented on the purpose of the bankruptcy process and said, "The purpose and object of the *Bankruptcy Act* is to equitably distribute the assets of the debtor and to permit his rehabilitation as a citizen, unfettered by past debts. The discharge, however, is not a matter of right, and the provisions of Sections 142 and 143 plainly indicate that in certain cases the debtor should suffer a period of probation."[23] Justice Estey's comment relates to a prior act, but similar provisions are in the current statute (see section 172).

> **Unconditional discharge not granted if bankruptcy offence is committed**

Note that the discussion here has focused primarily on the bankruptcy of an individual. The primary difference with a corporation is that there is no discharge after the bankruptcy unless the corporation is able to repay all of the money owing. That of course is highly unlikely, there being very little likelihood of a bankruptcy in the first place in those circumstances. A Division II proposal under the *Bankruptcy and Insolvency Act* as mentioned is not available to a corporation, but corporations often try to restructure using a Division I proposal. Larger companies also often restructure using the *Companies' Creditors Arrangements Act,* and if their proposal is approved, or they reach an arrangement with their creditors and properly fulfill those obligations, the corporation will then be free to carry on its business, avoiding bankruptcy altogether. The obligations of the debtor to supply appropriate information and documents apply to the corporation as well. The corporation must supply someone who is familiar with the situation to answer the questions that would otherwise have been put to an individual debtor by the trustee, the creditors in a creditor meeting, or the receiver or court. A company will often face dissolution after the bankruptcy process, though this usually is not worth the trouble. Still, disgruntled shareholders and creditors may have further rights under both winding-up acts and the various company acts and legislation in place at both the provincial and federal levels. They also may have claims against the directors and other officers of the corporation under those statutes.

> **Corporations not discharged after bankruptcy**

> **Corporations may use proposals and arrangements to avoid bankruptcy**

> **Corporations normally do not survive bankruptcy**

Corporations that go into **receivership** are often not involved in bankruptcy at all. When a creditor loans such a corporation significant funds, they usually include in the agreement the right, in the event of default or some other triggering event, to appoint a receiver to take over the business without the necessity of going through the bankruptcy procedure. Such an assignment of assets to a receiver is not actually a bankruptcy, but the effect can be every bit as devastating to the business. The rights of creditors to appoint such receivers have been limited to some extent by the recent revisions to the *Bankruptcy and Insolvency Act* relating to proposals and the provisions of the *Companies' Creditors Arrangements*

> **Receivers may be appointed by creditors under security agreement**

---

23. *Industrial Acceptance Corp. v. Lalonde,* [1952] 2 S.C.R. 109 (S.C.C.) at 120.

*Act.* Further restrictions on the conduct of such receivers are set out in section XI of the *Bankruptcy and Insolvency Act.* Today, secured creditors in these circumstances will have to give the debtor reasonable notice before the appointment of a receiver or taking possession of the goods used as security. Whether the receiver is appointed by the creditors directly or they go to the trouble of getting a court order, failure to give reasonable notice can be devastating to the debtor and impose significant liability on the creditor when it is improperly done.

Legislation also exists to assist in the "orderly payment of debt." If the account owed is less than $1000, or if the debtor obtains the consent of the creditors, the debtor can obtain a consolidation order from the court, making arrangements to consolidate all the debts and pay all the creditors back at one rate with one regular payment. Government agencies available to assist in this process can be helpful to both the debtor and the creditor. In fact, the Division II consumer proposals provisions under the *Bankruptcy and Insolvency Act* have largely replaced this process. And since this particular aspect of the Act (part X) is voluntary, the service is made available in only a few provinces.

**Orderly payment of debt provisions don't apply in most provinces**

It must be remembered that the creditor is in the business of making money, not destroying the debtor. If the debtor cannot pay, the creditor gains nothing by harassment. The two main purposes of the *Bankruptcy and Insolvency Act* and the other legislation discussed in this section are to ensure that the creditor realizes as much of the amount owed as possible, and to rehabilitate the debtor. The legislation also provides punishment for fraudulent activities by the debtor and provides a uniform system of laws throughout Canada. The idea is to restore the debtor as a productive working member of the community as soon as possible.

# Summary

### Security

- Gives a creditor some assurance that he or she will be paid even when other creditors are not
- Conditional sales agreement—the creditor retains title while giving the debtor possession of the goods
- Chattel mortgage—the debtor gives up title to the creditor while keeping possession; in the event of default, the creditor may retake the goods
- Assignment of book accounts can also be used as security

### *Personal Property Security Act*

- Allows both chattels and intangible forms of personal property to be used as security
- The security must first attach, but the priority is established by perfection (involving registration or taking possession of the property)
- In the event of default, the creditor can retake the goods and resell them and/or sue for the debt. In some situations, the creditor must choose one or the other but cannot do both
- The debtor has the right to be notified of sale and to redeem the property

### The guarantee

- A guarantee is a contingent liability in which someone agrees to be responsible when a debtor fails to pay, whereas an indemnity involves co-responsibility for the debt

- If a guarantor is required to pay the creditor, he or she steps into the shoes of the creditor and can seek redress from the debtor
- The guarantor usually has the same defences as the debtor
- Changes to the agreement by the creditor and the debtor may release the guarantor

## Other forms of security

- *Bank Act* security covers growing crops and goods being manufactured
- Floating charges used by corporations permit inventory turnover
- Builders' liens protect subtrades and suppliers
- The property owner is required to hold back a portion of payment
- Cheques and promissory notes are often used with credit transactions
- Advantaged position of innocent holder in due course attractive to creditors
- Letters of credit used to secure credit in international trade

## Related legislation

- *Bulk Sales Acts* protect unsecured creditors from sale of business assets
- Fraudulent preferences and transfers can be reversed

## Bankruptcy

- Two main objectives are to protect creditors and to rehabilitate the bankrupt
- Can take place voluntarily through assignment or involuntarily through a receiving order
- Involves the transfer of the debtor's assets to a trustee in bankruptcy who sells the assets and distributes the proceeds to the creditors
- After meeting certain qualifications, the debtor can apply to be discharged
- Absolute discharge relieves responsibility for most prior debts
- Discharge may be automatic for first-time personal bankruptcy
- Division I proposal is used to protect commercial debtors from action by creditors; where the proposal is properly performed bankruptcy is avoided
- Division II proposal is used to protect consumers with debts less than $75 000 and provide an alternative to bankruptcy
- Large corporations can ask courts for protection from creditors under the *Companies' Creditors Arrangements Act*
- Assets go first to secured creditors, then to preferred creditors, then to general creditors
- Suppliers of goods can reclaim them within 30 days of delivery
- Bankruptcy offences punishable by no discharge or prison

---

## QUESTIONS

1. Distinguish between the following
   a. A chattel mortgage and a mortgage on real estate
   b. A chattel mortgage and a conditional sale
   c. Real property and personal property
   d. Chose in action and chattel

2. What significant problem associated with the practice of taking goods as security is alleviated by the registration requirements introduced by legislation? Describe the resulting obligations on all parties.

3. What obligations are imposed on the secured creditor who retakes goods used as security when a debtor defaults?

4. In what ways was the passage of the *Personal Property Security Act* a significant departure from the traditional treatment of secured transactions?

5. Distinguish among security contract, attachment, and perfection, and explain the significance of each step. Explain how it is accomplished.

6. In the event of a default, explain what the rights of a secured party are and what limitations there are on those rights.

7. What kinds of property can be used as collateral under the *Personal Property Security Act*?

8. Explain the rights of debtors after they have defaulted and the secured party has taken possession of the collateral.

9. Explain the position of the secured creditor in relation to the debtor and other creditors in the following situations in which assets have been used as security. Indicate provincial variations in your response.

   a. The amount still owing to the secured creditor is less than the value of the asset used as security.

   b. The amount still owing to the secured creditor is greater than the value used as security.

10. What obligations does the guarantor of another person's debt incur? What protection is available to guarantors in subsequent dealings between the creditor and debtor?

11. When a debtor defaults on a loan and the guarantor is required to pay, what rights does the guarantor have in relation to the debtor?

12. Distinguish between a *Bank Act* security and other forms of security and explain the reason why this form of security was created.

13. What happens upon default when a floating charge has been used to secure a debt? How does this form of security affect the priorities among types of creditors?

14. What significant difficulty facing the supplier of goods and services in the construction industry is overcome by the creation of the builders' lien? Explain the role of the holdback.

15. Explain why cheques and promissory notes are often used in association with credit transactions.

16. What is the difficulty associated with the assignment of contractual rights that is overcome when a negotiable instrument is used?

17. Explain the nature and use of a letter of credit and distinguish between a standby letter of credit and a normal letter of credit.

18. Define the objectives of bankruptcy legislation and distinguish between an assignment and a receiving order, with an explanation of the process involved in each case.

19. Distinguish between bankruptcy and insolvency and explain the role of the trustee in the bankruptcy process.

20. Explain what is meant by a settlement under the *Bankruptcy and Insolvency Act*, and describe how such a settlement is dealt with.

21. Distinguish between Division I and Division II proposals and explain the advantages of making such a proposal.

22. Explain what is meant by a bankruptcy offence and the possible consequences of committing one.

## CASES

### 1. *Re Purschke and Avco Financial Services Canada Ltd.* (1984), 43 D.L.R. (4th) 464 (Alta C. of Q. B.).

Sandra Harris entered into a chattel mortgage with a bank in 1985. The bank registered this chattel mortgage, but the serial number was recorded incorrectly. Ms. Harris then granted another chattel mortgage to Avco in 1986, which was properly registered. Before Avco registered the mortgage, they contacted the bank for a credit check on Ms. Harris and were told that the bank had a chattel mortgage already on the vehicle. After Avco registered their chattel mortgage, they contacted the bank telling them that they had done a search, found the incorrect number, and had registered their mortgage ahead of the bank. Avco seized the motor vehicle, and after correcting the serial number the bank challenged Avco's right to the car. Explain the arguments available on both sides.

### 2. *Finning Tractor and Equipment Company Limited v. Mee* (1980), 110 D.L.R. (3d) 457 (B.C.S.C.).

In April 1976, Morrill and Sturgeon Lumber Company signed a conditional sales agreement with Finning Tractor to purchase a new Caterpillar wheel loader. The agreement was guaranteed by Mee. The purchaser defaulted after some payments were made. Finning chose to seek payment from the guarantor instead of seizing the tractor under the conditional sales agreement. Explain the liability of the guarantor in these circumstances. Would your answer be any different if you learned that Finning had neglected to register the conditional sales agreement and therefore had lost its priority against other secured creditors?

### 3. *Bank of Montreal v. Duguid* (2000), 185 D.L.R. (4th) 458 (Ont. C.A.).

Mr. Duguid is a school principal and participated in a tax-shelter investment scheme in California. This required a loan of money from the Bank of Montreal, with a promissory note given as security. His wife signed the promissory note as a guarantor. The scheme was very risky and highly speculative. The bank knew this, the wife did not, and the bank officers failed to inform the wife about the risk. Although it was normally the bank's policy to request that people in the position of Mrs. Duguid obtain independent legal advice, this was not done in this instance. The marriage broke up, the loans were defaulted on, and the bank is now demanding that the wife honour the guarantee. Explain the arguments on both sides.

Would it make any difference to your answer to know that the wife was a successful real estate agent?

### 4. *Canadian Imperial Bank of Commerce v. Shire* (2000), 80 B.C.L.R. (3d) 285 (B.C.C.A.).

Mr. Shire and Mr. Konja were equal shareholders in and operating a business called Vogue Marketing, located in British Columbia. Their wives were not involved. Needing operating capital for the business they borrowed money from the Canadian Imperial Bank of Commerce, supported by a guarantee signed by both couples and secured by a mortgage on their two residences. There followed some involved financial dealings between Vogue Marketing and the bank as the business struggled along, but eventually the business failed and the bank sought to foreclose against the residence owned by the Shires. In fact, as part of those complicated dealings the bank had discharged the mortgage against the property owned by the Konjas, who had left for Ontario. Another complication was that the loan secured by the guarantees and mortgages was not to exceed $200 000, and the bank had allowed the company's indebtedness to grow in excess of $245 000. The Shires had, in fact, paid more than $100 000 but failed to pay any more. Explain the arguments available to the Shires as the bank takes steps to foreclose and take their home.

Would it make any difference to your answer to know that there was a paragraph in the agreement allowing the bank to discharge and otherwise deal with securities as it "may see fit"?

### 5. *Engels v. Merit Insurance Brokers Inc.* (2000), 17 C.B.R. (4th) 209 (Ont. Sup. Crt.).

Mr. Engels was an insurance agent who ran into serious financial difficulties, which forced him to merge with Merit Insurance Brokers Inc. He also was given a personal loan by Merit with the understanding that he would pay it back out of commissions earned. But his financial problems continued, and he found it necessary to make an assignment in bankruptcy. Before he was discharged he told Merit that he felt morally bound to repay the loan they had given him and would do so despite the bankruptcy.

The question here is whether he is still obligated to pay after being unconditionally discharged from the bankruptcy, or whether he is now entitled to those commissions earned despite the debt. Consider the arguments on both sides. Consider as well the argument raised by Merit that the reason why they didn't contest the discharge was because of the assurance they had received that they would still be repaid.

### 6. *Bank of Montreal v. Giannotti* (2000), 51 O.R. (3d) 544 (Ont. C.A.).

Mr. Gianottie was a major player in real estate development but was caught when the market experienced a downturn. He owed more $2.5 million to 30 creditors when the Bank of Montreal forced him into bankruptcy. During the process he was uncooperative and withheld from his trustee information about a family trust. During the discharge hearing he was entering into another business venture, in violation of the provisions of the *Bankruptcy and Insolvency Act*. The Bank of Montreal is opposing his request for discharge. Explain the arguments available to them and what alternatives might be available in these circumstances. In your answer consider the purpose and objective of the bankruptcy process.

# Employment, Agency, and Insurance

**B**usiness activity, in addition to the production of products or services, normally involves interaction with customers, suppliers, creditors, and others. These activities are carried out by employees or other representatives, and the legal rules and principles associated with these relationships are the subject of this section. Chapter 11 deals with the master–servant relationship, or employment. It looks at the responsibilities that employees and employers have to each other. Statutes that set standards and establish the rights of such workers, as well as the special labour legislation controlling the collective bargaining process, are reviewed. Chapter 12 examines the agency function, where one person represents another in transactions with a third. The law of agency is much more significant than is sometimes appreciated, since in the corporate environment all transactions must be entered into by such representatives. This chapter concludes with an overview of insurance, an area of law that often involves interaction with agents.

# 11

# Employment

**CHAPTER HIGHLIGHTS**

- Distinctions between employees, agents, and independent contractors
- Employment relationships and common law rights
- Legislation impacting employment
- Collective bargaining and labour unions

A contract for employment is one of the most important in which a person will become involved. This chapter is devoted to exploring the different legal ramifications of the employment relationship.

### Case Summary 11.1

**Dishonesty Justifies Dismissal:** *Saumer v. Genie Office Services Ltd.*[1]

The plaintiff, Judy Saumer, was employed by the defendant placement agency, Temporarily Yours, as a service coordinator, filling clients' short-term positions with temporary employees. She was promoted to branch manager in 1987 and was responsible for the overall running of the branch as well as maintaining direct contact with clients. On returning from her annual vacation, the plaintiff found that her personal effects had been removed from the office, and her employer promptly advised that she was dismissed from her position. Saumer then commenced a wrongful dismissal suit, seeking damages.

A witness for the defendant, Ms. Braun, countered that the plaintiff had been dismissed for cause. She claimed that the plaintiff had lied to and cheated a major client, thus destroying the trust the client had in the firm. Ms. Braun had assumed the plaintiff's responsibilities while she was away on vacation. It was then that she discovered that the plaintiff had failed to provide a temporary employee for a major client, Gulf Canada, and had then attempted to deceive the client by denying that any order had been placed. The truth was unravelled, however,

---

1. (1991), 119 A.R. 204 (Q.B.).

when Gulf contacted a particular employee and that individual revealed that the plaintiff had called her about filling Gulf's position. Ms. Braun had also discovered many other instances where the plaintiff had failed to perform required duties. The court held that these failures to follow up with clients did not amount to sufficient grounds to justify dismissal without notice. But the manner in which the Gulf account was handled, including deception and lies, gave the employer good reason to lose confidence in the plaintiff as manager of the business. Accordingly, dismissal without reasonable notice was justified. The wrongful dismissal action was dismissed.

# What Is Employment?

Employment involves one person doing work for another, but not all such relationships are classed as employment. The work of independent contractors, such as doctors, lawyers, plumbers, and the like, must be distinguished from employment. Such independent contractors work for themselves and act independently, providing a specific service for the person they contract with, whereas an employee is said to be in a master–servant relationship, acting under the direction of the master.

Agency is a third type of business relationship, where one person acts as a go-between in relationships between others, and will be discussed in detail in the next chapter. Each of these relationships imposes different legal rights and obligations on the parties; understanding which body of rights governs a particular relationship can be of vital importance.

**Not all work is employment**

AB

## The Control Test

The traditional method of determining whether an employment relationship exists is to assess the degree of control exercised by the person paying for the service. A person who is told not only what to do but also how to do it is classed as an employee. But if the person doing the work is free to decide how the job should be done, the position is more likely that of an independent contractor. For example, if Fong hires Kirk to paint a house, Kirk could be either an independent contractor or an employee. If Fong tells Kirk what tools to use, when to work, and how to perform the job, then Kirk is an employee. If Kirk supplies the tools and determines what time to start work and the best way to perform the job, then Kirk is probably an independent contractor. Whether the person is paid a wage or salary or is paid by the job is also taken into consideration in determining employment. Courts will also look at who owns the tools used and who profits or runs the risk of loss from the work performed.

**Employee controlled by employer**

The employment relationship involves a contract in which the employee agrees generally to serve the employer, who in turn has the right to supervise and direct. On the other hand, an independent contractor agrees to do a particular job, not to enter a general service relationship. In other words, employees work for their employer, whereas independent contractors work for themselves. In Case Summary 11.2, it was clear to the court that Mr. Spencer was working for Tim Hortons and not for himself.

**Independent contractor works independently**

## Case Summary 11.2

### Control Suggests Employment—But It's Not the Only Test:
*Spencer v. Tim Hortons;*[2] *Wolf v. Canada*[3]

Spencer drove a courtesy bus for Tim Hortons, transporting seniors and children for promotional purposes. His contract stipulated that "spare drivers are considered self-employed," and no deductions were made from his pay for income tax, unemployment insurance, or any other benefits. His services were abruptly terminated, without notice and without a reason being given. It was evident at trial that the event that triggered the firing was Spencer's alleged authorization, given to the servicing company retained by the defendant, to have the lugs on a wheel of the bus changed. This act disobeyed the policy that servicing required prior approval from Ms. Hoffer; she was unavailable when the problem arose, so the lugs were changed without her consent.

The first issue that the court had to resolve was whether Spencer was an employee at all. Only employees can seek damages for wrongful dismissal. After noting that the defendant had complete control over how the plaintiff's work was carried out, and noting that the plaintiff was paid hourly and was not in business on his own account, the judge declared that an employment relationship did exist. The minor act of disobedience was insufficient to warrant dismissal, and so damages for wrongful dismissal were awarded.

Contrast this with the *Wolf* case, where a mechanical engineer specializing in aerospace contracted with one company, Kirk-Mayer of Canada, and took on a project with a second, Canadair Limited. The level of control was minimal, as once Wolf knew what was requested of him he could approach completion of the project as he saw fit. In consideration of higher pay, Wolf took all the risks—he was provided neither health care insurance nor a pension plan. He had no job security, no union protection, no hope for promotion. The Court referred to an earlier Supreme Court of Canada ruling where Justice Major stated:

> ...the central question is whether the person who has been engaged to perform the services is performing them as a person in business on his own account. In making this determination, the level of control the employer has over the worker's activities will always be a factor. However, other factors to consider include whether the worker provides his or her own equipment, whether the worker hires his or her own helpers, the degree of financial risk taken by the worker, the degree of responsibility for investment and management held by the worker, and the worker's opportunity for profit in the performance of his or her tasks.
>
> It bears repeating that the above factors constitute a non-exhaustive list, and there is no set formula as to their application. The relative weight of each will depend on the particular facts and circumstances of the case.[4]

In Wolf's circumstances, considering the control he exercised over how the work was done and his bearing all the risks, the Court concluded that he was an independent contractor.

---

2. (1995), 167 A.R. 248 (Prov. Ct.).

3. [2002] 4 F.C. 396 (F.C.A.).

4. *671122 Ontario Ltd. v. Sagaz Industries Canada Inc.*, [2001] 2 S.C.R. 983, at para. 47, 48.

## The Organization Test

In recent years, the courts have supplemented the control test with the organization test. Even if there is little direct control, where the individual is an integral part of the organization, working only for that company and subject to group control, that person is likely an employee.[5] On the other hand, if that person is free to offer services to others and bears the risks of profit or loss if work is not completed in a timely manner, he may be an independent contractor as in the *Wolf* case, above.

It is important to note that, at least for the purposes of establishing vicarious liability, a person can be an independent contractor for most purposes but an employee or a servant in some specific instances.[6] This ruling has prompted the courts to find employment relationships in areas that were traditionally considered purely independent. Jones could be a plumber acting as an independent contractor for Smith for most of the job, but while digging a drainage ditch at Smith's direction he could be considered an employee for that purpose. If someone was hurt, Smith could be found vicariously liable for Jones' careless conduct in digging that ditch.

Individual statutes may provide a definition of employment for the purposes of that statute, but there is no general legislated definition. And so, when a court is dealing with vicarious liability or wrongful dismissal, it must turn to the principles enunciated in precedents to determine whether an employment relationship exists.

It is also important to note that while a person cannot be an independent contractor and an employee at the same time, the same is not true of an agent. **Agents** can be independent contractors or employees. A sales clerk in a store is both an employee and an agent; and a person selling insurance is likely an independent contractor but is also functioning as an agent for their client. It's important to keep these categories separate, as the liability of the parties will likely be determined by the relationship between them.

The legal principles governing the independent contractor are embodied in the general rules of contract law already covered in Chapters 5 to 8. This chapter will examine the law of master and servant, the federal and provincial legislation, the trade union movement, and collective bargaining.

# The Law of Master and Servant

Over the years, the common law courts developed special rules to deal with the unique problems associated with employment, which was then referred to as a master–servant relationship. Today, employment law is governed primarily by the general provisions of contract law, supplemented by these special rules as well as a number of statutes that further define the responsibilities and obligations of the parties.

The main responsibility of the employer, in addition to payment of wages, is to provide a safe workplace and good working conditions for the employee. Some

*Organization test supplements control test*

*Definition of employment broadened*

*An employee can be an agent*

*An agent can be independent*

*Obligations of employer include:*
• *payment of wages or salary*
• *safe working conditions*

5. John G. Fleming, *The Law of Torts*, 8th ed. (Sydney: The Law Book Co. Ltd., 1992), p. 372.
6. *Cooperators Insurance Association. v. Kearney*, [1965] S.C.R. 106.

types of jobs are inherently dangerous, as in construction, and the employer is obligated to minimize the danger, usually by promoting safe work practices; erecting protective fences, barriers, and nets; and requiring the use of proper safety equipment. The employer must hire competent people. If it can be shown that the employer hired a careless or incompetent worker who caused injury to others, the employer may be held accountable. Jobsite health and safety requirements and injuries caused by other workers are specialized areas covered by occupational health and safety legislation and workers' compensation legislation; both will be discussed below.

The contract of employment usually includes a commitment by the employer to pay a specific wage or salary. That agreement will often also set out bonus arrangements, benefit packages, and the repayment of reasonable expenses incurred.

**Obligations of employee:**
• Work competently
• Honesty and loyalty
• Punctuality
• Act in employer's best interests
• Fiduciary obligations may apply

The employee also has obligations to fulfill. The employee must possess the skills claimed and exercise them in a reasonably competent and careful manner. The employee has an obligation to follow any reasonable order pertaining to the employment and must treat the property of the employer carefully. The employee must be honest, loyal, and courteous; an employee who does the work required but acts in an insubordinate or disloyal way can be fired. Similarly, an employee must be punctual and work for the time specified in the contract. If the employee uses company time or facilities without permission, he or she may be disciplined. With some types of jobs, there may also be an obligation to act in the best interests of the employer. This is referred to as a **fiduciary obligation** and is usually imposed only on senior-level employees.

An employee who is also a fiduciary is automatically subject to certain obligations toward an employer. These include a duty to act in good faith, make full disclosure, and not take corporate opportunities for one's own benefit. For example, in the *Felker* case,[7] where the employee secretly engaged in negotiations to become the sales agent for a second company and did not advise or offer his employer this opportunity to represent the second company, the court found cause for that employee's dismissal. Failure to disclose this activity and to secure prior consent justified the dismissal.

**General contract law applies to employment**

Although employment contracts are often not formal or written documents, it is always good advice to put the contract in writing, clearly stating the provisions that are important for the parties. These provisions may include the rate of pay, the hours of work, and a description of what services are required and for what period. As with other contracts, all the ingredients necessary for a contract to exist must be present. Employers often try to impose new one-sided employment contracts on their employees well after the commencement of employment. These contracts often include terms adverse to the employee, such as restrictive covenants or terms limiting the period of notice to be given upon termination. When imposed after the fact, these provisions are often not binding because of a failure of consideration. The employment contract is illustrated in Figure 11.1.

**Restrictive covenants must be reasonable**

When **restrictive covenants** are included in the original contract, committing the employee not to work in a particular geographic area or in a particular industry after leaving the position, they have to be for a reasonable time and area. If too broad, these covenants will not be enforced. Further, such covenants must be

---

7. *Felker v. Cunningham* (2000), 191 D.L.R. (4th) 734 (Ont. C.A.), leave to appeal to S.C.C. refused, [2000] S.C.C.A. No. 538.

## Figure 11.1 The Employment Contract

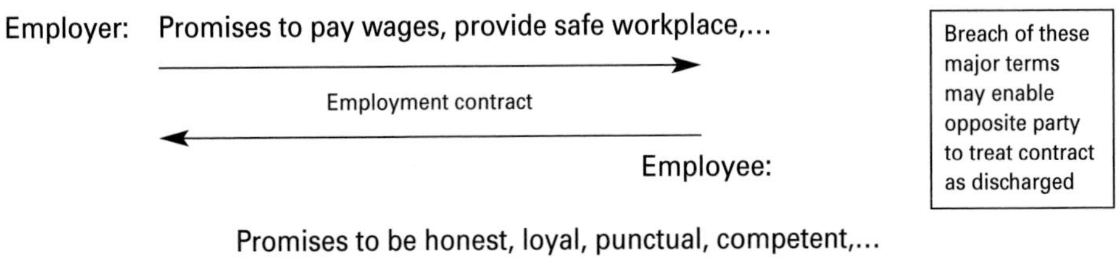

Employer: Promises to pay wages, provide safe workplace,...

Employment contract

Employee:

Promises to be honest, loyal, punctual, competent,...

> Breach of these major terms may enable opposite party to treat contract as discharged

the most appropriate way of protecting the employer's interests, and not be against the public interest. For example, if an employer invents a special production method, the secrecy of which could be maintained only by requiring that the employees commit themselves not to work in a similar industry for a reasonable period of time, a restrictive covenant in the contract of employment to that effect would likely be valid. But in general, the courts are reluctant to enforce restrictive covenants in employment contracts because of the danger of denying the employee the ability to earn a livelihood and because of the normally weaker bargaining position of the employee.

## Case Summary 11.3

### Injunctions Sought to Enforce Promises Not to Compete: *Herff Jones Canada Inc. v. Todd;*[8] *Lyons v. Multari*[9]

Todd entered into a sales-representative agreement with the respondent, whereby he agreed to solicit schools and colleges for the purpose of selling class rings, medals, awards, and yearbooks supplied by the respondent. After six years, Todd severed the relationship and went to work for the competitor Jostens. By doing so, he breached a promise that he would not compete with his former employer. The respondent sought and obtained an injunction from the trial judge, preventing Todd from "soliciting or contacting directly or indirectly any of those schools or accounts who were customers" of the respondent as of May 20, 1994, for a period of four years.

Todd appealed, arguing that the trial judge erred in deciding that the restrictive covenant in the sales representative agreement was valid. Prohibiting an employee from working for a competitor for four years does, at first glance, appear excessive. However, the Court of Appeal found the trial judge had applied the correct tests: (1) The covenant was reasonable as between the parties. Its duration, four years, was reasonable in light of the fact that Todd would have been entitled to a split commission for three years after leaving the respondent had he not breached the restrictive covenant. Further, Todd had developed a special relationship with the customers, so the proprietary interest of the respondent would be jeopardized if Todd could approach them on the competitor's behalf. Nor did the covenant cover too large a geographical area. Todd had simply promised not to compete in the area formerly serviced by him on behalf of the respondent. (2) The covenant was also reasonable with regard to public interest.

---

8. (1996), 181 A.R. 236 (C.A.).

9. (2000), 50 O.R. (3d) 526 (C.A.), leave to appeal to S.C.C. refused, [2000] S.C.C.A. No. 567.

Contrast the above with the *Lyons* case, where the plaintiff oral surgeon took on a new associate and the two signed a short, handwritten contract containing a non-competition clause. The defendant oral surgeon therein agreed not to compete for three years within a five-mile area. After 17 months he gave the agreed 6 months' notice and opened his own oral surgery practice in the same city. The Court of Appeal determined that it was not appropriate to enforce a non-competition clause if a non-solicitation clause would adequately protect the employer's interests. A non-solicitation clause prohibits a departing employee from soliciting clients, patients, or customers of his previous employer. A non-competition clause does more—it attempts to keep the former employee out of the business.

These cases suggest that not only must the non-competition clause be reasonable as between the parties (not overly broad geographically or in terms of time), but the party trying to enforce the same must show that the clause is necessary to protect some proprietary interest. Otherwise, the court might regard the clause as being too restrictive or unnecessary and simply refuse to enforce it.

# Termination

**Contract may stipulate amount of notice to be given**

An employment contract may provide for its own discharge (as when the contract is for a fixed term, say one year, and that term expires), or the parties can mutually agree to bring it to an end. However, most contracts of employment are for an indefinite period of time with no reference to notice requirements. In general, such contracts of employment can be terminated by either party giving reasonable notice, by the employer giving the compensation that should have been earned in that notice period (pay in lieu of notice), or immediately with just cause.

• Otherwise, reasonable notice of termination required of both employer and employee

Just as the employee is not bound to the job and can leave after giving reasonable notice, so too is the employer free to terminate the employment relationship for no specific reason as long as sufficient notice is given. Note, however, that the employer's right to terminate even with proper notice is restricted somewhat by provincial and federal human rights legislation and by the *Charter of Rights and Freedoms,* which prohibit such action when it amounts to discrimination on the basis of gender, religion, colour, physical disability, or other protected ground.[10]

• But note human rights violations

## Reasonable Notice

**What constitutes reasonable notice varies with circumstances**

**Courts consider:**
• Length of service
• Type of job
• Age of employee
• Qualifications
• Availability of similar employment
• Bad-faith conduct

The problem for employers is that reasonable notice, especially where long-term employees are involved, can be quite significant. The courts impose notice periods on the basis of such factors as length of service, the type of job, the employee's age and qualifications, and the nature of the job market.[11] In some cases involving long-term senior managers, the required notice period may exceed two years. Bad-faith conduct in the manner of dismissal is another factor that is properly compensated for by an addition to the notice period.

---

10. *Canadian Charter of Rights and Freedoms,* ss. 15 and 28, Part I of the *Constitution Act 1982,* being Schedule B to the *Canada Act 1982* (U.K.), 1982, c. 11, and, for example, *Human Rights Code,* R.S.O. 1990, c. H.19, s. 5.

11. *Bardal v. The Globe and Mail Ltd.* (1960), 24 D.L.R. (2d) 140 (Ont. H.C.J.).

## Case Summary 11.4

### Bad-Faith Conduct Draws Further Damages: *Wallace v. United Grain Growers Ltd.*[12]

A subsidiary of United Grain Growers decided to update its printing operations. The marketing manager, Mr. Logan, met with Mr. Wallace to discuss the possibility of employment. Mr. Wallace had the type of experience the respondent sought, having worked for 25 years for a competitor that used the type of press contemplated. Mr. Wallace expressed reluctance to leave his current employer without some guarantee of job security. Mr. Logan assured him that if he performed as expected, he could continue to work for the company until retirement.

Mr. Wallace's performance with the new employer was a great success. He received compliments from his employer days before he was summarily discharged without explanation in 1986. Mr. Wallace sued for wrongful dismissal. In its defence, the respondent claimed Mr. Wallace had been dismissed for cause. These allegations were maintained until trial. They caused the plaintiff so much distress that he was forced to seek psychiatric help. His attempts to find similar employment were largely unsuccessful.

The Supreme Court of Canada restored the trial judge's award of damages in the amount of 24 months' salary in lieu of notice. In light of Mr. Wallace's advanced age (59 years), his 14-year tenure as the company's top salesman, and his limited prospects for employment, a lengthy notice period was warranted. Another factor that the Court declared relevant was the fact that the plaintiff was induced to leave previous secure employment and had been guaranteed job security. Although the trial court found there was insufficient evidence to establish that Mr. Wallace had been hired for a fixed term, ending at his retirement, the Court found that, subject to his satisfactory performance, he had been guaranteed job security. This breach also factored in the amount of notice appropriate in the circumstances.

Of particular interest, though, were the Supreme Court's comments on bad-faith conduct in the manner of dismissal. To ensure that employees receive adequate protection, employers ought to be held to an obligation of good faith and fair dealing in the manner of dismissal, breach of which will be compensated for by adding to the length of the notice period. At a minimum, "employers ought to be candid, reasonable, honest and forthright with their employees and should refrain from conduct that is untruthful, misleading, or unduly insensitive."[13] The Court found that injuries, such as humiliation, embarrassment, or damage to one's self-worth and self-esteem, might all be worthy of compensation, depending on the circumstances of the case. These intangible injuries may lead to difficulties in finding alternative employment, a tangible loss that warrants an addition to the notice period or may merit compensation in and of itself.

Even seasonal employees, who are fired at the end of a season and then repeatedly re-hired, may be entitled to reasonable notice if not recalled.[14] Short-term or probationary employees may be entitled to extended notice periods if the employee has not been informed of the basis on which his performance will

---

12. [1997] 3 S.C.R. 701.

13. (at para 99).

14. See *Levy v. Ken-Wo Country Club* (2001), 194 N.S.R. (2d) 213 (N.S.S.C.), where the golf course groundskeeper was not recalled after 24 seasons with that employer.

## Reducing **Risk** 11.1

What the foregoing highlights is that legal advice should be sought if an employer wishes to terminate an employee without cause. Adequate notice must be given. If the amount of notice has not been agreed upon by the parties, either in the employment contract or through subsequent mutual agreement, then reasonable notice must be given.

If the employer has concerns about the employee continuing to work during the notice period, pay in lieu of notice can be given instead (i.e., a severance package). A lawyer can advise as to the length of that notice, determined by reviewing precedents, and costly litigation may thus be avoided.

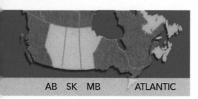

AB   SK   MB        ATLANTIC

be evaluated or was persuaded to leave another job but then is terminated after a short time. Similarly, if an employer fosters employee loyalty by promising job security, that employer may be required to provide even greater notice of termination to its employees than would otherwise be the case.[15] Trade unions generally include terms in their collective agreements as to when an employee can be terminated and what notice is required. Also, minimum statutory notice periods are set out in employment standards statutes and will be discussed below.

### Just Cause

**Notice not required when there is just cause**

Where there is just cause, there is no requirement upon an employer to give any notice. An employee can be dismissed without notice for such things as serious absenteeism, consistent tardiness, open disobedience, habitual negligence, incompetence, harassing other employees, drinking on the job, or immoral conduct on or off the job that reflects badly on the employer. Even swearing at the employer has been determined to be serious misconduct sufficient to justify dismissal. Such conduct may be used to defend a wrongful dismissal action, even if it is discovered after the employee has been dismissed. In the *Saumer* case in Case Summary 11.1, it was the employee's dishonesty that justified the dismissal. Such dishonesty need not be tolerated by the employer, no matter what the plight of the employee is. When dismissing employees for dishonesty, or behaviour such as fraud or theft, great care must be taken to ensure that the accusations are accurate and the evidence firm. The courts have awarded significant damages for wrongful dismissal, augmented by punitive damages, when such charges have not been substantiated.[16] Also, care should be taken to ensure that when a person is dismissed, the real reason for the termination is not discrimination. The human rights tribunals of the various jurisdictions are very active in prosecuting such violations.

### Case Summary 11.5

**Off-Duty Misconduct May Be Cause for Dismissal: *Hyland v. Royal Alexandra Hospital*[17]**

Professionals have to be careful if they act within "grey areas" of the law. Mr. Hyland, a chartered accountant, lost his job when it was discovered that he had

---

15. *Singh v. BC Hydro and Power Authority* (2001), 95 B.C.L.R. (3d) 238 (C.A.), leave to appeal refused, [2002] S.C.C.A. No. 45.

16. See *Clenndenning v. Lowndes Lambert (B.C.) Ltd.* (1998), 41 C.C.E.L. (2d) 58 (B.C.S.C.), varied (2000), 4 C.C.E.L. (3d) 238 (B.C.C.A.) where the trial court awarded an additional 36 months' salary as damages for the bad faith of the employer. On appeal, this award was reduced as the employer's honest belief that it had cause for dismissal negated bad faith.

17. (2000), 267 A.R. 329 (Alta. Q.B.).

acted dishonestly in purchasing a new car for personal use. He had a co-worker's wife, who was a Treaty Indian, buy the car so as to avoid payment of GST. The plaintiff then paid her $250 for her trouble and bought the car from her. For the car to be GST-exempt, it would have to be delivered to a reserve. This was not done, yet no GST was paid by either of the purchasers or the dealer.

The employer hospital defended the wrongful-dismissal action claiming it had grounds to be concerned. Mr. Hyland was the hospital's internal auditor. He had been hired to maintain compliance with tax law and his manipulation of "loopholes" reflected poorly on his employer, a public institution. The employer claimed Mr. Hyland's actions reflected a lack of the judgment required of an internal auditor. The court agreed. Representations made in the bill of sale were dishonest in that the intermediary never "owned" the car. She did not take possession of it, did not choose it, and did not pay for it. The transaction was a sham concocted to avoid taxes. This case demonstrates that misconduct even off the job may constitute conduct justifying dismissal, particularly where one's position demands a certain level of integrity and accountability.

Should what one does on one's own time constitute grounds for dismissal? Will this information temper how you act on a Saturday night?

## Disabled Workers

In the past, employees who became seriously ill, even though not "at fault," could be discharged without notice if they could no longer perform their job. The employer did not have to pay for work not done. In effect, the employment contract was frustrated. Today, however, there is a legislated duty to accommodate disabled workers who are still able to work, and human rights commissions are very willing to rule against employers who too quickly fire workers because of illness or disability. The employer must take great care to comply with the provisions of both the applicable human rights legislation and the workers' compensation legislation designed to protect disabled or injured workers.

**Illness may constitute frustration of contract**

Disability is a prohibited ground. In enforcing the prohibition of discrimination against the disabled, the courts have ruled that employers have a legal duty to take reasonable steps to accommodate an employee's individual needs. However, this legal duty does not apply if the only way to resolve the problem will cause the employer *undue hardship*; that is, hardship that is substantial in nature. To deal with this problem, most businesses offer some form of illness and long-term disability insurance or policy as part of their benefits package.

## Disobedience and Incompetence

Although an employee is entitled to refuse to work because of dangerous working conditions, failure to perform a reasonable order is also grounds for dismissal without notice. Disobedience justifies dismissal. Incompetence is also just cause for dismissal; however, employers are well advised to let employees know when the level of performance is unacceptable as soon as it becomes apparent and provide an opportunity for improvement. It may appear to be easier to let the matter go, but the employer may then be faced with the argument that the employer's conduct and acceptance of the employee's performance led that employee to believe that the level of performance was appropriate. This argument will be especially difficult to overcome if bonuses or wage increases were given to the employee in the past despite the poor performance.

**Problem where incompetence tolerated**

## Layoffs

**Layoff or termination**

When an employer simply runs out of work for the employee to do, that is not just cause for termination, and reasonable notice is still required. Even when the layoff is only temporary, the employee may be entitled to treat it as termination and demand the appropriate notice and compensation. In the absence of such reasonable notice or just cause, the employee can sue the employer for wrongful dismissal. Provisions in collective agreements often cover layoffs and recalls, and several provinces have included provisions covering temporary layoffs in their employment standards legislation.

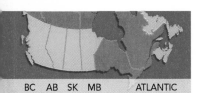

BC  AB  SK  MB          ATLANTIC

For example, Ontario's *Employment Standards Act*[18] stipulates that if an employee has been laid off for a period longer than the defined "temporary layoff" (generally 13 weeks) employment terminates, and the employer must pay the employee termination pay. However, if wages or other payments are made to or for the benefit of the employee during the layoff, the length of the temporary layoff can be extended to 35 weeks. (Each province will have different rules in this area, so refer to the specific provincial law in effect where the employee is working.)

## Wrongful Leaving

Employees are also required to give reasonable notice upon leaving, although what constitutes reasonable notice is usually considerably less. Unless the employee is in a key position, such as senior executive or salesperson, it is usually not worth the effort to sue when an employee leaves without giving proper notice. But key employees may be required to give substantial notice just like employers. Employees are entitled to leave without notice if the employer commits a serious breach of contract first. So if the employer gives an unreasonable or dangerous order, if the working conditions are dangerous and the employer refuses to correct them, or if the employer involves the employee in illegal or immoral activities, the employee may be entitled to "quit."

**Employees can leave without notice if contract breached by employer first**

**Employees may be sued for breach of duty**

But in most cases, where former employees are sued, it is for breach of fiduciary duty or for disclosing confidential information. Ordinary employees do not have a fiduciary duty, and unless there is a valid restrictive covenant in their employment contract preventing them from doing so, they are free to compete with their former employer as soon as they leave.[19] That competition, however, must start after they leave. Employees cannot gather information, copy customer lists, or solicit customers before termination. If they do, they can be sued. Similarly, if the departing employee takes confidential information and misuses it, that conduct is also actionable.[20] Managers and other executives do have a fiduciary duty to their employer and may find themselves somewhat restricted in what they can do even after they leave their employment. It is much preferable for the employer to set out such restrictions clearly in the original employment contract.

---

18. S.O. 2000, c. 41, s. 56.

19. See *Gertz v. Meda Ltd.* (2002), 16 C.C.E.L. (3d) 79 (Ont. Sup. Ct. J.), where Gertz's wrongful-dismissal action succeeded whereas the employer's claims of breach of fiduciary duty and of confidentiality were dismissed. Gertz took certain knowledge about the industry and client needs with him, but the Court held that a mere employee's duty of fidelity to the employer ceases with termination of employment.

20. See *CRC-Evans Canada Ltd. v. Pettifer* (1997), 197 A.R. 24 (Q.B.); aff'd (1998), 216 A.R. 192 (C.A.), where two former, key employees set up a competing corporation and used confidential information from the former employer in bidding against that party. They were ordered to pay $305 507.72 in damages for breaching their duty to serve their employer honestly and faithfully, and for breach of their fiduciary duty.

## Case Summary 11.6

### Even Employees Can Be Required to Give Lengthy Notice:
### *Tree Savers International Ltd. v. Savoy*[21]

Savoy and Deringer were employees of Tree Savers, a relatively small company working in the oil industry. After giving Tree Savers' management two weeks' notice, they left and incorporated a company in competition with Tree Savers. Savoy and Deringer had been key employees at Tree Savers, and when they left they took some documents with them, including lists of contacts. Ducharme, who gave them financial aid and advice, and the company they created, Trojan, were also defendants. The Court had to decide whether Savoy and Deringer were in violation of their fiduciary duty to their former employer. The answer was yes, and an injunction was issued ordering them to stop their offending conduct. The Court decided that because the two men were senior key employees they should have given their employer 18 months' notice, and the damages awarded were calculated on this basis. Ducharme was also found liable for inducing them to breach their contract.

## Constructive Dismissal

When an employer demotes the employee or otherwise unilaterally changes the nature of the job, this may constitute constructive dismissal, and the employee can sue for wrongful dismissal. Sometimes this is done inadvertently; sometimes it is done in order to humiliate or make an employee uncomfortable so that the employee will voluntarily leave. But looking at this from a contractual perspective, one party cannot simply impose a change in the terms of a contract without first securing the consent or agreement of the other party. In essence, the employer is simply refusing to perform the original contract when it demotes an employee.

As with harassment or sexual harassment, even where the problems are caused by other employees the employer is still responsible, and this may constitute constructive dismissal. For example, in the *Stamos* case, where an employee suffered stress-related health issues as a result of another employee and resigned, the Court found that the employer's failure to defuse the hostile work environment constituted constructive dismissal.[22] Where there is constructive dismissal, the employee has an obligation to mitigate, possibly to the extent of accepting the new position offered by the employer. Of course, the employee is not obligated to accept such a position where it would cause undue humiliation or otherwise create an impossible working situation, especially if bad relations have been created because of the way the termination took place.

**Constructive dismissal— employer breaks contract when nature of job is changed without consent**

Promoting one employee is fine, but demoting another without cause may prompt a costly lawsuit. An employee may be constructively dismissed even when offered a comparable position. Consider the *Weselan* case,[23] where an employee was relocated and given a similar position. The new job, however, involved a substantial daily commute at cost of time and approximately $34 000 per year. This meant his working conditions and net remuneration would be substantially dif-

---

21. (1992), 120 A.R. 368 (C.A.).

22. *Stamos v. Annuity Research & Marketing Service Ltd.* (2002), 18 C.C.E.L. (3d) 117 (Ont. Sup. Ct. J.).

23. *Weselan v. Totten Sims Hubicki Associates (1997) Ltd.* (2001), 16 C.C.E.L. (3d) 184 (Ont. C.A.), varied on issue of costs, [2001] O.J. No. 5145 (Ont. C.A.).

ferent, so the employee was constructively dismissed. The law simply requires reasonable steps to be taken to mitigate damage. One does not have to suffer a substantial loss in order to mitigate damages.

### Remedies for Wrongful Dismissal

**Compensation based on notice that should have been given**

In a wrongful dismissal action, the damages awarded are usually based on what the employee would have received had proper notice been given. If a person is fired and is given only one month's notice when he should have received five months' notice, he will be awarded the difference, including any benefits and pension rights to which he would have been entitled. But the employee also has

**Obligation to mitigate losses**

an obligation to mitigate and so must try to find another job.[24] Any damages awarded will be reduced by what is earned from that other employment.[25] In rare circumstances the court will also take into account a person's damaged reputation or mental distress, and sometimes will even award punitive damages where appropriate. It is normally the employer, often a corporation, that is sued for wrongful dismissal, but the individual manager implementing the decision may also be sued where defamation or some other actionable wrong has taken place.

**Employer must have clear evidence of misconduct**

It is evident that great care must be exercised when dismissing an employee for incompetence or misconduct. An employer must have the clearest evidence of the misconduct or incompetence and with the latter must demonstrate that the employee has been given a reasonable opportunity to improve. Failure to substantiate just cause will likely result in a successful action by the employee for wrongful dismissal and may include an award of punitive damages and compensation for mental distress.

Damages are the appropriate remedy for wrongful dismissal, and it is rare for the court to order that an employee be given back the job. Reinstatement is more common when collective agreements are involved, where the decision is made by an arbitrator rather than a judge. Some statutes, such as the *Canada Labour Code*,[26] provide for reinstatement in non-union situations. Still, reinstatement is rare.

## Reducing **Risk** 11.2

Employers are often surprised to learn of the lengthy notice requirements for termination in Canada. Including specified notice entitlements in the contract of employment will go a long way to solving the problem. But when this is done, it is vital not to make that contracted notice period less than the minimum specified in the employment standards legislation of the province. Otherwise, the contract clause may be void and the employer required to pay a much higher amount calculated on the common law notice period.

Employers must avoid the temptation to manufacture reasons to justify dismissal without notice or to make the employee so uncomfortable they will quit. The courts today are much more willing to find constructive dismissal and assess higher damages if there is evidence of false statements, defamation, a poisoned work environment, and damage to the employee's reputation. The sensible way to approach the problem is to negotiate with the employee. Typically, the employee will settle for less when he realizes that he will avoid significant legal costs.

---

24. Efforts to mitigate damages need only be those expected of a reasonable person. See e.g. *Bradbury v. Newfoundland (Attorney General)* (2001), 207 Nfld. & P.E.I.R. 181 (Nfld. C.A.).

25. But see *E.C. & M. Electric Ltd. v. Alberta (Employment Standards Officer)* (1994), 7 C.C.E.L. (2d) 235 (Alta. Prov. Ct.). Whereas under common law a duty to mitigate exists, under Alberta's *Employment Standards Code*, no such duty is imposed on the employee. Money earned from other employment need not be deducted from the statutory severance pay.

26. R.S.C. 1985, c. L-2.

# Liability of Employer

Although not directly at fault, an employer can be held liable for torts committed by an employee during the course of employment. This is the principle of vicarious liability discussed in Chapter 4. Because the employer benefits from the work of the employee, the employer is held responsible for losses caused by the employee while working. The employer's liability is limited to those activities that take place during the course of employment. This includes not only incidents arising during working hours but also any conduct that takes place as part of the employment activity. If Pawluk, while delivering a letter to his employer's client on his way home, injures a pedestrian, both Pawluk and his employer would be liable. The negligent act occurred during the course of employment, even though it did not happen during working hours. But if Pawluk injures the pedestrian when he goes out to do his personal banking during working hours, the employer would not be liable. In this case, Pawluk is "on a frolic of his own," and the injury has not taken place in the course of his employment.

> **Employer liable for torts committed by employee while on the job**

As a general rule, there must be an employment relationship for vicarious liability. This is why the tests discussed above for determining whether an employment relationship exists are so important. (Some exceptions to this requirement will be discussed in the next chapter.) Several jurisdictions have legislated vicarious liability in special situations. For example, in Alberta, British Columbia, and some other provinces, the owner of a motor vehicle is vicariously liable for any torts committed by the person driving the vehicle with the owner's consent. The driver "is deemed to be the agent or servant of the owner of the motor vehicle and to be employed as such, and is deemed to be driving the motor vehicle in the course of that person's employment."[27] This section actually expands the potential liability of an employer that allows its employees to drive its vehicles, beyond the normal scope of vicarious liability. Under vicarious liability, the employer escapes liability if the employee negligently hurts the plaintiff while "on a frolic of his own." The statute, on the other hand, deems the driver to be driving in the course of his employment, whether he's driving for a job-related purpose or not. In the *Morad* case,[28] for example, the employer was held liable when an employee borrowed the company vehicle and then deliberately ran over some third party who owed him money!

> **Vicarious liability and motor vehicles**

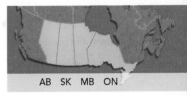

AB  SK  MB  ON

Although the employer has the right to turn to the employee for compensation when found vicariously liable, this is usually a hollow remedy, the employee being in no financial position to pay such compensation.

Employers often try to separate portions of their operations from the actual business they conduct. Cleaning and office management, as well as sales and product service, may be contracted out. This is done to reduce the number of employees, thereby reducing administrative costs, leaving the organization free to concentrate on what it does best. It may also reduce the risk of the employer being found vicariously liable when injuries take place. Avoiding vicarious liability is more likely when great care has been taken to make sure the people doing those jobs are truly independent. But even then, the courts may still find a sufficiently close relationship to impose vicarious liability on the employer for the wrongful acts committed by these supposedly independent workers. The risk of

---

27. *Highway Traffic Act*, R.S.A. 2000, c. H-8, s. 181. See also *Motor Vehicle Act*, R.S.B.C. 1996, c. 318, s. 86.

28. *Morad v. Emmanouel* (1993), 9 Alta. L.R. (3d) 378 (Q.B.).

such liability should be planned for in the operation of the business. Liability insurance is typically advisable.

# Legislation

As a consequence of the relatively weak position of individual employees in the employment relationship, employees have tended to band together to exert greater pressure on the employer. Such collective action is now governed by legislation and will be discussed under Collective Bargaining later in this chapter. A considerable amount of legislation has also been passed that is designed to protect employees, whether unionized or not, by setting minimum standards of safety, remuneration, hours of work, and other benefits. Conditions of employment normally fall under the provincial jurisdiction. Most provinces have concentrated their employee welfare legislation into one statute, generally called the *Employment Standards Act* or *Labour Standards Act*, which sets minimum standards in connection with:

- Wages
- Overtime, work hours, and rest periods
- Vacation and holiday entitlements
- Maternity and parental leave
- Termination and severance pay

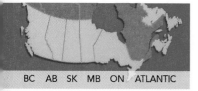

BC   AB   SK   MB   ON   ATLANTIC

**Both federal and provincial legislation apply**

Some also provide for bereavement and sick leave.

There are substantial differences in the details. For example, general minimum wage in Alberta in June 2003 was set at $5.90, whereas in neighbouring B.C. it was $8.00. Employment standards legislation varies with each jurisdiction. Consult this textbook's provincial supplement for specific information relevant to your particular jurisdiction.

But there are a number of activities, such as banking; the military; activities on Native reserves; the post office; telephone and broadcast companies; and airlines, railroads, and steamships that fall under federal jurisdiction. The employment relationship in those sectors is governed by the federal *Canada Labour Code*,[29] Part III sets out employment standards. Since it applies across the country, its provisions will be reviewed here to illustrate employment standards.

## Employment Standards

### Case Summary 11.7

**Statutory Notice May Not Suffice: *Machtinger v. HOJ Industries Ltd.*[30]**

This case involves two employees, Mr. Machtinger and Mr. Lefebvre, who were terminated from their employment with only four weeks' notice despite the fact that they both had been employed for a number of years. The notice given corresponded with the statutory minimum under the *Employment Standards Act*, even though their actual contracts required even less notice to be given. By the Court's determination, if common law applied they would be entitled to more than seven months' notice. Both employees brought a wrongful dismissal action against the

29. R.S. 1985, c. L-2.

30. [1992] 1 S.C.R. 986.

employer, demanding compensation. The problem for the Court was to decide whether the four weeks' notice was enough.

The Supreme Court of Canada held that any contractual term that did not comply with the minimum standards set out in the *Act* was a nullity, and therefore the minimal notice provisions found in the contract were void. The Court then observed that although the notice given satisfied the requirements of the *Employment Standards Act,* that was merely a minimum standard. Since common law required more than seven months' notice in such circumstances, that longer notice requirement prevailed. Complying with the statutory minimum was not good enough in this case.

Notice periods less than the common law standard can be set out in employment contracts, but unless they are more generous than the minimum statutory period they will be void. The employer will then have to comply with the longer "reasonable notice" provisions found in common law. The statutory provisions set a minimum standard, thus agreements that waive the protections or remedies available under this legislation may likewise be declared void. Where the parties have agreed to a higher standard, or where a higher standard is imposed by common law, that higher standard will normally prevail.[31] But even the minimum statutory provisions do not treat all employees equally. The government may exempt certain employments or modify certain provisions in respect of an employment. In other words, employers may be excused from paying minimum wage to managers or students, and overtime may be calculated differently for persons engaged in different lines of work. (Note that details as to payment of wages, minimum wage, deductions from pay, hours of work and overtime, vacation and holiday entitlements, maternity and parental benefits, employment of minors and bereavement and sick leave are located in this text's provincial supplements.)

**Statutes set out minimum standards**

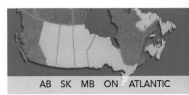

AB  SK  MB  ON  ATLANTIC

## Termination[32]

As under common law, the *Canada Labour Code* recognizes that no notice is required where the dismissal is for cause; otherwise, notice of termination is necessary. Where the *Code* and common law differ is in the remedies available for wrongful dismissal. The *Code* does not consider the nature of the employment, but only its length, when determining adequate notice and severance pay. Employees who have completed three months or more of continuous employment are to receive two weeks' notice of termination (except where the dismissal is for cause). Additionally, employees who have been employed for more than 12 months are entitled to severance pay of two days' wages for each completed year of service, plus five days' wages. The *Canada Labour Code* also provides that when a person has been laid off for a period longer than three months he may be able to treat this layoff as a termination and claim termination pay and severance pay. (There are exceptions, as where payments are made to the employee during the layoff.)

**Termination entitlements determined by length of service**

**Layoffs may trigger termination pay**

Most jurisdictions have passed similar legislation, but the provisions vary substantially; it is thus necessary to review the provisions of the relevant statute to determine the entitlements of a particular employee.

31. *Canada Labour Code*, R.S. 1985, c. L-2, s. 168. Note that similar provisions are found in provincial acts.

32. *Ibid.*, ss. 230–237.

## Issue Estoppel

Employees who face termination have a real concern. Case law makes it impera-
tive that employees seek legal advice before filing a complaint under employment
standards legislation. By simply applying for these minimal benefits, one may lose
the ability to later sue for damages for wrongful dismissal. If an employment standards officer or inspector determines that the complainant was terminated for
cause, not only will the complainant's claim for termination pay under the statute
fail, but also if the employee later tries to sue for damages for wrongful dismissal
the court may decide that the issue was already settled.[33] This is because the
employment standards officer or inspector has already decided that the termination was not wrongful. **Issue estoppel** may cause the court to dismiss the wrongful
dismissal suit altogether without even hearing the details. Such were the results in
the *Fayant* and *Wong* cases,[34] where the pleadings were struck out after issue estoppel was successfully raised.

**Choosing to file complaint
may later preclude ability
to sue**

## Complaints[35]

Rather than incur the costs of litigation, employment standards legislation
enables employees to file a complaint with the government, and then the investigation and determination is made by civil servants. Note that time limitations vary
between employment standards statutes and may well be as short as a few months.
Under the federal legislation the inspector may dismiss the complaint if it is
unfounded, but this determination may be appealed. If the inspector determines
that earnings are due to the employee, the inspector may order payment to be
made. If the employer is a corporation, the individual directors may be liable personally for up to six months' wages per employee.

## Human Rights

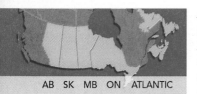

AB   SK   MB   ON   ATLANTIC

An area of employment law that is becoming much more significant is the area of
protection of employee rights. With the passage of the *Charter of Rights and
Freedoms,* as well as federal and provincial human rights legislation, employers are
required not only to ensure that they do not discriminate in their hiring and
employment practices but also to take active steps to ensure that these basic rights
are protected. Although the *Charter* does not apply directly to most employment
situations, it does have an important indirect effect, since federal and provincial
human rights statutes must be consistent with the provisions of the *Charter.*
Indeed, as mentioned in Chapter 1, the courts have gone so far as to read into
human rights statutes protection for homosexuals, where no such provision was
originally included.[36] Human rights legislation has an impact on employment by
prohibiting discrimination on the basis of race, national or ethnic origin, colour,
religion, gender, sexual orientation, and in some cases age, marital status, family
status, physical or mental disability, and pardoned criminal convictions.

**Federal and provincial
human rights legislation
prohibit most forms
of discrimination in
employment**

---

33. *Rasanen v. Rosemount Instruments Ltd.* (1994), 17 O.R. (3d) 267 (C.A.), leave to appeal to
S.C.C. refused, [1994] S.C.C.A. No. 152.

34. *Fayant v. Campbell's Maple Village Ltd.* (1993), 146 A.R. 175 (Q.B.); *Wong v. Shell Canada*
(1995), 174 A.R. 287 (C.A.), leave to appeal to S.C.C. refused, [1995] S.C.C.A. No. 551.

35. *Canada Labour Code*, ss. 251–260.

36. *Vriend v. Alberta*, [1998] 1 S.C.R. 493.

## Case Summary 11.8

### Fired Because of One's Relatives: *B. v. Ontario* (*Human Rights Commission*)[37]

A's employment was terminated when his wife confronted his boss, B, accusing B of sexually assaulting her daughter. In essence, A was fired because of who he was related to. A complaint was filed with the Ontario Human Rights Commission, alleging discrimination on the basis of family status and marital status. The Supreme Court of Canada later determined that these prohibited grounds were broad enough to include discrimination based on the identity of the complainant's spouse or family member. Since the complainant suffered differential treatment on the basis of a prohibited ground, discrimination was established.

Where violations occur, human rights tribunals have been established to hear complaints. These tribunals have the power to investigate, levy fines, and even order reinstatement of employees if they find that they have been terminated in violation of some human rights provision or forced to quit because of harassment.

**Tribunals hear complaints**

The *Canadian Human Rights Act,* for example, prohibits discrimination with regard to any term or condition of employment on the basis of person's race, religion, and so on. It specifically prohibits the refusal to hire or the firing of any person on the basis of one of the prohibited grounds.[38] For example, to discriminate against a woman because of pregnancy would constitute gender discrimination. Employers, thus, cannot fire or demote an employee because of pregnancy. Also, an employer's refusal to permit an employee to breastfeed in the workplace may constitute discrimination on the basis of gender.[39] Furthermore, employers should refrain from asking women at job interviews whether they are pregnant or plan to have children, for the legislation also addresses discrimination during pre-employment inquiries.

Job advertisements and application forms must be reviewed by employers to ensure that they do not directly or indirectly express a limitation or preference based on race, colour, gender, or other prohibited ground. The forms used cannot require an applicant to furnish information concerning their gender, age, marital status, and so on. Accordingly, unless a *bona fide* occupational requirement exists that would justify such an inquiry, employers should refrain from requesting photographs or requesting that the applicant's gender, previous name, marital status, date of birth, or religion be supplied in the application form.

Employers have an obligation to take steps to accommodate employees with disabilities.

Harassment is a form of discrimination that occurs when one subjects another person to unwelcome verbal or physical conduct because of their colour, gender,

**Harassment also covered**

---

37. (2000), 50 O.R. (3d) 737 (C.A.), affirmed, [2002] S.C.J. No. 67.

38. *Canadian Human Rights Act,* R.S.C. 1985, c. H-6, s. 7.

39. *Re Carewest and H.S.A.A. (Degagne)* (2001), 93 L.A.C. (4th) 129 (Alta.).

age, or other characteristic. Unwanted physical contact, jokes, or insults are harassment when they negatively affect the working environment. Note that interaction between supervisor/subordinates even outside the workplace can be employment-related harassment. If the supervisor's conduct creates a perception that continued employment is dependent on sexual interaction with that person, then that supervisor has engaged in harassment.[40] Sexual harassment is just one example. Even when the harassment comes from other employees, the employer can be held responsible if it has failed to take adequate steps to protect the employee. It is, thus, vital for employers to be proactive and to take positive steps to develop anti-harassment and anti-discrimination policies, clarifying that such conduct will not be tolerated. These policies should also spell out what disciplinary steps might be taken.

### Case Summary 11.9

#### Should the Employer Be Liable? *Robichaud v. Canada (Treasury Board)*[41]

The Supreme Court of Canada had to determine whether the employer was responsible for the sexual harassment committed by another employee. Mrs. Robichaud worked as a lead hand in a cleaning operation for the Department of National Defence, and a supervisor subjected her to unwanted sexual attention. Such behaviour amounts to discrimination on the basis of gender because it differentiates adversely against an employee on the basis of her gender. The Court also found that the employer, under the *Canadian Human Rights Act*, was liable for the discriminatory acts of its employees that were committed in the course of their employment, much like vicarious liability in common law. The case indicates the approach taken by courts when faced with sexual harassment.

In fact, this precedent has been followed when applying provincial legislation to instances of sexual harassment. In the *Katsiris* case,[42] the corporation owning the restaurant was held liable for the harassment committed by its employee. That case also addressed whether the CEO of the corporation should be personally liable. Since it was not shown that he knew of the sexual harassment, liability was not imposed on him personally. Should officers be held liable as well as the corporate employer? What factors should a court consider in these cases?

**Duty to accommodate**

This positive obligation on the employer to protect employees from wrongful conduct of others in the workplace has been taken further. Employers now have an obligation to take steps to accommodate employees with disabilities and special needs. This may extend to changing the physical work environment to accommodate the visually impaired or wheelchair-bound or to allow workers with chronic illness, such as AIDS, or partial disability, to do lighter work or work only part-time.[43] Schedules may require adjustment to accommodate different religious holidays, so long as the request does not cause the employer undue hardship.[44]

---

40. *Simpson v. Consumers' Association of Canada* (2001), 57 O.R. (3d) 351 (C.A.), leave to appeal to S.C.C. refused, [2002] S.C.C.A. No. 83.

41. [1987] 2 S.C.R. 84.

42. *Katsiris v. Isaac* (2001), 204 Sask. R. 52 (Q.B.).

43. See the updated Canadian Human Rights Commission Policy on HIV/AIDS, online: Canadian Human Rights Commission **http://www.chrc-ccdp.ca/Legis&Poli/aids-sida.asp?=E**.

44. See *Ontario (Human Rights Commission) v. Roosma* (2002), 21 C.C.E.L. (3d) 112 (Ont. Sup. Ct. J.), where releasing employees from Friday night shifts to accommodate these employees' religious beliefs would cause undue hardship. Such accommodation was therefore waived.

Employers may find their rules being challenged as discriminatory. Rules requiring employees to be of a certain stature may discriminate against certain racial groups. Rules requiring uniforms or hard hats to be worn may discriminate against certain religious groups. These rules may, however, be saved if the employer establishes them to be *bona fide* (or genuine) occupational requirements. The hard-hat rule may prevail, even if it violates a religious right to wear a turban, if safety concerns justify its use. But for the requirement to be a *bona fide* one, it must relate to a necessary part of the job. Also, where the rule adversely affects a particular group the employer must take reasonable steps to accommodate the disadvantaged group.

## Case Summary 11.10

### Duty to Accommodate and Adverse-effect Discrimination: *Meiorin* [45]

This is a leading case for determining whether a particular occupational requirement is reasonable and justifiable. Here, Ms. Meiorin, who worked as a firefighter, failed a running test designed to measure aerobic fitness; consequently, she was terminated after three years of service. Minimum fitness standards for firefighters had been introduced by the government. The issue before the arbitrator was whether the running test component was discriminatory on the basis of gender, as it measured aerobic capacity and women have lower aerobic capacity than men, despite training. It was argued that this amounted to *adverse-effect discrimination* against Ms. Meiorin. This type of discrimination involves a *generally applicable rule* that has a *particular adverse effect* on one group (women) because of a prohibited ground (their gender). In these circumstances, where a rule is shown to have a discriminatory effect, the employer can continue to apply the rule only if it is justifiable as a *bona fide* occupational requirement.

The Supreme Court of Canada enunciated a three-part test to evaluate if an occupational requirement (meeting the fitness standard) is justified. In fact, the Supreme Court stated that the categorization of discrimination as adverse effect or direct effect was no longer appropriate and substituted a three-step test. Once the complainant shows that the standard is discriminatory, the employer must prove:

**1.** that there is a rational connection between the test and performance of the job;

**2.** that the test was adopted under an honest and good-faith belief that the standard was necessary; and

**3.** that the standard is reasonably necessary to accomplish the employer's legitimate purpose. This implies that the employer may need to show that it is impossible to accommodate the employee without the employer suffering undue hardship.

The test requires employers to accommodate different members' capabilities before adopting a "standard" or occupational requirement. Before setting the aerobic standard, and setting it so high that most women cannot attain it, it must be shown that such a level of aerobic capacity is necessary to do the job. If it is unnecessary, then the standard cannot be saved as a genuine or *bona fide* occupational requirement.

---

45. *British Columbia (Public Service Employee Relations Commission) v. British Columbia Government and Service Employees' Union (B.C.G.S.E.U.)*, [1999] 3 S.C.R. 3.

No credible evidence was shown to establish that the prescribed aerobic capacity was necessary for either men or women to perform the work of a forest firefighter. The employer also failed to show that it would experience undue hardship if a different standard were used. Accordingly, reinstatement of the claimant was ordered, and she was compensated for her lost benefits and wages. This case underscores the need to be vigilant in setting occupational standards or requirements, for they may be challenged if they have a discriminatory impact on a particular individual or group. What about requiring employees to wear a particular uniform—say, a hat that prevents individuals from wearing turbans? Can such rules be similarly challenged? What arguments can be advanced by either side? How would a court rule in light of this precedent?

**Pay equity**

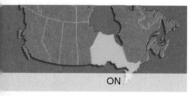

ON

Some jurisdictions have passed **pay equity** statutes requiring equal pay for work of equal value.[46] These provisions usually benefit women, who have traditionally been paid less than men for similar jobs, but they may place considerable hardship on the organization that must bear the extra expense. Most notably, in the *Public Service Alliance of Canada* case,[47] the federal government was required to pay more than $3.3 billion to some 230 000 current and former employees for 13 years' back pay with interest! The Canadian Human Rights Tribunal ruled that the federal government had failed to abide by section 11 of the *Canadian Human Rights Act* by allowing a wage gap between men and women doing clerical work—work of equal value.

**Correction of past imbalance**

Discrimination in the workplace has prompted the passage of various **employment equity** acts as well.[48] Organizations may be required to take steps to correct employment situations where there has been a tradition of racial or gender imbalance, such as in nursing and engineering. This usually means giving preferential treatment to those job applicants or candidates who belong to underrepresented minority groups. The resulting **reverse discrimination** directed at individuals in the overrepresented group is also distasteful. Programs that are intended to correct these historical imbalances in the workplace are sometimes called **affirmative action** and are specifically authorized under section 15(2) of the *Charter of Rights and Freedoms*.

**Mandatory retirement at 65 permitted**

**Mandatory retirement** also raises human rights issues. Forced retirement at 65 years is often justified as good social policy, opening up new jobs for the youth. But from the point of view of the retiree, it can be a disaster. Although discrimination in employment on the basis of age is usually prohibited, retirement at 65 years is generally exempted in provincial employment standards or human rights statutes. Where "age" is defined as being 18 or older and less than 65, one who faces age discrimination in the form of forced retirement at age 65 may have no remedy. The Supreme Court of Canada has held that where such a mandatory retirement policy is allowed under provincial human rights legislation it does not violate the provisions of the *Charter of Rights and Freedoms*, being a reasonable exception under section 1.[49] But if an employer tries to impose a retirement policy commencing at a younger age (for example, 60 for firefighters) it can be

46. *Canadian Human Rights Act*, R.S.C. 1985, c. H-6, s.11.

47. *P.S.A.C. v. Canada (Treasury Board)*, [2000] 1 F.C. 146 (T.D.).

48. For example, see *Employment Equity Act*, S.C. 1995, c. 44.

49. *Dickason v. University of Alberta*, [1992] 2 S.C.R. 1103.

saved only if the employer establishes the policy as being justifiable in the circumstances of its workplace.[50]

As the rules with respect to discrimination in employment change, employers should be particularly vigilant in developing policies that give same-sex couples the same benefits as others, that accommodate disabled workers, and that prevent the various forms of harassment that can take place in the workplace.

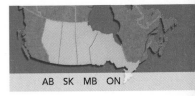

## Workers' Compensation[51]

Common law was often unable to provide an appropriate remedy for an employee injured on the job. This was especially true when the accident resulted from the employee's own carelessness. All provinces and the federal government have enacted workers' compensation legislation that provides a compulsory insurance program covering accidents that take place on the job.[52] The legislation sets rates of compensation to be paid for different types of injuries and establishes a board that hears and adjudicates the claims of injured employees. The system is essentially a no-fault insurance scheme, in which benefits are paid to injured workers, or to their families in the event of death, and careless conduct on the part of the worker will not disqualify an injured employee from receiving compensation. The program is financed by assessments levied by the provincial workers' compensation boards against the employers; the amount levied varies with the risks associated with the industry involved. Some employees, such as casual workers, farmers, and small business employees, are often excluded, but British Columbia has extended workers' compensation coverage to almost all workers in the province.

**Worker's compensation compulsory insurance coverage**

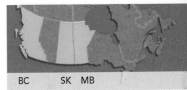

A significant aspect of workers' compensation legislation in most jurisdictions is that the worker gives up the right to any other compensation. The worker can no longer sue the employer (or the party who caused the injury, if he also contributed to the plan), being limited to the benefits bestowed by the workers' compensation system.

**Worker gives up right to any other compensation and cannot sue**

Compensation is also limited to injury or disease that arises in the course of the employment. This can sometimes be a problem where it is difficult to establish that a disease, such as emphysema or a heart condition, was caused by the work of the employee. Compensation is typically paid to the employee, but where an employee dies as a result of injuries sustained on the job, payments are to be made to her dependants,[53] which may include same-sex partners.[54]

## Health and Safety

Related to workers' compensation legislation, in that they work to reduce compensation claims, are statutes controlling health and safety conditions in the workplace. Health and safety requirements are sometimes embodied in general

**Provision of safe workplace**

50. See: Policy on Discrimination Against Older Persons Because of Age, online: Ontario Human Rights Commission **www.ohrc.on.ca/english/publications/age-policy.shtml**.

51. Further information on workers' compensation in Canada is available through the Association of Workers' Compensation Boards of Canada, online: **http://www.awcbc.org**.

52. See, for example, Alberta's *Workers' Compensation Act*, R.S.A. 2000, c. W-15, *Workers' Compensation Regulation*, Alta. Reg. 323/2002. The federal legislation is entitled the *Government Employees Compensation Act*, R.S.C. 1985, c. G-5.

53. *Government Employees Compensation Act*, R.S.C. 1985, c. G-5, s. 4.

54. For example, see *Workplace Safety and Insurance Act, 1997*, S.O. 1997, c. 16, s. 22.

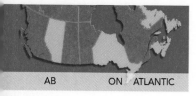

AB    ON  ATLANTIC

labour statutes, as in the *Canada Labour Code*.[55] Some jurisdictions deal with health and safety in a separate statute, as in Ontario's *Occupational Health and Safety Act*.[56] The main thrust of these statutes and their related regulations[57] is to:

**1.** Provide safer working conditions, by requiring fencing of hazardous areas, safety netting, proper shielding of equipment, environmental control, and so on.

**2.** Ensure safe employment practices, such as requiring the supply and use of hard hats, goggles, and protective clothing.

**3.** Establish programs to educate both the employer and the employee on how to create a safer working environment for all concerned.

**Safety boards ensure regulations are adhered to**

These objectives are facilitated through the establishment of a board with the power to hear complaints and enforce correction. Officers are empowered to enter the workplace without a warrant, and when they encounter dangerous conditions (such as lack of fencing or shielding), poor safety practices (such as failure to use hard hats or safety lines), or environmental contamination (caused by hazardous chemicals, fumes, or dust), they can order the problem corrected or can shut the job site down altogether. The offending business can be prosecuted for violations, especially where injury or death results. These provisions are effective only if the fines are significant, and Ontario, for example, has increased the maximum fines levied and extended liability to make directors of corporations personally responsible for harmful and dangerous practices.

## Employment Insurance

**Employment insurance is federal jurisdiction**

The federal government was given jurisdiction over insurance coverage for unemployed workers by an amendment to the *Constitution Act (1867)* in 1940.[58] Under the *Employment Insurance Act,* both employers and employees pay into a government-supplemented fund,[59] and laid-off employees are entitled to receive payments for a specific period of time. This is not a fund where the employee is entitled to get back what he has contributed. Rather, the payments are insurance premiums, and an employee is entitled to receive only what is set out in the statute and regulations. This amount is based on the number of weeks worked before the claim and the amount of wages received. Workers who voluntarily leave their employment or are involved in a strike or lockout are generally not entitled to receive employment insurance benefits. Those who cannot work because others are on strike will receive benefits, provided they otherwise qualify. A severance package from the employer will also limit eligibility, and no benefits will be paid until the severance period is over. Benefits are also paid under the *Employment Insurance Act* to those who are unable to work because of illness or disability and due to pregnancy and adoption. Workers may appeal any decisions made, such as entitlement to benefits, to an administrative body set up under the legislation. The rights of individuals before such administrative tribunals were discussed in Chapter 3.

**Employee must meet qualifications to receive benefits**

---

55. R.S. 1985, c. L-2, Part II.

56. R.S.O. 1990, c. O.1

57. These statutes are supplemented by numerous regulations, such as Alberta's *Chemical Hazards Regulation*, Alta. Reg. 393/88, and *Noise Regulation*, Alta. Reg. 314/81.

58. *Constitution Act, 1940*, 3-4 Geo. VI, c. 36 (U.K.).

59. *Employment Insurance Act*, S.C. 1996, c. 23.

## Reducing **Risk** 11.3

Adhering to the employment standards legislation and dealing with government regulatory bodies can impose considerable hardship on employers, straining their management resources. Dealing with health and safety and workers' compensation issues are a fact of life, and enforcement provisions usually put enough pressure on the employer so that there is adherence. The same is true with employment insurance and taxation. But human rights standards, including provisions against direct and indirect discrimination and harassment, as well as employment standards, such as minimum wage, hours of work, overtime, holidays, maternity leave, and so on, are usually only enforced when someone makes a complaint. Employees who want to keep their jobs usually do not make such complaints. These complaints then come after the fact, often after the employee or group of employees have been working in those conditions, sometimes for years. Penalties imposed can be significant. Ideally, the employer will develop carefully crafted policies and develop training for all, especially those in key decision-making positions, to make sure that these pitfalls are avoided. When jobs are advertised and potential employees interviewed, great care should be taken to avoid stating qualifications or asking questions that could be construed as discriminatory. Questions relating to a person's place of birth, race, religion, age, language, arrest history, gender, sexual preference, child care arrangements, marital status, or medications being taken should be avoided. Care should also be taken to avoid practices that could be considered discriminatory in promotions, benefits, and bonuses. Clear policies, designed to prevent harassment or discrimination by other employees, should be designed and implemented, with the policy and penalties being made clear to all.

## Other Legislation

Many other statutes affect the employment relationship. Most jurisdictions have legislation controlling the apprenticeship process and trade schools.[60] Pension benefits are controlled by legislation. Some jurisdictions have legislation controlling the licensing of private employment agencies and restricting the types of payments they can receive from their clients. And, as has been discussed in other chapters, legislation such as the *Bankruptcy and Insolvency Act* and the *Mechanics'* or *Builders' Lien Acts* provide security to the worker in the payment of wages. All jurisdictions have legislation dealing with special categories of employees, such as teachers and public servants.

## Collective Bargaining

A significant portion of the legislation affecting employment relates to the collective bargaining process. But because the percentage of unionized workers in Canada has declined over the past few decades, those laws have changed in response to the diminished political strength of the unions. Trade unions today are fighting to hold onto what they have gained and resisting the further weakening of their position. Since the time of the industrial revolution in the United Kingdom, workers have banded together in an attempt to overcome poor working conditions and low wages. A considerable amount of confrontation and violence flared up between unions and employers, especially at the point in time when the unions first attempted to organize or unionize the workforce. In North America, earlier governments and courts treated efforts to organize workers as criminal conspiracies, and the activists were severely punished.

**Consequence of weaker unions**

Over the years, trade unions gained grudging acceptance, if not respectability, and legislation passed in the first half of the 20th century allowed them to play an increasingly significant role in the economy. The first important piece of legislation passed by the United States Congress in 1935 was known as the *National*

**Legislation designed to reduce conflict**

---

60. For example, see Alberta's *Apprenticeship and Industry Training Act*, R.S.A. 2000, c. A-42.

*Labor Relations Act* or the *Wagner Act*.[61] The Act reduced conflict by recognizing an employee's right to be a member of a union and eliminating the employer's power to interfere in any way with the organizational process. A trade union successful in persuading more than 50 percent of the employees to join was recognized as the official bargaining agent for all the employees in that workforce. The employer was then required to negotiate with the trade union in good faith. The primary objectives of the *Wagner Act* were to promote labour peace and to give some stability and structure to the field of labour relations in the United States.

## Legislation

**Canada followed example of American legislation**

After a considerable amount of labour strife in Canada, the federal government passed the *Wartime Labour Relations Regulations* by an order-in-council.[62] This order incorporated most of the provisions set out in the *Wagner Act*, and after the war, most Canadian provinces added the provisions of this federal regulation to their provincial statutes. The Canadian legislation, in addition to controlling **recognition disputes** (disputes arising between unions and employers during the organization process), included provisions that reduced conflict in interest disputes and rights disputes. An **interest dispute** is a disagreement between the union and employer about what terms to include in their collective agreement. A **rights dispute** is a disagreement over the meaning or interpretation of a provision included in a collective agreement. Another type of dispute that can arise is a **jurisdictional dispute**, which is a dispute between two unions over which one should represent a particular group of employees or over which union members ought to do a particular job. For example, should carpenters or steel workers put up metal-stud walls in an office building? The employer is usually caught in the middle in jurisdictional disputes and has little power to affect the situation.

**Types of disputes—recognition, interest, rights, jurisdiction**

**Both federal and provincial legislations cover collective bargaining**

The federal collective bargaining legislation is embodied in the *Canada Labour Code*.[63] This legislation covers those industries over which the federal government has jurisdiction, such as railroads, shipping, air transportation, broadcasting, and dock work. Each provincial government has passed collective bargaining legislation covering sectors over which it has jurisdiction. These acts are variously called *Labour Codes, Trade Union Acts, Labour Relations Acts, Industrial Relations Acts*, and *Labour Acts*. The statutes cover most labour relations situations arising within the jurisdiction of the provinces as set out in section 92 of the *Constitution Act (1867)*. Some types of activities, such as public services, schools, and hospitals, have unique federal or provincial legislation specifically designed to cover labour relations within that industry.[64]

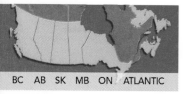

BC   AB   SK   MB   ON   ATLANTIC

**Labour tribunals regulate process**

In all jurisdictions, special labour relations boards have been established to deal with disputes associated with the collective bargaining process. These bodies take the place of courts. It is important to remember that although they quite often look and act like courts, they are not. Rather, they are part of the executive branch of government, and as such, they can be used as an instrument of government policy. Labour relations boards have the advantage of expertise in labour

---

61. (1935), 49 Stat. 449.

62. 1944, P.C. 1003. (Because of the war emergency, the federal government had the power to pass general legislation for Canada.)

63. R.S.C. 1985, c. L-2.

64. See, for example, Alberta's *Public Service Employee Relations Act*, R.S.A. 2000, c. P-43.

matters. Resolution of disputes by such tribunals is usually accomplished quicker than would be the case in the courts. Administrative tribunals are discussed in more detail in Chapter 3.

Important questions arise with respect to union membership, collective bargaining, and the *Charter of Rights and Freedoms*. Is there a constitutional right to belong to a union, to strike, or even to bargain collectively? Earlier, the Supreme Court of Canada held that there was not. These rights had been created by statute, and the limitations imposed by government were held not to have violated section 2(d) of the *Charter* guaranteeing freedom of association. However, recent case law suggests a different direction has been taken by the Court.

**No constitutional right to belong to a union**

## Case Summary 11.11

### Agricultural Workers Strike at the Government: *Dunmore v. Ontario (Attorney General)*[65]

In 1994, the NDP Ontario government enacted the *Agricultural Labour Relations Act (ALRA)*, giving collective bargaining rights to agricultural workers. When the Progressive Conservative government then repealed the *ALRA* in 1995, it effectively excluded agricultural workers' rights both under the repealed *ALRA* and the *Labour Relations Act (LRA)* of the province. Section 3(b) of the *LRA* provides: "This Act does not apply to a person employed in agriculture, hunting or trapping." Agricultural workers claimed that the statute repealing the *ALRA* and the resultant exclusion from the *LRA* infringed their freedom of association guaranteed by section 2(d) of the *Charter*. The Supreme Court of Canada agreed.

The *LRA* was to safeguard the exercise of the right to associate, not parcel it out to some classes of workers, excluding others. An argument could be made that by allowing some workers, but not all, to associate violated equality rights protected by section 15 of the *Charter*. The Court, however, preferred to deal with the constitutional challenge by focusing on section 2(d). Without the protective regime of either the *ALRA* or the *LRA*, agricultural workers would not be able to organize. Accordingly, section 3(d) of the *LRA* and the statutory provisions repealing the *ALRA* were both found unconstitutional. The violation of section 2(d) being significant, the Court decided it could not be justified under section 1. Although the Supreme Court did not declare that provinces *must* pass legislation that protects the freedom of association, the decision does require the statutory freedom to organize. By specifying that agricultural workers could not organize under the *LRA*, unless a statute like the *ALRA* was put in place, agricultural workers' freedom to associate would effectively be curtailed.

Labour rights have been gained politically and political action must be relied on to retain them. Relying on the courts to advance these rights is a gamble. As it currently stands, section 2(b) of the *Charter*, guaranteeing freedom of expression, protects picketing to some extent.

Canadian labour statutes vary considerably from jurisdiction to jurisdiction. Reference herein will generally be made to the federal legislation that has application across the country. Province-specific information is available in the provincial supplements.

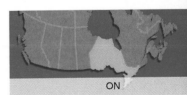

ON

---

65. [2001] 3 S.C.R. 1016.

# Organization of Employees

## Certification

While in some Canadian jurisdictions it is possible for employers to voluntarily recognize a trade union as the bargaining agent for their employees, the most common method of union recognition in Canada results from the certification process adopted from the *Wagner Act* of 1935. For a union to obtain certification as the **bargaining agent** for a group of employees, referred to as the **bargaining unit**, it must apply to the appropriate labour relations board for certification and satisfy the board that a certain percentage of the workforce are members of the union.

Under the *Canada Labour Code* if the applicant can show that 50 percent of the workforce has joined the union, it can apply for and shall receive certification. If the union has less than 50 percent support, but more than 35 percent, a representation vote is then held, and a majority vote supporting the union is necessary for it to obtain certification. In some provinces, the labour relations boards also have the power to certify without a vote, but the union must show that it has the support of a greater portion of the workforce.

**Certification of bargaining unit adopted from *Wagner Act***

**Majority of workers must be members of union**

## Bargaining Agent

Once certified, the trade union has exclusive bargaining authority for the employees it represents, and a unionized employee loses the right to negotiate personally with the employer. The resulting contract between union and employer is binding on all the employees in the designated unit. It is important, therefore, to determine whether the workforce the trade union intends to represent is an appropriate bargaining unit before certification is granted. Labour relations boards discourage bargaining units that are either too small or too large or that contain groups of employees with conflicting interests. Management employees are, thus, excluded. Also, to obtain certification, the trade union cannot be guilty of any discriminatory practices. A union that has applied for certification and has failed must wait a specified period before trying again.[66]

**Only union has right to bargain for employees**

## Unfair Labour Practices

The primary objective of labour legislation is to create an orderly process for the organization and recognition of trade unions, eliminating the conflict that often takes place in such circumstances. Prohibited unfair labour practices include threats or coercion of employees by either the union or management. For example, in the *Convergys* case,[67] the employer implemented a policy prohibiting disclosure of employee contact information to union organizers, and threatened dismissal for violating this policy. Surveillance cameras, positioned near the entry to the workplace, enabled the employer to monitor union organizers' activities. Further, a security guard was posted at the entrance whenever union officials appeared to hand out leaflets. The employer was ordered to stop these unfair labour practices and to schedule paid staff meetings where the union could meet with staff, without employer surveillance.

**Rules of conduct reduce conflict**

---

66. Each jurisdiction may specify a different waiting period. In Alberta, for example, the period is 90 days. See *Labour Relations Code*, R.S.A. 2000, c. L-1, s. 57.

67. *Re Convergys Customer Management Canada Inc.*, [2003] B.C.L.R.B.D. No. 62 (BCLRB).

The employer cannot threaten dismissal for joining a trade union or require that an employee refrain from joining a trade union as a condition of employment. Once the organization process has begun in most provinces, the employer cannot change conditions or terms of employment in order to influence the bargaining process. In some jurisdictions, in face of such an unfair labour practice, if the labour relations board concludes that a vote would not reflect the true feelings of the employees, it can grant certification without a vote. This is rarely done and will take place only where there is clear evidence of intimidation interfering with the reliability of the voting process.

Requiring that an employer not coerce or intimidate employees does not eliminate the employer's right to state his or her views during the electioneering process that precedes a certification vote. Freedom of expression as set out in the *Charter of Rights and Freedoms* requires that as long as such statements are merely statements of opinion or fact and do not amount to threat or coercion, they are permitted. But it is an unfair labour practice for an employer to participate in, or interfere with, the formation or administration of a labour union. Consequently, employers cannot contribute financially or otherwise provide support to a labour union, undermining the independence of the union.

Trade unions, even in the process of organizing the workers, do not have the right to trespass on the employer's property or to organize during the employees' work time. However, employers will sometimes allow this so that they can at least know what is going on. Once the trade union has successfully completed the certification process, it becomes the certified bargaining agent for all the employees in the bargaining unit, and the employer must recognize it as such and bargain with it. The trade union can then serve notice on the employer requiring the commencement of collective bargaining. Employers often wish to join together to bargain collectively with a trade union. In some jurisdictions, such **employers' organizations** can also be certified (or designated to be the "employer" authorized to bargain with the union),[68] creating bargaining agents that are stronger and better able to negotiate with large unions on behalf of their members. These employers' organizations are usually found where there are a number of small employers, such as in the construction industry. In a similar fashion, local trade union organizations are often affiliated with much larger, parent unions which strengthen the local bargaining units by providing funds to support a prolonged strike and making available research and other expertise to assist in negotiations.

Unfair labour practices are not limited to the organization process. It remains vitally important to ensure that the union remains independent from employer domination even after certification and to ensure that it can carry on its union activities free from harassment by the employer.

**Threats, coercion, dismissal —unfair labour practices**

**In some provinces, unfair labour practices can result in certification without vote**

**Employer retains right of free speech**

**Employer organizations help employers bargain with unions**

## Bargaining

### Collective Agreements

Once a union is certified as the bargaining agent for the bargaining unit, that trade union has exclusive authority to bargain on behalf of the employees in the unit. Employees can no longer strike their "own deal" with the employer. In a

68. *Canada Labour Code*, R.S.C. 1985, c. L-2, s. 33.

recent Ontario decision,[69] the Board found that an employer program, designed to reward good performance by awarding non-cash gifts, violated the collective agreement (compensation above scheduled wage) and breached the requirement that the employer recognize the union as the exclusive bargaining agent. By unilaterally implementing this program, the employer was compensating select employees above the wage scales set in the collective agreement. This interfered with the union's exclusive right to negotiate matters of wages, benefits, and other terms of employment.

**Either party can give notice to commence collective bargaining**

Any time after a trade union is certified, either party can give notice, requiring bargaining to commence, usually within 10 to 20 days,[70] depending on the jurisdiction. In those situations where the union has been certified for some time and a collective agreement is already in place, this notice cannot be given until shortly before the expiration of the old agreement, usually three to four months.[71]

**Parties must bargain in good faith**

Once this notice has been given, the parties are required to bargain or negotiate with each other, and in most jurisdictions, the bargaining must be "**in good faith**." Whatever the term means, the parties must at least meet with a willingness to explore compromises and try to find an area of agreement. It does not mean that either party has to agree to the other's terms. Some provinces have adopted the wording used in the federal legislation, requiring the parties to make "every reasonable effort" to reach an agreement.[72]

### Case Summary 11.12

**Employer Must Bargain in Good Faith:** *Royal Oak Mines Inc. v. Canada (Labour Relations Board)*[73]

The employer operated a mine in the Northwest Territories and put forward an offer to contract with its unionized employees. The offer was rejected, and a bitter 18-month strike followed in which a number of workers died. Some employees were dismissed, and the company, when pressured as part of the eventual settlement package to at least provide for due process in the dismissals, steadfastly refused. After attempts at mediation, an industrial inquiry commission, and intervention by the Minister of Labour, there was still no settlement to the strike. The union went to the Canadian Labour Relations Board, complaining that the employer failed to bargain in good faith. The Board agreed. It ordered the employer to renew the original offer made before the strike. The employer refused and appealed the Board's decision. The Supreme Court of Canada upheld the Labour Relations Board's right to find that the employer had not bargained in good faith and upheld their right to impose the settlement.

But should a board be able to force an offer to be re-tabled? If so, isn't the board indirectly imposing terms into the eventual collective agreement? The Supreme Court of Canada held that if there is a requisite nexus or connection between the terms imposed and the breach of good faith bargaining duty, specific terms can be so imposed.

69. See *Re Toronto Hydro and Canadian Union of Public Employees, Local 1* (2002), 103 L.A.C. (4th) 289 (Ontario).

70. Twenty days under federal legislation, *Canada Labour Code*, R.S.C. 1985, c. L-2, s. 50.

71. Four months under federal legislation, *Ibid.*, s. 49.

72. *Ibid.*, s. 50.

73. [1996] 1 S.C.R. 369. See also *Allsco Building Products Ltd. v. United Food and Commercial Workers International Union, Local 1288P,* [2000] N.B.J. No. 6 (C.A.), which followed this decision.

## Ratification

Once a bargain has been reached, it is presented to the union membership and, where appropriate, to the employer's board or to an employer's organization for ratification. When both sides ratify, there is a binding collective agreement. The agreement is a contract, but because of the modifying legislation, it must be viewed as a special form of contract with unique features, such as the method of its enforcement. In most jurisdictions, while bargaining is proceeding the employer is not permitted to change the terms and conditions of the employment, such as wages, benefits, or hours of work.[74] When it is clear that the parties cannot reach an agreement, it is possible in some jurisdictions for the Labour Relations Board to impose a first contract, although this option is seldom used.[75]

**Agreement must be ratified**

## Mediation (Conciliation)

Mediation, sometimes called conciliation, has been provided for in the various Canadian jurisdictions. When negotiations begin to break down, either party has the right to apply to the appropriate government agency for the appointment of a **conciliator**[76] or **mediator**. This person then meets with the two parties and assists them in their negotiations. The hope is that communications between the two parties will be greatly facilitated by this third-person go-between. The parties are prohibited from taking more drastic forms of action, such as strike or lockout, as long as a conciliator/mediator is involved in the negotiations.

**Mediation assists negotiation process**

Some provinces provide for a two-tiered process of conciliation, with first a single officer and subsequently a conciliation board consisting of three mediators, but the function is essentially the same. Federally, the Minister must choose between appointing a single conciliator or establishing a conciliation board.[77] It is only after the conciliator or conciliation board have removed themselves from the process, by booking out of the dispute and by filing a report, that the parties are allowed to proceed to strike or lockout. In some jurisdictions, conciliation is a prerequisite to strike or lockout.[78] Although conciliators have no authority to bind the parties, they do have the power to make recommendations that will be embarrassing to an unreasonable party. Note that in many jurisdictions, a conciliator can be imposed on the parties by the Labour Relations Board, even when neither party has requested one.[79]

Under federal legislation, the parties can choose to take to an arbitrator any matter respecting renewal, revision, or the entry into a new collective agreement.[80] Arbitration differs from conciliation in that the arbitrator does have the power to make a decision binding on the parties. Alternatively, legislation may empower labour relations boards to impose a first contract where the parties themselves cannot reach an agreement.[81]

74. *Canada Labour Code*, R.S.C. 1985, c. L-2, s. 50(b).

75. *Ibid.*, s. 80; *Labour Relations Code*, R.S.B.C. 1996, c. 244, s. 55; *Labour Relations Act, 1995*, S.O. 1995, c. 1, s. 43.

76. *Canada Labour Code*, R.S.C. 1985, c. L-2, s. 50(b).

77. *Ibid.*, s. 72.

78. *Ibid.*, s. 89.

79. *Ibid.*, s. 72(2).

80. *Ibid.*, s. 79.

81. *Ibid.*, s. 80.

# Contract Terms

**Contract must be for at least one year**

The completed collective agreement must satisfy certain requirements, such as having a term of at least one year. If the parties have placed no time limit on the agreement, it will be deemed to be for one year.[82] Where the labour relations board has settled the terms of the collective agreement, its term will be for two years.[83] Collective agreements may have an automatic renewal clause so that if no notice to bargain is given at the appropriate time, the contract will automatically be renewed, usually for another year. Retroactivity is generally a matter to be negotiated by the parties; but if the new collective agreement is to apply retroactively, any changes in terms (such as a new rate of pay) will take effect from the date the old agreement expired. The parties often do not reach an agreement until well after the old collective agreement expires. If the new one then takes effect retroactively, even with this one-year minimum requirement in effect, the new contract will last only a few months. It can be readily seen why every province has taken the approach that any agreement for a period shorter than one year is unworkable.

## Arbitration

**Interpretation of contract disputes to be arbitrated through grievance process**

All collective agreements must contain provisions for the settlement of disputes arising under the agreement. This is usually accomplished through a **grievance procedure** ultimately leading to arbitration. The contract will set out a process involving a series of structured meetings where the parties can negotiate a settlement. When no settlement can be reached, the matter is submitted to an arbitrator (or panel of arbitrators), who will hold a hearing and make a decision that is binding on both parties. This grievance process is used to resolve disputes not only over the interpretation of the contract provisions but also as a response to individual employee complaints of violations of their rights by the employer.

**Decision of arbitrator binding**

While both arbitration and mediation/conciliation involve the intervention of an outside third party, the distinction is that the parties are not required to follow the recommendations of a mediator/conciliator but the decision of the arbitrator is binding. Arbitration, therefore, is a substitute for court action. Each party is given an opportunity to put forth its position and present its evidence before the arbitrator makes a decision. Arbitrators are not required to follow the stringent rules of evidence that normally surround judicial proceedings, and their decisions can, in some jurisdictions, be appealed to the labour relations board or to the courts. Some provinces, on the other hand, do not permit appeals, so that the decision of the arbitrator is final. The collective agreement replaces any individual contract that may have existed previously between the employer and employee, so all disputes between the parties must be handled by the grievance procedure and arbitration. This method of dispute resolution is compulsory. It is not permissible for the parties to indulge in strikes or lockouts or to use the courts to resolve a dispute over the terms of the contract once a collective agreement is in force.

**No strike when contract is in force**

---

82. *Ibid.*, s. 67.
83. *Ibid.*, s. 80(4).

## Case Summary 11.13

### Disputes Arising from Collective Agreement Must Be Arbitrated: *Strathcona Steel Manufacturing Inc. v. Oliva*[84]

Oliva, a member of a union that had a collective agreement with Strathcona Steel Inc., was dismissed, allegedly for cause. His union decided not to proceed with a grievance on his behalf, so Oliva commenced a wrongful dismissal action through the courts. Similarly, Protz was dismissed by her employer, Zeidler Forest Industries Ltd. Protz initiated a grievance, abandoned it, and commenced an action seeking damages for wrongful dismissal. In a third case, Rusel, a member of SAIT's academic staff association, was advised that his position had been abolished. He was paid 13 weeks' salary in compliance with the collective agreement. After accepting the payment, Rusel commenced an action claiming he was entitled to two years' salary in lieu of notice. In all three cases, collective agreements were in place, and yet the chambers judges determined that the courts had jurisdiction to entertain the claims.

The Court of Appeal, however, followed the precedent set by the Supreme Court of Canada in the *Ste. Anne Nackawic*[85] case, where Justice Estey summarized the law as follows, at p. 718:

> The collective agreement establishes the broad parameters of the relationship between the employer and his employees. This relationship is properly regulated through arbitration, and it would, in general, subvert both the relationship and the statutory scheme under which it arises to hold that matters addressed and governed by the collective agreement may nevertheless be the subject of actions in the courts at common law.

Accordingly, the jurisdiction of the courts to deal with claims involving the "interpretation, application, or operation of a collective agreement" has been effectively ousted by the provisions of the *Labour Relations Act* and the *Technical Institutes Act*, both of which require collective agreements to contain a method of resolving differences. The intention of such legislation is to provide for a speedy and more informal resolution of industrial disputes, outside the court system.

## Other Terms

In addition to the terms specifically relating to conditions of work, rates of pay, vacations, termination, and the like (which are the main object of the collective bargaining process), there are various other terms that often appear in collective agreements. The federal government and some provinces have passed legislation requiring collective agreements to cover how technological changes in the industry will be handled.[86] Throughout Canada, the parties can agree to terms that provide for union security. One is the **union shop clause**. This clause simply requires that new employees join the union within a specified period of time. A second arrangement used, particularly in such industries as construction or longshoring, may require that the employee be a member of the union before getting the job. This requirement is called a **closed shop clause**. A third option enables employees to retain the right not to join a union but they are still required to pay

**Agreement must provide for technological change**

**Union shop and closed shop provisions**

84. (1986), 74 A.R. 46 (C.A.), leave to appeal to S.C.C. refused, (1987), 78 A.R. 200 n (S.C.C.).

85. *Ste. Anne Nackawic Pulp & Paper Co. v. Can. Paper Wkrs.' Union, Loc. 219*, [1986] 1 S.C.R. 704.

86. *Canada Labour Code, supra* note 98 at ss. 51–55.

**Agency shop, check-off and maintenance of membership provisions**

union dues. This arrangement is referred to as the **Rand Formula** or the **agency shop**. Fourthly, the collective agreement may contain a **check-off provision**, which means that the parties have agreed that the employer will deduct union dues from the payroll. A fifth option, **maintenance of membership**, requires those who are already union members to pay dues and maintain their membership, but new employees need not join the union.

## Strikes and Lockouts

**Job action may involve lockout, strike, work to rule**

Some sort of job action will probably result if the parties cannot agree on what terms to include in the agreement. A **lockout** is action taken by the employer to prevent employees from working and earning wages. A **strike** is the withdrawal of services by employees. Although a strike usually consists of refusing to come to work or intentional slowdowns, other forms of interference with production may also be classified as strikes. For example, postal employees announced just before Christmas 1983 that they would process Christmas cards with 10-cent stamps on them despite the fact that the appropriate rate was thirty-two cents per letter. This action was taken to draw attention to the fact that certain commercial users of the postal system got a preferential bulk rate not available to the public. The courts declared that the action was a strike, and since a strike would have been illegal under the circumstances, the union reversed its position. Employees can pressure an employer by strictly adhering to the terms of their agreement or by doing no more than is minimally required. This behaviour is called **work to rule** and will often prompt a lockout. Strikes and lockouts are both **work stoppages** but are initiated by different parties.

**Strike or lockout can occur only between contracts in an interest dispute**

Since the main objective of modern collective bargaining legislation is to reduce conflict, the right to strike and the right to lock out have been severely limited. It is unlawful for a strike or lockout to occur while an agreement is in force. Strikes and lockouts can take place only after the last agreement has expired and before the next one comes into effect.[87] Any strike or lockout associated with the recognition process or involving jurisdictional disputes between two unions is also illegal and must be dealt with through the certification process described above. Only when the dispute is part of the negotiation or bargaining process and concerns the terms to be included in the collective agreement (an interest dispute) is a strike or lockout legal.

If a collective agreement is in place and a dispute arises as to the terms (a rights dispute), it must be resolved through the grievance and arbitration process described above. Any strike associated with such a dispute is illegal.

**Must bargain in good faith first and vote before strike**

**Proper strike notice must be given**

Even when the dispute concerns what will go into the new agreement (an interest dispute), there are still some limitations on strike action. The old contract must have expired and the parties must have attempted to bargain in good faith. A vote authorizing strike action must be taken, and a specified period of notice must be given, for example, 72 hours in Alberta, in British Columbia, and under the *Canada Labour Code*.[88] The employer must give the same notice to the employees when a lockout is about to take place. No strike or lockout can take place until a specified period of time has passed after a conciliator has made a report to the Minister of Labour. Even then, in some areas, a further cooling-off

---

87. *Ibid.*, s. 88.1.

88. *Ibid.*, s. 87.2.

period may be imposed. In some jurisdictions, the employer is prohibited from hiring replacement workers during a strike. This restriction puts considerably greater pressure on the employer to settle the dispute and goes some way in reducing the violence associated with such labour–management confrontation. The federal government has amended the *Canada Labour Code* to partially prohibit the use of such replacement workers.[89]

## Picketing

Once a strike or lockout has taken place, one of the most effective techniques available to trade unions is picketing. But, as with striking, the use of picketing is severely limited and controlled. Picketing involves strikers standing near or marching around a place of business trying to dissuade people from doing business there. Picketing is permissible only when a lawful strike or lockout is in progress. Employees who picket before proper notice has been given, or somewhere not permitted under the labour legislation, are in violation of the law. A picketer responsible for communicating false information to those who might cross the picket line can be sued for defamation.

**Right to picket limited by legislation**

But when the information communicated does not try to discourage people from crossing the picket line or dealing with the employer, the action may not qualify as picketing.

### Case Summary 11.14

**Leafleting and Picketing Distinguished:** *United Food and Commercial Workers, Local 1518 (U.F.C.W.) v. KMart Canada Ltd.*[90]

The UFCW represented employees who were locked out from the KMart department stores in Campbell River and Port Alberni. They decided to escalate the dispute by handing out leaflets to customers in KMart stores in the Vancouver and Victoria area, explaining the nature of their complaints against the company and encouraging them not to shop at KMart. In British Columbia, the legislation prohibits secondary picketing (picketing at a location other than where the employees work), and the Court was asked to decide whether this leafleting qualified as prohibited secondary picketing. The Supreme Court of Canada held that it did not. The Court determined that "the distribution of leaflets did not interfere with employees at the secondary sites, nor was there any indication that it interfered with the delivery of supplies. The activity was carried out peacefully, and it did not impede public access to the stores. Neither was there any evidence of verbal or physical intimidation." Some customers may have been persuaded not to deal with the stores, but this was a consequence of leafleting rather than picketing.

The Court distinguished between picketing and leafleting and held that *leafleting* was an expression of free speech and as such was protected by section 2 of the *Charter of Rights and Freedoms*. Because the *Code*'s definition of picketing was overly broad, including leafleting, it was struck down. The prohibition against secondary picketing was also an interference with free speech, but it was justified under section 1 because of its interference in commercial relations.

---

89. *Ibid.*, s. 94 (2.1).

90. [1999] 2 S.C.R. 1083.

**Violence not permitted**

Picketing must be peaceful and merely communicate information. Violence will not be tolerated. A tort action for trespass may follow the violation of private property, and if violence erupts the assaulting party may face criminal and civil court actions. When picketing goes beyond the narrow bounds permitted in common law and legislation, the employer can resort to the courts or labour relations boards to get an injunction to limit or prohibit the picketing. Where the number of picketers used may be excessive, as with mass picketing, this goes beyond simple information communication and becomes intimidation. The employer can then apply to have the number of picketers restricted.

**Strong tradition of union solidarity makes picketing effective**

Although picketing limited in this way may seem to be an ineffectual weapon, there is an extremely strong tradition among union members and many others never to cross a picket line. Others simply wish to avoid the unpleasantness of a confrontation. Employers must deal with other businesses that employ union members, and these workers generally will not cross the picket line. It eventually becomes very difficult for an employer to continue in business surrounded by a picket line.

**Some provinces permit secondary picketing**

Just what locations can be legally picketed varies with the jurisdiction. Employees in every jurisdiction can picket the plant or factory where they work. In some jurisdictions, such as New Brunswick, picketing can be extended to any place at which the employer carries out business.[91] Where such **secondary picketing** is allowed, the striking employees are able to picket not just their own workplace but also other locations where the employer carries on business. In any case, unrelated businesses cannot be legally picketed, even if they are located on the same premises as the one struck, as might be the case, for example, in a shopping mall. Of course, whether the picketing is directed toward such an unrelated business in a given dispute is a question for the court or board to decide. But the more extensive the picketing, the more effective the economic pressure placed on the employer.

**No legal obligation to honour picket line**

Anyone has the legal right to cross a picket line. Customers are free to continue doing business with an employer involved in a strike or lockout; suppliers are free to continue supplying goods and services to the employer if they can persuade their employees to cross the picket line; and the employer has the right to continue normal business activities. Unfortunately, picketers can lose sight of these basic rights when they think their picket line is not being effective. As a result, a considerable amount of intimidation, coercion, violence, and injury still take place despite all the precautions introduced into the labour relations system in Canada.

## Public Sector and Essential Services

**Public-sector employees have limited rights to job action**

The discussion thus far relates to people employed in private industry. However, many people are employed either as part of the public sector or in service industries that are considered essential to society, such as hospitals, and police and fire departments. Employees falling into these categories are treated differently from those employed in private industry, and special legislation governs their activities. Although labour issues and disputes in these occupations are virtually the same as those in the private sector, the government and the public regard the position of public service employees as quite different. Strikes by police, firefighters, hospital

---

91. *Industrial Relations Act*, R.S.N.B. 1973, c. I-4, s. 104.

## Reducing **Risk** 11.4

Some employers will feel threatened by the prospect of a union organizing its workforce. Often, emotional rather than economic factors come into play, employers not wanting to give up their right to manage or to surrender any control to trade unions. This is true especially at the organizational stage and is the main reason the employer's role at that level has been minimized. The certification process, supervised by government, has reduced conflict at that stage. Employers are well advised to exercise care, especially in a newly unionized situation, to avoid unfair labour practices and other situations that poison the atmosphere because of ill-thought-out tactics and strategies.

workers, schoolteachers, and other public servants are usually considered inappropriate by members of the public.

Every province has special legislation to deal with these groups. Most provinces permit collective bargaining to some extent, but only a few allow public-sector employees to participate in strikes and picketing, the others substituting some form of compulsory arbitration of disputes.[92] Of course, in all labour disputes, including private ones, the government retains the right, either by existing statute or by the passage of a specific bill, to impose a settlement or an alternative method of resolving the dispute, such as compulsory arbitration.

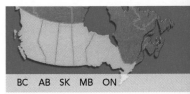

BC  AB  SK  MB  ON

## Union Organization

Trade unions must be democratic organizations, in which policy is established by vote and executives and officers are elected. Members can be expelled or disciplined for misbehaviour, such as crossing picket lines after being instructed not to by the union executive. Expulsion can be devastating for a worker, since many collective agreements provide for a **union shop** in which all employees must be members of the union. Some jurisdictions have passed legislation stipulating that a person who loses his or her union membership for reasons other than failure to pay dues will be able to retain employment.[93] There are some employees whose religious beliefs prevent them from joining or contributing to such organizations as trade unions, which presents a real dilemma in a union shop situation. Some governments have passed legislation exempting such individuals from joining unions; dues are still deducted but are paid to a registered charity instead. The other terms of the collective agreement still apply.[94]

**Unions can expel for misbehaviour**

Trade unions are subject to the human rights legislation in place in their jurisdiction. In some jurisdictions, the labour legislation provides that they can be denied certification[95] or lose their status as a trade union if they discriminate. Unions have an obligation to represent all their members fairly.[96] Employees who feel unfairly treated by the union or who feel that the union is not properly representing them in disputes with employers can lodge complaints before the Labour Relations Board, and the union may find itself required to compensate the wronged employees.

**Trade unions controlled by labour relations boards and courts**

---

92. *Ibid.*, s. 96.

93. *Canada Labour Code*, R.S.C. 1985, c. L-2, s. 95(e).

94. *Ibid.*, s. 70(2).

95. *Ibid.*, s. 25(2).

96. *Ibid.*, s. 37.

Trade unions were once considered illegal organizations with no status separate from their membership and therefore no corporate identity. Most provinces have passed legislation giving a recognized trade union the right to sue or be sued on its own behalf, at least for the purposes outlined in the labour legislation.[97]

# Summary

### Employee

- Provides general service to employer.
- Must follow direction, be honest, competent, and loyal.

### Independent contractor

- Contracts to do a specific job.

### Agent

- Acts on behalf of or represents a principal.

### Employer

- Vicariously liable for the acts of the employee during the course of employment.
- Must also provide a safe working place, direction, and wages.

### Termination

- Duration or term of employment, together with amount of notice of termination, may be contractually agreed upon.
- Otherwise, both parties are obligated to give the other reasonable notice.
- Reasonable notice depends on length of employment, age of employee, requisite qualifications, availability of similar work, whether employer acted in bad faith.
- No notice required when there is just cause for dismissal, such as dishonesty, misconduct, disobedience, or incompetence.
- Wrongful dismissal is dismissal without cause and without proper notice.
- Employee must mitigate losses by trying to find other employment.
- Constructive dismissal—consequence of unilateral demotions or unilateral changes to terms of employment.

### Legislation

- Employment standards legislation controls minimum wage, hours of work and overtime, termination, child labour, maternity and parental leave.
- Human rights legislation prohibits discrimination in the workplace.
  - Addresses ancillary issues such as harassment.
  - Requires positive action to accommodate disabled workers and others facing discrimination.
- Occupational health and safety legislation—sets health and safety standards.
- Employment insurance legislation—an insurance scheme that provides benefits to those who are unemployed.
- Workers' compensation legislation—an insurance scheme that provides benefits to those who are injured on the job.

97. See, for example: *Labour Relations Code*, R.S.A. 2000, c. L-1, s. 25.

## Collective bargaining

- Controlled by legislation.
- Certification process controls the organization and recognition of bargaining units.
- Job action possible only when that bargaining process breaks down.
- Strikes allow persuasive picketing but no physical confrontation.
- Once the contract is in place, any disputes arising under it must be dealt with through an arbitration process provided for in the agreement.
- Public sector—often subject to different rules.

---

## QUESTIONS

1. Distinguish among an employee, an independent contractor, and an agent.

2. Explain how a court will determine whether a person is an employee rather than an independent contractor.

3. Summarize the employer's obligations to the employee and the employee's obligations to the employer under common law.

4. Explain what is meant by a restrictive covenant and what factors determine whether it is enforceable or not.

5. What is the proper way to terminate an employment contract that is for an indefinite period of time?

6. How is the appropriate notice period to terminate an employment relationship determined?

7. Under what circumstances can an employee be dismissed without being given notice? When can an employee leave employment without giving notice?

8. What risk does an employer who ignores an employee's incompetence over a period of time face?

9. What factors will a court take into consideration when determining compensation in a wrongful dismissal action? Indicate the various types of remedies that may be available to the plaintiff.

10. Explain what is meant by "vicarious liability." Describe the limitations on its application.

11. Describe how the employment standards legislation protects basic workers' rights.

12. Explain how human rights legislation applies to areas of employment.

13. Explain what is meant by a duty to accommodate in the field of human rights and how that can affect employers.

14. Explain the object and purpose of workers' compensation legislation and how those objectives are accomplished. If a worker is injured on the job and is not covered by workers' compensation, what course of action need he take to secure a remedy?

15. What is the significance of the *National Labor Relations Act (Wagner Act)* in Canada?

16. Compare and contrast recognition disputes, jurisdiction disputes, interest disputes, and rights disputes.

17. Explain the difference between mediation/conciliation and arbitration. Describe how these tools are used in Canadian labour disputes.

18. Once a collective agreement is in place, what effect will it have on the individual rights of employees? How will it affect the employer?

19. What kind of disputes are strikes and lockouts limited to? How are the other types of disputes between union and employer dealt with?

20. Distinguish between a strike and a lockout. Describe the type of job action that can constitute a strike.

21. Explain what steps must take place before a strike or lockout is legal.

22. Explain what is meant by picketing, when it can take place, and the limitations that have been placed on picketing in different jurisdictions.

23. What is the legal position of a person who wishes to cross a picket line?

---

## CASES

### 1. *Clare v. Canada (Attorney-General)*, [1993] 1 F.C. 641 (F.C.A.).

Clare was an employee of the federal government, who was fired from his job for incompetence after 23 years of service. After a number of years of satisfactory service in various capacities with the federal public service, the plaintiff received an unsatisfactory evaluation in his performance appraisals for three consecutive reviews. On the basis of this performance, the plaintiff was fired from his position.

During that time, his wife had suffered from a series of major illnesses and nearly died. He was also having serious problems with his son, including physical confrontation. As a result, Clare was experiencing an extreme amount of stress in his life. In addition to his personal troubles, he had a personality conflict with his immediate supervisor that introduced work-related stress. During this period, Clare was receiving counselling and had asked to participate in a federally sponsored program designed to help employees experiencing these kinds of difficulties. The plaintiff sought reassignment, which was refused; and so, after 23 years of service, he was fired from his position.

Explain the legal position of the parties and whether the dismissal was justified in the circumstances. Would your answer be different if it were established that he had experienced family problems over his entire work history with the department, that several of his transfers from one department to another had been to accommodate a "problem or troubled employee," and that his performance had never been fully satisfactory?

### 2. *Queen v. Cognos Inc.*, [1993] 1 S.C.R. 87.

Cognos Inc., a computer software corporation located in Ottawa, hired Mr. Queen. Queen had been working at a secure, well-paying job in Calgary. Cognos hired Queen to develop an accounting software package, but, two weeks later, the corporation decided to shift research funds into a more successful product. Queen was then given a number of fill-in jobs, but his employment was terminated 18 months later. Queen sued for "wrongful hiring." He argued that Cognos made a false representation when it was hiring him, as he was not told that senior management had not yet approved the project for which he was hired. Discuss the likely decision of the Supreme Court of Canada. If Queen was successful with his claim of wrongful hiring, explain the resulting implications for employers with respect to the information which must be disclosed to job applicants.

## 3. *Straton Knitting Mills Ltd. and Clothing and Textile Workers*, [1979] O.L.R.B. Rep. August 801, File No. 0278-79-R (OLRB).

When the union in question tried to organize the workers at the respondent's premises, the co-owner held three meetings with the employees in an attempt to dissuade them from joining the union. He told them it was not necessary for them to have a union, that it would be divisive, that they would have to pay union dues, that there was the possibility of a strike, and that it might result in the loss of contracts for the company, which would mean less work for the employees. The company also changed the pay scale, which resulted in higher wages. A petition was circulated to oppose the union, but there was some suggestion that the management was behind it. Part of the message that got through to the employees was that the employer did not want a union and that if it came, there would be layoffs, short weeks, and perhaps closure of the business. What course of action would you recommend to the union in these circumstances?

# 12

# Agency and Insurance

## CHAPTER HIGHLIGHTS

- The agency relationship
- The rights and responsibilities of an agent and a principal
- The implications of a fiduciary relationship
- Vicarious liability and the recourse available to the third party
- Insurance policies and the rights of the insurer and insured
- Consequences of contracts of utmost good faith

Fraudulent misrepresentation is one of the few circumstances in which a principal will be held vicariously liable for the acts of an agent, even in the absence of an employment contract between them, provided that the agent is acting within the authority he has been given by the principal. Such an agency relationship can have a tremendous impact on the principal. How agency relationships are created and the obligations that arise between the parties are the topics covered in this chapter.

### Case Summary 12.1

#### Vicariously Liable for Fraud: *Steinman v. Snarey*[1]

Mr. Snarey was a "well-respected agent" working for the Mutual Life Assurance Company of Canada when he was approached by a customer who wanted to take advantage of one of the investment opportunities offered by the company. Mr. Snarey persuaded the customer to part with $16 000 by way of a cheque made out to Mr. Snarey. The customer was told that his money was going into an "investment vehicle offered to the public by Mutual Life." Actually, the company did not offer this kind of investment plan and never had. This was simply a scheme used by Mr. Snarey to cheat a trusting customer out of a considerable amount of money. When the customer discovered the fraud, he turned to the Mutual Life Assurance Company for compensation. In the resulting action, it was determined that Mr. Snarey had devised and conducted a fraudulent scheme. Because he was

---

1. (1987), 26 C.C.L.I. 78 (Ont. Dist. Ct.), aff'd (1988), 32 C.C.L.I. xliii (Ont. Div. Ct.).

an agent of Mutual Life with the actual authority to enter into this general type of transaction with the company's customer, the company was vicariously liable for his conduct and had to pay compensation to the client.

The subject of agency is a vital component in any discussion of business law. The legal consequences that stem from an agency relationship are of utmost concern to businesspeople because at least one of the parties in most commercial transactions is functioning as an agent. Agency law is the basis of the law of partnership, and an understanding of it is essential for coming to terms with corporate law. These subjects, partnerships and corporations, will be dealt with in the next two chapters.

An agent's function is to represent and act on behalf of a principal in dealings with third parties. Although by far the most common example of agents representing principals is in the creation of contracts, agents also find themselves involved in other types of legal relationships. Real estate agents do not usually have the authority to enter into contracts on behalf of vendors, but they function as agents nonetheless because they participate in the negotiations and act as go-betweens. Other professionals, such as lawyers and accountants, may make representations or act on behalf of their clients or principals. The term **agency** refers to the service an agent performs on behalf of the principal. This service may be performed as an employee, as an independent agent, or gratuitously. When an agent is acting independently, the business performing the service is often called an agency, such as a travel agency, employment agency, or real estate agency.

The discussion in this chapter focuses on the law of agency, and in most cases no distinction will be made between people functioning as agents as part of an employment contract and those acting independently. In any case, it is important not to think of the agency function found within an employment relationship as just another aspect of that employment. The duties and obligations imposed on agents go far beyond the employment relationship and must be understood as a separate function or set of obligations.

*Agent represents and acts for principal*

*Agency refers to service performed by an agent*

# The Agency Relationship

The agency relationship can be created by an express or implied contract, by estoppel, by ratification, or gratuitously, the key element being the granting of **authority**.

## Formation by Contract

Usually, an agency relationship is created through a contract, called an **agency agreement**, between the agent and the principal; thus, general contract rules apply. This should not be confused with the contracts agents enter into on behalf of their principals. The agency contract can cover such things as the authority of the agent, the duties to be performed, and the nature of payment to be received. It may be imbedded in a contract of employment or establish an independent agency relationship. Generally, there are no additional formal requirements for the creation of such a contract. Thus, although it is a wise practice to do so, the agency agreement need not be in writing, except in those jurisdictions where the *Statute of Frauds* requires it or where it is to last longer than one year, as was dis-

**Agency relationship usually created through contract**

**Basic rules of contract apply to agency contracts**

cussed in Chapter 6. Under the *Bills of Exchange Act,*[2] where the agent is to sign cheques or other negotiable instruments the granting of the agent's authority must also be in writing. Although there may be other advantages in doing so, it is not necessary that the agency agreement be under seal, unless the agent will be sealing documents on behalf of the principal as part of his or her agency function. An agency agreement in writing and under seal is called a **power of attorney.**

All the elements of a contract, such as consensus, consideration, legality, intention to be bound, and capacity on the part of both parties, must be present for an agency agreement to be binding. The lack of any one of these elements may void the agency contract, but that will not affect the binding nature of any agreement the agent enters into on behalf of the principal. Thus, if Clarke is underage and acts as Jiwan's agent in the sale of Jiwan's car to Skoda, the agency contract between Clarke and Jiwan may be voidable because of the incapacity of Clarke. But the contract between Jiwan and Skoda for the purchase of the car is still binding. Only when agents are so young, drunk, insane, or otherwise incapacitated that they do not understand what they are doing does the contract between the principal and third party become doubtful on the basis of incapacity or lack of consensus.

**Consent only essential requirement of agency**

The actions of an agent may be binding on the principal even when the agent is acting gratuitously. Only consent is necessary, which explains why, in the above example, the contract for the purchase of the car is binding between Jiwan and Skoda despite the infancy of the agent, Clarke. Still, most agency relationships are based on contract, either expressly entered into by the parties or implied from their conduct. Often, these are simply employment contracts.

# Authority of Agents

Most disputes that arise in agency relate to the extent of the authority of the agent in dealing with third parties. An agent's authority can be derived from the principal in several ways.

## Actual Authority

**Actual authority express or implicit**

The authority specifically given by the principal to the agent and usually set out in the agency agreement is called the agent's **actual authority**. This actual authority may be **expressly** stated by the principal or **implied** from the circumstances, such as from the position the agent has been given. In the example used to introduce this chapter, the contract entered into by Mr. Snarey was just the kind of contract he was authorized to conclude with his clients. Because of this actual authority, the principal was liable for his fraud. A person who is hired as a purchasing agent

### Figure 12.1 The Agency Agreement

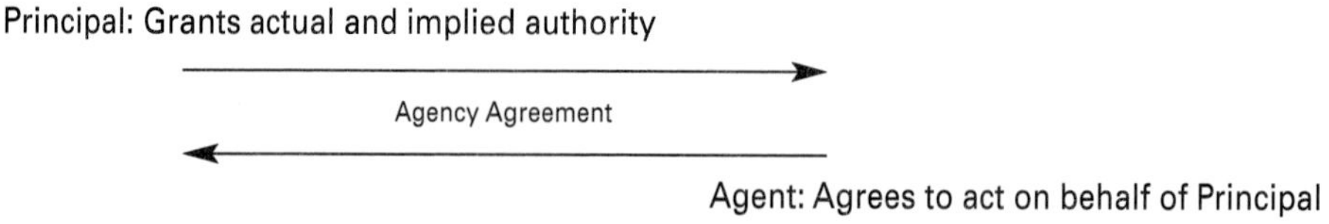

Principal: Grants actual and implied authority

Agency Agreement

Agent: Agrees to act on behalf of Principal

2. R.S.C. 1985, c. B-5.

has the authority to carry out the customary and traditional responsibilities of purchasing agents as well as the duties necessarily incidental to that function. Of course, if the principal has specifically stated that the agent does not have certain powers, no such authority is implied. Still, even where actual or implied authority is absent, there may be apparent authority.

Any written agency agreement should carefully set out the authority of the agent, eliminating, as far as possible, the need for any implied authority. An agent who exceeds this actual authority may be liable to the principal for any injury caused by his conduct. But no matter how much care is used in drafting an agent's actual authority, the principal may still be bound by the agent's conduct that falls within his apparent authority.

## Apparent Authority—Authority Created by Estoppel

When a principal does something by conduct or words to lead a third party to believe that an agent has authority, the principal is bound by the agent's actions, regardless of whether there is or is not actual authority. Even when the principal has specifically prohibited the agent from doing what he did, the principal will be bound because of the agent's apparent authority. This is an application of the principle of estoppel. **Estoppel** is an equitable remedy that stops a party from trying to establish a position or deny something. It is available to address an injustice. It would not be fair, for example, for a principal to hold out his agent as having certain authority and later try to establish that the agent had no such actual authority, so as to avoid being liable for the agent's acts. When a principal states, "George is my agent and has my authority," estoppel applies. Even if the statement is wrong, when a principal leads a third party to believe the agent has authority in this way, that principal is said to have "held out" that the agent has authority to act on his or her behalf. If a third party has relied on this representation, the principal cannot then claim that the agent had no authority.

> *Apparent authority presumed from actions of principal*
>
> *Estoppel applies when principal indicates that agent has authority*

### Case Summary 12.2

#### Portrayal of Authority Sufficient: *CMLQ Investors Co. v. Cajary Building Corp.*[3]

Must there be some actual authority before apparent authority can be shown to exist? The answer is, apparently, no. In the *CMLQ* case, the trial judge determined that: (1) the appellant, through its conduct, clothed a solicitor, Mr. Solomon, with apparent authority to renegotiate a mortgage between the appellant and the respondent; and (2) that Mr. Solomon effectively renegotiated the term of the appellant's mortgage from five years down to three. The appellant now tried to avoid this change, arguing that as a prerequisite to the existence of apparent authority, the respondent had the onus of proving that an actual principal/agent relationship existed at all, as between the appellant and Mr. Solomon. The appellant claimed that because the respondent failed to show Mr. Solomon had actually been retained to act as CMLQ's solicitor, as evidenced by a formal retainer, there could be no apparent authority. The Court of Appeal dismissed this argument. Agency by estoppel depends not on the actual relationship that

---

3. (1999), 127 O.A.C. 284 (Ont. C.A.).

exists between principal and agent; rather it depends on the way that relationship is presented to third parties. CMLQ's conduct suggested Solomon had authority and so the renegotiated mortgage was binding on the appellant. What lesson can be learned here? Ever heard the phrase "presentation is everything"?

The most important example of the application of estoppel is in the field of agency. It is important not to confuse this principle of estoppel with equitable or promissory estoppel, as described in Chapter 5. **Equitable estoppel** involves a promise or commitment to do something in the future. Here, we are dealing not with a promise but with a claim or a statement of fact made by the principal.

**Agent acting on apparent authority will bind principal**

Although the principal may look to the agent for compensation, so long as that agent has acted within his apparent authority, the principal is still bound in contract with the third party. If Pedersen employed Mohammed as sales manager of his used car dealership, it would be reasonable for customers to assume that Mohammed had the authority of a normal manager to sell cars and to take trade-ins. If after receiving instructions from Pedersen not to accept trades over $2000 without his express approval, Mohammed were to give Kim a $5000 trade-in for a 1995 Mercedes, Pedersen would still be bound by the deal. Pedersen put Mohammed in that position and led Kim to believe that Mohammed had the ordinary authority and power of a sales manager. The agent acted within his apparent authority, and the contract was binding on the principal. If, however, the agent had sold Kim the entire car lot, this would be beyond both his actual and apparent authority and would not be binding on Pedersen.

**Previous acceptance of agent's actions**

A principal can also be bound by the actions of an agent that would normally be beyond the agent's authority if the principal has sanctioned similar actions in the past. Kim's chauffeur Green would not normally be expected to have the authority to purchase automobiles on behalf of his principal. But if he had done so several times in the past and Kim honoured the deals, the dealer, Pederson, would be entitled to assume that the next purchase was authorized as well and Green had apparent authority. Even if Kim specifically told Green not to buy any more cars, and Green in violation of those instructions purchased another car from Pederson, the contract would be binding on Kim because of apparent authority. The existence of this apparent authority is based on the statements and conduct of the principal, not the agent. When the misleading indication of authority comes from the agent rather than the principal, and the action is otherwise unauthorized, the third party will have no claim against the principal.

**Actions of principal create apparent authority**

**Reasonable person test used to determine existence of authority**

The **reasonable person test** has a significant role to play in determining the existence of apparent authority. The usual authority associated with the position in which an agent has been placed is based on this test. The reasonable person test is also used to determine whether the third party should have been misled into believing that the agent had authority by the statements and conduct of the principal.

### Case Summary 12.3

**Reasonable Assumption to Conclude Authority Exists:**
*Gooderham v. Bank of Nova Scotia*[4]

This case demonstrates how apparent authority can result in a principal being bound by the actions of its agent. Mrs. Gooderham and her late husband went to

4. (2000), 47 O.R. (3d) 554 (Sup. Ct. J.).

the Bank of Nova Scotia for a $55 000 mortgage and the Bank's representative, Braun, provided them with an application for mortgage life insurance. The insurer under the policy was Canada Life. Canada Life would need to approve an application only if the applicant answered yes to a question in the health questionnaire form. The Gooderhams had answered yes. The Bank failed to forward this application form to Canada Life. Had the Bank done so, Canada Life would have denied coverage. Instead, the Bank conveyed premium information to the Gooderhams and collected premiums for several months. Mr. Gooderham then died and Canada Life denied coverage, claiming the Bank was not its agent.

The Court awarded judgment to the Gooderhams, concluding that Braun had apparent authority to represent Canada Life. When the Bank conveyed premium information to the Gooderhams and collected premiums, it was reasonable for the Gooderhams to assume that the Bank had authority to represent the insurer.

When a principal puts an agent in a position so that it appears to others that they have authority to make certain commitments, they have that authority, even though it has not been actually given. This is the very nature of apparent authority. It shows how important it is, for public and private institutions alike, to carefully define the authority of those acting for them and then take steps to ensure that their agents act within those boundaries.

## Case Summary 12.4

### Conduct of the Principal Is a Critical Consideration: *LeRuyet v. Stenner*[5]

In contrast to the *Gooderham* case, the Court found that there was no apparent authority in the LeRuyet case. LeRuyet approached Stenner seeking assistance with investments. In accordance with Stenner's recommendations, LeRuyet gave Stenner $130 000 to purchase a Great West annuity. Stenner defrauded LeRuyet, showing him false documents and failing to actually purchase the annuity. Stenner was convicted. To recover his loss, LeRuyet claimed Great West was vicariously liable for its agent's acts. The main issue was whether Stenner acted as Great West's agent. The agency agreement did not give Stenner actual authority to bind Great West to a contract. The case rested on whether there was apparent authority. Stenner did not display any connection to Great West, not using Great West business cards or operating from Great West premises. The only involvement by Great West was that they allowed licensed agents to present their annuities for sale and LeRuyet saw the Great West logo on the documents Stenner had shown him. There being no representations made by Great West that would lead a reasonable person to assume that Stenner acted as an agent of Great West, the Court dismissed the claim of apparent authority.

To determine whether a principal is bound in contract with a third party by the actions of an agent, a person must first ask, "Was the agent acting within the actual authority given by the principal?" If the answer is yes, then there is a contract, provided all the other elements are present. If the answer is no, then the question to ask is, "Did the principal do anything to lead the third party to believe that the agent had the authority to act?" In other words, was the agent acting with

**Was the action of the agent authorized by principal?**

5. (2001), 93 B.C.L.R. (3d) 163 (S.C.)

apparent authority? If the answer is yes and the third party relied on that apparent authority, there is a contract between the principal and the third party. It is only when the answer to both these questions is no that there is no contract, and the third party must look to the agent for redress.

Most people find it difficult to understand the difference between implied and apparent authority, and in most cases the distinction is not important. But to clarify, when a principal has specifically stated that the agent does not have authority, no authority can be implied. In spite of such a declaration, however, there may still be apparent authority because of the principal's comments or conduct in relation to the third party (estoppel). The principal has led the third party to believe that the agent has authority and now cannot deny that fact.

## Ratification

**If principal ratifies unauthorized contract, it is binding**

A principal can still ratify a contract even if the agent has acted beyond both actual and apparent authority. The first time Kim's chauffeur bought a car on Kim's behalf, there would likely have been no apparent authority, since this is not normally a chauffeur's job. If Kim liked the car, however, he could ratify the contract and the deal would be binding on the dealer. The effect of such ratification is to give the agent authority to act on behalf of the principal retroactive to the time of the sale. The result can seem unfair because the principal is not bound when an agent goes beyond the authority given, but if the principal chooses to ratify, the third party is bound and can do nothing to change that.

In fact, the power of the principal to ratify must meet the following qualifications:

**Third party can set time for ratification**

1. The third party has the right to set a reasonable time limit within which the ratification must take place. In the case of a chauffeur buying a car without authority, the dealer cannot simply repudiate the contract but could give the principal a short time to ratify by saying, for example, "You have until noon tomorrow to decide." In the United States, once the third party repudiates, it is too late for the principal to ratify. This may indicate the future direction in Canada, but the courts have not adopted this approach as of yet.

**Agent must have been acting for a specific principal**

2. The agent must have been acting for the specific principal who is now trying to ratify. A person cannot enter into a contract with a third party while purporting to be an agent and then search for a principal to ratify. The customer would be free to repudiate the purchase, since the would-be agent did not have a particular principal in mind when entering into the contract. There is no one to ratify the agreement.

**Principal must be capable of entering into contract**
• when it is entered into
• when it is ratified

3. The principal has to be fully capable of entering into the contract at the time the agent was claiming to act on his or her behalf. A principal who did not have the capacity to enter into the original deal because of drunkenness or insanity does not have the power to ratify upon becoming sober or sane. This requirement of capacity can be a problem where pre-incorporation contracts are involved. Often, promoters who are planning an incorporation will enter into contracts, such as the purchase of property on behalf of the proposed corporation, assuming that once the corporation is formed it will ratify the agreements. But because there is no corporation at the time the contract is entered into there can be no ratification, leaving the promoter personally liable for any losses suffered by the third party. Legislation in some

jurisdictions has modified this principle to allow a corporation to ratify such pre-incorporation contracts.[6]

**4.** The parties must still be able to perform the object of the contract at the time of the ratification. For example, if an agent enters into a contract on behalf of a principal to insure a building against fire, the principal cannot ratify the agreement after a fire. There is no building to insure when ratification is attempted, so there can be no contract. Furthermore, the contract the agent enters into must not make any reference to the need for ratification. If the contract includes such terms as "subject to principal's approval" or "subject to ratification," it becomes merely an agreement to enter into an agreement. The contractual requirement of consensus is not satisfied, and there is no contract.

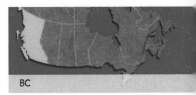

BC

Ratification can work against the principal in other ways. The principal can inadvertently ratify by knowingly accepting some sort of benefit under the agreement. If Kim's chauffeur bought a new Rolls Royce on Kim's behalf without the actual or apparent authority to do so, Kim would normally not be bound by such a contract. However, if Kim were to use that car in some way, such as driving it to work before returning it to the dealer, Kim would have accepted some benefit under the contract and thus ratified it. Kim would be bound to go through with the purchase of the automobile, provided that at the time he received the benefit, Kim knew that the purchase was made on his behalf.

**Ratification can take place inadvertently**

## Case Summary 12.5

### Delay in Repudiating Unauthorized Act Treated as Ratification: *Community Savings Credit Union v. United Association of Journeymen and Apprentices of the Plumbing and Pipefitting Industry of the United States and Canada, Local 324*[7]

Does ratification have to be express or given in writing? Evidently not. In this case, mere acquiescence was sufficient to constitute ratification. The labour union's business manager acted without actual authority when he pledged $80 000 of the union's funds as security to induce the Credit Union to finance construction of a building. Financing was advanced. Months later, the business manager disclosed his unauthorized actions to the union's Board and the Board did nothing about it. The business manager then advised the Credit Union that the union had disavowed further financial responsibility for financing the project. When the Credit Union lost confidence in the project and demanded payment from the union under the indemnity agreement, the validity of the pledge was brought into question. Although the business manager acted without actual authority, the failure of the Board to notify the Credit Union of the same, upon learning of these unauthorized acts, was sufficient to constitute ratification. The pledge was thus enforceable against the union.

Can failure to repudiate constitute a representation? When is one well advised to speak up?

6. For example, the Canada *Business Corporation Act*, R.S.C. 1985, c. C-44, s. 14.

7. (2002), 22 B.L.R. (3d) 311 (B.C.C.A.).

# Agency by Necessity

Consent is at the heart of agency law. Both principal and agent must consent to the conduct. Without authority (apparent or actual) or ratification, the principal cannot be bound. Only when there is agency by necessity will the court impose an agency relationship on the principal, despite the clear lack of consent.

When communication systems were less reliable than they are now, it might have been important for the captain of a ship to decide to sell a cargo that was spoiling, without waiting for instructions from his principal. The owners of the perishable goods could not later attack the sale as being unauthorized and demand the return of the cargo or compensation from the captain. In this circumstance, the ship's captain was authorized to act by the principle of agency by necessity. Today, communication can be instantaneous, and agency-by-necessity normally would not arise. Note that for agency by necessity to apply, there must be some duty or responsibility placed on the agent to care for those goods. Merely finding another person's property in danger does not, in and of itself, create an agency-by-necessity relationship.

**Agency by necessity rarely used today**

## Case Summary 12.6

### Whose "Necessity" Is It? *Canadian Pacific Forest Products Ltd. v. Termar Navigation Co.*[8]

The ship carrying the defendant's lumber was struck by a large wave, causing the load to shift. The ship thus had to stop in Portugal to have the lumber discharged and restowed before it could be delivered at its destination in England. The shipper claimed that these costs of discharging and restowing the lumber were incurred on behalf of, and were thus payable by, Canadian Pacific Forest Products Ltd. The shipper alleged it incurred these costs as an agent by necessity. The Court dismissed these claims, characterizing these costs simply as expenses the shipper had to incur to get the job done. The shipper could not assert it incurred those costs as an agent by necessity when they were merely a risk or cost the shipper should have considered as a cost of completing its contractual obligations.

## Exception in Family Relationships

It is common for a spouse to have the actual or even apparent authority to act on behalf of their spouse when dealing with merchants, especially for the purchase of necessities and other household goods. When the marriage breaks down, those merchants who, because of past dealings, have been led to believe a person has authority to act for a spouse, may rely on that apparent authority. In the absence of notice to the contrary the authority continues, even when the spouse has been specifically prohibited from making such purchases.

In some circumstances, authority can be implied by operation of law against the will of the other party. A wife who is deserted by her husband is presumed to have the authority to bind him to contracts with third parties for the purchase of necessities. But this must be viewed in the light of modern family law legislation. For example, in Alberta, as long as there are no arrears owing under an alimony order the defendant spouse is not liable for necessities supplied to the other spouse.[9] In Ontario, spouses and same-sex partners can be held liable for the pur-

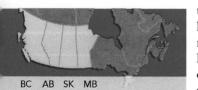

BC  AB  SK  MB

---

8. [1998] 2 F.C. 328 (F.C. T.D.), aff'd [2000] F.C.J. 450 (F.C.A.).

9. *Domestic Relations Act*, R.S.A. 2000, c. D-14, s. 19.

## Reducing **Risk** 12.1

A businessperson who deals through an agent runs a risk of that agent entering into contracts that are not authorized. Whether this is done by mistake or intentionally, the effect on the businessperson can be significant. To avoid the problem, the principal should make the limits of that authority absolutely clear to the agent and include those limitations in a written agency agreement, where practicable. The principal should also, where practical, make the limits of the agent's authority clear to the customers or third parties with whom that agent will deal. Customers should also be notified immediately upon the termination of that agent's authority, otherwise it will continue because of the principle of apparent authority.

chases of necessities made by the other partner, so long as the purchases were made during cohabitation and the spouse or same-sex partner has not notified the third party that this authority has been withdrawn.[10] In some jurisdictions, this principle has been abolished altogether.[11]

# The Rights and Responsibilities of the Parties

## The Agent's Duties

### The Contract

When an agency agreement has been created by contract, the agent has an obligation to act within the actual authority given in that agreement. An agent violating the contract but exercising apparent authority can be sued for breach and will have to compensate the principal for any losses suffered. Failure on the part of the agent to fulfill any other obligation set out in the agreement will also constitute an actionable breach of contract. Of course, if the specified act is illegal or against public policy, there is no obligation to perform.

An agent owes a **duty of care** to the principal. The agent must not only have the skills and expertise claimed but also must exercise that skill in a reasonable manner. For example, if Khan hires Gamboa to purchase property on which to build an apartment building, Gamboa must not only stay within the authority given but also must exercise the degree of care and skill one would expect from a person claiming to be qualified to do that type of job. If Gamboa buys a property for Khan and it turns out to be zoned for single-family dwellings, such a mistake would be below the standard of reasonable performance one would expect from someone in this type of business, and Gamboa would be liable to compensate Khan for any loss.

**Agent owes duty of reasonable care**

Agents often have considerable discretion in carrying out agency responsibilities as long as they act to the benefit of the principal. However, an agent cannot go against the specific instructions received, even if it might be in the principal's best interests to do so. If a stockbroker is instructed to sell shares when they reach a specific price, the broker must do so, even though waiting would bring the principal a better price.

**Agent must perform as required by principal**

Agents have a duty to act in the best interests of their principals.

10. *Family Law Act*, R.S.O. 1990, c. F. 3, s. 45.

11. See Saskatchewan's *Equality of Status of Married Persons Act*, S.S. 1984-85-86, c. E-10.3, s. 5.

### Case Summary 12.7

**Failure to Follow Instructions Can Be Costly:** *Volkers et al. v. Midland Doherty Ltd.*[12]

Mr. Volkers, a knowledgeable investor, was assured by the representatives of Midland that he could give instructions to Mr. Hill, or any other trader, and they would be followed. On February 28, Volkers determined that he wanted to purchase a substantial number of shares in Breakwater Resources Ltd. After receiving instructions, Mr. Hill made the appropriate purchase. Later that day, Mr. Volkers decided to purchase additional shares in that company and phoned to give instructions to Mr. Gurney to make the purchase first thing the next morning, since Mr. Hill had left for the day.

Mr. Gurney arrived at 7:00 a.m. but because of some doubts about the wisdom of the trade delayed making the purchase until Mr. Hill arrived about two hours later. Unfortunately, trading in Breakwater shares had been stopped before Mr. Hill's arrival, and when it came back on the market, it had doubled in price. Mr. Volkers suffered substantial loss and sued.

It was argued that Mr. Gurney had a duty to act in the best interests of his client, and since this was what he was doing, there should be no liability. But the appeal court held Mr. Gurney had been given specific instructions to purchase the Breakwater shares first thing in the morning, and his duty was to do so, or to tell Mr. Volkers that he did not so that Mr. Volkers could make other arrangements. Although the agent was obligated to do what he thought was best for the client, the agent bore an even greater obligation to keep Mr. Volkers informed. Mr. Volkers was the one to make the decision, not Mr. Gurney. This case illustrates that it is an important aspect of the agent's duty to the principal to follow instructions.

## Delegation

**Agent cannot delegate responsibility**

Generally, the agent has an obligation to perform the agency agreement personally. An agent is not permitted to delegate responsibility to another party unless there is consent to such delegation, either express or implied by the customs and traditions of the industry. Even then the primary agent has the responsibility to see that the terms of the agency agreement are fulfilled. The authority of an agent is commonly delegated to sub-agents, when that agent is a corporation or large business organization, such as a law firm, bank, real estate agency, or trust company.

## Accounting

**Agent must turn money over to principal**

The agent must turn over any monies earned pursuant to the agency function to the principal. If the agent acquires property, goods, or money on behalf of the principal, there is no entitlement to retain any of it other than the authorized commission. Even when the agent has some claim against the funds, he cannot keep them. If the third party owes money to the agent and pays money to the agent intended for the principal, the agent cannot intercept those funds on his own behalf but must pay over any money collected to the principal. To facilitate this process, the agent also has an obligation to keep accurate records of all agency transactions.

**Agent must account for funds**

---

12. (1985), 17 D.L.R. (4th) 343 (B.C.C.A.), leave to appeal to S.C.C. refused, (1985), 17 D.L.R. (4th) 343 n.

## Fiduciary Duty

### Case Summary 12.8

#### Conflicting Interests: *Ocean City Realty Ltd. v. A & M Holdings Ltd.*[13]

Mrs. Forbes was a licensed real estate salesperson working for Ocean City Realty Ltd. She was approached by Mr. Halbauer to find a commercial building in downtown Victoria. After some investigation, Mrs. Forbes approached the owners of a building to determine whether it might be for sale. The owner of the property, A & M Holdings Ltd., entered into an arrangement with her, whereby they agreed to pay a commission of 1.75 percent if she acted as their agent in selling the building. After some negotiations the sale was concluded for $5.2 million, but unknown to the seller, Mrs. Forbes had agreed to pay back half her commission to the purchaser, Mr. Halbauer. When A & M discovered the secret deal between Mrs. Forbes and Mr. Halbauer, they refused to pay any commission.

Mrs. Forbes had a fiduciary obligation to act in the best interests of her principal, A & M, but she argued that A & M got what it expected and her sacrifice only ensured that the deal went through. That did not hurt A & M but helped it. The Court held, however, that one of the key elements in the duty of a fiduciary is to disclose all pertinent information with respect to the transaction that would be considered important by the principal. In this case, the knowledge that she was paying part of her commission back to Mr. Halbauer was important to A & M, and it may have determined whether it would go through with the deal or not. In effect, A & M thought that Mr. Halbauer was paying one price, when, in fact, he was paying less for the property. A & M was entitled to this information, and it may have influenced its decision. Therefore, the fiduciary obligation of the agent had been breached, and the agent was entitled to no commission at all.

One may be sympathetic with the position of Mrs. Forbes in Case Summary 12.8. She only paid over part of her commission to Mr. Halbauer to preserve the deal. But who was she acting for? If she did not reduce her commission, the property may have been sold by another real estate agent to somebody else, and she would have received nothing. Thus, it is clear that she was acting in her own self-interest above the interest of the principal. This case strongly illustrates the nature of fiduciary duty; a person owing that duty must submerge personal interests in favour of the interests of the principal he or she represents.

Further, a positive duty of **full disclosure** exists. The agent cannot arbitrarily decide what would likely influence the conduct of the principal and what would not. For example, in the *Krasniuk* case,[14] the agent assumed, incorrectly, that she was obligated to forward only written offers to the vendor. She unilaterally turned down the verbal offers for $135 000 and $137 500. Later, when the same purchasers submitted a written offer for $130 000, the vendor, unaware of the earlier offers, accepted it. The agent had breached its fiduciary duty by failing to disclose this information, so no commission was payable. Had the vendors been aware of the earlier offers, they may have accepted them or at least countered the subsequent written offer. Similarly, in the *Ocean City* case described in Case Summary 12.8, it was Mrs. Forbes' failure to fully disclose the special deal she had made

**Agent must disclose information**

---

13. (1987), 36 D.L.R. (4th) 94 (B.C.C.A.).

14. *Krasniuk v. Gabbs* (2002), 161 Man. R. (2d) 274 (Q.B.).

with the purchaser that was her undoing. When an agent profits from a breach of the duty to disclose, the court's reaction is stern and uncompromising.

Because the principal puts trust in the agent, the principal may be vulnerable; accordingly, the law imposes a fiduciary duty obliging the agent to act only in the best interests of the principal. The relationship is often referred to as an **utmost good faith relationship**, in which the agent has an obligation to:

- keep in strict confidence any communications that come through the agency function;

- act in the best interests of the principal, even if the agent may lose some personal benefit;

- not take advantage of any personal opportunity that may come to his or her knowledge through the agency relationship; and

- disclose to the principal any personal benefit the agent stands to gain. Only with the informed consent of the principal can the agent retain any benefit. If there is a failure to disclose, the principal can seek an accounting and have any funds gained by the agent in such a way paid over to the principal.

**Agent cannot act for both principal and third party without consent of both**

An agent cannot act for both a principal and a third party at the same time. It would be very difficult for an agent to extract the best possible price from a third party on behalf of a principal when the third party is also paying the agent. The common practice of agents accepting gifts, such as holidays, tickets to sporting events, and liquor, is an example of the same problem. If the principal discovers the agent accepting payment from the third party, the principal is entitled to an accounting and the receipt of all such funds and will likely have just cause to terminate the relationship. Only where full disclosure has been made at the outset and permission given can the agent profit personally in this way.

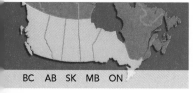

BC   AB   SK   MB   ON

In real estate transactions, the agent usually acts for the seller. This can cause problems for the purchaser, who often does not realize this and expects the agent to protect their interests as well. In some western provinces, this difficulty is largely overcome by requiring the purchasers to have their own agent acting for them and splitting the commission.

**Agent must not profit at principal's expense**

Another problem sometimes arises where an agent, who is hired to purchase goods or property, sells to the principal property actually owned by the agent as if it came from some third party. This is a violation of the agent's fiduciary duty; even if that property fully satisfies the principal's requirements, there must be full disclosure.[15] The reverse is also a breach, where the agent buys for himself what he has been hired to sell to others. An example would be where a real estate agent hired to sell a house recognizes it as a good deal and purchases it for himself, perhaps through a partner or a corporation. The agent then has the advantage of a good price, knowing how low the principal will go, and getting the commission as well. This is not acting in the best interests of the principal, and the agent would be required to pay back both profits and commission to the vendor of the property.

**Agent must not compete with principal**

It also follows that the agent must not operate his own business in competition with the principal, especially if a service is being offered. Nor can the agent also represent another principal selling a similar product. Finally, the agent must not collect any profits or commissions that are hidden from the principal, but is

15. *G.L. Black Holdings Ltd. v. Peddle* (1998), 226 A.R. 302 (Q.B.), aff'd (1999), 244 A.R. 376 (C.A.).

## Reducing **Risk** 12.2

When professionals or independent businesses offer their services to others, a relationship of trust is created that leaves a client vulnerable, so a fiduciary duty is owed. The person providing the service must put the interests of the client ahead of his or her own and follow the instructions given. It is sometimes difficult to keep personal interests and the interests of customers and clients separate, but failure to do so is asking for trouble. It is vitally important that a professional or businessperson in such a position learn the nature of their fiduciary duty and make sure they honour it.

to pay over all the benefit resulting from the performance of the agency agreement. Such a breach of fiduciary duty by an agent who is also an employee will likely constitute just cause for dismissal.

## Duties of Principal

### The Contract

The principal's primary obligation to the agent is to honour the terms of the contract by which the agent was hired. If the contract is silent as to payment, an obligation to pay a reasonable amount can be implied on the basis of the amount of effort put forth by the agent, as well as the customs and traditions of the industry. If the agreement provides for payment only on completion, there is no implied obligation to pay for part performance. Thus, if an agent is to receive a commission upon the sale of a house, even if the agent puts considerable effort into promoting a sale, there is generally no entitlement to commission if no sale occurs. Unless there is agreement to the contrary, the agent is normally entitled to compensation for reasonable expenses, such as phone bills and car expenses.

> **Principal must honour terms of contract and pay reasonable amount for services**

If the agency agreement is vague about the extent of the agent's authority, the courts will usually favour an interpretation that gives the agent the broadest possible power. Thus, if Jones is hired as a sales manager for a manufacturing business and is given authority to enter into all sales related to the business, a court will likely interpret it to include authority to sell large blocks of product but no authority to sell the plant itself. When the power to borrow money is involved, however, the courts take a much narrower approach. Thus, if Klassen were hired as a purchasing agent with "all the authority necessary" to carry out that function and he found it necessary to borrow money to make the purchases, the courts would not imply an authority to borrow without getting additional approval from the principal. It is necessary for an agent to be given specific authority to borrow money on the principal's behalf in order to proceed.

> **Principal must reimburse agent's expenses**

> **Ambiguous authority will be interpreted broadly**

> • except when power to borrow money is in question

## Undisclosed Principals

In normal circumstances, the agent is not liable to the third party. The contract is between the principal and the third party, and the agent is not a party to it. Sometimes, however, principals do not want a third party to know who they are, and the agent will act without identifying the principal. When an agent makes it clear that she is acting as an agent for a principal who does not want to be identified, the third party can still elect to enter into the agreement but there will be no recourse against the agent. In the event of a breach, the third party must seek out the identity of the principal and look to that individual for redress. But if the agent fails to state that she is acting for someone else and signs the documents as

**Third party can sue agent or principal if principal undisclosed**

if she is the principal, the agent is directly liable to the third party. If an agent acts for an undisclosed principal in a way consistent with either being an agent or the main contracting party, the third party has a choice. For example, when the agent signs a purchase order in a way consistent with being an agent for the purchaser or the actual person purchasing the goods, the third party can sue either the agent or, upon learning the identity, can sue the principal instead. The injured party cannot sue both; once the choice is made, the third party is bound by it.

To avoid the problem of an undisclosed principal, a person acting as an agent should be extremely careful to make it clear that they are acting in an agency capacity. This is normally done by writing "per" immediately before the signature of the agent. For example, if Sam Jones were acting for Ace Finance Company, he would be well advised to sign:

Ace Finance Company
per *Sam Jones*.

## Case Summary 12.9

### No Liability under Contract When Agent Makes It Clear He Is Acting as Agent: *Q.N.S. Paper Co. v. Chartwell Shipping Ltd.,*[16] *Logistec Stevedoring Inc. v. Amican Navigation Inc.*[17]

Chartwell provided stevedoring services for Q.N.S., which operated a chartered ship. Although Chartwell never mentioned specifically who it was acting for, Chartwell made it clear at all times that it was acting as an agent on behalf of others in their dealings with Q.N.S. The deal fell through. Q.N.S. sued Chartwell. The Supreme Court of Canada had to decide whether this was an undisclosed principal situation where the agent could be successfully sued. The Court held that because Chartwell had made it clear at all times that it was functioning as an agent, there was no personal liability for that agent on the contract. Chartwell consistently emphasized that its sole responsibility was as an agent. It identified itself as "Managing Operators for the Charterers" or "acting on behalf of principals" or signed "as agent only."

In a subsequent case, *Logistic v. Amican*, Amican claimed it too had acted as agent and should not be personally liable for payment of the contracted price. The Federal Court reviewed the correspondence and communication between the parties and, although Amican occasionally signed "as agent for Pegasus Line S.A.," this was not done consistently. Rather, in several communications the tone suggested Amican was the principal. Thus both Amican and Pegasus were jointly and severally liable to the third party. An agent cannot be held personally liable for a contract that it enters into with a third party if it makes it clear he is acting as an agent, even though he does not disclose the identity of the principal. But it appears the onus of making its agency clear lies upon the agent.

Apparent authority does not apply where the principal is undisclosed, since no representations of authority have been made by the principal. A contract binding on the principal and third party results only when the agent is acting within the actual authority given. Even then, not all contracts with undisclosed principals are binding on third parties, as the third party may succeed in having the contract set aside. When the identity of the undisclosed principal is important

---

16. [1989] 2 S.C.R. 683.

17. [2001] F.C.J. No. 1009 (T.D.).

to the third party—in a contract involving personal services, for example—the third party would be able to repudiate upon discovering that the deal had been made with an agent rather than with the principal. Similarly, in the case of *Said v. Butt*,[18] a theatre refused to sell a ticket to someone on opening night because he had caused a disturbance in the past. That person arranged for a friend to acquire the ticket on his behalf but was refused admittance even though he had a ticket. He sued for breach, but the court held that in this situation, the identity of the party was obviously important, and the court did not enforce the contract.

**Third party can repudiate when identity of undisclosed principal important**

Undisclosed principal relationships are often used when well-known companies are assembling land for new projects. Agents approach property owners in the area to obtain options on their properties. The options are exercised only if a sufficient number of property owners are willing to sell at a reasonable price. The undisclosed principal approach is used to discourage people from holding out for higher prices once they find out who is really buying the property.

If the existence of an agency is undisclosed, the third party can sue only the agent. Similarly, the agent may sue under the contract when the principal is undisclosed. The agent only loses the right to enforce the agreement when the principal chooses to act like a principal and takes steps to enforce the agreement. The principal can enforce the contract, unless the identity of the parties is an important factor in the contractual relationship, as discussed above (for then the third party may choose to set aside the contract altogether).

A third party can choose to sue either the agent or the disclosed but unnamed principal, but the third party is bound by this choice only once the identity of the principal has been determined. Normally, a principal can ratify a contract when an agent has exceeded his authority, but this is not possible when an undisclosed principal is involved. Ratification can take place only when the agent is claiming to act for a principal, so it follows that an undisclosed principal cannot ratify the acts of an agent.

**Only identified principal can ratify**

To further complicate matters, where the contract is made under seal (sealed by the agent) the undisclosed principal cannot be sued. Only parties to a sealed document can have rights or obligations under it.

## The Third Party

### Case Summary 12.10

**Misrepresentation or Breach of Warranty of Authority: *Salter v. Cormie*[19]**

Mr. Salter was employed by a corporation as its treasurer and chief financial officer. He also owned a block of shares in the corporation. Mr. Salter was fired by the directors, one of whom also acted as the corporation's lawyer and is a defendant in this case. In the negotiations to settle, the defendant made an offer on behalf of "a group of individuals" to purchase the shares held by Mr. Salter.

The offer was accepted; a deposit was paid, and a few of the shares were transferred, but in general, the contract was not performed. Eventually, the shares were de-listed and became worthless. This action was brought against the corporation's lawyer who negotiated the contract to settle, as well as the lawyer's firm. The defendant claimed that despite what was said he was not representing a

18. [1920] 3 K.B. 497.

19. (1993), 108 D.L.R. (4th) 372 (Alta. C.A.).

specific principal, only that there was an intention to form a group to purchase the shares. The judge said that if the group did exist, they would be liable, and if it did not, the lawyer would be liable on the basis of breach of warranty of authority. Since the lawyer took the position that the group did not exist and that he was an agent acting on its behalf, he and his firm were liable to Mr. Salter.

**Third party can sue agent for unauthorized acts**

When an agent does not have the authority claimed, either actual or apparent, that agent may be sued by the third party for breach of "warranty of authority." This action is founded in contract law and is the most common example of an agent being sued directly by the third party. Also, an agent who intentionally misleads the third party into believing that she has authority when she does not may be sued by the third party for the tort of deceit. Furthermore, agents who inadvertently exceed their authority can be sued for negligence.

**Remedies in tort available for fraud or negligence**

It is important to distinguish between the tortious liability of the agent based on fraud or negligence and a contract action based on breach of warranty of authority. Where a breach of warranty of authority action is brought, the damages will be limited to those that were reasonably foreseeable at the time the contract was entered into or those that flow naturally from the breach (that is, the damages awarded for breach of contract). If, unknown to the agent, the goods were to be resold at an unusually high profit that was lost because of the breach of warranty of authority, the agent would not be liable for those losses, since they were not reasonably foreseeable. However, if the third party could establish the agent's fraud or negligence, the lost profits might be recovered from the agent because they are the direct consequence of the tortious conduct—and in tort law, damages are awarded to compensate for the loss caused.

## Liability for Agent's Tortious Conduct

As discussed in Chapters 4 and 11, an employer is *vicariously liable* for the acts an employee commits during the course of employment. When an agent is also an employee of the principal, the principal is vicariously liable for any tortious acts committed by the agent in the course of that employment. The difficulty arises when the agent is not an employee but acts independently. In 1938, the Supreme Court of Canada held that the principle of vicarious liability is restricted to those situations in which a master–servant relationship can be demonstrated.[20] This issue is currently before the Supreme Court of Canada and one hopes its decision will clarify matters. The case in question, *Thiessen v. Clarica Life Insurance Co.,*[21] is summarized in the provincial supplements.

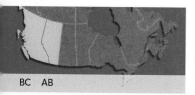

BC   AB

**Vicarious liability limited to employment**
• but definition of employment may be broadened

The courts have been expanding the definition of employment. Fleming points out that "the employment of a servant may be limited to a single occasion, or extend over a long period; it may even be gratuitous."[22] Even if the relationship involves a person who is essentially an independent agent, that agent may be functioning as an employee or servant in a given situation; thus, the courts may impose vicarious liability on the principal by simply asserting that the agent is also an employee. With such a broad definition of employment, judges will have little

---

20. *T. G. Bright and Company v. Kerr,* [1939] S.C.R. 63.

21. (2002), 219 D.L.R. (4th) 98 (B.C.C.A.).

22. John G. Fleming, *The Law of Torts*, 8th ed. (Sydney: The Law Book Co. Ltd., 1990) at 371.

difficulty imposing vicarious liability on principals when the circumstances warrant. Of course, the principal can then look to the agent for compensation for any losses incurred.

There are some situations in which vicarious liability will apply even if the agent is acting independently. The courts appear willing to hold the principal responsible for theft or fraudulent misrepresentation by an agent, even when no employment exists. In the example used to introduce the chapter, it made no difference whether Mr. Snarey was an employee or was acting as an independent agent; because fraud was involved, the principal was liable for the agent's wrongful conduct. Whether other wrongful conduct, such as negligence, will give rise to the imposition of vicarious liability on the principal for the acts of independent agents remains to be seen. Until recently, liability for negligence has been limited to those situations where the wrongful conduct takes place as the agent performs the specific act they have been engaged to do.

**Vicarious liability where independent agent deceitful**

A principal can also be found directly liable for his own tortious conduct. If the principal has requested the act complained of, has told the agent to make a particular statement that turns out to be defamatory or misleading, or is negligent in allowing the agent to make the particular statements complained of, the principal may be directly liable. In the case of *Junkin v. Bedard*,[23] Junkin owned a motel that was sold to a third party through an agent. Junkin provided false information regarding the profitability of the motel to the agent, knowing that the agent would pass it on to the purchaser, Bedard. The agent did so, and Bedard bought the property. Bedard later discovered the falsification and sued Junkin for fraud. Because the agent had innocently passed the information on to Bedard, Junkin alone had committed the fraud, even though the agent had communicated the information. Here, the principal was directly liable for his own fraud. If the agent had fabricated the false information, the principal would have been vicariously liable for the agent's fraud. As is the case with employment law, vicarious liability makes the principal responsible, but it does not relieve the agent of liability for his own tortious conduct. Both can be sued, but the principal can then seek compensation from the agent.

**Direct liability if principal is origin of fraud**

**Vicarious liability—both parties liable**

## Termination of Agency

Since the right of an agent to act for a principal is based on the principal's consent, as soon as the agent is notified of the withdrawal of that consent that authority ends. When the agent is an employee, the relationship is usually ended with appropriate notice, as discussed in Chapter 11. But even where employment may

---

### Reducing **Risk** 12.3

Since most business is done through agents, businesspeople must take care to understand the exposure they have to liability for their agents' conduct. That liability may be based in contract or tort, and both are derived from the duties and authority given. Whether the agent is independent or an employee, care should be taken to carefully define his or her authority and to make sure that the agent stays within those specified parameters. Even then, liability may be incurred when agents do in a careless manner what they are authorized to do. The key here is to minimize exposure, not to eliminate it. In the end, the best practice is to ensure that agents are reliable, trustworthy, and well trained.

---

23. [1958] S.C.R. 56.

**Termination as per agreement**

continue, the authority to act as an agent will end immediately upon notification of the agent. Sometimes, the agency agreement will set out when the agent's authority will end. If the agency relationship was created for a specific length of time, the authority of the agent automatically terminates at the end of that period. Similarly, if the agency contract created the relationship for the duration of a particular project or event, for example, "for the duration of the 2004 Olympic Games," the authority ends when the project or event ends.

**Requirement of notification**

When the principal wants to end the agent's authority to act, simple notification is usually sufficient, for there is no requirement that the notice be reasonable, only that it be communicated to the agent. This applies to the termination of authority to enter into new contracts on the principal's behalf, not necessarily to the right to continued payment, which may be based on other contractual considerations. If the activities the agent is engaged to perform become impossible or essentially different from what the parties anticipated, then the contractual doctrine of frustration may apply, terminating the agent's authority. Similarly, an agent's authority to act on behalf of a principal is terminated when the actions the agent is engaged to perform become illegal. If Cantello agreed to act as Jasper's agent to sell products in a pyramid sales scheme, that authority would have been terminated automatically upon passage of the *Criminal Code* provision prohibiting such activities.[24]

**Frustration may terminate agency, as will requests to perform illegal tasks**

**Death, insanity, or bankruptcy will terminate agency**

An agent's authority to act on behalf of a principal can be terminated in several other ways, as Table 12.1 shows. The death or insanity of a principal will automatically end the authority of an agent. When the principal is a corporation, its dissolution will have a similar effect. An agent will lose authority when a principal becomes bankrupt, although other people may assume such authority under the direction of the trustee. How third parties are impacted by termination of agency varies. Certainly, as far as termination of authority on the basis of agreement is concerned, unless the principal notifies the third party of such termination, the actions of the agent may still be binding on the principal on the basis of apparent authority. Though it is not entirely clear, this may also be the case when the principal becomes insane. However, in the case of bankruptcy or death of the principal, or dissolution of the principal corporation, the agent's actual and apparent

### Table 12.1 Other Ways to Terminate an Agent's Authority

| | Impact on Agent's Actual Authority | Impact on Agent's Apparent Authority |
|---|---|---|
| Death of principal | Ceases | Ceases |
| Bankruptcy of principal | Ceases[1] | Ceases |
| Dissolution of principal corporation | Ceases | Ceases |
| Insanity of principal | Ceases | Unclear—possibly continues[2] |
| By mutual agreement | Ceases | Continues until the third party is notified of termination[2] |

1. Other people may assume this authority under the direction of the trustee.
2. Since apparent authority continues, the principal must actively *notify* third parties that the agent's authority has been terminated. Only then does apparent authority cease.

---

24. *Criminal Code*, R.S.C. 1985, c. C-46, s. 206.

authority ceases. Because of the lingering effect of apparent authority, it is vitally important for a principal to take steps to notify current and potential customers, as well as other people and businesses that they may have dealings with, regarding the termination of the agent's authority.

## Enduring Powers of Attorney

As stated above, loss of sanity on the part of the principal will terminate an agency; consequently, authority to act under a power of attorney terminates when the principal loses capacity. This is problematic, especially where society is aging and many individuals may desire to appoint someone as their agent or decision maker with power to act in the principal's stead after the principal loses capacity. In the past, it was necessary for family members (or others) to apply to the courts for an order appointing them as the trustee of the person who had lost capacity. These applications could be expensive and time consuming, especially if the family was divided as to who should act as trustee. The process could also be a humiliating one for the principal involved, whose loss of mental capacity would be openly examined in a public setting.

To remedy some of these difficulties, provinces have passed legislation to allow individuals to execute **enduring powers of attorney,** vesting powers similar to those given to trustees to the person chosen to act as one's attorney. These powers typically are exercisable after the principal loses mental capacity. The attorney generally can make all financial decisions on behalf of the donor. Through use of an enduring power of attorney, a person can decide, in advance, who to entrust with the future handling of his financial affairs. It is now also possible for individuals to exercise some control over who will make health care decisions and similar personal decisions for them.

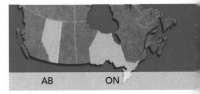

## Specialized Agency Relationships

Many examples of specialized services offered to businesses and the public are essentially agencies in nature, such as those of travel agents, real estate agents, lawyers, accountants, stockbrokers, financial advisers, and insurance representatives. Some of these agents do not enter into contracts on behalf of their clients but negotiate and act on their clients' behalf in other ways. For example, a real estate agent neither offers nor accepts on behalf of a client. In fact, the client is usually the vendor of a property, and the agent's job is to take care of the preliminary matters and bring the purchaser and vendor together so they can enter into a contract directly. Nonetheless, few would dispute that these real estate agents are carrying out an essentially agency function and thus have a fiduciary obligation to their clients. The important thing to remember is that the general provisions set out above also apply to these special agency relationships, although there may be some exceptions. For example, in most of these specialized service professions, the rule that an agent cannot delegate usually does not apply. The very nature of these businesses requires that employees of the firm, not the firm itself, will act on behalf of the client.

**General principles apply to specialized agencies as well**

Most of these specialized agencies are fulfilling a service function and are governed by special statutes and professional organizations. For example, the real estate industry in each province has legislation in place that creates commissions or boards that govern the industry. The commissions require that anyone acting for another in the sale of property be licensed or be in the employ of a licensed real estate agent. Bodies that license their members often provide training, and discipline them when

**Special statutes and professional organizations**

required. It is beyond the scope of this text to examine these professional bodies in detail; students are encouraged to examine the controlling legislation, as well as to seek information directly from the governing professional bodies. Most of them are concerned about their public image and are happy to cooperate.

Often, agencies perform a service to their customers that involves not only representing those customers but also giving them advice. Because of the specialized expertise provided, customers are particularly vulnerable to abuse should such agencies try to take advantage of them. The governing bodies hear complaints and go a long way toward regulating the industry and preventing such abuses. But abuses still occur, and victims should know that they have recourse based on the fiduciary duty principles set out here as well as remedies in contract and tort discussed before. Such fiduciary duties, in fact, may be imposed on other professional advisers, even when their duties do not extend to being agents.[25]

# Insurance

The insurance industry is one where agents play an integral role. Appreciation of agency law assists in determining what duties are owed and to whom. Most insurance is purchased through the services of an agent. But in the context of insurance, **agents** generally act on behalf of insurance corporations, handling and selling the products of several corporations at once. **Brokers**, on the other hand, are retained by the insured to ascertain the insurance needs of the insured and secure the necessary coverage. Their duties are thus owed to the insured, as principal, and must follow the instructions of the insured. Insurance agents owe important obligations to their principals (the insurance corporations), but they also owe a duty of good faith to the customer; thus, agents will be held liable if they fail to provide the insurance coverage asked for or otherwise fail to properly service the client's needs. Customers are increasingly successful in suing agents for negligence and breach of the duty of good faith when such mistakes are made.

People will also often find themselves dealing with insurance **adjusters**, who are employees or representatives of the insurance corporation charged with investigating and settling insurance claims against the corporation after the insured-against event takes place. It is important to remember when dealing with adjusters that they are not normally looking after the interests of the person making the claim, but the insurance corporation instead. There are also many independent people working in the industry available to assist both parties—to arbitrate disputes, to mediate, and to otherwise ensure that the interests of whomever they represent are protected.

The balance of this chapter examines insurance law and how it impacts the insured, the insurer and the agent or broker.

**Agent normally acts for insurance company**

**Broker negotiates terms of insurance for the insured**

**Adjuster values the loss for the insurance company after the insured-against event takes place**

### Case Summary 12.11

**Policy's Terms Determine Coverage:** *Omega Inn Ltd. v. Continental Insurance Co.*[26]

The Omega Inn Ltd. operated a restaurant in Nanaimo, B.C., that burned down in December 1985. It carried both fire insurance and business interruption insur-

25. *Hodgkinson v. Simms*, [1994] 3 S.C.R. 377.

26. (1988), 55 D.L.R. (4th) 766 (B.C.C.A.).

ance with the defendant Continental Insurance Co., and applied for payment with respect to the loss. But Continental Insurance Co., suspecting arson, possibly at the hands of the plaintiff, refused to pay for some six months, while the cause of the fire was being investigated. After it did pay, it took a further four months to rebuild, causing a total of 10 months' interruption in the operation of the business. Continental Insurance Co. refused to pay the business interruption insurance for the 10-month delay. It claimed that the policy required it to pay only for the "length of time as would be required with the exercise of due diligence and dispatch to rebuild, repair, or replace such part of the described property as has been destroyed or damaged, commencing with the date of such destruction or damage...." This was only the four months it took to rebuild, not the 10 months claimed.

Omega, of course, claimed that the extra six months was caused by the failure of the insurance company to honour the policy and so should be included as part of the interruption in business caused by the fire. Although the trial judge agreed with Omega, awarding payment based on a 10-month interruption period, the British Columbia Court of Appeal overturned the lower court decision. The policy was clear and required payment only for the time the business would be interrupted while diligent effort was being made to rebuild. That obligation should not be affected by the fact that the insured did not have the funds to rebuild. "In my opinion, the impecuniosity of the plaintiff cannot be laid at the door of the insurer because it failed to pay more promptly. Its obligation and the full extent of its obligation, with respect to the business loss interruption coverage under the policy, was to pay for such length of time as would be required with the exercise of due diligence and dispatch to rebuild."[27]

Fire insurance and business interruption insurance usually go together, and this case shows their nature and how they work. It also forcefully points out the obligation on the insured to get back into business as soon as possible. Insurance is an important consideration when one holds property, in any of its forms. Insurance was designed to provide compensation for damaged, lost, or stolen property but now also includes such areas as liability and life insurance, as well as business interruption insurance.

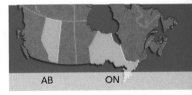

**Insurance spreads risk**

Spreading the risk reduces cost. Premiums paid cover the anticipated losses, the cost of administration, and a profit for the insurance company. The industry is regulated by the federal *Insurance Companies Act*.[28] This statute requires all non-provincial insurance corporations to be registered and sets out other matters, such as the amount of reserves that must be retained to cover eventual claims. All provincial jurisdictions have similar insurance legislation. These provincial and federal statutes can be viewed as a type of consumer protection legislation in the field of insurance.

**Industry regulated by statutes**

Insurance companies use standard form contracts, the wording of which varies considerably between corporations. Government controls help to ensure that the terms do not give unfair advantage to the insurance corporations, but individuals should take care that the terms meet their needs. Each type of coverage has a different standard contract, and when modifications are made, they are

**Standard form contracts are used and must be carefully examined**

27. *Ibid.*, 768.

28. S.C. 1991, c. I-11.8.

attached as supplemental provisions called **riders**. Changes to already existing agreements are made by attaching an **endorsement.**

## *Contra Proferentum* Rule: Ambiguities Construed as Against the Insurer

The courts recognize that most insurance contracts are drafted by the insurer. Often, insurance contracts contain exclusions enabling the insurer to avoid liability for certain losses. But what if the contractual terms are ambiguous? In whose favour should the contract be interpreted?

Application of the *contra proferentum* rule allows the court to choose an interpretation that favours the insured. Coverage will be broadly construed while exclusions will be narrowly interpreted. The courts will apply an interpretation that favours the insured, rationalizing that it is possible for the insurer to choose language that would not have left the issue of coverage open to doubt.

### Case Summary 12.12

***Contra Proferentum* Rule Applied: *Heitsman v. Canadian Premier Life Insurance Co.*[29]**

The insured's widow sued for death benefits under a policy of accidental death and dismemberment insurance. The insured died after suffering a heart attack while trying to free himself from an overturned tractor-trailer following a motor vehicle accident. Medical experts testified that the heart attack was brought on by the stress, emotional and physical, resulting from the accident. The stress would not have been fatal were it not for the deceased's pre-existing heart problems. The Court determined that both the pre-existing condition and the stress caused by the accident contributed to the death. Neither one was the proximate cause. The insurance policy included an exclusion of liability for loss of life caused by sickness or disease. The Court found the clause ambiguous. It was not clear whether the parties had excluded payment for a death where one of its causes was accidental, the other a pre-existing disease. The *contra proferentum* rule was applied, and the exclusion was narrowly interpreted; thus, judgment was issued to the widow.

## Property Insurance

**Co-insurance clause may reduce coverage**

The predominant form of property insurance covers losses to buildings and their contents due to fire. **Co-insurance** clauses are included in most fire insurance policies requiring that the insured maintain a certain percentage of coverage

### Reducing Risk 12.4

There is great danger that a business does not arrange for adequate coverage. Fire insurance, for example, will not normally cover damages caused by nuclear contamination, war, or insurrection, without a special rider to that effect. Similarly, burglary insurance would not cover shoplifting or theft by employees. Natural disasters, such as earthquakes or floods, are excluded from most standard form policies, at least in relation to some types of property loss. Most insurance contracts require insured parties to maintain certain safety and security standards to protect themselves against the risk of fire and theft. It is good practice to read the policy carefully and ask questions as to what is and is not covered.

---

29. (2002), 4 B.C.L.R. (4th) 124 (S.C.).

or bear some of the risk of loss themselves. Thus, in a policy with an 80 percent co-insurance clause, if the policy coverage were for less than that portion of the actual potential loss (say, only $60 000 coverage on property worth $100 000), the insured would have to assume a portion (20 percent in this example) of any covered loss that occurred.

On the other hand, even if you overinsure a property, you cannot collect more than the loss. People may mistakenly think that if they have two policies covering the same risk, they can collect on both. A basic principle of insurance law is that you can recover only what you have lost, and so no matter how many policies you have, the total you can collect from all of them is no more than you have lost. If you take out two policies for $100 000 each on a house and suffer $50 000 damage in a fire, you can only collect $50 000 from either insurer, or each insurer will pay you $25 000. You will not be entitled to collect $50 000 from each insurer, despite the fact that you have paid premiums to both. It becomes important, then, for the insured to have coverage that is at least close to the maximum potential loss and to obtain coverage for all types of loss, including fire, theft, natural disaster, and so on.

**Overinsurance wasteful**

Sometimes the reason an insured has overlapping insurance is coincidental (as when both parents have dental insurance for their children under their respective employer's group insurance); sometimes this is required by the insurer. Where there is more than one policy covering a loss, the contracts of insurance may indicate which is the primary insurance and which is excess coverage. In the *Family Insurance Corp. v. Lombard Canada Ltd.* case,[30] the issue of contribution among insurers was complicated as both policies contained "other insurance" clauses that declared the policies to be "excess insurance" to any other insurance coverage. Rather than looking outside the policies or to surrounding circumstances for guidelines, the Supreme Court of Canada held that the policies were clear and unequivocal—each claimed to be the excess policy. Thus the equitable principle of contribution demanded that the insurers each bear the burden equally. **Contribution** requires that where two or more policies exist, the insurers are to contribute to compensating the insured. Generally, this is done in accordance with contractual terms and the courts are called upon to interpret the contracts and determine degrees of contribution.

**Insurance companies to contribute as spelled out in their contracts**
• if degree of contribution unclear, equal sharing may be required

Further, when there is a situation of considerable risk to an insurance company, such as a large project that needs to be insured (for example, a new chemical plant), the corporation will often turn to other insurance corporations so that the risk is spread among them all. This pooling of risk is called **re-insurance** and is an important aspect of the industry.

**Insurance companies often re-insure**

## Business Interruption Insurance

Often, an ongoing business will find itself unable to function because of some unforeseen event that may or may not be covered by another form of insurance. For example, if Rampal operates a plant manufacturing widgets and the plant burns down, fire insurance and other forms of property insurance would normally cover the loss. Such insurance would not, however, cover the loss of profits suffered while the plant is not operational. Business interruption insurance will normally cover not only lost profits but also any added expenses incurred to bring the business back into production. Property insurance and business inter-

**Business interruption insurance covers lost profits**

30. [2002] S.C.J. No. 49.

ruption insurance together are an attempt to put the insured in the same financial position it would have been in had the fire or other damage not occurred.

## Life and Health Insurance

Life insurance provides security for a family or business against the death of the insured. Businesses take out life insurance against the death of key personnel to cover losses incurred from any disruption that may result from the death or illness of an executive or partner.

Death is inevitable, and so premiums are calculated on the basis of a prediction of how long a person of a certain age and health can be expected to live.

### Case Summary 12.13

**Consent Given—Insurable Interest Requirement Satisfied: *Chantiam v. Packall Packaging Inc.*[31]**

Mr. Chantiam was working as the plant manager for Packall Packaging Inc., when he consented to a "keyman" insurance policy being taken out on his life by the company. Under this type of policy, the employer is able to insure the life of important key employees so that if anything happens that results in a disruption of business it will have compensation through the insurance coverage. About two years later, Mr. Chantiam terminated his employment and started up a business in competition with Packall. He had assumed that the insurance policy had ended as well, but discovered that the company had maintained the policy and continued to pay the premiums. Mr. Chantiam brought this action, demanding that the policy be terminated or transferred to him.

Like other forms of insurance, there must be an insurable interest in the life being insured. In this case, the company had such an insurable interest in Mr. Chantiam's life at the time the policy was taken out. However, Mr. Chantiam argued that since circumstances had changed, the policy should be cancelled. The trial judge agreed with Mr. Chantiam, ordering that the policy be cancelled on the ground that it was not "in the public interest" that Packall be allowed "to continue insuring the life of its business competitor."[32]

But on appeal, the Court held that the appropriate time to determine insurable interest was when the policy was made, and it did not matter that circumstances had changed since. The policy was valid and the company was within its rights to continue it. An insurable interest is determined by the company being in a position to suffer a loss if the insured-against event were to happen. In this case, because of Chantiam's key position, there was no question that such an insurable interest was present at the time of the creation of the policy. Furthermore, the legislation involved stipulates that where the insured consents in writing to the creation of the policy, as happened here, that satisfies the insurable interest requirement. Since there was an insurable interest at the time the policy was created, there were no grounds to challenge the continuation of the policy by Packall.

31. (1998), 38 O.R. (3d) 401 (C.A.), leave to appeal to S.C.C. refused, [1998] S.C.C.A. No. 358.
32. *Ibid.*, at 403.

A person taking out life insurance, like other forms of insurance, must be able to demonstrate an insurable interest in the life of the person insured. For businesses, it is a prudent and common practice to insure the life of key personnel. Having that employee sign a written consent to the policy may satisfy the requirement of an insurable interest. This case illustrates that with life insurance, the question of insurable interest only relates to when the policy is taken out. Note that Manitoba has changed its legislation allowing a person to bring an application to the court to have the policy cancelled when that insurable interest is no longer present.[33] But in this case, Ontario (like other provinces) had no similar provision.

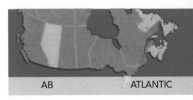

There are various forms of life insurance to meet the needs of different individuals. Term insurance provides only a benefit upon death, and the premiums are lower than whole life insurance, which provides coverage in the event of death as well as investment potential and retirement income. These are just two of several variations of life insurance available.

Health and disability insurance provides coverage during the life of the insured and is designed to pay health care expenses and provide an income for a person who is unable to earn a living because of illness or accident. Medical insurance can be arranged individually or as part of group coverage. Health care services in Canada are funded through the government-sponsored medical system, which is often supplemented by plans providing extended coverage. In most Canadian jurisdictions, disability insurance can be obtained on an individual basis with an insurance corporation, but it is more often acquired by large organizations as part of an employee benefits package.

**Health and disability insurance usually part of group coverage**

## Liability Insurance

When injury or damage is caused by a person failing in their duty to others, the wrongdoer can be sued for the loss. Such carelessness can take place anywhere, and it can happen when the person acts in a business, professional, or personal capacity. In some occupations, professional liability insurance is mandatory. In all cases, it is important to maintain appropriate insurance coverage to avoid potentially disastrous consequences. Personal liability insurance and motor vehicle insurance go a long way toward protecting individuals from potentially devastating claims against them.

Businesspeople must also insure against vicarious liability, which may be imposed on them because of the wrongdoing of employees. Liability insurance does not excuse the insured from responsibility, and it is quite likely that the insured will have to go through a lawsuit. However, in most liability insurance contracts, the insurance corporation arranges legal representation and covers the judgment up to the amount of coverage. The insured will be responsible for the amount of the judgment over the insured amount, and so it is important to maintain adequate coverage in this area as well. If Jones has liability insurance for only $500 000 and causes a $750 000 loss, he will be required to pay the $250 000 shortfall. Liability insurance will not cover you for your own wilful acts, such as assault, theft, or arson.

**Liability insurance covers negligence by self or employees**

**Only to extent of coverage**

Many people assume that if there is insurance coverage any injury or damage will be compensated regardless of fault, but with liability insurance the insurer will pay only where the insured was at fault. If there was no negligence or other

**Coverage only when insured is at fault**

---

33. *Insurance Act*, R.S.M. 1987, c. I-40, s. 155(4).

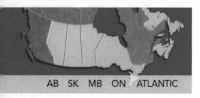

AB   SK   MB   ON   ATLANTIC

wrongful conduct on the part of the insured, the insurance corporation will not pay. Many argue for no-fault coverage in these circumstances. No-fault insurance is similar to workers' compensation in that the injured party is entitled to compensation, no matter who is responsible. Liability coverage has become so important in the operation of automobiles that several provinces have instituted compulsory automobile coverage, and some have or are considering going to no-fault schemes.

## Insurable Interest

**Must be insurable interest to avoid illegality**

For insurance not to be considered a wager, the insured must be able to demonstrate an insurable interest in what is insured. That means that when the insured-against event happens, the insured must have suffered a loss for which the insurance payout provides compensation. Insurance is only intended to put the person who suffers a loss back in the original position she would have been in had the event not taken place. The contract for insurance is a contract of indemnity. Consequently, except in the case of life insurance, the insured can recover only what he or she has actually lost, up to the limit set out in the policy. When the payout becomes a windfall, the insurance agreement is void as an illegal contract.

### Case Summary 12.14

**Insurance Void Due to Lack of Insurable Interest:** *Blue Seal Paving Stone Inc. v. Western Union Insurance Canada Ltd.*[34]

The requirement that an insurable interest exists is critical to the validity of a contract of insurance. One cannot insure someone else's property against loss, for one does not suffer a loss if that property is destroyed. Any payment on such a policy would be a windfall—like the proceeds from a bet. This explains why the insurance placed by Blue Seal was invalid. Mr. Girard owned and operated a car. Because of his driving record, Mr. Girard was considered uninsurable by conventional carriers. His wife, being principal shareholder in Blue Seal, took out insurance on the vehicle and did not disclose that her husband would be operating it. The premiums payable were thus significantly lower than when Mr. Girard insured it personally. Blue Seal's insurer refused to pay on the policy when the vehicle, having been driven by Mr. Girard, was involved in a collision. The insurer claimed, as accepted by the Court, that the insured, Blue Seal, had no insurable interest in the car. The Court dismissed the plaintiff's allegations that the car had been given to Mrs. Girard by her husband as a gift.

The Court relied upon other cases where parents of the driver insured their son's vehicle, claiming to be the owners.[35] The motivation to claim that the vehicle belonged to the parents was to secure insurance at a lower premium. Unfortunately, when their son was involved in a collision and was hurt, the insurers denied coverage due to the absence of an insurable interest. The message is clear. One can only insure property if one owns it or can demonstrate that one will suffer a loss if it is damaged or destroyed.

When a claim is made, the insured will be able to collect only up to the value of the insurable interest she has in the property insured. The insurable interest,

---

34. (2000), 269 A.R. 393 (Prov. Ct.).

35. See *Morrow v. Royal Insurance Co. of Canada* (1990), 42 C.C.L.I. 135 (Alta. Q.B.), aff'd (1992), 11 C.C.L.I. (2d) 86 (Alta. C.A.); *Lal v. Guardian Insurance Co. of Canada* (1992), 130 A.R. 147 (Q.B.).

then, is the amount she stands to lose if the insured-against event takes place. If Flynn owned a half-interest in a painting worth $150 000, she would have an insurable interest of $75 000. If Flynn carried an insurance policy of $150 000 on the painting and it was stolen, she would be able to collect only $75 000 for herself, even though she had insured it for the higher amount. Any other result would give Flynn a windfall, which is prohibited. (Were Flynn's painting to be stolen, she would likely collect the entire $150 000 but be required to hold the other $75 000 in trust for the person who owned the other half interest in the painting.)

It should be noted that when life insurance is involved, legislation defines in whose life one has an insurable interest. One evidently has an insurable interest in her own life, but also in the lives of one's spouse and other close relatives. A loss, economic, emotional and otherwise, is assumed if a close relation dies. Depending on the jurisdiction, where the lives of key business personnel are insured the written consent of that person may be required. The value of that insurable interest will be the amount of insurance coverage contracted for.

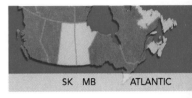

In the past, it was thought that because a corporation was a separate legal entity, the shareholder had no insurable interest in the assets of the corporation. The Supreme Court of Canada, however, has decided that shareholders do have an insurable interest in those assets. The Court held that it was not necessary for the person taking out insurance to actually have a legally enforceable interest in the property to insure it. It is enough that a relationship to the subject matter or a concern in it exists, such that a loss would be suffered if the insured-against event took place.[36]

**Shareholders now have insurance interests in assets of corporation**

## Contract of Utmost Good Faith

A relationship of *trust* exists between the insured and insurer, creating an *obligation to act in good faith*. An important aspect of that obligation is the duty on the part of the insured to disclose pertinent information, especially where it affects the *risk* assumed by the insurer. After all, it is the insured who knows, has possession of, or has access to the information relevant to that risk. Even after the contract is made, there is often a duty to notify the insurance company when circumstances change, as when an occupied building becomes unoccupied for a length of time.[37]

**Insured has duty to disclose changes in risk**

### Case Summary 12.15

**Punitive Damages Awarded to Deter Breaches of Good-faith Duty:**
*Al-Asadi v. Alberta Motor Association Insurance Co.*[38]

Insurance fraud is a serious problem and insurers are fighting back. The courts appear ready to assist, awarding punitive damages against those found trying to defraud their insurers. In the *Al-Asadi* case, the insured claimed that his car had been stolen and vandalized. He tried to collect the value of the vehicle from his insurer. The insurer had doubts as to whether the theft was staged, so it refused to pay. The insured sued, alleging breach of contract and a breach of the duty of good faith on the insurer's part, as it was implying that Al-Asadi was deceitful. The

---

36. *Kosmopoulos v. Constitution Insurance Company of Canada Ltd.*, [1987] 1 S.C.R. 2.

37. See, for example, *528852 Ontario Inc. v. Royal Insurance Co.* (2000), 51 O.R. (3d) 470 (Sup. Ct. J.), where the insured's failure to disclose a change of use, namely that the premises were left unoccupied, was a material non-disclosure that entitled the insurer to deny coverage.

38. [2003] A.J. No. 405 (Q.B.).

evidence brought forward by the insured was contradictory—he failed not only to prove bad faith on the insurer's part, but also to satisfy the court that someone else had stolen the car. The car had been vandalized, but by whom? By Al-Asadi? Quoting Justice Murray in the *Andrusiw* case,[39] the Court accepted that:

> The contract of insurance between an insurer and an insured is a contract of utmost good faith. Implicit is a term of the contract that the insurer has an obligation to deal with the claims advanced by the insured in good faith and an insured has an obligation to the insurer to put forward his claims honestly and in good faith. As such, breach of that obligation on the part of either party constitutes a separate an independent wrong for which compensation is paid. Thus, if either party acts in bad faith toward the other, that is an independent actionable wrong....

Putting forward a false insurance claim is acting in bad faith. Punitive damages and solicitor–client costs were awarded against the insured, Al-Asadi.

**Insurer's duty to process claims fairly**

Just as the insured has a duty to be honest in its dealings with the insurer, the insurer has a duty to process claims fairly. Where insurers have withheld payments without justification, damages, punitive damages, and solicitor–client costs have been awarded to the aggrieved insured. In the *Fowler* case,[40] for example, the insurer cut off disability payments to the insured even in light of medical evidence supporting the claim. The insurer's actions further exacerbated the insured's condition, by adding to the stress he was already under. Similarly, in the *Whiten* case,[41] the insurer's rejection of proof of loss without explanation was regarded as a failure of its duty of good faith. The insured had fled their burning house in their nightclothes, suffering frostbite as they watched their house burn down. After paying their living expenses for a couple of months, the insurer abruptly cut off payments. It raised a lame claim of arson, which was wholly discredited at trial. Punitive damages of $1 million were awarded by the jury, which evidently regarded the insurer's conduct as reprehensible.

**Duty to defend**

The insurer also has a duty to defend the insured in particular situations. Liability insurance is placed specifically because the insured does not wish to bear the cost of being liable to third parties for its negligence or other wrongful acts. But this duty only goes so far. An insurer will not have to fund defending an insured charged with committing intentional, criminal acts. In the *Scalera* case,[42] where the insured had a comprehensive general liability policy, the insurer was not required to defend the insured against charges of sexual assault.

## Disclosure

When applying for property insurance, the insurer will want to know what the property will be used for, whether it is for a business, whether it will be vacant for extended periods, and what kind of security and safety equipment is in place. For life, disability, or medical insurance, any injury, disease, or other health problems

---

39. *Andrusiw v. Aetna Life Insurance Co. of Canada*, [2001] 289 A.R. 1 (Q.B.) at para. 82.

40. *Fowler v. Manufacturers Life Insurance Co.* (2002), 216 Nfld. & P.E.I.R. 132 (Nfld. S.C. (T.D.))

41. *Whiten v. Pilot Insurance Co.*, [2002] 1 S.C.R. 595.

42. *Non-Marine Underwriters, Lloyd's of London v. Scalera*, [2000] 1 S.C.R. 551.

that may affect that person's health must be disclosed. These factors affect eligibility or the rates charged for insurance, and since the insurer usually has no way of determining this information by itself, it must depend on the honesty of the insured to disclose it. Failure to disclose information material to the loss may be misrepresentation and may result in the loss being unrecoverable. Even where it is not relevant to the loss, if it is a material misrepresentation it may cause the entire policy to be void. Legislation in some provinces upholds the insurance where the misrepresentation was innocent; but even in those jurisdictions if the misrepresentation or failure to disclose were done knowingly, the insurance policy cannot be enforced.

**Insured must disclose relevant information**

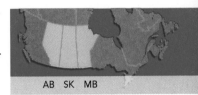

AB   SK   MB

### Case Summary 12.16

**Failure to Disclose Medical Condition Proves Deadly:** *Duong v. NN Life Insurance Co. of Canada*[43]

Life insurance policies had been taken out on the lives of Duong's spouse and son. There were material misrepresentations made in the applications with respect to the wife's health and medical treatment. Following the wife's death, the insurer denied coverage, conveying its position to the insured that the misrepresentations voided the policy. The insured argued that as the insurer continued to receive premiums after learning of the death and misrepresentations, it should be estopped from avoiding the contract. The Court disagreed. NN Life refunded the premiums and that was the extent of its obligations to the insured.

What lessons can be learned from this case? Whose obligation is it to be honest and forthcoming with information relevant to the risk?

## Subrogation

The right of subrogation gives the insurance corporation, once it has paid out a claim, the right to take over the rights of the insured in relation to whoever caused the injury or loss. The insurer steps into the shoes of the insured and can then sue whoever caused the loss as if it were the insured. Thus, where a neighbour carelessly allows a bonfire to get out of control causing Mrs. Kostachue's house to burn down, she would normally claim on her insurance and receive compensation. Her insurance corporation would then sue the neighbour for negligence and recoup what it can. In fact, if the neighbour had liability insurance, it would likely be his insurer that would ultimately pay. You should not assume when you are involved in an accident that just because the other person has insurance, you are protected. If it is your fault, that person's insurance company will seek to recover its loss from you.

In the *Personal Insurance v. Ross* case,[44] the insurer could not recover from the third party who ransacked the insured's apartment because the insurer had not completely indemnified the insured first. The insurer paid only $14 000 to the insured, whereas the damage inflicted was assessed at $31 000. Accordingly, the insured was able to retain any funds recovered from the third party under an order of restitution, to the exclusion of the insurer. An insurer can exercise its right of subrogation only if it completely indemnifies the insured first. This point was emphasized by the Supreme Court of Canada as illustrated in Case Summary 12.17.

---

43. (2001), 141 O.A.C. 307 (Ont. C.A.).

44. *Personal Insurance Co. of Canada v. Ross* (1998), 90 A.R. 233 (Q.B.).

### Case Summary 12.17

#### Subrogation Rights Not Violated If They Haven't Arisen: *Somersall v. Friedman*[45]

The respondents suffered serious injuries in an automobile accident caused by the other driver (the "tortfeasor") and were able to reach an out-of-court settlement. That settlement provided that the tortfeasor would admit fault at the trial and the injured respondents would not sue for more than the limits of his insurance. The agreement benefited all parties in that the tortfeasor would not face personal liability (he was underinsured) and the respondents would avoid a lengthy trial trying to establish fault. When the respondents sought to recover the remainder of their damages from their own insurer, coverage was denied. Instead, their insurer alleged a breach of contract, claiming that the insured had violated its subrogation rights. The Supreme Court of Canada found that the insured had not sufficiently interfered with the insurer's right of subrogation so as to deprive it of its contractual rights, for rarely is this right of subrogation of any value as against an underinsured motorist. Further, the Court clarified that right of subrogation did not arise until the insured had been fully indemnified, something that the insurer had not yet done. The insured could thus advance a claim for the deficiency as against their own insurer.

**Right of salvage**

**Depreciated rather than replacement value**

Insurance corporations will also normally have the choice to rebuild, repair, or replace what is damaged so that they can minimize their cost. They also have the right of **salvage**. If stolen goods are recovered, for example, they can sell those goods to recover their costs. When personal property has been lost, the insurer usually has to pay only the depreciated value of the goods, not the replacement cost, unless it has agreed otherwise. Most personal household insurance policies today provide for the replacement of destroyed or stolen goods at their full retail value. When a loss does take place, there is a general requirement on the part of the insured to report that loss to the insurance corporation right away so that the insurance corporation can take steps to minimize the damage. There might also be an obligation to report the matter to the police if a crime is involved or if the loss resulted from an automobile accident.

**Insured can't profit from wilful misconduct**

It should also be pointed out that the insured is not permitted to profit from his wilful misconduct. If the insured deliberately causes the loss, he will not be able to collect. Thus, if Fagan burns down his own house, killing his wife in the process, he will not be able to collect on the fire insurance and he will not be able to collect on his wife's life insurance, even where he is named as beneficiary. The **forfeiture rule** (that a criminal should not be permitted to profit from a crime) also extends to those who claim through the criminal's estate. In the above example, if Fagan were also to die in the house fire, his estate would not be able to collect on either policy.

## Bonding

While insurance coverage is not generally available for intentionally wrongful acts, such as assault, many businesspeople insist on some protection against losses

---

45. [2002] S.C.J. No. 60.

brought on by their employees or the people they deal with, who may act wrongfully, even wilfully so. Bonding is available in these circumstances, and it takes two forms. Usually, an employer will pay a fee to have an employee bonded against that employee's own wrongful conduct (**fidelity bond**). If the employee steals from the employer or a customer, the bonding corporation will be required to compensate the employer for that loss. It must be emphasized, however, that this does not relieve the bonded employee of responsibility. The bonding corporation can turn to the employee and collect from that party, which is what distinguishes bonding from normal insurance arrangements.

**Bonded parties still liable**

The second form of bonding, a **surety bond**, occurs when the bonding is designed to provide assurance that a party to a contract will perform its side of the contract. For example, in a large construction project the corporation doing the foundation may be required to put up a performance bond that it will finish the job at a specified level of quality and by a certain time. If it fails to complete or does not complete on time, the bonding company will be required to pay compensation. A standby letter of credit, as discussed in Chapter 10, can also be used for the same purpose.

# Summary

## Agents

- Act for a principal in dealings with third parties.

## Authority

- Actual authority is defined in the contract.
- Apparent authority.
  - When the principal has done something to lead the third party to believe that the agent has authority, even when such authority has been specifically withheld.
  - Even when the agent has exceeded both the actual and apparent authority, the principal may ratify the agreement.
  - Ratification works retroactively.
  - When the agent acts beyond all authority he or she can be sued (breach of warranty of authority).

## Agent's duties

- Involve performing terms of contract; providing an accounting of funds, and fiduciary duty.
- Cannot be delegated.

## Principal's duties

- To honour terms of contract and reimburse agent's expenses.

## Undisclosed principal

- Third party's recourse is against agent if existence of principal is not disclosed.
- Third party has a choice to sue the agent or the undisclosed principal to enforce the contract, once existence of the principal is revealed.
- Undisclosed principal cannot ratify contracts.

## Vicarious liability

- In the absence of an employment relationship, the principal may escape vicarious liability for the acts of the agent, except when fraud is involved.
- Principal may be vicariously liable if misconduct of agent applies to acts within agent's actual or apparent authority.

## Fiduciary relationship

- Exists between the agent and the principal.
- Agent has obligation to act in the best interests of the principal.
- Full disclosure by the agent is required.

## Termination

- The agency relationship is typically terminated by simple notification or as agreed in the agency contract.
- Bankruptcy, death, or insanity of the principal or, when the principal is a corporation, the dissolution of that corporation, will also terminate the agent's authority.

## Insurance

- Designed to spread the risk of loss.
- *Contra proferentum* rule: policy's ambiguities interpreted in the insured's favour.
- Property, business interruption, life, health, and liability are the primary forms of insurance available.
- Insured must have an insurable interest in the subject matter. Recovery limited to the extent of that insurable interest.
- Insurance is a contract of utmost good faith
  - Insured has a duty to fully disclose material facts and be honest.
  - Insurer has a duty to act fairly and to defend the insured.
- Liability insurance
  - Payment will be made only where the insured was at fault.
  - When a claim is paid, the company is subrogated to the rights of the insured.
  - Can salvage the property or take over the insured's right to sue a third party.

## QUESTIONS

1. What is the agent's function? Why is it important to understand the law of agency in business?

2. Distinguish among agents, employees, and independent contractors. Describe the relationship between them and the principals.

3. What is the significance of the agency agreement for the parties to it?

4. Explain what effect an agent's limited capacity will have on the contractual obligations created between a principal and a third party. What effect would the incapacity of the principal have on this relationship?

5. Distinguish between an agent's actual, implied, and apparent authority. Explain why this distinction can be important from the agent's point of view.

6. Distinguish between equitable (promissory) estoppel and ordinary estoppel. Explain the role estoppel plays in agency law.

7. Explain what is meant by ratification. Explain why the principal's right to ratify might be considered unfair to the third party.

8. Describe the limitations on a principal's right to ratify the actions of his or her agent. How can the principle of ratification be as dangerous to the principal as it is to the third party?

9. What effect does it have on the relationship between the principal and the third party when an agent writes on an agreement "subject to ratification"?

10. Agents owe a fiduciary duty to their principals. What are the requirements of that duty?

11. What options are open to a third party who has been dealing with an undisclosed principal if the contract is breached?

12. Does an undisclosed principal have the right to ratify an agent's unauthorized act?

13. Explain how the doctrine of vicarious liability applies in a principal–agent relationship.

14. How does the function performed by a real estate agent differ significantly from that normally performed in a principal–agency relationship? What governs the real estate agent's conduct?

15. Explain conceptually the purpose of insurance and why it is not void as an illegal contract. (See also Chapter 7.)

16. Distinguish between business interruption insurance and fire insurance. Why might a businessperson want to have both forms of coverage?

17. What kinds of things cannot be covered under a liability insurance policy? Indicate any other methods a person or business might use to ensure that the people they are working with perform their jobs properly.

18. Discuss the similarities and differences between insurance and a wager.

19. What is meant by an insurable interest, and how does it apply to the various types of insurance discussed in the chapter?

20. Explain what is meant by the right of subrogation. How may subrogation affect not only the insured but also the person who has caused the injury or damage? Indicate what other means the insurance corporations have to keep their damages as low as possible.

21. What is meant by bonding? In your answer, distinguish between bonding and insurance coverage.

---

## CASES

### 1. *Kisil v. John F. Stevens Ltd.* (1980), 42 N.S.R. (2d) 148 (S.C. (T.D.)).

Mr. and Mrs. Kisil bought a house through Buckley, an agent for the John S. Stevens firm. In the process of selling the house, Buckley assured the Kisils that there was no problem with the water in the well. They decided to buy the house, but Buckley kept them out of the house until after the deal's closing date. All this time, Buckley maintained that the condition of the well was good and that the water would clear up as soon as it was used a bit. In fact, the well had been improperly constructed and the water it produced was unfit for use. The Kisils sued Buckley and the real estate company. Describe the arguments that would form the basis of their complaint, their likelihood of success, and the remedies available. Explain as well the legal position of the vendor.

### 2. *Rockland Industries Inc. v. Amerada Minerals Corporation of Canada Limited,* [1980] 2 S.C.R. 2.

Kurtz was a salesman in charge of bulk sales and the manager of marketing who reported to Deverin, a senior vice-president of Amerada. Kurtz negotiated and concluded a deal with Powers and Leaderman, employees of Rockland Industries Inc., for the sale of 50 000 tons (45 360 tonnes) of sulphur. During the process of negotiation, Kurtz gave no indication of any qualifications on his authority. However, any sale of this magnitude had to be approved by an executive operating committee of Amerada and signed by the chairman of the board. After the deal was completed, Rockland's representative was informed of the limitations on Kurtz's authority but was also told that the operating committee had given approval and that the chairman of the board's signature was merely a rubber stamp. In fact, Amerada refused to deliver the sulphur, and Rockland had to acquire it from other sources. They were able to acquire only 25 000 tons and sued Amerada for damages. Explain the arguments available to both sides and the likely outcome.

### 3. *Raso v. Dionigi* (1993), 12 O.R. (3d) 580 (C.A.).

Guerino Sirianni was a real estate agent working for Joseph Leonardis Real Estate Ltd. His sister-in-law Raffaela was looking for some income property, and after some searching Sirianni entered into a deal with Mr. and Mrs. Dionigi, persuading them to list their property for sale with him and subsequently presented an offer to purchase from his sister-in-law, who used her maiden name (R. Raso in trust) so that the sellers would not know that he was related to the purchaser. Before the deal was to close, the Dionigis discovered the relationship between the agent and the purchaser and refused to go through with the deal. Sirianni sued for his commission and his brother and sister-in-law sued for specific performance.

Explain the arguments that are available to the sellers in response to these claims. How would your answer be affected by the knowledge that the brother and sister-in-law of Sirianni had disclosed to him that they were willing to pay between $250 000 and $300 000 for the property, and in the negotiations that followed this was not disclosed to the sellers? In fact, the first offer made by his brother and sister-in-law was only $270 000. The sellers eventually took $285 000 for the property, not knowing that the purchasers were willing to go to $300 000. The actual fair market value of the property was determined to be $285 000.

### 4. *Hammill v. Gerling Global Life Insurance Co.* (1990), 109 A.R. 254.

Mrs. Hammill obtained a life insurance policy in which she stated that she had been a non-smoker for the past 12 months. In fact, this information was incorrect. It was clearly established that she had smoked considerably during this period. She had taken out the policy in 1985 and was killed in an auto accident on February 2, 1986. Although her smoking in no way contributed to the accident, the insurer refused to pay the beneficiary under the policy. Explain the insurer's legal obligations in these circumstances.

# Organizations

One important characteristic of our modern commercial world is the effort that has been made by the legal system to facilitate the involvement of large groups of people in various business projects and activities. Partnership is the historical method of people joining together to carry on such business activities, and this, along with an examination of the sole proprietorship, is the subject of Chapter 13. Chapter 14 deals with the now more common method used, where people come together to participate in business, the corporation. Corporations are artificial persons, and their uniqueness results in a complex world of interaction among the company, shareholders, creditors, managers, and workers, and developing an understanding of these relationships is the objective of that chapter.

# 13

# Sole Proprietorship and Partnership

## CHAPTER HIGHLIGHTS

- Sole proprietorship, government regulations, and liability
- Partnership
- Rights and obligations of partners
- Advantages of partnership
- Dissolution of the partnership

Each of the different methods of carrying on a business has specific rules and obligations associated with it. It is vitally important that the parties to such business relationships clearly understand the legal implications of their associations, whether they are the owners of the business, employees, or outsiders involved in commercial transactions with it. This chapter is primarily devoted to an examination of the law relevant to partnerships. The following case illustrates how a sole proprietor will be personally liable for debts of a business, how a partnership can arise despite an intention to the contrary, and how a bankruptcy will dissolve an existing partnership.

### Case Summary 13.1

#### Is the Business a Sole Proprietorship or a Partnership? *Brer Rabbit Printing Co. v. Bosiak (c.o.b. Pegasus Printing)*[1]

Pegasus Printing owed Brer Rabbit Printing an outstanding amount for services rendered between August and November 1997. Brer Rabbit sued Mr. and Ms. Bosiak, as partners in Pegasus Printing. Ms. Bosiak declared personal bankruptcy and the claim against her was stayed. Mr. Bosiak applied to have the claim against him dismissed, on the grounds that his wife had been operating the business as a sole proprietor. The Court found that while the business was registered as a sole proprietorship for licensing, banking, insurance, and financial reporting purposes, the Bosiaks were understood to have been partners and were treated as such. This, however, did not assist Brer Rabbit, as Mr. Bosiak had declared bank-

---

1. [2001] B.C.J. No. 649 (S.C.)

ruptcy in October 1996, thereby dissolving the partnership. There was no evidence to demonstrate a partnership was re-established after that date. Therefore, the Bosiaks were not partners when the debt arose, and only Ms. Bosiak was liable for the debt in question.

# Types of Business Organization

There are essentially three major types of business organization (see Figure 13.1). The first, the **sole proprietorship**, involves an individual carrying on business alone. Employees may be hired and business may be carried on through the services of an agent, but the business is the sole responsibility of one person, the owner. A second method of carrying on business is called a **partnership**, where ownership and responsibilities, along with both profits and losses, are shared by two or more partners. As was the case with the sole proprietorship, the partnership may also employ others and act through agents. The third type of business organization is the incorporated company. Any type of business organization involving more than one person can be called a company; a **corporation**, however, is a legal entity. By statute, it has been given an identity separate from the individual members who make it up. Thus, contracts with a corporation are dealings with the corporation itself as if it were a person in its own right.

> **Sole proprietorship involves one person**
>
> **Partners share responsibilities**
>
> **Corporation is a separate legal entity**

There are other ways for people to work together to carry on a commercial activity. For example, a **non-profit society** can be set up under legislation such as the Alberta *Societies Act*.[2] This also creates a separate legal entity, but the procedure of incorporation and the obligations of those involved are quite different. There are also several ways in which these various types of business organizations can be combined. A **holding corporation** holds shares in other corporations. A **joint venture** involves several different incorporated corporations that band together to accomplish a major project. They may form a separate corporation or a partnership. The discussion in this chapter will be limited to an examination of sole proprietorship and partnership, while Chapter 14 will deal with corporations.

> **Societies are separate legal entities, but obligations differ**

## Figure 13.1 Types of Business Organization

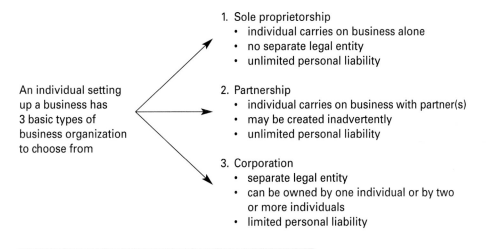

An individual setting up a business has 3 basic types of business organization to choose from

1. Sole proprietorship
   - individual carries on business alone
   - no separate legal entity
   - unlimited personal liability

2. Partnership
   - individual carries on business with partner(s)
   - may be created inadvertently
   - unlimited personal liability

3. Corporation
   - separate legal entity
   - can be owned by one individual or by two or more individuals
   - limited personal liability

2. R.S.A. 2000, c. S-14.

# The Sole Proprietorship

**Sole proprietorship carries on business in own right**

The sole proprietorship is simply an individual carrying on a business activity on her own. The sole proprietor makes all the decisions associated with the business and is the only one entitled to the benefits derived from the business. A sole proprietor also bears full responsibility for all the costs, losses, and obligations incurred in the business activity. Thus, there is no distinction between the personal assets of the sole proprietor and those of the business. They are all the assets of the proprietor and are available to creditors if things go wrong.

## Government Regulations

**Must adhere to licensing and governing regulations**

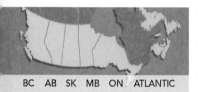

BC  AB  SK  MB  ON  ATLANTIC

The sole proprietor, like all other types of business organizations, must satisfy many federal, provincial, and municipal requirements in order to carry on business. Usually, the name of the business must be registered if it is different from the sole proprietor's name,[3] and a licence to operate obtained from the appropriate level of government. This licensing process is used to control or restrict certain types of businesses, such as door-to-door sales, credit information services, moneylenders, hotels, and cabarets. When the handling of food or dangerous commodities is involved, there are further provincial and federal regulations that must be obeyed. Sole proprietors must also satisfy local zoning bylaws, and if they have employees they are subject to employment legislation, such as workers' compensation, employment insurance, and income tax regulations. They are also required to remit Goods and Services Tax if the business income is more than $30 000 per year.

**Sole proprietor relatively free of outside interference**

As a general rule, sole proprietors are subject to fewer government regulations than partnerships and corporations. Only minimal records need be kept, and sole proprietors are usually not required to disclose information about the business to others. They must keep sufficient records to satisfy government agencies, such as Canada Customs and Revenue Agency. In essence, the sole proprietor has complete control and complete responsibility for the business activity.

A sole proprietor has complete control of and responsibility for the business.

## Liability

Sole proprietors do not have accountability to others and alone are responsible for making important business decisions. They can look only to their own resources to finance the business operation; they cannot sell shares and are restricted to their own credit standing when borrowing money to finance the business. The sole proprietor owns all the assets, receives all the profits of the business, and is responsible for all its debts and liabilities. This **unlimited liability** can be the most significant disadvantage of the sole proprietorship. When liability is incurred for breached contracts or torts, or where there is insurmountable debt, the whole burden falls on the sole proprietor. Under the principle of **vicarious liability**, the sole proprietor is responsible for any tort committed by an employee during the course of

---

3. See, for example, *Business Names Act*, R.S.O. 1990, c. B-17, s. 2(2).

employment. Although the sole proprietor's entire personal fortune is at risk, much of this risk can be offset by carrying adequate insurance. Any profit derived from a sole proprietorship is subject to personal income tax, while some tax advantages available to partnerships and corporations are not available to sole proprietors. These factors alone are often enough to encourage the businessperson to incorporate.

**Sole proprietor has unlimited liability but can purchase insurance**

Some individuals, notably professionals, such as doctors, dentists, lawyers, and accountants, cannot incorporate their practice and derive little advantage from doing so in those jurisdictions where professional incorporations are permitted.[4] They carry on business as sole proprietors or band together in a group as partners, or limited liability partners. These professionals must join the appropriate professional organization, such as the law society or medical association of the province. These **professional associations** are set up under legislation, with extensive power to regulate educational and professional qualifications and standards of behaviour and to establish methods of disciplining members for wrongful conduct or incompetence. Note that it is only the practice of the professional service that cannot be incorporated, and so these professionals obtain many of the advantages of incorporation by establishing companies that own the building, employ the office staff, and supply the management service and equipment to the professional.

**Professionals bound by certain rules**

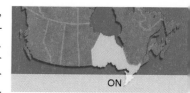

ON

# Partnership

A partnership is the simplest form of business in which people pool their resources and carry on business together with the object of making profit. This relationship is based on contract, and so basic contract law applies, with special provisions to deal with this unique relationship. Unlike a corporation, a partnership is not a separate legal personality from those making it up. However, the firm can enter into legal relationships so that it is not necessary to contract with each partner individually. This allows the partnership the convenience of functioning as a single business unit. It can own land, contract with others, and sue or be sued in its own name.

**Partnership—carrying on business together for profit**

**Partnership governed by contract law**

## Legislation

In 1890, as part of a similar trend in other areas of law in the United Kingdom, the vast body of case law governing partnership was summarized into one statute, the *Partnership Act.*[5] This legislation was adopted in all the common law provinces of Canada, where it has remained in place to the present day, with only a few alterations, such as the creation of limited liability partners. With some minor variations province to province, the law of partnership is basically consistent across Canada. For convenience, the Ontario legislation, the *Partnerships Act,* will be referred to in this chapter, and the sections discussed will refer to that statute.[6]

***Partnership Act* still used today**

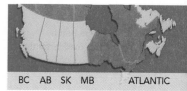

BC    AB    SK    MB                    ATLANTIC

---

4. See, for example, the *Regulated Accounting Profession Act,* R.S.A. 2000, c. R-12, which, in s. 38, provides that a shareholder or professional corporation is liable as if the business were carried on as a partnership or a sole proprietorship, and that the liability of an accountant is not affected if the practice is carried on by the individual as an employee and on behalf of a professional corporation.

5. (1890), 53 & 54 Vict., c. 39 (U.K.).

6. *Partnerships Act,* R.S.O. 1990, c. P-5. Note that Ontario is the only province for which the name of the partnership legislation is in the plural; all of the other provinces have a "Partnership Act."

# Creation of the Partnership

## Case Summary 13.2

### What Are the Damages for Breach of Fiduciary Duty? *Olson v. Gullo*[7]

Mr. Gullo entered into a verbal agreement with Mr. Olson to purchase and develop a 1000-acre (405-hectare) tract of land as an industrial park. They were both to contribute equal funding and their special skills—Mr. Gullo in real estate speculation and Mr. Olson in marketing and promotion. The pair had difficulty purchasing the designated land from the owners and eventually abandoned the project.

As it turned out, however, Mr. Gullo was able to maintain part of the deal by purchasing one 90-acre (36-hectare) parcel for himself, which he then sold at a $2.5-million profit. Mr. Olson, who was an employee of Mr. Gullo, found out about the deal, quit his job, and sued. It is interesting to note that Mr. Gullo died before the trial, but not before trying to have Mr. Olson murdered. Mr. Gullo's son carried on the defence of this action.

The first problem for the Court was to decide whether a partnership existed between the parties. The plaintiff relied on the oral agreement, the existence of which was flatly denied by the defendant. The Judge found that each was to contribute an equal share of the funds needed to acquire the land; that Mr. Gullo was to negotiate the purchases; and that Mr. Olson was to find interested investors and prepare promotional material. Thus, as they were carrying on business together with a view to making profits, their relationship was one of partnership. Mr. Gullo then had a fiduciary obligation to act in the best interests of his partner. When he secretly purchased the 90-acre parcel for himself, he did so in breach of that obligation.

The Court then had to find an appropriate remedy in the circumstances. At the trial level, the Court decided that the whole $2.5-million profit should be forfeited to Mr. Olson in order to discourage this kind of wrongful behaviour. If Mr. Gullo were allowed to keep half the profits, he would only be in the position he would have been in had he not committed the fraud in the first place, and there would be no consequence for his wrongful behaviour. This was overturned on appeal, with that Court finding that the nature of a partnership required the equal sharing of assets and profits. Mr. Gullo, despite his misconduct, was entitled to half the profits.

The case illustrates not only what is necessary for a partnership to exist and the essential nature of that partnership, but also the fiduciary obligation or duty between the partners to act in the best interests of each other.

**Partnership created by agreement or inadvertently**

A partnership is not always created by formal agreement between the partners. The *Partnerships Act* provides that a partnership is created when two or more people carry on business in common with a view toward profits.[8] A profit does not actually have to be made, only that profit is the object of the exercise. It should be noted that the sharing of gross returns from a business activity does not in itself

---

7. (1994), 113 D.L.R. (4th) 42 (Ont. C.A.); leave to appeal refused (1994), 116 D.L.R. (4th) vii (note) (S.C.C.).

8. *Supra* note 6, s. 2.

create a partnership. It is the sharing of the net proceeds after expenses have been deducted (the profits) from the enterprise that gives rise to the presumption of a partnership. The splitting of the commission on a sale by two real estate agents does not create a partnership, but when they split what is left after expenses the presumption of a partnership will arise.

The *Partnerships Act* sets out a number of other circumstances, which, though they involve the sharing of income, by themselves will *not* establish a partnership.[9]

**1.** Owning property in common, even when it is rented out for profit.

**2.** When a debt is repaid by the creditors taking a share of the debtor's profits. For example, Pallas owes Clegg $10 000, and Clegg agrees to let Pallas pay it back by paying 20 percent of the profits of Pallas's furniture store per month until repaid.

**3.** When the payment of an employee is based on a share of sales or profits, such as commission selling or profit-sharing schemes.

**4.** When the beneficiary of a deceased partner receives the deceased partner's share of the profits.

**5.** When a loan is made in relation to a business and payment of interest varies with the profit. For example, Pallas loans Clegg $10 000 to start a furniture business, and Clegg pays interest on that $10 000 principal by paying 10 percent of the store's profits per month.

**6.** When a business is sold and the payment of the good will portion varies with the profitability of the business. For example, Pallas sells Clegg a furniture business for $10 000 for the assets and 50 percent of the first year's profits for good will.

*Partnerships Act* lists exceptions

The question remains: What constitutes carrying on business together with a view to profit? When evidence indicates that there has been one of the following, a partnership will be presumed:

When partnership presumed

**1.** Joint contribution of capital to establish a business,

**2.** Intention to share expenses, profits, or losses, or

**3.** Joint participation in the management of a business.

If two people operate a restaurant together by sharing the work and expenses and jointly making decisions, the relationship is a partnership. It should be further noted that the *Partnerships Act* requires that the parties carry on a continuing business together. A single joint project, for example a school dance put on by two university students who combine their resources, would probably not be classed as a partnership. (If the students put on several dances, they would be in the "business" of providing this type of entertainment and, thus, would be in legal partnership, whether they looked at it that way or not.) Whether a business relationship is held to be a partnership will always depend on the circumstances.

Partnership must carry on continuing business

---

9. *Ibid.*, s. 3.

### Case Summary 13.3

**Does Co-owning Property Create a Partnership?** *A. E. LePage Ltd. v. Kamex Developments Ltd.*[10]

In this case, a number of people owned an apartment building together under the name of one of them, "M. Kalmykow in trust"; that is, in trust with the other owners as well. A corporation, called Kamex Developments Ltd., was created to control the property. The co-owners met monthly to discuss the property and what should be done including the possibility of sale. One of these parties, Mr. March, took it upon himself to list the property for sale under an exclusive listing agreement. He was not authorized to do so by the others. The property was eventually sold by a different agent, and under this agreement A. E. LePage claimed their commission of $45 000 on the basis that Mr. March was in partnership with the rest and therefore bound the partnership to the exclusive listing agreement. Looking at the nature of the agreement, the Court found that although all these people owned the property together, this was not enough to constitute a partnership, and so the others were not liable for the commission.

## Creation by Inadvertence

**Partnership can be created by conduct**

It is important to realize that the existence of a partnership relationship is a question of fact that a court can imply from the conduct of the parties. A partnership can therefore be created inadvertently. Because of the liability of one partner for the contracts and misdeeds of other partners, the finding of such a relationship can have significant consequences for that person. This must be a consideration whenever someone is involved in any kind of business activity with another. Failure to appreciate this possibility can have disastrous financial consequences when one partner incurs liability to a third party.

The partnership relationship is primarily one of contract, usually created by agreement, but this agreement often does not take a written form. The *Olson v. Gullo* case used to introduce this section is an instance where a court found that a partnership had been created by an oral agreement.

**But should be created by agreement**

In addition to setting out the responsibilities of partners to third parties, the *Partnerships Act* also sets out the rights and obligations of the partners to each other. But like the *Sale of Goods Act*, the *Partnerships Act* provisions, at least as far as the rights between the partners themselves are concerned, can be modified by the partnership agreement. It is important for the partners to enter into an agreement, preferably in writing, setting out the exact nature of the relationship between them.

## Written Contract Not Always Conclusive Proof

In a recent case,[11] the Supreme Court of Canada discussed the essential ingredients of partnerships and the preferred approach to determining whether a partnership exists. In that case, the partnership agreement, along with other documentation, indicated an intention to form a partnership. But the Court held

---

10. (1977), 78 D.L.R. (3d) 223 (Ont. C.A.); aff'd [1979] 2 S.C.R. 155.

11. *Backman v. Canada*, [2001] 1 S.C.R. 367.

that that was not sufficient, and ruled that a partnership did not exist, as the fundamental criteria of a valid partnership were not satisfied. On the other hand, in an Alberta case,[12] the Provincial Court held that the circumstances indicated the existence of a partnership, despite a provision, in the agreement between the two dentists, which specifically stated that there was not a partnership relationship.

A partnership agreement should deal with all of the matters important to the partnership, such as:

**Rights and obligations of partners can be modified by agreement**

- the duties of each partner,
- what type of work or talent each is expected to contribute,
- the amount of time to be committed to the business,
- how the profits are to be shared and how the capital is to be distributed,
- any limitations on the powers or authority of each partner,
- methods of resolving any disputes between the partners, and
- the circumstances in which the partnership will be dissolved.

It must be remembered that the rights of outsiders dealing with the partnership are, without notice, unaffected by any agreement between the partners. Outsiders' rights are determined by the provisions of the *Partnerships Act* and partnership law generally.

It should also be noted that a partnership relationship can arise because of **estoppel**. If one of the parties represents to a third party, either by words or by conduct, that another person is a partner and that representation is relied on, the existence of a partnership cannot be denied, even if it can be clearly demonstrated that the two were not carrying on a business together. The principle of estoppel applies to partnership just as much as it does to agency because each partner acts as an agent for the partnership.

**Partnership can be imposed by the principle of estoppel**

## Case Summary 13.4

### Does Holding Someone Out as a Partner Create a Partnership?
### *Poulos v. Caravelle Homes Ltd.*[13]

Mr. Lloyd owned and operated a truck purchased under a conditional sale agreement and used primarily to move mobile homes from one location to another, usually for dealers. Mr. Lloyd lived in British Columbia and was not licensed to deliver mobile homes from point to point in Alberta, just from Alberta to other locations. In an effort to remedy this problem he approached the principals of Caravelle with a scheme whereby they would purchase the truck. They declined this arrangement but agreed to a sham transaction in which they completed a bill of sale stating that Caravelle had purchased the truck for one dollar. They advanced money to pay Mr. Lloyd's arrears. They changed the insurance permits and other documents, which then showed Caravelle as the owner. Also, they added signs to the truck that indicated Caravelle was its owner. Whenever the truck stopped at weigh stations, Mr. Lloyd produced documents showing that the truck was owned by Caravelle. He continued his own independent trucking business separately from Caravelle. On one of the deliveries for Caravelle, to a business owned by Mrs. Poulos, Mr. Lloyd was careless in unhitching a mobile home,

---

12. *Foothills Dental Laboratory Ltd. v. Naik* (1996), 40 Alta. L.R. (3d) 434 (Prov. Ct.).

13. (1995), 32 Alta. L.R. (3d) 76 (Q.B.); rev'd on other grounds (1997), 49 Alta. L.R. (3d) 385 (C.A.).

and it slipped and pinned Mr. Poulos's arm causing him serious injury. Mr. Poulos sued Caravelle, claiming that Mr. Lloyd and Caravelle were partners. The Court decided that because Caravelle allowed the truck to be held out as owned by it, it was a partner of Mr. Lloyd and was vicariously liable for the injury caused when he delivered the mobile home.

## The Partner as an Agent

**Laws of agency apply to partnership**

Every partner is the agent of the other partners and so has the power to bind them in contract as long as the contract involves the business of the partnership.[14] To properly understand the law of partnership, this chapter must be read in conjunction with the material in Chapter 12 on agency. Even where the authority of a partner has been limited and the partner exceeds the power given, that contract will be binding if the third party is unaware of the limitation and the contract relates to the partnership business.[15] For example, Akbari and Carlson operated a shoe store in partnership, and Akbari, while visiting his regular supplier in Toronto, purchased 500 pairs of yellow patent-leather oxfords he was unable to resist for $5000. That contract would be binding on Carlson, even if the partnership agreement specifically set out that neither partner could make any purchase over $1000 without the other's approval. However, if Akbari bought a new boat during his trip to Toronto, this purchase would not be binding on his partner because the purchase could not be said to be made pursuant to the partnership business of selling shoes.

## Vicarious Liability

**Partners liable for each other's acts**

All partners are also vicariously liable in tort for both careless and intentional conduct of their partners in all business-related activities, including personal injury. Thus, if Agostino and Paradis were partners selling firewood, and Agostino negligently dropped a load of wood on a passing pedestrian, both Agostino and Paradis would be liable to pay compensation for the injury. There are many cases showing vicarious liability for intentional wrongs, such as an Ontario case in which the partners of a lawyer who fraudulently acquired $60 000 from his client were required to make good the loss, even though they were completely innocent.[16]

**Partners liable for breach of trust**

Partners can also be held responsible for the breach of trust of their partners, such as the misuse of their clients' money. In such situations, all the partners are responsible for compensating the victim's loss. Note, however, that under the *Partnerships Act* the other partners are liable only if they have notice of the breach of trust.[17]

**Partners liable for wrongful acts of employees**

Since a partnership can employ individuals, the principles set out in Chapter 11 on employment law apply. Partners are vicariously liable for the misdeeds of their employees committed in the course of their employment. They must also adhere to government regulations on workers' compensation, employment insurance, and income tax.

---

14. *Partnerships Act, supra* note 6, ss. 6, 7.

15. *Ibid.*, ss. 6, 9.

16. *Victoria & Grey Trust Company* (1986), 57 O.R. (2d) 484 (H.C.J.).

17. *Partnerships Act, supra* note 6, s. 14.

## Reducing **Risk** 13.1

For a businessperson, a serious risk associated with the law of partnership is the danger of becoming a partner inadvertently. This can come about by carrying on business together without realizing that a partnership has been created, or by allowing oneself to be held out as a partner by someone else. The danger is the liability imposed by such a partnership both in tort, on the basis of vicarious liability, and in contract, on the basis of each partner being an agent. This unlimited liability means a partner's entire fortune is at risk, and can lead to devastating results. Care should be taken to avoid the risk that an inadvertent partnership can create.

## Unlimited Liability

Like a sole proprietor, a partner's liability is unlimited, and her personal fortune is at risk to satisfy the claims of an injured party. With partners, however, they are liable not only for their own wrongful acts and those of their employees but also for the conduct of their partners. If the assets of a partnership are not sufficient to satisfy the claims of the creditors, the partners must make up the difference out of their own personal assets. This is done in the same proportion that they share the profits. Thus, if a partnership agreement provides that a senior partner gets 40 percent of the profits and each of the three junior partners gets 20 percent of the profits, the senior partner will bear 40 percent of the loss and the junior partners will each bear 20 percent of the loss.

**Partners share losses equally or proportionally by agreement**

Note that such a provision in the partnership agreement will affect only the relations between the partners. An outsider is not affected by any term in the partnership agreement that limits the liability of one of the partners and can collect all of what is owed from any partner. If one partner is particularly well off and the other partners have few personal assets, the injured party will look to the partner with significant assets for compensation once the assets of the partnership have been exhausted. That partner can seek contributions from the other partners on the basis of the partnership agreement if they have anything left to contribute.

**Third party can collect from any partner regardless of agreement**

In most provinces, partners are only **jointly liable** for the debts and obligations of the partnership, as opposed to jointly and **severally liable**.[18] This means that for someone to seek a remedy against all the partners, they all must be included in the original action, as there is only one cause of action. Thus, if only two of the three partners are sued and it later turns out that they do not have enough assets to satisfy the judgment, it is then too late to sue the third. It must be emphasized, however, that when liability arises because of wrongful conduct (tort) or because of breach of trust, this liability is both joint and several.[19] This means that it is possible for the injured party to sue one partner and still maintain the right to sue the other partners if the claim is not satisfied. In any case, when an action is brought against the partnership in the partnership name, the plaintiff will be able to enforce the judgment against any of the partners. The result of this vicarious liability is that all the partners are personally responsible for the injuries incurred to the extent of their entire personal fortunes.

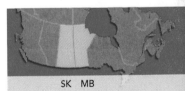

SK   MB

**All personal assets at risk**

A retiring partner remains liable for any wrongs committed or liability incurred during the partnership period. This liability also continues for acts committed after the dissolution of the partnership or the retirement of the partner, unless the third party has been given notice that the retiring party has left the

**Retiring partner remains responsible**

---

18. *Ibid.*, s. 10.

19. *Ibid.*, ss. 12, 13.

firm. The remaining partners or a new partner coming in can agree to take over these obligations in the partnership agreement, but the new partner is not automatically liable.[20] This is why such care is taken to notify colleagues and customers when the membership of a partnership changes.

### Case Summary 13.5

**Was the Loss Incurred in the Normal Course of Business?**
*McDonic v. Hetherington (Litigation Guardian of)*[21]

In 1985, two elderly sisters, Ms. McDonic and Ms. Cooper, on the advice of Ms. Cooper's son-in-law, retained Mr. Watt, a solicitor, to advise them on investments. Mr. Watt invested a considerable sum of money for them but failed to properly secure those investments. The result was that Ms. McDonic lost more than $230 000 and Ms. Cooper lost more than $10 000. Mr. Watt was sued and lost on the basis that he failed in his fiduciary duty to these clients. The problem here was for the Court to determine whether his partners were also liable for these losses on the basis of vicarious liability. The partners denied liability, claiming that this was misconduct on the part of Mr. Watt outside the scope of the business as Mr. Watt was acting as an investment adviser, not a lawyer, in these transactions. The lower Court agreed. However, the Ontario Court of Appeal decided that the partners were liable for the losses caused by their partner because Mr. Watt did what he did as a partner in the normal course of that partnership's business. The money went into a partnership trust account. It was dealt with like all other accounts, and the other partners actually dealt with those funds as well. In addition, he was liable as an agent acting within the apparent authority given by the other partners.

It is true that the transactions were not expressly authorized by the partners, but it is clear that he was acting within his apparent authority and, as such, made the other partners liable for his conduct. His office was part of the firm's offices, he used the firm's letterhead, and in making the investments for the sisters he used the facilities of the law office as well as the firm's accounts in the normal course of the firm's business.

## Registration

**Registration usually required**

Most provinces require that a partnership be registered. Some provinces, such as British Columbia[22] and New Brunswick,[23] require registration only when the partnerships involve trading, manufacturing, and mining. Alberta also requires registration of partnerships involving contracting.[24] Ontario prohibits partners from carrying on business or identifying themselves to the public unless the firm name has been registered. In addition, partners may not carry on business, or identify themselves to the public, under a name other than a firm name, unless the name has been registered. An exception is allowed for partners carrying on business or identifying themselves under a name that is composed of the names of the

20. *Ibid., s. 18.*

21. (1997), 142 D.L.R. (4th) 648 (Ont. C.A.); leave to appeal to S.C.C. refused [1997] S.C.C.A. No. 119.

22. *Partnership Act,* R.S.B.C. 1996, c. 348, s. 81.

23. *Partnerships and Business Names Registration Act,* R.S.N.B. 1973, c. P-4, s. 2.

24. *Partnership Act,* R.S.A. 2000, c. P-3, s. 106.

## Reducing **Risk** 13.2

All partners are liable to the extent of their personal fortune for the wrongful acts and mistakes of their partners. Case Summary 13.5 deals with the misuse of trust money in a law firm, but this is just one of the many examples that could be used where one partner's liability for the acts of another is present. We must use great care in choosing our partners and even then we face great risk of loss. This is one reason that incorporation has become much more popular as a method of doing business.

partners.[25] Registration may also be required when the partners are in limited partnerships or limited liability partnerships, as discussed below.

Failure to register properly can result in the imposition of a fine[26] but typically will prevent the unregistered partnership from maintaining an action[27] and cause joint liability to become joint and several liability.[28] Note that an unregistered partnership can still be sued, and so there are pressing reasons to register and no advantage in not doing so.

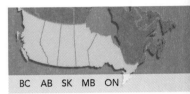

BC   AB   SK   MB   ON

## Rights and Obligations of the Parties

### Fiduciary Duty

Each partner has a fiduciary duty to act in the best interests of the other partners. This duty imposes an obligation to account for any profits that have been made or for any partnership funds or property used. A partner who uses partnership property for personal benefit without the consent of the other partners must pay over any profit made and reimburse the partnership for any deterioration of the property. Property brought into a partnership for the purposes of the business becomes the property of the partnership, even though the title documents might not reflect this ownership. The partner with title is said to hold the property in trust for the partnership. This was the situation in *Olson v. Gullo,* discussed in Case Summary 13.2, and why Olson had the right to one-half of the profits from the sale of the property that Gullo had secretly purchased. It also underlines why the appeal court found it necessary to reverse the lower court's decision to award all the profits to Olson. This was inconsistent with the true nature of the partnership where they shared the ownership of the property and thus the rights to the profits.

If a partner operates a similar business without consent, he will be required to pay over any profits made to the partnership, which will then be distributed normally to all the partners. That partner, however, will not be reimbursed for losses. If a partner in a restaurant in Vancouver were to open another in Victoria without consent, any profits made from the Victoria operation would have to be paid over to the partnership and then be distributed equally among them. However, any losses sustained would be borne by that partner alone.

Any information obtained through a person's position as partner must be used to the benefit of the partnership, not for personal use. If Noorami came across a deal for some mining claims because of his position as a partner in a mining partnership, he would be required to inform his partners about the

**Fiduciary duty exists between partners**

**Partners must account for any profits or use of property**

**Partners cannot compete with partnership**

**Information must be disclosed**

25. *Business Names Act, supra* note 3, s. 2.

26. In Alberta, for example, the fine may not exceed $500. See *Partnership Act, supra* note 24, s. 112.

27. *Ibid.,* s. 113.

28. *Ibid.,* s. 115.

opportunity. If he bought the claims for himself without his partner's consent, he would have to turn over any profits earned to the partnership but suffer any losses himself. In effect, the information he used was the property of the partnership.

### Case Summary 13.6

**Does a Partner Have to Account for Income from Other Sources?**
*Rochwerg v. Truster*[29]

The individual parties were chartered accountants who practised accountancy together in a partnership. One of the partners, Rochwerg, became a director of a corporation that was a client of the partnership. Rochwerg advised his partners of his directorship, but he did not disclose information regarding the shares and stock options to which he had become entitled. His partners sought an accounting of these benefits.

There was no written partnership agreement, so the Court of Appeal found that the mutual rights and duties of the partners were governed by the *Partnerships Act*. The Court held that Rochwerg owed his partners duties of disclosure, loyalty, utmost good faith, and avoidance of conflict and self-interest. While Rochwerg became director of the corporation because of his partnership, his acceptance of the directorship, and his activities of directorship, did not place him in a position of conflict with his partners, or in respect of his duties as partner. His entitlement to the shares and stock options, however, derived from his directorship in the corporation and formed part of his compensation as a director. Rochwerg was therefore obliged to disclose them to his partners, and to account for them.

Again, we see just how important fiduciary duty is. It is present when there is a relationship where one party places trust in another and is vulnerable if that trust is not honoured. Partnership is an important example of such a trusting relationship and of the imposition of the fiduciary obligations.

### Provisions of the Partnership Act

The rights and obligations of partners to each other are set out in the *Partnerships Act*, and these provisions apply except where modified by the partnership agreement.[30] Some of the provisions of the Act are as follows:[31]

**Profits and losses shared equally or modified by agreement**

**1.** The partners will share profits equally between them. Similarly, any losses incurred are shared equally between the partners. This provision is often modified by a partnership agreement, but outside third parties will not be affected by any agreement, as they can recover losses from any partner who has assets. That partner may then look to the other partners for reimbursement.

**Partners' expenses reimbursed**

**2.** The partners are entitled to reimbursement for any expenses they incur in the process of the partnership business. They are also entitled to be reimbursed for any money other than capital they have advanced to the partnership, before the other partners can claim a share of the profits. In

---

29. [2002] O. J. No. 1230 (C.A.). For a recent case that applied the *Rochwerg* decision, see *McKnight v. Hutchison,* [2002] B.C.J. No. 2211 (S.C.).

30. *Partnerships Act, supra* note 6, s. 20.

31. *Ibid.,* s. 24.

addition, the partner advancing such funds is entitled to the payment of interest on that money.

**3.** All partners have the right to take part in management. This provision is often modified by partnership agreements, which create different classes of partners, particularly in firms with a large number of partners.

*Partners participate in management*

**4.** A partner is not an employee and is not entitled to wages or other remuneration for work done, only to a share of the profits. To provide partners with a steady stream of cash flow, the firm may pay partners a monthly draw against the yet-to-be-calculated profits of the partnership.

*No salaries paid to partners*

**5.** No major changes can be made to the partnership business without the unanimous agreement of all the partners. No new partner can be brought into the partnership, nor can a partner be excluded from the firm without the unanimous consent of all the partners.[32] However, for the ordinary matters of the firm a simple majority vote is sufficient, unless the partnership agreement states otherwise.

*Unanimous agreement needed for major changes*

**6.** Partners do not have the right to assign their partnership status to some other party without the consent of the other partners. The benefits can be assigned, but the assignee will not have the right to interfere in the management or administration of the partnership business.[33]

*Assignment requires consent of other partners*

**7.** The business records of the partnership must be kept at the partnership office, and all the partners have the right to inspect them.

*Partners must have access to records*

As can be seen from this summary, the general principle governing a partnership relationship is that the partners function as a unit and have a considerable responsibility to look after each other's interests.

## Advantages of Partnership

Although the problems associated with a partnership may appear overwhelming, many of these difficulties can be overcome by proper insurance coverage. It should also be noted that a disadvantage to one person may be an advantage to another. For example, the unanimous consent required for important changes in a partnership may appear to interfere with effective management, but it does provide considerable protection to the individual partner. Such an individual partner cannot be outvoted by the majority, as is the case with a minority shareholder in a corporation. Similarly, the right of the individual partner to inspect all records of the business confers advantages not shared by minority shareholders in corporations to the same extent.

*Insurance coverage important*

*Unanimous consent protection*

It is also normally less expensive to set up a partnership than a corporation and less costly to operate a partnership because there are few formal requirements once the business has been established. For example, a corporation must keep certain types of accounting records, and file reports with the appropriate government agency. A partnership, on the other hand, has only the needs of the partners to satisfy in this regard. But, as with sole proprietorships and corporations, there are other government regulatory bodies that require records, such as

*Partnership less costly to form and operate*

---

32. *Ibid.*, s. 25.

33. *Ibid.*, s. 31.

## Reducing **Risk** 13.3

Businesspeople should not be too quick to discard partnership as a valuable method of carrying on business with others. From an individual point of view all partners have an equal say, and in all important matters there must be unanimity. This eliminates the "tyranny of the majority" problem usually associated with corporations. The disadvantages, such as unlimited liability, can be overcome, to a large extent, by obtaining appropriate insurance. Before a decision is made to incorporate, consideration should therefore be given to the pros and cons of using a partnership to carry on the business instead.

the Canada Customs and Revenue Agency, the Workers' Compensation Board, and the Employment Insurance Commission.

It should not automatically be assumed that, because of the unlimited liability and unwieldy management structure of partnerships, incorporation is a better way of carrying on business. Many of the apparent advantages of incorporation are illusory, and many of the disadvantages of partnership can be overcome. While it may be true that a corporation is the best vehicle for carrying on business in many situations, there are other situations in which a partnership is more appropriate. For a small business operating in a "low-risk" industry, for example, it may be advantageous to start up and then carry on business as a partnership until the business becomes profitable. This would enable the partners to personally take advantage of the business losses for tax purposes.

**Partnership may be only alternative for professionals**

Some activities, such as the practice of law, accounting, medicine, and dentistry, are not allowed by statute to be engaged in by corporations. A partnership is the only alternative when more than one of these professionals wishes to join together to carry on business. Note that in some jurisdictions it is possible for these professionals to carry on their practices as professional corporations. But many of the advantages of incorporation have been removed, including limited liability. This problem has recently been addressed by the passing of legislation allowing certain professionals to form limited liability partnerships. These are discussed below.

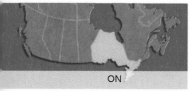

ON

## Dissolution of a Partnership

**Dissolution by notice**

Usually, a partnership is easy to dissolve, requiring only notice to that effect by one of the partners.[34] Such notice can be implied, as in the case where a partnership was terminated when one of the partners stopped driving a taxicab.[35] While it is an advantage to the leaving partner to be able to dissolve the partnership simply by giving notice to the other partners, it can be a considerable disadvantage, requiring the sale of the partnership assets and distribution of the proceeds to the partners. Usually, this is overcome by providing in the partnership agreement a mechanism whereby one partner can leave without causing the remainder of the partnership to dissolve.

**Dissolution by death, bankruptcy, or insolvency**

Subject to the partnership agreement, a partnership is dissolved by the death or insolvency of any partner.[36] This provision varies slightly from province to

---

34. *Ibid.*, s. 32.

35. *Singh v. Taggarh*, [2000] M.J. No. 237 (Q.B.).

36. *Partnerships Act, supra* note 6, s. 33.

province.[37] Dissolution can give rise to significant problems in ongoing, long-term partnerships of professional groups. Therefore, professionals will typically set out in partnership agreements that the death or insolvency of one partner will not dissolve the partnership and that, instead, the partner's share will be made available to the heir or creditor of the partner. Insurance coverage is often taken out to cover such a contingency.

British Columbia's partnership legislation is unique because it establishes that, when more than two partners are involved, the partnership will be dissolved only in relation to the partner who has died or become bankrupt. This provision can be modified by agreement, but its unique feature is that the death or bankruptcy of one partner will not bring to an end the whole partnership relationship in the absence of an agreement among the partners.[38]

A partnership that has been entered into for a fixed term is dissolved by the expiration of that term.[39] Similarly, a partnership that is entered into for a single venture or undertaking is dissolved by the termination of that venture or undertaking.[40] A partnership is automatically dissolved if the business engaged in by the partnership becomes illegal.[41] In addition, a partner can apply to the court to dissolve the partnership if any one of the following factors are present.[42]

> **Partnership established for specified time will end at expiry**

> **Partnership can be dissolved by request to the court**

**1.** When one of the partners has become mentally incompetent, or otherwise incapable of performing partnership responsibilities,

**2.** When the conduct of one partner is prejudicial to the partnership relationship, or the partner is otherwise in breach of the partnership agreement,

**3.** When it is clear that the partnership business can be carried on only at a loss, or

**4.** When it is just and equitable that the partnership be dissolved.

The effect of dissolution is to end the partnership relationship, oblige the partners to wind up the business, liquidate the assets to pay off any obligations to creditors, and then distribute any remaining assets and funds to the former partners. Individual partners should take care to give public notice of dissolution.[43] The law may require that such notice be filed with the partnership registration office or registrar of corporations, depending on the jurisdiction. For further protection, such notice should be sent to all regular customers of the business. Failure to do so may render each partner liable for the acts of the other partners even after dissolution. Note that although dissolution takes place, the partners still have the authority to act as partners and bind the firm by their actions in doing whatever is necessary to wind up the affairs of the partnership.[44]

> **Public notice may prevent liability**

---

37. In Alberta, for example, a partnership is dissolved by the death or bankruptcy of a partner, or by an assignment of a partner's property in trust for the benefit of his creditors. See s. 37 of the *Partnership Act, supra* note 24.

38. *Partnership Act, supra* note 22, s. 36(1)(b).

39. *Partnerships Act,* supra note 6, s. 32(a).

40. *Ibid.,* s. 32(b).

41. *Ibid.,* s. 34.

42. *Ibid.,* s. 35.

43. *Ibid.,* s. 37.

44. *Ibid.,* s. 38.

### Case Summary 13.7

**How Can You Avoid Liability for Partnership Debts?**
***The Bank of Montreal v. Sprackman***[45]

The members of a partnership had a falling-out and agreed among them that one of the partners (Mr. Sprackman) would retire from the partnership. A hand-written letter was drawn up and signed, stating that Mr. Sprackman's interest in the partnership and responsibility for liability would be taken over by one of the other partners, Mr. Dinardo. Mr. Dinardo subsequently sold his interest in the partnership to a third partner, Mr. Gotzaminis, who subsequently became bankrupt. When the partnership was active, arrangements had been made for a $3000 loan and an overdraft arrangement with the Bank of Montreal. Mr. Sprackman verbally advised Mr. Martin, the bank manager, that he was retiring and that his obligation was being taken over by Mr. Dinardo. Mr. Martin agreed to release Mr. Sprackman from the loan if he paid $1500, plus interest, which he did over some period of time. Unfortunately, neither side said anything about the overdraft, which amounted to $2899.66 at the time of Mr. Sprackman's retirement. This amount increased after Mr. Sprackman's retirement to $6029.82, including interest at 18 percent per annum. The bank then insisted on payment of this overdraft from Mr. Sprackman. One of the documents Mr. Sprackman had signed with the bank required that the overdraft arrangement would stay in force until "terminated by written notice."

The Judge was not impressed by the conduct of the bank personnel in this situation. They had allowed Mr. Sprackman to believe that the $1500 settlement extinguished all debt. This was not the case, as it was clear that his obligation for the overdraft remained until ended with written notice. The Judge reluctantly agreed that the bank was within its rights to demand payment and gave judgment accordingly. The 18-percent interest also was upheld, because this was the amount being paid on the overdraft when the firm was active and Mr. Sprackman was aware of this. The Judge did show his displeasure by refusing to award the bank costs in the action.

This case shows how important it is for the terms of a partnership agreement to be clear and for each partner to know exactly to what she is agreeing. It also shows how important it can be for a retiring partner to make a clean break. It was fully appropriate for the partner who was leaving to enter into a separate agreement with the bank settling his liability, but the partner was not sufficiently careful in entering into that agreement and making all those terms clear. The devil is in the details, and in this case, the devil got Mr. Sprackman.

## Distribution of Assets and Liabilities

**Debts paid out of profits first, then capital, then personal assets of partners**

Subject to the partnership agreement, when dissolving a partnership the debts must be paid first out of profits and, if they are insufficient, out of the capital the partners originally invested. If there is still not enough money to pay the debts, the creditors can then turn to the partners themselves, who are liable in the proportion in which they were entitled to share profits. On the other hand, once all creditors have been paid and the other obligations of the partnership satisfied, any assets still remaining are applied first to pay back the partners for advances

45. (1977), 78 D.L.R. (3d) 665 (Ont. H.C.J.).

and then to pay back the original capital investment. Any remaining funds are divided among the partners on the established basis for sharing profits.[46]

The dissolution of the partnership and the distribution of assets may be a problem, especially when some of the partners want to continue the business in a new partnership. To avoid this problem, the partners often agree in the partnership agreement to a different process than that described above. It should be noted that if one partner owes a debt to an outside creditor that has nothing to do with the partnership business, that creditor can claim against only the assets of that partner, including his or her share of the partnership assets left after all other claims against the partnership are settled.

## Limited Partnerships

Additions to the legislation governing partnership in every province provide for the creation of limited partnerships.[47] This measure gives some of the advantages of incorporation to partnerships. But partners can lose their status as limited partners if they fail to carefully adhere to all the requirements of the governing legislation, with the result that they are then deemed to be general partners with all the consequences inherent in that designation. The main advantage of a limited partnership is that it allows the partners so designated to invest money in a partnership but to avoid the unlimited liability that goes with being a general partner. The only loss a limited partner can incur is the original investment.[48]

**Limited partners liable only to the extent of their investment**

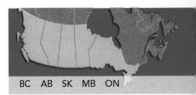

BC   AB   SK   MB   ON

If Kimmel and Ingram were general partners with Pak, a limited partner, and Kimmel were to negligently injure a customer to the extent of $300 000 damages, Pak would lose only his investment in the firm. Both Kimmel and Ingram would be liable for the entire $300 000, but Pak's liability would be limited to the amount he invested, even if the combined assets of Kimmel and Ingram were not enough to cover the loss.

The problem is that it is relatively easy for the limited partner to lose that status, thus becoming a general partner, with unlimited liability. In the preceding example, if Pak had allowed himself to be represented as a partner in the business, taken part in the control of the business, allowed his surname to be used in the name of the business, or contributed services to the partnership, he would have become a general partner and would have been required to pay along with Kimmel and Ingram, with no limitation on his liability.

To form a limited partnership, it is necessary to file a declaration at the appropriate government registry. This declaration will set out information such as the term of the agreement, the amount of cash and other property contributed, and the way profits are to be shared.[49] The name used by the limited partnership can contain the name of the general partners, but the surname of a limited partner cannot be included in the firm name unless it is also the surname of one of the

**Registration required to become a limited partner**

46. See *Partnerships Act, supra* note 6, s. 44, for the rules governing the distribution of assets on final settlement of accounts.

47. These additions vary from province to province. In Ontario, see the *Limited Partnerships Act,* R.S.O. 1990, c. L.16. In Alberta, see the *Partnership Act, supra* note 24, ss. 49–80. The discussion in the text refers to the Ontario legislation.

48. *Limited Partnerships Act, ibid.,* s. 9.

49. In Ontario, the specifics of what is to be included in the declaration are prescribed by the *Limited Partnerships Act General Regulation, R.R.O. 1990, Reg. 713.*

## Reducing **Risk** 13.4

As was discussed above, the rights and duties of partners can be modified in a partnership agreement. This applies to the relationship between general and limited partners as well. Limited partnerships are attractive to people because of favourable tax implications. To obtain these tax benefits, one big advantage normally associated with limited partnership, limited liability, may have to be sacrificed to a considerable extent through modifications set out in the partnership agreement. Often, these changes are not brought to the attention of prospective investors. Great care should be taken before entering into a limited partnership as such an investment vehicle, to ensure that you understand exactly what you are getting into.

general partners. It is not possible to form a partnership with only limited partners; there must be at least one general partner in the firm.

**Limited partners cannot take part in control of the business**

A limited partner can contribute money and other property to the business, but not services. A limited partner cannot take part in the control of the business, without becoming a general partner. The limited partner is not prohibited from giving the other partners advice as to the management of the business, but since it is often difficult to determine where advice stops and control of the business starts there is a considerable risk in doing so. When a business starts to fail, there is a great temptation for the limited partner to jump in to preserve the investment, but doing so raises the risk of becoming a general partner and should be avoided.

### Case Summary 13.8

**Is a Limited Partnership a Legal Entity?** *International Minerals & Chemical (Canada) Global Ltd. v. Canada (M.N.R.)*[50]

International Minerals & Chemical Global Ltd. ("International") and IMC Esterhazy Ltd. ("IMC") formed a limited partnership. International was the general partner, while IMC was the limited partner. International transferred its business to the limited partnership, and carried on the business as the general partner of the limited partnership. The issue was whether the formation of the limited partnership created a new "employer" for the purposes of deducting and remitting contributions under the Canadian Pension Plan and the Employment Insurance Plan. Revenue Canada took the position that the limited partnership was a new employer, as it was a "new legal entity."

The Tax Court of Canada held that a limited partnership is created solely by statute. Further, while a limited partnership is a business entity, it is not a "person," and is therefore not liable for anything related to the business. In this case, the general partner is a "person," and is thereby liable for everything related to the business. There was therefore no change in the employer upon the formation of the limited partnership.

## Limited Liability Partnerships

Historically, professionals have not been allowed to incorporate their businesses and have therefore carried on business using partnerships. This has caused increased concern as the size of professional partnerships has grown and the number and size of liability claims against professionals have increased significantly. Ontario addressed this issue in 1998, by introducing the limited liability

---

50. [2001] T.C.J. No. 293 (T.C.C.).

partnership (LLP).[51] Alberta did the same in 1999,[52] followed by Saskatchewan,[53] Quebec,[54] and Manitoba.[55] Other provinces are considering legislation to allow for LLPs. New Brunswick, for example, asked for comments from the public on its "Limited Liability Partnerships Discussion Report."[56]

BC   AB   SK   MB

In Ontario, an LLP is formed when two or more persons enter into a written agreement that designates the partnership as an LLP and states that the agreement is governed by the *Partnerships Act*.[57] An LLP may carry on business only for the purpose of practising a profession governed by legislation and only if that legislation expressly permits LLPs to practise that profession and the governing body of the profession requires the partnership to maintain a minimum amount of insurance.[58] The LLP must register its firm name before carrying on business.[59] The name of an LLP must contain as the last words or letters of its name the phrase "limited liability partnership" or one of its abbreviations ("LLP" or "L.L.P.") or their French equivalents.[60]

At this time, the only professions that are allowed to use LLPs in Ontario are accountants and lawyers. A limited liability partnership of lawyers must maintain professional liability insurance coverage for each partner at the level required to be maintained individually by each member who is a partner of the firm, namely $1 million per member.[61] In Alberta, members of an "eligible profession" may register as an LLP. An eligible profession is one that is regulated by legislation and that authorizes its members to carry on business through a professional corporation.[62] This includes accountants, chiropractors, dentists, lawyers, optometrists, and physicians.

The main advantage to professionals carrying on business in an LLP is that potential liability is limited. In Ontario, a limited liability partner is not liable for the liability of the partnership arising from the negligent acts or omissions of another partner, or an employee, agent, or representative of the partnership.[63] This does not apply to liability caused by the partner's own negligence, or the negligence of a person under the partner's direct supervision or control.[64] The result of these provisions appears to be that the partnership's assets are at risk

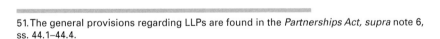

51. The general provisions regarding LLPs are found in the *Partnerships Act, supra* note 6, ss. 44.1–44.4.

52. See the *Partnership Act, supra* note 24, ss. 81–84.

53. See the *Partnership Act,* R.S.S. 1978, c. P-3, ss. 78–110.

54. See the *Act to amend the Professional Code and other legislative provisions as regards the carrying on of professional activities within a partnership or company,* S.Q. 2001, c. 34.

55. See *The Partnership Act,* R.S.M. 1987, c. P-30, ss. 67–88.

56. See the news release from Communications New Brunswick of April 25, 2002, "Public Consultations on Limited Liability Partnerships."

57. *Partnerships Act, supra* note 6, s. 44.1. LLP legislation varies from province to province. The discussion in the text is based primarily on the Ontario legislation.

58. *Ibid.,* s. 44.2.

59. *Ibid.,* s. 44.3(1).

60. *Ibid.,* s. 44.3 (3).

61. *By-Law 26,* By-Laws of the Law Society of Upper Canada.

62. *Partnership Act, supra* note 24, s. 81.

63. *Partnerships Act, supra* note 6, s. 10(2).

64. *Ibid.,* s. 10(3).

with respect to liability caused by negligent acts or omissions of partners, employees, agents, or representatives of the LLP, but the victim of the negligence may not pursue the individual assets of non-negligent partners.

These provisions apply, however, only to negligence. They do not apply to actions for other torts, breaches of contract, or breaches of trust. In Alberta, a limited liability partner will not be liable for the debts or liabilities of the LLP, or of another partner, which arise from the negligence or misconduct of the other partner or an employee of the LLP occurring in the ordinary course of carrying on the practice of the profession.[65] The innocent partner, however, will not be protected from losing her share in the partnership's assets. The LLP's insurance coverage will be available to satisfy any claims against the responsible partners, and all partners, including "innocent partners," will be liable for the ordinary debts of the partnership. The liability shield does not, of course, protect a limited liability partner from liability for her own negligence or misconduct. The protection also does not apply if the partner knew of the negligence or misconduct of others when it was committed and failed to take reasonable steps to prevent it. A limited liability partner will also be personally liable if the negligence or misconduct were committed by an employee of the LLP for whom the partner was responsible for supervising and the partner did not provide adequate supervision.[66]

The Saskatchewan legislation states that limited liability partners are liable for any partnership obligation for which they would be liable if the partnership were a corporation of which they were directors.[67]

Refer to Table 13.1 for a comparative summary of the different types of business organizations.

## Table 13.1 Comparison of Different Types of Business Organizations

| Type of Business Organization | Created by Registration? | Number of Participants? | Separate Legal Entity? | Unlimited Personal Liability? | Vicarious Liability? |
|---|---|---|---|---|---|
| *Sole proprietorship* | No, but registration of business name is usually required | 1 | No | Yes | Yes, for employees |
| *Partnership* | No; can even be created inadvertently | 2 or more | No | Yes | Yes, for employees and partners |
| *Limited partnership* | Yes | 2 or more; must be at least one general partner | No | Yes, for general partner | Yes, for employees and partners |
| *Limited liability partnership* | Yes | 2 or more members of eligible profession | No | Yes, except for "innocent" partners | Yes, for employees and partners |

65. *Partnership Act, supra* note 24, s. 12(1).

66. *Ibid.,* s. 12(2).

67. *Partnership Act, supra* note 53, ss. 80, 81.

# Summary

## Sole proprietors

- Carry on business by themselves with some government regulation.
- Have unlimited liability for their debts and obligations.

## Partnership

- Involves two or more partners carrying on business together with a view to profits.
- Controlled by partnership legislation and by specific agreement of the partners.
- Can be created by agreement but often comes into existence by inadvertence when people work together in concert in a business activity.
- Each partner is an agent for the partnership, and all partners are liable for the contracts and torts of the other partners and employees. That liability is unlimited, and all the assets of the partners, including personal assets, are at risk to satisfy such debts and obligations.
- Fiduciary duty
  - Partners must act in the best interests of the partnership.
- Changes
  - Partners must unanimously agree on major changes.
- Dissolution
  - Partners to give notice to that effect.
  - Upon death or bankruptcy of one of the partners, unless the partners have agreed otherwise in their partnership agreement.
- Limited partner
  - Liable only to the extent of the investment made in the business, but must be careful to protect that limited liability status.
- Limited liability partnerships
  - Now available for professionals who cannot incorporate their businesses.

## QUESTIONS

1. Distinguish among a sole proprietorship, a partnership, and a corporation.

2. What risk does a businessperson face in a sole proprietorship or partnership that is avoided in a corporation?

3. What advantages and disadvantages are associated with carrying on business as a sole proprietorship?

4. What advantages and disadvantages are associated with carrying on business as a partnership?

5. What distinguishes a partnership from other types of joint activities?

6. Distinguish between sharing profits and sharing revenues.

7. If two people enter into a business together with the object of making money but lose it instead, can the business still be a partnership?

8. Why must a person understand the law of agency in order to understand the law of partnership?

9. What danger exists when a third party is led to believe that two people are partners when, in fact, they are not? What legal principle is applied in this situation?

10. What is the significance of the existence of a partnership agreement for outsiders dealing with the partnership? What is the advantage of entering into a formal agreement?

11. Explain the different ways in which a person can become responsible for the acts of his or her partner and describe the limitations on this responsibility.

12. Describe the liability of retiring and new partners.

13. Partners have fiduciary obligations to each other. Explain what this means.

14. What will the consequences be if a partner operates a business similar to the partnership without the partners' consent, or if she uses information acquired through the partnership to her own advantage?

15. What events may bring about the end of a partnership prematurely? Under what circumstances might it be necessary to get a court order to end a partnership?

16. What will the normal effect be on a partnership when a partner dies or becomes insolvent? How is the law of British Columbia significantly different?

17. When a partnership is being dissolved and does not have sufficient assets to pay its debts, how is the responsibility for these debts distributed? How are excess assets distributed?

18. Explain the significance of being a limited partner.

19. What must a person do in order to qualify as a limited partner? What happens when a limited partner fails to meet one of these qualifications?

20. What is the main advantage of limited liability partnerships? In light of this, what does the law require, in an attempt to protect those who suffer losses through the actions of a partner or an employee of a limited liability partnership?

-------------------------------------------------------------------

## CASES

### 1. *Lampert Plumbing (Danforth) Ltd. v. Agathos,* [1972] 3 O.R. 11 (Co. Ct.).

Magoulas, the sole owner of Alpha Omega Construction Company, signed a contract with Agathos, the owner of a Toronto radio station, for advertising over a period of time. Magoulas was unable to pay, but Agathos continued to give him advertising in hopes that the business would get going to the point that he would be able to pay. Agathos also helped Magoulas out in his business, signed many contracts, and performed other acts on behalf of Magoulas, including writing cheques on his personal account. In January 1971, Kreizman, president of the plaintiff corporation, entered into a contract to supply the Alpha Omega Construction Company with certain plumbing and heating equipment. This contract was entered into at the construction company's premises. The person Kreizman dealt with was Agathos. Kreizman thought he was dealing with the owner of the business, and Agathos did nothing to dissuade him of this notion. In all the many subsequent dealings between these two parties, Kreizman continued to think that Agathos was the principal of the construction company. Agathos did nothing to correct that. It is clear that there was no partnership agreement or arrangement between Agathos and Magoulas and that Agathos was helping Magoulas out gratuitously, hoping for eventual payment under the advertising contract. Magoulas only partially paid for the supply and installation of the plumbing equipment. Lampert Plumbing sued Agathos as a partner for the unpaid funds. Explain the arguments available to both sides and the likely outcome.

## 2. *Boychuk v. Boychuk* (1975), 55 D.L.R. (3d) 751 (Alta. S.C. (T.D.)).

Two brothers operated a series of businesses, including a taxi service, bowling alleys, billiard rooms, school buses, and the rental of buildings. One of the brothers died without a will, and his wife brought an action for a declaration that the brothers were carrying on a business in partnership. The action was contested by the surviving brother. Some of the evidence showed that the brothers carried on their businesses together. There was also evidence that the taxis and buses were owned separately. The Court looked at the licences for the billiard rooms and the bowling alleys and saw that they were issued jointly to the brothers. In addition, income tax returns were filed as partners. The returns showed that they split the profits 50-50. Explain the arguments on both sides of the issue as to whether the brothers' relationship constituted a partnership.

## 3. *Barnes v. Consolidated Motors Co. Ltd.*, [1942] 1 D.L.R. 736 (B.C.S.C.).

Hall was negligently driving a motor vehicle when he struck and injured Mrs. Barnes. Hall was an employee of Distributors Used Car Branch, which was a business established by Consolidated Motor Co. Ltd. and Dan MacLean Co. Ltd. for the purpose of disposing of their used cars. J.M. Brown Motor Co. Ltd. later joined the business. The business had its own bank account, management, and employees, but until they were sold the cars remained the property of the company that supplied them. Hall was driving one of the cars owned by Consolidated to Distributors' premises when the accident took place. Mrs. Barnes sued all three car companies, claiming that they were in partnership with each other. Explain the arguments for each side. Discuss the likely outcome.

## 4. *Castellan v. Horodyski*, [1956] O.J. No. 286 (H.C.J.).

Horodyski and Lynkowski were partners in the operation of a hotel, which they sold to Castellan. One of the assets sold in this transaction was a heating boiler. Horodyski had made fraudulent misrepresentations about this boiler, which induced Castellan to enter into a contract for its purchase. Although Horodyski knew that what he said was false, Lynkowski was not aware of what was said or that there was any problem with the boiler. Shortly after Castellan's purchase, the boiler broke down and had to be rebuilt. Castellan sued both Horodyski and Lynkowski for the cost of rebuilding the boiler. Explain the legal position of the parties and the likelihood of success of the action.

**5.** *Haughton Graphic Ltd. v. Zivot* **(1986), 33 B.L.R. 125 (Ont. H.C.J.); aff'd (1988), 38 B.L.R. xxxiii (Ont. C.A.); leave to appeal refused, [1988] S.C.C.A. No. 212.**

Zivot wanted to launch a magazine, but the corporate organization that he set up to do it was quite complex. He incorporated a corporation called Lifestyle Magazine Inc. with himself as an employee. He then had Lifestyle enter into a partnership, called Printcast, with himself and several other partners. Zivot and the other partners were limited partners, whereas Lifestyle was a general partner. Haughton Graphic Ltd. supplied printing services to Printcast in order to produce the magazine, but was not paid. Haughton sued Zivot and another limited partner, claiming that because they took part in the control of the business, they ceased to be limited partners, became general partners, and were therefore liable for the indebtedness of the partnership. Would the Court agree with this conclusion? Explain the reasoning for your answer.

# Corporations

## CHAPTER HIGHLIGHTS

- The process of incorporation
- Separate legal entity or corporation
- Funding a corporation
- Duties of corporate officers
- Advantages and disadvantages of incorporation

The previous chapter dealt with the simpler methods of carrying on business: sole proprietorship and partnership. This chapter will examine the third method, the incorporated company. Since incorporation is, by far, the most common means of setting up a large business organization, exposure to the concepts and forms that regulate this important aspect of the commercial world is a vital part of the study of business law. In this chapter, we will examine the process and effect of incorporation, some features of incorporated bodies, and the rights and responsibilities of the various parties involved.

## Case Summary 14.1

### Is a Corporation a Separate Legal Entity? *Salomon v. Salomon & Co.*[1]

Incorporated

Mr. Salomon ———————————→ Salomon & Co.
(a separate legal entity)
- majority shareholder of Salomon & Co.
- loaned Salomon & Co. money and became a secured creditor
- operated business through Salomon & Co.
- business failed
- had priority over unsecured creditors

debt incurred ↓ ↑ sued by creditors

sued by creditors

Creditors of Salomon & Co.
- sued Salomon and Salomon & Co. for debts owed by Salomon
- successful against Salomon & Co.
- unsuccessful against Salomon

1. [1897] A.C. 22 (H.L.).

In this case, Mr. Salomon ran a successful shoe manufacturing business that he decided to incorporate. He set up a company in which he owned almost all the shares. He then sold the business to that company. Since the company had no assets to pay for the business, he loaned the company enough money to purchase the business from himself, securing the loan with a debenture similar to a mortgage on the company's assets. In short, Mr. Salomon loaned the company he "owned" enough money to purchase the business from him and had a mortgage on the assets of the business created to secure the loan.

When the business failed because of labour problems, the creditors turned to Mr. Salomon for payment. Not only did he refuse to pay, but as a secured creditor he had first claim on the assets of the company, leaving nothing for the unpaid creditors. In fact, the creditors had dealt only with Mr. Salomon and blamed him for their problems. They sued, claiming that he should not only be prevented from claiming ahead of them but also should be responsible for paying them if the company's assets were not enough.

The Court decided that since the company was a separate legal entity, it had a separate legal existence apart from Mr. Salomon and so he could indeed sell his assets to the company and could take security back. The end result was that Mr. Salomon was a secured creditor who stood in line ahead of the other unsecured creditors and thus had first claim on the remaining assets of the company. For the same reason, the Court held that Mr. Salomon was a person separate from the company and was in no way responsible for its debts.

This case graphically illustrates not only what is meant by a company or corporation being a separate legal entity, but also the consequences of limited liability on the part of the shareholder. This chapter will discuss the concept of the corporate entity and the legal benefits and responsibilities that result from the creation of a corporation.

# The Process of Incorporation

The concept of an incorporated company was developed in response to the need to finance large economic projects without the limitations associated with sole proprietorships and partnerships. What was needed was to have a large number of people participate in a venture without playing active roles in it. The incorporated company was the means to accomplish this end. The most significant feature of an incorporated company is that it has a separate legal personality from the people who own shares in it. The shares that represent an individual's interest in the incorporated company can be bought and sold; thus, the shareholders can be continually changing, while the company itself remains intact. This structure provides considerably more flexibility in meeting the needs of owners and directors and is a much more effective method of attracting capital.

**Corporation is a separate legal entity**

An early example of incorporation was when the monarch granted a royal charter to a town or university, thereby creating a separate legal personality. It was a natural step to extend that practice to commercial ventures. The Hudson's Bay Company is one of the earliest English commercial companies created by royal charter. Parliament also got involved by creating "special act companies" when ventures were considered important enough to be incorporated by their own special legislation.

**Royal charters created early corporations**

**Special-act companies were corporations**

At this stage, ordinary citizens could not incorporate, and so they created their own unofficial companies through contracts called **deeds of settlement**. Parliament eventually permitted incorporation for private business activities, but in the process it also had to accommodate the numerous voluntary contractual associations that were already in existence. The resulting legislation gave these companies formal status and the advantages of incorporation by allowing them to register at the appropriate government office and pay a fee.

Canada adopted many of the features of the British approach to incorporation. Both the federal and provincial governments have created many corporations through their power to pass special statutes. For example, the Canadian Broadcasting Corporation (CBC) and the Canadian Pacific Railroad (CPR) were created by special acts of Parliament. Some Canadian jurisdictions adopted the British practice of incorporation through **registration**. Other jurisdictions developed their incorporation process from the royal charter approach and created incorporated bodies through the granting of **letters patent**. A third approach which has been borrowed from the United States is based on the filing of **articles of incorporation**. Although there are technical differences between these three methods of incorporation, it is important to understand that the practical effect of each system is the same. Each method is described in more detail below.

**Three general methods of incorporation in Canada**

In Canada, it is possible to incorporate a corporation at the federal level or in each province. The choice should be made on the basis of what the corporation will be doing and where it will be done. If the activity is to be confined to a local area, it is likely that incorporation under the provincial legislation would be appropriate. Thus, a restaurant would be provincially incorporated. When the activity involves something that will be carried on in several provinces, such as a chain of restaurants, or generally across Canada, as with some service provided on the internet, the federal option might be preferable. Cost will be a major consideration. It is possible, even after choosing to incorporate provincially, to carry on business in other provinces as well, but the corporation will have to be registered in all of the provinces in which it does business, with corresponding fees paid in each jurisdiction. If a corporation has been federally incorporated, it can carry on business in any part of the country, although it must go through the formality of registering extra-provincially in each province.

**Federal and provincial corporations**

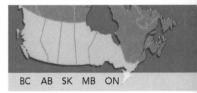

BC   AB   SK   MB   ON

## Registration

Incorporation through registration recognizes the contractual relationship between its members and grants them corporate status. In British Columbia and Nova Scotia, the jurisdictions in which the registration system is currently used, registering a "memorandum of association" and "articles of association" with the appropriate government agency, and paying the required fee, meets the requirements for incorporation.[2]

**Registration accomplished by filing memorandum and articles**

The **memorandum of association** serves the same function as a constitution in that it sets out important matters, such as the name of the company, the

**Memorandum is like a constitution**

---

2. The British Columbia government recently introduced new corporate legislation, the *Business Corporations Act*, S.B.C. 2002, c. 57. This statute comes into force on March 29, 2004, and replaces the existing *Company Act*. The new legislation continues the use of the registration method of incorporation, but with significant amendments.

authorized share capital (the total value of shares that can be sold), and, when appropriate, the objects of the incorporation.

The objects listed in the memorandum of association set out the purposes for which the company is created and also set out the limits of the capacity of the company to act. In British Columbia, "objects" are no longer permitted, but the law does permit the inclusion of "restrictions."[3] The memorandum is difficult to alter once it has been registered, so care must be taken in its design.

**Operational rules in articles**

The internal procedural regulations for governing the ordinary operation of the company are contained in the **articles of association** (not to be confused with the articles of incorporation used in other jurisdictions, discussed below). These articles deal with such matters as how shares are to be issued and transferred, requirements for meetings of the board of directors and of shareholders, voting procedures at those meetings, regulations covering borrowing, powers of directors and other officers, requirements dealing with dividends, regulations concerning company records, and how notice will be given to shareholders. The articles also set out the procedures for altering the articles, so there is considerably less difficulty in changing them than in changing the memorandum of association. But because the articles of association are filed along with the other incorporating documents, subsequent changes are more difficult than in the jurisdictions where the corresponding bylaws are considered internal documents and need not be filed.

This method of incorporation is accomplished by registration only; the registrar has no discretionary right to refuse incorporation except when the requirements set out in the legislation are not complied with. Companies created in a registration jurisdiction originally had their capacity to contract limited by their objects of incorporation. This has been modified by statute in both Nova Scotia and British Columbia. In British Columbia, the *Company Act* states that a company has "all the power and capacity of a natural person of full capacity."[4]

## Letters Patent

The letters patent method of incorporation is based on the practice of the monarch granting a royal charter. The process involves an applicant petitioning the appropriate government body for the granting of the letters patent. The government representative, acting by statute, grants a charter of incorporation to applicants who meet certain qualifications. Today, only Quebec and Prince Edward Island use this method of incorporation.

**Use of letters patent method declining**

The letters patent sets out the constitution of the new company and contains such information as the purpose for which the company is formed, the name to be used, the share structure, any restrictions on the transferability of shares, and the rights and obligations of the parties. The rules governing the ordinary operation of the company are set out in separate bylaws. In letters patent jurisdictions, companies have always had all the powers of a natural person to enter into contracts.

---

3. *Company Act,* R.S.B.C. 1996, c. 62, ss. 22, 23.

4. *Ibid.,* s. 21.

## Articles of Incorporation

The other provinces and the federal government have adopted a system of incorporation, developed in the United States, based on the filing of articles of incorporation and the granting of a certificate of incorporation. The articles of incorporation method has features of both the letters patent and the registration methods. As with letters patent companies, corporations under this system are primarily the creations of government rather than being based on contract. The articles that are filed are similar to a constitution or statute controlling the activities of the parties rather than a binding agreement between them. A corporation is granted a certificate of incorporation by filing the articles of incorporation and paying the appropriate fee. The articles of incorporation serve the same function and contain the same types of information as the memorandum of association and the letters patent in the other systems. The day-to-day operation is controlled through bylaws similar to the bylaws in a letters patent system, or the articles of association in a registration system. It is not necessary to file these bylaws when applying for incorporation. It is also important to note that in an articles of incorporation system, the government body assigned to grant certificates of incorporation has no general discretion to refuse a request for incorporation.

**Articles of incorporation method borrows features from each**

**Incorporation accomplished through granting certificate of incorporation**

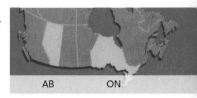

AB          ON

## Other Incorporated Bodies

Cities, universities, and other public institutions are incorporated legal entities that can sue or be sued in their own right. Under both federal and provincial legislation,[5] it is also possible to establish (incorporate) non-profit bodies, sometimes called "societies," or non-share capital corporations. These bodies are primarily cultural, social, charitable, and religious organizations, such as the Canadian Society for the Prevention of Cruelty to Animals (SPCA), the Canadian Red Cross Society, and the Canadian National Institute for the Blind (CNIB). The one thing these bodies have in common is the non-profit nature of their activities. The legal obligations and technicalities associated with these bodies are much simpler and more straightforward than those associated with corporations generally. Businesspeople often deal with such bodies and so should be aware of them and the statutes by which they are regulated. An examination of these non-profit organizations is beyond the scope of this text.

**Societies also incorporated**

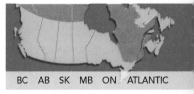

BC  AB  SK  MB  ON  ATLANTIC

# Separate Legal Entity

The original case on the existence of the company or corporation as a separate legal entity, which is still routinely cited, is the *Salomon* case discussed at the beginning of this chapter. The case recognized the separate legal existence of even a "one-man company." The decision emphasized that, when the incorporation process is completed, there are two legal persons: the shareholder and an incorporated company. Although the corporation does not exist except on paper and is only a "legal fiction," all the forces of law assume that it does exist as a legal entity separate from the shareholder, and that it can function in the commercial world. Shareholders often have difficulty understanding that they do not actually own the assets of the business and that the corporation they have incorporated

**Corporation a separate legal entity**

---

5. See, for example, the *Societies Act,* R.S.A. 2000, c. S-14.

## Figure 14.1 Separate Legal Entity

```
              buy shares              buys assets
Shareholders ──────────────▶ Corporation ──────────────▶ Assets
                          (a separate legal entity)
```

The shareholders own the shares of the corporation. The corporation (not the shareholder!) owns the assets it purchases.

does. Shares held in a corporation bestow the rights of control, but give the right to share in the liquidation of the assets (the right to participate in capital) only when the corporation is wound up. See Figure 14.1 for an illustration of the separate legal entity concept.

The problem is the opposite when dealing with a large corporation. It is difficult to think of Sears Canada Inc. and Imperial Oil Limited as a fiction or myth. It is easy to make the mistake of thinking of the corporation's assets, its warehouses and stores, or its shareholders as the entity. But just as Vandenberg's car is not Vandenberg, but an asset owned and used by her, so, too, is Sears Canada Inc. separate from its stores or shareholders. The large corporation, just like the small one, is a legal fiction, which is often referred to as the **corporate myth**.

**Courts will sometimes ignore separate legal entity**

It is also important to recognize that the status of separate legal entity for a corporation is a flimsy one, and businesspeople are often shocked to see the courts cast aside this aspect of the law governing corporations to get at the principals of the corporation. For example, the tax department will often deem several different corporations to be one person for tax purposes. Similarly, where the object of incorporation is to get around some government regulation or commit a fraud, the courts will ignore the separate legal entity aspect of the corporation, and "lift the corporate veil" to get at the directors, shareholders, or officers committing the fraud. The case discussed in Case Summary 14.2 illustrates a situation where the courts were willing to lift the corporate veil.

Nevertheless, the separate legal entity aspect of a corporation is tremendously important for commercial activities. It allows for the acquisition of capital without involving the shareholders in the operation of the corporation. It also allows the purchase and sale of their shares without interfering with the ongoing operation of the business. Like sole proprietorships and partnerships, a corporation is responsible for contracts made on its behalf, and for the torts of their employees, under the principle of vicarious liability. The corporation can even be convicted and fined for the commission of a crime. But it is the corporation itself that is liable, not the shareholders, who have limited liability. They can lose only their initial investment. It is this principle that protected Mr. Salomon in Case Summary 14.1. As a shareholder, he was not liable for the debts of the company. He was even able to claim ahead of the others, as a secured creditor of the company.

## Reducing Risk 14.1

Unfortunately, businesspeople often act as if the corporation is a real person. Managers often make decisions they find repugnant and which they would not otherwise make because they think that the corporation they serve is real. They draw a distinction in their minds between the corporate entity and themselves, as managers. While it is true that the legal duty of directors and officers is owed to the corporation, it must also be remembered that the corporation itself is merely a fiction. It has no mind or personality, and its existence cannot be used an excuse for immoral conduct.

Today, creditors can protect themselves by requiring directors or shareholders to sign a personal guarantee and become liable for the debt along with the corporation. A significant advantage of incorporation—that of limited liability—is, to a large extent, thereby lost. Furthermore, there are examples, such as the case discussed in Case Summary 14.2, where the courts are willing to lift the corporate veil. But, in most cases, the status of the corporation as a separate legal entity will be respected. This is an important institution in our commercial world, although it is important that businesspeople not take it completely for granted.

**Limited liability derived from separate legal entity**

## Case Summary 14.2

### Will the Court Lift the Corporate Veil in the Event of Fraud?
### *H&D Hobby Distributing Ltd. v. Svatos*[6]

Retail hobby goods and supplies were shipped by the plaintiff to Edmonton Hobby. A witness for the plaintiff testified that he had never heard anything about the defendant operating as a corporation. The defendant claimed that it was the corporation, not him, that was carrying on the business as Edmonton Hobby. The Court accepted the plaintiff's version of the facts. Most of the business dealings with the plaintiff made no reference to the corporation, and the business "...appeared more like the personal undertaking of a proprietor than a corporate obligation."

But even if the plaintiff knew that the defendant was operating through a corporation, there was improper conduct by the defendant in giving one creditor an unjust preference over the other creditors. The Court acknowledged that a corporation is a legal entity separate and distinct from its shareholders, who are therefore not liable for the corporation's liabilities. But here the Court would pierce the corporate veil and hold the defendant, who was the sole shareholder, director, and officer of the corporation, responsible for the improper conduct.

## Capacity

It was only in provinces using the registration system of incorporation where the capacity of the company to enter contracts was limited. That was more of a nuisance than anything else, and in the two provinces still using the registration system (British Columbia and Nova Scotia) the legislation was changed so that companies now have all the capacity of a natural person. Under the articles of incorporation statutes, it is stated that a corporation has the capacity and the rights, powers, and privileges of a natural person, subject only to the provisions of the legislation.[7] The problem of capacity to contract still may arise when dealing with corporations created by special acts of the legislature or Parliament, where those acts limit their activities to specified areas. When dealing with such a corporation, it seems that unusual care should be taken to check that there is no restriction on its capacity. Some legislation, including the federal statute, states that it is possible to set down restrictions on what the corporation can do,[8] but outsiders dealing with that corporation would be affected only in the unlikely event that they had specific notice of the limitation.[9]

---

6. (1998), 234 A.R. 376 (Q.B.).

7. See, for example, the *Canada Business Corporations Act,* R.S.C. 1985, c. C-44, s. 15(1).

8. *Ibid.,* s. 16(2).

9. *Ibid.,* s. 17.

## The Role of Agents

**Corporations must act through agents**

Since the corporate entity is a legal fiction, all of its activities must be carried out through the services of real people acting as agents. The principles of agency law set out in Chapter 12 are, therefore, extremely important when dealing with corporations. Directors and employees, from officers right down to clerks, may have actual or apparent authority to bind the corporation, depending on the nature of their jobs. Historically, a corporation could be protected from unauthorized action from such employees simply by filing with the incorporation documents a specific limitation on the actual authority of an agent. Today, these limitations on authority are no longer considered notice to the public, even when they are filed with the other incorporating documents.[10]

**Filed documents no longer notice of limited authority**

# Funding

An important attraction of the corporation is the ability to acquire capital from a large number of sources through the sale of shares. While the **share** gives the holder an interest in the corporation, that interest falls short of ownership. The corporation remains an independent personality, separate and apart from the shareholders or members who make it up. Owning shares gives the shareholder control of the corporation and, under certain circumstances, a right to the assets of the corporation upon dissolution.

**Issued shares usually less than authorized share capital**

Memorandum of association and letters patent jurisdictions require that the authorized share capital be set out in the incorporation documents.[11] This sets an upper limit on the shares that can be sold. This limit is usually set quite high to avoid the problem of having to go back and amend the incorporating documents. It is difficult to justify this limitation, and the articles of incorporation jurisdictions no longer require a limitation on the authorized share capital.[12]

## Par-Value versus No-Par-Value Shares

The practice of issuing par-value shares is declining. Such practice involves each share being given a specific value, such as $1, at the time of issuance. This can be misleading, as the marketplace quickly sets a value on those shares that is not reflected in that stated par value. The more common practice in Canada and the United States is to put no value on the share at all, making it a no-par-value share, and allowing the marketplace to determine the value. The articles of incorporation jurisdictions have abolished par-value shares altogether.[13]

**Common practice to issue no-par-value shares**

## Special Rights and Restrictions

The shares issued by a corporation are normally divided into different classes, usually called *common shares* and *special* or *preferred shares*. The rights and restric-

---

10. *Ibid.,* s. 17.

11. *Company Act, supra* note 3, s. 19.

12. See, for example, the *Canada Business Corporations Act, supra* note 7, where s. 6(1)(c) gives the incorporators discretion as to whether a maximum number of shares is set.

13. *Ibid.,* s. 24(1). British Columbia currently allows both par-value and no-par-value shares; *Company Act, supra* note 3, s. 19.

tions associated with special shares can be designed to accomplish many diverse objectives, but they usually give the shareholder preference when dividends are declared and are, therefore, called **preferred shares**. Usually, a preferred share will bear a promise to pay a specific dividend each year. This is not a debt, and the corporation is not obligated to declare a dividend, but once it does, the preferred shareholder has the right to collect first, before the common shareholders. These rights may be cumulative, and, if they are, when there has been a failure to pay the promised dividend for a number of years, the preferred shareholder has a right to receive any back payments before the common shareholders get any dividends. If Bandura has 100 preferred non-voting shares in a corporation that committed to pay a dividend of $10 per share per year, she may receive $1000 in dividends from that corporation in any given year. She cannot force the payment of the dividend, but she does have the right to payment before any dividends are paid to the common shareholder. This includes any failed dividend payments from prior years.

Shares of public corporations are traded on the stock exchange.

Usually, only common shareholders have the right to vote, but a preferred share usually gives the right to vote when the corporation fails to pay the promised dividend. There can be a right to vote, even without such a provision, when major changes that would materially affect the position of the preferred shareholder are proposed. For example, a proposal to change the rights or nature of the preferred share, or to sell the assets of the corporation, could not be adopted without allowing the preferred shareholders to vote.[14] Also, when a corporation is dissolved, preferred shareholders usually have the right to have those shares repaid before any funds are paid out to the holders of common shares.

**Different classes of shares can give some shareholders preference**

Since a variety of rights and restrictions can be incorporated into preferred shares, depending on the interests of the parties, it is important that these matters be negotiated before the shares are issued. When a closely held corporation

---

## Reducing **Risk** 14.2

It is relatively easy to incorporate a business. The process is now simplified to the extent that people can either do it themselves or purchase a simple off-the-shelf corporation, much like they can purchase a suit off the rack. But these approaches may result in a loss of some of the considerable flexibility that is available using the corporate form to carry on business. It is possible, by careful use of common shares, the creation of shares with special rights and restrictions, and shareholders' agreements, to cater to a great variety of different relationships and needs, giving different rights and obligations with unique advantages

to the various players. In addition, through holding corporations, corporations working together, and even corporations in partnership, there is no limit to the creative solutions that can be designed to deal with a variety of business problems and needs. Businesspeople should be aware that, just as a personally tailored suit has advantages over an off-the-shelf one, paying a lawyer to custom-design a corporation for their particular needs may well be worth the trouble and expense. Skimping to save a few dollars at the outset may cause expensive problems later on.

---

14. See s. 176 and s. 189 of the *Canada Business Corporations Act, ibid.,* which deal with class votes and extraordinary sales or leases of the corporation's assets, respectively.

is involved, it is common to include a restriction on the transfer or sale of the shares, such as requiring the approval of the directors before the transfer or sale can take place. (Closely held and broadly held corporations are discussed below.)

**Special shares used in estate planning**

Special shares are used for other purposes, such as estate planning, where two classes of shares can be created: one with a right to vote and with some control in the affairs of the corporation, but no right to dividends or to receive money upon dissolution, and the other with a right to dividends, but no right to vote. Such a division allows the holder of the voting shares to maintain control of the operations of the corporation, but to surrender the income and the beneficial interests of the corporation to any heirs.

## Borrowing

The corporation can also borrow funds, thus accumulating debt. This can be done by borrowing large sums from a single creditor, such as a bank, which usually requires a mortgage on the property of the corporation. It can also be accomplished through the issuing of bonds or debentures, either secured or unsecured, to many different creditors. The result, in either case, is the creation of a debtor–creditor relationship and an obligation that must be repaid. When shares are involved, even preferred shares, there is no legal obligation to pay dividends, but a failure to repay a debt constitutes a breach of the corporation's legal obligation. The creditor can execute against security, bring an action, and, once judgment is obtained, garnish or seize the assets of the corporation. If the corporation is unable to pay, bankruptcy will likely follow.

**Corporation borrows funds by issuing bonds**

Usually, the terms "bond" and "debenture" are used interchangeably, but in Canada a **bond** is normally secured by a mortgage or a floating charge on all assets of the corporation not already mortgaged or pledged, whereas a **debenture** is more likely to be unsecured. The corporation typically makes a debt commitment to a trustee, who then issues shares in the indebtedness to individual bondholders. These bondholders are entitled to a portion of the repayment at a set rate of interest, and are free to sell such claims to others, sometimes at a premium or discount, depending on the market.

**Bondholder has right to payment**

Shareholders are participants in the corporation, whereas bondholders are simply creditors. The corporation is in debt to the bondholder for the amount of the bond, but the corporation is not in debt to the shareholder for the price of the share. The bondholder can demand repayment and enforce that right in court, whereas a shareholder, even a preferred shareholder, has no similar right to demand payment of a dividend or repayment of the cost of the share.

**Bondholder has no right to vote**

On the other hand, while a shareholder can determine the operation of the corporation through the exercise of her voting power, a bondholder has no right to vote and cannot affect management decisions. In the event of a default, however, the bondholders usually have a right to take over the management of the corporation through the appointment of a receiver, similar to bankruptcy but without the requirement of court involvement. While the corporation remains solvent, however, the shareholders retain control through their voting power, and the bondholders only have the right to be paid on a regular basis. From the investor's point of view, the choice between shares at one end, bonds at the other, and preferred shares in the middle is likely to be simply a question of balancing risk and return. But in order to calculate the risks, a clear understanding of the legal differences between these vehicles as well as an understanding of their different tax implications is essential.

Most large corporations maintain a balance between common and preferred shares on the one hand, and various types of debt instruments, such as large loans and secured and unsecured corporate bonds, on the other. To illustrate, suppose Bowman wanted to incorporate a small manufacturing business. There are several ways to transfer the assets of the business to the corporation. Bowman might incorporate a corporation that would acquire the manufacturing business and any property associated with it in return for all the shares of the corporation. A better alternative, however, might be to have the corporation purchase the manufacturing business as well as any property associated with it from Bowman, giving him a bond secured by a mortgage on the property as security for the repayment of the debt.

Bowman owns all the shares of the corporation in either case. However, in the second case, instead of simply owning shares in a corporation with significant assets, Bowman is a creditor of that corporation. Because the debt will be secured, he will be in a better position to get his money back if the corporation eventually runs into financial difficulties. This is similar to the situation in which Salomon found himself in Case Summary 14.1. Before decisions are made with respect to these options, careful consideration must be given to the various tax implications of the choices. Refer to Figure 14.2 for a summary of the funding of corporations.

## Closely Held and Broadly Held Corporations

Traditionally, company law statutes in various jurisdictions recognized a distinction between broadly held and closely held companies, which were usually called *public* and *private companies*, respectively. In recent years, statutory provisions relating to these two classes of corporation have received considerable attention and have been significantly modified. In general, a closely held corporation is one in which there are relatively few shareholders. There are restrictions on the sale of shares, which cannot be sold to the general public openly or on the stock market. Closely held corporations are usually (but not always!) small corporations that are used to operate a family business. They are usually managed by the shareholders themselves. The closely held corporation is much freer of government regulations and control than the broadly held corporation. The special requirements for broadly held corporations are found not only in the appropriate incorporation statutes but also in the securities legislation of that jurisdiction.

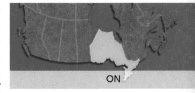

**Broadly held corporations more closely regulated**

**Figure 14.2 Funding of Corporations**

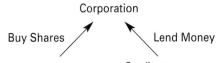

Corporation

Buy Shares        Lend Money

Shareholders
- buy shares from corporation
- common or preferred
- control corporation
- corporation not obligated to declare dividends
- share in liquidation of assets on winding up of corporation, after creditors paid

Creditors
- lend money to corporation
- secured or unsecured
- no control over management
- corporation has legal obligation to repay loans
- entitled to be paid before shareholders, on winding up of corporation

Using Alberta as an example, corporations in that province that offer shares to the public and that have more than 15 shareholders are called *distributing corporations*.[15] Such corporations have to satisfy the most stringent legislative requirements. For example, section 160 of the Alberta *Business Corporations Act* requires them to file financial statements with the Alberta Securities Commission. They must have an audit committee (section 171). They must provide greater access to corporate records (section 23). They cannot restrict the transfer of their shares, except to non-residents, or to enable the corporation to meet any requirement to allow them to obtain a business licence, to become a publisher of a Canadian newspaper, or to acquire shares in a financial intermediary (sections 48, 174). They must have at least three directors, two of whom must not be officers or employees of the corporation or its affiliates. A non-distributing corporation requires only one or more directors (section 101(2)). Legislative requirements for distributing corporations are found not only in the *Business Corporations Act*, but also in the securities legislation, the *Securities Act*.[16]

Non-distributing corporations with 15 or fewer shareholders have to comply with the least amount of government regulation and control. Non-distributing corporations with 16 or more shareholders that do not offer shares to the public do have to comply with more statutory requirements than those corporations with fewer than 16 shareholders, but not as much as distributing corporations.[17]

BC

# Corporate Officers

## Directors (Managers)

### Within the Corporation

### Case Summary 14.3

**To Whom Does a Director Owe a Duty of Good Faith?**
*Deluce Holdings Inc. v. Air Canada*[18]

Air Ontario was a small regional airline that had been owned and operated by the Deluce family for years out of London, Ontario. In 1986, a deal was struck with Air Canada whereby it acquired a majority interest in Air Ontario. (Air Canada had a 75-percent share and the Deluce family a 25-percent share through separate holding corporations.) Air Canada had the right to appoint seven directors to the board of directors of Air Ontario and the Deluce family was to appoint three. The deal also involved a separate shareholders' agreement, whereby Air Canada would have the right to buy out the Deluce interest when the employment of the last member of the family ended. Stanley Deluce was the chairman, and his two-year contract was not renewed when it expired. William Deluce, who was the vice-chairman and CEO, was subsequently asked to resign. When he refused, he was fired. This was a complicated action, but, basically, the Deluce family claimed oppres-

---

15. *Business Corporations Act,* R.S.A. 2000, c. B-9, s. 1(p).

16. R.S.A. 2000, c. S-4.

17. Such corporations must, for example, comply with s. 149 and s. 150 of the *Business Corporations Act, supra* note 15, regarding proxies and proxy solicitations, unless they are exempted by the Alberta Securities Commission.

18. (1992), 98 D.L.R. (4th) 509 (Ont. Gen. Div.).

sion on the basis that the seven directors appointed by Air Canada ganged up on the others, forcing William Deluce out. This would enable Air Canada to buy out the Deluce interest. This was done as a result of a general policy change, whereby Air Canada decided to acquire control of all its regional feeder airlines.

The case turned on the nature of the duty of the directors appointed by Air Canada. The Court found that the directors had a duty of good faith to act in the best interests of the corporation that they were directing, namely Air Ontario. The Court then examined the circumstances of the firing of William Deluce and found that the directors appointed by Air Canada, instead of acting in the best interests of Air Ontario, had acted on behalf of Air Canada so that they could buy out the Deluce family and take over the corporation. This was in violation of their duty and constituted oppression of the minority shareholders.

This case illustrates that directors owe a duty to the corporation of which they are directors, not to the interest group that appointed them. This can cause a serious dilemma to people acting as directors, especially when they owe their position to some other holding corporation whose interests they are expected to protect. This creates a classic conflict of interest. The case also shows the importance of shareholder agreements and the role they can play in creating specialized relationships and obligations between the parties.

The shareholders normally exercise control over a corporation through the election of directors at the annual meeting. Once the directors are elected, the shareholders have little real say in the operation of the corporation until the next election, but the expectation is that if they want to be re-elected, the directors will follow the wishes of the shareholders. Sometimes, a shareholders' vote will be held when decisions involving a fundamental change in the corporation are to be made or when required by the incorporating documents. Smaller (closely held) corporations are more often run like an incorporated partnership. The shareholders are usually the managers as well as the directors, and they participate in all important decisions.

**Shareholders choose directors**

For a person to serve as a director, he must be an adult of sound mind, and cannot be a bankrupt.[19] In most jurisdictions, the director no longer needs to be a shareholder.[20] Because many corporations in Canada are foreign subsidiaries, usually a significant proportion of the directors must be resident in Canada.[21]

A director owes a significant duty to the corporation to be careful. In common law, this duty was minimal, the director being liable only where there was some blatant or gross carelessness on his part. This standard has been significantly raised in most jurisdictions. The federal legislation, for example, now requires a director to exercise the care, diligence, and skill of a "reasonably prudent person" when exercising their powers and discharging their duties.[22]

**Director owes duty not to be negligent**

Directors also owe a **fiduciary duty** to the corporation.[23] This duty requires the director to act in the best interests of the corporation, to be loyal, to avoid

**Director owes fiduciary duty**

---

19. See, for example, *Canada Business Corporations Act, supra* note 7, s. 105(1).

20. *Ibid.,* s. 105(2).

21. *Ibid.,* s. 105(3) and (4). Note that the residency requirement for federal corporations was recently reduced from a majority to 25 percent.

22. *Ibid.,* s.122(1)(b).

23. *Ibid.,* s. 122(1)(a).

conflict of interest, and to otherwise act honestly and in good faith toward the corporation. Directors are not permitted to take personal advantage of opportunities that arise because of their positions as directors, nor can they start a business in competition with the corporation. Any gains made by directors from such dealings must be paid over to the corporation, but any losses must be borne by that director alone. When a director is personally involved in some transaction that the corporation may become involved in, the director must disclose that interest by making a declaration to the board of directors, avoid any involvement in the discussion of the matter, and abstain from voting on it.[24]

**Director owes duty to corporation, not to shareholders**

A major problem associated with director's **liability** is that they owe a duty to the corporation itself, not to the shareholders. This principle was clearly established in the case of *Foss v. Harbottle*[25] and has subsequently been incorporated into many statutes. Only the corporation can sue the director when this duty is violated. Since the directors decide what the corporation does, a decision to sue a director must be made by the directors, and they are not likely to decide to sue themselves.

**Derivative or representative action**

To solve this problem, many jurisdictions give even minority shareholders the right to bring what is called a **derivative action** (in some provinces, a **representative action**) against the directors or others on behalf of the injured corporation.[26] This change, along with the change in the nature of the imposed duty to be careful, has significantly enhanced the peril associated with being a director. It has even been argued that the fiduciary duty of a director extends to the creditors of the corporation in some limited situations.

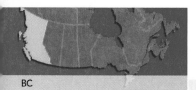

BC

### Case Summary 14.4

**To Whom Does a Director Owe a Fiduciary Duty? *400280 Alberta Ltd. v. Franko's Heating and Air Conditioning (1992) Ltd.*[27]**

The plaintiff and the defendant incorporated a sheet metal business ("Franko's Ltd."). The plaintiff provided the initial capital and directed work to Franko's Ltd. The defendant worked as an employee of Franko's Ltd. The defendant started to generate some work on his own, and incorporated another corporation against the plaintiff's wishes. The plaintiff, as a minority shareholder of Franko's Ltd., eventually brought an oppression action against the defendant. The Court held that, as a director of Franko's Ltd., the defendant owed it a strict fiduciary duty not to divert work away from it to his other corporation. The defendant breached this fiduciary duty. His actions were oppressive, unfairly prejudicial to, and in unfair disregard of the plaintiff as a shareholder in Franko's Ltd. The defendant was ordered to account for the plaintiff's share of the profits from the work that was diverted from Franko's Ltd., as well as the plaintiff's share of the assets owned by Franko's Ltd. that were used without the plaintiff's knowledge or consent.

**Directors may face personal liability**

In addition to these general duties, statutes in all jurisdictions set out many specific responsibilities and liabilities directors are subject to when they make specific prohibited decisions. For example, directors become personally liable if

24. *Ibid., s. 120.*
25. (1843), 67 E.R. 189, 2 Hare 461 (V-C).
26. *Canada Business Corporations Act, supra* note 7, s. 239.
27. (1995), 166 A.R. 241 (Q.B.).

they allow shares to be sold for consideration that is less than the fair equivalent of the money that the corporation would have received if the share had been issued for money.[28] Directors will also be personally liable if they allow transactions that are not permitted by the legislation, such as the purchase of shares, or the payment of dividends, by the corporation, if there are reasonable grounds for believing that the corporation would, after carrying out the transaction, be unable to pay its liabilities as they become due, or if the value of its assets would then be less than the value of its liabilities.[29] Finally, directors may be liable if they contravene specific responsibilities as set out in the legislation, such as the calling of annual shareholders' meetings.[30]

Directors (and officers and others who are deemed to be insiders) are prohibited from using "insider knowledge" to their own advantage or to the advantage of their friends or family. That is, directors who are aware of something about to happen that will materially affect the value of shares, bonds, or other assets of the corporation are prohibited from using that knowledge to their own advantage through dealing in these assets. There are strict disclosure requirements whenever an insider trades in the securities of the corporation. The misuse of insider information is prohibited by securities legislation, and an offender is subject to fines and imprisonment. The *Canada Business Corporations Act* also provides for personal civil liability of a director who commits insider trading.[31]

**Directors are "insiders"**

There are many other statutes that impose duties and responsibilities on directors. Directors of larger corporations, for example, face personal financial liability and even imprisonment if information is not provided to the Chief Statistician of Canada, as required by the *Corporations Returns Act*.[32]

## External Obligations

Various federal and provincial statues impose personal liability on the director in primarily three areas. Directors can be held personally liable when a corporation fails while owing workers unpaid wages.[33] Often, when a corporation is in trouble, directors will resign rather than face this risk. Sometimes, the corporation will agree to indemnify them, but if the corporation fails, such an agreement is useless. Insurance provides the best protection in these circumstances. Directors can also be held personally liable for breaches of employment standards legislation as well as workers' compensation and occupational health and safety legislation in place in the particular jurisdiction.

**Director's statutory duty for**

• wages

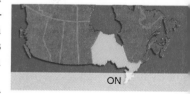

ON

A second area of personal liability for directors involves unpaid taxes. Under federal income tax legislation, the directors are personally responsible if back taxes are left unpaid.[34] In many jurisdictions in Canada, if foreign firms wish to

• taxes

---

28. *Ibid.,* s. 118(1).

29. *Ibid.,* s. 118(2).

30. *Ibid.,* s. 133(1).

31. *Ibid.,* s. 130. See *Tongue v. Vencap Equities Alberta Ltd.* (1996), 184 A.R. 368 (C.A.), where the Court found the directors of a corporation personally liable for damages for breach of fiduciary duty and insider trading, under the *Canada Business Corporations Act.*

32. *Corporations Returns Act,* R.S.C. 1985, c. C-43.

33. See, for example, s. 119 of the *Canada Business Corporations Act, supra* note 7, which makes directors of federal corporations liable for up to six months' wages payable to each employee of the corporation.

34. This includes liability for the corporation's failure to remit any prescribed amounts under the *Income Tax Act,* R.S.C.1985, c. 1 (5th Supp.) and the *Excise Tax Act,* R.S.C. 1985, c. E-15.

operate they must have local resident directors.[35] Local businesspeople are often expected to act as token directors but are not actually expected to participate in the decision-making process of the corporation. Many take these positions not realizing their exposure, and if the corporation fails, leaving unpaid taxes and other obligations, the personal liability can be ruinous.

### Case Summary 14.5

**When Are Directors Liable for Unpaid Taxes?** *Axford v. Canada*[36]

Axford was the sole shareholder and director of a corporation. The corporation failed to remit to Revenue Canada income tax, GST, and source deductions of its employees. The corporation was assessed for these, and the related interest and penalties. The corporation did not pay the required amount, so Revenue Canada assessed Axford for it. The Court held that Axford was involved in the corporation's affairs and knew of its financial difficulties. He was therefore under a positive duty to act when Revenue Canada demanded payment. Axford did not take any action, and thus did not exercise due diligence to prevent the corporation's failure to pay Revenue Canada. He was personally liable for the amount owed to Revenue Canada.

• environment

The third area involves environmental regulation. Complicated statutes impose personal liability on directors for damages caused by the corporation to the environment.[37] Contamination of property, pollution of the air, unexpected spills, and the cost of cleanup are examples of potential sources of a director's personal liability. In addition to potential fines and imprisonment, the directors may also face being personally responsible for the actual damages caused, or the costs of cleanup, in a civil action.

Usually, directors can escape liability only when they can show that they acted with "due diligence."[38] What constitutes **due diligence** varies with the situation, but, in general, directors must show that they kept themselves informed of what was required of the corporation and what the corporation was doing to comply and that they did all that was reasonable to avoid the problem.

• other

Individual liability has also been imposed on directors for offences under consumer protection legislation, the federal *Competition Act*, securities legislation, and provincial human rights codes. It is important to note that many of these statutes not only contemplate fines, but also provide for imprisonment in extreme situations. Usually, both criminal and civil responsibilities may be imposed on the corporation itself, as well as on its directors and officers.

It should also be remembered that when the commission of a tort, such as misrepresentation or deceit, is involved, a director may be held personally liable if he was the one who committed the wrong. The corporate structure is some-

---

35. *Canada Business Corporations Act, supra* note 7, s. 105 (3) and (4), discussed above in note 21.

36. [2002] T.C.J. No. 597 (T.C.C.).

37. For example, see s. 280 of the *Canadian Environmental Protection Act, 1999,* S.C. 1999, c. 33, which states that where a corporation has committed an offence, any officer, director, or agent of the corporation who "directed, authorized, assented to, acquiesced in, or participated in" the commission of the offence is also guilty of the offence and liable to the punishment provided for the offence.

38. *Ibid.,* s. 283. Section 280(2) states that a director must take "all reasonable care" to ensure that the corporation complies with the legislation.

times no protection to the person who actually commits the tort. The decisions on this issue have been inconsistent, but the following statement appears to accurately state the law:

> ... there will be circumstances in which the actions of a shareholder, officer, director or employee of a corporation may give rise to personal liability in tort despite the fact that the impugned acts were ones performed in the course of their duties to the corporation. Where those actions are themselves tortuous or exhibit a separate identity or interest from that of the corporation so as to make the act or conduct complained of their own, they may well attract personal liability....[39]

## Officers and Senior Executives

### Case Summary 14.6

**Do Officers Owe a Fiduciary Duty to the Corporation?** *Roper v. Murdoch*[40]

Catalina Productions Inc. was involved in several high-profile programs, including "Let's Make a Deal," "The Tom Jones Show," and a game show called "Pitfall." It instituted negotiations with Richard Deacon, a well-known Hollywood personality, to produce a television news program called "Micro Magic," which involved microwave cooking and celebrity guests.

At the initial stage, the negotiations were handled by Catalina's owner, McLennan, and then handed over to Armstrong, the vice-president of programming. Unfortunately in this case, because of financial problems and chaotic conditions at Catalina, the negotiations fell through, and on September 9 a letter was received by Deacon's agent cancelling the deal.

On that same day, Northstar Productions Inc. was incorporated by Armstrong and Murdoch, formerly Catalina's vice-president of marketing, who had resigned from Catalina in late August. Northstar concluded a deal with Deacon and his agent to produce the new "Micro Magic" show. That agreement contained virtually the same terms as the handshake agreement Deacon had entered into with McLennan and Catalina. The project went ahead, and during the year 1981–82 Northstar produced the show.

In this case, Murdoch and Armstrong had been executives and, as such, owed a fiduciary duty to Catalina. Armstrong had been in the planning stages of "Micro Magic" while at Catalina, and Murdoch in his position at Catalina was certainly aware of the project. The situation became even more complex because Catalina went into bankruptcy, and the trustee assigned any rights it had arising out of television production to Roper, who brought this action against Armstrong and Murdoch.

The Court held that Armstrong and Murdoch, because of their positions with Catalina, owed a fiduciary duty to Catalina. It was clear from the evidence that on the day they resigned, Armstrong and Murdoch had it in mind to produce "Micro

---

39. *Blacklaws v. Morrow* (2000), 261 A.R. 28 (C.A.), leave to appeal refused, [2000] S.C.C.A. No. 442, para. 41. For a case where a director was found to be personally liable in tort, see *ADGA Systems International Ltd. v. Valcom Ltd.* (1999), 43 O.R. (3d) 101 (C.A.), leave to appeal refused, [1999] S.C.C.A. No. 124.

40. (1987), 39 D.L.R. (4th) 684 (B.C.S.C.).

Magic." This opportunity came to them because of their corporate positions, and they were prohibited from taking personal advantage of it. The Court required them to pay any profits they made from the deal to Roper, the successor of Catalina.

This case shows clearly the fiduciary duty imposed on the officers and directors of a corporation and also how that duty continues after their resignation from the corporation. It is also interesting to note that the right to sue did not die with the bankrupt corporation, but was subsequently exercised by a complete stranger to these dealings, the assignee, Roper.

**Similar duties owed by senior management**

Although directors are legally responsible for management, in a large corporation they usually appoint a managing director or CEO, who is given overall responsibility, along with a managing committee of the directors, to run the affairs of the corporation. The day-to-day operation of the corporation is assigned to others who report to the CEO. These officers may include a president, treasurer, secretary, and other senior executives, such as vice-presidents and managers, as deemed appropriate for the organization. In general, these officers and managers are in a fiduciary relationship to the corporation, similar to that of the directors. They owe the same types of general obligations and duties of care and competence to the corporation as the directors, but may be held to an even higher standard. In the case of statutory obligations, they may have to pay any wages and taxes owing. They may be held personally liable for judgments against the corporation in human rights and consumer complaint actions as well as costs for cleaning up any environmental damage caused by the corporation.[41] The legislation usually imposes the same obligations on officers as those imposed on directors. The *Roper* case shows the nature of fiduciary duty as well as how that duty can continue even after the employment relationship has ceased.

## Promoters

**Promoters also owe duties**

**Disclosure required**

A **promoter** is someone who participates in the initial setting up of the corporation or who assists the corporation in making a public share offering. Provincial securities statutes control the sale of shares to the public, whether through the stock exchange or other means. A **securities commission** is established to prevent fraud and to encourage a free and efficient market in corporate shares and other securities. This requires the complete disclosure of as much information as possible. To accomplish this, a proper prospectus must be issued when shares are to be sold to the public. The purpose of the **prospectus** is to disclose all pertinent information of interest to investors about the corporation and its business operations. The corporation and the promoters are responsible to ensure full disclosure and that there is no misrepresentation in the prospectus. In addition to any civil liability, significant fines and jail sentences may be imposed when there is not full disclosure or when misrepresentations take place.

---

41. For example, the personal liability described in s. 280 of the *Canadian Environmental Protection Act 1999, supra* note 37, extends not only to directors, but also to officers and agents of the corporation.

The securities commission is also charged with controlling other forms of abuse, including insider trading, where officers or people holding significant percentages of the shares of a corporation trade in those shares using their insider's knowledge to anticipate a rise or fall in prices. The securities commission also controls abuses by providing for the licensing and regulation of all those involved in the selling and marketing of shares and other securities, including brokers, sales personnel, and the issuers of the shares (the corporations) themselves.

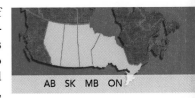

AB  SK  MB  ON

Whether promoters are officers of the corporation or not, they, like directors and other officers, owe a fiduciary duty to the corporation. When property is acquired with the intention of incorporating a corporation and then selling that property to it, the promoter has a duty to act in the best interests of the corporation. The promoter cannot sell the property to the corporation at an excessive profit, must divulge the original price paid, and must not participate in the decision to purchase from him. The promoter has a fiduciary duty to the corporation and a duty to disclose any personal interest in deals in which the corporation is involved.

**Fiduciary duty**

### Case Summary 14.7

#### When Is a Promoter Personally Liable? *1080409 Ontario Ltd. v. Hunter* [42]

Garth Drabinsky incorporated 1080409 to purchase the subject property. He later decided to sell the property. He entered into an agreement with Hunter, but the purchase and sale agreement was in the name "Furama Investments." Furama was not incorporated. Hunter did not have sufficient funds, so the deal did not close. 1080409 later sold the property to a third party, but at a lower price than Hunter had agreed to pay. 1080409 sued Hunter for the difference in net proceeds.

The Court found that Hunter was personally liable, pursuant to s. 21(1) of the *Ontario Business Corporations Act*. Hunter had signed the agreement on behalf of a corporation before it came into existence. He could have expressly provided in the purchase and sale agreement that he was not personally bound by the agreement, but he did not do so.

### Reducing **Risk** 14.3

Promoters will often purchase property on behalf of a corporation before it has been incorporated and then have the corporation ratify the agreement after incorporation. Such ratification of pre-incorporation contracts is invalid in common law, since the corporation did not exist at the time the promoters were claiming to act on its behalf. Although this approach may be legally sound, it is not practical from a business point of view, and many jurisdictions have made legislative changes permitting the later-incorporated corporation to ratify a pre-incorporation contract.[43] The result is that the contract is valid and binding on the corporation once it is so ratified. Of course, if the corporation does not ratify, or if a pre-incorporation contract is signed in a jurisdiction where the corporation cannot ratify, the promoter remains solely liable for any losses, since there was no authority to act. Businesspeople should try to avoid personal liability for pre-incorporation contracts. They may be able to do so by including a provision in the contract exempting them from any resulting liability.

42. [2000] O.J. No. 2603 (Ont. Sup. Ct. J.).

43. See *Canada Business Corporations Act, supra* note 7, s. 14.

## Shareholders

### Case Summary 14.8

#### Can a Minor Shareholder Commence a Lawsuit on Behalf of the Corporation? *Richardson Greenshields of Canada Ltd. v. Kalmacoff*[44]

Two security corporations were involved in this case, Security Home Mortgage Investment Inc. ("Security Home") and Security Home Financing Ltd. ("the Advisor"). Security Home was controlled by a small group of individuals holding 85 percent of the common shares. That same group largely owned the shares in the Advisor, which had a contract to manage and run the operation of Security Home. A large number of preferred shares in Security Home had been sold on the open market through the agent, Richardson Greenshields of Canada Ltd. These special shareholders only had the right to vote with respect to the management contract. Security Home ran into financial difficulty but renewed the management contract of the Advisor anyway. Because renewal of the Advisor's management contract also required the approval of the preferred shareholders, Richardson Greenshields obtained enough proxies from them to override that decision, and the contract was terminated.

It was at this point that the basis of the complaint arose. Instead of that being the end of the matter, the directors of Security Home, in order to thwart the spirit of the direction given them by the preferred shareholders, simply hired the people employed by the Advisor as managers for Security Home. In effect, they were doing exactly the same jobs they were doing before, but now they were employed directly by Security Home instead of by the Advisor. In response to this, Richardson Greenshields bought 100 shares of Security Home on the open market and brought a derivative action in the name of and on behalf of Security Home against its directors.

The question in this case was whether Richardson Greenshields had the right to bring such a derivative action, since it had acquired the shares after the conduct complained of. The Court of Appeal decided that the issues involved were significant, that it did not matter when Richardson Greenshields obtained the shares, and that, as a shareholder, it had the right to ask the Court for permission to commence a derivative action against the directors of the corporation. Permission was granted.

The Court's decision did not decide the merits of the dispute; it simply authorized the action to proceed. However, the case does illustrate some very important points. First, it shows how "preferred" shares can be set up with rights and obligations different from those of common shares and what the effects of those differences can be. It also illustrates how different corporate entities can be used and intermingled to accomplish different purposes, as was the case here with Security Home and the Advisor having essentially the same investors owning common shares in each. For our purposes, the most important point to note is the right of a disgruntled shareholder to overcome the tyranny of the majority and bring an action on behalf of the corporation against those who have, for their own ulterior purposes, made decisions not in the best interests of the corporation.

**Shareholder has few responsibilities**

One of the main attractions of incorporation is that shareholders have few obligations to the corporation or other shareholders, other than not to use insider knowledge for their own purposes. Unlike the director, the shareholder usually has no duty to act in the best interests of the corporation, although obli-

---

44. (1995), 22 O.R. (3d) 577 (C.A.), leave to appeal to S.C.C. refused, [1995] S.C.C.A. No. 260.

gations can be imposed on shareholders if they hold enough shares to be classi-fied as "insiders." The number of shares required to qualify as an insider varies from one jurisdiction to another,[45] but shareholders who have been classified as insiders have the same obligation as directors not to use insider information to their own benefit or to the benefit of friends or relatives.

## Rights

Shareholders do have significant rights and remedies. Certain records must be kept at a designated corporate office and made available to the shareholders.[46] These records must include:

- the documents of incorporation;
- lists of all the shareholders;
- lists of transactions or changes in relationship to the shares;
- lists of officers, directors, and debenture holders; and
- minutes of shareholders' meetings.

Some corporate records, including the minutes of directors' meetings and the actual financial records ("the books"), are not available to shareholders. Otherwise, such information could not be kept from competitors. Nonetheless, much important information is contained in documents that are accessible to anybody who holds a share in the corporation.

**Shareholder has right to see records and reports**

Shareholders are entitled to receive copies of annual financial statements of the corporation and the auditor's report, if any.[47] The financial statements of broadly held corporations must be audited.[48] An **auditor** is an unbiased outside accountant,[49] whose responsibility is to ensure that the financial statements use generally accepted accounting practices and are accurate. The auditor's duty is to the shareholders, not to the directors, and the auditors have access to the corpo-ration's books to ensure the accuracy of their conclusions.[50] Shareholders who have some doubts about the accuracy of these audited statements can have an inspector appointed to examine the auditing process.[51]

The shareholders also have considerable power to affect the decisions made by the corporation. An **annual general meeting** of shareholders must be held, where the shareholders are given an opportunity to vote for the directors of the corporation, making the directors directly answerable to the shareholders for their actions. Advance notice of this meeting, including the appropriate financial statements, must be given to the shareholders. Any major changes that will affect the nature of the corporation must be placed before the shareholders to vote on before the decisions are implemented. If necessary, a special meeting can be called for this purpose. The incorporating documents or bylaws of the corpora-

**Shareholders have the right to vote**

---

45. Section 131(1)(d) of the *Canada Business Corporations Act, supra* note 7, together with s. 40 of the *Canada Business Corporations Act Regulation,* S.O.R./2001-512, states that any person who beneficially owns, or exercises control or direction over, at least 10 percent of the outstanding voting shares of a corporation is considered an "insider."

46. *Canada Business Corporations Act, ibid.,* ss. 20, 21, 138(4).

47. *Ibid.,* s. 159.

48. *Ibid.,* ss. 163, 169(1).

49. *Ibid.,* s. 161.

50. *Ibid.,* s. 170.

51. *Ibid.,* Part XIX.

tion may provide for the right of shareholders to vote in other situations as well. Shareholders at these meetings can put forward proposals concerning any matter for the decision of the other shareholders, but management may refuse to submit a proposal if it appears that it is self-serving or is in some way an abuse of the process. It must be remembered that each vote is based on the number of shares held. Thus, someone holding a majority of the shares will always be able to out-vote minority shareholders.[52]

**Proxy can be passed to someone else**

Shareholders can pass their right to vote at the annual general meeting to someone else, in the form of a **proxy**. These proxies can be very important when groups of shareholders band together to effect a particular result or to determine which directors are elected at the annual general meeting. The rules for the creation and operation of proxies are quite strict because of the potential for abuse.[53] For example, for federal corporations, proxies (with some exceptions) cannot be solicited except by a circular in a form prescribed by regulation.[54] A proxy holder who fails to comply with the directions of the shareholder is liable to a fine of up to $5000 and/or imprisonment for up to six months.[55]

The bylaws or articles set out how many votes each shareholder is entitled to, but this may vary with the type of shares held. Holders of **common shares** are usually entitled to one vote per share. **Preferred shareholders** usually cannot vote, unless the promised dividend has not been paid. A shareholder holding a significant portion of the shares can usually force the calling of an extra meeting,[56] while someone with fewer shares, if she has good reason, can apply to the court for the same purpose.[57] However, the majority shareholder is still protected, as a majority vote or greater is necessary to decide all matters once the meeting is held.

**Preemptive rights entitle shareholder to be offered any new shares first**

In many jurisdictions, shareholders have the right not to have their proportion of shares diluted by the sale of more shares to others. If there are 1000 shares outstanding and Pantaz has 500 of them, he owns 50 percent of the corporation. If the directors decide to issue 500 new shares and none are offered to Pantaz, his interest will be reduced to a one-third portion. In smaller corporations, this is usually avoided by including, in a separate shareholders' agreement, a provision requiring that a sufficient number of the new shares be offered to the existing shareholders first so that they may retain their proportionate share of the corporation. Such a right is called a *preemptive right*. In most jurisdictions in Canada, preemptive rights exist only where actually granted in the incorporating documents or shareholders' agreements.[58]

---

52. Most of the requirements regarding annual general meetings are set out in Part XII of the *Canada Business Corporations Act, ibid.* But see also s. 106 (3), requiring the election of directors by shareholders at the annual general meeting of the shareholders, and Part XV, dealing with fundamental changes, which must be approved by special resolution of the shareholders (i.e., by at least two-thirds of the votes cast). It should be noted that the amendments to the federal legislation in 2001 resulted in many changes to the rules governing annual general meetings. In particular, shareholder meetings for federal corporations may now be held by electronic means, and voting may be carried out by using telephonic or electronic communications facilities—see ss. 132 and 141.

53. The rules relating to proxies are set out in Part XIII of the *Canada Business Corporations Act, ibid.*

54. *Ibid.,* s. 150.

55. *Ibid.,* s. 152(4).

56. *Ibid.;* s. 143 states that the holders of not less than five percent of the issued shares may cause a meeting to be called.

57. *Ibid.,* s. 144.

58. *Ibid.,* s. 28.

## Case Summary 14.9

### Do Shareholders Owe a Fiduciary Duty to Anybody?
***Bell v. Source Data Control Ltd.*[59]**

Bell, Stewart, Williamson, and Wilmot were minority shareholders in Source Data Control Ltd. (SDC), each having a 10-percent interest. James Hood was the majority shareholder, holding a 60-percent interest in the corporation. The corporation was successful for a number of years, but then Hood became distracted because of personal problems. The business deteriorated. Relations among the shareholders became difficult, and finally, the minority shareholders wanted out. For several years, McLean-Hunter Ltd. had expressed an interest in purchasing SDC, and Williamson offered to sell his 10-percent interest to it for $200 000. McLean-Hunter refused, saying it was only interested if it could get majority control. Later, Hood offered to sell his shares to McLean-Hunter and demanded $2.1 million. (At that rate, each minority shareholder's 10-percent interest should have been worth $350 000.) After considerable negotiation, it was agreed that McLean-Hunter would pay this price for Hood's shares but a much lower percentage price for the minority shares (the $200 000 initially offered by Williamson). Hood met with the minority shareholders without telling them what he was getting for his shares, or even that he was selling. He told them of the weak financial condition of the corporation and how poorly things were going. Without any suggestion from him, they told Hood they wanted $200 000 each for their 10-percent interests. At one stage, after the deal had been made but before it was executed, Hood was specifically asked what he was getting, but he refused to divulge any information to the minority shareholders. The deal closed, and when the minority shareholders discovered that Hood was getting much more proportionally for his shares than they were, they brought this action claiming that Hood had violated his duty to them.

At the trial, the judge found that there was not fraud, or a breach of trust, and that the minority shareholders had not placed any reliance or trust in Hood. It was the minority shareholders who suggested the $200 000 figure, as they wanted out of the corporation as quickly as possible. It was also found that it was not unreasonable for McLean-Hunter to be willing to pay a premium to the majority shareholder, to obtain a controlling interest. Thus, the action was dismissed. On appeal, two of the three judges agreed with the trial judge's decision, and thus the minority shareholders lost their action. The Court found that there was no fiduciary duty between the majority shareholder and the minority shareholders (or a director and the minority shareholders) to disclose any of this information. Hood was therefore not in violation of any duty because no duty existed. Note, however, that there was a strong dissenting opinion.

This case nicely illustrates that while shareholders may have an obligation not to misrepresent or commit fraud, there is no general fiduciary duty that requires them to disclose information or otherwise act in the best interests of the corporation or other shareholders.

These shareholder rights may seem significant, but to a minority shareholder such power may be an illusion. In large corporations with great numbers of shares distributed, an individual shareholder's rights may be very diluted, and the

**Weak position of minority shareholders**

59. (1988), 66 O.R. (2d) 78 (C.A.).

only practical recourse may be to sell the shares. In small, closely held corporations there is usually a restriction on the sale of shares. The "locked-in" shareholder may be unable to sell those shares and unable to influence the course of the corporation because of the overriding control exercised by the majority shareholder.

## Shareholder Protections

**Derivative or representative action**

To protect the shareholder from abuse in these circumstances, the statutes have provided several safeguards, the most important of which is the shareholder's right to sue the directors on behalf of the corporation when the directors have done something actionable. The right to **derivative** or **representative action** exists in British Columbia, Nova Scotia, and those jurisdictions that use the articles of incorporation method of incorporation.[60]

To succeed in these jurisdictions, a shareholder must show that it is in the interests of the corporation that the action be brought. In the *Richardson Greenshields* case in Case Summary 14.8, the directors used a technicality to thwart the rights of the preferred shareholders to their detriment and that of the corporation. Richardson Greenshields, as a shareholder, was seeking permission of the Court to bring an action on behalf of the corporation against those directors who were unwilling to bring an action against themselves.[61]

### Case Summary 14.10

**When Do Shareholders Have the Right to Bring a Derivative Action?**
***Primex Investments Ltd. v. Northwest Sports Enterprises Ltd.*[62]**

Northwest Sports Enterprises Ltd. ("Northwest") owned the Vancouver Canucks hockey team and created a wholly owned subsidiary, Northwest Arena Corp., for the purpose of building an arena in downtown Vancouver. Northwest also explored the possibility of getting an NBA franchise for Vancouver. Eventually, Mr. Griffiths, who was the president of Northwest, pursued this opportunity on his own. He made arrangements to obtain an NBA franchise for Vancouver with the cooperation of the McCaw Group. This required that Northwest sell its interest to the new organization. The directors of Northwest, with Griffiths abstaining, agreed to this new arrangement. A few of the minority shareholders, however, did not like the deal. One of them brought this action seeking permission to bring a derivative action against Griffiths and the other directors for violation of their fiduciary duty with respect to Northwest. The Court granted leave for such a derivative action, noting that Griffiths had violated his fiduciary duty by taking advantage of a corporate opportunity. The other directors who were refusing to sue on behalf of Northwest were in no position to do so, since they would be suing themselves. This was an appropriate situation for a derivative action.

60. See, for example, *Canada Business Corporations Act, supra* note 7, s. 239.

61. See *McAskill v. TransAtlantic Petroleum Corp.,* [2002] A.J. No. 1580 (Q.B.) for a recent judicial review of the case law on derivative actions.

62. [1996] 4 W.W.R. 54 (B.C.S.C.); rev'd in part, [1997] 2 W.W.R. 129 (B.C.C.A.); leave to appeal to S.C.C. refused, [1997] S.C.C.A. No. 4.

In other circumstances, the shareholder might be able bring an **oppression action**. For example, the directors might arrange for the sale of shares just to weaken the voting position of a particular shareholder, or, if the shareholder is also an employee, the directors might fire the shareholder to force the sale of the shares. In some jurisdictions, "complainants" have the right to go to court to seek an order for relief from oppression if this type of abuse takes place. Under the federal legislation, current (or past) shareholders, directors, and officers, along with any other person (including a creditor) who, in the discretion of the court, is a proper person, may seek relief from the court on the basis of oppression or unfair prejudice.[63] The court may then make any order it thinks fit, including granting a restraining order, appointing a receiver or receiver-manager, appointing new directors, ordering compensation, or ordering liquidation or dissolution of the corporation.[64] The oppression action is becoming more common, due to the wide discretion it allows the courts in granting remedies to complainants.[65]

*Shareholders have right to relief from oppression*

Sometimes, minority shareholders are adversely affected by a decision that is beneficial to the corporation as a whole. In the past, there was no recourse. In many jurisdictions, however, the injured minority shareholder now has the right to file a **dissent**.[66] Such dissent procedures are implemented when fundamental changes to the corporation adversely affect the shareholder and require that her shares be purchased at a fair price.

*Dissent provisions provide relief for shareholders*

### Case Summary 14.11

**When Can Minority Shareholders Force the Corporation to Buy Back Their Shares?** *Re 85956 Holdings Ltd. and Fayerman Brothers Ltd.*[67]

For several years, Sidney and Joseph Fayerman operated a wholesale/retail merchandising business through Fayerman Brothers Limited in Prince Albert, Saskatchewan. Because of their failing health and increased competition, it was decided by the directors, and approved by the majority shareholders, not to purchase any more inventory but to simply sell off what they had. The minority shareholders opposed this. When the decision was made to continue the sell-off without replacing inventory, the minority shareholders asked that their shares be purchased at a fair value. The request was refused, and so this action was brought to force the share purchase at a fair price on the basis that the minority shareholders were dissenting. The Saskatchewan legislation, like many incorporation

63. *Canada Business Corporations Act, supra* note 7, s. 238.

64. *Ibid.,* s. 241.

65. For a case where a creditor successfully used the oppression remedy, see *Bird v. Mitchell,* [2002] O.J. No. 4398 (Sup. Ct. J.). An employee was granted judgment using the oppression remedy in *Downtown Eatery (1993) Ltd. v. Ontario* (2001), 54 O.R. (3d) 161 (C.A.); leave to appeal refused, [2001] S.C.C.A. No. 397. For a case where the Court found that there was oppression of, and unfair prejudice to, the interests of the shareholders, see *218125 Investments Ltd. v. Patel* (1995), 33 Alta. L.R. (3d) 245 (Q.B.).

66. *Canada Business Corporations Act, supra* note 7, s. 190. This is a very significant shareholder power, but it is available only in limited circumstances, such as when a decision is being made to amend the articles of incorporation in order to restrict the issue or transfer of shares, or to restrict the type of business the corporation can carry on. It is also available when amalgamation with another corporation is involved or when a significant portion of the assets of a corporation is going to be sold or leased.

67. (1986), 25 D.L.R. (4th) 119 (Sask. C.A.).

statutes, had a provision that when "a sale, lease, or exchange of all or substantially all the property of a corporation other than in the ordinary course of business of the corporation" takes place and a shareholder does not approve such a sale, the dissenting shareholder can force the purchase of his shares at a fair price. The problem in this case was whether the choice not to replace the inventory changed this from being a sale done in the ordinary course of business, thus triggering the dissent provision.

The Court held that a sale in the ordinary course of business required the replenishing of the inventory. Not to do so amounted to a sale of all or substantially all the assets of the corporation, and the dissent provisions were triggered. The Court found that the corporation was required to buy out the minority shareholders, paying a fair market price for the shares.

This case illustrates how the dissent provision works and under what circumstances a minority shareholder is entitled to this protection. It is interesting to note that the corporation retained its real estate holdings. Still, this was considered a liquidation of the assets of the corporation, and the minority shareholders were entitled to have their shares bought out.

## Dividends

**Shareholders have no right to dividends**

Shareholders have no legal right to force the payment of a dividend, although they can require payment if one has been declared by the directors. Their recourse is political, and if the directors fail to declare a dividend when the shareholders expect one, they are likely to be voted out at the next shareholders' meeting. However, the shareholders cannot go to court and sue for a dividend even where preferred shares are involved, with the commitment to pay a specific dividend each year. Such preferred shareholders can force payment before any dividend is paid to the common shareholders and, where this right is cumulative, can also require the payment of any prior unpaid dividends before any dividend is paid to the common shareholders. The rights associated with the shareholders' position are rights of control, information, and protection, but there is no corresponding right to a specific return on the funds invested. Many provisions are in place to protect the position of shareholders, but it is important to balance these rights against some important drawbacks for shareholders.

For an illustration of the concept of corporate structure, see Figure 14.3.

### Figure 14.3 Corporate Structure

## Reducing **Risk** 14.4

Small, closely held corporations whose shareholders are also directors and managers of the corporation are often little more than incorporated partnerships. Often, the individuals will also be full-time employees of the corporation. When these individuals have a falling out, the problems can go far beyond what can be remedied or even what has been anticipated in the legislation. An individual shareholder may lose not only her job as director and manager, but also her full-time employment, and she may not be able to sell her shares. In such circumstances, the importance of a properly drawn up *shareholder agreement* cannot be overemphasized. Usually, the agreement will include a provision whereby one shareholder must buy out the other if these types of events or other forms of dissatisfaction occur. Provisions relating to employment are often included in such agreements as well. Shareholder agreements are very important and they can be used to set out many important obligations between the parties, much as a partnership agreement does in a partnership relationship.

# Pros and Cons of Incorporation

## Advantages

There are several advantages associated with incorporation, most of which are derived from the concept of the separate legal personality of the corporation.

### Limited Liability

As illustrated in the *Salomon* case described in Case Summary 14.1, shareholders are not liable for the debts and other obligations of the corporation because the corporation, as a separate legal person, is responsible for its own wrongful conduct. Where the corporation's assets are not enough to pay the unsatisfied creditors, they cannot turn to its shareholders for the difference. Shareholders can lose only what they have invested.

**Liability of shareholder limited to investment**

#### Case Summary 14.12

### Is a Subsidiary Corporation a Separate Person? *Sun Sudan Oil Co. v. Methanex Corp.*[68]

In 1981, two large oil corporations, Sunmark Worldwide Services Inc. and Ocelot Industries Ltd., created two subsidiaries, Sun Sudan Oil Company, Inc. ("Sun Sudan") and Ocelot Sudan Exploration Corporation ("Ocelot Sudan"), respectively, to explore for oil in the Sudan as a joint venture. When, after considerable exploration, the point came that Ocelot Sudan was to put more funds into the project according to the agreement, it was unable to do so. Sun Sudan sued the parent corporation, Ocelot Industries, not the subsidiary. The Court had to decide whether the parent corporation was responsible for the debts of its subsidiary. The Court determined from the evidence that there was no fraud on the part of Ocelot Sudan or any of the parties and that a substantial effort had been made to provide funding. Also, there were good and valid reasons for creating the subsidiaries, not the least of which was to reduce risk and insulate the parent corporations from liability. The Judge found that because of the *Salomon* principle, each corporation had a separate legal personality and the parent, Ocelot

---

68. (1992), 134 A.R. 1 (Q.B.).

Industries, was not responsible for the debts of the subsidiary, Ocelot Sudan. He pointed out that these were sophisticated businesspeople who knew they were dealing with limited liability corporations and concluded there was no wrongdoing; thus, the separate legal liability element was in effect.

**Limited liability lost when guarantee given**

This limited liability, although attractive and often the primary reason for choosing to incorporate, is often only an illusion. When dealing with a closely held corporation, banks and other major creditors will usually insist on a **personal guarantee** from the major shareholders or other principals, which effectively eliminates any advantage of limited liability for those asked to sign such a guarantee.

**Liability of shareholder limited to investment**

Still, limited liability will protect shareholders from unexpected corporate obligations, such as vicarious liability for torts committed by employees or the failure to properly perform contractual obligations. Also, suppliers of materials usually do not obtain any personal commitment from shareholders, so they cannot seek compensation from them if the corporation becomes insolvent. For example, if a person operating a grocery business incorporates a corporation and borrows money from the bank for business purposes, that bank will probably insist on a personal guarantee from the shareholder. A supplier of groceries, however, would normally have no such personal commitment. If the corporation becomes insolvent, the shareholder will have to pay the bank because of the personal guarantee, but the shareholder will not be obligated to the supplier, who must look to the corporation for payment. This is because the contract for the goods supplied was with the corporation, rather than with the shareholder. If an employee of the corporation negligently injured a pedestrian while delivering groceries, the corporation would be vicariously liable for that injury, not the shareholder.

**In rare cases, court will lift the corporate veil**

Even this amount of limited liability is not certain. As the *H & D Hobby* case discussed in Case Summary 14.2 illustrates, in rare cases the courts are willing to look behind the corporate veil and hold the principals liable for the obligations of the corporation. This is especially true when there is any taint of wrongdoing or avoidance of obligations that ought to be honoured.

## Taxes

Although tax reforms did away with many of the differences between the federal income taxes paid by sole proprietors, partners, and corporations, because the system is so complex there still may be advantages available to the individual taxpayer through incorporation. At the very least, the shareholder can leave the funds in the corporation and use it as a vehicle of investment, thus deferring some taxes until a later date. In addition, as many provinces have not followed the federal lead, there may still be significant provincial tax advantages to be gained through incorporation.

**Tax advantages gained through incorporation**

However, federal and provincial income tax laws are extremely complicated. It is possible that incorporation will backfire and that the process will lead to more income tax being payable rather than less. When losses are experienced, as is normally the case with a new business, the taxpayer is better off if the business is not incorporated so that these losses can be applied directly against personal income. Great care must be exercised in the process of tax planning for any business, and a prudent businessperson will seek expert advice in these circumstances.

## Succession and Transferability

Because a corporation is a separate legal entity and a mythical person, it does not die unless some specific steps are taken to end its existence. When a partner dies, the partnership will usually come to an end. The death of even a 100-percent shareholder will not affect the existence of the corporation, although the loss may have practical implications, especially when the shareholder is involved in the ongoing operation of the business. The share is simply an asset in the hands of the shareholder. Like any other asset, it therefore forms part of the deceased's estate and, in most cases, is simply distributed to the heirs.

Thus, where two people hold 50 percent each of the shares of a corporation and they are killed in an air crash, the corporation continues and the shares would form part of the estates of the deceased. The heirs would therefore usually become the new shareholders. If the two people were carrying on business as partners, however, the partnership would automatically be dissolved.

When a partner leaves a partnership, the process is complex, often requiring the dissolution of the partnership. Shares in a corporation, however, usually can be transferred at will without reference either to the other shareholders or to the corporate body. This free transferability of shares is one of the attractive features that led to the creation of the corporate entity in the first place. It provides an effective method for the contributors of capital to restrict their relationship with the corporation. When closely held corporations, which often have the same kinds of relationships as partnerships, are involved, this free transferability of shares is significantly restricted.

It is often said that a corporation cannot die, but actually there are several things that can cause a corporation to be dissolved.[69] The ultimate end for a corporation going through the bankruptcy process is dissolution by operation of law. Minority shareholders or creditors can bring application to the court to have a corporation dissolved because of oppression or some other inappropriate conduct by the other shareholders or directors. The shareholders themselves can vote to bring the corporation to an end when they feel it is appropriate, filing articles of dissolution or a statement of intent to dissolve at the appropriate registry office. But the most common way is for the corporation simply to fail to file the required annual returns. After a year, the corporation will be considered inactive and removed from the registry. Such corporations can later be revived by filing the missing returns, along with articles of revival and any other required documentation.

## Obligations of the Participants

Unlike partners, shareholders are generally free of any obligations or duties to the corporation or other shareholders. There is no fiduciary duty to act in the best interests of the corporation or even to refrain from carrying on business in competition with the corporation.

The extent of this freedom of action can be illustrated by the activities of some environmental groups. They acquire a few shares in the large corporations they consider a threat to the environment, with the express purpose of using the special privileges available to shareholders (such as rights to information and to

**Corporation does not die**

**But can be dissolved**

**No duty on shareholder in a corporation**

69. See Part XVIII of the *Canada Business Corporations Act, supra* note 7, for the legislative provisions relating to the liquidation and dissolution of federal corporations.

attend shareholders' meetings) in the battle against the polluting corporation. Even when the interests of the environmental group are diametrically opposed to, and interfere with, the profit-making ventures of the corporation and other shareholders, there is no obligation to act otherwise. Only when people acquire sufficient shares to be classed as insiders, or become directors or officers, or when an individual has a majority of the shares, are certain restrictions placed on their activities. These restrictions usually take the form of rules, which prevent the shareholders from abusing their positions of power within the corporation and causing injury to other investors.

### Management

**Managers and shareholders separate**

In a sole proprietorship, the business is controlled by the proprietor; in a partnership, each partner is entitled to participate in the business decisions of the partnership; in a corporation, however, it is common to separate the managers from the owners. The shareholders elect a board of directors that controls the business. The directors, in turn, can hire professional managers who have the expertise to make sound business decisions on behalf of the corporation. The shareholders do not have to devote time or attention to managing, but they can change the management by electing different people to the board of directors if they are unhappy with the decisions being made.

## Disadvantages

A corporation is not always the best method of carrying on business. Many of the characteristics outlined above as advantages can just as easily be seen as drawbacks from another person's perspective.

It is helpful to compare incorporation with partnership to illustrate some of the disadvantages of incorporation. Partners who wish to change important aspects of their partnership arrangement need only reach an agreement to that effect. In the case of a corporation, however, the incorporating documents themselves may have to be altered, which is an involved and expensive procedure. A partner in a minority position may have considerable power. In a partnership, one partner can veto a proposal supported by 10 others. A minority shareholder

---

### Reducing **Risk** 14.5

Businesspeople usually assume that the best way for them to carry on their business is through incorporation. While that may, in fact, be the case, consideration should also be given to the alternatives. Sole proprietorship and partnership are the only real alternatives discussed in this text, although if the enterprise is not for profit or does not involve an ongoing business, there are other possibilities. For example, societies are used for non-profit activities, such as charities, clubs, and religious organizations, and where property is shared, cooperatives and joint tenancy arrangements might be appropriate alternatives.

Even the choice between partnership and incorporation is not always clear. The unlimited liability of a sole proprietorship or partnership can be overcome by appropriate insurance. The tax advantages of incorporation have,

to a large extent, been eliminated or extended to sole proprietorships and partnerships as well. The unique power of a single partner to veto the decisions of the other partners can be built into a corporation by a carefully drawn shareholder agreement. Many of the disadvantages that professionals experience because they are required to carry on their profession as partners can be overcome by creating a management corporation to manage the practice, or by creating a limited liability partnership.

The point is that there are many different options and many different combinations available to a businessperson when structuring the tools used to carry on the business. Expert advice should be sought and careful consideration given to the options earlier, rather than later, in the process.

in a corporation may be unable to alter unsatisfactory decisions and may not even be able to sell her shares.

In closely held corporations, the free transferability of shares is restricted either through shareholder agreements or by limitations placed in the incorporating documents themselves. Often, shareholders are required to get approval of a sale of their shares, or offer their shares first to the other shareholders. As with partnerships, the reason people organize themselves into small, closely held corporations is often because of the individual skills each shareholder brings to the corporation. These shareholders are usually employees as well, and their contribution to the operation of the business is often vital to its success. Free transferability of shares in such circumstances might be a significant threat to the corporation, especially if the shareholder withdraws his or her services when the shares are sold.

A corporation is the most expensive way to operate a business. The initial incorporation process is costly, and the ongoing operation of a corporation involves more expense than that of sole proprietorships and partnerships. There are more formal record-keeping requirements and generally more government control exercised with a corporation.

It is important to note as well that there are many variations on the corporate approach to business. Often, corporations are set up that merely hold shares in other corporations. Corporations may join other corporations or individuals in joint ventures or partnerships, usually for some major project or activity. Corporations may license others to use their products, software, or other forms of intellectual property, such as patents or copyrighted materials.

It is also common to see small business enterprises that are part of a larger organization through **franchising**—business arrangements based on contracts of service and the supply of products between the larger and the smaller units. Fast-food restaurant chains are often set up this way. Many difficulties can arise in such relationships, and the changing nature of contract law and corporate responsibility is softening the normally narrow approach to these businesses. For example, the good-faith requirements that are now being read into business contracts put franchisees in a much more favourable position than they have formerly been.[70]

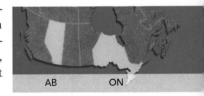

## Termination of the Corporation

Corporations can be dissolved in several ways. The process can be voluntary, by following the winding-up procedure found in the corporate law statutes or, in some jurisdictions, in a separate winding-up act.[71] If the corporation owns sufficient assets, it may be worthwhile to follow this process, but often it is not worth the expense.

Dissolution can take place either voluntarily or involuntarily, and the procedure can be induced internally, by the directors or shareholders, or externally, by the creditors. Occasionally, a court will order a corporation to be dissolved when a minority shareholder has been unfairly treated. If there are more debts owing

---

70. Alberta (*Franchises Act,* R.S.A. 2000, c. F-23) and Ontario (*Arthur Wishart Act (Franchise Disclosure), 2000,* S.O. 2000, c. 3) have enacted legislation governing franchising.

71. The liquidation and dissolution of federal corporations are dealt with in Part XVIII of the *Canada Business Corporations Act, supra* note 7.

to the creditors than the corporation has assets to cover, the common procedure is bankruptcy, and the end result is usually the dissolution of the corporation. Under the current bankruptcy legislation, it is possible for the corporation to make a proposal to the creditors and, if accepted and followed, the corporation will continue.

The process of distributing the assets upon winding up the corporation is set out in the various statutes and will not be dealt with here. It is important to note, however, that the directors have a considerable obligation not to allow any of the assets of the corporation to get into the hands of the shareholders until the creditors have been satisfied.

One of the most common ways for corporations, especially small, closely held corporations, to come to an end is for the principals simply to neglect to file the annual return. A federal corporation must, for example, file an annual return within six months after the end of the corporation's taxation year.[72] If it fails to do so, a certificate of dissolution may be issued for it.[73]

## Case Summary 14.13

### Does It Matter If a Corporation Is Dissolved? *602533 Ontario Inc. v. Shell Canada Ltd.*[74]

This action arose from a claim by the numbered corporation against Shell with respect to the installation of allegedly defective underground tanks. The plaintiff was seeking damages "for breach of contract, misrepresentation, deceit, breach of warranty, and negligent failure to warn and a declaration holding Shell responsible for any environmental damage caused by its conduct." John Pangos had been operating the service station in question through the corporation for about five years, when it was discovered that the underground tanks were leaking. The corporation commenced the action against Shell in February 1990.

However, the corporation had been dissolved by operation of law for non-compliance under the *Corporations Tax Act* in 1988. This was unknown to Pangos and was not remedied by reinstating the corporation until 1996. The point made by Shell in its application to dismiss this action was that at the time the statement of claim was issued there was no 602533 Ontario Inc., and so the non-existent corporation could not have commenced the action. To further complicate matters, the limitation period within which an action against Shell must have been commenced expired before the corporation was revived.

The Court dismissed the action against Shell, and that decision was upheld on appeal. The corporation could not bring an action against Shell when it was dissolved, and although the revival of the corporation restored any rights that the corporation had when it was dissolved, that was subject to any rights that had been acquired by the other party during the dissolution period. The expiration of the limitation period was a right Shell had acquired after the corporation was dissolved and could not be overcome by the corporation's revival in 1996.[75]

---

72. *Canada Business Corporations Act Regulations, 2001*, S.O.R./2001-512, s. 5.

73. *Canada Business Corporations Act, supra* note 7, s. 212.

74. (1998), 37 O.R. (3d) 504 (C.A.).

75. For a case where an action commenced on behalf of a corporation that had been dissolved was declared a nullity even though the relevant limitation period had not expired, see *M.C.M. Contracting Ltd. v. Canada (Attorney General)*, [2002] Y.J. No. 108 (Y.T.S.C.).

The case shows how careful businesspeople must be to make sure they comply with government regulations. In this case, the consequence was dissolution of the corporation. Such a dissolved corporation no longer exists legally and thereby loses the right to bring an action on its own behalf. The case also shows that such a dissolved corporation can be resurrected by following the appropriate procedure, but sometimes even that process cannot overcome the consequences of allowing the corporation to become dissolved in the first place.

Often, when a corporation is to go out of business, a decision must be made whether to sell the shares of the corporation or to sell its assets. If its shares are sold, the corporation continues as before. The debts and other obligations continue, but problems may arise if the purchaser decides to make changes in wages and contracts with suppliers. Because the corporation continues, the contracts stay in place and continue to bind the corporation, even with new ownership. When the corporation's assets are sold, on the other hand, the purchaser is not affected by the contractual or other obligations of the corporation selling those assets, unless those assets are encumbered. If the assets in question have been used to secure a debt, the secured creditor has first claim against the assets. Any purchaser of a business would be well advised to search the title of the assets for such liens and charges before entering into the transaction.

**Selling the shares or selling the assets**

As explained in Chapter 10, some provinces have bulk sales statutes in place to protect creditors from the sale of all, or substantially all, the assets of the debtor. Any debts or other obligations that have been incurred by the selling corporation remain those of that corporation. After the assets are sold and the corporation no longer has a business, the corporation can be wound up.

## Summary

### Corporation
- A fiction or a myth that has a separate status as a legal person from its shareholders.
- Methods of incorporation in Canada are registration, letters patent, and articles of incorporation.
- Shareholders are not liable for the debts of a corporation; they can lose only what they have invested (limited liability).
- Special statute corporations' capacity may be limited.
- Funding may be derived from the selling of shares (which may be common shares or shares with special rights and restrictions), or through borrowing (which involves the sale of bonds and debentures, secured or unsecured).
- Broadly held corporations have more stringent government controls and greater reporting requirements than closely held corporations.

### Directors/officers
- Have a fiduciary duty.
- Must act in the best interests of that corporation.
- Must avoid conflicts of interest.

## Shareholders

- Very few duties to the corporation or other shareholders unless they have sufficient shares to be classed as insiders.
- No right to sue the director when she acts carelessly or wrongfully in carrying out her duties, as the duty of the director is owed to the corporation, not to the shareholder.
- In many jurisdictions, the shareholder can bring a derivative or representative action against the director on behalf of the corporation.
- No right to demand dividends.

## Advantages of incorporation

- Limited liability.
- Tax benefits.
- Ease of transferring shares.
- Separate management and ownership.

## Termination of corporation

- The corporation does not die with the death of shareholders.

---

## QUESTIONS

1. What is meant by a corporation having a separate legal identity?

2. Distinguish among companies and corporations that have been created by special acts of Parliament, by royal charter, by registration, by letters patent, and by filing articles of incorporation.

3. Explain the significance of the memorandum of association in a registration jurisdiction. Contrast it with the role of articles of incorporation and of articles of association.

4. Explain how the liability of a shareholder is limited.

5. Explain why the concept of a par-value share is misleading and why the use of such shares has declined.

6. What is meant by a "preferred" share? Contrast this with the "common" share. Explain why the term "preferred shares" is misleading.

7. Does a shareholder, whether preferred or common, have a right to a dividend? Explain.

8. What is the significant difference between a bondholder and a preferred shareholder, both of whom are entitled to a specified payment each year?

9. Distinguish between closely held and broadly held corporations and explain the differences in terms of the provisions in place in your jurisdiction.

10. Set out the nature of the duties owed by a director of a corporation. To whom are these duties owed? Who else in the corporate organization owes similar duties?

11. Explain why it is becoming increasingly difficult to get prominent individuals to serve as directors of Canadian corporations.

12. Explain any duties shareholders assume. Summarize the rights of the shareholders in relationship to other shareholders, the management, and the directors of the corporation.

13. Explain what is meant by a proxy and why proxies can be so important at a corporation's annual general meeting.

14. Explain the advantages of free transferability of shares and how and why this right is often modified by shareholder agreement.

15. Set out and explain some of the disadvantages associated with the corporate method of carrying on business.

16. How can a corporation be terminated?

-------------------------------------------------------------------

## CASES

### 1. *Troost v. Ewanchuk*, [2002] A. J. No. 1171 (Prov. Ct.).

Ewanchuk operated a renovations business through a corporation. Troost signed a "proposal" for renovation work. The proposal was in the name of the corporation. Troost testified that Ewanchuk never mentioned the corporation and, in fact, Ewanchuk required the funds to be made payable to him personally. Ewanchuk never finished the work, as he was sent to jail for unrelated crimes. Troost sought return of the funds he had paid. Ewanchuk claimed he was not liable because the contract was between Troost and the corporation. Explain whether Troost should be successful with his action against Ewanchuk.

### 2. *Re Graham and Technequip Ltd.* (1981), 32 O.R. (2d) 297 (H.C.J.), aff'd (1982), 139 D.L.R. (3d) 542 (Ont. Div. Ct.).

Graham was one of four shareholders in Technequip, and, according to the shareholders' agreement, he was a director and an employee as well. At one directors' meeting, the other three directors fired Graham from his position as director and from his employment. He retained only his status as a minority shareholder. What courses of action are available to Graham in these circumstances? Explain the likely outcome. How would your answer be affected by the knowledge that Graham was not adequately performing his duties as either employee or director and that the shareholders' agreement had a buyout provision Graham could have implemented but chose not to?

### 3. *W. J. Christie & Co. Ltd. v. Greer* (1981), 9 Man. R. (2d) 269 (C.A.).

Greer was a longstanding employee of the plaintiff corporation and had held the positions of director and executive officer for 10 years. Greer left Christie and went on to establish his own corporation, Sussex Realty & Insurance Agency Ltd. In the process, Greer approached several customers of Christie's and persuaded them to transfer their business to the new corporation. In this action, Christie sued Greer for his conduct. Explain the arguments available to both parties and the nature of the compensation Christie would obtain, if successful.

### 4. *Re Keho Holdings Ltd. and Noble* (1987), 78 A.R. 131 (C.A.).

Twenty investors came together and incorporated Keho Holdings Ltd., buying 100 shares each at one dollar a share. One member of that group, Oliver, voluntarily directed the corporation's affairs and did so very successfully, taking the corporation's value up to $6 million. Oliver bought out some of the other shareholders and eventually acquired a 66-percent or greater controlling interest in the corporation. He then exercised control over those voting shares to his own personal advantage. The first complaint was that he used his position to structure the directors in such a way as to give him complete control over the corporation and its assets. He appointed himself, his two sons, and an ally, A. S. Cameron, as directors; the people representing the minority shareholders were completely frozen out. The second complaint was that Oliver had the shareholders grant him stock options for 12 500 shares of common stock priced at $1 per share. These shares were selling at $72 a share. This was supposedly done in recognition of his voluntary service to the corporation over the prior 25 years. The third complaint was that Oliver and the directors under his control voted to borrow $258 000 from the bank and then loaned that money to Gyron Petroleum Ltd. at 12-percent interest without any security. Gyron was Oliver's wholly owned corporation.

Explain whether these complaints are valid and what course of action is available to the minority shareholders in these circumstances.

## 5. *Dilorenzo v. Canada*, [2002] F.C.J. No. 1644 (F.C.A.).

Dilorenzo immigrated to Canada from Italy. He started working in the construction industry at age sixteen. He had no formal education. He incorporated his business, and was the sole director of the corporation. He stated that he had never been involved in the paperwork of the corporation, and that he hired accountants, lawyers, and office workers because of his lack of expertise. The corporation failed to remit GST to the federal government. Dilorenzo argued that he should not be personally liable for the GST, because he had shown due diligence in respect of the payment of the taxes. Explain whether Dilorenzo should be found personally liable for the corporation's unpaid GST.

## 6. *Montreal Trust Co. of Canada v. Call-Net Enterprises Inc.* (2002), 57 O.R. (3d) 775 (Ont. Sup. Ct. J).

Call-Net was in a proxy battle with one of its dissident shareholders, Crescendo. Call-Net entered into an agreement with its senior executives which said that a change in control would be deemed to have occurred if any person acquired the right to control or direct 35 percent or more of the combined voting power of the corporation in any manner. Crescendo accumulated proxies which, together with the shares it owned, were in excess of 35 percent of the voting shares. But the meeting for which the proxies were obtained was not held, and the proxies were therefore not used. Some of the executives claimed that a change of control had occurred. Call-Net claimed that no such change had occurred. Explain whether the executives were correct in their assertion that a change of control had occurred. Be sure to consider what a proxy is, and the power a proxy gives to the proxy holder.

# Property

Property rights have always played an important role in our legal system and have always been a vital concern of business. Property is traditionally divided into personal property and real property. Chapter 15 first looks at both tangible and intangible personal property and then examines real property, concluding with a discussion of residential tenancies and mortgages. Chapter 16 is devoted to a discussion of intellectual property, which, in modern times, has become a very important example of intangible personal property. The final part of Chapter 16 is an overview of the law with respect to computers and the internet, which involves intellectual property concerns as well as other aspects of law.

# Personal and Real Property

This chapter will examine both personal and real property.

# Introduction

**Ownership and possession separated**

**Real property—land and buildings**

**Chattel—tangible property**

**Chose in action—intangible property**

**Intellectual property deals with ideas and creative work**

While people usually think of property as a physical object, such as a boat, car, or land, "property," more correctly, refers to the relationship existing between the item and the individual who owns it. When a person says he owns a boat, it is descriptive of the nature of the interest he has in the boat rather than the boat itself, and this distinction must be kept in mind as we examine the nature of the different interests in property. Although ownership or title is the highest form of property right to a particular item, other lesser forms of interest are also possible. In our legal system, ownership or title can be separate from possession. Thus, one person might be in possession of something that belongs to someone else.

The term "real property" refers to land and things permanently attached to the land, such as buildings. The essential characteristic of real property is that it is fixed and immovable. Personal property, on the other hand, is movable and can be divided into two categories. **Chattels (or goods)** are tangible personal property, consisting of movables that can be measured and weighed. An intangible right is a claim one person has against another, such as a claim for debt, and is called a **chose in action,** which is, in effect, a right to sue. Bonds, share certificates, and negotiable instruments are examples of choses in action.

A special category of intangible personal property is now called **intellectual property**: **copyright** gives an author control over the use and reproduction of his or her work; **patent** gives an inventor the right to profit from his or her inventions; **trademarks** protect the name or logo of a business; **industrial designs**, **confidential information**, and **trade secrets** are other examples of intellectual property.

**Case Summary 15.1**

**A Taxi Licence Is Personal Property: *Re Foster***[1]

Foster had a taxi licence that he used as security in financial arrangements with several different people. These four creditors all claimed priority with respect to that licence. The court held that although the licence was subject to regulation, it still represented a valuable asset, and therefore it was a form of intangible personal property known as a chose in action. The security aspects of this case were discussed in some detail in Chapter 10.

Many aspects of both tangible and intangible personal property have already been discussed throughout the text. This chapter will focus on tangible personal property (goods or chattels) and real property. Intellectual property is discussed in Chapter 16, with a concluding discussion on computers and the internet.

# Personal Property

## Chattels

Chattels are movables, such as baggage, clothes, radios, animals, and boats. Even construction cranes and locomotives are chattels. **Real property**, on the other hand, is land and things fixed or attached to the land. A chattel can become part of the real property when it is attached to the land, and this can lead to a conflict with respect to who has first claim to it. When a person buys and installs a furnace or a hot water heater in their home, the item that was a chattel becomes a **fixture**. Who has first claim will usually be determined by whoever installed the item, for what purpose, and to what degree it is affixed. If, after buying a new hot water tank, Gauthier loses the house because he cannot make his mortgage payments, the mortgagee would have a claim to the hot water tank only if it has been installed. It then has become part of the real property. If Gauthier bought the water tank on credit, then two creditors have conflicting claims and the matter is now resolved by statute, primarily the *Personal Property Security Act* discussed in Chapter 10.

There is considerable confusion over when a chattel that has become a fixture can be removed from the property. Normally if the owner of land has affixed a chattel he or she has the right to remove it (**severance**). Difficulty arises when third parties, such as creditors or tenants, become involved and claim the property. Generally, when a chattel has been affixed to real property, it becomes part of that real property and cannot be removed. However, if a tenant of a commercial property attaches fixtures to enhance trade or carry on business, he has the right to remove those trade fixtures when leaving. In residential or commercial tenancies, non-trade fixtures attached for the comfort, convenience, or taste of the tenant, such as mirrors or paintings, can also be removed. Of course, when those fixtures have been incorporated into the property in such a way that they clearly are intended to stay or where their removal will cause damage, they must stay.

In any case, these fixtures can be removed only during the term of the tenancy. When the tenant moves out at the end of the tenancy and takes the mirrors,

**Chattels are movable things**

**Things fixed to the land become real property**

**Chattels attached become part of the real property**

**Trade fixtures can be removed by tenant**

---

1. (1992), 89 D.L.R. (4th) 555 (Ont. Gen. Div.).

light fixtures, loose rugs, and display cases that had been installed by the tenant, the landlord usually has no complaint. But the tenant can't come back later, after the tenancy has ended and the landlord has retaken possession. It is then too late to reclaim the fixtures, which have now become part of the landlord's property. Of course, any provisions in the lease to the contrary override these general provisions.

## Finders Keepers

**A finder gets good title against all but original owner**

When a person finds a watch or ring in a park, they have the right to that item against everyone except a prior owner. If that finder were to hand it to the police or the lost-and-found centre and the rightful owner could not be found, that finder would be entitled to it. Only the rightful owner, her heir, or someone having a proprietary interest in it, such as a secured creditor, could demand it from the finder.

If the goods are found on private property, however, the owner of that property normally has a right to the item. Only if it is found on a public portion of that property, such as the public part of a restaurant, store, or shopping mall, will the finder have first claim. And even then if the finder is an employee of the restaurant the employer gets the item subject to a claim by the original owner. Note also that whether the owner of the restaurant or the finder gets the goods there goes with it an obligation to exercise some care in looking after them. This obligation is based on the law of bailment.

### Case Summary 15.2

**Where the Finder Was Not the Keeper: *Weitzner v. Herman*[2]**

Mrs. Weitzner's husband died suddenly in a fire. She sold their home of 38 years, which was then demolished; in the process, the contractor found a fire extinguisher hidden in the basement crawlspace containing $130 000. Mr. Weitzner had operated a scrap business from the home, often taking cash but making no deposits in the bank. The Court found that he had put the money there. His sudden death prevented him from telling anyone about the hidden funds. The contractor had no claim to the money, since he was working for the Hermans and they had not given up any claim they had to the demolition materials. The Hermans were entitled to the funds against all except the original owner. As his heir, Mrs. Weitzner was entitled to all of the $130 000. "Finders keepers" is not always the case.

## Bailment

**Bailment created by giving goods to bailee**

A bailment exists when one person takes temporary possession of personal property owned by another. The owner giving up possession is called the **bailor** and the person acquiring possession the **bailee**. Although chattels are usually involved, intangibles, such as bonds, share certificates, or negotiable instruments can also be the subjects of a *bailment*. For a bailment to take place, the bailor must

2. (2000), 33 E.T.R. (2d) 310 (Ont. Sup. Ct.).

deliver the property to the bailee, making it clear that that the possession is only to be temporary, with the chattel to be returned at the end of the bailment period. Leases and rentals, goods left for repair, storage or transport, and simple borrowing of goods are examples of bailment.

Determining whether the goods have been delivered is not as easy as it may seem. When a car is left in a parking lot and the keys are given to the attendant, a bailment has taken place because control and possession have been given to the car lot. But when a person drives onto a lot, parks the car, and takes the keys with her, there is no bailment. This is just a licence to use the parking space, and the control and possession of the car stay with the driver. During the bailment, the title to the goods remains with the bailor, and only the possession goes to the bailee. Normally, a bailee cannot give the goods to someone else (a sub-bailment), unless there is permission to do so or where it is the custom of the industry, as might be the case where an automobile needing repairs is left with one mechanic who then transfers it to other specialists as needed.

When **fungibles**, such as timber, oil, and wheat, are placed in the care of a bailee, they can become indistinguishable from similar items being stored for others. In fact, the exact goods need not be returned, only goods of a similar quality and quantity. This situation is still a bailment and is treated under bailment law.

> With fungibles, the same goods need not be returned

The primary concern of bailment law is the liability of bailees for damage done to goods in their care. Bailees are responsible for any wilful, negligent, or fraudulent acts of themselves or their employees that cause injury or damage to the goods, although the standard of care used in establishing that negligence will vary with the type of bailment created.

## Bailment for Value

Bailments are either gratuitous or for value. Bailment for value involves a mutual benefit or consideration flowing between the parties. Usually, the relationship is commercial, and the bailor pays the bailee to repair, store, or transport the goods. But a bailment for value can also arise where a friend stores something, such as a piano, for another in exchange for the right to use it. The standard of care required in such circumstances is simply the ordinary standard for negligence—that is, the amount of care that would be expected from a prudent person looking after such goods in similar circumstances.

> Bailment for value—both parties receive benefit

> Bailee has a duty to care for the goods

The amount of care that should be exercised will vary with both the value of the goods and their nature. More care would be expected where delicate or valuable items were involved, such as china or a rare violin, but where heavy-duty machines were being stored, the standard of care would be much lower.

### Case Summary 15.3

**Containers Lost in a Storm: *Amo Containers Ltd. v. Mobil Oil Canada, Ltd.*[3]**

In this case, Amo supplied containers to Mobil, which used them to transport goods to the oil rigs off the east coast of Canada. The particular containers in question were being transported when the vessel sank with the loss of all on board. In this action, Amo, as bailor, was suing Mobil, as bailee, for the loss of its containers.

---

3. (1989), 62 D.L.R. (4th) 104 (Nfld. C.A.).

The Court held that, since the goods were in the care of the bailee, Mobil, and Mobil was in the best position to determine what happened, they must show that they were not negligent. Since it failed to meet that onus, Mobil was liable for the loss.

The law of bailment applies when personal property, even a large item, is used by another. This case shows that the principles of bailment can be quite significant in commercial relationships. Here, the bailment was one for value, and the obligation was on the bailee (the person or company holding the goods) to establish it was not negligent. It could not do so, and Mobil was liable for the loss.

## Care Required with Bailment for Value

**Duty may be determined by contract or common practice**

If the bailment is based on a commercial relationship, the provisions of the contract and industry practice will be taken into consideration in determining the standard of care required. In the *Amo Containers* case, the standard of care imposed on Mobil was based on the customs and traditions of the industry, but because the ship and containers were lost the onus was on Mobil to prove they had not been negligent. Reversing the onus in this way is rarely done in our legal system, but with bailment the bailee who has the care of the goods is often the only one who can establish what happened.

## Exemption Clauses

**Exculpatory clauses may limit liability**

Contracts of bailment often contain exculpatory or exemption clauses that limit the liability of the bailee. An example of such a clause is, "Goods left on the premises are entirely at the risk of the owner. The proprietor assumes no responsibility for any loss, whether caused by damage, loss, or theft of those goods." The parties are free to include such clauses, but, as was discussed in Chapter 8, courts interpret them narrowly, since they favour one side. To be enforceable, such clauses must be clear and brought to the attention of the customer at the time they enter into the contract.

## Common Carriers

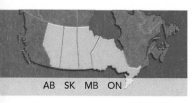

AB SK MB ON

**Common carrier has duty of insurer**

A particularly heavy standard of care is imposed on innkeepers and "common carriers" (trucking and bus companies, railroads, airlines, and even pipelines). Common carriers must be distinguished from private companies or individuals that transport for a particular bailor. These private carriers are merely bailees for a value and have the obligation of a reasonably prudent person in the circumstances. A common carrier offers general transport services to the public and undertakes the standard of an insurer, which means that if the goods are damaged or destroyed while in its care, the carrier is liable even when not at fault. But even a common carrier will not be liable when the damage was the result of some problem with the goods themselves or caused by some failure on the part of the shipper. If an animal dies in transit because of a previously contracted disease, or goods are damaged as a result of some problem with packaging or by spontaneous combustion, there is no liability. A common carrier is also not liable where the damage is caused by an act of war or some condition of nature, such as flood or earthquake. Most common carriers limit their liability by contract and include a term such as "Not responsible for lost or stolen goods or damage over $50." Again, to be valid and binding on both parties, such a provision must be clearly brought to the attention of the shipper at the time the contract is entered into.

## Reducing Risk 15.1

The law of bailment involves all those situations where one person's property is left in the care of another. This affects not only service industries, such as restaurants and hotels, but also repairers, mechanics, and the storage and transportation of goods. Businesspeople face a high stan- dard of care toward these goods, and it is wise to both insure against loss and limit liability through use of an exculpatory clause included in the service contract or posted so that it is clearly visible on the premises.

Insurance is usually made available to offset this limitation. Common carriers are controlled by specific statutory provisions regulating their industry.

## Innkeepers' Liability

In common law, innkeepers are also treated like insurers and responsible for the lost or stolen goods of a guest, unless it can be shown that they were lost because of some act of God or negligence on the part of the guest. To succeed, the guest must show that the establishment qualifies as an inn, offering both food and temporary lodging (transient-type accommodation).

**Innkeeper has duty of an insurer**

Most jurisdictions have significantly reduced the innkeepers' liability by statute so that they are liable only when it can be proven that they or their employees were at fault. In most provinces a copy of the appropriate section of the statute must be properly posted in the various rooms, otherwise the liability reverts to the common law standard. In Ontario, the innkeeper's common law liability has simply been reduced to $40. Most statutes require the innkeeper to accept a guest's valuables and put them in a secure place, assuming liability for them.

**Liability may be reduced by statute**

## Gratuitous Bailment

A gratuitous bailment occurs when only one side receives a benefit. Historically, when the bailee received the benefit (as when a friend borrows your car), the standard of care imposed was much higher than where the bailment was for the benefit of the bailor (as when you store furniture as a favour for a friend). Today the courts seem to be moving toward imposing the same standard of care no matter who benefits (see Figure 15.1).

**Gratuitous bailment**
• when bailee benefits, duty high
• when bailor benefits, duty less

Remember that even with these simple bailment cases the onus often shifts to the bailee. Thus, once the bailment and damage to the goods has been established, the bailee must show that he or she was not negligent.

## Figure 15.1 Historical Level of Care Required of Bailor

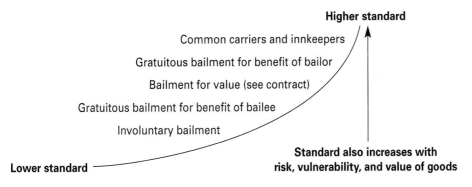

### Involuntary Bailment

### Case Summary 15.4

**Even Involuntary Bailees Have a Duty: *McCarthy v. Matthews*[4]**

Mrs. McCarthy left her belongings behind when her mortgagee foreclosed on and eventually sold the house she had been living in. A cleaning crew getting the property ready for sale disposed of them under instructions from the mortgagee. When Mrs. McCarthy returned to collect her things and found only a few items left she refused to take them and sued. The Court held that the mortgagee, who had been informed that the property belonged to Mrs. McCarthy, was an involuntary bailee "and was therefore under duty to exercise that degree of diligence which men of common prudence generally exercised about their own affairs." When he treated the property as abandoned he failed in this duty and was liable for Mrs. McCarthy's loss. Mrs. McCarthy was contributorily negligent having failed to take the few remaining goods when she had the chance.

This case involved an involuntary bailee, and so the duty was minimal and yet was still breached by the mortgagee.

**Involuntary bailment— duty low**

When someone leaves a coat in a restaurant or at a friend's house, or picks up a watch found on the sidewalk, an involuntary bailment has been created. Exercising control by putting away the coat or picking up the watch creates the bailment. As soon as you exercise that control, the obligations of a gratuitous bailee for the benefit of the bailor arise, and there is a duty to take care of those goods. The responsibility as bailee is to keep the coat safe and return it to the bailor. Generally speaking, if the goods are returned to the wrong person or discarded, as in the McCarthy case, the bailee is responsible.

### The Rights of the Bailee

**Contract terms prevail**

The terms set out in the contract govern a bailment for value. Such provisions as the terms of payment, the requirement of insurance, and any exculpatory clauses are binding if they have been properly brought to the attention of the parties. An unpaid bailee has a common law right to a lien if he has repaired or otherwise worked on the goods, but there is no corresponding common law lien where the goods are just stored, as with a warehouse, or transported. Today, statutes have been passed, giving common carriers, repairpersons, storage facilities, and other bailees for value the right to retain the goods until payment is

**Except where modified by statute**

arranged. This statutory lien includes a right to resell, after giving the bailor appropriate notice and an opportunity to reclaim the goods. When it is the bailor who has not been paid, as with rented tools or furniture, they can reclaim their goods and seek normal contractual remedies. Where no price has been agreed upon, the bailor is entitled to recover a reasonable payment on the basis of the principle of *quantum meruit,* as discussed in Chapter 8. Where consumers are involved, care must be taken to adhere to the consumer protection legislation, as discussed in Chapter 9.

---

4. [1988] B.C. Div. 2768-01 (B.C. Prov. Ct.).

# Real Property

The need to understand the law of real property (land and buildings) extends beyond business relationships, accommodation being one of life's essentials. Whether shelter is obtained through ownership, rental, or even squatting, the relationships created are governed by real property law. Everyone needs accommodation, either rented or owned, and a significant industry has developed to serve the property needs of business and non-business interests; that is, the provision and management of space and the purchase and sale of property. The material in the rest of this chapter is necessarily abbreviated, but it will serve as an introduction to the most significant aspects of the law of real property: interests in land and their transfer, landlord and tenant relationships, and mortgages.

## Legal Interests in Land

### Real Property

The term "real property" includes land and anything affixed to it, such as buildings and chattels that are permanently attached. As far as the areas above and below the surface are concerned, only the portion that the owner can permanently use or occupy is now considered part of that property, and even this space will probably be restricted by local zoning regulations, which will limit the type of building that can be erected as well as the type of activity that can take place. A landowner has no complaint when an airplane flies over the property, but power lines or an overhanging building that permanently incur into this air space would give rise to a right to sue. As for the sub-surface rights, usually the Crown has retained the mineral rights, and the oil and gas rights. Property owners generally have no complaint when these rights are granted to others, and mine tunnels or oil wells are developed under their property. In these cases, the property owner is entitled to compensation for surface disturbance, in the form of access roads, shafts, and so on, but not to a share of the profits coming from the minerals, oil, or gas. Mineral, oil, and gas rights are important topics with their own body of law and no attempt will be made to deal with them in this text.

**Real property is land or anything attached to land**

**Interest in Land.**   The current law of real property is rooted in the ancient feudal system of England, in which people held rather than owned their land. The king actually owned the land, and the right to possession of it, called an **estate in land**, was granted on the basis of some obligation of service to the king. The original estates in land, which were numerous and based on the type of obligation owed to the king, have been reduced to a few significant types, known today as *estates in fee simple, life estates,* and *leasehold estates.*

**All land owned by Crown**

**Fee Simple.**   The greatest interest a person can have in land today and what we think of as ownership is an estate in fee simple. Although the Crown (the federal or provincial government) technically still owns the land, a fee simple estate gives the right to use or sell the land subject only to any local restrictions which have been imposed by agreement or legislation. This right to sell the land free from interference is why we consider fee simple equivalent to ownership in Canada today.

**Fee simple comparable with ownership**

Still, the "owner" of land is subject to government and municipal regulations with respect to what the property can be used for, the nature and description of the buildings that can be erected on it, and the health, sanitary, and appearance standards to be maintained. The property may even be expropriated under certain circumstances.

**Life estate divides fee simple**

**Life Estate.** Whereas a fee simple estate can be inherited, a life estate is more restrictive and cannot be willed to others. Both types of estate give exclusive possession of the property to the holder, but upon the death of the life tenant, the property reverts back to the original owner of the fee simple or that owner's heirs. This right to take back the property or **reversionary interest** may be transferred to a third party, who is then called the **remainderman** and has a right to the remainder of the fee simple after the death of the life tenant. Life estates are not particularly common in Canada and are usually used to ensure that some member of the family, such as a spouse, is cared for to the end of their life. The holder of a life estate has special responsibilities and must pay for normal upkeep, pay fees and taxes, and not commit "waste"—that is, not do anything to harm the value of the reversionary interest, such as cut down trees or damage the house. The uncertainty associated with the life estate and the difficulty in selling or otherwise dealing with the land in question makes a life estate very unattractive from a business point of view. See Figure 15.2 for an illustration of the rights of parties with a life estate.

**Dower and homestead rights protect spouse**

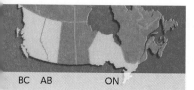

In many provinces, interests similar to life estates are created through the operation of law. **Dower rights** were intended to protect women who lost any individual claim to property when they married. Dower provided the wife a one-third interest in the husband's land as a matter of right, but this also interfered with the free transferability of property. Dower rights were also lost when the couple divorced. Because of these and other problems, dower rights have been modified[5] or replaced by other statutory protections. Today, these claims are protected in most provinces by **homestead rights**[6] or in family law statutes that give the spouse a claim to a substantial portion of all family assets in the case of marriage breakdown.[7] These family law considerations are beyond the scope of this text but can have a significant impact on businesspeople.

**Figure 15.2 Rights of Parties with Life Estate**

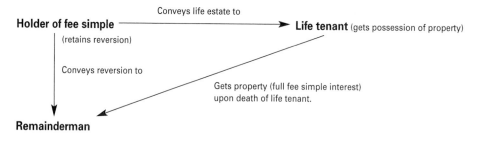

5. *Dower Act*, R.S.A 2000, c. D-15.

6. *Homesteads Act, 1989*, S.S. 1989–90, c. H-5.1.

7. *Family Relations Act*, R.S.B.C. 1996, c. 128, s. 56.

**Leasehold Estates.**   Fee simple estates and life estates are described as free-hold estates because a person has exclusive possession of the property for an indeterminate time. Leasehold estates or leases are limited to a specific period of time, after which the property reverts back to the landowner. These leases may be short or long term or may take the form of a periodic tenancy. This means that there is no definite termination date; rather, the term is an automatically renewable monthly or yearly tenancy, as when a person rents an apartment on a month-to-month basis without a lease. The tenancy arrangement continues until the landlord or tenant notifies the other that it is to end. This topic of leasehold interests is generally called *landlord and tenant law* and will be discussed in a separate section of this chapter.

**Leasehold estates determined by time**

• but may also be periodic

## Lesser Interests in Land

Unlike freehold and leasehold, there are several lesser interests in land that do not convey the right to exclusive possession of the property. An **easement** gives a person the right to use a portion of another's land, usually for a particular purpose. The **right of way** is one of the most common forms of easement that allows a person to cross another's land, usually to get to their own property or to reach another point of interest, such as a lake or the sea. The owner of the property cannot interfere with the right of the holder of an easement to cross his property, but it should also be noted that the person with the right of way cannot stop, park his car, or build some permanent structure on the property. The property that has the advantage of the right of way is called the **dominant property,** and the property subject to it is called the **servient property**. Another form of easement involves a permanent incursion onto the property, where, for example, someone has been given permission to have part of a building hang over onto the neighbour's property. **Statutory easements** give utilities or other bodies similar rights to run power lines or sewer lines across private property.

**Easement gives right to use of land—not possession**

**Must be dominant and servient tenement**

Other lesser interests include **licences**, where a person is given permission to use another's land. An example would be the invitation to the public to attend at a shopping mall. Licences can also be created by contract, as when a hotel rents a room for the night, but the rights created are not true interests in the property and do not run with the land.

Where such use continues unabated over a long period of time, in some provinces this can become a permanent enforceable right as illustrated by the right of way obtained in the *Caldwell v. Elia* case in Case Summary 15.5. Acquiring such a right over property through use is called an *easement acquired by prescription*, and to avoid this happening the landowner must periodically exercise some control over the portion of land in question, such as blocking off public access from time to time.

**Property rights may be acquired by prescription**

A right to actual possession of land can be acquired in the same way. This is called acquiring possession through *adverse possession* and occurs when someone has had possession of land for a significant number of years in an open and notorious fashion, tolerated by the actual owner. The actual number of years needed varies with the jurisdiction. Several Canadian jurisdictions, specifically those using a land titles system, have abolished both the right to an easement by prescription and the right to acquire land by adverse possession.[8]

• or by adverse possession

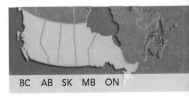

BC  AB  SK  MB  ON

---

8. *Land Title Act*, R.S.B.C. 1996, c. 250, s. 24 and *Limitation Act*, R.S.B.C. 1996, c. 266, s. 12.

### Case Summary 15.5

#### Rights Can Be Obtained by Use: *Caldwell v. Elia*[9]

Walsh and Caldwell owned cottages next to each other near Lake Simcoe in Ontario. There was a gravel road going though the Walsh property, which had been used for 20 years by both parties as well as a third property to access their cottages. There was also a right of way through Caldwell's property that had never been used. Walsh blocked off access to the road, insisting that the others use the right of way on Caldwell's property. Caldwell sued, claiming a right to an easement by prescription, but Walsh countered that the right of way made use of the road unnecessary. The appeal court found that the fact that they had reasonable access another way had nothing to do with it. They had used that road openly for more than 20 years and thus had acquired a right to use it by prescription. The road could not now be closed off.

Easements by prescription are not based on need but on use, and this case illustrates that fact as well as the nature and significance of such an easement. But many would argue that this principle caused an injustice in this case, needlessly causing a loss in the value of the Walsh property. What do you think?

Another lesser interest in land involves contracts to take trees, gravel, soil, peat, sand, or some other valuable commodity from the land. These are referred to as a **profit à prendre.**

**Restrictive covenant may bind future owners**

Another important right is a **restrictive covenant**. When someone sells land to another, they can place restrictions on the use of that land that will bind all subsequent holders. These restrictive covenants are typically restrictions as to the type of buildings that can be put on the property relating to their height, shape, and style, restrictions as to how the property may be used, such as for residential, commercial, or light industrial, and even restrictions as to whether children are allowed, although such a provision may be challenged under the provincial human rights law.

Although these are lesser interests in land, they run with the land, meaning that they are tied to the property itself rather than to the owner of it and bind not only the original purchasers but also any subsequent owners. They are better viewed as an interest in land rather than as a simple contractual relationship, and so the rule of privity of contract does not apply.

**To bind future owners these covenants must be negative**

For such restrictions to bind subsequent owners of the property, they must be negative rather than positive obligations. Thus, a requirement that no building more than three storeys be constructed on the property is a negative covenant and will bind future owners, but requiring that a building be built within a certain time period imposes a positive obligation to do something and will bind only the initial purchaser. A **building scheme** involves the same restrictive covenants being placed on all the properties in a large development. Building schemes take on many of the attributes of zoning bylaws because the developers have imposed basic rules governing the construction and use of property in the development, just as a municipality would normally do through zoning bylaws.

9. (2000), 30 R.P.R. (3d) 295 (Ont. C.A.).

## Case Summary 15.6

### Positive Covenants Do Not Bind Future Owners: *Durham Condominium Corporation No. 123 v. Amberwood Investments Limited*[10]

WHDC Harbour Development Corporation subdivided land into two parts and sold the first-phase portion to Amberwood, which built a high-rise and certain recreational facilities. The agreement anticipated that WHDC would also build a high-rise, which would support those recreational facilities, and in the meantime that WHDC would pay a portion of their operating expenses. This agreement was registered and contained a provision that the obligations were to run with the land. WHDC ran into financial difficulties, and the mortgagee sold the phase-two property to Durham pursuant to a power of sale in the mortgage. Durham refused to pay the interim expenses associated with the recreational facilities, and this action was brought by Amberwood to enforce that agreement. The Court held that since this was a positive obligation requiring Durham to make payments, such an obligation would not run with the land and would not bind a subsequent owner who had acquired ownership through a power of sale. This was the case even though the obligation was registered and stated it would run with the land.

For a restrictive covenant to bind future owners of property it must be negative in nature. Had the provision required Durham not to erect a building more than 10 storeys, this would have been binding since it was negative in nature, requiring the owner *not* to do something rather than to do something.

## Tenancy in Common and Joint Tenancy

When two people own property together in a tenancy in common, they both have an undivided half interest in the land. The two share the property, and if one dies that person's heirs inherit their interest. People can also share ownership of property in a joint-tenancy relationship, but here if one dies the other will be left with the whole property. In effect, both individuals own the entire property outright, and when one dies the survivor continues to own the entire property. Where one joint owner of property dies there is no inheritance, which avoids many of the problems encountered when property becomes part of the estate, such as probate fees and estate taxes. This is why joint tenancy is so attractive to couples holding property together.

Where property is owned jointly and one of the parties does not want the other to get their interest it is possible to "sever" the joint tenancy. Severance must take place before death and is accomplished by one of the parties acting toward the property in some way that is inconsistent with the joint tenancy continuing. Selling their interest in the property to a third party, for instance, would sever the joint tenancy, creating a tenancy in common between the other party and that purchaser. But bequeathing the joint interest to someone else in a will does not work, since the will operates after death and after the rights of the survivor have been established. Creditors can also bring applications to the court to partition or sever a joint tenancy so that the debtor's half of the property can be sold to pay the debt.

**Owning property together may be joint or in common**

**Only joint ownership creates right of survivorship**

**Joint tenancy can be severed**

---

10. (2002-03-20), ONCA C35155 (Ont. C.A.).

To avoid the creation of a joint tenancy, terms such as "held jointly" or "joint ownership" should not be used in the title document. When such words do not appear, the creation of a tenancy in common is presumed.

## Case Summary 15.7

### An Intention to Change a Joint Tenancy Is Not Good Enough: *Tompkins Estate v. Tompkins* [11]

Mr. and Mrs. Tompkins owned their home as joint tenants, but when their marriage broke down they had not finalized any arrangements before Mr. Tompkins died—although they had discussed the sale of the home and even involved their lawyers, who wrote "without prejudice" letters. This action was brought to determine whether Mrs. Tompkins was still entitled to the house by right of survivorship.

The Court held that the joint tenancy had not been severed and that Mrs. Tompkins was entitled to Mr. Tompkins' interest in the home. There must be a transfer or an agreement to change a joint tenancy into a tenancy in common. In this case, there was no transfer of the property, and although an agreement was being negotiated, it had not been completed when Mr. Tompkins died. An intention to sever had been demonstrated, but no severance had, in fact, taken place by the time of his death.

A surviving joint tenant acquires the other joint tenant's interest in the property upon the death. When relationships change the joint tenancy can also be changed, but the change requires some positive action on the part of the parties, and a demonstrated intention to do so is not good enough. Did the technicality of the law work an injustice in this case?

## Other Interests in Land

**Option gives right to purchase**

When an offer is made for the purchase of land, like other offers it can be revoked at any point before acceptance. Such an offer can be made irrevocable when the offeree pays some additional consideration to keep the offer open for a specified period. This is called an **option agreement**, and when land is involved it conveys with it significant rights, giving the offeree a right to purchase the land at a specified price, which can, in turn, be sold to someone else. Leases often contain an option to purchase, which must be registered against the title to bind subsequent purchasers of the property. Registration is discussed below.

## Reducing **Risk** 15.2

Shared property can be both a boon and a thorn in the side of the people who own it and those they deal with. Partners often find it efficient to own business property jointly so that if one dies the other acquires the whole property without having to deal with the estate and reducing taxes. On the other hand, it can be more difficult to enforce a judgment when property is co-owned, especially where the co-owner is a spouse who is not party to the debt. Great care should be taken to understand exactly what the rights of all the parties are when transactions involving such shared property interests are involved. For instance, it may be very attractive for partners to own assets jointly, but where this is the case and a person dies, that property does not go to his estate and is not available to his heirs. That may be an appropriate result if planned for and other arrangements are made to provide for the family, but it may be a tragedy if the implications of such a relationship were not fully understood.

---

11. (1993), 99 D.L.R. (4th) 193 (B.C.C.A.).

When a person purchases land, paying for it by a series of instalments, this is secured by either a mortgage or less commonly by an **agreement for sale**. An agreement for sale is like a conditional sale of personal property, in the sense that title to the property does not transfer to the purchaser until the last payment is made. In the event of a default, the seller can reclaim the land that he has title to. In the interim, the agreement for sale bestows a significant interest in the property on the purchaser, including the right of possession. The agreement for sale also must be properly registered to protect the interest against subsequent claims against the property.

A more common way of financing the purchase of property is through a **mortgage.** The creditor lends the borrower money to make the purchase, and the title of the property is conveyed (transferred) to the moneylender as security, to be reconveyed upon receipt of the last payment. Note that title doesn't actually transfer in all jurisdictions. Mortgages are not restricted to financing the purchase of property but can be used to secure loans for any purpose. Because the use of mortgages is so common and important special rules have been developed, and these will be examined in more detail in a separate section of this chapter.

**Security given through mortgage or agreement for sale**

## Transfer and Registration of Interest in Land

The first stage in the purchase of property, whether it be commercial or residential, involves the creation of an **agreement of purchase and sale**, sometimes referred to as an interim agreement between the vendor and purchaser. It is important to understand that this is the contract governing the transaction and great care must be taken in its creation. All of the terms and special conditions must be properly set out at this stage and will govern the relationship between vendor and purchaser. If you as purchaser wish to not be bound until you can arrange acceptable financing, or sell your house, or until the house passes a proper inspection, or if you require something to be done to the property such as connection to a sewer or a repair of the roof, you must carefully state that as a condition in the contract. It will be too late to insist on it later. Your lawyer will search the title to ensure all is in order and at the appropriate time the transaction will "close"—at that point the property transfers from vendor to purchaser.

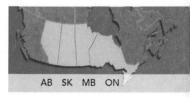

AB   SK   MB   ON

Historically, land was transferred by grant. The document used to accomplish this transfer had to be under seal and was called a **deed of conveyance**, now shortened simply to *deed*. A problem with this system was that there was no way to keep track of the various deeds that would accumulate with respect to a particular property over the years. It was impossible to be certain that good title to the property had been transferred by the most current deed, without inspection of all the past documents. Two different solutions to this problem were developed, and either one or the other has been adopted in all Canadian jurisdictions.

**Grants give title to property**

Both systems require the registration of documents, but the more traditional approach does not affect the rights of the parties, which are determined by the registered documents rather than the process. This is called the **registration system;** the registry is merely a repository of documents that provides assurance to the parties that they will not be affected by any unregistered documents. The purchaser's lawyer must still "search the title" by examining the title documents and establishing a chain of valid deeds to determine whether the seller has good title. This usually means going back over the documents for a set period of time (40 years) to make sure no mistakes have been made. Anything before that period is presumed to be correct. To add to the confusion, many interests in land may exist

**Registration imposed to assist ascertaining title**

at the same time all needing registration, including the fee simple, lease interests, easements, and judgments.

**Some provinces guarantee title**

The western provinces, the territories, and some areas of Ontario and Manitoba have taken the registry system one step further and adopted a **land titles system**, where the title to real property is guaranteed. In this system, once registration has taken place in a central registry a certificate of title is created and registered that is binding on all parties. The government guarantees that the information on that certificate of title is correct. This information sets out the declared owner of the property as well as any mortgages, easements, or other interests that might be held by others. The key to understanding this system is that the certificate of title determines the interest of the parties listed on it to the land specified.

For example, in British Columbia the *Land Titles Act*[12] states that the **certificate of title** is conclusive evidence in any court that the person named on the certificate is the holder in fee simple of that property and that is the end to the matter. For this reason Mrs. Hill lost her home in the case discussed in Case Summary 15.8. Both systems require registration, but in the registration system it is up to the parties to sort out the legal relationships derived from those registered documents, whereas in the land titles system the certificate of title determines the interests. New Brunswick has also adopted a modified system of guaranteed title, and other Atlantic provinces intend to follow their example.

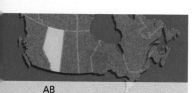

AB

In both registry and land titles systems, great strides are being made to modernize the process using advanced data compilation technologies. This has already introduced significant changes in data storage, and more changes can be expected in the future. One very important change is in the process of filing the documents, which now can be done electronically in many jurisdictions.

### Case Summary 15.8

**Certificate Guarantees Title:** *Paramount Life Insurance Co. v. Hill*[13]

Mr. Hill sold the property he and his wife owned to his business partner and had his partner arrange for a loan with Paramount Life Insurance Company on the basis of a mortgage on the property. Neither the partner nor the Insurance Company knew that he had forged his wife's signature on the documents. The facts became apparent when Hill died and Paramount foreclosed when they no longer were receiving mortgage payments. Mrs. Hill fought the foreclosure action claiming she was still entitled to the property because of the fraudulent sale. But because this happened in a land titles jurisdiction (see later in this chapter) where title is guaranteed, and because the partner and Paramount were innocent of any wrongdoing, the Court found that the business partner had obtained good title to the property and that the mortgage granted was good. A certificate of title had been granted to the partner, which determines ownership against all other parties. Mrs. Hill was the victim of her husband's fraud and lost the property.

This case illustrates the difference between the land titles system and the system of land registry used in other parts of the country, where the validity of the forged document could be challenged and Mrs. Hill would have retained her home.

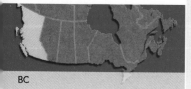

BC

---

12. R.S.B.C. 1996, c. 250, s. 23(2).

13. (1986), 34 D.L.R. (4th) 150 (Alta. C.A.).

## Reducing **Risk** 15.3

Often the most important transaction a person will be involved in is the purchase of a home. Still, many treat the purchase of a computer or automobile with more deliberation. This purchase should be taken with great care. Remember that the purchase agreement (sometimes called the interim agreement) is the contract governing the transaction and is binding on the parties. The actual transfer documents that are completed later are just the execution of that contract. Great care should be taken with the terms of that contract and any conditions should be fully understood and carefully worded. The purchaser should make sure of their finances, have their own lawyer involved at an early stage, and deal with a trusted real estate agent and banker. It is also important to have the house properly inspected by a competent independent professional so that any problems can be factored into the purchase price. The lawyers will search the title to make sure all is in order, and often it will also be necessary to have the property surveyed to determine its proper boundaries.

## Condominium Legislation

Because traditional real property law did not recognize the difference between the land and the buildings affixed to it, it was incapable of handling the modern practice of creating ownership in suites stacked vertically in an apartment building or attached townhouses. All the Canadian provinces have passed legislation allowing fee simple interest in individual units in a condominium structure. But because condominium ownership involves a combination of unit and common ownership, many unique rights and responsibilities apply. Although individuals may own their separate units, all common areas, such as the halls, reception areas, and laundry facilities are owned in common.

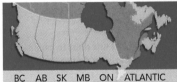

BC   AB   SK   MB   ON   ATLANTIC

**Condominium legislation allows vertical title**

**Condominium interest involves some shared property**

The condominium association is a corporate body and functions in a way similar to a municipality, company, or society, holding regular meetings with each member (those owning apartments in the development) having a vote. Bylaws are passed that outline the rights and duties of members. Although these bylaws must conform with statutory requirements, they can still create hardship where rules are put in place that interfere with what would normally be considered a right of ownership, such as prohibitions on pets or children. The condominium association will also levy a fee on each member to pay for such things as repairs, the cost of management, and other services. If these fees are not paid, the condominium corporation has a right to place a lien on the title of the member and force a sale, if necessary, to recover the funds. When unexpected repairs occur, these fees or levies can be substantial. In British Columbia, there has been a particular problem with "leaky condos," the repair of which has required many condominium owners to pay levies sometimes in excess of $50 000, causing many to lose their homes. Each member of the condominium owns his or her own suite and the normal rules of real property apply; the suites can be sold, mortgaged, or rented, but the interest the member has in the common area goes with that conveyance and so do the responsibilities associated with it. The condominium structure is not limited to residential apartments but can be applied to commercial properties, townhouses, or even separate, physically unconnected units or vacation properties.

**Rules must be obeyed and fees paid**

A **cooperative** is a less common method of acquiring accommodation. Like with a condominium, all the members of a cooperative have shares in the apartment building. However, their rights to their individual suites are based on the terms of the contract and the bylaws of the cooperative, as opposed to a specific real property interest in the suite itself. In this case, the real property interest in all the suites and the common areas is held by the cooperative, which is a company composed of the members holding shares in it and the members do not have title to the specific suite that they occupy.

**Apartments can be owned through cooperatives**

There are some disadvantages to condominium and cooperative ownership, such as submission to the bylaws and the monthly fee, but there are also significant advantages. This form of ownership is the only viable alternative to renting an apartment. Although a monthly fee must be paid which can change, there is no danger of a rent increase since the unit is owned by the member. Also, members can share facilities such as swimming pools and other recreational areas that normally would not be available to an individual homeowner. In condominiums or cooperatives, residents can be required to leave if they violate the bylaws. For example, buildings can be designated as adults-only or pet-free, and couples can be required to leave if they have pets or children. (Although such provisions may violate human rights legislation.)

## The Landlord–Tenant Relationship

### Leasehold Estates

**Tenant has right to exclusive possession during period of lease**

**Registration and writing requirements for leases**

**Terms of lease can modify obligations**

**Leasehold interests run with the land**

A leasehold estate lasts for a specific or determinable period of time, usually ending on a specified day or at the end of a specified period. It also may take the form of a **periodic tenancy** where the specific period (usually a month) is automatically renewed. Unlike a **licence**, which does not convey an exclusive right to the property, the lease gives the tenant the right to use the property to the exclusion of all others for the period of time stated in the lease agreement. If Jones were to rent a hotel room for a month this would normally be a licence since the hotelkeeper has the right to come in the room, make the beds, clean the room, do any repairs, and even move Jones to another location if it is deemed appropriate. But if Jones were to lease an apartment for a month he would have the exclusive use of it and the landlord could not enter without permission unless some arrangement to do so had been set out in the lease agreement.

The general requirements of contract law apply to leasehold estates.

As with other business relationships, the general requirements of contract law apply to leasehold estates. Even though it is wise to do so, a lease for three years or less need not be in writing. In most jurisdictions, however, leases over three years must be evidenced in writing to satisfy the *Statute of Frauds* or its equivalent.[14] A written lease should set out the premises covered by the lease, the parties to it, the consideration or rent to be paid by the tenant, the duration of the lease, and any other special provisions the parties may have agreed to.

Leases, like freehold estates, are interests that run with the land. Privity of contract does not apply, and so, when a landlord sells the property, the prior lease binds the new owner. Also, if the landlord mortgages the property after the lease is made and defaults, the creditor is subject to the lease arrangement, and if the property is seized or resold, the lease must still be honoured. Registration of long-term leases is required to ensure these rights are protected.

14. R.S.O. 1990, c. S.19, s. 3.

Like other contracts, a landlord who contracts with an infant, a drunk, or a mentally incompetent person runs into all the problems associated with incapacity, as discussed in Chapter 6, and the resulting contract may not be binding. Historically, frustration, as discussed in Chapter 8, did not apply to land.[15] Many jurisdictions have changed this with respect to residential tenancies so that if the property is destroyed or damaged, rendering it unusable, the contract will be discharged by frustration and the tenant's obligation to pay rent will cease. In Ontario, for example, the *Tenancy Protection Act* states that the "doctrine of frustration of contract and the *Frustrated Contracts Act* apply with respect to tenancy agreements."[16]

**Statutes apply frustration to some tenancies**

Most jurisdictions have introduced special legislative provisions determining the rights and obligations of landlords and tenants in residential relationships. Commercial tenancy law has also been modified by statute to a lesser extent. This legislation varies from province to province, so no attempt will be made to make a comprehensive summary of these statutory provisions except to indicate some of the more interesting provisions in place.

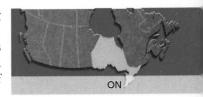

## Types of Tenancies

Property may be leased for a specific period or time, such as for "one year" or "ending September 5," or it may be a periodic tenancy with no set duration. When such an agreement has a set duration, it is a term lease, entitling the tenant to exclusive possession of the property for the specified period. Where the lease allows the tenant to **assign** the lease and she does so, all rights and claims in relationship to the property are given up to the new tenant. However, if the property is **sublet**, the tenant retains a reversionary interest, giving the tenant the right to retake possession at the expiration of the sublease. Usually, leases contain provisions allowing for such assignment or subletting with the permission of the landlord, "which shall not be unreasonably withheld." This gives the landlord some say in who takes possession of the property but does not allow unreasonable interference.

**Property may be sublet**

A **periodic tenancy** has no specific termination date; rather, it involves a specific lease period that is automatically renewed in the absence of notice to the contrary. The period involved can be weekly, monthly, or yearly, but the most common is the month-to-month tenancy. Without notice bringing the relationship to a close, a periodic tenancy will continue indefinitely. Any notice to end the periodic tenancy must give one clear period of notice unless otherwise specified in the lease. Thus, in a month-to-month tenancy, notice must be given before the end of one month to take effect at the end of the next. If Nilsson rents an apartment from Delgado in a month-to-month tenancy and pays his rent on the first of each month, the lease period ends at the end of the month. Notice to terminate must be given on or before the last day of the month to take effect at the end of the next month. If notice is given on the day the rent is paid to terminate at the end of that month it will not be effective because the lease period has already begun. This requirement has caused considerable problems and is an area that has been modified by statute with respect to residential tenancies in many jurisdictions.

**Periodic tenancy usually month to month**

**Notice period is one clear rental period**

15. *Paradine v. Jane* (1647), Aleyn 26 (K.B.).

16. *Tenant Protection Act, 1997*, S.O. 1997, c. 24, s.10.

# Rights and Obligations of the Parties

**Obligations may be modified by statute**

In common law, commercial and residential tenancies were treated the same way, but all provinces have passed statutes modifying these rules. These changes apply primarily to residential tenancies, where the rules have been significantly modified. The following comments apply primarily to commercial tenancies. The unique rules associated with residential tenancies will be discussed under a separate heading. You should refer to the specific legislation in effect in your jurisdiction.

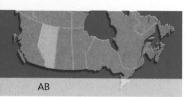

AB

**Lease sets out rights of the parties**

It is important to remember that leasehold tenancies are based on contract and the following discussion relates to the rights and obligations of the parties where they have not been modified by unique terms set out in the lease. Normally a lease will set out a description of the premises—the parties, the rent to be paid, and the term of the lease. Other terms that are often included in commercial leases relate to what use the property can be put to and who is responsible for the payment of utilities, taxes, repairs, and insurance. In special situations, such as services or retail stores in shopping malls, provisions may prohibit the operation of a similar business close to the tenant. In the shopping mall situation, rent is sometimes fixed as a percentage of sales. Long-term commercial leases often include an option for the review of the rent at set periods or for its renewal.

**Landowner must provide vacant premises**

## Vacant Possession.
The landowner has an obligation to ensure that the premises are vacant and ready for occupancy at the time the lease period is to start. A failure to deliver vacant possession is often caused by construction delays or an over-holding prior tenant and compensation is normally based on how much it costs the tenant to find other accommodation in the interim.

**Landlord must not interfere with the tenant's use of property**

## Quiet Enjoyment.
A landlord is obligated to give a tenant quiet enjoyment of the premises. This does not mean that the tenant has to be happy or like the premises, only that the landlord must ensure that nothing happens to interfere with the tenant's use of the property. Where Cho leases office space in a new building to Coglan, but the construction is not complete, causing noise and vibration that interferes with Coglan's business, this would be a breach of his right to quiet enjoyment of the lease. Where Coglan's office is on the 10th floor and the elevator is not yet installed; where the entranceway is blocked by construction; or where the central heating is not yet working in the winter are also examples of what would be a breach of quiet enjoyment.

### Case Summary 15.9

**You Must Be Able to Use the Premises: *Shun Cheong Holdings B.C. Ltd. v. Gold Ocean City Supermarket Ltd.*[17]**

Gold Ocean City Supermarket Ltd. leased premises from Shun Cheong Holdings B.C. Ltd. to operate a grocery store. Unfortunately, there was seepage of a "smelly greasy fluid" from above that interfered with the operation of the store. After several complaints with no correction of the problem, the grocery store simply abandoned the lease. The question was whether the landlord could bring an action

---

17. (2002), 216 D.L.R. (4th) 392 (B.C.C.A.).

against Gold Ocean City Supermarket Ltd. for breaching their lease and obtain as a remedy the payment of the remaining rent. At trial the Court held that there had been a breach of the tenant's fundamental right of quiet enjoyment and that the abandonment of the lease was justified. The Court of Appeal agreed that a breach of quiet enjoyment had taken place because the smelly liquid made "further performance of the lease impossible or deprived the lessee of substantially the whole benefit of the lease."

This case shows the significant nature of the implied covenant of quiet enjoyment.

**Repair of Premises.**     The landlord has no general obligation to deliver premises that are clean or in good repair. The tenant takes the property the way it comes, and if he or she wants it in better condition the cost is the responsibility of the tenant. Only when the premises are in such disrepair that it amounts to a breach of quiet enjoyment can the landlord be held responsible. In the example above, Coglan would have no complaint if the premises were not painted or the carpet was threadbare when he moved in, unless a provision to provide better facilities was in the lease. But if the structure of the building is in such poor repair that it is no longer capable of supporting a wall or a floor and a resulting cave-in would make the office unusable, that would be a breach of the covenant of quiet enjoyment. Usually, the parties specify changes to these obligations in the lease agreement but there are also many situations in which the courts will imply contractual obligations because of the circumstances. For example, when a tenant rents only part of a building, the court will assume that the landlord has an obligation to provide heat, unless otherwise stated in the lease. But when the tenant leases the entire building, that obligation may be assumed to fall on the tenant.

*No general obligation to repair*

**Termination.**     A lease that ends on a specific date, or is for a specified period of time, ends when specified, unless there is an agreement to extend it. But when a periodic tenancy is involved (for example, month-to-month), notice to terminate must be given. If the tenant fails to leave after the lease has expired or after being given the appropriate notice, a **tenancy at sufferance** relationship is established. Where the landlord permits the over-holding tenant to stay it is called a **tenancy at will**. In these circumstances the landlord is entitled to compensation, but if the normal rent payment is made there is a danger of creating a periodic tenancy requiring more notice before the tenant can be ejected.

*Proper notice must be given for periodic tenancy*

## Tenants' Obligations

The tenant cannot withhold rent when the landlord fails to make repairs, as those obligations are considered to be independent of each other. In these circumstances, the tenant can ask the court for an order of **abatement** that will reduce the rent to be paid to compensate for the landlord's breach of the lease obligation. The tenant has no obligation to repair normal wear and tear or even to make serious repairs when they occur, unless they are caused by waste (his or her own action). The landlord should be notified of any serious problems, but in common law, the landlord has no obligation to make these repairs unless failure to do so would interfere with the quiet enjoyment of the tenancy. If Coglan rents an office from Cho and the rug on the floor wears out over the years, Coglan

*Tenant must pay rent*

would be under no obligation to replace it. But neither would Cho, since the landlord is not required to provide premises of any standard of fitness for the tenant. Of course, the landlord and tenant can agree otherwise, and in most lease agreements one of the parties assumes the responsibility for keeping the property in good repair.

**Tenants not responsible for normal wear and tear**

A tenant does have an obligation to make repairs when undue wear and tear takes place because the premises are used in a way not agreed to in the lease. The landlord can also evict the tenant. If Coglan rents premises from Cho to be used as an office and instead it is used for manufacturing furniture, Cho could demand payment for any excessive wear and require Coglan to vacate the premises, no matter how long the lease had to run.

**Tenant can remove her fixtures before termination of lease**

When a tenant attaches something (a fixture) in such a way that it is clearly intended to become a permanent part of the building or will cause damage to remove it, they are not permitted to remove it when they leave. If Coglan installed modern wiring and added a staircase to the second floor of his rented office, these fixtures would become permanent and he could not remove them when he left. Trade fixtures, on the other hand, such as shelving, display counters, machinery, decorative artwork, and signs can be taken away by the tenant who attached them. But they must be removed when the tenant leaves. If they are left by the tenant, they become part of the real property, and the tenant cannot come back later to recover them.

## Remedies

**Landlord can sue for compensation when lease breached**

**Breach of Lease.**    When the rent is not paid, the landlord can sue for the overdue rent. When some other breach occurs, the landlord may sue for damages and, in serious cases, may require the tenants to vacate the premises. This is called **forfeiture**, and when unpaid rent in a commercial lease is involved no court order is needed, and forfeiture may be accomplished by the landlord simply changing the locks. When the tenant is in breach of some other term of the lease, such as the use of the premises or repair, the landlord must first give the tenant notice to end the breach and time to do so. When eviction is necessary, the services of a law enforcement officer, such as a sheriff, must be obtained, which can be a costly and time-consuming process. Residential tenancy statutes usually limit the availability of eviction as a remedy.

When the landlord does retake the property for failure to pay rent prior to the end of the lease term, the tenant can pay the arrears and apply to the court to have the lease reinstated. This **relief against forfeiture** is an equitable principle similar to a right to redeem an interest in real property after a mortgage has been foreclosed, which will be discussed below.

When the tenant abandons the premises, the landlord retains the right to payment of rent for the duration of the lease period. It should be noted that the landlord is normally not obligated to mitigate this loss, at least in commercial tenancies, by finding a new occupant for the premises until the expiration of the lease period.

**Landlord can seize tenant's property when lease breached**

The landlord also has the right to seize any property left by the tenant and hold it until the rent is paid or to sell the tenant's property to pay the rent owing. This is called **distress**, and when done often causes confusion, because by so doing the rent is paid and the lease continues. The landlord cannot treat the lease as ended and also distrain the tenant's property. This power to seize the tenant's property is usually significantly limited or eliminated in residential tenancy legislation.

The landlord can also seek contractual remedies in the form of damages when the lease is breached. This usually amounts to the rent due but also may be compensation for the cost of repairs when damage is done to the premises.

**Monetary compensation available for breach of lease**

The courts will also issue an injunction when either tenant or landlord carries on some activity inconsistent with the terms of the lease. Thus, when a tenant uses the premises for a purpose different from that contemplated in the lease, the landlord can get an injunction to prevent the misuse of the property.

**Also injunctions in some limited circumstances**

The remedies available to the tenant for the landlord's breach of the lease are more limited. The tenant is generally entitled either to sue the landlord for compensation for any injury suffered because of the breach or to seek an injunction. The tenant is not entitled to withhold rent to force the landlord's compliance with the lease obligations. But if the landlord's breach is significant enough to qualify as a breach of a major contractual term, the tenant may be entitled to treat the lease agreement as discharged and vacate the premises voluntarily, thus terminating the lease. For example, if the lease agreement requires the landlord to provide heat and water and those services are turned off, this would probably be a significant enough breach for the tenant to terminate the agreement. In any case, the tenant always retains the right to seek a court order that the lease be declared as ended or the tenant's obligation to pay rent be reduced because of the landlord's breach.

**Tenant has limited remedies**

It is a principle of tort law that the occupier of property, including a tenant, is responsible for any injury caused to people using the property. The landlord may also be liable if the landlord is responsible for repairs under the lease and the tenant has notified the landlord but the repairs are not made. The landlord may also be responsible for injuries to the tenant or the tenant's employees when such repairs are not made and injury results.

**Occupier's liability on tenant**

## Case Summary 15.10

### Tenant Responsible for Injury to Customer: *Barnett-Black v. Silad Investments Inc.*[18]

Mr. Silad leased a laundromat and had to pay a customer $27 000 when she was injured by a falling fluorescent light fixture. The question was whether the landlord or the tenant was liable. Under the *Occupiers' Liability Act*, it is clear the tenant occupier is responsible to the person using the premises, and because there was no provision in the lease making the landlord responsible for repairs, the Court held that the tenant had no recourse to the landlord for the damages he had to pay. This case shows how important it is to specify in a lease agreement which party will be responsible for repairs.

## Reducing **Risk** 15.4

One of the most important transactions not directly associated with the focus of a business is the acquisition of physical space to carry on the activity. Whether it is office space, a manufacturing plant, or a warehouse, the space is usually leased rather than purchased outright. It is vitally important that the tenant understand the terms of the lease agreement; that appropriate modifications are made to it; and that the lease provides for the possibility that the facility needs of the business might change in the future. Aside from not fully understanding what they are agreeing to, a common failing for tenants is to commit themselves for an extensive period without the flexibility to change as the business grows or declines. Great care should be taken when entering into these commercial leases to ensure that provisions are added or modified providing for as much flexibility as possible.

---

18. (1990), 74 D.L.R. (4th) 734 (Ont. Gen. Div.).

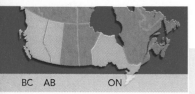

BC  AB          ON

## Residential Tenancies

## Case Summary 15.11

### The Effects of a Lease-Breaking Party: *Applewood Lane West Ltd. v. Scott et al.*[19]

Thomas Scott and Dave Hinds were tenants, and informed their neighbours and friends that they would hold a series of "lease-breaking parties" to get out of their one-year lease. Several noisy parties lasting well into the morning were held. Neighbours complained, police attended, and finally the landlord was driven to give them notice to vacate within five days. They left a month later without paying that month's rent. The landlord retook possession of the premises and made necessary repairs but was unable to rent until several months later. The landlord sued to recover the damages from the two tenants, and they applied for the return of their security deposit. The question was whether in evicting their tenants the landlord gave up any claims to rights they had under the lease.

The Court of Appeal found that the conduct of the tenants constituted abandonment of the lease on their part. The tenants, not the landlord, had breached the lease, therefore the landlord was entitled to lost rent as well as the cost of repairs and was successful in his action.

This case illustrates the special nature of a residential landlord–tenant relationship and underscores the need for the special legislation in place to deal with those relationships.

**Residential tenancy rules modified by statute**

**Some jurisdictions impose rent controls**

AB

**Notice periods increased**

Most jurisdictions have introduced special statutes to significantly modify common law where a tenant rents or leases premises for the purposes of acquiring living accommodation. These Acts are like consumer protection statutes, altering the rights and obligations of the landlord and tenant. In some cases, they also introduce rent controls and establish administrative tribunals in the form of a rentals person or rent-review commission to handle disputes that normally would fall under the jurisdiction of the courts. Generally, the removal of landlord and tenant disputes from the courts has been advantageous to both landlord and tenants. The rights of the parties before such administrative tribunals were discussed in Chapter 3. In many cases, the residential tenancy legislation restricts how often a rent increase can be imposed and sometimes restricts the increase to a given percentage or provides guidelines for the calculation of such increases. This type of control is very controversial, and legislative changes occur regularly as one provincial government is replaced by another. Readers are encouraged to study the current legislation in their own jurisdictions to determine what kinds of controls may be in effect.

Notice periods have also been increased by legislation. Only one clear month had to be given as notice of rent increases or for termination of a monthly periodic tenancy under common law. This has been increased up to three months for rent increases and terminations depending on the jurisdiction. Many provinces have extended the termination notice period still further when the landlord requires the premises for some specific purpose, such as for personal use or for conversion to condominiums.[20] Often, these statutes require the landlord to give

---

19. (1987), 35 D.L.R. (4th) 287 (Man. C.A.).

20. *Residential Tenancy Act*, R.S.A. 1980, c. R-15.3, s. 12.

notice even when the lease is for a specific term. In most cases, the notice required of the tenant is only one month, and no reasons are necessary.

Also, these residential tenancy statutes usually impose an obligation on the landlord to keep the property in good repair, to live up to the local health and safety bylaw standards, and to maintain the services that have been provided, such as laundry facilities and parking. The cost of such services is generally considered to be part of the rent, and so the landlord will not be permitted to get around the rent-increase restrictions by taking these services out of the monthly rent and charging for them separately. The landlord's right to enter the premises without notice is usually restricted to those situations where the tenant has abandoned the premises or in the case of an emergency. The landlord can enter for purposes of inspection or to do repair work but must give notice, and even this access is restricted to normal daylight hours. Most residential tenancy statutes require that a tenant be given a copy of a written lease before its provisions are binding.

*Landlord obligated to repair and maintain premises*

*Landlord's right to enter restricted*

## Case Summary 15.12

### Statute Overrules Lease: *Pinheiro v. Bowes*[21]

This case involves a lease entered into between a landlord and tenant of a residential premises. The lease contained a provision indicating that in the event of termination 30 days' notice would be given. The tenant stayed until the lease expired and then continued to stay from month to month. In 1993, the tenant served one month's notice on the landlord pursuant to the provisions of the lease for termination. This was rejected by the landlord, who insisted on two months' notice as set out in the *Landlord and Tenant Act* in force in the province. The Court decided that the provisions of the Act applied and could not be waived. The tenant was required to pay another month's rent. Such legislation usually favours the tenant, but note that in this instance it was the landlord who benefited.

Where a security deposit is taken, as in the *Applewood* case discussed in 15.11, the legislation usually restricts the amount to a half of one month's rent depending on the jurisdiction. Usually interest must be paid as well.[22] In most provinces, the landlord can retain this amount to cover damage to the premises or for rent owing. But in others, including Ontario, the deposit is made to secure the payment of the last month's rent rather than provide security for damage. In those jurisdictions, the tenant obtains repayment simply by not paying the last month's rent after giving notice of leaving.

*Amount of security deposit restricted by statute*

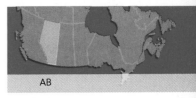

AB

The statutes also usually impose a duty on the landlord to mitigate, and so, when the tenant abandons the premises, the landlord must try to re-rent rather than let the lease run out and retain the security deposit or seek out the tenant for further payment. Landlords of residential premises in many jurisdictions are not permitted to seize the personal property of tenants for unpaid rent (common law distress), but may be allowed to take goods that have been left after the tenant has abandoned the property.

*Landlords must mitigate losses*

Tenants are required to maintain reasonable health and cleanliness standards and repair any damage they cause other than normal wear and tear. It may be possible for a tenant to assign or sublet the lease, but the landlord is usually given

21. (1993), 109 D.L.R. (4th) 315 (Ont. Gen. Div.).

22. *Residential Tenancies Act*, R.S.N.S. 1989, c. 401, s. 12(2).

the right to veto this course of action as long as the consent to sublet or assign is not unreasonably withheld. Note as well that these statutes make frustration applicable to residential tenancies. If the premises is destroyed or made uninhabitable, the tenant is discharged from any obligation to pay rent.

Although these changes to common law are significant, they should be viewed as a form of consumer protection legislation designed to prevent serious abuses that have occurred in the past in landlord and tenant relationships.

## Mortgages

**Mortgage involves transfer of title as security**

A mortgage is a form of security usually involving large sums used to purchase the property in question or for some other purpose. The borrower temporarily transfers the title in the property to the creditor as security for the funds advanced. Upon proper repayment the creditor re-conveys the title, but if there is a default the creditor has first claim on that property before other creditors.

The terminology used to designate the parties to such transactions can be confusing. The person who conveys the title (grants the mortgage) is the one borrowing the money and is called the mortgagor. The creditor is on the receiving end of the transfer of the title and is called the mortgagee.

**Debtor is mortgagor, creditor is mortgagee**

Originally, the creditor actually took possession of the land, but this was inconvenient and the practice soon developed where the creditor was given title but the debtor kept possession of the property, hence the term **mort (dead) gage (pledge)**. In the event of default, the creditor could take possession of the property on the basis of the title held as security. But since the mortgage was separate from the debt, this allowed the creditor to take possession and still demand payment of the defaulted loan. Subsequent developments of the law of mortgages, especially in the Courts of Chancery, were intended to overcome these problems and have resulted in a unique body of law.

### Equity of Redemption

The law relating to mortgages is a significant example of how the Courts of Chancery stepped in to relieve the harshness or unfairness of common law. In common law, the mortgagor not only lost the property upon default, but still had to pay the money owed. The Courts of Chancery recognized the unfairness and allowed the debtor to reclaim the property even after default by paying the money owed plus any expenses involved. This right to redeem became known as the **equity of redemption**, and it bestows on the mortgagor an interest in the land that goes beyond the basic contractual responsibility. If Nagai has property worth $100 000 and owes $60 000 on a mortgage to Dhillon, in the event of default where Dhillon retakes the property Nagai's right to redeem the property is worth $40 000 less any costs involved. Today, we often use the shortened term **"equity"** to refer to the value left in any asset a person owns after they subtract what they owe. Thus, if I own a car worth $12 000 and I owe $5000, I will have $7000 equity in that vehicle.

**Mortgagor retains right to redeem after default**

### Foreclosure

But this right to redeem causes problems for the creditor, who is always in danger, even years later, of the mortgagor exercising his right to redeem and reclaiming the property.

The solution devised by the Courts of Chancery was to set a time limit within which the mortgagor's right to redeem must be exercised. If the mortgagor failed to pay within that time, an order would be made which forever foreclosed the mortgagor from redeeming the property. This combination—a right to redeem on the part of the mortgagor and a right to obtain foreclosure on the part of the mortgagee—has worked well and is the system in place in Canada today.

**Mortgagee can foreclose the right to redeem**

The process of obtaining foreclosure has two stages. Upon default, the mortgagee makes an application asking the court to set a time limit within which the mortgagor must redeem (called an **order nisi**). This time limit will vary with the circumstances and from jurisdiction to jurisdiction, although it is usually not more than six months. If the property is not redeemed within the designated period, the mortgagee returns to court and asks for a final order of foreclosure (an **order absolute**). This order, once obtained, prevents any further exercise of the equity of redemption on the part of the mortgagor. Note that even then the court usually retains a discretionary right to reopen the redemption period if the circumstances warrant. (See the *Namu* case in Case Summary 15.13.) But once the property has been resold, or is in a land titles system where a new certificate of title has been issued subsequent to an order absolute, the original owner no longer has a right to redeem the property.

**Foreclosure is a two-stage process**

### Case Summary 15.13

#### Redemption Allowed Even after Foreclosure Complete: *355498 B.C. Ltd. v. Namu Properties Ltd.*[23]

In 1995, Namu Properties Ltd. sold a townsite property on the British Columbia coast to EuroPacific Properties Ltd. with a mortgage back to the vendor. They also acquired a foreshore lease from the provincial government. They ran into financial difficulties at the outset and were unable to make proper payments on the mortgage. As the mortgagee went through the foreclosure process they were very patient, granting extensions of time and adjournments; finally they applied for and were granted an order absolute of foreclosure, but even then the mortgagee agreed not to file it in the land registry if the appropriate payments were made. They were not, and the order absolute of foreclosure was filed at the appropriate land registry. Several months later, the mortgagor tried to redeem and was refused. In this application, the mortgagor was asking the court to reopen the order absolute and allow them to redeem the property. The mortgagee took the position that it was too late to do that. The Court held that they had discretion to allow redemption even after the order absolute had been registered and allowed the redemption of the mortgage by the mortgagor.

A mortgage is a transfer of the property interest to the creditor as security for the loan. The equitable right to redeem is a recognition of the security nature of that interest, giving the mortgagors a right even after default to reclaim their property upon payment of what is owed. The process of foreclosure (the order nisi and then the order absolute) puts an end to that right to redeem so that the security can be realized after allowing an appropriate time for the right to redeem to be exercised. This case shows how those various interests work and also the power, discretion, and willingness of the court to recognize the right to redeem even after an order absolute has been registered in the

23. (1999), 171 D.L.R. (4th) 513 (B.C.C.A.).

land registry, especially when the mortgagor has a substantial equitable interest in the property.

In a registration jurisdiction the document filed actually transfers title to the mortgagee, but in a land titles system the certificate of title remains in the name of the mortgagor. The interest of the mortgagee is merely noted as a charge against the property, much as an easement or a leasehold interest would be. But the rights bestowed are those of a mortgagee under common law and so the mortgagee (chargeholder) has the right in the event of default to start the foreclosure process. In the event of the property not being redeemed before the time limit specified, the mortgagee has the right to have a new certificate of title created in their name. Although the method of recording the relationship in land titles jurisdiction might be different, the effect is the same.

**In land titles system jurisdictions, a mortgage is registered as charge on title**

## Second Mortgage

The mortgagor's right to redeem is a valuable interest in land and can be used to secure further debt. When the debtor transfers this equity of redemption to another creditor to secure further debt, it is called a second mortgage. Since the title itself was transferred the first time the property was mortgaged and the right to redeem is an equitable remedy created by the Courts of Chancery, any subsequent mortgages after this first mortgage are called *equitable mortgages*. But even after a second mortgage is created, the mortgagor has a similar right to redeem by paying off the second and first mortgages. Thus, the mortgagor retains the right to redeem. In this way, third, fourth, and fifth mortgages can be created. The mortgagor always has a right to redeem any mortgage interest that has been created.

**Mortgagor can use right to redeem to secure a second or third mortgage**

It should be obvious that the more mortgages involved, the weaker the security, so anything beyond first, second, and third mortgages is rare. To illustrate, if Redekop financed the purchase of a new home valued at $150 000 with a first mortgage with Johal for $90 000, he would retain an equity of redemption worth $60 000. He could then borrow a further $35 000 from a second mortgagee using that equity of redemption as security. And Redekop would retain a right to redeem the property from the second mortgagee valued at $25 000 ($150 000 – $90 000 – $35 000 = $25 000). There is no reason why Redekop could not grant a third or fourth or additional mortgage on the property if somebody were willing to take the risk.

Because the first mortgagee has the right to foreclose in the event of default, stripping the mortgagor and any subsequent mortgagee of any interest in the property, the position of a second or third mortgagee involves considerably more risk. They must be prepared to pay off any interest above them to protect their investment. In this example, if Redekop defaults the second mortgagee must be prepared to pay off the first mortgage (pay off Johal the $90 000 owing) in order to protect the $35 000 secured by the second mortgage). This puts any subsequent mortgagees in a very vulnerable position. As a result, higher rates of interest are charged for second and third mortgages.

**Power to foreclose increases risk to second mortgagee**

In a land titles jurisdiction, the first, second, and subsequent mortgages are listed on the certificate of title as charges against the property, and the order of priority is established by the order in which they have been registered. In other registry jurisdictions, the rights of mortgagees will also be determined by the time of registration of their interest at the appropriate land registry office rather than by the order in which they were created. The prompt registration of mortgages is

**In land titles system, mortgages are listed as charges on certificate**

## Figure 15.3 The Creation of Multiple Mortgages

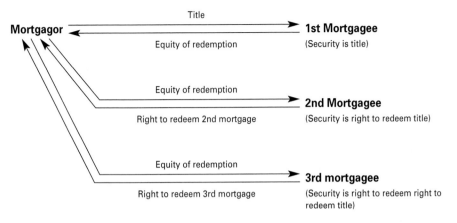

Note that where there is default, the third mortgagee must pay off the second and first mortgagees to recover title.

vital in both systems. The whole purpose of a registration system is to notify people who are acquiring interest in the land of other claims against the property. Thus a properly registered interest will take priority over one that is not properly registered or one that is registered subsequently. If Redekop grants a first and second mortgage and both are properly registered in that order, the first mortgage will have priority. But if the first mortgagee fails to register its mortgage before the second, the first will lose its priority. This advantage can be lost, however, if the second mortgagee has notice of the first mortgage. They can no longer be said to be acting in good faith. See Figure 15.3 for an illustration of the creation of multiple mortgages.

## Types of Mortgages

Mortgages are usually used to finance the purchase of property either for residential or commercial purposes. But mortgages can also be used to finance other private as well as commercial activities. When used to secure a loan for some other business venture, usually in conjunction with a promissory note and sometimes involving a third-party guarantee, they are known as collateral mortgages. A review of secured transactions and creditors' rights as discussed in Chapter 10 is recommended.

**Mortgages for shorter term amortized over long term**

Although a mortgage may be amortized over a 30- or 40-year period, which is the length calculated for repayment, the mortgage term is much less, usually one, two, or five years. The mortgage agreement expires at the end of that term and the entire amount left owing on the mortgage becomes due. The mortgagor must then pay it off or negotiate a renewal of the mortgage, usually at a different interest rate. This can work to the advantage of either party, depending on whether the interest rates have gone up or down. Some people use open-ended mortgages, wherein the mortgage continues and a varying rate of interest fluctuating with changes in the banks' prime rate is charged. The mortgage may require only one payment at the end of its term, but usually payment is required by monthly or bi-weekly instalments.

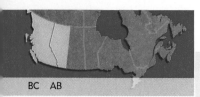

BC   AB

## Remedies upon Default

### Case Summary 15.14

**The Dangers of Being a Second Mortgagee:** *Regional Trust Co. v. Avco Financial Services Realty Ltd.*[24]

Mr. and Mrs. Foster owned property on which they had first and second mortgages. The first mortgage was to Regional Trust and the second was to Avco. They ran into financial difficulties and made arrangements with Avco to transfer their title to Avco in the form of a quitclaim deed. Avco took over their position, making payments to Regional Trust for about a year and then defaulting. Regional Trust exercised their right to sell the property under the power of sale and then sought payment of the deficiency of $6500 from Avco.

When Avco assumed title to the property they had also assumed the obligations. They stepped into the shoes of the Fosters, and when the property was sold for less than what was owed Avco was required to pay the difference. This loss was caused by the sudden drop in the market, which Avco had not anticipated, but the effect was that Avco ended up losing much more than they had actually loaned to the Fosters.

Had Avco remained as a second mortgagee they would have no responsibility to Regional, and both Avco and Regional would have had a claim against the Fosters for any shortfall from the sale of the property. But by taking over the position of the Fosters, Avco also assumed their obligations. This case illustrates not only the nature and distinctions between first and second mortgages and the rights associated with exercising a power of sale, but also graphically illustrates the danger associated with the second or third mortgagee positions.

**Mortgagor must also pay insurance, taxes and keep property in good repair**

Failure to make proper payments is just one of the ways a mortgagor can be in default. Mortgage contracts in addition to the obligation to make such payments usually include an obligation on the mortgagor to insure the property, to pay property taxes, and to otherwise preserve the condition of the property (not commit waste). This ensures that the value of the assets is preserved, protecting the security. When second or third mortgages are involved, a provision making the failure to pay a prior mortgage a default will also be included. Although the most common method of breaching a mortgage agreement is failure to make the appropriate payments, a breach of any of these terms will constitute default. The following is a summary of the types of remedies available to the mortgagee in the event of such default. Of course, the possibility of a negotiated settlement should always be explored.

There is no sense in incurring the legal expense of court action if the defaulting mortgagor can be persuaded to surrender the property, participate in a joint sale, or rehabilitate his or her position by accepting a different repayment schedule. But even when there is a willingness to negotiate, it might be important for the creditors to protect their positions by obtaining a court order. The adversarial remedies discussed below are almost always time-consuming, especially with an uncooperative mortgagor, and when payments are not being made the amount owing including interest can quickly grow. When this happens, creditors often

24. (1984), 5 D.L.R. (4th) 670 (Ont. H.C.).

will only partially recover what they are owed and the mortgagor will get nothing. Where a default does take place, an **acceleration clause** is usually included in the mortgage contract, providing that upon default all that is owed becomes due and payable. But legislation normally requires the creditor to notify the mortgagor of the default and give a specified period of time to repay any arrears and costs and reinstate the mortgage. If such repayment is not made, the mortgagee can proceed to obtain the following remedies.

**Suing on the Covenant.**    As with other types of contracts involving security, the creditor has the right to sue on the promise to repay rather than seek other remedies, such as foreclosure. It should be noted that in several jurisdictions, the right to foreclosure is lost when the mortgagee follows this course of action because the two remedies are inconsistent. Once foreclosure has taken place and the mortgagee wants to sue on the covenant, he or she must be prepared to re-convey the property back to the mortgagor. If the property has been sold after foreclosure and the amount recovered is less than is owed, it is too late for the mortgagee to sue for the deficit. They no longer have the property to re-convey to the mortgagor. Several provinces, including British Columbia, have incorporated into legislation this prohibition against suing after foreclosure. Note that where the power of sale is exercised or a judicial sale takes place, the mortgagee still has the right to sue for any shortfall.

**Creditor can sue for breach of contract**

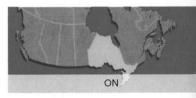
ON

**Possession.**    The mortgagee also has the right to take possession of the property upon default of payment. The problem with this course of action is that any profits earned through the property must be accounted for and given to the mortgagor upon redemption. Nor is the mortgagee entitled to compensation for any expenses incurred in looking after the property, such as the cost of a caretaker. If any damage is done to the property while the mortgagee is in possession, the mortgagee is responsible to compensate the mortgagor upon redemption. The mortgagee will generally not seek an order of possession of the property if it appears that redemption is likely because of the responsibilities involved. Only when the property has been abandoned or is in danger of deterioration for some other reason will this course of action be used.

**Right to take possession upon default**

**Foreclosure.**    This remedy was discussed earlier, but it must be pointed out that its availability varies with the jurisdiction. For example, foreclosure is only available in Manitoba and some other provinces after attempts to sell the property by the court fail.[25] In Nova Scotia the property is sold rather than foreclosed. In other jurisdictions, the process of foreclosure is the usual course embarked on by the mortgagee in the event of default by the mortgagor. However, in the process, all interested parties, including the mortgagor and second and third mortgagees, must be notified of the foreclosure, giving them opportunity to seek other remedies, which usually results in the property being sold rather than foreclosure.

**Foreclosure most common remedy sought**

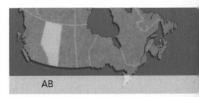
AB

25. *Real Property Act*, R.S.M. 1988, c. R-30, s. 138(2).

## Case Summary 15.15

### Second Mortgagee Retains Right to Sue: *Der Bach v. Mueller* [26]

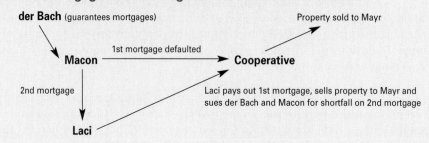

Macon owned a condominium and granted a first mortgage to Cooperative Trust Company and a second mortgage to Frank Laci. In both cases, der Bach guaranteed or co-signed the mortgage debt. Macon defaulted on the mortgages and the property was sold to Mayr. The first mortgagee foreclosed, and the second mortgagee then paid off the first mortgagee and assumed the position of first mortgagee. The purchaser, Mayr, paid out sufficient funds to cover the amount of the first mortgage and the amount owing to Laci, and now Laci, the second mortgagee, wished to proceed by way of personal judgment against Macon and the guarantor, der Bach. The question for the Court was whether the second mortgagee, when he or she buys out the first mortgagee, retained the right to sue on the personal covenant. The answer was yes, and der Bach and Macon, the debtors, had to pay the shortfall. The foreclosure by the first mortgagee forced the second mortgagee to buy out that first mortgage, and the second mortgagee assumed those rights, but he did not lose the contractual rights he had with respect to the second mortgage; that is, the right to sue on the covenant to repay. Compare this to the *Foster* case in Case Summary 15.14, where the second mortgagee took over the position of the mortgagor instead of the first mortgagee.

**Contract usually provides for right to sell property upon default**

**Court-ordered sale common**

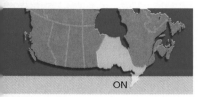

**Power of Sale and Judicial Sale.**   In almost all cases, the contract embodying the mortgage will contain a term called a "power of sale" giving the mortgagee the right to sell the property upon default without going to court first. In some jurisdictions this power is commonly exercised, but in many others an application will be made instead for an order for a judicial sale. This important but often misunderstood remedy involves an application to the court by the mortgagee, and sometimes another creditor or even the mortgagor, for an order that the property be sold under the court's supervision with the object of realizing as much money as possible from the sale for the parties.

The actual procedure varies from province to province. In some jurisdictions, the property is sold at public auction in the case of both a judicial sale and a power of sale. The sale is advertised; tenders are invited; and sometimes, a reserve bid is included to make sure the interests of the parties are protected. In other jurisdictions, the responsibility to conduct the sale will be given to the party who has the incentive to obtain the highest reasonable price, usually the second or third mortgagee depending on the value of the equity. The property is sold through a real estate agent in the normal way; when a purchaser is found, the parties, in the case of a judicial sale, return to the court, and the court gives its

26. (1987), 46 D.L.R. (4th) 320 (B.C.C.A.).

consent to the sale. It is important to understand the effects of this remedy. If the first mortgagee goes to court and asks for foreclosure, the judge will grant a specific redemption period, such as six months, during which time the mortgagor may arrange refinancing and redeem the property. The problem is that at the same time an order to sell the property may be made, usually at the request of the second or third mortgagee. This order is designed to protect the financial position of the second or third mortgagee, by selling the property before the foreclosure can take place. Thus, the person who acquires the order for the judicial sale obtains the right to have the property sold, not in six months, but immediately. The timing of the sale varies with the jurisdiction and the process involved, but it must take place before the end of the redemption period, thus shortening the period given to the mortgagor to redeem the property.

**Court will authorize sale during redemption period**

In some provinces, an attempt must be made to sell the property before the foreclosure route can be taken. In every province, the mortgagor has the right to sell the property during the redemption period as long as the purchase price is high enough to cover the amount owed to the mortgagee. If the property has been sold by judicial sale or using the power of sale in the contract, and the total amount of money realized from the sale is less than the total amount owing on the mortgages, including accumulated interest and other costs, the original mortgagor will get nothing and will be still liable to pay any outstanding amounts owing to the creditors.

**Where judicial sale mortgagee can sue for deficit**

This, of course, was the problem in the *Regional Trust Co. v. Avco* case discussed in Case Summary 15.14. Avco, by accepting the quitclaim, had put themselves in the position of the original owner of the property, and when not enough money was obtained from the sale of the property to cover the amount owing to Regional, they were responsible for the shortfall. One of the disadvantages of being a second or third mortgagee in the event of default is the necessity of taking over the property to protect your investment. The case illustrates that there may be even more dangers when that course of action is taken. In some provinces, a mortgagor does not have to pay a deficit where residential property is involved.

### Case Summary 15.16

**Suing for a Shortfall: *Bank of Montreal v. Allender Investments Ltd. et al.*[27]**

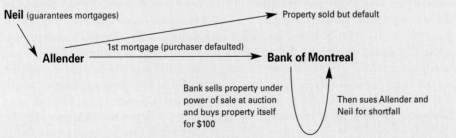

Allender Investments borrowed $46 000 from the Bank of Montreal, secured by a mortgage and also guaranteed personally by Neil. Allender sold the property but the purchaser defaulted, with the result that the bank exercised its power of sale under the mortgage. The property was sold at auction for only $100 to the Bank of Montreal, the mortgagee being the purchaser. The bank then sought to recover the shortfall of $45 711 from the original mortgagor or the guarantor,

27. (1983), 4 D.L.R. (4th) 340 (N.B.Q.B.).

Mr. Neil. Neil challenged the sale, claiming that the bank had failed in a duty owed to get the best price possible for the property. The Court found that the bank would lose this right only if they failed to proceed as required under the mortgage covenants or statutes or if they acted negligently in the sale itself. Here, they acted properly. The sale by auction was in no way negligent and they were still entitled to recover the deficit from the defendants. The Judge also pointed out that the bank would not be making a windfall as the defendants still had the right to redeem the property upon payment of what was owed.

The power of sale gives the mortgagee the right to have the property sold in the event of default, and so long as they follow the provisions in the mortgage contract and statutory requirements and do not act negligently in the process of the sale they will retain the right to recover any deficit. This is true even when the amount recovered is nowhere near the actual market value of the property.

On the other hand, in the case of *Bank of Nova Scotia v. Barnard*,[28] the Court found that there was negligence in the sale and refused to allow the mortgagee to recover a deficit owing. The property had been appraised (for a quick sale) at a price below its true market value and sold at that price. There was a duty to take reasonable steps to obtain the market value of the property upon resale, and while that price may not be obtained, a reasonable process should be in place to accomplish that goal. Getting a below-market-value appraisal for a "quick sale" and listing it at that low price amounted to negligence and barred recovery for a deficit on the sale.

The power of sale allows the mortgagee to sell the property to recover on the security. Any shortfall can also be recovered, but only if the sale has been exercised without negligence, making a reasonable attempt to get market value for the property. Do you think that auctions are a reasonable way to attempt to get market value, and that the Bank of Montreal acted reasonably in the first case?

**Where judicial sale excess to mortgagor**

Of course, any excess from the sale after costs must go to the mortgagor or subsequent mortgagees. The remedy of foreclosure, on the other hand, involves the seizure of the property and obtaining title rather than the payment of compensation. When this remedy is used and the property is sold later for more than is owed, the mortgagee is not required to pay over any excess to the mortgagor. In the example used above, Redekop financed the purchase of a home valued at $150 000 with a $90 000 first mortgage with Johal and a $35 000 second mortgage. If because of default Johal initiated the foreclosure process, the second mortgagee could either take over the payments and foreclose himself or ask for an order for judicial sale at the same time that Johal first goes to court to begin the foreclosure process. If the property is sold Johal will recover his $90 000 plus interest and costs, and any excess will go to pay the second mortgagee. In the unlikely event that there is still some left, it will be paid to the mortgagor. But if there is a shortfall and the first mortgage or the second mortgage is only partially covered, those creditors will look to the mortgagor for repayment. In addition to losing his house, Redekop will also be required to pay Johal or the second mortgagee, which may jeopardize any other assets he possesses.

On the other hand, if there is only a first mortgage involved and Redekop defaults, Johal will likely proceed with the foreclosure process, obtaining first an

---

28. (1984), 9 D.L.R. (4th) 575 (Ont. H.C.).

## Reducing **Risk** 15.5

Business and personal leases and mortgages are some of the most intricate of legal relationships, and people are well advised to acquire the services of a lawyer when they enter such relationships. Unfortunately, because these are common transactions, the parties are often less vigilant and do not appreciate just what they are getting into. This becomes especially apparent when there is a default and the complex rights and obligations come into play; in par-ticular, when second and third mortgages are involved. The court's power to sell the property (thus shortening the time given to the debtor to redeem), the speed at which the costs and interest eat up any equity, and the responsibility for any shortfall all combine to create very involved and difficult problems for the parties. Great care should be exer-cised before entering these relationships.

order nisi setting the redemption period and after the expiration of that period obtaining an order absolute of foreclosure. If Johal then sells the property for more than was owing, Redekop cannot recover the excess and Johal will obtain a windfall. To avoid this loss, Redekop will make great efforts to refinance and redeem his title in the property or sell during the redemption period. In most sit-uations, therefore, the property is either redeemed by the mortgagor or sold under the supervision of the court.

Where all payments have been properly made and no default has taken place, the mortgagor is entitled to have that mortgage discharged. A discharge transfer-ring the property to the mortgagor is filed at the appropriate land registry, pro-viding notice that the legal title has been re-conveyed and the mortgagee no longer has any interest in the property. In a land titles system, a notice of dis-charge is filed at the land registry, and the mortgage charge is removed. Depending on the terms of the mortgage agreement, the mortgagor may have the right to pay off the mortgage or a portion of it prior to the expiration of the mortgage term. In many cases, under the terms of the agreement the mortgagor will have to pay an additional amount to compensate the mortgagee for the inter-est that will not be earned because of the early payment, especially if interest rates have gone down. This may be an important consideration when the property is to be sold and the purchaser will not be assuming the mortgage.

**Mortgage is discharged through proper payment**

# Summary

### Personal property

- Tangible, movable property—chattels
- Intangible property—a chose in action
- Chattels can become fixed to real property, but where they are trade or tenant fixtures, they can be removed when the tenant leaves, if this can be done without damage
- Bailment—when property owned by one person is temporarily in the possession of another; imposes an obligation to look after that property; depends on contractual terms or on who benefits from the bailment when there is no contract

### Real property

- Land and things attached to it
- Estate—right to exclusive use of the land
- Fee simple estate—complete ownership of the land

- Life estate—right to the land for life
- Leasehold estate—right to the land for a specific period
- Lesser interests—easements, restrictive covenants, and, in some cases, licences
- Joint tenancy—when one of the parties dies, the other takes the whole property by right of survivorship
- Tenancy in common—separate interests remain apart even with death
- Registration system—only deposited documents affect the title
- Land titles system—government provides a certificate of title that is conclusive proof of the interests affecting the title of the land
- Leasehold estates involve landlord and tenant relationships
- Commercial tenancies are governed primarily by common law, with the rights of the parties set out in the lease
- Residential tenancies have been significantly modified by statute; notice must be given by the landlord to increase rent or terminate a lease; parties have limited obligations to repair or pay security deposits; rent controls are in place in some jurisdictions

## Mortgages

- Title to property transferred to a creditor/mortgagee as security for a loan
- Debtor/mortgagor retains a right to redeem the property
- Equity of redemption can also be mortgaged, creating an equitable second or third mortgage
- Upon default, the creditor seeks a foreclosure order, which ends the mortgagor's right to redeem; second mortgagee usually seeks an order for judicial sale of the property to ensure some payment before the operation of the foreclosure order takes effect

## QUESTIONS

1. Indicate how personal property can become real property. Discuss why a determination of why and when this has happened may be significant.

2. What is a fixture, and under what circumstances can someone other than the owner of real property remove fixtures?

3. Explain what is meant by the saying "finders keepers" in terms of who is entitled to property that has been found.

4. Discuss the different ways in which a bailment may be created and the nature of the duty imposed on the bailee in each circumstance.

5. Distinguish between the obligation placed on a bailee for value and that imposed on a common carrier or innkeeper.

6. What does the purchaser get when he or she buys a house?

7. Distinguish between personal and real property.

8. What is meant by a fee simple estate in land?

9. Explain the rights and obligations of reversion and remainder when discussing a life estate.

10. Explain and contrast life estates and leasehold estates.

11. What is meant by an easement? Give examples and explain why an easement is called a lesser interest in land.

12. Explain the significance of dominant and servient tenements when dealing with easements.

13. What is meant by a restrictive covenant? Under what circumstances will such a covenant be binding on subsequent landowners? How does this relate to a building scheme?

14. Contrast a tenancy in common with a joint tenancy and indicate how one can be changed to another. Why is the distinction important?

15. How can failure to properly register a mortgage or deed affect the initial parties to an instrument in a registration jurisdiction? What happens when an innocent third party becomes involved?

16. How is a leasehold right different from the rights of a resident created under a licence agreement?

17. Under what circumstances must a leasehold interest be evidenced in writing? Why?

18. What is a periodic tenancy? How does it compare with an ordinary lease arrangement? What special problems come into play with periodic tenancies, which are not present with term leases?

19. Explain what is meant by a landlord's obligation to ensure a tenant's "quiet enjoyment."

20. What is meant by mortgage, equity of redemption, and foreclosure? Distinguish between the mortgagor and mortgagee.

21. Compare the terms "equity of redemption" and "equity in property."

22. What is mortgaged when a second or third mortgage is created? Explain how the risk of a second or third mortgagee is greater than that of the first mortgagee.

23. How is the registration of mortgages handled differently under a land titles system of land registry as opposed to the registration system in place in the rest of Canada?

24. Why is the time of registration of a mortgage significant in all jurisdictions in Canada?

-------------------------------------------------------------------

## CASES

### 1. *Punch v. Savoys Jewellers Limited et al.* (1986), 26 D.L.R. (4th) 546 (Ont. C.A.).

Mrs. Punch owned a very valuable antique ring, which was in need of repair. She took it to Savoys Jewellers, who then sent it by registered mail to Walkers, a Toronto jeweller. By the time Walkers had repaired the ring there was a postal strike in progress, so they used Rapidex, a branch of the Canadian National Railway, to transport the ring back to Savoys with their agreement. There was a provision on the bill of lading limiting Rapidex's liability for "negligence or otherwise" to $50. Walker put a $100 value on the bill of lading, when in fact the ring was worth about $11 000. The ring was never delivered, and Mrs. Punch sued Savoys, Walkers, and CN for the loss. CN had no record of what happened and was not able to show whether the ring had been lost or stolen.

Explain the nature of the duty owed by Walker, Savoys, and CN to Mrs. Punch and the likely outcome of her action against them for the recovery of the value of the ring.

## 2. *National Trust Co. v. Chriskim Holdings Inc.* (1990), 66 D.L.R (4th) 213 (P.E.I. S.C.).

A bank and a restaurant were located on adjoining properties. The company operating the restaurant wanted to expand by extending the restaurant into a lane that it thought it owned but which, in fact, was owned by the bank. The restaurant only had a right of way across it. Unwittingly, the owners of the restaurant started the expansion but soon discovered their mistake. They sent a letter to the bank offering to pay an annual rental of $1 per foot. When the bank did not accept this offer, instead of stopping they continued with the construction. The bank sued. The restaurant countersued; it seems a mistake had been made when the bank was built and it encroached slightly onto the property owned by the restaurant. The restaurant had been leasing the property since 1983 and had purchased it in 1987. Before this time, however, the former owner had used that right of way since 1952. The bank building had been at its location since 1967.

Explain the rights and obligations of the parties to each other in these circumstances and the arguments available to each in defending their positions. Would your answer be any different if this had taken place in a land registry jurisdiction rather than in a land titles jurisdiction?

## 3. *Re Ramsay and Heselmann* (1983), 148 D.L.R. (3d) 764 (Ont. H. C. of J.).

The appellant was the owner of a property consisting of 12 furnished rooms, one of which was rented to the respondent. Rent was paid weekly. The respondent failed to make proper payments, and the appellant seized her clothing and personal effects as security for the non-payment of rent. (The *Innkeepers' Act* allows an innkeeper or boardinghouse-keeper to seize goods in this way. The *Landlord and Tenant Act* [R.S.O. 1980, c. 232] does not allow a landlord a similar right.)

The respondent brought this action, applying for a declaration that her goods and personal effects had been wrongfully seized. Explain the arguments on both sides and the likely outcome of the case.

## 4. *North Bay TV & Audio Ltd. v. Nova Electronics Ltd. et al.* (1983), 148 D.L.R. (3d) 764 (Ont. H. C. of J.).

North Bay TV was the landlord, and Nova was the tenant operating a store selling audio and electronic equipment. They entered into a five-year lease agreement in 1981. In 1982, business started to go bad for Nova. They were late paying their rent in April and paid only partial rent in May and June. They failed to pay their rent in July altogether or make even partial payment for their share of the utility services supplied to the building. This caused North Bay's representative, Mr. Stanfall, to call Nova about the lapses. Mr. Smith and Mr. Becock were the principals involved in Nova. Mr. Becock informed Mr. Smith that he understood the landlord was intending to close the premises down, and he suggested to Mr. Smith that they remove as much inventory as possible that evening, which they proceeded to do. They removed three station-wagon loads of electronic goods from the store. While they were doing this, Mr. Stanfall arrived, confronted them, and asked them what they were doing. The tenants told him they were moving out of the premises. When the tenants had left, Mr. Stanfall closed the shop door with a sign saying that the store had been closed by landlord, and anyone taking anything from the premises without permission of the landlord would be prosecuted. The next morning, they changed the locks.

Explain the rights and remedies available to each party. Who has terminated the lease? Who is entitled to any goods still on the premises? Would your answer be affected if you understood that several months later the landlord re-let the premises at a higher rent than they were receiving from Nova?

## 5. *Kiceluk v. Oliverio*, [2001] ABQB 704 (Alta. Q.B.).

Ms. Kiceluk was a tenant and caught her heel in a crack in the cement, causing her to fall down a flight of stairs, severely breaking her ankle. This took place in a common part of the property. She sued the landlord claiming that he had been notified of the damaged cement and had promised to fix it but had not done so. Mr. Kiceluk claimed $55 000 damages from the injury. What should be the outcome of this action?

Would your answer be different had the damaged cement been in the tenant's apartment and the landlord had not been notified about it?

## 6. *Sterne v. Victoria & Grey Trust Co.* (1985) 14 D.L.R. (4th) 193 (Ont. H.C. of J.).

Mr. Sterne owned a hobby farm, with a first mortgage held by Victoria & Grey Trust. Mr. Sterne was unable to make payments when they became due. The mortgagee commenced sale proceedings under their power of sale as set out in the mortgage. They obtained two appraisals, one for $190 000 and the other for $195 000. The mortgagee advertised the property, received an offer of $185 000, and sold it for that price. During this time, Mr. Sterne had listed the property and had received an offer for $210 000, but the offer had conditions and the closing date was several months away, so the mortgagee went ahead with the deal for $185 000.

Explain the rights of the parties in these circumstances. Would your answer be any different if you learned that at the time of the sale, the mortgagee was aware of other appraisals that placed the value of the property as high as $240 000 and also that the property was listed only as "work" property, not as a hobby farm, and then only in the local newspapers?

# 16

# Intellectual Property, Computers, and the Internet

## CHAPTER HIGHLIGHTS

- Forms of intellectual property
- Legal protection of intellectual property
- Electronic technology and its effects on commerce
- The internet—its advantages and drawbacks
- Regulation of the internet
- Legislation affecting electronic commerce

Intellectual property law attempts to balance the protection of the product of a person's mental effort on the one side and the free flow of new and innovative ideas, which stimulate the advancement of the commercial environment, on the other. Its primary focus is on the rights and responsibilities of individuals in relation to ideas, information, and other creative works, and how others use those products of the mind. Often these interests collide dramatically as we enter the digital information age with the explosion of computers, software, and internet technology.

# Intellectual Property

Intellectual property must be contrasted to other forms of personal property. When a chattel is stolen or destroyed, it is no longer available for the use of the original owner. When an idea is taken and used by somebody else, or confidential information is wrongfully communicated to another, the idea or information does not change. It is still available to the original holder, although its value might be considerably diminished.

As computer data storage and internet information transmission expand, intellectual property law has grown significantly in importance. The development of law has not kept pace with this information and technological explosion, but existing laws go a long way in establishing rights and obligations, and many recent changes have been made by both Parliament and the courts.

Most legislation protecting intellectual property is federal, with copyright and patent legislation being exclusively granted to the federal government in the

*Constitution Act (1867)*.[1] Other important federal statutes include the *Trade-mark Act* and the *Industrial Design Act*. Confidential information, trade secrets, and passing-off will also be discussed in this chapter.

## Case Summary 16.1

### Grad Student Finds Thesis Marketed for Profit Online

A Canadian academic surfing the internet was startled and angered to find her master's thesis marketed for US$69.50 on Contentville.com, an American website. Graduate students submit copies of their work to the National Library of Canada when they complete their degrees, often without knowing their work could be sold for profit to others. "I never gave permission for them to use it. It was like it was stolen," the author claimed. In fact, students fill out a form giving the library permission to reproduce their work to facilitate scholarly research. The library in turn contracted with UMI Dissertations Publishing to perform this service and UMI made part of their catalogue available to Contentville. People wishing to purchase contacted Contentville and were turned over to UMI, which sent the requested copy to the buyer and collected the fee.

"We are simply attempting to broaden the access to dissertations," says Bill Savage of UMI. He notes the catalogue was already available to scholarly societies and libraries, as well as to UMI's own website."[2] Since this time, Contentville has agreed to remove Canadian dissertations and theses from their websites.[3]

# Copyright

The federal *Copyright Act*[4] gives the owner of the copyright a monopoly over the use of the created work, prohibiting copying or reproduction of the work without permission. Only the actual work itself is protected, not the ideas or thought behind it. Thus, the actual expression of an idea in a book is protected, but someone else is free to express those same ideas in a different way.

*The work is protected, not the idea*

The federal government has the power to make law with respect to copyright. The *Copyright Act*, originally passed in 1928, has recently undergone significant changes. These changes were required because of technological advances, including the ease of reproducing written, musical, visual, and computer works. Massive copying of books, records, tapes, CDs, videos, and computer programs is now not only possible but also common. This is especially true on the internet—compression software and CD and DVD burners have made the wholesale copying of recorded music so widespread it has seriously affected the viability of the recorded music industry.

## Matters Covered

Only original work that is the product of an artist's or author's own work or skill is entitled to copyright protection. Note that it is the expression that has to be original, not the idea. For example, judges' decisions are compiled into collections such as the *Dominion Law Reports* published by Canada Law Book. The publisher

*To be copyrightable, work must be original and the product of the author's skill*

---

1. *Constitution Act (1867)*, section 91, ss. 22, 23.

2. Adapted from Chris Tenove, *National Post*, Aug. 15, 2000, A4.

3. *Lawyers Weekly*, Vol. 20 No. 16 (Sept. 1, 2000).

4. R.S.C. 1985.

**Table 16.1 Areas Included in the *Copyright Act***

| | |
|---|---|
| **Literary works** | including tables, computer programs, and "literary compilations" such as poems, stories, and articles (books). |
| **Dramatic works** | include shows (movies, videos, television, and theatre) and mime performances, including choreography and scenery. |
| **Musical works** | include musical composition with or without words. |
| **Artistic works** | include paintings, drawings, charts, maps, plans, photos, engravings, sculptures, works of artistic craftsmanship, and architecture. |

*In addition to these works copyright protection has also been extended to*

| | |
|---|---|
| **Performers' performances** | including performances by actors, musicians, dancers, and singers |
| **Sound recordings** | including CDs, tapes, and other methods for reproducing sound. |
| **Communication signals** | such as radio and TV created by a broadcaster |

Note that there is considerable overlap, and someone's creative work might qualify for copyright protection in more than one of these categories.

simply adds headnotes and annotations. The compilation was held to be original work and the service operated by the Law Society of B.C. supplying photocopies of these judgments to lawyers was held to be a violation of the publisher's copyright.[5]

The categories of copyrightable materials have recently been expanded; Table 16.1 summarizes the areas that are now included in the *Copyright Act*.

Basically, copyright is intended to protect the expression of an author's work in any permanent or fixed form. A difficult problem involves whether computer software should be protected by copyright law or by patent. This matter was resolved by the 1988 amendment to the *Copyright Act,* which now specifically provides copyright protection for computer software and hardware. A particular problem with computer programs is the difficulty in distinguishing between what constitutes the idea behind the software and its expression. It is now settled that where one product has the same look and feel in its operation as the other an infringement of copyright has taken place, even where the actual computer code is completely different. Note as well that a specific statute has been enacted to protect the design of the integrated circuit expressed in the computer chip itself.[6] The actual three-dimensional design has to be registered, and the protection granted is for a period of 10 years.

**Computer programs protected**

## Creation

**Copyright comes with creation of work**

In Canada, the creation of the work generates copyright protection automatically. There is no need to register or even publish the work. Still, registration may be wise, since it establishes when the copyright was created and the presumption that the person named in the registration is the owner of the copyright. Although

5. *CH Canadian Limited v. The Law Society of Upper Canada* (2002), 212 D.L.R. (4th) 385 (Fed. C.A.).
6. *Integrated Circuit Topography Act,* S.C. 1990, c. 37.

not specified in the Canadian legislation, there is a practice (following the provisions of the Universal Copyright Convention) of notification of copyright that generally takes the following form:

Copyright © 2004 Pearson Education Canada Inc., Toronto, Ontario

The United States and other countries that are parties to the copyright conventions discussed below recognize valid Canadian copyright, and so registration is not necessary. However, notification as set out above is required; where the copyright is not registered, the remedies available for infringement may be significantly restricted.

For a person to obtain copyright protection in Canada, he or she must be a citizen or resident of Canada or a citizen, subject, or resident of one of the countries that adhere to the *Berne Copyright Convention* or the *Universal Copyright Convention* (UCC)—international agreements that set out common rules of conduct in matters concerning copyright. They will also be protected if their country is a member of the World Trade Organization (WTO). The federal minister can extend this protection to other countries.

Other countries, for example the People's Republic of China, do not have the same traditions of protection of artistic and literary works as in Western countries, and the disregard for intellectual property protection in such countries has been a major stumbling block in the further development of trade relations.

## Ownership

Copyright is usually associated with the author or creator of the work, but where it is done pursuant to employment the employer normally has the copyright. A contractor usually retains copyright, but this is often changed by contract. Once the copyright has been created, the owner can assign or license it (all or in part) to someone else. A court will presume the copyright is held by the creator unless there is evidence to show otherwise. Even when the owner of the copyright has assigned it to someone else, the author will continue to have **moral rights** in the work. This gives the author the right to the integrity of the work; that is, the right to demand that his name continue as author and that the new owner not change the work in such a way as to degrade it and bring harm to the reputation of the author. In 1982, an Ontario court granted an injunction to a respected sculptor when, to celebrate Christmas, Toronto's Eaton Centre put red ribbons around his sculptures of flying geese. Since the 1988 amendments, these moral rights of the authors and artists have been incorporated into the *Copyright Act*. While the Act prohibits the assignment of moral rights, the author of the work can waive them.

**Copyright can be assigned but moral rights retained**

### Case Summary 16.2

### Even Students Are Entitled to Copyright Protection: *Boudreau v. Lin*[7]

Paul Boudreau was a part-time MBA student who was working for a high-tech firm. He wrote a paper for a course based on information gathered there and incorporated suggestions from his professor. The professor and a colleague published the paper under a different title with only a few revisions, naming themselves as authors. Boudreau discovered his paper published in a case book and brought an action for copyright infringement against the professor and the uni-

7. (1997), 150 D.L.R. (4th) 324 (Ont. Gen. Div.).

versity. The court found that the student was the author and holder of the copyright. The Court rejected the professor's claim that the student's name had been omitted in error. The university was deemed to have knowledge of the infringement, and thus shared liability with its employee. The removal of the student's name and changed title blocked the professors' claim of fair dealing. The inclusion of the paper in a case book defeated the university's claim that it was for use in private study. Also, the author's moral rights were infringed, because they had interfered with the integrity of the work. The Court noted, "Plagiarism is a form of academic dishonesty which strikes at the heart of our educational system. It is not to be tolerated from the students, and the university has made this quite clear. It follows that it most certainly should not be tolerated from the professors, who should be sterling examples of intellectual rigour and honesty."

In the academic environment it is not always clear who can claim copyright. This is especially true where university facilities and grants are involved. But in this case there was no doubt that others had taken credit for the student's work. The case shows not only how copyright is established and what is meant by moral rights, but also the narrow scope of the defences of fair dealing and private use. It also gives rise to the question as to what extent students ought to have intellectual property rights in the work they do for credit in university and college programs. What do you think?

Copyright gives the owner control over the work, except for the moral rights, which remain with the author. No one else can perform, copy, publish, broadcast, translate, or otherwise reproduce the work without the permission of the owner of the copyright.

**Copyright holder has complete control over rights for author's life plus 50 years**

This protection extends for the life of the author plus 50 years, with some exceptions, such as photographs and government publications, where the protection is limited to 50 years from the creation of the negative or document. Note that in the United States the protection period is now for life plus 70 years, which will provide added protection for Canadian works being used in the U.S.

Infringing copyright includes situations where a person tries to obtain a benefit from the sale, reproduction, distribution, performance, broadcast, or other commercial use of the work. Plagiarism involving the copying of another's work and claiming authorship is also a violation of copyright. The moral rights of an author are infringed when someone else claims authorship or if the work is mutilated or modified in such a way that the reputation of the author is harmed. Where moral rights have been infringed, the author can seek an injunction or compensation even though someone else owns the copyright, provided the author has not waived his or her moral rights.

**Exceptions**

Quotations from the work that are not extensive and are attributed to the author do not amount to an infringement of copyright. The *Copyright Act* specifically states that fair dealing for the purpose of "research or private study, criticism or review and news reporting" does not infringe copyright.[8] Educational institutions, library archives, and museums are specifically mentioned in relation to this exception. There is considerable debate as to just what these words mean, and certainty will be established only when courts rule on specific practices. It is likely, however, that where the reproduction, even for classroom or study purposes, is so

8. *Copyright Act*, ss. 29, 29.1, and 29.2(2)(a).

extensive as to deprive the author of the market for the product it would be an infringement of the copyright. Teachers can write materials on the board or include them in exams and not infringe the Act. They can also record and keep for a limited period of time radio, newspaper, and television material. Teachers can also project materials on a screen unless commercially available slides are available for that purpose. People who have reading or hearing disabilities can make copies to assist them, such as converting the work to Braille. People can make one backup copy of their computer programs. And, interestingly, anyone can make a recording of music tapes, records, and CDs for their own private use. Royalties are charged on blank tapes and other recording media to compensate artists and producers for this exception.

## Case Summary 16.3

**Copyright Protects Videotapes:** *Tom Hopkins International, Inc. v. Wall & Redekop Realty Ltd.*[9]

The managers of Wall & Redekop were impressed with a set of videotapes titled "How to Master the Art of Listing and Selling Real Estate" that had been prepared by the plaintiff. In 1981, they obtained a used copy of the tapes, made 10 copies, and distributed them to their various offices. When the plaintiff was informed of this, they wrote to Wall & Redekop complaining about the infringement. Wall & Redekop immediately called in the 10 tapes and erased them. The plaintiff was awarded damages, not only for a violation of copyright but also for the tort of "conversion," wherein ownership in something is wrongfully taken over by another.

## Remedies

The normal remedies available in a civil action, including an injunction, are available when a copyright is infringed. Sometimes, an **interlocutory injunction** is given before the actual trial to prevent further damage. This is an interim measure, and a permanent injunction may or may not be granted at trial. Often, the effect of the interim remedy may be so devastating to the offender that no further action need be taken. To obtain an interlocutory injunction, the plaintiff must establish a *prima facie* case that there has been an infringement of copyright and that if the injunction is not granted, irreparable harm will be suffered that could not properly be compensated for by an award of damages at the trial. The **balance of convenience** must also be in the plaintiff's favour. This refers to which side will suffer the greatest damage if the injunction is granted. Where a small business seeks an interim order to stop the production and sales of a much larger operation, it will not be granted if the order would cause that business more damage than the small one would suffer if the injunction were not granted. Courts are generally reluctant to grant interlocutory injunctions.

> Interlocutory injunctions may be granted before trial

Sometimes, a court will issue an order before trial that the offending material be seized. This is called an **Anton Piller order**. This is an *ex parte* procedure, in which the evidence must be seized by surprise before the goods or relevant documentation can be hidden or destroyed. The court will issue such an order only where there is clear and compelling evidence of the infringement of copyright, the danger of significant damage to the plaintiff, and some indication that sur-

> Anton Piller order provides for seizure of goods

---

9. (1985), 20 D.L.R. (4th) 407 (B.C.C.A.).

Schools have a limited right to reproduce works used for study.

**Permanent injunction granted at trial**

**Damages can compensate for loss**

**Accounting requires handing over profits**

**Punitive damages may be available to punish wrongdoer**

**Statutory damages now available**

**Fine and imprisonment available for infringement**

***Criminal Code* may apply**

prise is needed to protect the evidence. The seizure of the offending works before trial is now provided for in the *Copyright Act* itself.[10]

After the trial, one of the most important remedies is the **permanent injunction** prohibiting the production, sale, or distribution of any of the infringing products. If the copyright has not been registered and the defendant were unaware they were violating copyright, the only remedy under the act is an injunction, often with an order to surrender the offending documents. The court may also award a remedy of damages or an accounting. An award of **damages** is calculated to compensate the victim for the losses suffered, including the lost profits that would have been earned had the copyright not been infringed. An **accounting** is often given where it would be difficult to determine what actual damages have been suffered. This remedy requires that any profits made from the sale or rental of the offending product be paid over to the victim, even if this amount exceeds the damages suffered by the plaintiff. The court may also award **punitive damages** in cases of flagrant violation to punish the offender rather than simply to compensate the victim of the infringement. In any case, it must be noted that the limitation period in which an action must be commenced is three years, from the time the person learned of the infringement rather than from when it actually occurred.

One of the purposes of the recent revision of the Act is to make enforcement of its provisions more equitable. To that end, a simplified or summary procedure has been introduced, making enforcement much easier and less costly. In addition, the courts can now in their discretion award statutory damages in the range of $500 to $20 000 simply on the basis of affidavits. One of the serious problems of the old legislation, which is overcome by this provision, was the difficulty of proving actual losses.

In addition to these civil remedies, the *Copyright Act* provides for penalties of up to a million dollars in fines and five years in jail for the most serious cases. The provisions set out in the *Criminal Code*, such as those sections prohibiting theft and fraud, may also apply to infringement of copyright cases.[11]

## Reducing **Risk** 16.1

The victim of copyright infringement should exercise great care when deciding what remedy to seek. An interlocutory injunction may seem attractive, but if the matter is not settled or the action fails at trial the party who obtained the interlocutory injunction may be held responsible for the losses caused to the enjoined business. Where an accounting is granted and the infringer's profits are nil, the award will also be nil even though there may have been considerable damage. The standards of proof are much higher in a criminal case and the prosecutors may not feel there is enough evidence to prove the case. All of these factors must be weighed, including the likelihood of success and the defendant's ability to pay before determining how best to proceed. Of course, the need to protect one's intellectual property may outweigh all of these considerations.

10. *Copyright Act,* s. 38 (1)(b).

11. *Criminal Code*, R.S.C. 1985, c. C-46.

## Case Summary 16.4

### Criminal Conviction under the *Copyright Act*: *R. v. AFC Soccer* [12]

When a manufacturer discovered that knock-off soccer jerseys were being sold on the internet they complained to the RCMP. The source was traced to AFC Soccer, which was producing the offending jerseys and selling them at a much lower price than the originals. The police searched AFC's shop and seized 1118 items of clothing as well as various records and documents. AFC was charged and convicted under section 42(1)(a) of the *Copyright Act,* which provides criminal penalties for copyright infringement. A fine of $45 000, about one-third of the gross revenues, was levied against the infringing company.

It is important to understand that the unauthorized copying of artwork, photographs, computer programs, compact discs, videotapes, or even designs on clothing can result in a criminal conviction as well as copyright infringement even though the original is unaffected.

## The Copyright Board

The *Copyright Act* establishes a board with broad powers to handle disputes between individuals and otherwise supervise and regulate the industry. The board's functions range from setting and reviewing fees and royalties for use of copyright materials to arbitrating disputes. Several associations have been created that represent the owners of copyright when they enter into licensing arrangements with others and to assist in the collection of royalties. SOCAN (Society of Composers, Authors, and Music Publishers of Canada) performs this service in the music industry, and Access Copyright (Canadian Copyright Licensing Agency, formerly CANCOPY) serves a similar function in the literary field, entering into general licensing agreements. They collect royalties and fees for works to be photocopied or digitally reproduced, and pay the funds collected to the authors and publishers. These bodies can also launch civil actions on behalf of their members in the event of copyright infringement.

## Patents

A patent is a government-granted monopoly, giving only the inventor the right to produce, sell, or otherwise profit from a specific invention. Unlike copyright, the patent protection extends to the idea or concept expressed in the invention. To qualify, the invention must be new, in the sense that no one else has been given a patent for it and that it has not been disclosed to the public in Canada or elsewhere more than a year prior to application. This includes disclosure in an academic paper. The invention must also be the original work of the inventor. Thus, a person could not take an invention found in another country and patent it in Canada as his own. The invention must be unique and distinguishable from other products. It must have some utility or perform some useful function. It must also be possible to construct and use it on the basis of the information supplied to the patent office.

**Must be original invention to be patentable**

---

12. (2002), 22 C.P.R. (4th) 369 (Man. P.C.).

### Case Summary 16.5

**Selling Product Was Fatal to Patent:** *Baker Petrolite Corp. v. Canwell Enviro-Industries Ltd.*[13]

Canwell Enviro-Industries developed a chemical formula to sweeten the sour smell associated with "sour gas" natural-gas wells. They started selling the product (W-3053) on December 10, 1987. The following year, on December 23, 1988, they made an application for a patent on the process in the U.S., followed by an application for one in Canada on December 19, 1989. This application was opposed by Baker Petrolite, which had developed a similar product. The Federal Court of Appeal held that they were not entitled to a patent because of disclosure more than a year before the application for the patent. The product had been sold to the public, and although Canwell didn't actually disclose the formula, if a person with the appropriate skills could, by analyzing the product, determine its active components and develop a similar product disclosure had taken place and a patent could not be given.

The case deals with complex engineering data and formulas, but the point made is simple. If you produce and sell a product incorporating a patentable idea that can be discerned though careful examination of the product (reverse engineering), the idea is no longer novel. If that disclosure takes place more than a year prior to the patent application the application will be denied. Do you think that this decision is consistent with the objectives of patent law?

**Theories, concepts, or obvious improvements are not patentable**

You cannot patent a scientific principle or abstract theory, such as Newton's discovery of gravity;[14] nor can you patent obvious improvements to other products, inventions designed for illegal purposes, things that cannot work, and things generally covered by copyright law. But a non-obvious improvement on an already existing invention is patentable. It is clear that lower forms of life such as plants and bacteria are patentable, but until recently there was great debate whether Canada would follow the American approach and allow higher forms of life, such as genetically modified animals, to be patented. The Supreme Court of Canada has now determined that higher life forms cannot be patented in Canada. This case involved a genetically altered mouse with special value in cancer research.[15] There is still a possibility that this decision will be changed by specific statutory amendment to the *Patent Act.*

**What can and can't be patented**

In Canada, as a general rule, computer programs cannot be patented and are now covered by copyright legislation, but such patents have been granted in the United States and may be available in limited situations in Canada in the future. Recently the Americans have allowed business methods patents (BMPs), which create a patent monopoly on a particular process or model of carrying on business. This has had a great impact on innovation, especially where internet businesses are concerned. In Canada there is no right to patent methods of carrying on business as yet, but Canadian firms doing business in the U.S. or even selling products there could be sued for patent infringement for their business practices taking place in Canada. U.S. patents have been issued for business

---

13. (2002), 211 D.L.R. (4th) 696 (F. C. A.).

14. *Patent Act,* R.S.C. 1985, c. P-4, s. 27, ss. 8.

15. *Harvard College v. Canada (Commissioner of Patents)* (2003), 219 D.L.R. (4th) 385 (S.C.C.).

methods including distribution models, inventory management, service delivery models, training methods, financial models, and models for sharing information.

## Creation

Unlike copyright, the patent must be registered before conferring rights on the inventor, and so it is vital that a patent be applied for right away. If someone else beats you to it, you will not only lose the right to patent but also be prevented from producing or otherwise using or profiting from the invention. Employers are entitled to patent the inventions of their employees, and the holder of a patent can assign that patent to others. Joint patents can be obtained when two people have worked on the same invention.

**Patent must be applied for and registered**

The process of obtaining a patent is complex, requiring that patent records in the United States and Canada be searched to see if a patent already exists, and then submitting an application with supporting documentation and the proscribed fee at the appropriate patent office. These documents include a petition, specifications, claims statements, an abstract, and a drawing that set out not only what the invention is supposed to do but also enough information so that someone looking at them could build and use the item. The patent office then assigns an examiner, who may require further submissions from the applicant, and when all conditions have been met the patent will be granted. If there are opposing applications, the patent will be granted to the person who first made an application. This process is usually handled by a registered patent agent with both a legal and an engineering background and may take two or three years to complete.

Pursuant to international agreements, once a Canadian patent has been granted application can be made for patents in other jurisdictions, but priority in those countries will be based on when the application was first made in Canada. The reverse is also true, and the Canadian patent office will grant a patent to a foreign applicant who applies in his or her own country before the Canadian applicant applies here. There is a limited period of time after obtaining the Canadian patent to make an application for a foreign patent, and so this should be done without delay.

**Date of application in own country determines priority**

Once the patent has been issued, the patent number should be put on the manufactured item to which it applies. The use of "patent pending" has no legal effect but the phrase is put on goods to warn that a patent has been applied for. A patent gives its holder a monopoly for a maximum period of 20 years from the date of application, but it requires that the inventor publicly disclose how to make the item in documents that are open to public inspection. Secrecy is surrendered in exchange for the 20-year protection, the idea being that others will be stimulated to produce new inventions because of the disclosure of that information (this is the reason a patent won't be issued on an invention that has already been disclosed). The granting of the patent gives the patent-holder exclusive rights to manufacture, sell, and profit from the invention for those 20 years, and it even protects someone who merely develops an improvement of the product, providing that variation meets the general requirements of a patentable invention, as discussed above.

**Patent grants monopoly for 20 years but requires disclosure**

Because a patent protects the idea rather than its expression, another person would not be able to produce a simple variation of the product without breaching the patent. An infringement of patent may take place by an unauthorized person manufacturing, importing, selling, or otherwise dealing with or using the invention. The patent holder is entitled to the same remedies that would be available in any civil action, including injunction, damages, and accounting, as discussed above under the heading of Copyright.

### Case Summary 16.6

#### How Far Should Patent Protection Go? *Monsanto Canada Inc. v. Schmeiser*[16]

Using genetic engineering, Monsanto developed a specific strain of canola seed that was resistant to Roundup, a herbicide also produced by Monsanto. Farmers planting the seeds would also use Roundup, which would kill all other plant forms leaving the modified canola plants unscathed. Part of the agreement was that farmers would purchase new seeds every year and not plant seeds from last year's crop.

Mr. Schmeiser did not purchase his seeds from Monsanto, but noticed that some of his own crop was resistant to Roundup. He collected seeds from that section and planted them the next year, giving his entire crop this resistance to Roundup. Through tests on the canola crop grown on Schmeiser's farm (likely through illegally obtained samples), Monsanto determined that his plants contained the genetically engineered genes they had developed and sued him for patent infringement. Even though Schmeiser used seeds growing on his field, the Federal Court of Appeal held that he was infringing on the Monsanto patent and ordered an injunction and damages.

Had he simply collected seed from his entire crop and planted in the normal way he may have been okay, but he targeted the seeds that were specifically resistant to Roundup. That violated the Monsanto patent and it didn't matter how the Roundup-resistant canola had originally gotten on his property or even whether he actually used the herbicide Roundup to take advantage of it. It also didn't matter in this civil action whether Monsanto had gathered the evidence illegally. The Court could rely on it, and did.

Do you think that justice was done in this case? Hasn't Schmeiser suffered from this intrusion? Are there other legal arguments that Schmeiser could rely on against Monsanto? Note that this case has been appealed to the Supreme Court of Canada.

Often, the holder of the patent does not have the resources to manufacture or otherwise exploit the invention and will license its manufacture to another company. Where an important invention is involved, there is provision for compulsory licences to be granted with the payment of royalties, even over the objections of the inventor.

It should be noted that by a 1987 amendment to the *Patent Act* drug manufacturers were given more control over the production and sale of their products. This stopped the practice of competitors capitalizing on the research and development of those manufacturers and producing much cheaper "generic drugs." A

### Reducing Risk 16.2

A business should take great care to protect its intellectual property in any form. Whether a process or product is developed by an independent contractor, a consultant, or an employee, a provision in the contract creating that relationship should designate who is entitled to the patent copyright or other form of intellectual property developed. Otherwise, when the relationship ends it is quite possible to find that process being sold to and used by a competitor.

---

16. (2002), 218 D.L.R. (4th) 31 (F.C.A.).

Patent Medicine Prices Review Board was also established with broad powers, including the power to reduce the sale price of patented medicines and pharmaceuticals.[17] The period of patent protection in this area has also been extended to 20 years.

## Trademarks

A **trademark** is any term, symbol, design, or combination of these that identifies a business service or product and distinguishes it from a competitor. Registered trademarks are protected by the federal *Trade-marks Act*.[18] Examples of protected trademarks are such words as "Kodak" and "Xerox"; symbols such as the arm and hammer used on that company's baking soda box; combinations of words and symbols, such as the apple logo on computers; and even the distinctive design of a product's container, such as the Coca-Cola bottle. Trademarks also include the special marks used by some organizations, such as the Canadian Standards Association, to indicate quality or certification. A business is normally worth much more than the total of its tangible assets. Its reputation and ongoing relations with customers and product identification are known as **good will**. The name and trademarks associated with the business are to a great extent the embodiment of that good will. The object is to protect the value of the good will and prevent people from misleading others by using the trademark words or symbols for their own purposes and to prevent the trademark's value from being diminished through association with inferior products.

Symbols or designs of business protected as trademarks

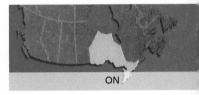

An unregistered trademark is entitled to protection under the common law, but for a trademark to be protected under the Act it must be registered. As part of the registration process, it is published in the *Trade-mark Journal*, and if someone feels that it does not qualify, they can oppose the registration. Once registered, the trademark gives its owner an exclusive right to use it throughout Canada for 15 years (renewable). The registration also establishes a presumption of ownership, so that in an action for infringement a defendant claiming otherwise must produce strong evidence to that effect.

**Purpose to protect consumer deception**

**Registration protects trademark**

A trademark can be any word, design, symbol, or packaging that distinctively identifies a business or product. It cannot be obscene or scandalous or just a sound or a colour, although a distinctive colour may be part of the trademark. Nor can it be anything that resembles the insignia, crests, or other symbols of royalty, the government, or government agencies, such as the RCMP; service organizations, such as the Red Cross; or even names, portraits, or signatures of individuals, without their consent. There is also a prohibition against using any marks, symbols, or designs that resemble a well-known one, which would cause confusion with the products or services of that other body. Normally, simple surnames cannot be registered, and so people can use their own surnames in their business without fear of violation. Only where the name has become associated with another product, such as McDonald's hamburgers or Campbell's soup, will the applicant run into problems. And, traditionally a word that is descriptive of what the product is used for, such as "food" or "cleaner," can't constitute the trademark because it does not distinguish the product. This can cause great difficulty with domain names on the internet, which have to have that characteristic

17. *Patent Act Amendments*, R.S.C. 1985 (3d Supp.), c. 33.

18. R.S.C. 1985, c. T-13.

to assist the browser. Also, a trademark can't be a functional aspect of the design of the product. For example, the studs on the tops of Lego blocks are functional in that they are used to connect one block to another. Because they were functional rather than a distinctive mark the federal court refused to recognize them as an unregistered trademark.[19]

## Restrictions

### Case Summary 16.7

**What's In a Name?** *Upper Beach Village Ltd. v. Upper Beach Village Estates Ltd.*[20]

The plaintiff carried on a real estate business as "Upper Beach Village Limited," and a competitor started a similar business in the area. It was at first called "Upper Beach Village Estates Limited"; after complaints from the plaintiff, this was changed to "Upper Beach Estates." Still not satisfied, the plaintiff brought a passing-off action seeking an interlocutory injunction to prevent the defendant from using that name. The Judge found that the term "upper beach" was descriptive of the area in which they were working rather than distinctive, and refused to grant an injunction. The injunction was refused also on the grounds that there was no evidence that the plaintiff would suffer any irreparable harm if the injunction were not granted. Note that this was a passing off-action rather than a breach of trademark, but the principles are the same. Do you think that the name of the original company deserved more protection?

### Case Summary 16.8

**Court Rules Lexus Can Be Both a Luxury Car and a Fruit Juice**[21]

Lexus Foods, a Quebec company that produces canned fruit and vegetables, has won a legal battle against Toyota Motor Corp. The car manufacturer went to the Federal Court of Canada to stop the Quebec company from using the name Lexus, arguing that most Canadians would associate the name with its luxury car.

The Federal Court of Appeal had to decide whether the registrar had been correct in registering Lexus Foods trademark despite Toyota's opposition. The Court decided that people were unlikely to confuse a can of fruit juice with a luxury car. "It is hard to see that anyone about to buy some of the canned fruit juice of the appellant would even entertain the thought that the Japanese automobile manufacturer of Lexus was the source of this product," Justice Allen Linden wrote in his reasons for the Court's decision. He also commented that trademark protection must be related to "certain wares or services" because confusion is less likely when the products in question are markedly different.

**Trademark lost through common usage**

Trademarks can lose their status through common use. Aspirin, trampoline, Kleenex, and linoleum are examples of terms that have lost their unique status in either Canada or the United States because people use them to describe the general type of product.

---

19. *LEGO Canada v. Ritvik Holdings* (2002), FCT 585 (Fed Crt. T.D.).

20. (2000), as reported in *Lawyers Weekly*, Vol. 20, May 2000 (Ont. S.C.).

21. *Toyota Jidosha Kabushiki Kaisha v. Lexus Foods Inc.*, [2001] 2 F.C. 15.

Applying for trademark registration is a complicated process requiring the services of an expert, and, once registered, there is an obligation to use the trademark. Failure to do so can result in the loss of the trademark through abandonment. Also, it is common practice whenever the trademark appears to mark it with the symbol "®", indicating that the trademark has been registered. An unregistered trademark can be marked with "TM."

The object of trademark protection is to preserve the value of the good will associated with it by preventing others from using the mark to mislead others into thinking they are dealing with the owner of the trademark when they are not. To enforce that right, the owner must show not only that they own the copyright but also that the public would likely be confused by the wrongful use of the trademark causing damage to the owner.

If the action to protect a trademark is successful, the types of civil remedies available are the standard ones, discussed under copyrights and patents. A very effective remedy in the appropriate circumstances is an order giving the owner of the trademark custody of the offending goods. An action can be brought in the federal court when the infringed trademark has been properly registered under the Act, or the trademark can be enforced in the provincial courts whether or not it has been registered.

**Remedies same as copyright infringement**

In addition to the federal *Trade-marks Act*, this area is also covered by common law in the form of a passing-off action. A **passing-off action** is founded in tort and prevents a person from misleading the public into thinking it is dealing with some other business or person when it is not. The court can order compensation be paid or that the offending conduct stop. This remedy is available even when an unregistered trademark is involved.

**Common law passing-off action gives similar protection**

For a passing-off action to succeed, it is necessary to establish that the public was likely to be misled. The plaintiff must show that the offending party used its mark, name, or other feature associated with its business in association with its own operation, causing confusion in the minds of the public with at least the potential of causing damage to the owner of the copyright. It would be an actionable passing-off for an independent hamburger stand operator to put golden arches in front of his place of business so that people would assume they were part of the McDonald's chain. But if a person were to use an attractive logo developed by someone else but not yet registered or used in association with any business, a passing-off action would not succeed because the logo had not become associated with any business and the public could not be misled. Note that if the trademark is registered that is a complete defence to a passing-off action.[22]

**Public must be misled**

## Industrial Designs

Registering a unique shape, pattern, or ornament under the federal *Industrial Design Act* can protect a unique design or pattern that distinguishes a manufactured article, such as the Coca-Cola bottle.[23] To be protected, the design must be registered within one year of being published, and every item (or label or packaging) should be marked with the letter "D" enclosed in a circle and the name of the registered owner, or its normal abbreviation. Failure to mark the item in this way will limit remedies for infringement to an injunction if the defendant did not know of the registration. Most products with a distinctive shape or pattern can be

*Industrial Design Act— reproduced artistic designs must be registered*

---

22. *Molson Canada v. Oland Breweries Ltd.* (2002), 214 D.L.R. (4th) 473 (Ont. C.A.).

23. *Industrial Design Act*, R.S.C. 1985, c. I-9.

## Reducing Risk 16.3

Intellectual property is fast becoming the most important asset of many businesses. Companies, not realizing the value or potential of these assets, often fail to properly protect or exploit them. Some large companies have discovered they have untapped resources in their trademarks and other intellectual property that they have not taken advantage of because they were not directly related to their primary business objectives. Even where companies license or otherwise deal in software and other intellectual property assets they often fail to keep track or do proper audits and therefore lose significant revenue and royalties. As businesses realize the importance and value of intellectual property, more resources will be devoted to protecting and exploiting it. The right to use such resources is often abused by others. Outsiders often manage to register a business's domain name or logo—or even its business concept—and then try to sell them back for exorbitant prices. A company's exclusive right to a logo can also be lost through lack of use or not exercising proper control over its use. It is vital that businesses turn their attention to their intellectual property resources, determining the extent of those resources and taking steps to protect and exploit them.

registered and will receive protection for a period of 10 years, provided all the requirements of the Act are met.

The Act is intended to protect attractive and distinctive patterns or shapes, as opposed to useful ones. In 1964, in a case before the Exchequer Court, a uniquely designed sofa was deemed to be protected by an industrial design registration.[24] As with copyrights, patents, and trademarks, the product involved must be original and not a copy of some product already on the market, and the resulting interest can be assigned to others. Many of the unique designs appearing on computer displays, such as the appearance of a particular icon, may best be protected under this statute.

## Confidential Information

Confidential information is given in circumstances where it is clear that the information is intended to remain confidential and not be disclosed. In business, it may be necessary that confidences be kept by insiders, such as managers, investors, and employees, as well as outsiders, such as contractors, consultants, and suppliers. The disclosure of confidential information can prove as devastating to a company as interference with other forms of intellectual property, and so its protection is a vital concern of business. For information to be confidential it must not be generally known and not already disclosed to others. In fiduciary and

**Duty to keep confidence**

other trust relationships, there is a common law duty not to disclose such information or to use it for personal benefit. Such a duty usually arises because of a special relationship, such as principal and agent, partnership, employer and employee or contractor, business and consultant, or between officers and their corporation. The duty not to disclose or misuse confidential information is not restricted to fiduciary relationships. It can also arise in other situations, for example pursuant to express or implied contracts between the parties, as was the situation in Case Summary 16.9.

---

24. *Cimon Ltd. v. Benchmade Furniture Corp.* (1964), 1 Ex. C.R. 811.

## Case Summary 16.9

### A Drink by Any Other Name: *Cadbury Schweppes Inc. v. FBI Foods Ltd.*[25]

Cadbury Schweppes

Shares sold to

Duffy-Mott

Licensing agreement (supplied formula and some ingredients)

Caesar Canning

Supplied formula and
Some ingredients

Contracted with FBI to produce product in the rest of Canada

FBI Foods

(Cadbury cancels contract and then Creaser and FBI develop competing product)

Caesar Canning contracted to produce Clamato juice for Duffy-Mott in Canada. They then contracted with FBI Foods to produce the product in parts of Canada where they did not operate. The contract with Duffy-Mott included a term not to produce a similar product for five years after the agreement was terminated. Duffy-Mott provided a recipe to Caesar Canning and FBI Foods for the juice and certain pre-packaged herbs and spices needed to produce the unique flavour.

Cadbury Schweppes bought out Duffy-Mott and terminated the agreement. Caesar Canning and FBI Foods had an employee develop a replacement product called Caesar Cocktail, which the court determined copied the Clamato juice recipe. "It is beyond doubt that without the formula and process information about Clamato, Mr. Nichlason could not have developed Caesar Cocktail personally. He did not have the necessary skills." Even though they could have developed their own product within the 12 months notice they were given, they chose instead to copy the Clamato recipe. The Court found that the information in question was confidential; that it had been communicated in confidence; and that the party to whom it was communicated had misused it. These three elements established that a breach of confidence had taken place.

The Supreme Court of Canada decided that given the long delay (11 years) and the relative unimportance of the confidential information, an award of damages (based on 12 months' production) was a more appropriate remedy than the permanent injunction ordered by the lower court.

This case shows what constitutes a breach of confidential information. The information was given in a manner that indicated it was intended to remain confidential, so there is an obligation to keep it so. The case also provides an interesting insight into the way the court determines appropriate remedies.

One of the most significant legal settlements in Canada arose out of such a duty by LAC Minerals Ltd. not to use information obtained in confidence from International Corona Resources Ltd. The case is very complicated but, in essence, Corona had obtained land claims in the Hemlo District of northwestern Ontario. Representatives of LAC entered into discussions with representatives of Corona with the prospect of a joint venture or partnership. In the process of

---

these discussions, information was given in confidence to LAC to the effect that Corona did not own the surrounding gold claims but was in the process of negotiating for them. When negotiations broke down between LAC and Corona, LAC independently purchased the surrounding claims and made huge profits from the resulting mines. The court held that this was a violation of the duty imposed on LAC not to disclose or use the information for its own benefit, as a result of the special circumstances in which it was obtained. A trust relationship had been established and the information gained because of it was intended to remain confidential. When the information was used for LAC's gain at Corona's expense, it was a violation of that duty of confidentiality.[26] In both the *LAC Minerals* case and the *Cadbury* described in Case Summary 16.9, the courts found that the duty to keep information confidential arose when information was disclosed in circumstances that showed it was to remain confidential. The unauthorized use of that information was a breach of that duty of confidentiality.

## Trade Secrets

**Duty of confidentiality covers trade secrets as well**

A **trade secret** is a particular kind of confidential information that gives a businessperson a competitive advantage. Customer lists, formulas or processes, patterns, jigs, and other unique features unknown to competitors are trade secrets. Successful actions for the wrongful disclosure of trade secrets have been brought in such varied matters as recipes for fried chicken and soft drinks, formulas for rat poison, methods to flavour mouthwash, processes for making orchestral cymbals, and even the techniques prescribed in a seminar to help people quit smoking. A trade secret has the additional requirement that it be valuable to the business and not readily available to any other user or manufacturer. Customer lists available through government publication cannot be classed as trade secrets, nor can a process involved in the manufacturing of a product that is plainly discoverable simply by examining or disassembling the product.

It should be noted that it is the conveying of the private information that is wrongful. There is no proprietary right in the idea or information itself. If Deng operated a company manufacturing tiddlywinks and had a secret process by which they could be produced more cost-effectively, which he failed to patent, and one of Deng's employees were to give that information to a competitor, it would be a wrongful disclosure of a trade secret. But if the competitor were to develop the same or a similar procedure independently, Deng would have no complaint, since he has no proprietary right in the idea or process.

**Employees must not disclose trade secrets or confidential information**

While an employee may be required either expressly or by implication in the employment contract not to disclose trade secrets and confidential information that he or she acquires in the process of employment, the employee can use the general skills and knowledge he or she gains on the job in another employment situation. An employee working in a guitar-manufacturing factory who acquires the skills of a luthier would not be expected to refrain from using any of those skills if he or she were to work for another manufacturer. However, specific processes or jigs used to make guitars might qualify as a trade secret. It is sometimes difficult to draw the line, and in such circumstances it would be wise for the first manufacturer to include a **restrictive covenant** in the employment contract (a non-competition clause).

26. *LAC Minerals Ltd. v. International Corona Resources,* as reported in *The Globe and Mail,* November 19, 1986.

Although the courts are reluctant to enforce such covenants against employees, if the covenant is reasonable, and limited to an appropriate time and area, it may be enforceable. At the least, it will likely discourage the employee from seeking subsequent employment with a competitor. In any case, it is good policy to specifically include prohibitions and consequences in an employment contract dealing with the disclosure of confidential information and other forms of intellectual property of the employer. Consultants and other outside contractors should also be required to sign such an agreement.

From a practical point of view, the owner of secret information can best maintain its confidentiality by informing the employee or other confidant that he or she is in a position of confidence and is expected to keep the information private. It is good policy to require them to sign a non-disclosure statement with respect to that specific information. Where practical, this can be incorporated onto the envelope or file folder containing the information, with the requirement that all who work with that material sign for it below the non-disclosure statement. It is now common for businesses using co-op students on special projects in conjunction with their colleges or universities to also require such agreements.

**Employees, consultants, and contractors should sign non-disclosure agreements**

It is important to specify what information is confidential and what is not. Even the most honest employee can innocently disclose such information if he or she does not know it is confidential. No liability will be imposed for the disclosure of information if a person could not have been expected to know it was intended to be confidential. Steps should also be taken to minimize the number of people to whom the information is given or who have access to it, and to mark all distributed copies "Confidential."

**Specify what is confidential**

Care should be taken not to take this too far. If too much is marked confidential, the notification loses its effect. In addition, a person cannot be accused of wrongful disclosure of information if it has been widely distributed and is no longer confidential. It should also be noted that while in Canada the law related to trade secrets is founded on common law and equity, in some parts of the United States statutes have been passed to govern this area (*Trade Secrets Act*). Whenever those jurisdictions are involved, care should be taken to be aware of and comply with the appropriate statutes.

## Remedies

Where someone wrongfully discloses information causing harm, the normal remedies of injunction, damages, and accounting discussed above may be available. The court, however, is reluctant to grant an injunction that will prevent an employee from earning a living, unless it is clear that the injunction is necessary to prevent the disclosure of confidential information. This usually happens when the employee goes to work for a competitor. Damages or an accounting are also

**Disclosure must harm confider**

**Remedies similar to copyright infringement**

---

### Reducing **Risk** 16.4

When a business has trade secrets and other forms of confidential information to protect, it should take great care to impress upon their employees and those they do business with the importance of keeping it confidential. It is vital to make employees, consultants, and outside contractors aware of their obligation of confidentiality in employment and service contracts as well as policy manuals and other forms of reminders. It is also important to identify just what is to be kept confidential. Even the most loyal employee cannot be expected to keep a confidence that he does not know is a secret. Employees should again be reminded of their obligations with respect to confidentiality when their employment comes to an end.

available when confidences have been breached in this way. Even punitive damages have been awarded. Whether the confidant used the information personally or passed it on to someone else who used it to the detriment of the first party, either or both offending parties can be sued.

**Non-disclosure provisions in employment contracts**

**Suing for inducing breach of contract**

Contract and tort law may be used to give increased protection to the various forms of intellectual property. Non-disclosure provisions in employment and service agreements will provide grounds for remedies such as dismissal, damages, accounting, or injunction in the event of breach. While it may not be worth the trouble to seek damages from an employee, when the employee has been enticed away and persuaded to disclose the information to a rival business the employer can sue the competitor for the tort of inducing breach of contract. Although this tort was first developed to prevent one employer from luring away the employee of another, it has been expanded to many different kinds of contractual relationships and even to some relationships not based on contract. To succeed in such an action, the plaintiff is not required to establish malice on the part of the defendant, but it must be clear that the interference was intentional.

# Computers and the Internet

The internet has established an attractive new medium for business that is international in scope and almost unlimited in its potential. It is used and exploited for positive and negative purposes by companies and individuals alike. Laws and regulatory processes are working hard to catch up with an area that has been marked by phenomenal growth. Many argue that the internet should be left unfettered by laws and regulation so that it might be free to realize its vast potential. But after 15 or so years, the attempts at self-regulation are seen as a failure and there is considerable demand that some form of formal controls be imposed.

**Formal regulation of the internet required**

Canada's Chief Justice Beverley McLachlin remarked that the internet has operated outside the scope of the law, and, "If we are to use these modern 'outlaws' with confidence and safety and realize their enormous potential for increasing world prosperity, we must find ways to bring them within the protective regulatory umbrella of the law." She went on to say that combating computer fraud and hacking requires countries to coordinate their legal approaches. "There is but one alternative—international co-operation backed up by international law."[27]

Creating laws to regulate the internet presents some unique challenges that have yet to be overcome. Many of them are related to the intellectual-property topics discussed earlier in this chapter, but before we revisit them it is important to discuss more generic business concerns. One of the greatest problems relates to jurisdiction. You will recall from our examination of contracts that business relationships are affected by the location of the parties and when and where a contract was made. The internet has further blurred those markers. Another difficulty with the internet is that often the identity of the person or business being dealt with is uncertain. Also, the devices to protect consumers from unscrupulous business dealings or to guarantee payment from people who benefit from another person's ideas or a business's products are inadequate or non-existent. The internet provides access to a wealth of information; so, another important

---

27. Schmitz, Cristin, "McLachlin calls for regulation of the Internet," *Lawyers Weekly*, Vol. 20 No. 2 (May 12, 2000).

question is how to protect the rights to that information. Because the technology has the means to store and replicate data, questions of privacy and security are also pressing. Existing laws go a long way to establish rights and obligations for the parties doing business online, but the protection and enforcement of those rights can be an insurmountable problem. There is no doubt that there is a need to regulate the use of electronic technologies; while they have the power to do much good, they can also wreak havoc if left unchecked. In the rest of this chapter we will discuss the issues related to electronic commerce and the laws that have been enacted in Canada to regulate the area, and also will suggest some areas where more regulation is needed. As Chief Justice McLachlin, referring to the internet, further affirmed: "People can get hurt, without legal recourse. Business transactions may fail, without remedy. Ultimate uncertainty, the great threat to economic development—looms in prospect."[28] Electronic commerce is a broad topic; we will focus primarily on the internet and related matters.

**Lack of enforcement a major problem**

## Implications for Tort Law

### Defamation

Most of the concerns related to the internet can be examined in the context of topics already discussed in the text and applied to this new medium of communication. Because the internet provides direct and inexpensive access to a massive audience, torts related to the spoken word such as deceit, negligent misstatement, and defamation are primary concerns. A major contributor to the problem is that there is no intervener (editor or publisher) to monitor the communication; people can say whatever they want, however they want to say it. We must also distinguish between individual-to-individual communications (email) and those published on a broader scale, such as in chat rooms or on websites generally. Where the communication is found to be defamatory, the first question to be determined is which rules will apply. If communication over the web qualifies as broadcasting, the defamation even where communicated orally would be considered libel rather than slander, since most provinces have enacted legislation to that effect. In Ontario such internet communication to mass audiences has been likened to television or radio and determined to be broadcasting. Justice Helen Pierce of the Ontario Superior Court declared, "I conclude therefore that placing material on the internet, via a website, where it may be accessed by a large audience, constitutes broadcasting within the meaning of the *Libel and Slander Act.*"[29]

**Defamation on the internet is libel**

Thus, if the information is in the form of an online newspaper or journal the rules of libel will apply, but if the communication is between two individuals, as in an email message or vocal communication, there is still some question as to whether this will be considered libel or slander. Another problem relates to whom an injured party can sue. If the author is known and lives in the same jurisdiction there is little difficulty, but where the author is unknown, uses a false name, or resides in another jurisdiction with different rules, where can you sue? If you don't have access to the author, can you sue the service provider or website operator for defamation? What happens where an offensive email is intercepted and sent to others? It is now clear that an internet service provider (ISP) can be

**ISP can be forced to disclose source**

28. *Ibid.*

29. *Bahlieda v. Santa,* [2003] O.J. No. 1159 (Ont. S.C.).

forced to disclose the source of such material,[30] but even that may not be helpful where they are in a different jurisdiction or without resources. It is likely that these intermediaries will be liable for the defamation only if they encouraged the offending behaviour, or if they knew or ought to have known of it and failed to remove it after notification.

**ISP will be liable only where they fail to remove after notification**

### Case Summary 16.10

**When Can a Court Hear a Case Involving Defamation on the Internet?**
*Dow Jones v. Gutnick;[31] Young v. New Haven Advocate*[32]

Two recent cases illustrate the problems when dealing with defamation over the internet. In *Dow Jones v. Gutnick*, Gutnick sued in Australia, where he resided, for defamation in an article published by Dow Jones over the internet, originating in New Jersey. The High Court agreed with Gutnick that since the article was read and the damage to his reputation was done in Australia that was the appropriate place to sue. In *Young v. New Haven Advocate*, a U.S. appeal court decided essentially the opposite. In that case, Young, a prison warden residing and working in Virginia, brought an action in that state against the *New Haven Advocate* for publishing a defamatory article over the internet, originating in Connecticut. The Court held that the fact that the defamed person lived and worked in Virginia and his reputation was damaged there was not enough. There also had to be some evidence that the offending party did something to focus on Virginia readers (targeting), and since this wasn't proven they declined to take jurisdiction. It will be interesting to watch the direction taken by Canadian courts.

### Nuisance

Although the courts have been reluctant to create new categories of torts, they have been willing to provide remedies where an already established type of tort is committed in some new way. For example, in the case of *Motherwell v. Motherwell*,[33] the Alberta court found that a nuisance had been committed even though the interference was perpetrated from a distance over the telephone. It is likely that the same will hold true for the internet and courts will be willing to expand existing tort law to encompass these new technologies, or statutes will be passed to expand or modify the common law where current tort law proves inadequate. This has already happened with respect to the law of defamation (discussed above) and breach of privacy, which has been made an actionable tort in several jurisdictions.

**Current tort law likely to adapt to new technology**

### Negligence and Misrepresentation

While defamation may be the obvious concern for regulators, there are many other ways that users can be injured by improper communications over the internet. Where careless recommendations, advice, or tips are given injury can result. Who will be responsible? Now, any fool, charlatan, or well-meaning humanitarian can give advice over the internet without any check on its validity. Whether this

**Advice may be unreliable on internet**

---

30. *Irwin Toy Limited v. John Doe* (2000), 12 C.P.C. (5th) 103 (Ont. S.C.).

31. [2002] H.C.A. 56 (H.C. Aust.).

32. *Young v. New Haven Advocate,* [2002] CA4—QL 2856 (U.S. Court of Appeals, Fourth Circuit).

33. (1976), 73 D.L.R. (3d) 62 (Alta. C.A.).

advice relates to prescription drugs, diet, financial tips, natural remedies, or household hints, there is no regulation and no test with respect to reliability. It is likely that the adage "buyer beware" is even more applicable to internet resources, and consumers will have to use a healthy dose of skepticism and seek additional opinions before relying on the information obtained there. The principles of misrepresentation and negligent misstatement will apply to the internet just like any other form of communication, but the problems of jurisdiction and whom to sue will cause the same kind of formidable obstacles. From a business point of view, professionals dispensing information should include disclaimers, specific instructions for use, and restrictions. Liability may be avoided by establishing a process for creating a contract that lists restrictions and disclaimers. People using the information should be required to indicate their agreement with the instructions and restrictions. Still, there will be an expectation that the information will be accurate and kept reasonably current, and where injury is caused by outdated or inaccurate information liability may still be imposed.

**Disclaimers may help protect business**

## Product Liability

Companies that sell their products over the internet will still be held liable under the law of contract or negligence if that product causes injury. If the purchaser is the injured party they can sue the seller in contract. If someone else is injured a negligence action against the manufacturer would be appropriate. In many jurisdictions consumer protection legislation has been passed allowing even non-purchasers to sue sellers or manufacturers for breach of contract, as was discussed in Chapter 9. The problem with internet transactions is again determining jurisdiction. If the injured party must sue in a distant or third-world country it is doubtful that it would be worth the trouble.

**Injured party can sue for negligence**

**Product liability rules will apply to internet purchases**

**Problem will be where goods are sold and manufactured**

# Internet Transactions

Most internet transactions involve contracts, and their validity should not be affected by the fact that they were made over the internet. But internet transactions do create some special problems. An advertisement is normally just an invitation to treat, but if the terms are complete and specific and provision is made for the web surfer to click on a button on the screen to accept those terms and make the purchase, it will likely qualify as an offer. If the retailer wants the advertisement to remain an invitation, they must make it clear in the advertisement that it is merely an invitation to treat. They might want to do this to retain control over the process, or to make the website more passive in order to avoid being found to be carrying on business in a particular jurisdiction and being subject to that jurisdiction's law.

## Consensus

An offer accepted by email or on a website will also be effective so long as the basic requirements of acceptance are met. A purchaser of a product, whether in a store or online, will be bound only by those terms of the agreement of which he has notice. When purchasing software in a store it is common to find the actual product sealed in shrink-wrap, which when opened indicates acceptance of the terms set out on the package itself. When a person buys software over the internet, or the licence to use it, the purchaser is usually required to indicate that they have read and accepted the seller's terms and conditions before accepting. Clicking the "I Accept" button is the equivalent of removing the shrink-wrap. This

**Clicking "I Accept" button accepts terms**

Internet ad with "click-wrap" may be offer

is called "click-wrap," and the contract is binding as soon as that button is clicked. When a product has been ordered, there is now a binding contract and it remains for delivery to be made by the supplier. Where software is involved, it is usually downloaded as soon as the "I Accept" button is clicked. Unlike other products, software is usually provided in the form of a licence rather than a purchase. This gives the customer a limited right of use and by following this process the seller has a remedy if the purchaser produces unauthorized copies or otherwise misuses the product. The buyer must take care to read these terms and understand them before accepting.

Postbox rule will likely not apply to online communications

Another problem relates to the application of the postbox rule. As you will recall from Chapter 5, if it is appropriate to answer by mail an acceptance is effective when and where posted. This was an exception to the rule that an acceptance had to be received to be effective. The courts have not been willing to extend this exception to instantaneous forms of communication such as telephone, telex, and fax. But what of email and web-based communications where there can be some delay before transmission or reading? It is doubtful that the courts will extend the postbox rule to these forms of communication either. Recent statutes in various jurisdictions provide that such communication will be effective when it reaches the information system of the recipient, even though there may be some time before it is actually read. These problems can be avoided by the retailer or other businessperson specifying in the offer or website advertisement that an acceptance will not be effective until received, no matter what form of communication is used, and also specifying the law of which jurisdiction will apply to the transaction.

## Capacity

Difficult to be sure whom you are dealing with over the internet

It is also not possible when using online communications to determine the capacity of the person with whom you are dealing. A business may not even be incorporated as claimed. Children and people with limited mental faculties often have access to computers and the internet. For this reason it is particularly important that buyers beware and sellers include appropriate restrictions and disclaimers.

## Writing

Statutes to make electronic document equivalent to written ones

Another problem arises in those few contracts needing a written record or signature. Requiring a written record is of course always a good policy, and, while electronic records can be easily altered, sophisticated methods have been created to try to ensure the authenticity of electronic signatures and evidence. Where actual writing is required this must be generated separately from the internet transaction. Many jurisdictions have passed legislation making electronic communication the equivalent to written documents, and some have adopted processes for providing electronic identification. Many land registries have created computer databases of their registration system that now allow lawyers to transfer properties and register interests online. Saskatchewan has adjusted the fees charged to reflect the replacement of the former labour-intensive system with a less costly electronic one. In many jurisdictions, however, it is still necessary to print a document, sign it, and return it to the other party to provide the required evidence in writing. This problem may be solved eventually simply by redefining the term "writing" and the definition of "signature." The federal *Personal Information Protection and Electronic Documents Act* sets out a definition of an electronic signature and how it may be used in federal government documents; it may well

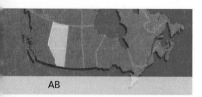

AB

become the model for similar legislation recognizing electronic or digital signatures in the provinces.[34]

Several provinces have adopted the provisions of the *Uniform Electronic Commerce Act* (UECA), a model statute created by the Uniform Law Conference of Canada. This model has no legal status until adopted in whole or in part by provinces. Ontario and Nova Scotia have adopted variants of this statute and now have provisions in place validating such electronic documents and signatures. Other provinces will undoubtedly follow. In effect, such statutes "strengthen confidence in e-commerce by, among other things, ensuring that electronic contracts, documents and signatures have the same legal effect as those signed on paper, and set up rules for automated transactions and for correcting mistakes made on a computer."[35] For example, the Ontario Act recognizes electronic signatures for all documents except wills and negotiable instruments.

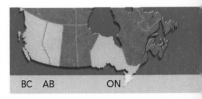

BC  AB          ON

## Sale of Goods and Consumer Protection

Canadian contract law can offer some protection, but deceitful practices and fraud are ongoing concerns for those transacting business on the internet. The internet is perilous even for those who are careful. The author of this chapter, despite exercising considerable caution, fell victim to such a scheme. After unsuccessfully bidding on a portable computer on eBay, he was approached through email by another seller with a similar model at an attractive price. After checking the seller's business website and eBay references, a deal was struck and payment arranged. The product was to be put into the hands of United Parcel Service (UPS), after which point payments were to be made in cash through Western Union. A UPS tracking number was provided along with a photocopy of the label and bar code showing the package had been sent, and payment was made as arranged. The product never arrived. Upon the author's investigation, a UPS representative stated that companies are given a series of labels and tracking numbers and that in fact they are not an indication that goods have been shipped. Phone calls and emails to the company went unanswered. The website disappeared from the internet, and no trace could be found of the sellers at the New York street address given on the website. Hindsight shows that there were many warning signs, but it is likely that many consumers would be taken in by such a scheme. In fact, the author has since discovered that the "gentleman" behind this particular scam has been not only operating to his great advantage for some time, but also bragging about his deceptions. The name he used on eBay was Ken, and the reader should beware of him and others like him who seek to use the internet for such purposes.

A hard lesson learned: many online sellers can not be trusted. Money should never be sent without independent verification that the goods are shipped. Services provided by Paypal and other third-party guarantors try to ensure the validity of these transactions, but it is surprising how clever unscrupulous sellers can be in getting around these protections. It is doubtful whether statutory intervention or other forms of government regulation will ever completely prevent such abuses.

**Current law will apply to online transactions**

**It is dangerous to trust internet retailers**

34. Geist, Michael, *Internet Law in Canada,* 3rd ed. (Toronto: Captus Press) 652.

35. Flaherty, Jim. From the announcement introducing the Ontario statute by Attorney General as reported in *Lawyers Weekly,* Vol. 20 No. 8 (June 23, 2000).

Amendments to provincial legislation have been made or proposed to facilitate the sale of goods online and to protect both buyers and sellers. For example, Ontario and Nova Scotia have enacted the *Uniform Electronic Commerce Act* validating internet transactions and legitimizing such things as electronic signatures and computer-to-computer transactions. In most instances the *Sale of Goods Act* and consumer transaction provisions discussed in Chapter 9 will apply to electronic transactions as well. The *International Sale of Goods Act,* also provincial legislation, comes into play when transactions cross national borders. Special provisions to deal with the internet are being drafted, including amendments to accommodate the new technology. Vendors will be required to provide:

- their identity and address;
- a description of the product or service;
- all taxes, costs, charges and fees;
- method of payment and cost of borrowing;
- warranty limitation and cancellation policies;
- a printed record giving proof of sale; and
- arrangements for complaints, exchanges, and refunds.

**Consumer protection statutes coming for internet**

Consumer protection legislation, already in place in several jurisdictions imposing special restrictions on mail-order transactions, will likely be extended to internet transactions. Among the recommended changes are the right to cancel an order when the product is not delivered within 30 days and a cooling-off period. In this way consumers will receive online protection similar to other consumer transactions. This will require local courts to have jurisdiction, and the implementation of many of the recommended changes set out in the above paragraph. Private information provided by the customer must also be protected. Mechanisms for handling complaints should be efficient and reasonably available.

Provincial securities regulations will also apply to trades on the internet, but amendments will likely be enacted to apply special provisions to electronic trading. The internet seems to attract an unusual number of frauds and get-rich-quick schemes, and so it will be a considerable challenge for government regulators to develop effective methods of controlling these abuses.

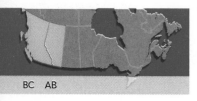

BC AB

## Electronic Money

Negotiable instruments cannot be created or transferred online since their essential nature is a unique written document. There are, however, electronic substitutes. Credit and debit cards have begun to replace the use of negotiable instruments in both commercial and consumer transactions. Access and stored-value cards, where value is embedded in a chip on the card and reduced as it is used, are also available in some areas. Many credit card transactions and most debit cards no longer require a signature, substituting the PIN (personal identification number) as the essential element of identification. While automated banking machines and credit, debit, and access cards have made life more convenient, they have also provided ample opportunity for criminals to gain illegal access to our funds. Many jurisdictions have passed consumer protection legislation limiting a cardholder's liability, placing most of the responsibility for credit card loss on the banks. With clever new schemes appearing daily, we must use extra caution in protecting our PIN and other personal information, for it is clear that the cost of these losses will be passed on to the bank's customers in one way or

**Credit cards, debit cards, and other forms of electronic money replacing negotiable instruments**

another. The issue of fraud relating to electronic funds is a serious one that affects consumers and businesses alike. As the incidents increase in frequency and magnitude, everyone must take precautions.

## Criminal Activity and Other Abuses

In addition to the problems related to the fraudulent uses of electronic technologies and the outright piracy of computer programs, businesses must contend with computer viruses that interfere with the operation of programs and corrupt or destroy data. Hackers can steal telephone services and access confidential or secret information through misuse of the telecommunications systems and computers of other businesses. This has become particularly easy with the growing use of wireless networks. Outright piracy of computer programs, tapes, and videos is already a huge problem. Other common internet and computer offences include pornography, theft, gambling, criminal defamation and harassment, pedophilia, hate literature, and other human rights violations.

**Criminal offences proliferate on internet**

General *Criminal Code* provisions such as theft and fraud, and specialized provisions prohibiting the unauthorized use of computers (section 342.1) and mischief relating to computer data (section 430 (1.1)), as well as the specific offences included in the copyright and trademark acts are used to deal with these problems. Also, sections 183 and 184 of the *Criminal Code* prohibiting the interception of private communications apply to the internet as well as to more traditional methods of communication. But, as was pointed out in our discussion of intellectual property, relying on criminal prosecution is not a very reliable way to protect a business from these activities. Matters are made worse by the international nature of the internet and other forms of electronic communication and data transfer, which requires international cooperation to prosecute. It is hoped that the recommendations made in a recent international treaty on cybercrime now being implemented in various jurisdictions will eventually lead to much greater control and regulation of electronic communication.[36]

### Enforcement

The authorities are to be commended for several successful prosecutions, extending from hackers such as the infamous cybervandal "Mafia Boy" to recent pedophilia and child pornography convictions. But law-enforcement agencies are overwhelmed, and businesses cannot count on help from that quarter for effective prevention. Civil litigation is often not much more attractive. Although the person bringing the action is in control of the process, there are many inherent disadvantages. For example, determining the identity of perpetrators is often impossible, and even then they usually have limited resources, making a civil action a waste of time and money.

Businesses often find themselves tied to these criminal activities through the actions of their employees. Employees use company computers to carry on activities against the company, other employees, and outsiders, often bringing civil and criminal liability to the company. To avoid such liability the company must take active steps to establish a comprehensive communications systems policy. The use of computers must be monitored, and employees must be taught what they can

**Business must develop programs to control employee conduct on computers**

---

36. Schmitz Cristin, "Government Plans Massive Expansion of 'Lawful Access'," *Lawyers Weekly*, Vol. 22 No.18 (Sept. 13, 2002).

and cannot do on their computers. In addition, active measures must be taken to protect the business from this kind of attack by outsiders or disgruntled former employees.

## Security

Usually, the best solution is a defensive one. Internet technology has outstripped the law, and businesses must take active steps to protect their data and their communications. Effective security is vital, but because of the growing vulnerability of the systems this measure must go much further than simply changing passwords frequently. For example, with the common use of wireless networking it is now a simple matter to drive down the street in any business district in a modern city and access those networks from the car—either for a sinister purposes with respect to a particular target, or simply to get a free ride onto the internet or accessing a company's long-distance communications. The solution requires encryption of data and the use of special programs supplied by several different manufacturers to protect from viruses and hackers; these programs also require constant updating. There is an ongoing contest between the hackers and those creating viruses, worms, and other destructive devices on the one side and those trying to develop effective defences on the other.

**Encryption of data and other defences best protection**

## Jurisdiction

Jurisdiction with respect to the internet is an important area of concern, and the already-developed rules referred to as **conflict of laws** may require modification to effectively handle these disputes. The problem is to determine which court will have the right to hear a case when the parties reside in different jurisdictions. When a retail business advertises or offers a product or service over the internet, does it face the risk of being sued or prosecuted in every area that the internet message is seen? Are they subject to the variations of tort, contract, criminal, or consumer protection law in all of those jurisdictions? Web messages go into every jurisdiction in the world, but it is now generally accepted that there has to be something more than information delivery or mere advertising to give a particular court jurisdiction to hear a complaint. A passive website will usually not create a problem in any particular jurisdiction where it is read. There must be a special link or connection or degree of interactivity to have a local court take jurisdiction. Without that special connection, the courts in a particular province may refuse to hear a case.

**Special link or connection needed to give court jurisdiction**

### Case Summary 16.11

**Ontario Court Had No Jurisdiction in Domain Name Dispute:**
*Easthaven v. Nutrisystem*[37]

This case involves a dispute over the use of the name "Sweet Success." The defendant, Nutrisystem, had several registered trademarks under that name in the U.S. As is so often the case, the plaintiff, Easthaven, acquired the internet domain name "sweetsuccess.com" from a body that issues such domain names, setting the stage for the confrontation. At first, Nutrisystem negotiated with Easthaven to acquire the name, but when negotiations broke down both compa-

37. (2001), 202 D.L.R. (4th) 560 (Ont. S.C.J.).

nies resorted to litigation. Nutrisystem brought action in the U.S. seeking control over the name but this action failed. An arbitration panel appointed under the rules of Internet Corporation for Assigned Names and Numbers (ICANN) found that Easthaven had not acted in bad faith and was entitled to the domain name sweetsuccess.com.

In the meantime, Easthaven had commenced an action in Ontario to acquire control of the disputed domain name and for damages. But the Ontario Court found that there was no real or substantial connection between Ontario and the domain-name dispute. Nutrisystem was an American company and was not active in Ontario. The plaintiff was a Barbados company. Only the domain-name supplier had their head office in Ontario, but they also operated out of the U.S. in Delaware. The Court held that the domain name was intangible intellectual property having no physical existence and so could not be said to be located in any specific location. There was no transaction or activity of any substantial or continuous nature that took place in Ontario, therefore the Ontario Court had no jurisdiction to hear the case. In the end, Easthaven got what they wanted since Nutrisystem had also failed in their U.S. action to wrest control of "sweetsuccess.com" away from Easthaven.

The case is instructive in that it illustrates the serious problem of conflicting rules associated with trademark law and the issuance of internet domain names. This will be discussed further below, but for the discussion here the case illustrates the requirements needed to establish jurisdiction when dealing with internet disputes. There must be some special or unique connection to a particular jurisdiction before the court will have the authority to hear the case.

A Canadian may find him- or herself being prosecuted for an activity that is against the law in one jurisdiction but perfectly acceptable in another. These cases often involve moral issues, such as gambling and the distribution of pornography, where different community standards contribute to this variation in laws. This has become a serious problem with the borderless nature of the internet blurring international boundaries and where the origin of the service provider or the business is not always obvious. It is no longer sufficient to simply follow the rules of one's own jurisdiction, and a business must take great care to determine just where they are doing business and the laws that apply in that jurisdiction. Some countries are even attracting business by making themselves a safe haven for such activities. There are currently international efforts being made to rationalize this area, but it is unlikely that universal rules will be developed that will be acceptable to all of the various players. Another related problem is how to enforce a judgment obtained in one jurisdiction in another where the offender resides or may have assets. Treaties often allow for the enforcement of one court order in another jurisdiction, but these usually require the conduct being actionable in both areas.

*Safe havens provide protection for internet companies*

In order to avoid these problems the parties should make their own rules specifying in their contract what law is to apply. Where business is solicited disclaimers should be included similar to product warranties, such as "Void where prohibited by law," or "Only available to residents of Canada." If a website is created to do business in another jurisdiction, the law of that jurisdiction will apply to the transactions unless it is clearly stated otherwise in the contract. But even with that precaution, the content of the website may still be an offence in that jurisdiction.

## Reducing **Risk** 16.5

A business offering a service or product over the internet that is at all questionable should take care to offer those services only in jurisdictions where they are permitted and provide notification accordingly. They should also declare the law of which jurisdiction applies to the transaction and establish the contracting process in such as way that the contract is actually accepted in the jurisdiction where the business resides. They should also take care to include appropriate disclaimers of liability in their contracts. The key is to not have a website that allows any degree of interactivity in those prohibited jurisdictions. Still, if the material is offensive some localities may try to prosecute.

A business will avoid these pitfalls only as they take proactive steps to anticipate and provide for these contingencies before they happen: "The nightmare of costly and difficult multi-jurisdictional conflict of laws disputes demands a creative solution, particularly for the mid-size to small business person or individual."[38]

Offshore gambling over the internet provides a particular problem with respect to jurisdiction. Is the activity happening in this country or where the operators reside? Where is the bet made? While the activity may be criminal in Canada it is usually permitted in the jurisdiction where the operators reside, making enforcement of Canadian laws and extradition impossible. The selling of securities also poses particular problems when done online. Securities regulations control abuses such as insider trading, fraud, and other unfair practices, and strictly control the flow of information requiring complete disclosure by the parties.

**Trading in securities closely controlled in whatever form**

Trading in securities over the internet is subject to all of the normal restrictions and regulations imposed for any sale of securities in Canada. Anyone making offerings over the internet must comply not only with the rules of where they reside but also those in place in Canada.

## Regulation

**More regulation coming**

Since the tragic events of September 11, 2001, it is clear that the freewheeling unregulated nature of the internet will no longer be tolerated; unfortunately, there is both an upside and a downside to that kind of freedom. As a result, our rights to privacy and freedom are being drastically curtailed, with internet communications being a primary target. That, combined with abuses ranging from unreliable medical, financial, and other advice to various frauds and scams, makes it impossible for governments to resist regulatory intervention. For example, the proliferation of *spam,* which is unsolicited bulk email advertising, now represents more than 30 percent of internet traffic. Various worms and viruses continue to do untold damage. This is why the chief justice of the Supreme Court of Canada commented on the need to haul in the reins on the internet, as quoted at the beginning of this section. Governments, of course, also realize the attraction of collecting fees and taxes, as discussed below.

Certainly, federal and provincial taxes, including sales taxes (PST) and goods and services taxes (GST), will be payable on products, services, and information sold on the internet, and income tax will be payable by companies residing and doing business in Canada. But it is difficult to determine residency and to trace the origin of products, especially where even Canadian products can be sold from other countries in order to avoid taxes. Goods delivered to Canadian customers

---

38. Carrington, Victoria, "Internet Needs Fast, Fair Dispute Resolution Process," *Lawyers Weekly,* Vol. 20 No. 27 (November 17, 2000).

are subject to taxes and duties as they enter the country, but it is not possible to exercise such control when software or services are downloaded from the internet. Canadian content rules, generally administered by the Canadian Radio-television and Telecommunications Commission (CRTC), have been at least temporarily set aside with regard to the internet, largely because it is impossible to enforce them. In some areas, such as gaming and lotteries, federal and provincial regulations are applied and both the originator of the contest and the service provider will be held liable if they are found to infringe these regulations. These services are, however, usually provided by companies operating from sympathetic offshore locations, making enforcement extremely difficult. Although there are several examples of statutes that apply to companies doing business on the internet, most internet transactions and communications remain unregulated.

**Difficult to enforce such regulations**

Another major problem is to determine who is subject to these controls and who can be held responsible for violations. An internet-based business involves many players including the retailer or business providing the service, the website developers and operators, the internet service providers, and even the advertisers, product manufacturers, and deliverers. An example of an ISP responding to non-legal pressure involved a home furnishing company's attempt to advertise by sending out bulk e-mails (spam). This practice was thwarted when their service provider deactivated their site after receiving complaints from other users who received the unsolicited e-mails. When the home furnishing company sought an injunction to force the ISP to reinstate the service, claiming irreparable harm, the court refused. It found that the ISP had included a term in the contract restricting this kind of activity and were within their rights to enforce it by discontinuing the company's account when after notification they refused to stop.[39] It will likely take a combination of government regulation, the application of traditional law, and this kind of self-regulation by the major players to finally strike the appropriate balance in these new and challenging areas of electronic communication.

**ISP may be responsible to stop abuses**

## Dispute Resolution

It has been suggested that the problems with monitoring the internet make it a prime area for the use of alternative dispute resolution mechanisms, thereby avoiding the bureaucratic red tape that would come with government regulatory bodies. In some particularly troublesome areas independent dispute resolution processes have already been initiated. For example, the National Arbitration Forum has been very effective in handling internet domain-name disputes. Also, negotiation and mediation services such as "eResolution" or "Cybersettle.com" are now available online with the same savings in time and money that have characterized the alternate forms discussed in Chapter 2. So far these online services deal mostly with domain-name disputes, but they will likely expand to handle other disputes arising from the use of the internet.

**ADR used to settle internet disputes**

## Security and Privacy

Although breach of privacy is not recognized as a tort in common law, privacy and confidentiality concerns have become a particular problem. Modern businesses are particularly vulnerable as information becomes much easier to access, accumulate, and sort. Internet transactions usually require the exchange of pri-

39. *1267623 Ontario Inc. v. Nexx Online* (1999), 45 O.R. (3d) 40 (Ont. Sup. Ct.).

**Voluntary protection of privacy has failed**

vate information, and the misuse or resale of this information without consent is a growing concern. The hope of self-regulation in this area was misplaced. It is clear that with the increasing value of intercepted, confidential data taken from stored computer files or from online communications there is greater temptation to acquire that data in any way possible. The data can reveal a person's browsing and buying habits as well as other personal information. It is now reluctantly acknowledged that increased business and consumer protection is needed.

Many users don't realize that information from electronic mail and other internet communications can easily be intercepted and become public, or redirected to competitors or others who will misuse it. Or it can simply be collected by the company being dealt with and subsequently misused. In the past there was some anonymity in the vast amounts of data collected, but today this information can be sorted and arranged in such a way that individuals with specific buying habits can be identified and targeted by advertisers, charities, and others seeking

**Private data often sold for profit**

to do business with them. It is common for this gathered data to be sold without the subjects being aware or giving consent. The internet service provider or business being dealt with may use the information to provide better service, but it is more likely that it will get into the hands of shady entrepreneurs who inundate users with emails and pop-ups promoting legitimate and illegitimate services and products. Protecting rights of privacy is an immense challenge, and the best advice is for users to refrain as much as possible from giving out their private information online. Encryption of the information and data communicated is advisable, but even then there is no guarantee that it will be secure from a motivated hacker. This area is now regulated by the *Personal Information Protection and Electronic Documents Act*,[40] which applies to all jurisdictions in Canada except

**Some provinces moving to pass privacy legislation**

where the provinces have passed "substantially similar" legislation. This gives the provinces a choice of having the federal legislation apply or passing their own statute. Quebec has had a privacy act in place since 1994. At the time of writing Ontario has introduced a draft privacy act (*Privacy of Personal Information Act*), and British Columbia is considering enacting such legislation.

The federal legislation provides that:

> 4.1.3 An organization is responsible for personal information in its possession or custody, including information that has been transferred to a third party for processing. The organization shall use contractual or other means to provide a comparable level of protection while the information is being processed by a third party.

> 4.1.4 Organizations shall implement policies and practices to give effect to the principles, including:

> (a) implementing procedures to protect personal information;
> (b) establishing procedures to receive and respond to complaints and inquiries;
> (c) training staff and communicating to staff information about the organization's policies and practices; and
> (d) developing information to explain the organization's policies and procedures.

---

40. S.C. 2000, c. 5.

4.7.1 Personal information shall be protected by security safeguards appropriate to the sensitivity of the information. The security safeguards shall protect personal information against loss or theft, as well as unauthorized access, disclosure, copying, use, or modification.

The Act was implemented in three stages, and by January 1, 2004, it applied to all organizations that disclose personal information in connection with commercial activities. The rules are there, but governments still face the seemingly insurmountable challenge of enforcing these new regulations because of the borderless nature of the internet. Self-regulation remains important, as does the creation and implementation of international treaties.

**Federal statute protects privacy**

As mentioned above and in Chapter 4, a particular problem relating to privacy is the unauthorized interception of communications between individuals. This is now a criminal offence in Canada. Encryption helps, but is no guarantee. As discussed in Chapter 4, links connecting internet sites are commonplace but are sometimes misused to redirect customers from one website to a competitor's. Sometimes, embedded software devices called "cookies" that trace a user's internet activities are misused, giving others the capacity to read private information. This information can be used by the ISP to provide more efficient service, and by retailers for marketing purposes, or it can be used to incriminate a person who has been downloading and inappropriately using websites. Users should remember that the information stored in computers is more permanent than paper, and even when we delete that information someone with the appropriate expertise can readily recover it. Eventually, it is likely that regulations will require notice and consent before such private information can be gathered, as well as disclosure of how it will be used and the right to check its accuracy. Again, the problem will be enforcement.

**Computer data vulnerable**

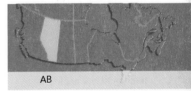

AB

## Employment

Employers are particularly vulnerable to the misuse of their computer resources by employees. Employees can tamper with company data directly, and they can also expose the employer to criminal and civil liability as they use company equipment in their dealings with outsiders. The challenge is to monitor the use of computers in the workplace. The employer will be responsible for data transmissions that result in intentional or careless violations of intellectual property rights, privacy rights, or even the criminal law in local or foreign jurisdictions. The employer must be concerned with the security of not only their own information but also that of their customers and others.

The ease of communicating by email has led to casualness and carelessness, and employees often don't realize that their messages may be defamatory, reveal private or confidential information, or eventually be used to create a digital trail that would expose illegal activity. The circulation of confidential, hateful, discriminatory, or defamatory material, or the practice of using company computers to harass other employees, will also put the company at risk. A message intended for one person may in error be sent to another, or upon receipt could be intentionally reproduced and broadly distributed, greatly increasing the potential for damage. Often these messages are sent anonymously or in the name of someone else, but they can be easily traced back to the employer's computer. Emails are deceptive; they are not nearly as private as they appear. They are susceptible to unauthorized access, and unlike paper, which can be destroyed, the evidence remains

**Employee's use of computers can expose employers to risk**

**Monitoring of employees' computer use may be only viable solution**

in the computer even after it has been erased. It is vital that an employer retain control of its data, its computers, and its communications.

**Employers should inform employees of surveillance**

**Employer must have a viable electronic communication and data policy in place**

Employees—sometimes with the company's blessing—may also photocopy copyrighted material without permission or use pirated software. To protect itself, the company must show that there are effective policies and programs in place to prevent these abuses. Monitoring employees' email and their internet use can be effective, but it also raises privacy concerns; the company should advise employees that these activities are being monitored. This will eliminate any expectation of privacy and will encourage employees to use discretion. This situation, again, begs for a comprehensive company policy and education program with respect to electronic communications, confidentiality, and data storage.

## Intellectual Property

**Current copyright and trademark law applies to the internet**

The internet and other forms of electronic communication and information manipulation have had a significant impact in the area of copyright, trademarks, and confidential information. Canadian copyright law specifically protects computer software and also protects original works including those published on the internet. Trademark law will apply to domain names and website logos. Again, it is one thing to have these laws and another thing to enforce them. A business must do all it can to protect its own interests. Where software products are involved, contractual terms including limitations on use must be clearly specified and acknowledged before downloading, or clearly indicated on the packaging with clear notification that breaking the seal commits the purchaser to those terms. Domain names should be acquired and trademarks registered. Copyrighted material should also be registered and accompanied by a notification that it cannot be reproduced or used without permission.

41. Turban, Efraim, Jae Lee, David King, H. Michael Chung, *Electronic Commerce: A Managerial Perspective* (Upper Saddle River, NJ: Prentice Hall, 1999), p. 353.

Copyright law provides the owner of electronic material with the legal right not only to prevent unauthorized copying, but also to rent it and otherwise control its use. Today most software is licensed with severe restrictions on how it can be used and how copies may be made. Registration of copyright, although not required in Canada, is recommended to provide protection internationally and to establish a proprietary interest in work produced.

While the misuse of software causes difficulty, a much greater problem is the unauthorized copying of music, movies, and the written word found online. The ease of reproducing information in all forms on the internet has led users to think they can do anything they want with it. This has led to massive illegal copying and to dramatic legal steps being taken to stop the process. The ease of downloading free music using file-sharing software programs may have been a boon to music lovers, but it came at a great expense to the producers and musicians who have, through successful lawsuits, stopped much of this improper copyright interference. The Napster trial and other high-profile cases have shown that the courts will not tolerate such abuse. However, the problem continues, with vast amounts of music still being improperly copied. As soon as one site is shut down another that uses different technology is created. Hopefully, the two sides will eventually reach a compromise so that we can take advantage of these tremendous technological advances in a way that will benefit all the players.

**Copying music a massive problem that has resulted in serious litigation**

The same problems exist with illegally copied movies, games, and other forms of entertainment. A business that uses the internet not only must be concerned with what the technology allows them to do and how profitable it will be, but also must consider what they are allowed to do legally. It is important to understand that the principles of copyright, trademarks, and other forms of intellectual property embodied in the law are not limited by clever and novel technological innovation. The close to $300-million settlement that MP3 had to pay to record companies over their disputed service is an example of just how costly failing to consider these legal risks can be.

In Canada software is protected primarily under copyright legislation, although there are many situations where patent law will apply to software embedded in a particular invention or application. There is also a unique Canadian statute protecting the design of an integrated circuit embodied in a computer chip.[42] But most disputes with respect to intellectual property and the internet involve copyright and trademark legislation.

A major area of confrontation involves the use of trademarks on the internet. Brand names and company logos are important company assets and have become even more important as they continually flash across a computer screen. Keeping them in the conscious or subconscious mind of the web browser is a key marketing tool. These assets are protected by trademark, and unauthorized use of a name or mark is against the law. The posting of material on a website invites viewing, and so merely accessing such sites does not violate the trademark. Communication by itself is not an infringement, but when the viewer downloads the visual or sound sequence and prints it, creates a link, or otherwise uses it to enhance his or her own website without permission, an actionable infringement has taken place. While people thought the freewheeling nature of the internet allowed them to use information in any way they wanted, it is now clear that the traditional rules of trademark and copyright law apply. As always, the problem is with enforcement.

**Viewing a website is no violation but downloading information from it may be**

---

42. *Integrated Circuit Topography Act*, S.C. 1990, c. 37.

## Reducing Risk 16.8

Rights to names and trademarks present a complex problem on the internet. Private companies such as Network Solutions Inc. have been given the responsibility of issuing domain names to applicants on a first-come, first-served basis. To facilitate browsing these names should be closely related to the product or service provided, with the attendant danger that competitors will acquire the name or a similar one first and will divert browsers to their own site. It is wise to apply not only for trademark registration but also for all variations of domain names that are likely to be associated with one's service, product, or website as one of the first things done in establishing a business.

The granting of domain names has led to considerable conflict. Like a trademark, a domain name identifies the user, but because of their descriptive nature domain names have been subject to considerable abuse. While trademarks are usually limited to local areas, because of the worldwide nature of the internet each domain name can be used only once. This has led to numerous conflicts over the acquisition and use of the same or a similar name. To make matters worse, cybersquatters (users who buy up certain names just to sell them to others) have tied up domain names that a browser would associate with well-known companies. For example, shortly after Vancouver was granted the 2010 Olympic Games several domain names, including **www.2010-wintergames.com** and **www.Vancouver2010-Olympicgames.com**, were registered and put up for sale on eBay. The Vancouver Olympic officials take the position, which is supported by current trademark law, that anyone acquiring these domain names will not be able to use them because the use of any name that can be confused with registered Olympic domain names is actionable. It is important to remember that the registration of domain names and their use on the internet will not overrule trademark law, as discussed in this chapter. Where trademarks are infringed it will be no defence to show a registered domain name. This is another example of the internet being subject to more general legal principles.

**Domain name disputes often solved by trademark law**

Controls have been introduced to try to stop this kind of abuse. A person wishing to claim a particular domain name or web address applies to the Domain Name Registry operated by the Canadian Internet Registration Authority (CIRA), which for a small annual fee will issue the name if it is available. If someone else already owns it, the parties can negotiate its purchase or an application can be made to reverse the original registration on the basis that this new claimant has a better right to the name. Dispute-resolution mechanisms are now in place to resolve these conflicts, and a name issued to one party can be rescinded on the basis that the registration was improper because of bad faith. The CIRA, which handles such disputes in Canada, defines bad faith as obtaining the name to resell at a profit, to prevent someone who has a greater right from using it, or to disrupt another's business.[43] The comparable U.S. organization is ICANN; this was the body that found Easthaven's registration of the domain name "sweetsuccess.com" was not done in bad faith in the *Easthaven v. Nutrisystem* case discussed in Case Summary 16.11.

**Issued domain name may be reversed because of bad faith**

The ease with which people can transfer material from one website to another—or link to other websites, even bypassing that website's homepage—is also a cause for concern. The homepage may contain advertising, disclaimers, agreements for use, copyright limitations, and fee schedules. Trademarks and

43. Cotter, John C., "CIRA Cybersquatting Dispute Resolution on the Way," *Lawyers Weekly,* Vol. 21 No. 29 (Nov. 30, 2001).

logos can be easily copied and used, and it may be difficult to track down the person responsible for the infringement. This was the problem acknowledged and remedied by the Federal Court in the *Imax Corp. v. Showmax* case described in Case Summary 16.12.

## Case Summary 16.12

### And Now for a Showstopper: *Imax Corp. v. Showmax Inc.*[44]

Imax Corp. applied for an interlocutory injunction for trademark infringement against Showmax Inc., a company based in Montreal that opened a large-format motion picture theatre. Showmax promoted its grand opening on banners, in magazines, and on its website. The website used a framing device to show multiple windows on its homepage. One of the windows linked browsers to the Old Port of Montreal website, which, in turn, contained information and advertising regarding the Imax theatre at the Old Port of Montreal. The plaintiff argued that the arrangement of framing and linking would cause the viewer to think that Imax was responsible for or was connected with Showmax. The Federal Court of Canada agreed that there was evidence that the website might lead consumers to believe that the Showmax theatre was operated and controlled by the same entity that controlled the Imax theatres. This evidence of confusion was sufficient to lead to the loss of "name, goodwill, and reputation." The Judge concluded that this was a serious issue with the possibility of irreparable harm, and therefore granted the interlocutory injunction. This case illustrates that laws governing copyright and trademark infringement will be applied to internet communications, and website managers must be careful that their links and frames do not mislead browsers as to the source of the information. It also illustrates how an injunction—and particularly an interlocutory injunction, which is granted before the actual trial—can be an important remedy when such an infringement takes place.

Although voluntary compliance has not been very effective, web users often do impose sanctions on each other and report offenders to service providers or groups who patrol illegal activities on the net. This is known as "netiquette" and is a form of self-regulation provided by the services of Usenet. For example, spammers have had their accounts discontinued by their internet service providers after complaints from such organizations.[45] Another example of self-regulation is the code of ethics and standards of practice established by the Canadian Direct Marketing Association, with which its members must comply.

It is clear that a substantial amount of business is now being done online and that this will continue to increase. Complete self-regulation is a failed dream, and governments will continue to impose ever more effective regulations. There will be more comprehensive international treaties, leading to a more unified approach to law creation and enforcement. Businesspeople not only must understand the law with respect to electronic commerce and internet communication but also must anticipate where it will likely be going, to avoid pitfalls that could be disadvantageous to the future business.

44. (2000), 5 C.P.R. (4th) 81 (Fed. T.D.).

45. *1267623 Ontario Inc. v. Nexx Online* (1999), 45 O.R. (3d) 40 (Ont. Sup. Ct.).

# Summary

## Intellectual property

- Protected by both federal legislation and common law
- Copyright protects literary, artistic, dramatic, and other works from being copied or used by unauthorized parties for the author's life to the end of the calendar year, plus 50 years. Producing the work creates the copyright
- Registration ensures international protection
- Remedies include injunctions, Anton Piller orders, damages, and accounting of profits
- Patent—registration gives international monopoly protection on the use of an invention for 20 years
- Trademark—registration protects certain terms, symbols, and designs associated with a business or product, prevents deception of consumer, and protects good will. Passing-off action may provide similar protection
- Industrial designs are protected by federal legislation
- Confidential information
- In common law, an employee or associate under a fiduciary obligation is prohibited from disclosing confidential information including trade secrets
- Damages or an injunction may be awarded when such confidences are breached

## Computers and the internet

- Voluntary compliance falls short and more regulation of the internet is needed
- Problems posed with respect to identifying source of defamation and other torts and enforcement out of jurisdiction
- Existing law including product liability and consumer protection will also apply
- Internet users are particularly vulnerable to scams and fraud
- Current criminal law applies but may be difficult to enforce
- Self protection is safest defence, including encryption, supervision of employees, and security
- Determining jurisdiction is a problem. Courts need some special local connection
- Federal and some provincial protection of privacy statutes as well as some provincial electronic commerce acts now in place
- ADR used to solve domain-name disputes
- Employers now monitoring employee email and computer use
- Current copyright and other intellectual property statutes apply to internet
- Use of domain names often conflict with trademark law, which will prevail

## QUESTIONS

1. What two principles do the law of intellectual property try to balance?

2. Explain how a copyright is obtained and the qualifications that must be met to obtain such protection.

3. Discuss the significance of the 1997 amendments to the *Copyright Act.*

4. Summarize the nature of the protection given to the holder of a copyright and indicate what remedies are available to enforce such rights.

5. Discuss under what circumstances an Anton Piller order would be given and indicate how this remedy might be more valuable than other remedies that might be available.

6. What is the purpose of patent law, and why is registration required for protection?

7. What kinds of things are protected by the trademark legislation, and how is that protection obtained or lost?

8. What kinds of material are intended to be protected by industrial design? How is this protection obtained?

9. How does the duty of confidentiality arise, and what protection or remedies are available to the confider?

10. Indicate how criminal law, tort law, and contract law can be used to protect intellectual property. How effective are such alternatives?

11. What are some of the problems enforcing intellectual property regulations when the medium for transmitting information is the internet?

12. Why has it become necessary to regulate the internet?

13. How does the current law of tort, contract consumer protection, and intellectual property affect internet communications?

14. Explain the role played by private bodies and ADR in regulating the use of the internet.

15. Explain the relationship between the use of domain names and trademark law. How are disputes between different domain-name claimants resolved?

16. How does federal and provincial legislation contribute to the protection of privacy and the increase of security on the internet?

17. Describe abusive conduct that takes place on the internet and the criminal law provisions that are intended to prevent it.

18. Explain the problems created by the internet with respect to jurisdiction and what factors courts now use to determine whether they will hear a case.

19. What steps should a company take to protect themselves and their data from internal and external threats?

------------------------------------------------------------------------

## CASES

### 1. *Spiro-flex Industries v. Progressive Sealing Inc.* (1982), 32 D.L.R. (4th) 201 (B.C.S.C.).

Mr. McLeod designed a new pump coupler (a device used in a circulating water pump), which he intended to produce and sell. But he could not produce a special spring used in the device and so had to turn to others. He produced freehand sketches of the product as well as directions and specifications and went to different manufacturers to have it made. He entered into an agreement to have the product marketed and provided a photograph of the device to illustrate a brochure. Once the device was on the market, several companies made copies of the coupler, including the people he originally asked to produce the device and some of those involved in the production of the brochure. Explain McLeod's rights against those parties.

### 2. *Thurston Hayes Developments Ltd. v. Horn Abbott, Ltd.* (1985), 6 C.I.P.R. 75 (F.C.A.).

The plaintiff was the developer of the board game "Trivial Pursuit," which had been on the market successfully for several years. The defendants brought out a new board game with the same approach but which involved a different subject matter and called it "Sexual Pursuit." The board used was essentially the same, the box the game came in was similar, and the games were even played the same way. Explain the nature of the complaint the plaintiff has, any legal action that can be taken to protect his rights, and the likely outcome.

### 3. *Ciba-Geigy Canada Ltd. v. Apotex Inc.* (1992), 95 D.L.R. (4th) 385 (S.C.C.).

Ciba-Geigy had the right to manufacture in Canada the product Metoprolol, a drug used for treating hypertension and angina. Under the *Patent Act* then in place, other manufacturers could acquire a licence and manufacture and sell the product in Canada. These versions are known as generic drugs. Apotex and Novopharm both obtained licences and, in the process, produced a drug with the same appearance as that produced by Ciba-Geigy. They used the same shape, size, and colour. Even the dosages were the same. In fact, these drugs were interchangeable with the original product. Given that these companies have the right to produce generic drugs that are similar and useable for the same purpose, is there any complaint Ciba-Geigy can use against these imitators? Would your answer be affected by the fact that only doctors and pharmacists are aware of the differences and the ultimate consumer would not notice the difference?

### 4. *Allen v. Toronto Star Newspapers Ltd.* (1997), 152 D.L.R. (4th) 518 (Ont. Gen. Div.).

Jim Allen, a photographer, took a photograph of Sheila Copps, MP, wearing leathers and sitting on a motorcycle. It was used on the cover of *Saturday Night* magazine, which had employed Allen to take the picture. Allen sold the picture on two other occasions. It became a matter of some controversy. The *Toronto Star*, without the photographer's permission, published the picture, including the cover, in their newspaper as part of a news story. No objections were raised by *Saturday Night* magazine. What options are available to Jim Allen, and what defences are available to the *Toronto Star*?

### 5. *R. v. Weir* (1998), ABQB 56 (Alta. Q. B.).

Mr. Weir had a computer and was communicating on the internet. His internet service provider was doing some repair work requiring them to access his email and in the process discovered what they took to be child pornography as an attachment to a particular email message. They notified the police, who obtained a warrant and at his residence confiscated computer equipment and disks containing the original email and other material they assessed to be child pornography. Mr. Weir was charged, and in his defense he claimed that the internet service provider had no right to intercept his private email. Therefore, the warrant was wrongly obtained and the evidence should be thrown out. There is no question that this right to privacy exists with respect to first-class surface mail, but should it be extended to email? What do you think?

### 6. *Black v. Molson Canada* (2002), 60 O.R. (3d) 457 (Ont. S.C.J.).

Black obtained the use of the domain name "Canadian.biz" through proper registration with the intention of using it with respect to a website catering to Canadian businesses and entrepreneurs. This site was not yet established as it awaited resolution of the dispute over who had the right to the use of this domain name. Molson produced a product called "Molson Canadian" and claimed that only they were entitled to the use of the domain name on the basis that it was identical to their trademark. They demanded its transfer from Black, and when he refused Molson complained to the National Arbitration Forum, the body that dealt with these kinds of issues. They agreed with Molson, concluding that the name had been registered in bad faith by Black, who had no legitimate claim to its use, and ordered its transfer to Molson. Black brought this application to the court to have that decision overturned. Who do you think should be entitled to use this domain name and why?

**abatement** a court order to reduce the rent to be paid to compensate for breach of lease by landlord

**absolute privilege** exemption from liability for defamatory statements made in some settings (such as legislatures and courts), without reference to the speaker's motives or the truth or falsity of the statement.

**abuse of power** acting beyond the jurisdiction set out in the legislation or making an unreasonable decision

**acceleration clause** a contractual term that comes into effect when there is a failure to make an instalment payment

**acceptance** one party agrees to the terms of the offer made by another

**accord** both parties in agreement on some change in the contract

**accord and satisfaction** agreement to end a contract, with extra consideration to be supplied by the party benefiting from the discharge

**accounting** court-ordered determination of the injuries suffered; agent must pay over money or property collected on behalf of principal; court order that any profits made from wrongdoing be paid over to victim

**accounts receivable** funds owed to a business for goods or services provided to customers

**actual authority** authority given to agent expressly or by implication

**adjusters** employees or representatives of the insurance corporation charged with investigating and settling insurance claims against the corporation after the insured-against event takes place

**administrative law** the rules and regulations governing the function and powers of executive branch

**administrative tribunals** government decision makers (committees, commissions, tribunals or individuals) who act as judges or referees

**adverse possession** a right to actual possession can be acquired by non-contested use of the land

**affidavit evidence** evidence based on statements made by witnesses out of court but under oath

**affirmative action** programs intended to correct racial or gender imbalances in the workplace

**agency** the service an agent performs on behalf of a principal

**agency agreement** creates an agency relationship between principal and agent

**agency by necessity** consent to act as an agent is implied when there is an urgent reason

**agency shop** (*see* **Rand formula**)

**agent** represents and acts on behalf of a principal in dealings with third parties

**agreement for sale** purchase of land by instalments

**agreement of purchase and sale** first stage in the purchase of real property; also referred to as an interim agreement between vendor and purchaser

**agreement to sell** goods and title transferred at some time in the future

**annual general meeting** a meeting where shareholders vote for directors and on other important resolutions

**anticipatory breach** repudiation of contract before performance is due

**Anton Piller order** court order to seize offending material before trial

**apparent authority** conduct of principal suggests to third

**appeal** a formal process whereby a higher court will reexamine a decision made by a lower court

**appearance** document filed by the defendant indicating that the action will be disputed

**arbitration** parties in a dispute elect or are contracted to submit their claims to a panel which makes a binding decision on their behalf

**articles of association** sets out the procedures for governing a corporation in a registration jurisdiction

**articles of incorporation** a method of incorporating based on U.S. approach used in some jurisdictions in Canada

**assault** an action that makes a person think he is about to be struck

**assignment** the transfer of rights under a contract to another party

**attachment** under the PPSA where value has been given pursuant to contract and creditor now has a claim against assets used as security

**attachment of debt** court order that monies owed to the judgment debtor

(defendant) be intercepted and paid to the judgment creditor (plaintiff)

**auditor** unbiased outside accountant with responsibility to ensure that financial statements for a corporation are properly done

**authority** the right or power to act or to make a decision

**bailee** person acquiring possession of personal property in a bailment

**bailment** when one person takes temporary possession of chattels owned by another

**bailor** the owner giving up possession of property in a bailment

**balance of convenience** determination of who will suffer the greatest injury if the damage were allowed to continue

**bankruptcy** process by which an insolvent person voluntarily or involuntarily transfers assets to a trustee for distribution to creditors

**bargaining agent** a body certified to act on behalf of a group of employees or employers

**bargaining unit** group of employees who have been certified

**battery** unwelcome physical contact

**bearer instrument** a negotiable instrument made payable to the bearer

**bias** prejudice; in order to be unbiased, the decision maker must be impartial and have no personal interest in the decision

**bilateral contract** a contract in which both parties assume an obligation

**bilateral discharge** both sides agree to terminate the contract or to disregard a term of the contract

**bill** the form in which legislation is introduced into Parliament or legislature

**bill of exchange** instrument where drawer directs the drawee to pay out money to the payee; drawee need not be a bank, and the instrument may be made payable in the future

**bill of lading** a receipt for goods in the care of the shipper

**bill of sale** a written agreement which conveys title from seller to buyer

**bona fide purchaser for value** innocent third party who has paid full value for goods under claim by creditor

**bonds or debentures** a share interest in the indebtedness of a corporation; a bond is normally secured, but a debenture is not

**book accounts** accounts receivable that can be used as security for a loan

**breach** failure to live up to conditions of a contract

**broadly-held corporations** a corporation that is publicly traded on the stock market; also called a distributing corporation in some jurisdictions

**brokers** agents retained by the insured to ascertain their insurance needs and secure the necessary coverage

**building scheme** restrictions placed on all the properties in a large development

**business interruption** a form of insurance to protect the insured if business is interrupted

**"but for" test** had it not been for the act of the defendant, the injury would not have occurred

**canon or church law** legal system of the Catholic Church that contributed law in relation to families and estates

**capacity** the freedom to enter into a contract is sometimes limited by a person's ability to understand or fulfill its terms

**causation** determining whether the act actually caused the injury

**caveat emptor** "let the buyer beware"; purchaser must examine, judge and test for herself

**certificate of title** conclusive evidence as to the owner of a property

**certified cheque** means of transferring funds by cheque where payment is, in effect, guaranteed by the bank

**certiorari** a court order overturning a decision and making it null and void

**chambers applications** interim applications and questions (before the actual trial) are brought before the judge in a more informal setting for a ruling

**champerty** an agreement to allow a third party to share in the proceeds of a litigated claim; generally, a sale of the right to sue is discouraged

**Charter of Rights and Freedoms** a document entrenched in the Canadian Constitution in 1982 listing and guaranteeing fundamental human rights

**chattels** tangible, movable personal property that can be measured and weighed; also known as goods

**check-off provision** employees agree to have employer deduct union dues from payroll

**cheque** negotiable instrument; a bill of exchange drawn on a bank, payable on demand

**chose in action** the thing or benefit that is transferred in an assignment; intangible personal property, such as a claim or the right to sue

**circumstantial evidence** facts or evidence that lead one to infer the existence of other facts

**civil law** the legal system used in most of Europe based on a central code, which is a list of rules stated as broad principles of law that judges apply to the cases that come before them

**civil litigation** the process of one party suing another in a private action, conducted in a small claims or superior trial court

**closed shop** only workers who are already members of the union can be hired

**closely-held corporations** a corporation in which there are relatively few shareholders; referred to as "non-distributing corporations" in some jurisdictions

**collateral** goods or property used to secure a debt

**collateral contract** a separate contractual obligation that can stand alone, independent of the written contract

**common law** the legal system developed in Great Britain based on judges applying the customs and traditions of the people and then following each other's decisions

**common law courts** the historical English court of common pleas; the court of king's bench and the exchequer court

**common shares** a share to which no special rights or privileges attach

**compliance audit** the process of entering, inspecting and investigating private property to ascertain that owners are living up to environmental standards

**conciliator** a neutral third party who facilitates discussion between parties to a dispute to encourage and assist their coming to an agreement; also known as a mediator

**conditional sale** the seller provides credit to the purchaser, holding title until the goods are paid for

**conditions** major terms of a contract

**conditions precedent** conditions under which the obligations will begin; also called "subject to" clauses

**conditions subsequent** conditions under which the obligations will end

**Confederation** the process that united the British colonies in North America as the Dominion of Canada in 1867

**confidential information** private information, the disclosure of which would be injurious to a business; a type of intellectual property

**confirmed letter of credit** a document, ratified by the lender, that secures or guarantees the financial aspects of a trade transaction

**conflict of laws** if there is overlapping jurisdiction, federal law prevails and provincial law goes into abeyance; it also refers to the area of law dealing with disputes with those in other jurisdictions

**conglomerate mergers** merger of companies not in direct competition

**consensus** when both parties understand and agree to the terms of a contract

**consent** a defence to an assault charge; can be expressed or implied

**consideration** the price one is willing to pay for promise set out in the offer

**construction approach (to fundamental breach)** a way to ascertain the meaning of a written contract; a finding by a court that an exemption clause does not limit liability

**constructive dismissal** demoting an employee may be the same as dismissal

**consumer transactions** involve goods or services purchased by individuals for personal use and not for resale or for business purposes

**continuing guarantee** creditor can advance further funds without affecting the obligation of the guarantor to pay in the event of default

**continuing trespass** permanent incursion onto the property of another

**contract** a voluntary exchange of promises creating obligations which, if defaulted on, can be enforced and remedied in the courts

**contribution** in the context of insurance, is a requirement that where two or more policies exist, the insurers are to contribute to compensating the insured

**contributory negligence** a failure to take reasonable care, which contributes to the injury complained of

**control test** defines employment in terms of authority and service

**conversion** intentional appropriation of the goods of another person

**cooling-off period** allows purchasers time to change their minds and rescind a contract

**cooperative** company composed of members holding shares in it; method of acquiring residential accommodation

**copyright** gives author control over the use and reproduction of the expression of creative work; type of intellectual property

**corporate myth** a corporation is a legal fiction

**corporation** a business organization that is a separate legal entity from the owners

**counterclaim** a statement of claim by the defendant alleging that the plaintiff is responsible for the losses suffered and claiming back against the plaintiff for those losses

**counteroffer** a new offer is proposed before acceptance of a standing offer

**Court of Chancery** court developed as a supplement to the common law courts; sometimes referred to as Court of Equity

**crimes** wrongs that affect society as a whole

**crumbling skull rule** defendant is not responsible for an inevitable loss by plaintiff; must be used in conjunction with thin skull rule

**damages** monetary compensation to victim

**debenture** often used interchangeably with "bond," it is an acknowledgment of debts by a corporation; normally involves more than one creditor

**deceit** the fraudulent and intentional misleading of another person, causing injury

**declaration** the court declares the law applicable to a particular case

**declaratory judgment** the power of the court to declare what the law is in any matter brought before it

**deed of conveyance** document transferring an interest in property

**deeds of settlement** early means of setting up a company

**defamation** a published false statement to a person's detriment

**defence of justification** when defamatory statement is the truth

**delegation** entrusting someone else to act in one's place; an agent normally cannot turn his responsibilities over to someone else

**deposit** money prepaid with the provision that the funds are to be forfeited in the event of a breach

**deregulation** the dissolution of agencies created to monitor and enforce certain standards; corporations are encouraged to self-regulate

**derivative action** the right of shareholders to sue the directors on behalf of an injured company; sometimes called representative action

**devolution of powers** the process of transferring power from one level of government to another

**digital watermarks** a method of ensuring the authenticity of a website

**direct sales** sales made to consumers at their dwellings or places of business. Also known as **door-to-door sales**.

**director's liability** corporation (and certain creditors) can hold directors responsible for failure to live up to duties

**discharged by agreement** agreement by parties that a contract is ended

**discovery** process with two parts: discovery of documents (discovery of records), where documents/records that are in the hands of each side and may be used at trial are made available to the other side; and examination for discovery, where each party has the opportunity to cross-examine the opposite party, under oath, before the trial

**dissent and appraisal** when major changes adversely affect minority shareholders, they can indicate their oppositon and force the company to buy back the shares at a fair price

**distinguishing the facts** the process judges use to decide which case is the binding precedent

**distress** landlord can seize any property left by tenant and hold it until the rent is paid or sell it to pay rent owing

**dividends** payments to shareholders out of company profits

**Division I proposals** an alternative to bankruptcy, created by the Bankruptcy and Insolvency Act, whereby the debtor secures some time to reorganize its affairs and make a proposal for partial payment that will satisfy its creditors; if the creditors reject the proposal, the insolvent debtor is deemed to have made an assignment in bankruptcy from the day the notice of intention was filed, and the normal bankruptcy procedures follow

**dominant property** property that has the advantage of an easement

**door-to-door sales** same as **direct sales**.

**dower rights** protection of the rights of spouse; have been modified or abolished in most jurisdictions

**down payment** money that must be returned to the purchaser in the event of a breach

**drawee** person or institution ordered to pay out the amount indicated on the instrument

**drawer** person creating the negotiable instrument

**due diligence** doing everything reasonable to avoid the problem leading to legal liability

**duress** force or pressure to enter into a contract

**duty** an obligation to live up to a reasonable standard

**duty of care** an obligation to take steps to avoid foreseeable harm; an essential element for establishing liability in the tort of negligence

**easement** the right of a person other than the owner to use a portion of private property

**easement acquired by prescription** free use of land without interference over a number of years gives a right to the use of that land

**electronic commerce** retail selling using the Internet

**employee** a person working for another who is told what to do and how to do it

**employers' organizations** bargaining agents representing groups of employers

**employment equity** correction of employment situations where there has been a tradition of racial or gender imbalance

**encryption coding** technological innovations to protect privacy and security on the Internet

**endorser** person who signs the back of a cheque usually assuming the obligation to pay it if the drawee or maker defaults

**enduring power of attorney** the power to act as the donor's trustee or representative following the donor's lack of capacity

**equality rights** are among the basic rights provisions in the Canadian Charter of Rights and Freedoms; include the right not to be discriminated against on the basis of grounds such as gender, age, religion, race, or colour, and the guarantee of equality before the law

**equitable estoppel** when a gratuitous promise to do something in the future causes a person to incur an expense, the promisor may be held liable for those expenses if they fail to live up to the promise; also known as promissory estoppel

**equity** legal principles developed in Courts of Chancery to relieve the harshness of the common law; and value left in an asset after subtracting what the owner owes

**equity of redemption** mortgagor retains an interest in land even after default

**error of fact** making an incorrect conclusion with respect to the facts in the matter in dispute

**error of law** incorrectly stating the legal interpretation or effect of the statute or common law

**errors and omissions insurance** insurance to protect holder should the holder cause injury by negligence

**estate** all the property the owner has power to dispose of, less any related debt; also an interest in land

**estoppel** an equitable remedy that stops a party from trying to establish a position or deny something

**evidence in writing** any document that provides information or proof

**examination for discovery** lawyers from opposing sides question the plaintiff and defendant in a civil suit under oath—their responses can be entered as evidence; a method of making all relevant information known to both sides before trial

**examination in aid of execution (examination in aid of enforcement)** court-ordered review of judgment debtor's finances to arrange for payment of the judgment

**executed contract** when both parties have performed or fulfilled their obligations under the contract

**executive branch** part of government comprised of the Queen acting through the prime minister, cabinet, deputy ministers and government departments and officials; also known as the Crown

**executory contract** when an agreement has been made but there has been no performance

**exemplary damages** damages designed to deter and punish; also known as punitive damages

**exemption clause** an attempt to limit liability under an agreement (also exclusion or exculpatory clause)

**express authority** the authority of the agent as actually stated by the principal

**express contract** clear verbal or written statement of an agreement

**fair comment** defence available when defamatory statements are made about public figures or work put before the public

**fair hearing** a hearing conducted in accordance with the rules of procedural fairness; person affected negatively by a decision has a right to receive proper and timely notice of all the matters affecting the case and be given a chance to put forward her side

**false imprisonment** holding people against their will and without lawful authority

**fee simple** highest interest in land, equivalent to ownership

**fidelity bond** insurance against an employee's wrongful conduct

**fiduciary duty** a duty to act in the best interests of other partners (e.g., a business associate or a corporation)

**fiduciary obligation** a duty to act in the best interests of another; senior or key employees may owe a fiduciary obligation to the employer

**fixture** a thing permanently attached to land or building

**floating charge** a security not fixed on any particular goods until default

*force majeure* **clause** contract term anticipating some catastrophic event that will interfere with performance of the contract

**foreclosure** court process ending the mortgagor's right to redeem

**forfeiture** when lease is breached the landlord may terminate the lease and require the tenant to vacate the property

**forfeiture rule** a criminal should not be permitted to profit from a crime

**formal contract** an agreement under seal

**franchising** arrangements based on contracts of service and the supply of products between larger and smaller units of one organization

**fraudulent misrepresentation** misleading words said knowingly or without belief in their truth, causing injury

**fraudulent preference** defaulting debtor pays one creditor over another

**fraudulent transfers and preferences** fraudulent attempts by debtors to keep their property out of the hands of creditors

**frustration** some outside, unforeseen event makes the performance of the contract impossible

**full disclosure** obligation to reveal all details of a transaction

**fundamental breach** breach of a fundamental aspect of the contract that is not covered by an exclusion clause; a breach that goes to the very root of the contract

**fundamental freedoms** among the basic rights in the Canadian Charter of Rights and Freedoms; include freedom of conscience and religion, of thought and belief, of opinion and expression, and of assembly and association

**fungibles** goods which are identical with others of the same nature, such as timber, oil and wheat

**garnishment** court orders that monies owed to the judgment debtor by third parties be paid into court and applied towards judgment debts; a portion of the defendant's wages may be so directed to payment of the judgment

**general damages** compensation for incalculable losses such as pain and suffering

**golden rule** rule for interpreting a statute requiring that the normal meaning of the terms be applied

**good faith** the decision maker must act with honesty and integrity

**good will** a business's reputation and ongoing relations with customers and product identification

**goods** tangible, movable personal property that can be measured and weighed; also known as chattels

**gratuitous promise** a one-sided deal that the courts will not enforce

**grievance process** procedure for settling disputes arising under a collective agreement

**guarantee** a written commitment whereby a guarantor agrees to pay a debt if the debtor doesn't

**guarantor** assumes obligation to pay if the debtor doesn't

*habeas corpus* a court order to bring an arrested person before a judge to determine if that person is being improperly detained

**heard by decision maker** all the evidence must be heard by the individuals making the decision

**holdback** person owing funds must retain a specified percentage to be paid later when paying out in construction contract

**holder in due course** an innocent third party entitled to collect on a negotiable instrument in spite of any claims of the original parties

**holding corporation** owns shares in other corporations

**homestead rights** give spouse a claim to a substantial portion of family property upon divorce

**horizontal merger** one competitor buys out another

**illegal consideration** a promise to commit an unlawful act or to do anything forbidden is not valid consideration and will not be enforced by a court

**illegal contract** one that is void because it has an unlawful purpose

**implied authority** the authority of the agent as implied by the principal

**implied contract** an agreement inferred from the conduct of the parties

**in camera hearings** part of trial proceedings closed to the public

**inadvertence** unintended; two people working together may be held liable for one another's actions even if they did not intend for form a partnership

**indemnity** a primary obligation of a third party to pay a debt along with the debtor

**independent contractor** a person working for himself who contracts to provide specific services to another

**inducing breach of contract** encouraging someone to break her contract with another

**industrial design** unique shapes or patterns that distinguish manufactured articles; type of intellectual property

**infant** a person under the age of majority

**injunction** court order to stop offending conduct

**injurious falsehood** defamation with respect to another's product or business; also known as product defamation and trade slander

**innocent misrepresentation** a false statement made honestly and without carelessness by a person who believes it to be true

**innuendo** an implied statement that is detrimental to another

**insanity** when a person cannot understand the nature of his acts

**insider knowledge** information that affects share pricing that is not publicly known; directors, officers and large shareholders cannot profit by improperly using confidential knowledge about the company

**insolvency** where a person is unable to pay her debts as they become due

**insurable interest** a real and substantial interest in specific property

**insurance riders** modifications to a standard insurance contract

**intellectual property** personal property in the form of ideas and creative work

**intention** desire or aim; parties must intend an agreement to be legally binding; must intend to assume the obligations of the agreement

**interest dispute** disagreement about the terms to be included in a new collective agreement

**interim agreement** binding contract that will subsequently be put into a more formal document

**interlocutory injunction** court order issued before a trial to stop an ongoing injury

**interpretation statutes** statute terms that direct the court to interpret legislation in specific ways

**invitation to treat** invitation to engage in the bargaining process

**involuntary assignment** assignment of rights that takes place involuntarily, as in the cases of death and bankruptcy

**issue estoppel** being stopped from litigating an issue again as it has already been determined in an earlier trial or hearing

**joint liability** parties who are liable all together; partners may face joint liability for debts of the firm

**joint tenancy** shared ownership with right of survivorship

**joint venture** several corporations join together to accomplish a major project

**jointly liable** being liable together with others for the same debt

**judicial branch** part of government comprised of courts and officers of the court

**judicial review** power held by the courts to review decisions made by administrative decision makers

**jurisdiction** legal authority and scope of power; the Constitution Act (1867) delegated responsibility for matters to federal or provincial governments, thus giving them distinct jurisdiction to create laws in those areas

**jurisdictional dispute** a disagreement over who has authority; in the labour context, a dispute between two unions over which one should represent a group of employees, or over which union members ought to do a particular job

**just cause** valid reason to dismiss an employee without notice

**laches** undue delay; neglect or omission to assert a right or claim

**land titles system** registration system that guarantees title to real property

**last clear chance** the last person capable of avoiding the accident is responsible

**law** the body of rules that can be enforced by the courts or by other government agencies

**law merchant** laws developed by the merchant guilds and source of common law relating to negotiable instruments such as cheques and promissory notes

**lease to purchase** credit purchase where goods transfer to lessee at end of lease term

**leasehold estate** tenant has exclusive possession until a specific date

**legal rights** among the basic rights provisions in the Canadian Charter of Rights and Freedoms; include rights such as the right to life, liberty, and security of the person; and security against unreasonable search and seizure and arbitrary imprisonment and detention

**legality** the object of the contract must not be against the law

**legislative branch** part of government comprised of Parliament and legislatures, including the cabinet and prime minister or premiers

**letter of credit** commitment by the importer's bank that the price stated will be paid upon presentation of documentation confirming delivery

**letters patent** method of incorporating granted by government when company is set up in some jurisdictions in Canada

**liability** the situation of being potentially or actually subject to some obligation

**liability insurance** covers negligence by self or employees

**libel** the written or more permanent form of a defamatory statement

**licence** a non-exclusive right to use property; permission to use another's land that can be revoked

**lien** charge giving the creditor the right of seizure when goods are passed on to third parties; a claim registered against property in order to force payment of a debt

**life estate** an interest in land ending at death

**limitation periods** rules requiring that legal action be undertaken within a specified time of the offending conduct taking place

**limited liability** liability is restricted to capital contributed; a corporation shields shareholders, directors and officers from liability

**limited partnership** partners liable only to the extent of their investment

**liquidated damages** a remedy requiring party responsible for a breach to pay a stated amount

**lockout** employer prevents employees from working

**maintenance of membership** requirement in collective agreement that union members pay dues and maintain their membership, but new employees need not join the union

**mandatory retirement** forced retirement from employment generally at 65 years

*mandamus* a court order directing that a specific act be performed

**mediator** a neutral third party who facilitates discussion between parties to a dispute to encourage and assist their coming to an agreement; also known as a conciliator

**memorandum of association** constitution of a corporation in a registration jurisdiction

**merchantable quality** goods that are free of defects that, if known, would impact the price

**mini-trials** corporate executives stage a form of trial to consider the issues, arguments and legal opinions that would influence a judicial decision

**mischief rule** rule requiring that an ambiguous term be interpreted in the most reasonable way or according to the intention of the act

**misfeasance** wrongful conduct

**misrepresentation** a false statement of fact that persuades someone to enter into a contract

**mistake** a misunderstanding about the nature of an agreement that destroys consensus

**mitigation** victims of a breach must make effort to lessen the loss

**moral rights** author's right to prohibit the owner from changing original to degrade it

**mortgage** means of securing loans; title of property is held by the money-lender as security in some jurisdictions; in other jurisdictions, a mortgage is simply a charge against title

**necessaries** the essential needs required to function in society

**negligence** an unintentional careless act that results in injury to another

**negligent words** careless words that cause economic loss

**negotiable instruments** substitutes for money that bestow unique benefits; vehicles for conveniently transferring funds or advancing credit

**negotiation** direct communication between the parties to a dispute in an effort to resolve the problems without third-party intervention; transferring negotiable instruments to third parties

**netiquette** a code of conduct for on-line commercial activities

*non est factum* "it is not my act"—a party is unaware of the nature of the contract

**non-disclosure** silence constitutes misrepresentation only when there is a duty to disclose

**nonfeasance** failure to help when situation required it

**non-profit society** separate legal entity with different rules for incorporation than corporations

**novation** when a party to a contract is substituted by another

**offer** a tentative promise to do something if another party fulfils what the first party requests

**oppression action** action against the directors who have offended the rights of creditors or minority shareholders

**option agreement** a subsidiary contract putting a condition on an offer; consideration given to hold an offer open for acceptance

**order absolute** final order of foreclosure ending the right to redeem

**order bill of lading** consignee retains right to receive goods at their destination

**order nisi** an order establishing the time limit within which the mortgagor can redeem his interest

**organization test** whether or not service-provider is part of employee's organization

**par value** a share with a stated value at issuance (most shares are now no-par-value)

**paramountcy** when a matter is covered by both federal and provincial legislation and there is a conflict, the federal legislation takes precedence

**parliamentary supremacy** the primary law-making body is Parliament or the provincial legislatures in their respective jurisdictions, and statutes take priority over the common law

**parol contract** a simple contract that may be verbal or written, but is not under seal

**parol evidence rule** courts will not permit outside evidence to contradict clear wording of a contract

**partially executed contract** when one party has performed and the other has not

**partnership** ownership and responsibilities of a business shared by two or more people, with a view towards profit

**party and party costs** court costs determined by a tariff establishing what opposing parties in a civil action ought to pay

**passing-off action** prevents someone from misleading the public into thinking it is dealing with some other business or product when it is not

**past consideration** something completed before an agreement is made; it is not valid consideration

**patent** government-granted monopoly prohibiting anyone but the inventor from profiting from the invention; gives inventors the right to profit from their inventions

**pay equity** principle or statute requiring equal pay for work of equal value

**pay in lieu of notice** an amount paid to a dismissed employee rather than notice to terminate

**payee** the person designated on the instrument to receive the money to be paid out

**payment into court** the defendant estimates the true value of the claim and deposits it with the court; if the decision is for less than the deposit the plaintiff will be penalized through payment of additional costs

**perfected** registering a security or taking possession of the collateral used to secure a debt

**performance** when both parties have completed the terms of a contract

**periodic tenancy** automatically renewing tenancy with no specific termination date

**permanent injunction** prohibits production, sale or distribution of infringing products; granted at trial

**personal guarantee** a guarantee which, when signed by major shareholders and other principals of a closely-held corporation, has the effect of eliminating any advantage of limited liability

**personal property** chattels (tangible, movable things); also known as personalty

**picketing** job action during a legal strike when employees circulate at the periphery of the jobsite to persuade others not to do business with struck employer

**pleadings** the documents used to initiate a civil action, including the statement of claim, the statement of defence and counterclaim and any clarification associated with them

**pledge or pawn** creditor or pawnbroker takes possession of an item as security and holds it until repayment

**postbox rule** mailed acceptance is effective when and where it is dropped into a mailbox

**power of attorney** an agency agreement in writing and under seal

**precedent** in a common law system, judges are required to follow a decision made in a higher court in the same jurisdiction

**preferred shareholders** normally can only vote when dividends have not been paid

**preferred shares** give the shareholder preference when dividends are declared along with other benefits

**prerogative writs** the remedies the court may apply if it finds that an administrator has acted beyond its jurisdiction, made an unreasonable decision or not followed the rules of natural justice

*prima facie* **case** where a court finds that circumstantial evidence establishes a case "on the face of it"

**principles of fundamental justice** principles set by tradition and convention that protect the right to a fair hearing by an impartial decision maker acting in good faith

**priority** registered lien has first claim (over other interests) to goods used as security

**privacy** the right to be let alone, to protect private personal information, and to be free of physical intrusion, surveillance, and misuse of an image or name

**private law** the rules that govern our personal, social and business relations, which are enforced by one person suing another in a private or civil action

**private nuisance** the use of property in such a way that it interferes with a neighbour's enjoyment of theirs

**privative clause** terms in a statute that attempt to restrict the right of judicial review

**privity of contract** contract terms apply only to the actual parties to the contract

**procedural fairness** a hearing must follow accepted standards

**procedural law** determines how the substantive laws will be enforced; the rules governing arrest and criminal investigation, pre-trial and court processes in both criminal and civil cases are examples; law can also be distinguished by its public or private function

**product defamation** defamation with respect to another's product; also known as injurious falsehood

**product liability** manufacturers owe a duty when users are injured by their products

**professional associations** organizations for professionals that are set up under provincial legislation; have extensive power to regulate educational and professional qualifications and standards of behaviour and to establish methods of disciplining members for wrongful conduct or incompetence

**professional liability** a person who puts himself forward as an expert must live up to the standard expected of a reasonable expert

*profit à prendre* contracts to take resources off the land

**prohibition** an order not to proceed with a hearing or other administrative process

**promissory estoppel** when a gratuitous promise to do something in the future causes a person to incur an expense, the promisor may be held liable for those expenses if they fail to live up to the promise; also known as equitable estoppel

**promissory note** a promise to pay the amount stated on the instrument

**proof of claim** document filed with bankruptcy trustee establishing validity of a creditor's claim

**prospectus** public document disclosing relevant information about a corporation

**public law** includes constitutional law that determines how the country is governed and the laws that affect an individual's relationship with government, including criminal law and the regulations created by government agencies

**public policy** although some acts may not be illegal, the court will not encourage them by enforcing contracts that are socially distasteful

**punitive damages** compensation for damages in excess of plaintiff's actual losses to punish the wrongdoer for outrageous or extreme behaviour; also known as exemplary damages

**purchase money security interest** a security interest which is registered within a specified time

**qualified privilege** exemption from liability for defamatory statements made pursuant to a duty or special interest, so long as the statement was made honestly, without malice, and circulated only to those having a right to know

*quantum meruit* "as much as is deserved"; reasonable price paid for requested services; sometimes called a quasi-contract

**quasi-contract** contractual relationship involving a request for goods and services where there is no agreement on price before the service is performed; courts impose obligation to pay a reasonable price; also known as *quantum meruit*

**quiet enjoyment** landlord must ensure that nothing interferes with tenant's use of the property

**quiet possession** goods must be usable by the purchaser

*quo warranto* remedy to prevent exercise of unlawful authority

**Rand formula** option in collective agreement enabling employees to retain the right not to join the union, but they are still required to pay union dues; also known as agency shop

**ratification** majority agrees with terms of collective bargain; principal confirms a contract entered into by his agent

**real property** land, buildings and fixtures attached to land or buildings

**reasonable foreseeability test** determines what a person should have anticipated would be the consequences of her action

**reasonable notice** must be calculated in terms of position and time served

**reasonable person test** establishes the judicial standard of socially acceptable behaviour; standard to determine the existence of apparent authority

**reasonable standard of performance** implied term of contract with a professional that he can be held to the standards of the profession

**receiving order** court ordering the transfer of debtor's assets to a trustee

**receivership** proceeding in which a receiver is appointed for an insolvent corporation, partnership or individual to protect its assets for ultimate sale and distribution to creditors

**recognition disputes** disputes arising between unions and employers while union is being organized

**rectification** court corrects the wording of a mistake in the contract

**referral selling** purchaser supplies a seller with a list of friends or acquaintances; when sales are made to those people, purchaser is given benefits

**registration** a legislated requirement for incorporating a company in some jurisdictions in Canada

**registration system** a means of registering and tracking property deeds

**regulations** supplementary rules passed under the authority of a statute and having the status of law

**regulators** government agencies including ministries, departments, boards, commissions, agencies, tribunals and individual bureaucrats at the federal, provincial and municipal levels

**relief against forfeiture** when a landlord retakes a property for failure to pay rent prior to the end of the lease term, the tenant can pay the arrears and apply in the court to have the lease reinstated

**remainderman** third party with the right to the fee simple after the death of a life tenant

**remoteness** determining whether the damages were too far removed from the original negligent act; a breaching party is only responsible for reasonably expected losses

**repossession** creditor takes possession of goods used as collateral and resells them to recover the amount owed

**representative action** the right of shareholders to sue the directors on behalf of an injured corporation; sometimes called a derivative action

**repudiation** one party indicates to the other that there will be a failure to honour the contract (expression can be expressed or implied); third party can refuse to go through with contract if the identity of the undisclosed principal is important

**res ipsa loquitur** the facts speak for themselves

**rescission** returning the parties to the position they were in before the contract

**restrictive covenant** seller imposes restrictions on what the purchaser can use the land for; in employment law, it is a commitment not to work in a certain geographical area for a designated period of time

**reverse discrimination** prejudice or bias exercised against a person or class for purpose of correcting a pattern of discrimination against another person or class

**reversionary interest** upon death of life tenant, ownership reverts to original owner

**revocation** withdrawal of an offer before acceptance (must be communicated to the offeree)

**right of way** type of easement that allows the crossing of another's land

**right to redeem** after collateral is repossessed by creditor the debtor has

a right to reclaim them upon proper payment

**rights dispute** disagreement about the meaning of a term in a collective agreement

**riparian rights** common law right given to people living near rivers and streams to have the water come to them in undiminished quantity and quality

**risk** potential loss due to destruction or damage to goods

**Roman civil law** source of civil law; provided the common law with concepts of property and possessions

**royal assent** the final approval of the representative of the British Crown for a bill to become law in Canada

**rule of law** unwritten convention inherited from Britain which recognizes that although Parliament is supreme and can create any law considered appropriate, citizens are protected from the arbitrary actions of the government

**rules of evidence** courts will only accept evidence gathered according to rules established by the courts

**sale** title and goods are transferred immediately

**salvage** that portion of goods or property which has been saved or remains after a casualty such as fire or other loss

**satisfaction** a substitute in consideration accepted by both parties

**secondary picketing** striking employees picket not just their own workplace but also other locations where the employer carries on business

**secured transaction** collateral right to debt giving the creditor the right to take back the goods or intercept the debt owing used as security in the event of a default

**securities commission** provincial agency that serves as watchdog on stock market

**seizure of property** court authorizes property of the defendant to be seized and sold to satisfy the judgment

**self-defence** a person can respond to an assault with as much force as is reasonable in the circumstances

**self-induced frustration** when one of the parties to a contract causes or fails to prevent a frustrating event; treated as a breach of contract

**seller's lien** seller who holds the goods has a lien against defaulting purchaser

**sentencing circles** meetings to suggest sentences in cases involving Aboriginal offenders and victims

**separate legal entity** a corporation exists separately from the people who created it

**service contracts** an agreement to perform a beneficial service

**servient property** the property subject to an easement

**settlements** transfer of assets where nominal or no consideration is involved

**several liability** each partner can be sued separately

**severance** a chattel affixed by owner can be removed by owner

**share** the means of acquiring funds from a large number of sources to run a corporation; an interest in a corporation held by an investor

**shared mistake** both parties make the same mistake

**shareholder agreement** protects the rights of shareholders in relations with the corporation

**simple contract** written or verbal agreement not under seal

**site audit** the process of examining a site to determine its state of environmental contamination

**slander** spoken defamation

**sole proprietorship** an individual carrying on business alone

**solicitor and client** *costs* costs based on what a lawyer ought to actually charge his client

**spamming** generating and sending unsolicited advertising via the Internet

**special damages** monetary compensation awarded by court to cover actual expenses and calculable pre-trial losses

**specific performance** court orders a breaching party to live up to the terms of the agreement

**standard form contract** contract with fixed terms prepared by a business

**standby letter of credit** commitment by the importer's bank that the price stated will be paid upon presentation of documentation confirming delivery; used as a guarantee

**stare decisis** a principle by which judges are required to follow the decision made in a similar case in a higher court

**statement of claim** the document setting out the nature of complaint and facts alleged forming the basis of the action

**statement of defence** response to a statement of claim by the defendant

**statutes** legislation passed by Parliament is law in the form of statutes

**statutory assignment** an assignment that meets certain qualifications; assignee can enforce a claim directly without involving the assignor

**statutory easements** give utilities or other bodies rights to run power or sewer lines across private property

**stop orders** an order to stop offending conduct

***stoppage in transitu*** seller retains the right to stop the shipment in event of default

**strict interpretation** courts need only apply legislation where the meaning is clear

**strict liability** liability without fault

**strike** employees withdraw services

**"subject to" clauses** terms making a contract conditional on future events

**sublet** lease executed by lessee of land or premises to a third person for a shorter term than that which the lessee holds

**subrogation** the right of insurer upon payment to take over the rights of the insured in relation to whoever caused the injury

**substantial performance** the parties have performed all but a minor term of the contract

**substantive law** establishes both the rights an individual has in society and also the limits on her conduct

**suing on the covenant** creditor can sue for breach of contract

**surety bond** insurance in case a party to a contract fails to perform

**tenancy at sufferance** tenant who fails to leave after lease has expired must compensate landlord

**tenancy at will** when landlord permits an over-holding tenant to stay

**tenancy in common** two people with undivided half interest in land

**tender of performance** one of parties attempts to perform but is prevented by the other party

**thin skull rule** we take our victims as we find them, even those with unique physical or mental conditions

**tort** an action that causes harm or injury to another person

**trade secrets** information that gives a business competitive advantage

**trade slander** defamation with respect to another's product or business; also known as injurious falsehood and product defamation

**trademark** protects the symbols or designs associated with a business

**trespass** being on another's property without permission or legal right

**trespass to chattels** direct intentional interference causing damage to the goods of another

**trespass to person** intentional physical interference with another person; also known as assault and battery

**trust** one person transfers property to a second person obligated to use it to the benefit of a third

**trustees in bankruptcy** licensed professionals who, for a fee, assist the debtor in the bankruptcy process

***ultra vires*** beyond the jurisdiction, power or authority of a decision maker

**unconscionable transaction** one of the parties to a transaction is under extreme disadvantage; merchants take advantage of disadvantaged customers

**undischarged bankrupt** debtor whose assets have been transferred to a trustee but who has not yet been released from the obligation

**undisclosed principal** when the agent doesn't make it clear she is working for a principal she can be held liable for the contract

**undue influence** a special relationship that induces a person to enter a contract

**unenforceable contract** a binding contract that the courts will not enforce, such as a contract that does not satisfy the Statute of Frauds

**unilateral contract** a contract formed when someone voluntarily completes the stipulated act

**unilateral discharge** non-binding agreement to discharge that only benefits one of the parties

**unilateral mistake** only one of the parties is mistaken about the terms of the contract

**union shop** new employees must join the union

**unjust enrichment** one party stands to make a windfall at the expense of the other

**unlimited liability** business owner or partners are liable for all debts incurred by the business to the extent of their personal resources

**utmost good faith** another term for fiduciary duty

**vacant possession** owner has obligation to provide premises that are empty and ready for occupancy

**valid contract** an agreement legally binding on both parties

**vertical merger** merger of a supplier and a retailer

**vicarious liability** employer is liable for the injuries caused by employees during the course of their employment

**vicarious performance** another qualified person may perform the obligations under the contract

**void contract** not a legally binding agreement because an essential ingredient is missing

**voidable contract** one of the parties has the option to end the contract

***volenti non fit injuria*** voluntarily assuming a clear legal risk

**voluntary assignment** an assignment of assets to a trustee in bankruptcy for the benefit of creditors, made voluntarily by a debtor

**warranties** minor terms of a contract

**without prejudice** words that, when used during negotiation, are a declaration that concessions, compromises, and admissions made by a party cannot be used against that party in subsequent litigation

**work to rule** employees perform no more than is minimally required; a job action used to pressure an employer

**work stoppages** strikes (initiated by employees) and lockouts (initiated by employers)

**writ of summons** the written judicial order by which legal actions are commenced

**wrongful dismissal** dismissal without reasonable cause or notice

# Table of Statutes

*Note: The page numbers given at the end of each entry in parentheses refer to pages in this book.*

# Table of Cases

*Downtown Eatery (1993) Ltd. v. Ontario* (2001), 54 O.R. (3d) 161
(C.A.), leave to appeal refused, [2001] S.C.C.A. No. 397
(p. 489*n*)

*Doyle v. Canada (Restrictive Trade Practices Commission)*, [1985] 1
F.C. 362 (C.A.), leave to appeal to S.C.C. refused (1985), 21
D.L.R. (4th) 366 n (S.C.C.) (pp. 94–95)

*Dr. Q. v. College of Physicians and Surgeons of British Columbia*, 2003
S.C.C. 19 (pp. 99–100)

*Dunmore v. Ontario (Attorney General)*, [2001] 3 S.C.R. 1016 (p. 389)

*Duong v. NN Life Insurance Co. of Canada*, (2001), 141 O.A.C. 307
(Ont. C.A.) (p. 433)

*Durham Condominium Corporation No. 123 v. Amberwood Investments
Limited*, (2002-03-20) ONCA C35155 (Ont. C.A) (p. 513)

*Eastern Power Limited v. Azienda Comunale Energia and Ambiente*,
(1999) 178 D.L.R. (4th) 409 (Ont. C.A.); leave to appeal to
S.C.C. refused (June 22, 2000) Doc. 27595 (pp. 197, 210)

*Easthaven Ltd. v. Nutrisystem.com Inc.* (2001), 202 D.L.R. (4th)
560 (Ont. Sup. Ct.) (pp. 56*n*, 566–567, 574)

*E.C. & M. Electric Ltd. v. Alberta (Employment Standards Officer)*
(1994), 7 C.C.E.L. (2d) 235 (Alta. Prov. Ct.) (p. 376*n*)

*Ed Learn Ford Sales Ltd. v. Giovannone*, (1990) 74 D.L.R. (4th)
761 (Ont. Gen. Div.) (p. 282)

*Edelweiss Credit Union v. Beck*, (1991-06-13) B.C.S.C. F882657
(B.C.S.C.) (pp. 243–244)

*Edwards v. Tracy Starr's Shows (Edmonton) Ltd.*, (1987), 61
Alta.L.R. (2d) 233 (C.A.) (p. 181)

*Egerton v. Finucan*, [1995] O.J. No. 1653 (Gen. Div.) (p. 143)

*85956 Holdings Ltd. and Fayerman Brothers Ltd., Re*, (1986), 25
D.L.R. (4th) 119 (Sask. C.A.) (pp. 489–490)

*Elite Bailiff Services Ltd. v. British Columbia*, (2003) 223 D.L.R.
(4th) 39 (B.C.C.A.) (pp. 284–285)

*Elliott v. Freisen et al.* (1982) 136 D.L.R. (3d) 281 (Ont. H.C.);
aff'd (1984) 6 D.L.R. (4th) 388 (Ont. C.A.); leave to appeal
refused (1984) 6 D.L.R. (4th) 388 n (S.C.C.) (p. 141*n*)

*Engels v. Merit Insurance Brokers Inc.*, (2000) 17 C.B.R. (4th) 209
(Ont. Sup. Crt) (p. 362)

*Entores Ltd. v. Miles Far East Corp.*, [1955] 2 All E.R. 493 (C.A.)
(pp. 197, 198)

*Family Insurance Corp. v. Lombard Canada Ltd.*, [2002] S.C.J. No.
49 (p. 427)

*Fancy, Re*, (1984) 8 D.L.R. (4th) 418 (Ont. S.C. Bktcy.)
(pp. 355–356)

*Fayant v. Campbell's Maple Village Ltd.* (1993), 146 A.R. 175
(Q.B.) (p. 380)

*Felker v. Cunningham* (2000), 191 D.L.R. (4th) 734 (Ont. C.A.),
leave to appeal to S.C.C. refused, [2000] S.C.C.A. No. 538
(p. 368)

*Ferme Gérald Laplante & Fils Ltée. v. Grenville Patron Mutual Fire
Insurance Co.* (2002), 217 D.L.R. (4th) 34, 61 O.R. (3d) 481
(C.A.) (pp. 81, 292)

*Fibrosa Spolka Akeyjna v. Fairbairn Lawson Combe Barbouk Ltd.*
[1943] A.C. 32 (H.L.) (p. 280)

*Finning Tractor and Equipment Company Limited v. Mee* (1980) 110
D.L.R. (3d) 457 (B.C. S.C.) (p. 361)

*First City Capital Ltd. v. Hall*, (1993) 99 D.L.R. (4th) 435 (Ont.
C.A.) (pp. 339–340)

*First City Capital Ltd. v. Petrosar Ltd.*, (1987) 42 D.L.R. (4th) 738
(Ont. H.C.) (p. 258)

*528852 Ontario Inc. v. Royal Insurance Co.* (2000), 51 O.R. (3d)
470 (Sup. Ct. J.) (p. 431*n*)

*578722 Ontario Inc. v. Dowma Ltd.*, Ontario Provincial Court,
Feb. 16, 1988, as reported in *Lawyers Weekly* Vol. 7 (1988)
(Ont P.C.) (p. 342)

*Foakes v. Beer* (1884) 9 App. Cas. 605 (H.L.) (pp. 203*n*, 276*n*)

*Folley v. Classique Coaches* (1934) 2K.B. 1 (C.A.) (p. 201*n*)

*Fontaine v. British Columbia (Official Administrator)*, [1998] 1
S.C.R. 424 (p. 152*n*)

*Foothills Dental Laboratory Ltd. v. Naik* (1996), 40 Alta. L.R. (3d)
434 (Prov. Ct.) (p. 447*n*)

*Foster, Re*, (1992) 89 D.L.R. (4th) 555 (Ont. Gen. Div.)
(pp. 330, 503)

*400280 Alberta Ltd. v. Franko's Heating and Air Conditioning
(1992) Ltd.*, (1995), 166 A.R. 241 (Q.B.) (p. 478)

*Fowler v. Manufacturers Life Insurance Co.* (2002), 216 Nfld. &
P.E.I.R. 132 (Nfld. S.C. (T.D.)) (p. 432)

*Francis v. Canadian Imperial Bank of Commerce* (1994) 120 D.L.R.
(4th) 393 (Ont. C.A.) (p. 210)

*Fraser Jewellers (1982) Ltd. v. Dominion Electric Protection Co.* (1997)
148 D.L.R. (4th) 496 (Ont. C.A.) (p. 271*n*)

*Freeth v. Burr* (1874) L.R. 9 C.P. 208 (Crt. C. P.) (p. 271*n*)

*Gee v. White Spot Ltd. and Pan et al vs. White Spot Ltd.*, (1986) 32
D.L.R. (4th) 238 (B.C.S.C.) (pp. 295, 309)

*Gerle Gold Ltd. v. Golden Rule Resources Ltd.*, (1999) 2 F.C. 630
(T.D.), varied, [2001] 1 F.C. 647 (C.A.) (p. 94)

*Gertz v. Meda Ltd.* (2002), 16 C.C.E.L. (3d) 79 (Ont. Sup. Ct. J.)
(p. 374*n*)

*Gilbert Steel Ltd. v. University Construction Ltd.*, (1976) 67 D.L.R.
(3d) 606 (Ont. C.A.) (pp. 200, 201, 202, 205)

*G.L. Black Holdings Ltd. v. Peddle* (1998), 226 A.R. 302 (Q.B.),
aff'd. (1999), 244 A.R. 376 (C.A.) (p. 416*n*)

*Gold Key Pontiac Buick (1984) Ltd. v. 464750 B.C. Ltd.* 2000
B.C.C.A. 435 (B.C.C.A.) (p. 330*n*)

*Gooderham v. Bank of Nova Scotia*, (2000), 47 O.R. (3d) 554
(Sup. Ct. J.) (pp. 408–409)

*Goodfellow Inc. v. Heather Building Supplies Ltd.*, (1996) 141 D.L.R.
(4th) 282 (N.S.C.A.) (p. 327)

*Graham and Technequip Ltd., Re*, (1981), 32 O.R. (2d) 297 (H.C.J.),
aff'd (1982) 139 D.L.R. (3d) 542 (Ont. Div. Ct.) (p. 499)

*Gregorio v. Intrans-Corp.*, (1994) 115 D.L.R. (4th) 200 (Ont.
C.A.); additional reasons (1994) 15 B.L.R. (2d) 109 (note)
(Ont. C.A.) (p. 274)

*Hadley v. Baxendale*, (1854) 156 E.R. 145 (Ex. Ct) (p. 283)

*Haig v. Bamford*, [1977] 1 S.C.R. 466 (pp. 159, 167)

*Haig v. Canada* (1992), 9 O.R. (3d) 495 (Ont. C.A.) (p. 21*n*)

*Halifax (County) v. Giles*, (1994) 111 D.L.R. (4th) 614 (N.S.C.A.)
(p. 194)

*Halpern v. A.G. of Canada*, (2003), 65 O.R. (3rd) 161 (C.A.)
(pp. 27–28, 32)

*Hammill v. Gerling Global Life Insurance Co.* (1990), 109 A.R. 254
(p. 438)

*H&D Hobby Distributing Ltd. v. Svatos*, (1998), 234 A.R. 376
(Q.B.) (pp. 471, 492)

*Hardman v. Falk*, [1955] 3 D.L.R. 129 (B.C.C.A.); aff'd [1955] 1
D.L.R. 432 (B.C.S.C.) (p. 215)

*Harry v. Kreutziger* (1979) 95 D.L.R. (3d.) 231 (B.C.C.A.)
(pp. 323–324)

*Harvard College v. Canada (Commissioner of Patents)* (2003) 219
D.L.R. (4th) 385 (S.C.C.) (p. 548*n*)

*Haughton Graphic Ltd. v. Zivot* (1986), 33 B.L.R. 125 (Ont.
H.C.J.); aff'd (1988), 38 B.L.R. xxxiii (Ont. C.A.); leave to
appeal refused [1988] S.C.C.A. No. 212 (p. 464)

*Hayward v. Mellick* (1984) 5 D.L.R. (4th) 740 (Ont. C.A.)
(p. 263)

*Hedley Byrne & Co. v. Heller's Partners Ltd.*, [1963] 2 All E.R. 575
(H.L.) (p. 159)

*Heitsman v. Canadian Premier Life Insurance Co.*, (2002), 4
B.C.L.R. (4th) 124 (S.C.) (p. 426)

*Henthorne v. Fraser*, [1892] 2 Ch. 27 (Eng. Ch. D.) (pp. 197, 198)

*Hercules Management Ltd. v. Ernst & Young*, [1997] 2 S.C.R. 165
(p. 168)

*Herff Jones Canada Inc. v. Todd*, (1996), 181 A.R. 236 (C.A.)
(p. 369)

*H.F. Clarke Ltd. v. Thermidaire Corp. Ltd.*, [1976] 1 S.C.R. 319
(S.C.C.) (p. 286)

title and risk, 296–299
transfer of goods, 295–296
transfer of title, 297–299
writing, requirement of, 296
salvage, right of, 434
same-sex marriages, 32
sample, 302–303
satisfaction, 275
seal, use of, 184, 206–207
sealed documents, 184, 206–207
second mortgage, 528–529
secondary picketing, 398
secured creditors, 63, 326, 352–353
secured debt
accounts receivable, 328
*Bank Act*, 340
bills of exchange, 343
bonds, 341
builders' liens, 341–342
certified cheque, 342
cheques, 342
collateral, retention of, 335
"consumer purchase," 343
debentures, 341
floating charges, 341
guarantees, 336–340
holdback, 341–342
leases, 328
letters of credit, 343–344
negotiable instruments, 342–343
personal property, 326–327
personal property security, 327–332
*Personal Property Security Act*, 329–336
promissory notes, 343
redemption right, 334
repossession, 334
resale of seized goods, 334–335
rights and remedies on debtor's
default, 333–336
securities commission, 482–483
security, 566
seizure of property, 62–63
self-defence, 134–135
self-induced frustration, 279
sentencing circles, 52
separate legal entity, 466
separate legal identity, 469–471
servient property, 511
settlement (litigation), 58, 203
settlements (in bankruptcy), 354–355
severally liable, 449
severance, 503
sexual harassment, 382
sexual orientation, and discrimination, 32
shared mistake, 236–237, 278
shared property, 514
shareholders
annual general meeting, 485–486
common shares, holders of, 486
derivative action, 488
dilution of shares, 486
dissent, 489
dividends, payment of, 490
election of directors, 477
financial statements, 485
limited liability, 492
"locked-in," 488
minority shareholders, 488, 489, 495

obligations, 485, 493–494
oppression action, 489
preemptive rights, 486
preferred shareholders, 486
protections, 488–489
proxy, 486
records, access to, 485
representative action, 488
rights, 485–488
voting rights, 486
shares
authorized share capital, 472
common shares, 473
described, 472
dilution of, 486
dividends, 490
for estate planning, 474
no-par-value, 472
par-value, 472
preemptive rights, 486
preferred shares, 473
rights and restrictions, 473–474
silence
acceptance, 195
and misrepresentation, 245
simple contracts, 184
Simplified Procedure (Ontario), 59
slander, 141
*see also* defamation
SOCAN (Society of Composers, Authors,
and Music Publishers of Canada), 547
sole proprietorship
described, 441, 442
government regulations, 442
liability, 442–443
professional associations, 443
professionals, 443
unlimited liability, 442–443
vicarious liability, 443
solicitor-client costs, 61
"special-act companies," 466
special damages
breach of contract, 282
described, 61
in tort law, 132
specialized agency relationships, 423–424
specific performance, 61, 62, 286–287
standard form contract, 193, 426
standard of care
bailment, 506
breach of, 150–152
children, liability of, 151–152
common carriers, 506–507
cost, effect of, 151
expertise and, 151
innkeepers' liability, 507
professional liability, 165–166
reasonable person test, 150
risk of injury, effect of, 151
standards of practice, 166
*stare decisis*, 6–7, 8, 69
statement of claim, 57, 65
statement of defence, 57
Status Indians, and capacity, 218
*Statute of Frauds*, 226–228, 229
statutes
*see also* legislation
enactment, 15

interpretation statutes, 89
judicial review, modification of, 102
procedural fairness, modification
of, 92
as source of law, 9
*Statutes of Canada*, 15
statutory assignment, 259
statutory easements, 511
statutory interpretation
golden rule, 88
interpretation statutes, 89
mischief rule, 88
plain meaning, 88
rules of, 88
strict interpretation, 89
*stoppage in transitu*, 303
Streamlined Procedures (Alberta), 59
strict interpretation, 89
strict liability, 160–161, 162
strikes, 396–397
"subject to" clause, 276
subject-to clauses, 188
sublet, 519
subrogated rights, 340, 433–434
substantial performance, 266
substantive law, 3, 54
Sunday shopping, 22–23
sunset clause, 21
Superintendent of Bankruptcy, 347
Supreme Court of Canada, 53
surety bond, 435
surrogate courts, 50

**T**
tax advantages of incorporation, 492
Tax Court of Canada, 53
taxation (of lawyer's bill), 72–73
temporary layoff, 374
tenancy at sufferance, 521
tenancy at will, 521
tenants
obligations, 521–522
remedies, 523
tender, 266–267
tenders, 192
termination of employment
constructive dismissal, 375–376
disabled employees, 373
disobedience, 373
and employment standards, 379
evidence of misconduct, 376
incompetence, 373
issue estoppel, 380
just cause, 372
layoffs, 374
mitigation, 376
reasonable notice, 370–372, 376, 379
undue hardship for employer, 373
wrongful leaving, 374
thin skull rule, 154
third parties
and agency law, 419–420
and partnerships, 449
and undisclosed principals, 417–419
ticket offences, 116
title
approval by acceptance, 298
bill of lading, 296